Dreams of a More
Perfect Union

Dreams of a More Perfect Union

ROGAN KERSH

✳

CORNELL UNIVERSITY PRESS
ITHACA AND LONDON

First published 2001 by Cornell University Press

Printed in the United States of America

Library of Congress Cataloging-in-Publication Data

Kersh, Rogan.
   Dreams of a more perfect union / Rogan Kersh.
      p.   cm.
   Includes bibliographical references and index.
   ISBN 0-8014-3812-8 (acid-free paper)
   1. United States—Politics and government—18th century.   2. United States—
Politics and government—19th century.   3. Nationalism—United States—History
—18th century.   4. Nationalism—United States—History—19th century.   I. Title.
JK31 .K47   2001
320.54′0973′09033—dc21

                                                         00-010766

Cornell University Press strives to use environmentally responsible suppliers and materials to the fullest extent possible in the publishing of its books. Such materials include vegetable-based, low-VOC inks and acid-free papers that are recycled, totally chlorine-free, or partly composed of nonwood fibers. Books that bear the logo of the FSC (Forest Stewardship Council) use paper taken from forests that have been inspected and certified as meeting the highest standards for environmental and social responsibility. For further information, visit our website at www.cornellpress.cornell.edu.

Cloth printing   10 9 8 7 6 5 4 3 2 1

Sail on, O Union, strong and great!
Humanity with all its fears,
With all the hopes of future years,
Is hanging breathless on thy fate!

—H. W. Longfellow,
"The Building of the Ship"

Contents

CONTENTS

Preface

UNION SQUARE, UNION STATION, Union College, the Union League Club. These and thousands of other familiar U.S. landmarks, along with more than six hundred towns and cities bearing the name, testify to a once vital theme in American popular discourse. Few of those who today pass through, disembark at, or otherwise inhabit these places are likely to recognize the Union appellation as meaningful, much less as stating a profound aspiration to political unity. But from the late colonial period to the early Gilded Age, American leaders and ordinary citizens constantly expressed—in everyday talk and grand administrative planning, as well as in place names and architecture—their dreams of a "more perfect" national union.

Beginning in the mid-1880s Americans' references to union declined sharply. So did the public testaments they left behind: of the eight states admitted since 1890, and the four lands that remain U.S. territories today, just two included a (single) Union town or county, each established well before statehood. In succeeding years the practice was in fact reversed, as former Union cities, streets, and so forth were renamed or dismantled.[1] This change in part reflects a general twentieth-century interest, among citizens of the United States as well as other countries, in grand questions of global import—rather than in what holds people together in a republic. More recently, however, Americans have returned to issues concerning their shared national life, including how to secure a significant degree of unity among a diverse, often fragmented people. U.S. history is often invoked in these debates but usually in idealized versions of a formerly vibrant union: present dreams about past dreams. By treating historical evidence instead as a record of the relation between public vernacular and institutions, this book's

---

1. For a detailed account of one such occurrence, in Portland, Oregon, see Paxton 1990. On older union references, see Wilbur Zelinsky (1988, 128–29), whose catalogue of American city names includes some six hundred Unions, fourth on the list after Washington, Lincoln, and Franklin. Union ranks first among U.S. counties named for "patriotic and inspirational terms," and is the most popular street name as well.

sustained attention to Americans' complex understandings of national union may provide some useful illumination for the present.

＊

Many hands aided in this book's making. I owe most thanks to Rogers Smith, whose numerous suggestions for improvement—and, just as important, example as a scholar and teacher—contributed in ways I'm still realizing. David Mayhew's encyclopedic knowledge of U.S. history saved me from a great many errors (those which remain are entirely my doing, of course), and his willingness to read and reread versions of a study far removed from his own research remains a source of grateful wonder. I also benefited immensely from detailed comments on the entire manuscript from David Waldstreicher, Jim Morone, and Wayne Fields. Much-appreciated advice on various portions also came from Bruce Ackerman, Marshall Berman, Shelley Burtt, Elizabeth Cohen, David Ericson, Alan Gibson, Jim Gorman, Jessica Goulden, Russell Hanson, Ralph Ketcham, Andrew Koppelman, Karl Kronebusch, Stephen Macedo, Suzanne Mettler, Mark Schlesinger, Garrett Ward Sheldon, Steven Smith, Jeff Stonecash, Alan Trachtenberg, and C. Vann Woodward. For timely research assistance, thanks to Rebecca Bohrman and A. Lanethea Mathews.

Little insight into past American political talk would be possible without newspaper and manuscript collections, and the libraries that sustain them. Thanks therefore to Kate Ohno and her colleagues at the Franklin Papers; Kevin Pacelli and his able staff at Sterling Library's microfilm collection, Yale University; Karen Renninger at the Library of Congress; and staff members at the American Antiquarian Society, British Library, Charleston (S.C.) Public Library, Huntington Library, National Archives, New Haven Historical Society, New Jersey Historical Society, South Carolina Historical Collection, and the university libraries of Brown, Dartmouth, Duke, Harvard, Pennsylvania, Princeton, UCLA, Syracuse, Virginia, and Wake Forest.

Roger Haydon, Alja Kooistra, and Peter Agree at Cornell University Press were vital sources of advice and counsel in the work's final stages; thanks to them and to the copy editor, Evan Young. I'm also grateful to Muriel Bell for her early encouragement about the manuscript's potential. Thanks to Robert Goodin and two anonymous readers for the *Journal of Political Philosophy,* where portions of chapter 2 appeared as "Liberty *and* Union: A Madisonian View." Similarly, thanks to Nicholas Xenos and two readers for *Polity,* which recently published parts of chapter 1. Generous fellowship support from the Mellon Foundation, the Luce Foundation, Yale University, and Syracuse University helped keep me going, intellectually and physically, over the years it took to complete this book.

My original interest in political history and ideas I owe to my father, Earle Kersh, whose inquisitive, open-minded approach to the past has been a lifelong inspiration. I was further stimulated in these pursuits by three extraordinary college teachers: Charles Lewis, Don Schoonmaker, and especially Jim Barefield, the last of whose continuing ruminations on topics from southern U.S. history to the virtues of Venetian *prosecco* have been an invaluable source of instruction. Most recently, my awareness of the possibilities of union—in ways delightfully surpassing the political—has been enhanced immeasurably by the shining example of Elizabeth Cohen, to whom this work is lovingly dedicated.

ROGAN KERSH

New Haven, Connecticut, and Syracuse, New York

Dreams of a More Perfect Union

Introduction

The Union is an ideal nation which exists, so to say, only in men's minds and whose extent and limits can only be discerned by the understanding.

—Alexis de Tocqueville, *Democracy in America,* 1840

INTERPRETATIONS OF THE Constitution's opening clause—"We the People of the United States, in Order to form a more perfect Union"—typically emphasize its first three words, given the democratic promise they imply. But no less dramatic are the pledges that follow. Thirteen disparate, squabbling states were in fact United, the document serenely declared. Moreover, the weak bonds joining the diverse American populace—a people separated into isolated "island communities," historians now insist—would be made "more perfect" by the Constitution's ordination. Modern accounts of American political history largely miss the import and audacity of these claims; most observers at the time found them absurd. "They have no centre of union and no common interests," sniffed one Tory observer. "They can never be united . . . they will be a disunited people 'till the end of time."[1]

This book reconstructs ideas of national union in American political thought from the colonial era into the 1890s. Treatises by the dozen view U.S. history through the prism of other foundational values, especially liberty, equality, and democracy.[2] But union was equally prized by the country's leading thinkers and politicians. "Union" and "unite(d)" appear more than almost any other political word in the *Federalist Papers:* the term is used fully four times as often as "liberty," "rights," or "America(n)," for example.[3] And union's appeal remained central in American political ideas, in all sections of the country, for a century after the founding era. Prominent figures including the still familiar (Daniel Webster, Frederick Douglass, Ralph Waldo Emerson, John C. Calhoun, Abraham Lincoln) and now mostly forgotten (postwar southern political leader Benjamin

---

1. "Island communities" is from Wiebe 1967, xiii, 4–5; Dean of Gloucester Cathedral quoted in Smith 1980, 3.
2. In the 1990s alone, book-length studies of *liberty* in American history include Foner 1998; Clark 1994; Ericson 1993; Handlin and Handlin 1986–94; Konig 1995; Treadgold 1990; and Davis and Mintz 1998 (a documentary history, organized around freedom's progress and regress). On *equality* as American ideal and practice, see, e.g., Pole 1993; Fuchs 1990; Smith 1997 (on the complex history of equal citizenship); Davis 1990; Condit and Lucaites 1993; and Klinkner and Smith 1999. Leading recent interpretations of U.S. history in *democratic* terms include Morone 1990; Ackerman 1991 and 1998; Sandel 1996; Gebhardt 1993; Lind 1995; and Burstein 1999.
3. See Engeman et al. 1988, s.v. "Union" and other cited terms.

Hill, black reformer Maria Stewart, California newspaper editor Philip Bell) all expressed a powerful commitment to strengthening unity. The American masses also extolled their national union in terms often surpassing the esteem they expressed for their local communities. Consider two pieces of evidence from the 1860s: the voluntary, even eager decision of thousands of young northern men, presumably encouraged by wives, parents, and other supporters, to risk life and limb in union's name during the Civil War; and, less familiarly, southerners' surprisingly swift reassertion, at the conclusion of the war, of their dedication to a united America.

This widespread fealty to national union remained potent into and after Reconstruction. But in the mid-1880s union began disappearing from meaningful use, and by century's end the term was a political anachronism. What explains the lasting appeal of unionist ideas, and their eventual decline from rhetorical favor? Who promoted the value, and why? What forms did American conceptions of a "more perfect" union take, and what were the constituent materials?

My investigation of these questions is rooted in a detailed study of American national-union ideas, from colonial times to the late nineteenth century. Like other cherished goods, union was a focus of continual debate, its meaning and purposes contested by successive generations of elites, their followers, and people on the margins of the civic culture. Reconstructing these conflicts requires close attention to how the ideal was initially adopted, popularized in virtually every sector of the polity, deployed in the service of ends ranging from abolition to railroad building to states' rights, and eventually abandoned. Tracing the rise and fall of union—as a core value, as rhetorical window dressing in the service of other aims, as a basis for major state endeavors—provides the book's animating purpose. Such extensive attention to this concept is justified by its vital importance in U.S. political history. The idea of union was the chief rhetorical means by which Americans sought to express shared ideals and a common identity, without invoking strong nationalism or centralized governance.

Asserting union's centrality in American political history raises an obvious question: Why has this theme been overlooked? I begin by investigating inattention among political theorists and historians to "union" as such, then turn to an overview of the concept's place in U.S. history. A short section on how examining union ideas helps illuminate other areas of national life follows: these areas include political-institutional development over time, and pressing present concerns about national identity. I then address the issue of defining this protean and highly contested concept, and conclude by briefly outlining the book's chapter-by-chapter investigation into the American dream of a more perfect union.

N.B.

MISREADING UNION

Political scientists and historians have noted, mostly in passing, the presence of union ideas in U.S. history, usually among the Revolutionary and Civil War generations. But few have addressed the term's significance—what sort of "union" was intended, by whom, and for what purposes.[4] Nor has its abrupt disappearance from political talk, a little more than two decades after the Civil War's close, been chronicled, much less explained. Such oversight is curious, considering modern scholars' fervent interest in other foundational American ideals, and in the ideological traditions claimed to influence these—and considering the current outpouring of works examining social capital, civil society, and other sources of the shared values said to have shored up the nation since its shaky beginning.[5]

At least three reasons account for the relative obscurity of union ideas in modern studies. First, many scholars' interests lie far from union or other consensus themes. John Higham describes American historical writing over the past four decades as "a fragmented, ethnocentric literature that has told us little about the relations of races, ethnic groups, and other minorities to one another or about the character of the nation as an inclusive society." Sustained efforts to specify the multitudinous diversity of America's past inevitably leave less room for (and heighten skepticism about) accounts of what citizens held in common. U.S. history as it is currently portrayed, writes Gordon Wood, "turns out to be one long story of different peoples struggling to identify themselves."[6] As noteworthy, however, is that many of these "peoples" (black, immigrant, southern, Catholic, and so forth) evidently prized their participation in the national whole. Unionist affirmations by elite and ordinary Americans deserve examination, given their prevalence into the late nineteenth century—however out of academic fashion such themes may be at present.

Second, since the 1960s most inquiries into American political theory—especially of the founding period—have been oriented around two rival ideological traditions: liberalism and republicanism.[7] These paradigms so thoroughly dominate the field that the requisite approach to any idea is to demonstrate its roots in one or the other. Yet in examining actors' motivations and meaning, it

---

4. Paul Nagel's *One Nation Indivisible* (1964) is the only scholarly treatment of American national union as such. Some studies of nationalism, federalism, or related themes treat the idea in limited detail; most notable among these are Beer 1993, esp. 341–78 (on James Wilson's account of social union); McWilliams 1973 (on fraternity in American political thought); Knupfer 1991 (on "constitutional unionism" and antebellum compromises); and Davis 1978. A few article-length studies investigate union ideas in part: see Mason 1950; Hutchinson 1959; Wilson 1967; Stampp 1978; Onuf 1986; Greenstone 1986; Conrad 1988; McCormick 1990; Diamond 1992; Eisgruber 1994; and Maletz 1998. Not one of these takes union as its principal subject; each is chiefly concerned with another aspect of U.S. political history (or, for Stampp and Onuf, historiography). Most writers simply cite Nagel by way of broader reference to the term. As this book was nearing completion, I came across James Lewis's fine chronicle of the importance of union ideas in Spanish-American diplomacy from 1783 to 1829 (Lewis 1998).

5. See, e.g., Sandel 1996; Etzioni 1993; Macedo 1999; Skocpol 1997a; Lind 1995; Barber 1998; or Seligman 1992, 81–91 (on "America as a model of civil society").

6. Higham 1999, 325; Wood 1998, 44.

7. Rodgers (1992) ably summarizes the field from the 1960s to early 1990s. More recently, a glance at any of the landmark works in American political thought cited in note 2 will demonstrate the continuing vitality of "paradigm wars," though modifications are apparent: Ackerman (1991, 1998) works in a "liberal republican" idiom, and Smith (1997) identifies an important third tradition, "ascriptive Americanism."

appears that civic-republican thinkers contributed no more than recessive strains to American ideas of political union, and that liberal philosophers had limited influence as well. Instead of a blend of Sparta and Locke, the concept's origins among Americans owe most to other sources, as the chapters of this book testify.[8] Moreover, leaders like Madison, Webster, and Lincoln promoted national union in the service of goals often unrelated to the ends sought by republican or liberal thinkers. In Americans' understanding, citizens were joined by affective bonds rather than martial *virtu* or economic self-interest; individuals were encouraged to consider themselves as members of a national whole, not primarily as bearers of rights or members of autonomous local communities. Rather than comprehending union in terms of either strong-communal republican ideas or rights-based liberalism, American thinkers steered in other directions. At most they incorporated a few elements of republican and liberal principles, blending these with aspects of other paradigms. "Union" refers at bottom to a combination of diverse elements; in the U.S. intellectual context the term was aimed at bridging ideological and practical divides rather than advancing one or another tradition.

Recent studies of American political thought also tend to neglect conceptions of national union owing to an increasing emphasis on *local* community, promoted by theorists and political activists alike.[9] Many communitarian writers favorably contrast past Americans' republican outlook with the belated growth of a nationalist spirit, which has been temporally located anywhere from the constitutional convention to the Civil War or even the New Deal. Yet while communal ideas were in important ways locally rooted well into the nineteenth century, union's spreading appeal from the 1780s onward testifies to the simultaneous resonance of broader loyalties.[10]

Third, conceptual studies usually focus on topics that are still "alive," that is, deeply embedded in contemporary political conversation; hence there is a wealth of studies (see n. 2) on such vital concepts as liberty, equality, democracy, and so forth. "Union" in its old, nation-denoting sense ceased to be a significant term in American politics around 1890 and remained an anachronism for decades thereafter. Until very recently, the term appeared mostly in fusty forms, such as presidential State of the Union addresses or reenactments of Union Army triumphs and losses in the Civil War.

Though union's obscurity through much of the twentieth century likely contributes to modern scholarly disinterest, the idea's irrelevance arguably makes it a worthwhile object of conceptual study. Union's disappearance from meaningful use, following decades of centrality in U.S. political vernacular, provides a rare window into how an idea's value waxes, wanes, and finally vanishes over time.

---

8. Readers interested in the intellectual history of union ideas, or in debating American "inheritances" from other paradigms, may wish to consult Kersh 1996 (21–66), which examines political union in the philosophy of several classical and Enlightenment thinkers.

9. The conclusion to this book includes an overview of this localist emphasis.

10. Wiebe 1984; Bender 1978, esp. 82–89; Shain 1994.

In short, union might well bear careful examination even if it remained "extinct." But the concept's mini-renaissance in recent years makes understanding its history all the more valuable.

UNION IN AMERICAN POLITICAL HISTORY

American conceptions of political union were present from the early colonial period, officially beginning in 1643 with the formation of the United Colonies of New England, a confederation that endured for more than half a century. Another union was established by the British in 1685: it included the entire northern half of British America, from Maine through what was then known as the Jerseys. In an episode little remembered today, colonists staged a mini-revolution and overthrew this "Dominion." Numerous schemes for uniting two or more colonies were subsequently promoted by both American colonists and British officials, inspiring a growing commentary on the virtues of unity. In 1747, Benjamin Franklin asserted that "at present we are like the separate filaments of flax before the thread is formed, without strength because without connection, but UNION would make us strong and even formidable." By the 1750s, thanks to Franklin and others, the term was firmly ensconced in American political discourse. Bernard Bailyn's comment on "power" during the revolution applies equally well to "union" in the founding period and first three quarters of the nineteenth century: Americans "dwelt on it endlessly, almost compulsively; it is referred to, discussed, dilated on at length and in similar terms by writers of all backgrounds."[11]

What did the framers of the U.S. constitution intend when they invoked their national union and promised to make it "more perfect," a phrase that resounded long after ratification? Union advocates' goals ranged from engendering a stronger sense of national identity, originally defined against Britain, to recognition of Americans' common rights across the different states. Overshadowing most thinkers' specific aims, however, was a pragmatic, almost desperate desire for a *sustainable* union: a republic that would hold together and thereby more nearly approximate the "completion" of the U.S. constitutional project.[12] Tenuous interstate relations and mutual suspicion among Americans of different geographical areas led the founders, particularly James Madison, to develop an elaborate account of national union designed to secure popular support for (and commit elites firmly to) the project of uniting the whole.

Madison and most of his fellow framers promoted a voluntarist, balanced view of sustainable union, based on three pillars: U.S. territory; affective bonds

11. Franklin in Labaree et al. 1959–, 3:180; Bailyn 1967, 56. A fuller account of the New England Dominion is undertaken in chapter 1.

12. "More perfect" was not then the oxymoron it may now be. As Garry Wills notes, "In the eighteenth century, 'perfect' still had its root sense of 'completed.' . . . A perfect man had completed his maturing. A perfect report covered all of its subject" (1999, 71). Thus a "more perfect" union meant a more *complete* polity, compared to the painfully inadequate one established by the Articles of Confederation.

between citizens; and representative leadership, the latter buttressed by mutual state/society reinforcement. This three-part vision endured through much of the nineteenth century, though interpretations of the founders' unionist "legacy" certainly diverged in different regions of the country and over time. Two other general unionist perspectives also gained prominence during the antebellum years. One was conceived principally by antebellum nativists and states' rights southerners, and is here termed *ethnocultural* union. A "more perfect" union, explained Ohio political editor William Thomas, was a more homogeneous one: "a union of common American blood . . . of white men committed to the furtherance of Anglo-Saxon civilization throughout the globe."[13] Though Madison and his like-minded heirs, particularly Webster, argued against a *Herrenvolk*-style union emphasizing shared race/ethnicity, religion, and culture, it attracted enough adherents to contribute significantly to national discourse.

Other nineteenth-century Americans saw the promise of perfectable unity in moral terms, and promoted ideas of *principled* union. Some did so by relating union to other primary goods. As Andrew Jackson declared in his second inaugural address, in 1833: "Without union our independence and liberty would never have been achieved; without union they never can be maintained."[14] A smaller set of thinkers identified moral enrichment of national unity with greater political and social inclusiveness, and sought to expand beyond Anglo-Saxon males the constituent elements of the American national union. Lincoln is a notable example here; his view was buttressed (and partly informed) by less obvious unionists like Emerson and Douglass.

Ultimately, "a union of all Americans"—as the stock phrase had it—mostly remained an unfulfilled promise. But this principled aspiration was not as impotent as modern portraits of an unvarnished nativist, racist nineteenth-century republic imply. The expansive unionist rhetoric of orators like Daniel Webster, along with that of abolitionists stressing a more moral union, seems to have provided a source of inclusive hope to many members of marginalized groups, particularly African Americans. Although in practice the exclusionary notion that a national union could be limited to a small subset of citizens usually prevailed, visions of a more moral union demonstrably had force in U.S. political development as well.

Especially in the years immediately after the Civil War, a morally refined conception of union appeared within reach. But the term's older sustainable ("union at any cost") and ethnocultural meanings were reasserted, and dreams of a more genuinely inclusive union faded. By the early 1870s, New South progenitors had capitalized on battle-weary northerners' sentimental response to "the romance of reunion," in Nina Silber's felicitous phrase.[15] Southerners promised permanent unity in exchange for regional autonomy, limits on central-state activity, and

13. Thomas in Jourdan 1889, 26.
14. Lott 1994, 69.
15. Silber 1993.

restricted civil rights for blacks. With intersectional comity spreading among whites, especially as Reconstruction drew to a close, the gap between the ambitious promise of a principled union and post-Appomattox reality proved too great to bridge. Largely in response to this disappointment, some white intellectuals and most black Americans ceased using the term.

This study moves between the views of a few selected thinkers or actors, which are profiled at length, and a more general assessment of the patterns of union usage during a given period. The latter surveys draw especially on unionist references among America's "political class," the 15 to 20 percent of adults (predominantly white and male, in the period covered here) who published newspapers, held political offices, or were otherwise active participants. This still overlooks eight of every ten residents of the United States: focusing on how a particular political concept was understood makes it difficult to analyze the views of those only sporadically engaged with public affairs. But where possible, I trace the term's spread among less-involved and disenfranchised Americans as well, seeking to understand their use of unionist rhetoric. Union's continued relevance rested on the idea's widespread appeal, which required that many people disseminate and uphold it. Political ideas in the United States have long been thus democratized: "The entire point of American political theory from the beginning," writes Donald Lutz, "was to replace elite dominance with popular control, to ground politics directly in human experience rather than in philosophical utopias."[16] Lutz may overstate the case, given early unionists' effort to ensure gentry control of political activity including even language. But the force of his claim is affirmed in the range of actors featured in the pages that follow.

UNION'S EFFECTS AND IMPLICATIONS

My exploration of union's variegated meanings and uses gives rise to two related topics of concern. One involves the interplay of union concepts and U.S. institutional development. Ideas and institutions are usually studied separately by social scientists, a convention that too often obscures an important truth: ideas can have consequences, in their "confrontation with the world."[17] The relation between concepts and practical political effects is notoriously difficult to specify, to be sure. But identifying how Americans employed unionist themes in constructing the institutions of national governance contributes to our understanding of the latter process.

Union's eighteenth- and nineteenth-century grammar may seem a quaint throwback today, but the purposes it addressed resonate powerfully again as Americans (and people in many other places) struggle to determine whether a

---

16. Lutz 1992, 102–3 (on "political class"), quote at p. 110.

17. Rae 1981, 5: "The complexity that interests us does not arise *within* the abstract idea of equality but in its confrontation with the world."

unified political community in a modern large-scale, diverse polity is feasible or even desirable. This book's other secondary motif is to illuminate pressing contemporary concerns about American national unity in light of the past. I take up these two themes in the following sections.

Ideas and Institutions

In addition to reconstructing union as Americans variously conceived the term, this book attempts to trace the practical political effects of ideas of union. This effort rests on the claim that "[a]ctions and practices are *constituted* in part by the concepts and beliefs the participants themselves have."[18] Such an insight is hardly confined to academics in the present. Eighteenth-century political actors were well aware of words' power to persuade, compel, and exclude, as exemplified in this comment from the Whig thinker Lord Shaftesbury, in 1711:

> I must confess, I have been apt sometimes to be very angry with our language for having denied us the use of the word *Patria,* and afforded us no other name to express our native community than that of country, which already bore two different significations abstracted from mankind or society. Reigning words are many times of such force as to influence us considerably in our apprehension of things.[19]

How might a "reigning word" like union influence not only people's "apprehensions," but political activities? First and most basically, it is through concepts that the ground for action is established. Before a national community could be plausibly imagined, much less realized, swirling notions of shared identity, purposes, and so forth had to be given a common meaning and focus. Alexander Hamilton, summarizing the constitutional convention's aims in the *Federalist* (including, grandly, "to vindicate the honor of the human race"), concluded that "Union will enable us to do it."[20] Second, much as intellectuals today labor to inject communal phrases into national discourse—"new covenant," civil society, "a politics of meaning"[21]—efforts to unify the American colonies and then states depended in important ways on language to do so.

Notably, union ideas helped constitute the republic itself, which was called "the Union" as early as 1775. American revolutionaries turned first to words for mutual succor. They *declared* independence, capping an oratorical revolution only later confirmed in blood and iron, and insisted repeatedly that colonists' united resolve would ensure their success. The bulk of revolutionary activities—boy-

---

18. Connolly 1974, 36. Melvin Richter similarly describes concepts as "contested intellectual constructions, which both register and shape what changes and what persists in the structure of societies" (Richter 1990, 41). For conceptual studies of American political history, see Rodgers 1987 and the essays in Ball et al. 1989.
19. Shaftesbury 1963 [1711], 3:248.
20. Rossiter 1961, 91.
21. For a recent summary of such attempts, see Jensen 1998.

cotts, riots, economic exchanges, criticism of British officials, Tea Parties—were local in origin. Until reported widely and interpreted in context, these appeared a constellation of unconnected events. Describing them as the work of a "united" people was a primary source of interpersonal bonds. Similar discursive effects are apparent for decades thereafter, as union talk was a basic inspiration for Americans' spirit of common identity—even as the term's meaning shifted in various directions. A national imagined community, in Benedict Anderson's apt phrase, was fostered by the affective sentiments Americans professed for one another, extending and enhancing the sense of allegiance they expressed toward their amorphous collective whole.[22]

Declaring a national union and a united people was one matter; as Page Smith writes, "it was something vastly more complex to accomplish it."[23] In the struggle to secure a unified republic in practice, union talk was also instrumental. The first several numbers of the *Federalist*, as Hamilton noted in the initial paper, were devoted to explicating the "utility of the Union" to institutional objects like national defense, facilitating economic exchange, and adjudicating quarrels between the states.[24] Phrases like "cementing the union" subsequently were used to promote a range of national government activities before the Civil War. Among these administrative achievements were establishing national communication via the post office and, later, railroads and telegraph; expanding and defending U.S. territory; and undertaking huge programs of internal improvements, as public works were then termed. These add up to considerably more than the negligible production of a weak antebellum state. Also abundant were postwar connections between (re)union ideas and concrete institutional activities, such as Supreme Court efforts to delineate formally the nature of relations between states and the collectivity they created; and a sentimental unionism that may have prompted states to agree on a uniform national date for elections to the U.S. House of Representatives. It cannot be proved that union (or any other) ideas "caused" these outcomes, of course; but attention to the ways in which leading actors attempted to justify their actions testifies to union's influential place in political practice as well as theory.

In numerous ways, then, union ideas were a vital source of the "glue" that held "otherwise atomistic and self-interested individuals together in an organized society." Union rhetoric had a legitimate role in what Stephen Skowronek terms the "production of order, system, and equilibrium." Consider, by way of analogy, courts and political parties, the two main national institutions of nineteenth-century America. Like parties, the concept of union was a key source of intersectional ties, and served as both a symbol capable of inspiring mass political action (as the Civil War powerfully demonstrated) and a programmatic instrument. Exemplifying the latter function were the policies associated with Henry

22. Anderson 1983.
23. Smith 1980, xvii.
24. Rossiter 1961, 36.

Clay's "American System," defended by Clay and fellow Whigs as "the basis of our union." Like courts, union stood as a central *rhetorical* institution . . . deeply embedded in categories of political discourse."[25] Though scholars usually observe a separation between ideas and institutions, from the antebellum years through Reconstruction the notion of national union served purposes associated with both.

Was "the Union" merely a stand-in for the 1780s–1880s American national state? No, if we follow prevailing understanding and view the state as a legal and institutional apparatus that constitutes the central government. "Union" and "state" or "government" were generally kept separate in period speech, by Hamiltonian centralists and southern states' rights advocates alike. Common usage placed the Union above or beyond the local/state and federal governments, mediating between both. This balancing function, transcending sectional, regional, and other cleavages, became over time a definitional property of union. Appeals to unity provided a constraint on actors who were inclined to expand central-government regulatory and welfare activities, and also were voiced against efforts to emphasize the autonomy of individual states. When at the height of the nullification crisis Andrew Jackson opened John C. Calhoun's state-sovereignty "Jefferson Birthday Dinner" with the stern toast "Our Union: It must be preserved," the words held much more than metaphysical import for Calhoun and other secession-minded guests. "[A]n order to arrest Calhoun where he sat," wrote one attendee, "could not have come with more blinding, staggering force."[26]

Understanding union as period thinkers did, as a symbolic source of loyalty and a concrete instrument of political power, helps clarify key features of nineteenth-century nation building. The U.S. national state was not "enfeebled" in the sense many scholars describe, though its welfare and regulatory functions lagged far behind those of European countries. American leaders, citing the need for stronger national unity, linked state functions and local civil-society activities in a mutually supportive fashion, albeit one little endorsed in present political theory. Pre–Civil War administrative activity was no mere staging ground on the way to a fully realized national state, as is often claimed today;[27] rather, it reflected a deliberate commitment to a balanced, middle-level form of governance. Unionist ideas were an important ingredient in early political development, girding and underpinning emerging national institutions. Whether the result constituted a robust avenue to wider political participation, as some early Americans believed, or an inadequate, incoherent response to demands for national regulatory control, as political historians now assert, is taken up in the subsequent chapters of this book.

25. Shepsle 1989, 2; Skowronek 1993, 93; Hopkins et al. 1959–92, 8:242–44; Skocpol 1992, 371.
26. Sellers 1991, 315.
27. See, e.g., Bensel: "Other than . . . pleas for a return to 'the Constitution as it was,' *the modern state's inheritance from the antebellum was nil.* In that sense, then, an account of American state formation can begin with the Civil War with little lost in historical continuity or theoretical generality" (1991, ix; emphasis added).

Contemporary Relevance

With the American national fabric showing signs of strain today, practitioners and scholars alike are turning anew to questions of political unity. But contemporary ways of addressing the topic—by encouraging a more robust national
patriotism in some quarters, or by insisting on fuller protection of carefully specified group rights in others—seem disturbingly inadequate. Among conservatives promoting shared moral values, moderates invoking "a new union of cultural and economic nationalism in the interest of the transracial middle class,"
and leftists both Old and New bemoaning "the disuniting of America" and "the
twilight of common dreams,"[28] much current commentary poses society's "fundamental challenge" as "identify[ing] the sources of unity in a democratic multi-
nation state."[29] Particularly at issue in such searches are conceptions of national
membership and identity that can balance different allegiances within a reasonably coherent whole—much as past unionists once sought to do, with some success. Thus union ideas, to the extent they represented a more complex conception of unified yet distinct political identities, may be of service once again.

Mining the past for useful verities is an uncertain venture, of course.[30] Among
American political historians such exercises have been frequently mounted in
search of past national community, with at best mixed results. It is true that few
historians now describe the early United States as a consensual polity: exclusionary tendencies, mutual suspicions, and cultural differences between groups and
sections are all richly chronicled.[31] Still, wistful invocations of a cohesive American past, variously located at points ranging from the revolution (said to have
forged a "civic covenant . . . bonded by patriot blood") to the advent of industrialism, remain commonplace. Such portraits are generally juxtaposed with deep concerns about the modern possibility of maintaining a collective national whole.[32]

Although I acknowledge the perils of reasoning by historical analogy, I believe
that the history traced herein offers useful recommendations for the present.
Rather than exhibiting decisive evidence of a strong or weak communal past, the
study of union yields more nuanced lessons. An initial conclusion is that affirmations of shared values and interpersonal ties can themselves serve as bases of common sentiment, providing a foundation for more substantive policies of inclusion. Hence the potential strength of testaments by presidents and other national
leaders, pledging "the faith that our nation can summon from its myriad diver-

28. Lind 1995, 15; Schlesinger 1992; Gitlin 1995.
29. Kymlicka 1995, 192. A recent ambitious multiauthor study of "American political culture" was
titled *The State of Disunion* (Hunter 1996).
30. Compare Quentin Skinner's insistence that past philosophy "cannot be concerned with our
questions and answers, but only with their own . . . there are only individual answers to individual
questions" (1969, 50).
31. Smith 1997 (on ascriptive exclusion in the early republic); Bensel 1984 (on sectionalism);
Elazar 1972b, 93–125, and 1992, 193–97 (on distinct regional political cultures in the United States).
32. Sullivan 1982, 193. See the similar, if less purple, accounts of a unified early United States in
Pocock 1975, 506–52; Wills 1981, 258–67; Bellah et al. 1985, esp. 252–56; Morris 1987; Schlesinger 1992;
Rahe 1992; R. J. Ellis 1993, esp. 8–16; and Lind 1995, 21–36.

sity the deepest measure of unity," or urging "never before have we had such a blessed opportunity—and, therefore, such a profound obligation—to build the more perfect union of our founders' dreams."[33]

Yet such appeals often ring hollow, in part because modern political rhetoric rarely strikes authentic communal chords. Linguistic historian James Darsey describes current public speech as "almost apolitical, perhaps even antipolitical, in that it addresses the multitude as a mass of individuals, not as a political unity. Its appeal is not to *de cive* but to each person as a maker of his or her destiny. It is a rhetoric of disengagement."[34] This book illustrates that union ideas once were more persuasively promoted, even alongside individualist themes (as by Emerson, for example). On a different front, however, past American leaders usually extolled national unity without acting to bring it about. A recounting of missed opportunities, especially to realize the more inclusive polity implicit in the term, may provide useful illumination of similar present policies, and even help identify the roots of today's public fragmentation.

Further implications for the present arise from the chapters that follow. For one, the tendency among scholars and political practitioners to strictly separate the spheres of state and civil society may be misguided. Unionists during the first century of the nation's existence were inclined to advocate a mutual empowerment of national state and local associational groups, rather than contrasting the two. National administrative capacity was harnessed to ends we now view as the province of civil society—a policy then defended, again, in terms of enhancing union. Such a commitment appears even among states' rights southerners, before and after the Civil War.

Another implication concerns the demise of a central, multidimensional concept like "union." The term referred to a balance between conflicting interests, or a combination of separate elements; at times Americans juxtaposed this unionist understanding to concepts of "nation," which suggests a stronger homogenizing effect. Union's disappearance from common use left Americans with a diminished basis for discussing, much less alleviating, particular political dilemmas that had been subsumed in the term. Investigating the decline of this balancing concept highlights apparently intractable tensions (e.g., between individual rights and national obligations) in modern U.S. politics.

A further lesson of the past concerns the potency of religious talk in the public sphere. Even a "secular" value like national union drew meaning and strength from association with religious themes, as will be discussed. For those who consider religion to be too dangerously illiberal to serve as a source of national identity, the point is that *some* connection to popular vernacular is essential to a concept's widespread purchase. Opinion leaders who opt instead for constructing ideal

33. Quoted from Clinton's first inaugural address, *New York Times,* January 21, 1993, A11, and final State of the Union appearance, *New York Times,* January 28, 2000, A16. See also Clinton's late-term statement that "If I could give America just one gift, it would be the ability to be *one America." Washington Post,* October 30, 1999, A9 (emphasis added).

34. Darsey 1997, 184.

speech communities based on rational deliberation, or even for spinning lapsarian tales of golden fraternal ages in the past, do little to inspire stronger bonds between citizens. Meanwhile, as countless episodes in the nation's past testify, those bonds may be constructed by others, often in cruelly exclusionary ways.[35]

This history leads many moderns to regard union talk with skepticism or even distaste. Wayne Fields notes that "union . . . is a thing we are sometimes inclined to distrust," especially in an age keenly aware of fraternal nationalism's dangerous excesses.[36] As is detailed throughout this book, past U.S. leaders often did neglect personal liberty—of women, blacks, Native Americans, dispossessed white men—in favor of achieving national unity, elevating that communal good above individual rights and otherwise failing to transcend the prejudices of their time. Yet the visions of Madison, Webster, Douglass, Lincoln, and others explored in this book also suggest that the history of American political thought—alongside its ascriptive themes—includes benign, even inspiring accounts of national unity that were well tested in practice. Those trying to promote political and social integration in the American (or any other) nation would be well served to recall the constructive ideas of our predecessors, even as we continue to address their shortcomings.

DEFINING THE TERMS OF UNION

Attempts to describe American ideas of union in a concise definition are likely to fail. The term was variously used to denote bonds among people, within and across state lines; collections of Americans, gathered in everything from self-help associations to national political parties and eventually a Union Army; the territory they occupied, commonly called "the Union" during the nation's first century; a desirable national value, ranked alongside liberty or equality; and a federalist system of government. (It also had important connotations in other realms, from religious to marital, but political union is the focus here.) Union signified both inclusion and alienation: it served as the primary referent for patriotic belonging among many Americans, but others—especially blacks—invoked the term to contrast national ideals with unsalutary practice. As Eric Foner remarks of liberty, it is "pointless to attempt to identify a single 'real' meaning against which others are to be judged."[37] Understanding the term's multiple uses in American political history thus begins not with an abstract definition or ideal type, but with the term's linguistic origins.

Like the majority of English words, "union" derives from Latin. The original *unus,* "one," spawned in Late Latin *unio,* "unity," which initially applied to a group of people combining for religious or martial purposes. That linguistic stem

35. A thorough accounting of ascriptive nationalist appeals from colonial times to the early twentieth century is in Smith 1997.

36. Fields 1996, 19.

37. Foner 1998, xiv.

produced a group of related English terms, which are used interchangeably in this study: union, unite, united, unity. "Community" is a relatively distant cognate, deriving from the Latin *communis*, "common." Interestingly, "nation" has an entirely different stem: *natio* in ordinary usage referred to a collection of people related by birth, usually a group of foreigners.

"Union" appeared among English speakers sometime in the thirteenth century, and by the 1400s had acquired a specific political sense, referring to domestic relations among citizens.[38] When Shakespeare wrote a century and a half later of "the unity and married calm of states," few in his audiences would have tripped over the trope.[39] In Elizabethan political usage union had *legal* and *binary* connotations: separate states, or citizens of a polity, were "united" when they contractually declared themselves to be. The thirteenth-century Union of Kalmar joining Scandinavian nations, the political unity existing among Welshmen or Englishmen, the United Netherlands—each was conventionally counted as a political union because (some of) their constituent members agreed that it was one, and sealed the arrangement in formal legal terms. The result was binary, in that potential members were either included in the legally defined union or considered outsiders. This straightforward account left open more interesting particulars, however. How was a union established in the first place? Who decided when a union was formed, or who was included; and when was a *union* achieved, as opposed to a mere league or confederation?[40] How much active dissent was required to dissolve an arrangement like Kalmar—or England's unions with Scotland and Wales? Conversely, how strong must interpersonal ties be to sustain unity within a nation?

These questions were addressed by several writers and speakers in the Atlantic realm, helping shape a familiar rhetoric of political union. During debates on Anglo-Scottish relations in 1646, a Parliamentary member exclaimed, "let us hold fast that union which is happily established between us; and let nothing make us again two, who are in so many ways one; all of one language, in one island, all under one King, one in religion, yea, one in covenant, so that in effect we differ in nothing but in name—as brethren do."[41] Related theoretical treatments included John Locke's depiction of the associative obligations incurred among members of a polity, descending from a consensual national founding; and James Harrington's close union of virtuous citizens, bound by a passionate love of country. Both these conceptions may be at least vaguely traced among Americans contemplating the subject during and after their revolution. But the ideas informing the usage of the term in the United States include sources not often recognized by conventional scholarship, and were mingled in ways better

38. Oxford English Dictionary, 2d ed., s.v. "union."
39. *Troilus and Cressida*, act 1, scene 3., in Staunton 1874, 5:307.
40. Meaningful distinctions were then (and are still) made in English among various collective designations. See, e.g., Safire (1991, 18), who ranks eleven such terms based on the strength of the bonds they denote. "Union," he writes, signifies the "strongest" ties among a people or group of states.
41. Marquis of Argyll, quoted in Murdoch 1998, 23.

described in metallurgical terms—creating a fundamentally altered alloy—than in terms of weaving together separate doctrinal strands, a favored motif among conceptual historians.

Nationalism, Federalism, and Union

Studies of nationalism and federalism in the U.S. context are important sources of inspiration for the present work, and in many ways union ideas exist at the intersection of these two "isms." Yet neither fully describes the concept of union. Although union ideas were integral to the constitution of an American nation, meaningful analytic distinctions between union and nationalism are evident in the U.S. past. "Nation," after all, was long an abhorrent term to many Americans. Well into the 1860s, writes Elizabeth Meehan, the "equivalent of 'the F-word' was 'the N-word.'" While public speakers during and after the founding period used both terms interchangeably, union was seen as an alternative source of national identification among a sizeable body of the population. Only after the Civil War would sentiments like "This is a Nation, not simply a Union" be voiced, testifying to a substantive distinction between the two.[42] As for federalism, this innovative division of governing authority describes an important institutional feature underlying unionist ideas but says little or nothing about why the notion of union was so appealing to Americans of all persuasions (including both "Federalists" and "anti-Federalists") or what it signified beyond a method of balancing and sharing power.

Nationalist and federalist principles, along with their leading modern interpreters, appear repeatedly in the pages that follow. But this work's specific focus on union frequently points in directions not typically explored by theorists of either nationalism or federalism. This is partly because both are complex, analytically sprawling concepts in their own right,[43] and their specification is sometimes only tangentially related to American unionists' concerns. Moreover, at times union ideas are in direct conflict with nationalism and/or federalism. In most of Europe, for example, a strong central state was a hallmark of nineteenth-century nationalism: hence the astonishment of a Hegel or Marx (and some modern scholars) at Americans' vigorous expressions of national identity despite a lack of supporting centralized administration.[44] Even Americans' earliest conceptions of union, in seventeenth-century experiments like the United Colonies of New England, featured substantial barriers to centralized administration. The constitutional union established by the American founders in 1789 was organized as a power-sharing arrangement, enabling joint authority within a flexible system of

---

42. Meehan 1996, 107; Delaware writer Howard Jenkins, cited in Hyman 1967, 460.

43. For a succinct overview of nationalist theory over the past thirty years or so, emphasizing continued vagueness in scholarly treatments of nationalism, see Tambini 1999. A similarly useful summary of the federalist "paradigm" is in Elazar 1996. See also, on the complex legal characterization of federalism, Powell 1993b.

44. On the "marriage of nation and state," see, e.g., Gellner 1983; Breuilly 1982; van Creveld 1999, 193–205 (quote at p. 195).

N.B.

partnership and mutual checks between states and nation. Among most nation-builders, from the French Revolution's leaders through to Mazzini and other nineteenth-century revolutionaries into our own time, circumscribed central authority was seen as an unfortunate byproduct of internal fragmentation and a source of future divisions (Mazzini, e.g., saw the U.S. polity as dangerously friable).[45] Romanticism, another prominent source of nationalist consciousness elsewhere, similarly had weak purchase among most U.S. political thinkers. Liah Greenfeld lists the "basic tendencies" of "Pieto-Romantic" nationalism, including rejection of modernity, renunciation of individual autonomy, yearning for violent social transformation, and "emphasis on the primacy of intellectuals." None of these, it may safely be said, was a salient feature of nineteenth-century American thought.[46]

While unionist themes at times contradicted nationalist or federalist theory, this work's focus on union also illuminates aspects of the latter persuasions in useful ways. For example, a basic dichotomy in much federalist writing concerns how to draw explicit lines between localist authority, exercised through self-governing civil society arrangements, and national power usually wielded by governing elites. Recognizing past American unionists' attempt to harmonize state functions and civil-society activity helps resolve this dilemma, as explored in detail in later chapters.

The United States, like all nations, was constructed over time, a process requiring rhetorical affirmation and reproduction. That activity is often the concern of the following pages, which trace the conceptual as well as practical creation of one "united American people." Some of the best work in nationalist studies is based on such a conceptual approach, and I build on those insights here.[47] But where theorists of nationalism see these inventions as molded primarily by the central state, or by insistence on a single ethnicity,[48] I hope to show that building an American union was a process featuring a much wider range of contributors.

More generally, Americans' distinctive unionist self-conception is impossible to comprehend if union talk is viewed simply as a marker for (or minor subspecies of) nationalism or federalism. Students of historical political thought distinguish carefully between most other core concepts, after all: democracy and equality are superficially synonyms—and were often registered as such in the early republic—but a massive literature points out their nuanced differences. Similar value lies in treating union separately from "nation" or "federal." Identifying these semantic differences is inevitably an interpretative act, inasmuch as few speakers in the early republic bothered to distinguish consistently between union, government, nationalism, and federalism. Many people applied these terms indis-

45. Mazzini's negative view of the U.S. system, and of federalism generally, is well chronicled in Haddock 1999, 323, 328–32.
46. Greenfeld 1992, 154–60, 184–86, 360–95 (quote at pp. 386–87).
47. E.g., Anderson 1983.
48. On "ethnic" nationalism, see especially Smith 1986, 13–18, 22–33, 153–73 ("Without ethnie and ethnicism, there could be neither nations nor nationalism," [156]); Greenfeld 1992, 11–12; or Staub 1997, 214–15, 223–25.

criminately; others were only slightly more precise, as when an Indiana writer declared "Union means what I wish it to mean [in my writing], no more or less."[49]
The chapters that follow try to sort out intentions and applications as clearly as
possible.

✳

This study of American union ideas proceeds chronologically, beginning with
the colonial period.[50] Chapter 1 explores the concept's early foundations among
colonial and revolutionary-era thinkers, tracing union's evolution to two separate
sources—Christian accounts of congregationalist unity, and an anti-British
spirit that inspired attempts to define the colonies as a political entity separate
from the "motherland." Most constituent features of European nations' development—common ethnicity, universal historical traditions and rituals, a national church, public education systems, economic integration, a dominant central state—were absent in the late-eighteenth-century United States. Union's
promoters offered early visions of an inclusive national civic culture, one that was
differentiated from the British identity most colonists held dear and was capable
of attracting the allegiance of German and other non-Anglo immigrants.

The next three chapters review attempts to define and create a more perfect
union during, respectively, the founding, Jacksonian, and antebellum/Civil War
eras. James Madison's tripartite understanding of sustainable union, centered on
territorial, affective, and representative sources, remained salient into the 1850s.
Despite sweeping social and political changes, figures as diverse as Emerson and
Daniel Webster were essentially faithful to Madison's unionist view. Amid antebellum clashes over slavery, tariff rates, and other burning issues, however, "sustainable" increasingly took on an unconditional meaning, whereby national
union was preserved at any price. Separate unionist understandings also developed, with various groups insisting on pushing a restrictive ethnocultural basis
for national belonging: chapter 3 outlines this history. Others, particularly African Americans and some white abolitionists, sought to reconceive the term as a
moral instrument, adapting the immense popularity of union ideas to antislavery ends. Chapter 4 recounts this development among black leaders, especially
Douglass, and assesses Lincoln's reinterpretation of the term. Lincoln advocated
a more forthrightly moral unionism while jettisoning the notion that Americans
in different sections exhibited anything like "affection" for one another, replac-
ing it with a strict insistence on rule of law. Together these three chapters demonstrate that union came to be a sacrosanct principle among Americans of virtually all backgrounds and mind-sets, if for widely varying reasons and in the
service of very different ends.

Also under investigation in the book's middle section are two points about the

49. *Indianapolis Tribune*, August 19, 1838.
50. This temporal organization is primarily for analytical convenience: different periods in U.S.
history overlap and spill across chapters in conformity with the ideas and events the book chronicles.

development of America's administrative state. Chapter 3 assesses the ways in which antebellum federal activities, from expanding networks of roads and canals to an elaborate pension system for Revolutionary War veterans, were defended in unionist terms. In subsequent chapters I trace the contrast between union ideas' widespread popularity and the meager efforts of public officials to create national union along "more perfect" institutional and moral lines.

Union ideas retained high popular salience after the Civil War, even among many former southern Confederates. Investigating applications of the concept after 1865 helps explain aspects of American political history that otherwise seem jarringly incongruous, especially against a backdrop of liberal or strong-communitarian traditions. One such paradox is how the North's military triumph, heralded as the crowning achievement of American nationhood, could be so swiftly followed by an abandonment of many of the supposed fruits of victory. Chapter 5 examines this phenomenon through the prism of union's enduring appeal. It appears that desires for reunion came to overshadow such other goods as civil equality and economic justice; association of these values with federal guarantees to blacks was countered, in important part, by a surge of anti-federal rationales that were justified as essential to maintaining a reunited country. It may be true that, as Eric Foner argues, "The Union's triumph [in the Civil War] consolidated the northern understanding of freedom as the national norm," but within a few years southerners had successfully restored a prewar, balanced understanding of union as a competing standard.[51]

This reassertion of "the Union as it was," chiefly by white southerners, ultimately hastened the concept's departure from the realm of purposeful political talk. Toward the end of Reconstruction, as detailed in chapter 6, African Americans and Radical Republicans were the first groups to abandon the term, recognizing (and signaling) an end to hopes for a more moral union. Two other factors later turned most other Americans away from national-union talk of all varieties, beginning in the mid-1880s: a wave of "new immigrants" from southern and central Europe, and Gilded Age class conflicts in the United States. Mass immigration sparked increasing resistance to the idea of a common, affectively united American people, and the growth of organized labor in response to class dissension and economic upheaval established a novel mass understanding of union as synonymous with *labor* unions. By the 1890s, the rhetorical and practical commitment by Americans to traditional ideas of political union had all but vanished. Partly as a result, unqualified versions of a celebratory nationalism, including imperialist trappings, appeared throughout the country.

This history of union's rise and fall deserves attention not only for its importance in U.S. political development. The concept has renewed relevance in the present climate of globalization, multiculturalism, and recalibrated governmental responsibilities. With Americans increasingly wrestling with questions of na-

51. Foner 1998, 97.

tional unity, this idea's time may have come again. Accordingly, in a concluding chapter past applications of union are examined in the context of present theoretical and practical efforts to conceive a stronger sense of national civic identity.

A NOTE ON METHOD

Various methodological approaches are combined in this book, in order to best reconstruct how a particular concept was understood and utilized by a broad range of the population across a substantial stretch of American history. I began by studying primary sources, imposing order on this process where possible; my hope was to avoid a list of citations that resembled, in one historian's rueful description, a "random scattering from hither and yon."[52] I relied on a large sample of newspapers, diaries, and official speeches—discussed further in a moment—for popular views, and studied several representative thinkers' collected papers for each period. I also drew on secondary monographs, attempting a measure of organization by reading prominent general histories, both recent and older works, of each period: Elkins and McKitrick as well as Miller for the Federalist era; Foner, Stampp, Franklin, Saville, and Ayers on Reconstruction and its aftermath; and so forth. The results of this approach are chronicled in the footnotes.

Second, I engaged in political-theory analysis of union ideas. Intellectual history is often told as a succession of battles between incommensurate and clearly defined rival paradigms. But Americans applied "union" as a political word almost willy-nilly, within ideological contexts themselves governed by myriad fault lines. Different conceptual applications rarely appeared in neatly opposing form. Hence I move between specific thinkers' accounts of union and the more general perceptions expressed by broader groups, providing diverse reconstructions of the word's principal manifestations.

Specialists in American political thought may be skeptical of my downplaying the influence of Anglo/European thinkers and paradigms on a vital American idea like union. I engage that issue at various points in the chapters below, attempting a middle course between two scholarly approaches to American political thought. Many theorists purportedly concerned with the founders' ideological outlook are so devoted to specifying sources and influences that the Americans "inheriting" European legacies recede into near passivity—the trees of American nuance disappear in a forest of expatriated paradigms. On the other hand, some reactions to a quarter century of debate over liberal and republican inheritance tend toward such conclusions as "to discover the Constitution, we must approach it without the assistance of guides imported from another time and place."[53] This pendulum has swung too far, overlooking the founders' actual

52. Saum 1980, vi.
53. Ackerman 1991, 3.

relationship to their intellectual forebears. The figures and ideas reviewed in chapters to come are treated not as unimpeachable influences, but as they appeared to eighteenth-century Americans: valuable sources for political consultation, but not especially relevant to a New World context, or requiring considerable adaptation before their application.

Along with analysis of union as a concept, I attempt to investigate its past applications in practice, among members of the population not often given to abstract theorizing. To that end, I also studied union usage empirically. I developed a database of union references, drawn from a comprehensive sample of newspapers, as described in the appendix. These organs are a useful guide to popular opinion as far back as the late colonial period. Widely read among America's developing "informed citizenry,"[54] they are our best available window on the attitudes and language of a large portion of the population. In a few instances I supplemented the newspapers with such other sources as congressional speeches or private diaries, both for variety's sake and to minimize any peculiarities of journalistic language. As it turned out, patterns of union usage differ little between newspaper and non-newspaper sources.

Armed with this sample, I counted references to union (and, in some periods, other national referents such as "nation," "country," "America," etc.) in editorial and news content for all newspapers and journals, based on a method outlined in the appendix. I then summed yearly totals for "union" references, and divided by total pages of editorial/news sampled for that year. This provided a running ratio of union usage, which is presented graphically at a number of points in the book. Other applications of my newspaper research appear as well, mostly in the form of illustrative quotations, but also as additional data sources. Overall, the exercise provided an informal sense of union usage across place and time, as I read through the papers.

*

Pelatiah Webster, concluding his "Dissertation on the [American] Political Union" in 1783, declared "'Tis now at our option, either to fall back into our original atoms, or form such a union as shall command the respect of the world, and give honor and security to all our people." More than two centuries later, Webster and a host of other unionist voices deserve rehearing. Union talk was often a combination of bombastic praise and maudlin sentiment, fitting Jürgen Habermas's characterization of "rhetoric" as "empty talk or ideologically distorted communication."[55] But this concept's power to move people to act politically was remarkable. Perhaps the most striking feature of the antebellum United States was

54. Brown 1996, 28–30, 44–46. See also Waldstreicher's account of newspapers as "constitut[ing] a national popular political culture" in Waldstreicher 1997, quote at p. 12, and see also pp. 45–46, 110–11, 227–29; Anderson 1983; and K. K. Smith 1999, 94–95, 124–27.
55. Webster 1783, 30; Habermas in Hohmann 1998, 362.

that it held together at all, given the enormous stresses and strains exerted by sectional, regional, and local differences, along with a host of divisive issues. Americans embraced the idea of union as a major source of continuing national coherence; for a time, with its aid, their aspirations were reasonably well fulfilled. How this initially became possible is the subject of the next chapter.

CHAPTER I

The Rhetorical Genesis
of American Political Union

I cannot but take notice how wonderfully Providence has smiled upon us by causing the several colonies to unite so firmly together against the tyranny of Great Britain, though differing from each other in their particular interest, forms of government, modes of worship, and particular customs and manners, besides several animosities that had subsisted among them. That, under these circumstances, such a union should take place as we now behold, was a thing that might rather have been wished than hoped for.

—Samuel West, "Sermon Preached before
the Honorable Council," 1776

America's . . . miraculous Union proves beyond all doubt [that] *saying* a thing is so can sometimes *make* it so.

—"A Mechanic," in *New-York Weekly Journal* (Albany), 1775

FORGING A POLITICAL union among thirteen diverse colonies grouped in four distinct regions—making one out of many—was the "chief problem" facing the revolutionary generation in the United States, and arguably its primary achievement. But how to explain the accomplishment? A half century after Hans Kohn called the "formation of an American nation out of so many disparate elements" a virtual "miracle," leading students of the period can point to little more resolution. "We do not really understand," writes Michael Zuckerman, how a "congeries of colonies which had displayed no previous gift for cooperation ever acted together so effectively in 1776 or stayed together afterward"—the fact, indeed, is "all but inexplicable."[1]

Efforts to explain Americans' original movement toward a unified polity nevertheless exist aplenty and usually follow disciplinary lines. Economists emphasize the importance of trade and other economic networks as sources of inter-

1. Arendt 1963, 152; Kohn 1944, 285; Zuckerman 1991, 170 (cf. Morone 1990, 53). Many observers at the time viewed matters similarly, such as one American marveling in 1774 at the "remarkable and unexpected union . . . throughout all the colonies." Quoted in Wood 1969, 102; cf. Smith 1980, 1–22. Note that this question about union's origins differs in emphasis from (though is invariably bound up with) historians' investigation into why the American colonists *rebelled* against Britain. It is possible that America could have won independence and still split into several smaller confederations.

colonial exchanges.[2] Political historians and social scientists note the binding force of events like war and tax increases, and sometimes of nascent American institutions.[3] Ideological historians reconstruct various paradigmatic "pattern[s] of ideas and attitudes" that informed colonists' steps toward union.[4] Though varying widely in their accounts of how the colonies came to be united, most of these studies focus on the years immediately preceding independence, not the earlier colonial past. As historian David Fagg writes, "It may be possible to view instances of cooperative action as presaging eventual union, but few historians will be convinced that the exploration of blind alleys from 1690 to 1763 made a major contribution to the dynamics of the American unity which emerged after 1763."[5] This attitude is widely shared. Most scholars insist that there was little significant national or even regional sentiment until the revolution and that colonial America comprised hundreds of intensely local communities linked (if at all) by fealty to Britain. Each town, concludes Kenneth Lockridge, was a "self-contained social unit, almost hermetically sealed off from the rest of the world."[6]

Yet across these homogeneous, fiercely autonomous "units," colonists advocated union with those outside their local community long before the independence movement was born in the 1760s. American officials proposed formally to unite several or all colonies as early as the 1630s; the United Colonies of New England, established in 1643, lasted more than forty years. Appeals to intercolonial union appear regularly in colonial newspapers, pamphlets, sermons, and other writings during the seventeenth and eighteenth centuries. Such references, many decades before any "nationalist" ideas were detectable among colonists,[7] represent a developing language of political unity. Though not originally a challenge to British rule, this union talk engendered serious friction between Britain and America during the revolutionary crisis and served as a vital unifying force in the early republic.

Reconstructing the *conceptual* development of union illuminates Americans' national-communal roots from a new explanatory direction. The initial unifica-

---

2. Summarizing a wide range of economic historical writing, James Shepherd (1988, 17) writes that Americans' "economic independence" was the "likely prerequisite" for political unity. See also Breen 1994, 448, 474.

3. See, e.g., Jack Greene's claim that political disagreements between England and British America, culminating in war, "push[ed] American resistance leaders in the direction of a permanent national continental union" (1986, 174). Other notable political-institutional arguments for union's origins are in Tucker and Hendrickson 1982; Rakove 1979; Onuf 1983; Koenigsberger 1989; and Draper 1996.

4. Bailyn 1967, 54; see also Edmund Morgan's earlier assertion that defense of bedrock constitutional principles bred a sense of solidarity among colonists (1963). Rodgers 1992 summarizes the explosion of subsequent writing on ideological bases of the U.S. republic.

5. Fagg 1971, 403; see also Steele 1998, 71–72. Affirms Gordon Wood in a related context: "many historians in the past several decades have ceased looking to the colonial period for the origins or roots of the United States" (1995, 693).

6. Lockridge 1970, 64; compare Robert Middlekauff: "The colonies at mid-[eighteenth] century apparently could not attain even rudimentary unity, or at least showed no desire to attain it" (1982, 28).

7. Compare, among many such accounts, Clark 1994, 57: "Powerful barriers checked the development of an American nationalism before 1776."

tion of a polity characterized by one early observer as a "logocracy—a republic of words"[8] can be better understood by exploring why Americans declared themselves united and their corporate body a union. Charting this concept's meaning in the colonial era, and its influence on political talk during the revolution, helps make sense of late-eighteenth-century pledges to form a "more perfect union." Preceding the growth of close economic ties or common institutions, the discourse of national union provided a way for British America's culturally diverse—and geographically dispersed—residents to conceive of themselves as one people.

This chapter analyzes the emergence of union as one of the republic's most important political concepts, from the early colonial period to 1776. My aim is not to retrace the history leading to independence and confederation but more specifically to understand how *union* came to be the term of American commonality and how colonial speakers applied it. Based on the nature and patterns of its usage, three conclusions are advanced below. First, union was established as a term for affective interpersonal relations and for interstate alliances early in the colonial period. Americans from Roger Williams to Benjamin Franklin, and many Britons as well, promoted unity among the colonies long before a split from Britain was even contemplated.

Second, a distinctive decline-and-surge pattern marks references to pan-American union during the revolutionary crisis (1763–76), in response to British Ministry efforts to suppress the term. This little-noted history testifies to the power of language to shape political realities. As early as the 1740s, British officials worried about the explosive potential of American efforts at closer unity. Amid the tumult following the Royal Proclamation (1763) and Grenville Acts (1764–65), British leaders sought to promulgate a very different meaning for union, as a codeword for colonists' subordinate place in the empire. Given these high stakes, many politically active Americans avoided the term in their public speech after 1765 or adopted England's prescribed usage. Only on the eve of revolution were joint colonial efforts again widely described in terms of union. By 1775, even anti-nationalists like Patrick Henry joined the chorus: "I am not a Virginian, but an American. . . . All distinctions are thrown down. All America is thrown into one united mass."[9]

A third, more general claim is that the origins of American national unity were in important part rhetorical, alongside the more exhaustively explored economic, institutional, and ideological sources summarized above. To be sure, this discursive approach resembles arguments that ideas chiefly inspired national unity. But American leaders did not derive union talk from reasoned commitments to Lockean liberalism, civic republicanism, or other paradigms. Instead they were spurred by two comparatively "irrational" influences: religious doctrine

---

8. Washington Irving in Rodgers 1987, 7. Wayne Fields (1996) similarly terms the U.S. republic a "union of words."
9. Henry quoted in Mason 1950, 506.

and, as the crisis crested, anti-British fervor. I contend that union resonated deeply in each of these discourses and that the term therefore gained pride of place where others—republic, empire, commonwealth, state, nation—instead might have.

In short, a real contest developed around union's meaning during the years leading to independence. This was less a clash of grand ideologies than a battle about who was "united" to whom: Americans to Britain, like child and mother, as Britons insisted? Or colonists with one another, as Americans claimed before 1763 and after 1774? The terms of union constituted a genuine ground of difference at a time when colonists shared the British understanding of most other core political values. This conceptual divergence helped fuel the much bloodier conflict that followed. My recounting of that development begins with the religious basis of union talk and then turns to the term's vital place in early American political discourse.

RELIGIOUS UNIONS

A familiar British American sermon text from Puritan to revolutionary times was *Zechariah* 11, which recounts Jerusalem's destruction through the parable of a shepherd pasturing his flock. Using a pair of staffs, "one [called] Grace and the other Union," the shepherd governs peaceably until the staff of Union is broken—representing divine rejection of God's chosen people because of their factional divisions. The message to colonial congregations was clear. "Remain as one people," sermonized a Boston minister in 1743, and "we shall be . . . our Lord's favored flock." Well into the 1750s, by far the most common invocations of union in British America were religious, heard from Anglicans, Presbyterians, and Separate Baptists in southern and middle colonies as well as from New England's Puritans and Congregationalists. Such usage, casually mingling church and state, dates from John Winthrop's "city on a hill" lay sermon aboard the *Arbella,* extolling "the unity of the spirit in the bond of peace" and urging that "we must be knit together in this work as one man." [10] To understand the conceptual development of American political union, we must turn first to religious rhetoric.

Religious Union in History
Early Christians, following Jewish practice, established "moral communities" among fellow worshipers, differentiated from their towns or villages and joined by bonds of exclusive communal fellowship. As Adam Seligman writes, this was

10. *Christian History,* March 19, 1743; Winthrop in Miller 1956, 79–84 (spelling modernized here, as throughout). David Hackett Fischer (1989, 190) sees "the importance of unity," both political and ecclesiastical, as "the leading theme of Puritan sermons" into the eighteenth century.

a novel conception of unity: "Cutting across existing solidarities of kith and kin, the message of the early Church was one of a social solidarity rooted only in a shared experience of the sacred. Christianity thus presented an alternative locus of social identity and of community that was rooted in the experience of grace. The bond established between communal members was one rooted not in primordial givens, but in an immediate connection to the fount of transcendental order." Such spiritual communions are today most commonly associated with Puritans, but other sects formed similar networks of friendship and exchange across geographic borders.[11]

According to basic Christian theology, *all* humans were bonded together. In biblical terms: "Ye are all the children of God. . . . There is neither Jew nor Greek, there is neither bond nor free, there is neither male nor female: for ye are all one in Christ Jesus." Protestant doctrine's expansively inclusionary ethic was restricted, at the same time. Much as later romantic-nationalist accounts of unity would limit a "people" to those sharing ethnic, racial, or cultural characteristics, religious communities included only the sectarian faithful. As Augustine testified: "What shall I say of the common good whose common pursuit knits men together into a 'united people,' as our definition teaches? Careful scrutiny will show that there is no such good for those who live irreligiously . . . a people devoid of justice is not such a people as can constitute a commonwealth." Augustine's principle was amply evident in practice, as the lines separating those within from those outside a religious union were often drawn sharply. A long history of crusades, wars, excommunications, and the like underscores the exclusionary principles animating unions of faith.[12]

Particularly relevant to American religious development are communities formed around a covenant. Covenantal bonds, dating originally from Judaism and adopted by Puritan thinkers in Tudor England, were a further innovation in joining bodies of believers, distinct not only from geographic or class connections but also from existing church arrangements. Again from Seligman: "Covenanting together, the Puritans also covenanted themselves off from the major existing institutional loci of solidarity—the Church, village, or parish—and so of those social identities which prevailed in English society. The growth of a new set of commitments, loyalties and identities . . . was a fundamental element in the construction of new loci of social life and individual identity."[13] American communities would adapt covenantal forms to political ends as well.

These various communal themes were described as "union," both in sermons and in Biblical sources. Religious historians identify at least five distinct meanings of union in traditional Christian doctrine, from incarnational union (Christ

---

11. Seligman 1998, 32. A good study of the "spiritual communion" among Puritans, including both American colonists and English clergy, is Bremer 1994.

12. Meagher 1978, 223. On the Christian "dynamic of noninclusion," see Chilton 1996, 136–39.

13. Seligman 1998, 33.

taking human nature and form) to spiritual unity between the believer and God, representing "the ultimate Christian goal of complete union with the Lord."[14] The roots of union talk run deep in Protestant Christianity, anchoring the term in the vocabulary of British America.

Colonial American Religious Unions

Every churchgoing or Bible-reading colonist regularly encountered testaments of union with God as the Edenic condition, lost through original sin, redemptively possible via divine salvation, and open to a broad swath of the elect. The step to valorizing social unity among members of a congregation, and even among all believers, was a natural one, and colonial religious leaders urged close ties among their followers and beyond. Roger Williams's repeated aphorism, "Union strengthens," referred to unity across different sects (rather plaintively, given Williams's own experience), and Jonathan Edwards produced long tracts praising union of a "religious people" as "one of the most beautiful and happy things on earth." Union's deep spiritual and interpersonal resonance ensured its wide appeal among colonial Americans anxiously inhabiting a "new world." The term was at the liturgical heart of practically every one of America's varied denominations, so that by the late seventeenth century union was firmly established as a core concept, evoking a broad relation of religious beliefs and practices. In 1760, the Connecticut minister Ezra Stiles enumerated fifteen separate "fundamental principles of Christianity and ecclesiastical policy, in which our churches are generally agreed." These together constituted, Stiles wrote, "the noble principle of unity."[15]

Religious British Americans of the seventeenth century utilized "union" in two principal ways. Many traditional religious leaders, especially in Massachusetts, advocated covenantal union of God and collected worshipers, gathered in hierarchically ordered towns and churches.[16] Other sects, particularly during and after the Great Awakening in the 1730s and 1740s, encouraged each believer's subjectively experienced "living Union to Christ."[17] These two conceptions were frequently in tension with one another, sparking some divergence around the desirable extent of "self-expression" and other points.[18] The contrast between congregational and personal religious unity mirrors, and likely helped to instantiate,

---

14. Ferguson and Wright 1988, 698–99.

15. Williams 1967 [1644], 6:280; Edwards 1747, 16; Stiles 1790 [1761], 9–63.

16. American covenant ideas originate with the Puritans, as Perry Miller extensively documents (1961 [1936], 21–26, 68–76, 133–46, 403–4); see also Kuehne 1996, 29–50. On versions among other sects, from Catholics to Quakers, see Elazar 1998.

17. Backus 1754, 18. On the tension between communal and individual religious doctrines in southern, mid-Atlantic, and New England colonies, see Calhoon 1991, 49–60.

18. Bushman 1967, 267; Mathews 1977, 32–33. Compare Miller's claim that covenantal duties were by the mid-eighteenth century increasingly rejected in favor of personal union (1961 [1936], 403–4). While accepting this pattern, others insist that the development was hardly linear: see Shain 1994, 84–85, 128–35, 199–240.

a communal-individual dichotomy observers at least since Tocqueville have noted as particularly pointed among Americans. But theologians were the primary disputants here. Most believers apparently found it reassuring to consider themselves both united to their fellow worshipers and personally connected to God.

Another theological tempest that helped popularize unionist language arose from a split among English Puritans, who had divided into two camps well before the English Civil War. Nationalists argued that the purified church should encompass the whole of Britain, as did the apostate Church of England; congregationalists or "Separatists" insisted that each church should constitute a particular, insular "union in itself." This divide between a close-knit separatist community of believers and the more expansive nationalist outlook reappeared in colonial New England, with Congregationalists on one side and Anglicans, Presbyterians, and, later, Catholics on the other.[19] Congregationalists and Presbyterians sought to settle their differences in 1691, following passage of the Toleration Act in England. The resulting compact was familiarly called the Union, and all parties to it—in principle, a majority of worshiping Americans—were instructed to term themselves United Brethren. Upon receiving the text of the agreement, Cotton Mather preached his stirring "Blessed Unions." Though within five years the compact fell apart, these disparate sects promoted very different ideas of unity using a common term—and described the agreement by which they sought to bridge their dispute in terms of union.[20]

A particularly influential source of connections across colonies was the Great Awakening. Boston minister William Cooper marveled in 1741 at the movement's "uniformity" in doctrine and "truly extraordinary" extent: "It is more or less on the several provinces that measure many hundred miles on this continent." Cooper also noted the Awakening's appeal among "all ranks and degrees: some of the great and rich, but more of the low and poor," including "some poor Negroes." A recent historical account confirms the Awakening's "intercolonial" nature: "Because itinerant preachers roamed the length and breadth of the colonies for more than five years, and because of the widespread distribution of printed materials, men and women in every corner of the colonies were aware of the revival and responded to it in some way."[21]

Most of the Awakening's leading revivalists, notably including Gilbert Tennent, Jonathan Edwards, George Whitefield, and James Davenport, specifically

19. For the Congregationalist side, see, e.g., Wise 1710 and 1717. Representative nationalist tracts are Morgan 1749 [1727] and Alison 1758. A useful account of the "fratricidal cacophony of 1640s Puritanism" in England, and its effects in New England, is Winship 2000 (quote at p. 70).

20. Bremer 1994, 249–52. In the 1760s and again after the revolution the episode recurred, with Presbyterians and Congregationalists forging a loose confederacy and then another "Plan of Union," ratified in 1801. See Bonomi 1986, 206–8; Finke and Stark 1989, 33–34.

21. Cooper in preface to Edwards 1741, 2–3; Lambert 1999, 254 (and see 88–124, 151–79, 153–54). On the complex of doctrines and movements comprising the Awakening, see ibid. or Larson 1999, which persuasively demonstrates the spread of revivalism among Quakers, including women preachers.

called for closer union among British Americans, in heavenly and also secular terms. Edwards's oft-preached and widely reprinted sermon "Explicit Agreement and Visible Union" promoted "A *civil* union, or an harmonious agreement among men in the management of their secular concerns." Looking back on the movement in 1760, Ezra Stiles warned that growing "differences and animosities" would "enervate and moulder down our cause" and reminded worshipers that restored "union and benevolence" could "strengthen and form it to defensible maturity."[22]

The Awakening also heightened disagreements among colonial American sects and between theologians. But even heated exchanges contributed to connections across geographical borders. As Sidney Ahlstrom writes, common efforts at "conversion and regeneration" served "as a bond of fellowship that transcended disagreements on fine points of doctrine and policy." The outcome was union's near universal currency among religious-minded colonists from Vermont to Georgia as a source of profound personal and collective meaning.[23]

Religious Roots of Political Union

The conceptual centrality of union in colonial religion inevitably colored American political conversation in an era "when almost every sermon was a political statement."[24] William Hubbard's election sermon of 1676 is a typical example: "[I]n the body politic, where it is animated with one entire spirit of love and unity . . . all the several members must and will conspire together to deny or forbear the exercise of their own proper inclinations, to preserve the union of the whole, that there be no schism in the body." Thirty years earlier the self-styled Cobler of Aggawam warned that "Experience will teach Churches and Christians . . . that it is far better to live in a state united, though a little corrupt, than in a state, whereof some part is incorrupt, and all the rest divided." The first colonial constitution, Connecticut's "Fundamental Orders," echoed church covenants in stating that "where a people are gathered tog[e]ther the word of God requires that to maintain the peace and union of such a people there should be an orderly and decent Government established according to God." Legal statutes in Virginia, as in other colonies, began with a like invocation: "For the preservation of the purity of doctrine and the unity of the church."[25] Throughout the seventeenth century, efforts to mount joint political activities were generally defended in religious terms.

22. Edwards 1747, 6; Stiles 1790 [1761], 5–6, 56–58, 63–65.

23. Ahlstrom 1972, 293–94; see also Peterson 1997, 236–38. On turbulent sectarian relations, see Cohen 1997, 697, 722; Clark 1994, 203–17, 339–81.

24. Stone 1992, 49. Ketcham (1974, 11) notes that sermons and "political polemics" were often intertwined and ranks the combination as the only "indigenous" examples of American writing. On the political import of sermons, see also Kuehne 1996, 79–84. On unity as the aim of Christian thought, notably that of Aquinas, see Beer 1993, 45, 51–53, 148, 179–80.

25. Hubbard 1676, 16; De la Guard 1969 [1647], 10; Trumbull 1850, 20, and 1876, 324. On the connection between early American politics and religious thought, see Lutz 1988, 52–75; Shain 1994.

The considerable influence of religious-union rhetoric on political talk affected social development as well. Common to most Protestant sects, at least in principle, was treatment of strangers as possible incarnations of Christ among the community. Only this attitude, Biblical teaching maintained, would permit "brethren to dwell together in unity." As travel and communication across colonies increased during the eighteenth century, many small communities viewed newcomers with deep suspicion. Religious doctrine served at times as a counterbalance. Contrary impulses to expel, include on strictly defined terms, or embrace strangers—each course promoted in the name of "true" unity—would be reflected in decades of erratic treatment of immigrants, minorities, and other "outsiders" at the hands of majority white, Protestant America.[26]

Religious exchanges were the leading source of communication between colonies during the seventeenth and eighteenth centuries. "Most denominations," writes historian John Ranney, "were intercolonial in their constituency; and in many churches [there developed] a strong movement for ecclesiastical unity, regardless of state lines." Ideas were transmitted through denominational conferences, reprinted sermons, itinerant preachers, and revival meetings. These exchanges served as an important early foundation of intercolonial unity, culminating in the Great Awakening described above. As Ralph Ketcham affirms, the movement had lasting political effects: "Though the Awakening had passed its peak by 1750 . . . the sense of communion of those who experienced it remained, and in the 1760s and 1770s, when Americans debated *national* loyalty and *political* purpose, the continuing impact of their earlier religious ferment was everywhere evident."[27]

Religious themes, in sum, were the foremost basis for early mentions of national union—both ecclesiastical and political. Tellingly, the first proposal to join all British American colonies was made (in 1697) by Quaker leader William Penn. Later religious thinkers developed elaborate treatises on "the noble principle of union," working out ideas of federal association among "ecclesiastical polities" that anticipated ideas instituted at the constitutional convention in 1787.[28] As the crisis with England developed, the prominent religious cleric Jonathan Mayhew urged Massachusetts lawyer James Otis to pursue "a communion of colonies" along the lines of "the communion of churches." Otis accepted the advice, proposing committees of correspondence as Mayhew suggested, and subsequently

26. Psalm 133:1 (the text goes on to compare union to other greatly desired goods, such as the "dew of Hermon, on mountains of Zion"). On how the "religious ideal of equality" influenced, especially after the Great Awakening, a "reconsideration of the Negro's external legal status," see Jordan 1968, 294–301 (quote at p. 296). But on colonial Protestants' destruction of slaves' African religious roots, see Butler 1990, 129–63.

27. Ranney 1946, 4; Hall 1994, 111–84; Ketcham 1974, 38.

28. Stiles 1790 [1761], 5, 120. In his "Discourses on Christian Union," originally preached in 1760 and reprinted for at least half a century, Stiles described "the fundamental principle" of American denominations' "union" in federalist terms: "none of our particular churches shall be subordinate to one another." Stiles did vest some "controlling power" in a "consociation," represented by a "supreme ecclesiastical tribunal." Ibid., 99–100.

convening the intercolonial Stamp Act Congress in October 1765.[29] These activities helped set in motion a complex interplay of rebellious acts and union talk,
explored later in this chapter.

POLITICAL UNION: ORIGINS AND EARLY DEVELOPMENT

Into the 1770s, heartfelt expressions of fraternal union among British Americans
were voiced primarily by religious thinkers. As a referent for colonists' political relations, the term was used in a far less ardent sense to denote cooperation
for purposes of defense, commerce, and the like. This usage was present among
American gentry as early as the 1630s when Connecticut officials proposed
a "united . . . consociation amongst our selves" of the New England colonies.
Formal institutional ties over the next century and a half were scant, owing to
a mixture of British opposition and intense intercolonial rivalry, epitomized in a
comment from New York governor Benjamin Fletcher. Visiting Connecticut in
November 1693, Fletcher bemoaned his neighbors' "Independent principle,"
grousing that "these small colonies . . . are [as] much divided in their interest and
affection as Christian and Turk."[30]

This lack of institutional attachments, along with the fact that most colonial
communal life remained centered within town units,[31] is likely what leads most
historians to overlook unionist ideas prior to the 1760s. But by the early eighteenth century "union" and "united" had nonetheless become common descrip-
tors for informal political connections among the colonies. When in 1754 Boston
physician William Clarke prepared "several small pieces" on "the nature of the
Union, that ought to be established among his Majesty's colonies on this continent," he could be confident of a knowledgeable and interested American readership.[32] Religious doctrine inspired unionist language, as we have seen; the other
chief contributor was British practice. Beginning with the England-Wales union
of 1536, various Britons—the Stuart and Hanoverian kings, notably, as well as
Oliver Cromwell—sought to unify different parts of the empire.[33] The most
successful collaboration, between England and Scotland, was termed the Union
of 1707. That Union is described in further detail below; note for now that Britons termed confederations of political bodies "unions" from the sixteenth cen-

29. Mayhew quoted in Thornton 1860, 44; on his influence with Otis, see Clark 1994, 368.

30. Brodhead 1858, 4:73. Foreign visitors thought likewise: English traveler Andrew Burnaby
(1904 [1775], 152–53) wrote after his 1759–60 trip that "fire and water are not more heterogeneous than
the different colonies in North America. Nothing can exceed the jealousy and emulation which they
possess in regard to each other." Connecticut official in Barck and Lefler 1958, 112.

31. Wood 1992, 57–92. Cf. Countryman 1986, 56–7; Bender 1978, 62–71. For a look at connections within one broader region, the Chesapeake, see Horn 1994, pt. 3 (on "the Social Web").

32. Clarke to Benjamin Franklin, in Labaree et al. 1959–, 5:271.

33. A good summary is in Murdoch 1998, 15–73.

tury onward and that British Americans (as one component of a "United Kingdom") carried the practice across the Atlantic.

A shared language served as an important cohesive force among the British American political class. Though the colonial population was already quite heterogeneous by the early eighteenth century, with immigrants from central and northern Europe arriving along with slaves from at least twenty different African tribes,[34] all official business and other exchanges among colonial leaders was conducted in English. J. R. Pole notes that "they used the language in essentially similar ways; there do not appear to have been marked differences of idiom."[35] Given the extraordinary importance of public speech in colonial America—one study notes that "talk became a primary focus of talk" among the colonists—such commonality mattered.[36] Cultural exposure, another source of common identity, helps explain this discursive unification: most educated colonists read the same British and European authors and worshiped in Protestant churches featuring similar doctrines. Most politically active Americans also shared a deep loyalty to England, which eventually would complicate the effort for separate unity but which did much to encourage colonists' sense of commonality into the 1760s.

By the eighteenth century, ample exposure to other colonies' activities was available from Vermont to Georgia. Newspapers, though strictly local in readership—no "national" journal would exist until John Fenno founded the *Gazette of the United States* in 1789—carried extensive coverage of events throughout and beyond British America. A typical four-page issue of an ordinary paper from 1745, the *Boston Weekly Post-Boy*, included news from Williamsburg, Virginia (lightning killed "a Colonel and his two daughters"); Philadelphia; Maryland; New York; Rhode Island; and the latest dispatches from the war in Nova Scotia. Readers of the *Post-Boy*, and of most other colonial organs, would see speeches reprinted from royal governors and other American officials, hear about Atlantic hurricanes and "Murder in the Carolinas," and learn the results of votes in Maryland's assembly and figures for boat traffic in New York. Detailed maps of all or several colonies—figuratively joining their residents—were occasionally published or printed in newspapers and frequently advertised for sale. Samuel Kernell traces newspapers' "national outlook" to the 1840s, but the tendency is evident more than a century earlier.[37]

Local editors usually doubled as the town or city printer, and in both roles were leading figures in every colony's political class. Many consciously saw their role as promoters of intercolonial connections and featured regular exhortations

34. Estimates for immigration by each ethnic group are in Fogleman 1998, 68–76.
35. Pole 1977, 74.
36. Kamensky 1997, 48.
37. *Boston Post-Boy*, September 2, 1745; other examples from issues of January 14 and June 17 of that year. Kernell 1986. A typical map offering (this one featuring Pennsylvania, New York, New Jersey, and Delaware) is in the *Pennsylvania Gazette*, July 23, 1752.

on the topic in editorial columns or reprinted such unionist icons as Franklin's famous "Join, Or Die" snake cartoon, which first appeared in a 1754 *Pennsylvania Gazette*.[38] The virtue of political concord, and the "very pernicious" nature of "factions and parties in a state, or any other society," as John Peter Zenger wrote in 1734, were a staple of editorial columns.[39]

As noted above, another important source of commonality was religion. Denominational connections transcended colonial boundaries, spreading first among Puritans and later through many other sects—witness the close ties between Lutherans, Moravians, and Reformed churches that extended from Pennsylvania throughout the South. Indeed, religious leaders were the first to effect intercolonial political connections termed "unions." In 1643, the four Puritan colonies in New England[40] extended their joint synod of churches, organized six years earlier to advance "Unity in the true worship of God," into a political organization, the "United Colonies." Also known as the Confederation of New England, it had limited powers, and members met only once or twice a year. Yet the organization endured for nearly half a century and inspired rhetorical flights such as Cotton Mather's declaration, after the agreement was signed, that they "became, in *fact* as well as name, UNITED COLONIES." Though little noted by modern historians, the United Colonies were once viewed as "help[ing] set the stage for the greater work of federation which was achieved before the end of the following [i.e., eighteenth] century."[41]

The United Colonies was disbanded by royal command in the 1680s. In 1685, a British Ministry substitute was introduced under the unpopular leadership of royal governor Edmund Andros. New York and New Jersey were brought in as members as well, so roughly half of existing British American territory (also including Maine and New Hampshire, which had traditionally been governed by Massachusetts) was politically unified in the late seventeenth century. Significantly, most colonists refused to call this collectivity a "union"; instead they applied the pejorative title "The *Dominion* of New England."[42] This body was under strict Crown control: elected assemblies in the four New England colonies were dissolved and replaced by a single royal governor empowered to achieve

---

38. *Pennsylvania Gazette*, May 9, 1754. The image later appeared on several colonial flags, currency notes in four colonies, and the first U.S. War Department seal. On this and other pictorial representations of the American colonies during the 1750s as "a singular body politic, as a united community that was distinct from the rest of the empire," see Olson 1994 (quote at p. 2), and Cook 1996.

39. *New-York Weekly Journal*, March 17, 1734.

40. Massachusetts, Plymouth, Connecticut, and Rhode Island.

41. On the Synod of 1637, see Ward 1961, 29–33 (quote at p. 30), and Mather 1855 [1702], 1:160. On the United Colonies, see Barck and Lefler 1958, 112–15 (quote at p. 115); Ward 1961; and Bancroft 1861, 1:421 ("even after it [the United Colonies] was cut down, [it] left a hope that a new and a better union would spring from its root").

42. Dominion was an established term in British officialdom, as in "the King's dominions." But English spokesmen usually referred to this arrangement in terms like "the union of all New England," while American opponents, in a series of pamphlets, angrily claimed that "this is a *Dominion* in virtue of our *Domination* by [Governor Andros]." See Andrews 1915, 66, 104.

"Immediate Dependence upon the Crown." This "forced union of the colonies," as Americans saw it, was heatedly protested and soon abandoned with the onset of England's "Glorious Revolution" in 1688. A group of American leaders met in Boston and issued a "Declaration" of colonial rights, which they then sent "to all the colonies in the Dominion, urging them to cast off the yoke." Governor Andros and his top military officers were jailed for nearly eight months, then sent home to England. The Dominion's overthrow is little remembered today but was once celebrated in New England as a mini-revolution anticipating that of 1776.[43]

The Dominion's failure by no means ended visions of a unified British America. Virtually every major political figure (and numerous religious, military, and commercial ones) involved with British America tried his hand at sketching a closer colonial union in the eighteenth century. Unionist schemes were launched by merchants seeking reduced intercolonial trade barriers, bureaucrats desiring streamlined colonial administration, and military commanders planning more secure boundaries and larger fiefdoms. Less plainly rational interest-maximizers also dreamed up plans of union, motivated by commitments to religious concord, civil peace, or solidaristic fellowship. As one historian summarizes: "a good deal of colonial intellectual activity from 1690 on was accounted for by projects of confederation of one sort or another."[44] Table 1 lists leading proposals for uniting several or all colonies.[45] The table indicates the year in which each plan was proposed and, in two cases, enacted; also summarized are each plan's primary purposes and (if considered by the British Ministry) reasons for failure.

The plans in table 1 testify to the presence of unionist talk and planning long before 1763, although most were little discussed among the majority of colonists. Their intended audience was colonial governors and assemblies, other opinion leaders, and the British Ministry, rather than the population at large. In short, no appeal for a more unified American people was made directly to that people.[46] If Americans were to join across colonial boundaries for even limited ends, it would be at the behest of their leaders, at home and in London. British ministers had ample reason to suppress most expressions of united feeling among the colonists, as shall be seen below.

At the same time, major plans like Penn's and Franklin's were reported in newspapers, and calls to unity for defense and commercial reasons were commonplace in the eighteenth century. Most politically aware Americans of the time would have read about, and likely discussed, possibilities of union between their own and neighboring colonies. In New England and the middle Atlantic,

43. Quotes in Koenigsberger 1989, 147–48; Barnes 1923, 248 (see ibid., 231–61, on Americans' "Revolution" against the Dominion; also Ward 1961, 314–43; Merritt 1966, 32–35).
44. Ranney 1946, 9.
45. Sources include Hart and Channing 1894; Ward 1971, 3–31; Brodhead 1858, 4:870–79; O'Callaghan 1855, 5:591–630; Bumsted 1974.
46. This was not out of the ordinary: Pole (1983, 117–36) shows that very few official colonial actions, including assembly debates or even votes, were communicated to the public.

Table 1. Prominent plans of intercolonial union, 1643–1763

United Colonies of New England, 1643–84	Among the four Puritan colonies, powers included war declaration (which occurred once, in 1675) and peace treaties; admittance of new members; and general intercolonial agreements/orders. Charter revoked by royal decree.
Dominion of New England, 1685–89	Crown-imposed replacement for Confederation was eventually rejected by colonies. Included New York and New Jersey as well.
	New York intercolonial congress (1690) among four colonies; met to coordinate policy in King William's War and continue joint military efforts. Planned but failed to meet again.
Penn's Plan of Union, 1697	First proposal to unite all (ten) colonies. Authority vested in central Congress, with jurisdiction over intercolony fugitives, commerce, and defense. No power to organize troops or levy taxes. Crown dismissed; plan faded without formal hearing.
	Charles D'Avenant: to unite northern colonies via a joint assembly and institute an intercolonial Trade Council (1698).
	Robert Livingston: three separate regional unions, formed for frontier defense and administrative coordination (1701).
	"A Virginian," probably Robert Beverley: unite mid-Atlantic and southern colonies (1701).
	Joseph Dudley, central military authority for New England: renew New England Confederation, possibly including New York and New Jersey (1702).
	Caleb Heathcote: "consolidate" all colonies to achieve self-financing (1715).
Earl of Stair Plan of Union, 1721	First British proposal to unite all existing colonies. Union with centralized authority over defense, taxes, postal system, trade regulation. Victim of administrative battles over details, though some colonial governors exchanged letters in support.
	Daniel Coxe: "Grand Council" plan to unite all colonies (1726).
	Martin Bladen: two-house legislature for military/trade purposes (1739).
	George Clinton, "Plan of American Union": common defense among New England/mid-Atlantic colonies; debated but rejected by British Ministry (1744).
	Archibald Kennedy: colonial union with strong ties to Indians, to be legislated by Parliament (1751). Franklin's 1754 plan in part a response to Kennedy's.

Albany Plan of Union, 1754	Common defense, related laws, taxes levied for support. Benjamin Franklin was the main author and promoter. Passed by Albany Congress, but no colony subsequently ratified, and Britain also opposed. Thomas Robinson, "Plan for Union of Colonies": British plan for defense (1754). Henry McCulloh, "Proposal for Uniting the Eng. Colonies": economic primarily—poll tax, supervised by commission, "Bills of Union" to pay provincial troops (1757).

Note: Major plans are at far left; lesser but still noteworthy proposals are indented.

they would also have noticed, and probably applauded, colonists' rejection of the Dominion. It is important to note that some sense of intercolonial community among Americans long predated their effort to split from Britain. Colonists' pre-1760s sense of shared interests and religious values constituted a nascent spirit of unity rather than an inclination to independence.

Pancolonial awareness of union ideas expanded in the 1740s, as we have seen, with the Great Awakening. Another boost in the concept's profile came in 1754 when several months of discussion culminated in a Continental Congress at Albany, New York, to which seven colonies sent representatives. Benjamin Franklin had the greatest hand in drafting the resulting Albany Plan of Union—appropriately so, since he had been encouraging closer unity among the colonies for years. Disputes among delegates to the Congress were overcome long enough to approve the Plan initially, but it then suffered wholesale defeat, being rejected by all voting colonies, vetoed by the Crown, and subsequently pilloried at town meetings around British America.[47] Franklin's disappointment was considerable: he complained to an English friend, Peter Collinson, later that year that "everybody cries, a Union is absolutely necessary, but when they come to the manner and form of the Union, their weak noddles are presently distracted. So if ever there be a Union, it must be formed at home [e.g., in England] by the Ministry and Parliament."[48]

With the failure of the Albany Plan, the boundaries of intercolonial union appeared clear. The term was familiarly used to denote political ties among the colonies ("Everybody cries, there must be a Union"), but these were minimal in practice until the 1760s. Colonial leaders' squabbling and an unwilling British Ministry combined to deny life to even tentative movements. Apart from Henry McCulloh's 1757 "Proposals for Uniting the English Colonies," largely ex-

47. On a 1755 Boston town meeting that criticized Franklin and other Plan advocates as "arrant blockheads," see Labaree et al. 1959–, 5:490. Ward (1971, 16) lists "particularistic objections" to the Plan from individual colonies, many of which anticipate battles in the constitutional convention. See also Anderson 2000, 77–85.

48. Labaree et al. 1959–, 5:453–54.

cerpted from an earlier manuscript, no prominent efforts at colonial union were mounted for a decade after Albany. By 1760 even the ever optimistic Franklin sounded resigned:

> However necessary a union of the colonies has long been, for their com-
> mon defense and security against their enemies, and how sensible soever
> each colony has been of that necessity, yet they have never been able to ef-
> fect such a union among themselves, nor even to agree in requesting the
> mother country to establish it for them. . . . If they could not agree to unite
> for their defense against the French and Indians, who were perpetually ha-
> rassing their settlements . . . can it be reasonably supposed there is any dan-
> ger of their uniting against their own nation, which protects and encour-
> ages them, with which they have so many connections and ties of blood,
> interest, and affection, and which, it is well known, they all love much
> more than they love one another? . . . I will venture to say, a union among
> them for such a purpose is not merely improbable, it is impossible.[49]

Franklin's seeming elegy in fact stated a novel, even subversive understanding of political union. Animated by a seemingly preposterous concern—what colonist in 1760 was contemplating separation from the "mother country"?[50]—Franklin proved to be an American Jeremiah, sounding a prophetic view. Later in the same essay, Franklin allowed that British "grievous tyranny and oppression" could inspire the colonies to unite.[51] Within a few years union would directly connote independence and a split with Great Britain. This possibility seemed so terrible that many Americans *avoided* employing "union" in this sense almost until their declaration of independence. Instead they adopted a formerly uncommon, British understanding of the term.

DISPLACEMENT: UNION USAGE IN THE "CRITICAL DECADE," 1764–73

Figure 1 demonstrates literate Americans' pattern of union usage between 1756 and 1780, based on a survey of newspaper references to the term and its coreferents ("United," modifying "Colonies" or "States"). As outlined in this book's introductory chapter and appendix, "union" and "united" references are depicted as a proportion of total newspaper pages examined. In 1766, for example, my sample of newspapers included sixty-seven pages of news content. Reading through

49. Ibid., 9:90. A short-lived attempt at a military union in 1758 is described in Anderson 2000, 221–24.

50. As Bumsted (1974) demonstrates, the handful of colonists who before 1763 discussed separation from Britain did so solely, and vehemently, to deny the possibility. That British officials on both sides of the Atlantic were already voicing alarm on these grounds is discussed below.

51. Labaree et al. 1959–, 9:90.

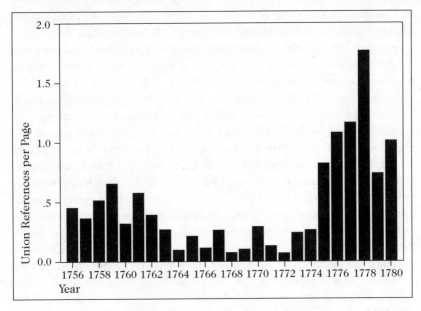

FIGURE I. Union references in American newspapers, 1756–80

these, I counted ten references to national union and related terms ("united colonies," "American unity," and so forth). The proportion of union references per page was thus 0.15 (10/67). The running total is an index of Americans' propensity to express national sentiments in the language of union.

Immediately apparent in figure I is a trough in references to pan-American unity during a period in which one would reasonably expect these to rise: the colonial crisis sparked by the Grenville Acts and subsequent events. The remainder of this section examines this precipitous drop in union talk during the "critical decade" leading to independence.

The American View: Intercolonial Union, or Union with England?

Benjamin Franklin's extensive contacts in England and America, along with his old printer's habit of attending closely to language, made him unusually sensitive to linguistic usage. Taking Franklin as representative (and as an influential leader) of the American elite's political thought during the 1750s to 1770s, we see patterns in references to intercolonial union in sharper perspective. Union appears in two different senses in Franklin's copious writings. One invokes union of the American colonies "for their mutual defense and security," among other aims.[52] A second usage denotes union between England (or Britain) and America, on the model of the English-Scottish accord of 1707. Franklin applied the

52. Ibid., 3:206.

first, intercolonial meaning as early as the 1740s, in keeping with longstanding British American practice. In 1747, for example, Franklin's "Plain Truth" pamphlet urged, "at present we are like the separate filaments of flax before the thread is formed, without strength because without connection, but UNION would make us strong and even formidable."[53]

Such calls to unify the American colonies abruptly disappeared from Franklin's lexicon during most of the resistance period, returning finally in 1775. Conversely, Franklin nowhere mentioned union between America and Britain until 1765, but he regularly employed this usage over the decade thereafter. In January 1766, Franklin wrote an English friend that "the measure [Britons] propose of a Union with the colonies is a wise one" and concluded "if such an Union were now established, which methinks it highly imports this country [America] to establish, it would probably subsist as long as Britain shall continue a nation."[54] Between 1765 and February 1775, Franklin mentioned (in private letters as well as public statements) "union" concerning the colonies fifty-one times: all but one reference was to unity between America and England, or to the Anglo-Scottish Union of 1707 as a model.[55] In contrast, between 1735 and 1764 his thirty-eight references to political union included none to unity between America and England. (His first extended discussion of the idea concerns *religious* unity, in keeping with this chapter's earlier argument.)[56]

A survey of principal American rebels turns up similar patterns in union references during the crisis. James Otis's pamphlet in response to the stamp and sugar duties concludes with an invocation of "the [1707] act of union" and a promise that American representation in Parliament would "firmly unite all parts of the British empire." At the 1769 signing of Virginia's nonimportation resolutions, the assembled company drafted a stern set of anti-British directives—and then drank a toast to "a speedy and lasting Union between Great-Britain and her Colonies." Daniel Dulany's "Considerations on the Propriety of Imposing Taxes" was perhaps the most notorious piece of colonial opposition writing in the 1760s, in part because of its warnings about "measures of prevention" and that "redress may be obtained" by the colonies, presumably acting in concert. Dulany coated

53. Ibid., 3:202. Compare his letter to James Parker in March 1751 (4:117–21), where Franklin gloomily summarizes the failed result of various attempts "to unite the several governments" in British America; his flurry of writings on union surrounding the Albany Plan (5:337–38, 353–55, 361–64, 387–97, 399–417, 426–28, 443–47, 449–51, 457–63); and various appeals to American unity from the mid-1750s to early 1760s (6:88, 140, 169–70, 231–32; 7:375–77; 9:90–95; and 10:405).

54. Labaree et al. 1959–, 13:23–24. Compare, e.g., 12:363 (writing to his son William late in 1765 that he had recommended to British officials "a thorough Union with America"); 19:96; 20:282–83 (Franklin, writing to Massachusetts assemblymen in July 1773, lists the mutual advantages of "a strict Union between the Mother Country and the Colonies"), 331, 386–87; and his December 1774 "Hints for Conversation" in 21:366–68, 380–86.

55. The single exception is in his July 1773 private letter to John Winthrop, which recommends "cultivating a harmony among the colonies, that their union in the same sentiments may give them greater weight." Franklin then immediately refers to "our Union with her" (England), "our mother tho' of late an unkind one" (20:330–31).

56. Labaree et al. 1959–, 2:65–66. These precise counts are possible thanks to a CD-ROM of Franklin's collected papers, an advance version of which was made available to me.

the pill with an appeal that "an *union* [be] established" between the colonies and Great Britain. A decade later, with Lexington and Concord only months away, James Wilson closed his "Considerations on Parliamentary Authority" by citing the "strict connection between the inhabitants of Great Britain and those of America": in these fellow subjects "this union of allegiance naturally produces a union of hearts. It is also productive of a union of measures through the whole British dominions."[57]

This sudden outburst of American paeans to their place in the Union of the British Empire, beginning as the imperial crisis broke out in 1763–64, accompanied a decline in references to pancolonial unity. Along with the evidence in figure 1, note that few of the leading calls to resist various British measures before 1775[58] include any mention of intercolonial union in even its weak Albany Plan sense, much less to denote a more cohesive, English-excluding set of bonds among the colonies.[59] Examples may be multiplied beyond these familiar opposition writings. Rhode Island governor Stephen Hopkins, an "ardent champion of colonial unity" before the crisis began and during it a regional leader of opposition to British authority, in his 1765 pamphlet on the controversy avoided the term altogether, a practice he maintained in public statements until 1775. George Washington, who before the Stamp Act used the term regularly to call for intercolonial defense—and who, as early as 1769, wrote about the colonies taking up arms against the British—after 1764 eschewed "union" with reference to the colonies until June 1775. To extend the point beyond elites, a collection of popular American patriotic songs and ballads of the period includes no reference to "union" or "united" in twenty-odd top "hits" from 1764–74. After 1775 there recur stirring lines like "an Union through the colonies will ever remain / And ministerial taxation will be but in vain."[60]

Why *should* we expect the term to appear in American arguments for intercolonial relations during the crisis?[61] Three reasons are pertinent. First, efforts at joint action—regularly termed "union" before 1763—were swiftly mounted between 1764 and 1774. Among these were the Stamp Act Congress, convened within weeks of the Act's promulgation; establishment of the intercolonial Sons

57. Otis 1764, 65; Virginia Assembly in Boyd 1950–, 1:31; Dulany 1765, 17, 47 (emphasis in original); McCloskey 1967, 2:745.

58. See, e.g., the pamphlets collected in Bailyn 1965, from Otis's "Rights of the British Colonies" (1764) through Jefferson's "Summary View of the Rights of British Americans" (1774). None includes a call for closer union among the American colonists.

59. Exceptions exist, though the two prominent examples may prove the rule. John Dickinson, a conservative among colonial spokesmen, in two of his 1767–68 "Farmer's Letters" propounds united action among the colonies and urges unity in his 1768 "Liberty Song," reprinted in Moore 1855, 37–39. Samuel Adams remained a fiery promoter of union throughout the crisis (see Cushing 1968, 2:47–48, 111, 179, 205, 212, 346; 3:15, 26, 32, 45, 141–44).

60. Quotes from Ward 1971, 17 (on Hopkins, see also Andrews 1931, 27; Bates 1898, 41); Washington in Abbot et al. 1983–93, 3:299, and compare 3:242, 359. Typical of Washington's usage before the crisis was his letter to Robert Morris, in 1756: "Nothing I more sincerely wish than a union to the colon[ie]s in this time of eminent danger . . ." (1:309; cf. 502–3). Ballad quote from Moore 1855, 105.

61. After all, studies of political concepts rarely focus on why a term disappears from political discourse, probably because most objects of conceptual analysis—power, liberty, rights, equality—remain very much alive.

of Liberty; the coordinated nonimportation policies of 1765, 1767, and 1774; a series of popular anti-British demonstrations and riots; and committees of correspondence and the Continental Congress that grew out of these. Colonists, as Richard Merritt demonstrates, "crossed the threshold of American common identity" during the 1760s. Calls for (and examples of) unified action were widespread, but the most obvious word for such efforts was missing, or otherwise engaged.[62]

Second, *British* officials, in writings well known among rebel leaders, frequently used "union" to describe intercolonial activity. Early in the crisis, former Massachusetts governor Thomas Pownall's *Administration of the Colonies* warned against "the danger" of the colonies "forming any Principle of Coherence with each other." Although the possibility seemed to him "trivial," Pownall did warn that "the particular danger here . . . is that of furnishing them with a principle of union" and consequently endorsed "the sure wisdom of keeping this disunion of council and imperium amongst them." The Stamp Act's principal drafter, Thomas Whately, was more succinct: "all Bonds of Union between them [must be] severed."[63] Such British concerns originated well before 1763. During consideration of the Albany Plan, the Leader of the House of Commons confided across branches to Whitehall's Lord Newcastle that "ill consequence[s]" were "to be apprehended from uniting too closely the northern colonies with each other, an Independency upon this country to be feared from such an union." Three decades prior, in 1722, Trenchard and Gordon devoted one of their popular *Cato's Letters* in part to possibilities of colonial union and independence. J. M. Bumsted locates British officials' fears on this score earlier still in the 1690s.[64]

The separate shocks following the Stamp Act, Townshend Acts, and Tea Act all issued in considerable rumbling among British ministers about the dangers of colonial union. In a typical 1766 Parliamentary debate on the Stamp Act's aftermath, one MP worried aloud that "the provinces of America . . . will unite in such a manner as to be superior to any power we can send against them." Colonists noticed the trend. As Joseph Galloway, then a Pennsylvania Assemblyman, declared in 1764: "An union [the Albany Plan] has been already rejected and such a one we shall now never enjoy. Our superiors think it convenient to keep us in another state."[65]

62. Merritt 1966, 126. Jack Rakove's authoritative study of the crisis concludes that intercolonial "union remained the paramount good" among Americans, though he does not consider the term's absence from period discourse (1979, 69; see generally 3–86. Cf. Maier 1974, 94, 221; Greene 1986, 157–65).

63. Pownall 1766, 63–65; Whately 1765, 98. Historian Ian Christie notes that Whately "felt that the political fragmentation of the colonies was a safeguard for the supremacy of the mother country—here he hinted at apprehensions also expressed by other people in official positions." Christie 1998, 305; cf. 319–20.

64. Olson 1960, 31; Trenchard and Gordon, Letter no. 106, in Jacobson 1965, 245–48. Rossiter (1953, 141) calls the *Letters* "the most popular, quotable, esteemed source of political ideas" among American colonists. Bumsted 1974, 537.

65. Parliamentary debate in Simmons and Thomas 1982, 2:297–98; Galloway in Boyd 1941, 20.

Third, to turn from primary evidence to an interpretive argument: among the principal claims of colonial scholars, especially over the past three decades, is that a "Great Transition" from classical to modern society occurred in America shortly after the revolution. The nature of this transformation remains disputed, but most participants concede that such a shift did occur during the last quarter of the eighteenth century. In Michael Zuckerman's summary account, during the revolution Americans "assumed that the republic could survive solely on a conception of the people as a homogeneous body and of the public good as a unitary entity to which the separate cares of separate citizens had steadily to be sacrificed." But "the advent of a very different set of commitments and conceptions" early in the Confederation period "admitted diversity and dissidence in politics" where before "republicans denounced political divisions among the people." The outcome, writes Zuckerman, was "ravag[ed] republican hopes for communal unity."[66]

If colonial and newly Confederated Americans spoke the classical, affective language of common good while their post-1787 successors favored commercial individualist doctrines, a communal term like "union" would seem the very heart of such classical talk. And the term was applied thus among civic humanists like Machiavelli, regarded by some as the original inspiration behind the Americans' idiomatic throne.[67] Hence we might well look for references to union among the "republican" rebels of 1764–74. Perplexingly, however, in practice the conceptual evolution of union appears to have moved in reverse. Until the revolution was at hand, the term was missing from colonists' "ritual reaffirmations of solidarity and shared purpose." Subsequently, especially after constitutional ratification "shattered the classical Whig world," the term's frequency of usage was scarcely matched by any other political word, a trend that increased into the Civil War era and beyond. Given that "cultures do not, as a rule, dismiss the words that allow them to say what they mean," union's absence during the crisis years appears a significant aberration.[68]

Thus *silence* marks one key aspect of union's place in American political language. This is not the only such instance in U.S. political history: Louis Hartz's *Liberal Tradition,* for example, explains the convictions of colonists, founders, and Progressives alike in terms of a missing feudal past.[69] Here, the absence of union talk may actually testify to the concept's centrality. As a referent for separate nationhood, union carried such explosive portent that it was avoided, tiptoed around, swept under the rug. Compare another compelling topic of the era:

66. Zuckerman 1991, 179, 184–85, 187–88; on the transition from classical to modern, see Wood 1969, vii–ix, 562, 606–15; Pocock 1975, 506–25; Rakove 1996, 151–52. Compare Progressives' view of the Revolution as a cooperative popular triumph destroyed by wealthy, commercial-minded Framers (Croly 1909, 30–35; 278–79; Beard 1935 [1913], chap. 1).
67. Pocock 1975, 506–26.
68. Zuckerman 1991, 180; Wood 1969, 605; Rodgers 1987, 19.
69. Hartz 1955; see also Greene 1986, 55–76 (on the "virtual absence" of formal attention to Parliament's relation to the colonies, the ensuing pages investigate "the meaning of this silence").

slavery. Nowhere in the Declaration or Constitution do "slave," "Negro," or related terms appear.[70]

With the significance of union's absence asserted, the question becomes why a common term, one familiar before 1764 and which after 1774 widely denoted pan-American solidarity, so rarely appeared in this context during the crisis years. Fear of retribution? Perhaps; yet agitated colonists hardly hesitated to damn the British from the outset of the imperial crisis. In 1764, Parliament and the Ministry were portrayed as "fatal" to colonial interests, and during subsequent outbreaks of opposition, they were routinely called "venal," "barbarous," "despotic," and the like.[71] John Adams's 1765 *Dissertation on the Canon and Feudal Law* set out an elaborate account of British perfidy. Such truculence, given England's relatively liberal tradition of free speech, was never explicitly forbidden by the Crown or its ministers in the Privy Council. In the case of union talk, however, such a ban effectively applied, for British leaders had already moved to claim the term as their own.

The British View: An Incorporating Union

Britain's relations to its American colonial "children," over the 150–plus years after the Jamestown settlement was established, oscillated between periods of neglect and intervention.[72] British officials' explicit efforts to establish closer relations between colonies and metropolis—especially between 1675 and 1720, and again from the mid-1740s until 1756, when attention turned to the Seven Years' War—were not described in terms of "union," however. Only with British attempts to assert closer control over the colonies after 1759 did union begin to undergo a dramatic shift in meaning. One early attempt to solidify this new usage among Americans came in 1762, when English officials sponsored a contest among University of Pennsylvania students for the best essay "on the reciprocal advantages arising from a perpetual Union between Great Britain and her American colonies." After the colonial crisis erupted soon thereafter, union subsequently appeared in the dress of harmony between Britain and America, along the lines of the Anglo-Scottish Union.[73]

The context for this latter usage was highly relevant to colonial Americans. England's attempts at forging political confederations with other members of the British Isles began in the sixteenth century and involved, in various combina-

70. As Maryland's Luther Martin noted at the Constitutional Convention, delegates "anxiously sought to avoid the admission of expressions which might be odious to the ears of Americans." Farrand 1937, 1:135. Jefferson's original draft of the Declaration did include a reference to slavery, as one of the "injuries and usurpations" visited on Americans by the King; Congress stripped this out as too provocative. See discussion in Boyd et al. 1950–, 1:413–14, 426.

71. See, e.g., *Georgia Gazette* (Savannah), September 19, 1765, and Edes and Gill 1769, 7. Other terms of dissension were utilized freely, such as "liberty," of which Kammen writes "no notion was invoked more frequently" after 1763 (1986, 17).

72. See Greene 1986; Barnes 1923, 4–26.

73. Contest cited in Labaree et al. 1959–, 10:143. On post-1759 British attempts to draw the colonies closer into the imperial sphere, see Knollenberg 1960.

tions, Scotland, Ireland, and Wales. Beginning with James I's 1603 uniting of the Scottish and English crowns, a century of edicts and diplomacy eventually led to an Act of Union between England and Scotland in 1707. A prominent feature of the resultant bipartite union was its "incorporating" character. The arrangement was not a dual-federalist one; Scotland retained some autonomy especially in its civil institutions, including the established Church of Scotland and legal and educational systems separate from England's. Such a "union state" model was an innovative move away from the traditional unitary-state conception, which held "parliamentary sovereignty as the supreme law, allowing no room for rival authorities above or below it."[74]

The Anglo-Scottish Union, plagued by dissent and popular disapproval in both countries, was a poor administrative model for binding other commonwealth members more closely to London.[75] Eventually it served as a *rhetorical* model, however. British leaders were slow to develop a coherent strategy of empire, as numerous commentators have detailed: Ira Gruber concludes that "what they had were less theories than metaphors."[76] Union was a long-established referent for federation among states. And, at least partly in response to perceived American attempts at independence, in the 1760s British public speakers increasingly referred to a "Union" of England and the American colonies, on the Scottish model.

The benefit of an incorporating union, Ministry officials explained to colonists, was an attentive, supportive English "parent" providing expanded social and commercial exchanges, as well as military protection. General Thomas Gage, arriving in America as military governor of Massachusetts, issued a proclamation containing both stern rebukes of colonial misbehavior and promises of enhanced "Union with the Colonies." Thomas Pownall, safely back in London after his turbulent turn as Massachusetts governor, wrote almost obsessively on themes of union and division. Concerned that the colonies might "form an alliance, and settle the union of their mutual interests," Pownall instead offered a vision of uniting "Great Britain, with all its Atlantic and American possessions, into one great commercial dominion." The American colonies, "united to the realm . . . [like] Scotland," would thereby "be guarded against having, or forming, any principle of coherence with each other." British official Andrew Oliver, writing to Thomas Hutchinson in 1769, ruminated at length about the best means of "perfecting" a "union between the head [England] and members [colonies]," reviewing Pownall's and other plans and concluding, "I think it must more and more prevail . . . the great difficulty will be in the terms of union." Another Ministry official, Thomas Crowley, drafted so many blueprints for uniting the Amer-

74. Keating 1998, 217–19. On the background and development of the Union, see Levack 1987; an overview of recent scholarship is in Szechi 1996.

75. Richards (1991, 74) writes that Scotland was simply "ignored by her larger partner over the first fifty years of Union." See also Riley 1978; Pryde 1950, 51–67.

76. Gruber 1969, 535; cf. Dickinson 1998, 68, 73–74, 81–83; Christie 1998, 304–5.

ican colonies to England that Franklin observed in 1773, "he seems rather a little cracked upon the subject."[77]

Though manifest intentions are lost to us now, there was likely more than coincidence behind Britons' spreading use of "union" during the crisis.[78] Constant reminders of colonists' filial dependence had order-keeping intent. This owed partly to concerns about "losing" the Americans, which as already noted were present at least as early as the 1730s. The mid-eighteenth century also marked a sharp rise in British nationalist feeling, as historians have recently demonstrated.[79] The strongest promoters of a heightened sense of Britishness saw Americans as part of a more tightly unified empire and insisted on closer ties between England and British America, as with Wales or Scotland. A similar analogy intertwining king and subject, "mother country" and child, had been asserted by monarchists like Filmer after the civil wars and Exclusion Crisis. (And England, despite the failed American effort, would revisit a unionist strategy with Ireland and Canada in subsequent years.)[80] Francis Bernard, in official dispatches to London from his governor's post in 1768, perhaps unwittingly summarized both British jingoism and British fears. Bernard invoked "the grandeur of the British Empire," then immediately warned that "if there is any danger of its falling to pieces, which surely cannot be too much guarded against, it seems to me that nothing can so effectively provide against so fatal an event, as binding the colonies to the mother country by an incorporating union."[81]

Into the early 1770s, American leaders responded in kind, embracing the idea of Anglo-American unity and avoiding mention of a separate intercolonial union. Jefferson recalled in his autobiography that the "only orthodox or tenable" view during the crisis "was that the relation between Great Britain and these colonies was exactly the same as that of England and Scotland."[82] Occasionally the impetus for this unionist usage was critical, to suggest that Scots through their Union enjoyed benefits that Americans deserved as well;[83] more commonly, col-

---

77. Gage 1933, 2:118; Pownall 1766, 35–36 (cf. 3–12, 35–39, 62–69, 87, 157–61, 198–202); Oliver 1773, 80; Labaree et al. 1959–, 20:386–87. See also Whately 1765, 39–41; Hutchinson 1936 [1773]; and various defenses of an incorporating union in Force 1837–46, 2:200–201 (Barclay 14–point plan for "A Permanent Union between Great Britain and Her Colonies," February 16, 1775), 397–99 (anonymous defense of Galloway Plan, April 1775).

78. Unionist rhetoric was not limited to the Ministry and its supporters: English radicals like Joseph Priestley declared that the Commonwealth's future depended "on UNION [among all member nations] and on LIBERTY." Bonwick 1977, 53.

79. Breen 1997, 16, 19–22; Colley 1992, 5–13, 30–33 (on religious patriotism), 85–98, 157–64. The problematic nature of "Britishness," then and since, is described in Kearney 2000, 16–17. Though I use "English" and "British" more or less interchangeably here, as did most Americans of the 1760s–70s, a thoughtful inquiry into the difference is in Langlands 1999, 1–18.

80. One 1798 pamphlet invokes five separate themes of unity (1707 Union, United Provinces, marriage, commercial partnership, common youth education) in urging the Irish to accept a union with England. "French control and intrigue," the author goes on to claim, explained Americans' earlier failure to realize "the advantages" of such "an incorporating union." Bushe 1798, 7–8, 16–18.

81. Bernard 1774, 60.

82. Jefferson in Mayo 1942, 50–51.

83. As Franklin wrote in 1766, "if we must, with Scotland, participate in your taxes, let us likewise, with Scotland, participate in the Union." Labaree et al. 1959–, 13:46; cf. Otis 1764, 61.

onists welcomed the new collaborative promises. Even Samuel Adams, busily spurring resistance efforts, paused to note: "So sensible are [the colonists] of their happiness and safety, in their union with . . . the mother country, that they would by no means be inclined to accept of an independency, if offered to them."[84] Why would the increasingly rancorous American colonists obediently reserve "union" for relations with England and not apply the term to their own expanding ties?

A plausible answer lies in Britain's potent hold over the colonies, both substantive and symbolic. Historian Jack Greene demonstrates that Americans' "mimetic" impulses were "increasingly intense" during the crisis years. Colonists' predisposition to "cultivate idealized English values and to seek to imitate idealized versions of English forms and institutions" were an outgrowth of "deep social and psychological insecurities, a major crisis of identity."[85] This "identity crisis," other scholars observe, resulted in large part from the series of humiliating actions by England from 1763 onward, which together indicated that Americans occupied a second-class status within the empire. In response, colonists initially labored to assure Ministry officials—and themselves—that they were loyal, willing Britons worthy of an incorporating union with the parent nation.[86]

At least in their own eyes, Americans remained culturally English into and after the revolutionary years.[87] Both dissident American leaders and loyalists had mostly been born and/or educated in England, and these colonists tended to replicate English forms down to their rhetorical styles.[88] In the 1760s and early 1770s, facing an apparent choice between continued ties with England and separate status outside the British Empire, colonists initially embraced the former, investing union ideas with the meaning preferred by Ministry spokesmen. That Americans accepted the "prohibition" on union as a descriptive term for their own relations is less surprising than it may at first appear.

Compared to other central political concepts of the period, union seems a special case. With values like liberty or equality, the colonists freely pointed out Crown and Ministry hypocrisy. But union was not an established principle of British political ideology, asserted on behalf of subjects' individual rights. A united empire remained an uncertain prospect in the mid-eighteenth century, to the deep concern of the officials charged with administering it. To denounce Anglo-American unity was a direct challenge to the concept of empire.[89] Already alert

84. Cushing 1968, 1:170; cf. 3:101–2, where Adams reversed the relation, asserting that "the being of the British nation, I mean the being of its importance . . . will depend on her union with America."

85. Greene 1969, esp. 343–47. See also Wood 1992, 165, 168.

86. See the excellent summary in Breen 1997, 27–35.

87. For an overview see esp. Fischer 1989, who sets out in extensive detail four sets of "British folkways" that shaped different regional cultures in British America, not only into the 1770s but also, in Fischer's argument, into the present day. See also Steele 1998, 80–82; Ketcham 1974, 3–21; and Greenfeld 1992, 403–21.

88. MacLaurin (1927) has an interesting discussion of such influence on Franklin's speech; see also Fischer's region-by-region accounts of "Speech Ways" (1989, 57–62, 256–64, 470–75, 652–55). On Franklin's Anglophilia, see Wood 1996, 48–50.

89. Along with the citations in note 76, see the introduction, along with essays by Ned Landsman and J. G. A. Pocock, in Robertson 1995.

to possibilities of colonial separatism hardly imagined by Americans before the 1760s, British ministers were quick to discourage tendencies toward intercolonial union—including rhetorical appeals. Colonists accustomed to London's relatively benign neglect objected to infringements on their self-determination, but they simultaneously feared the loss of imperial protection and identity. While loudly defending their liberties, they quietly set aside mention of intercolonial union. But as ties to England became seriously frayed, the term again took on the potent meaning British ministers had labored to eradicate.

UNION REDUX: USAGE, 1774–76

Into the 1770s, most British Americans appeared genuinely to desire reconciliation with the mother country. Even avid dissenters only sought redress of specific (usually economic) claims, within the context of a Scotland-style union. But a few influential colonists began to undermine the Parliamentary authority central to an incorporating union. Thomas Hutchinson's 1773 defense of the status quo before the Massachusetts House concluded with a familiar Ministry admonition: "It is impossible that there should be two independent Legislatures in one and the same state . . . the two Legislative bodies will make two governments as distinct as the kingdoms of England and Scotland before the union." John Adams's response on the House's behalf subtly shifted the locus of unity: "Very true . . . and if they [the two legislatures] interfere not with each other, what hinders but that being united in one Head and common Sovereign, they may live happily in that Connection, and mutually support and protect each other?"[90]

Adams and other colonial elites had come to envision a loose arrangement, along Scottish Union lines, of continued allegiance to the Crown along with free trade, American delegates in Parliament, and separate colonial judicial and executive authority. This expectation encountered ever greater Ministry intransigence. Such a negative response was inevitable, though most colonists failed to understand the underlying reason—which had relatively little to do with American concerns. For the British a system of sovereignty jointly shared by king, Parliament, and American assemblies implied a return to an independent monarch. England's unshakable commitment to parliamentary superiority, hard-won in 1688, posed for colonists a stark choice between submission and revolution.[91]

90. Hutchinson 1936 [1773], 269; Adams in Taylor 1977–89, 1:329. Other colonists soon followed Adams in writing Parliament out of the arrangement. Jefferson, in his legal history of English-American relations, explained that from the earliest "settlements . . . effected in the wilds of America, the *emigrants thought proper* to adopt that system of laws under which they had hitherto lived in the mother country, and to *continue their union with her* by submitting themselves to the same common sovereign, who was thereby made the central link connecting the several parts of the empire." Boyd et al. 1950–, 1:122–23 (emphasis added).

91. Koenigsberger 1989, 152 (cf. Dickinson 1998, 82–94). A quarter century later at the Virginia ratifying convention, James Madison saw matters similarly: "The fundamental principle of the Revolution was, that the colonies were co-ordinate members with each other, and with Great Britain, of

Whether or not colonists recognized this dynamic at the time, British policies in support of parliamentary power inflamed American opinion. As the crisis proceeded, colonists became painfully aware of their subordinate position within the empire. T. H. Breen summarizes their "sudden realization" in the early 1770s "that the British really regarded white colonial Americans as second-class beings, indeed, as persons so inferior from the metropolitan perspective that they somehow deserved a lesser measure of freedom." British promises of Anglo-American union, incorporating or otherwise, increasingly appeared hollow in the face of a string of policies and pronouncements seemingly designed to emphasize the degree of Americans' exclusion.[92]

As colonial resistance leaders arrived at this conclusion in 1773–74, their vision of a united British Commonwealth was reduced to a "network of separate republics, held together because they all shared the same constitutional monarch."[93] Ministry officials continued to proclaim parliamentary sovereignty as late as 1776, as in Lord Howe's haughty mention in a letter to Franklin of "the King's paternal solicitude for promoting the establishment of lasting peace and union with the Colonies," with details to be determined by Parliament. Franklin responded with a telling figure, "that fine and noble china vase the British Empire": he warned that "being once broken . . . a perfect re-union of those parts could scarce even be hoped for."[94]

From mid-1774 onward, awareness spread throughout the colonies of just how shattered Franklin's vase was. Twelve colonies sent delegates to the First Continental Congress, convened in September 1774 to "unite the colonies" in resistance to British "usurpation." Delegates stopped short of calling their collective body a union, instead adopting "the several colonies" or "the Association." Most also arrived at the Congress, as Neil York writes, "with remarkably similar charges: to restore the 'union and harmony between Great Britain and the Colonies.'" But such sentiment was fading rapidly. Within months John Adams dismissed the idea of "union [as an] incorporation of all the dominions of the King," instead advocating "a union of the colonies . . . and an American legislature." In Parliament, meanwhile, members lamented that "there is an end of all union [with America]."[95]

In such a climate, applying "union" to the colonists' own relations once again

an empire, united by a common executive sovereign, but not by any common legislative sovereign. . . . A denial of these principles by Great Britain, and the assertion of them by America, produced the Revolution." Elliot 1836, 4:589.

92. Breen 1997, 28–29.

93. Countryman 1986, 70. Cf. Wilson, "Considerations on Parliament . . . ," which advocated fealty to the king but rejected Parliamentary authority (in McCloskey 1967, 2:722–46).

94. Labaree et al. 1959–, 22:520. On British response to the colonists' distinction between parliamentary and monarchical sovereignty, see Bailyn 1967, esp. 225–29.

95. Congress proceedings in Ford et al. 1904–37, 1:63–80; cf. Boston Gazette, September 27, 1773, recommending a "congress of American states" to redress the fact that "no plan of union is yet agreed on between [Britain and America], the dispute continues, and everything floats in uncertainty." York 1998, 403; Adams in Taylor 1977–89, 1:310, 322; MP quoted in Simmons and Thomas 1982, 3:149.

became feasible. By 1775 Americans widely urged intercolonial unity, often in apocalyptic terms like Ebenezer Baldwin's: "A very little attention must convince every one of the necessity of our being united. If the colonies are divided or the people in the several colonies are very considerably divided, we are undone. Nothing but the united efforts of America can save us."[96] Rather than dependent "children," Baldwin and other colonists (invoking Locke, Hutcheson, and other British thinkers who drew analogies between familial and political relations) reconceived themselves as a separate, united "family" in their own right, "justifying political rebellion against the 'parent country' on the basis of natural development." References to colonists' "heroic" rejection of the Dominion of New England were exhumed and reprinted, evidence of a history of Americans' "independent minds."[97]

Some declarations of American union were still accompanied by appeals "that we may ever be united" to the Crown, a connection desirable not only for nostalgic reasons. Pauline Maier notes that restraint in advocating a separatist union "seemed essential . . . to gain time for the forging of American unity, upon which, everyone acknowledged, the success of their cause would depend." A complicated choreography was underway, with colonial leaders' calls for union arousing talk of independence, and cautionary warnings following in turn. In May 1775, the Second Continental Congress's "Olive Branch Petition" could still acknowledge the benefits of "the union between our Mother Country and these Colonies"—but entirely in the past tense. That same month, Edmund Burke declared in London that the "greatest" source of "sorrow" felt among Britons was that "there no longer subsist between you and us any common and kindred principles, upon which we can possibly unite." In response, Americans' anti-British cant intensified, even before the formal outbreak of war. Georgia's colonial congress denounced, in July 1775, "the unrelenting fury of a despotic Ministry, and . . . the most oppressive acts of a venal and corrupted Parliament," along with "the iniquity and cruelty [of] an array of mercenaries under an unfeeling Commander." The Georgia assembly concluded that this did have a "good effect, to unite men of all ranks in the common cause."[98]

Americans' renewed references to intercolonial union were not merely su-

96. Baldwin in Greene 1975, 219. Prominent among countless similar examples was a series of "Letters from London to a Gentleman," which ran in several colonial newspapers and which featured repeated exhortations to "let the Americans be united." The series is reprinted in Force 1837–46, vol. 2.

97. Barnes 1997, 598. See also Yazawa (1985, 87–110) on the "affective familial model of the empire" advanced by English spokesmen after 1760 and eventually rejected by colonists. Locke devotes long sections of his *Two Treatises* to comparing political societies and natural "families": see Locke 1988 [1690], esp. 303–18 (refuting "paternal power" in a polity), and also 183–94, 267–68, 345–47.

98. Arthur Lee in Maier 1974, 170n, 284; Force et al. 1837–46, 2:1870; Burke in Langford 1981–86, 3:277; *Georgia Gazette* (Savannah), July 12, 1775. Burke-style regrets among English writers were a staple in American newspapers for years to come. Papers from New Hampshire to North Carolina, for example, reprinted "Ludlow," writing in a 1778 *London Evening Post* that "a firm union and confederacy [with the United States] . . would perhaps be more beneficial to this country, than if we were established in our former claims to superiority." *North Carolina Gazette* (Wilmington), March 6, 1778; *New Hampshire Gazette* (Portsmouth), March 7, 1778.

perficial evidence of more important political or economic changes. Americans "draw strength and courage from talk of Union," a Tory official in Pennsylvania darkly reported home in 1775. The conceptual displacement traced above had been overcome, and a rhetorical forging of national unity was underway. Colonists increasingly imagined themselves as mutually dependent citizens rather than as subjects of the King. This entailed an independent American state, with John Adams applying power-balancing theory in its defense: "apply unto France, Spain, [and] Holland" for assistance, "and our Union would prevent a division by [England], of our united governments."[99]

By late 1774 American religious authorities also were again applying this potent term to political concerns, as churches sought to infuse the struggle against Britain with providential rhetoric. National unity was foremost among the "three ingredients necessary for [revolutionary] success" that Boston minister Charles Chauncy saw as "bless[ings] of the Almighty." Exulted his colleague Samuel West, "how wonderfully Providence has smiled upon us by causing the several colonies to unite so firmly together . . . though differing from each other in their particular interest, forms of government, modes of worship, and particular customs and manners, besides several animosities that had subsisted among them." Even traditionally Tory synods like New York's Presbyterians placed their religious "duty" to "maintain the union which at present subsists through all the colonies" ahead of loyalty to the Crown. Divine protection for colonists' nascent political bonds was invoked by secular figures as well, from Benjamin Franklin to Thomas Paine.[100]

In arguments opposing "virtual" representation, absolute Parliamentary supremacy, and eventually monarchical sovereignty, the justification for English spokesmen's "grand united Empire" was dismantled. The one-vote rejection, at the First Continental Congress, of a Plan of Union with Britain (proposed by longtime Franklin associate Joseph Galloway) was the last point at which reconciliation was formally contemplated. Expunging that vote and then the Plan itself from the Congress's minutes drove the point home. Franklin, by way of consolation, wrote Galloway that "I cannot but apprehend more mischief than benefit from a closer Union [with England]." Jefferson added to colonists' catalogues of British misdeeds the "exercise of . . . dividing and dismembering [our] country," a gross violation never before "occurr[ing] in his majesty's realm." By mid-1775 American Tories recognized the writing on the wall. Wrote Jonathan Sewall, shortly before fleeing to England: "It is now become too plain to be any longer doubted, that a Union is formed by a great Majority, almost throughout

---

99. *Pennsylvania Evening Post* (Philadelphia), January 25, 1775; Adams in Taylor 1977–89, 2:179. Christopher Brooks, in a study of American colonists' undertanding of "colony" and other terms during the crisis, similarly notes the importance of rhetoric in the rebellion: "Shifting the lexical ground . . . was the first step toward revolution." Brooks 1996, 242.

100. Chauncy and West quoted in Berens 1978, 67–68; Clark 1994, 359; Zuckerman 1977, 210; Paine 1969 [1791], 87–90.

this whole Continent." Daniel Leonard, writing as "Massachusettensis," concurred: "The colonies . . . are not of the same community with the people of England. All distinctions destroy this union; and if it can be shown in any particular to be dissolved, it must be so in all instances whatsoever."[101]

Shortly afterward came the first official American references since the 1750s to "United Colonies." A notable example was the "Declaration of Causes of Taking Up Arms," issued July 6, 1775, by the "Representatives of the United Colonies of North America." The concluding paragraphs, drafted by Jefferson and John Dickinson, exhibit lingering effects of Britain's rhetorical displacement. "Our [intercolonial] union is perfect," they wrote, adding quickly: "Lest this declaration should disquiet the minds of our friends and fellow-subjects in any part of the Empire, we assure them that we mean not to dissolve that Union [with the King] which . . . we sincerely wish to see restored."[102] This conceptual dissonance was cleared up a year later when in a more famous Declaration of grievances the Americans—now "United States"—announced all political connections to England null and void. "Manly spirit bids us to renounce forever these unfeeling brethren," Jefferson wrote in his original draft of the Declaration. "We must endeavor to forget our former love for them."[103] Assertions of union with Britain were thereafter rare among any but Loyalists in the former American colonies. In their place arose angry denunciations of British tyranny and calls to American union in response.

Along with the Declaration, reprinted in every Whig paper in the country, Thomas Paine's hugely popular *Common Sense* did much to bury the old usage and popularize the new. Anti-British and religious usage inform the pamphlet's stirring language. "'TIS TIME TO PART," exhorted Paine, denouncing English promises of filial unity as "farcical . . . the words have no meaning." "The time hath found us," he states at the work's heart. "The glorious union of all things prove[s] the fact. It is not in numbers but in unity, that our great strength lies . . . the whole, when united can accomplish [independence]." And the colonies responded: before the year was out all colonial assemblies had substituted for the traditional "God Save the King!" first "God Save the United Colonies!" and then "God Save the United States!"[104] Despite dissent (then as now) about the actual extent of colonial unity—such a "diversity of interests, inclinations, judgements, and conduct" existed among the colonies, Joseph Galloway stubbornly maintained in 1774, that "it will ever be impossible for them to unite in any general

101. Franklin to Galloway, in Labaree et al. 1959–, 21:509; Boyd et al. 1950–, 1:123; Sewall quoted in Greene 1975, 266; Adams and Leonard 1819 [1775], 62.

102. Boyd et al. 1950–, 1:217. The first recorded example in the Congress's records of "united colonies" appears in May 1775, in a letter from the Massachusetts Provincial Congress imploring more collective action among the colonies. Ford et al. 1904–37, 2:76.

103. Boyd et al. 1950–, 1:427.

104. Paine 1976 [1776], 87, 65–69, 100–101; cf. 83, 108, 122. By midyear 1775 even perennial go-it-alone Rhode Island would send delegates to Congress with instructions to pursue "the most proper measures for promoting and confirming the strictest union and confederation between the . . . United Colonies." Bates 1898, 63.

measure whatever"[105]—it is clear that rhetorical devotion to union spread rapidly throughout the colonial leadership in the mid-1770s. Observing his fellow members of the Second Continental Congress, Virginia's Richard Henry Lee proudly affirmed that "all the old Provinces not one excepted are directed by the same firmness of union."[106]

＊

These initial statements of political union among the colonies deserve careful attention. Americans had by no means simply returned, after a ten-year hiatus, to the weak self-defense understanding prevalent before the 1760s. Now the word was used to denote the whole American people in affective ways formerly reserved for religious relations. Union had powerful political connotations from 1775–76 on, erupting from a mixture of anti-British and religious sentiment. The resulting conceptual conflict—Americans blatantly reasserting the term Britons had employed to insist on continued interrelations—was a key register of defiance.

Union talk helped alleviate the anxieties of change, as countless revolution-era statements attest. The new union was claimed to be perfect, whole, or truly sacred in one sentence, then in danger of imminent disintegration in the next. "The management of so complicated and mighty a machine as the United Colonies requires the meekness of Moses, the patience of Job, and the wisdom of Solomon, added to the valour of David," sighed John Adams in April 1776.[107]

Such nervousness was evident in Americans' religious applications of union. Samuel Williams preached late in 1774 that the "influence of heaven" had provided "the means for establishing a firm and solid union among the colonies," although the outlook was otherwise "critical and dangerous to the last degree." To Jacob Duché, the first chaplain of Congress, "rude winds," "the billows of public or private adversity," and "all this load of misery" marked "this calamitous time," alleviated only "by such heavenly tempers and dispositions, as alone can testify [to] our vital union and communion."[108]

These religious appeals were as abstract as most early invocations of union ever got.[109] The revolutionary elite rarely engaged in philosophical ruminations of civic-republican, liberal, or other vintage, on unionist themes. This was partly because the problem of joining different states had received little systematic attention from British empire-builders. Unlike the rich British intellectual tradi-

105. Galloway in Jensen 1967, 384. Compare John Murrin's contemporary judgment: "native-born North Americans showed no interest in political union, much less independence" until the fact was forced upon them (1987a, 339, 344).
106. Smith 1976–, 1:337. Pauline Maier traces similar "enthusiastic affirmations of . . . American unity" among state and local conventions meeting to draft resolutions of independence (1997, 76).
107. Taylor 1977–89, 4:135.
108. Williams in Greene 1975, 384–85; Duché 1775, 34. On millennialism more generally, see Lienesch 1988, 186–203.
109. Or as historical as they ever got. As Americans sought to differentiate themselves from Britain, a history of Puritan piety was occasionally emphasized. See esp. Tuveson 1968.

tion undergirding concepts like liberty or natural rights, union was as much a slogan as it was a carefully specified theme. By the war's outbreak only the bare outlines of a conception of political union had emerged, describing "the Union" and means by which unity could be strengthened. Thus the *purposes* of promoting national union appear to have been straightforward: to oppose expected British retaliation; to aid in differentiating Americans from their cultural and, in many cases, biological forebears; and to glorify the God whose "Agency" secured, as Samuel Adams had it, "this Union among the colonies and warmth of Affection."[110]

Members of the American union included virtually anyone willing to help the revolutionary effort. For the moment, thorny problems of membership in additional communities, whether a home state or region or group based on shared interests, ethnicity, occupation, or gender, were muted: "loyalists vs. patriots" was the most salient distinction. Common standing as Americans was advertised by leading political spokesmen, to foster direct social and political ties among the people. To be sure, few nonwhite males held full civic membership, and the ascriptive sides of colonial religious communities—social exclusivity, intolerance, and the like—were in abundant display.[111] But women, resident aliens, American Indians, and free blacks all made welcome contributions to the new republic, especially its wartime needs. New Yorkers sought "peace and amity" with all "Indians . . . willing to unite their efforts" with the revolutionaries, language replicated in early federal treaties such as that the Continental Congress concluded with the Iroquois in 1775.[112] White women's works were extensive: they participated in consumer boycotts; raised funds for the army and quartered soldiers in their homes; spied on British troops and cared for American soldiers; articulated opposition themes in public statements, especially religious testaments; undertook virtually all "tasks normally performed by men," who were away at war; and, in at least a few cases, served (in disguise) as a soldier.[113]

Free blacks also joined the war effort and otherwise aided the unionist cause. At least partly in response, eight northern states abolished slavery during or soon after the war, beginning with Vermont. Though abolitionist sentiment expanded during the 1770s in the northern and mid-Atlantic colonies,[114] explicit references to union of whites and blacks were extremely rare. The few comments of this

110. Cushing 1968, 3:199.

111. For details see Smith 1997, 72–77. As he concludes, a "narrower, Anglo-Saxon-centered view left out too many colonial inhabitants whose support colonial elites desperately needed" (77).

112. *Goodell v. Jackson*, 20 Johns. R. 693 (N.Y.C.C. 1823), at 712; Ford et al. 1904–37, 14:104. For a much more critical view of the treatment of Native Americans during the revolution, see Jennings 1976; cf. Calloway 1995.

113. Evans 1975, 10–20, 303–34; Kerber 1989, 18–29; Breen 1994, 469 (quote); Kerber 1980, 35–67; Ulrich 1989, 211–12, 235–43. On black women, see Norton 1980, 196, 209–12, and Jones 1989. On women and other groups' civic membership in revolutionary times, see Smith 1997, 103–14; and Kerber 1995, 24, 27–28, and 1989, 29–42.

114. Most newspapers in New England and the middle colonies featured antislavery accounts, many infused with the patriotic spirit coloring the revolution. The *Connecticut Courant*, e.g., within the space of a few months ran two long abolitionist essays, one by "Antidoulious" (October 3, 1774)

type were often negative, as in this newspaper couplet from 1771: "Device and low cunning to commonly stand / Related in friendship and join hand in hand / Experience doth teach us that poor black and white / When blended together, as one, will unite!" While colonists' talk of universal liberty and equality seems cruelly hypocritical given the continued presence of black slavery, as Gordon Wood demonstrates, "Americans in 1775–76 began attacking [slavery] with a vehemence that was inconceivable earlier."[115]

Membership in this earliest American political union was a matter not of overt exclusion, as with citizenship laws, but of inclusion on varying terms, from full participation to subordination. Majority white men's rhetorical embrace of most other residents favorable to independence was partly a function of the American Revolution's radical heritage, as the growing emphasis on national unity was sometimes tapped as a moral weapon for change. New Jersey's legislative approval of female suffrage in 1790, for example, included this statement from one assemblyman: "We are united to [women], and they to us. . . . They therefore should vote, as men do."[116] Religious overtones still amply present in union talk during the 1770s also spurred antislavery and other inclusionary movements, though again on a limited scale. Morally charged applications of union became more common in the nineteenth century, after the term underwent considerable transformation in meaning.

Revolutionary Americans' relatively enlightened invocations of political unity owed less to a strong spirit of liberal toleration than to an obvious difficulty in promoting ethnicity or culture as the primary basis for national union. The rebels' strongest animus was expressed toward the British, and Americans—the vast majority of whom hailed from the British Isles in the 1770s, a demographic fact that remained true for another century—could hardly denounce that "people" as an inferior race. John Randolph reminded fellow Americans in 1774 that they were "descended from the loins of *Britons*, and therefore may, with propriety, be called the children, and *England* the mother of them. We are not only allied by blood, but are still farther united by . . . manners[,] religion, and language."[117] As Americans struggled to differentiate themselves from their putatively fellow Anglo-Saxons, a strong racial basis for their union would hardly serve the pur-

---

and the other a five-part series by Benjamin Rush beginning March 3, 1773. Southern papers, in contrast, included few editorial references to slavery at all, either for or against. As did some colonial northern papers, including Franklin's *Pennsylvania Gazette,* southern papers continued to print numerous advertisements seeking the capture and return of runaway slaves. The four October 1775 issues of the weekly *Georgia Gazette,* to take one typical example, featured 125 advertisements. Thirty-two, or 24 percent of the total, concerned runaway slaves (often more than one runaway per ad), and five (4 percent) advertised slaves for sale.

115. *Massachusetts Spy,* March 7, 1771; Wood 1991, 186–87 (see also Jordan 1968, 301–4, 308–11, and Foner 1998, 39). On African-American contributions to the Revolutionary War, and scattered support for black rights in response, see Brown 1867; Bradley 1998; and Klinkner and Smith 1999, 18–26 (though cf. Burrows and Wallace 1999, 400, on New Yorkers' later opposition to emancipation, on the grounds that blacks had "fought against us by whole regiments during the war").

116. As later recorded by a correspondent in the *Sentinel of Freedom* (Newark, N.J.), October 30, 1796. See also McCormick 1953, 93–100.

117. Quoted in Higham 1999, 302.

pose. Thus, in significant part, came the comparatively cosmopolitan nature of early conceptions of unity in the new republic.

Less clear than the purposes or agents of union were questions of *process*—how the unity now widely considered desirable might be effected and sustained. Debates over Britain's proposed incorporating union had been centered on matters of classification and principle: if the colonists and Ministry could reach accord on the location of sovereignty and on the character of colonial representation, a union based on the Anglo-Scottish example could be established. But efforts at purely American union presented novel institutional questions of establishing cooperation among a diverse people, historically displaying little interest in joint governance, whose main common trait was membership in the British Empire. American thinkers were only belatedly beginning to contemplate the problem in earnest. As Edmund Burke said of "American unity" in 1776: "It is a condition that confronts you, not a theory." [118]

For the moment, precisely specifying the new union of states remained a future concern, with the immediate patriotic and martial mandate clear enough. These ends were sufficient to promote the term's usage among the general American population in the years to come, providing a vital foundation for political development. No one concept's influence alone can account for the development of thirteen British colonies into a remarkably durable national union. But recounting that achievement without attention to the tense linguistic contest surrounding the term ignores a critical part of the story—enough to leave modern historians muttering about "miracles." Much as the Declaration helped many citizens overcome their fears of "that frightful word, Independence"[119] and imagine themselves as a separate people, asserting intercolonial unity buttressed the sense of fraternal purpose necessary to wage war successfully. And at a time when commercial and national-security institutions were still in their infancy,[120] the rhetorical assertion of unity was virtually the only source of strong cohesive ties.

After 1776, war with Britain was a powerful encouragement to Americans of all backgrounds, including many who paid no attention to union talk before the conflict, to imagine themselves as a united polity. But the conceptual basis for unionist commitments was under construction long before armed hostilities began. J. G. A. Pocock once noted that "men cannot do what they have no means of saying they have done,"[121] and the efforts of earlier colonists, particularly Franklin, to spur awareness of the benefits of colonial unity provided the rhetorical

118. Burke in Pole 1977, 55. See also Murrin 1987a, esp. 340 – 42.

119. Congressman Josiah Bartlett (N.H.), referring to his constituents' outlook, in a letter on New Year's Day 1776. In Smith 1976 –, 3:88.

120. On the emergence of an American market economy in the early nineteenth century, see Henretta 1991, esp. 34, and Gilje 1996.

121. Pocock 1972, 122. Cf. Bukovansky (1997, 210): "The U.S. polity had to be conceived of as a whole before it could be used as a venue for the pursuit of various interests or aims. The process by which American identity was conceptualized—and its underlying ideas—was as critical to the constitution of state identity as the existence of the territory and the people."

groundwork for Americans' transformation from British subjects to a separate united people. This concept was an important tool for leaders subsequently promoting the patriotic feeling to sustain war efforts.

The independence period by no means marked the end of struggles over the meaning and purposes of union. One writer suggested hopefully in 1776 that "the thirteen colonies [were] so happily united" that further tracts on the subject were no longer necessary.[122] For American unionists, instead, a long road—leading as often to disruption as to closer bonds—lay ahead.

122. Quoted in Maier 1974, 267.

cA Theory of Political Union Emerges, 1780s–1820s

> The advice nearest to my heart and deepest in my convictions is that the
> Union of the States be cherished and perpetuated. Let the open enemy to
> it be regarded as a Pandora with her box opened, and the disguised one,
> as the Serpent creeping with his deadly wiles into Paradise.
>
> —James Madison, "Last Political Will and Testament," 1834

WHEN WASHINGTON IRVING'S Rip Van Winkle stumbled home from the
Catskills around 1790 he returned to a transformed land, unable "to comprehend
the strange events that had taken place during his torpor." Even the names were
changed: Rip's old hangout (and the tale's symbolic center), the "King George"
village inn, had become the "Union Hotel." It was no coincidence that Rip's sleep
encompassed the two decades of independence, confederation, and constitutional ratification.[1] The story's figurative changes mirrored reality, as U.S. citizens in the 1780s found themselves committed, in binding legal terms, to building first a "perpetual union" and then a "more perfect" one.[2]

What did this entail? Most constitutional framers conceived national unity in
terms of close ties among American residents, cemented by a robust patriotic
sensibility, tighter connections between the states, and a stable set of institutions
securing the whole—though whether these were to be located primarily at the
federal or the state level was deliberately left vague. None of these features seemed
remotely "perfect" in the late eighteenth-century United States. Interstate and
interpersonal comity remained more assertion than fact, and ardent references to
"the Union" were backed by little administrative authority. During the war for
independence, the Second Continental Congress did raise an army, negotiate
treaties abroad, authorize each new state constitution, set tariffs and other commercial policies, and coin money. But with war's end congressional authority
dwindled, and by the mid-1780s Congress "had virtually ceased trying to govern."
Much of America's political class remained fiercely devoted to rhetorical defenses
of national union, but as the republic's viability dwindled concerns grew apace.

---

1. Neider 1975, 10, 14. In other tales Irving reiterated the point. "Legend of Sleepy Hollow," set
at the turn of the nineteenth century, begins "in a remote period of American history, that is to say,
some thirty years ago . . ." (33).
2. Viz. the "Articles of Confederation and Perpetual Union"; a "perpetual" union was invoked in
the first Article as well.

In 1786 Continental Congressman Theodore Sedgwick wrote home to Massachusetts that "even the appearance of a union cannot in the way we are now long be preserved. It becomes us seriously to contemplate a substitute."[3]

Facing a considerable gap between their unionist conceptions and reality, delegates to the constitutional convention defined "more perfect" in contrast with the Articles. A *sustainable* union was the goal in 1787, more perfect because it could be preserved. Recognizing the limits of political possibility, unionists including Madison, Washington, and the aged Franklin (who died a year after ratification) worked to bolster bonds between states and among their inhabitants, expanding central government powers to this end where they deemed it necessary and feasible. Anti-Federalists like James Winthrop ("Agrippa") and small-state supporters like Delaware's "Phocion" also advocated closer national union while opposing centralization as "the path to disunion."[4] Though historians have long viewed efforts to enhance political union during the confederation and constitution-making period as synonymous with expanding the national government,[5] this simple equation misreads Americans' conception of union and partly mistakes the nature of the constitutional struggle. Union did not signify strong centralization, except perhaps to a few especially avid nationalists.

Rather, union in the convention and ratifying debates served as shorthand for compromise, with the concept taking on a vital balancing role sustained in subsequent decades. Among the few points of agreement across multiple political divides was that the states must remain united, or disaster would follow. "I confess to you candidly," George Washington wrote in a 1785 letter, "that I can foresee no evil greater than disunion."[6] Widespread commitment to unity bridged deep divides over state sovereignty, finance, representation, administrative authority, slavery, and other highly charged matters. Among leading citizens of all persuasions union was a fulcrum of political talk in the 1780s; debaters agreed on its importance no matter how furiously they contested other issues. An inevitable result was that such an esteemed term lacked definitive content, lodging a dangerous ambiguity near the heart of American political institutions.

This chapter pursues two principal lines of inquiry. First, it continues into the early nineteenth century a recounting of union's meanings and purposes. After independence, the interest of most ordinary Americans in their common national fate declined, spurring leaders to promote a spirit of unity in response.

---

3. Wood 1969, 359 (and cf. 463–67; Jillson and Wilson 1994); Sedgwick in Henderson 1974, 394.

4. Storing 1981, 1:84; "Phocion" in Bailyn 1993, 2:526–32.

5. Morris 1987, esp. 245–322. Cf. Rossiter 1966, chap. 9, which details a "Nationalist Assault" at the constitutional convention; Murphy 1967; Rakove 1979; Wiebe 1984, 21–24, 34–41; McDonald 1985, 199–203, 284; Thomas 1991; Ackerman 1991, 27, 44; Banning 1995, 35–42, 140–46 (though cf. 296–97).

6. Chase 1985–97, 3:198. Most anti-Federalists also openly worried about disunion, though Patrick Henry complained about the "bugbear" of Federalist warnings "that the Union shall be dissolved" (in Ackerman 1998, 61).

Among the only ready means to this end was the *language* of union, expressed in public oratory, patriotic celebrations of independence and of the Constitution's ratification, and newspaper editorials. Gradually, inspired by these sources, the term again spread from elites to all classes. I explore this development in two separate sections in this chapter: the first treating opinion leaders' unionist commitment during the years between war and constitutional ratification and the second (at chapter's end) investigating union usage in the early republic.

Like any source of power, influential political words attract interested parties. As union's popularity grew, efforts were increasingly made to specify the term's meaning. A second thrust of this chapter is to reconstruct the early political theory of American union, focusing on the thought of James Madison. Facing the immense challenge of developing stable public institutions and social practices in a new nation, Madison wove together American territory, affective spirit among citizens, and representative leadership in explaining how disparate states—and people—could be united. The affective element in particular has received little attention among scholars of the early republic, though it influenced political ideas and even institutional structures for years thereafter. Yet its author was deeply ambivalent about the possibility of realizing closer interpersonal ties, a hesitancy that contributed to a tension between elite and popular governance that also long endured.

"A UNION AS LASTING AS TIME": CONCEPTUAL OVERVIEW

When the constitutional framers declared theirs a "more perfect" union, they drew (presumably consciously) on a rich phraseology. Cromwell famously promised, during the Glorious Revolution, to "conduce them [Englishmen] to such a knot [that] there shall be perfect union amongst them." In commemoration, a British commercial frigate built in the late 1740s, and still seaworthy during the revolutionary crisis, was called the *Perfect Union*. Tory sympathizer Joseph Galloway, angrily denouncing American rebels in 1775, complained that "none of them have been capable of offering the public any other more perfect system of union" than Great Britain's proposed incorporating union. Instead, charged Galloway, Americans were preparing "some deep-laid, dark [unionist] designs, which they do not care to unfold."[7] Now, fifteen years later, the "dark design" was fully apparent in the Constitution's opening line. The framers' intent was to encourage the American populace to view themselves as a more closely united people; a more perfect republic would result. Whether the people would cooperate was yet to be seen, however.

7. Merriman 1902, 2:230; Force 1837–46, 2:397. On the ship *Perfect Union*, see shipping notices in *Pennsylvania Gazette*, April 2, 1752; October 10, 1765. See also the discussion in the introduction, note 12.

Elites' Union

Mass patriotic euphoria greeted American victory at Yorktown in September 1781, a spirit that peaked twenty months later with the signing of a peace treaty in Paris. Subsequently, among the mass of former colonists, the commitment to political union spurred by the war ebbed steadily. As one authority summarizes, "few Americans were interested in collective public action before the revolution, only temporarily embraced it during the crisis, and returned to the pursuit of happiness in their individual lives rather than in the public realm." Examination of available workingman's newspapers confirms the point, as does postwar Americans' widespread indifference to elections of delegates to state ratifying conventions, with turnout below historical averages for local and statewide races. These were predictable developments, given fading anti-British fervor as the war concluded. A decade after it was written, Robert Beverley's 1775 lament already resembled a prophecy fulfilled: "Ambition, Resentment, and Interest may have united us for a Moment, but be assured . . . that that Union will soon be converted into Envy, Malevolence, and Faction, and most probably will introduce a greater degree of Opposition [to nation-building] than even now prevails against the Mother Country."[8] Far from substantiating some modern historians' claims that a "mobilized majority of American citizens" conferred "deep, broad, and decisive" support on the postwar effort for political union, it attracted mostly indifference.[9]

Against this tide, political leaders and other opinion shapers assiduously promoted the term after peace in 1783. Newspapers regularly featured subsequent unionist declarations. In a May 1786 editorial, one essayist, "Common Sense," deplored recent British perfidy and warned that "this is but a gentle beginning of what America must expect, unless she guards her union with nicer care and stricter honor. United, she is formidable. . . . Separated, she is a medley of individual nothings." Also typical was a New Jersey paper's front page in the same month, featuring two essays about the decline of American unity. The writer "Civis" bemoaned "the disunions that are now presiding in your infant republic" and proceeded through a long roster of associated dangers before frothily concluding, "my fellow citizens, [only] by union and perseverance, you may revive the dying sparks of freedom . . . and forever stand secure, though opposed by all the combined powers of the universe." Immediately following was an anonymous contribution titled "Perform or Not Promise," castigating "a love of gew-gawery"

---

8. Greene 1987, 5; on turnout, McDonald 1979 [1965], 319; Beverley in Kammen 1972, 83–84. Newspapers inspected for tradesmen and mechanics' union usage include the *American-Herald* (Boston), *New-York Journal*, and *Freeman's Journal* (Philadelphia), extant issues between 1775 and 1790. In my sample of available issues (I examined 162 pages with news content from the three) I found 21 references to national union, or 0.13 union references per page. This is well below the average for all papers (around one reference per page) during the period.

9. Ackerman 1991, 88n, 272–77. Samuel Beer's is a more balanced presentation of the "national idea" as a "democratic idea" from its beginning (1993, 1–2).

among Americans and reminding "my countrymen of New-Jersey" that they were "connected with the other states, and cannot be but affected with their situation. . . . Do you remember when we entered into an association, in which we pledged . . . in the common cause, with our lives and fortunes?"[10]

Constitutional ratification temporarily renewed Americans' patriotic spirit, and unionist references soared accordingly. A North Carolina newspaper declared, in July 1790, "The American Union Completed" and printed a poem in celebration, beginning "'Tis done. 'Tis finished! guardian Union binds, / In voluntary bands, a nation's minds." The *Salem Mercury*'s editor saluted the country's "narrow escape [from] the dreadful calamity of anarchy and disunion," contrasting "the enduring union" and its "national blessings." After 1787, even staunch anti-Federalist foes of centralization employed the term favorably. James Winthrop, one of the more rabidly antinationalist writers, devoted his Christmas Day 1788 number of "Letters of Agrippa" to the "grand principle of union" operating between the states. His animating force was not "power," the unifying engine of "despotick" regimes, but "commerce . . . a bond of union which applies to all parts of the empire." Such willing participation in creating national symbols seems inconsistent with anti-Federalists' commitment to decentralization. But for Winthrop, and colleagues like Patrick Henry, the aged Samuel Adams, and Melancton Smith, the term described a "natural principle of affection" between Americans of different regions, one "not requiring a Despot [i.e., stronger central government] to be fulfilled." Commercial interest and "friendship," combined with sharply limited federal powers, were sufficient to achieve a "great bond of union."[11]

As the leading historian of anti-Federalism affirms, by 1787 "the Union [had become] the decisive political entity, as was very widely recognized on both sides at the time." Having granted the importance of union and a "partial consolidation," anti-Federalists had to follow their opponents' logic at least partway toward ratification. Given "the desirable end of conciliation and unanimity," George Mason admitted to the Virginia ratifying convention, he would "make the greatest concessions" once "necessary amendments" were appended to the Constitution. At the same gathering Edmund Randolph maintained the "objections to the Constitution" he had expressed at Philadelphia but explained his influential decision to reverse his position and support ratification: "I never will assent to any scheme that will operate a dissolution of the Union . . . the Union is the anchor

10. *Political Intelligencer & New-Jersey Advertiser* (New Brunswick), December 30, 1783; *New-Jersey Journal* (Elizabethtown), May 31, 1786.

11. *State Gazette of North Carolina* (Edenton), July 2, 1790; *Salem Mercury* (Mass.) March 3, 1789; Storing 1981, 1:84–85; Smith in ibid., vol. 6; Henry in Bailyn 1993, 2:595–96; Adams in ibid., 1:446. Even in defeat, anti-Federalists like Maine's William Widgery glumly pledged to "endeavor to sow the seeds of union and peace" among constituents (Morris 1987, 305). Commentary on anti-Federalists' union allegiance is in Matson and Onuf 1990, 130–35; Ericson 1993, 29–50 (on anti-Federalists' "uneasy combination of political caution and nationalism"); Onuf 1988; Storing 1977, 24–37; a reminder that the two groups shared common ground in other principled respects is in Ketcham 1993.

of our political salvation; and I will assent to the lopping of this limb [his arm] before I assent to the dissolution of the Union."[12]

From a religiously imbued spring of anti-British sentiment during the revolution, union had become a chief political good among delegates at Philadelphia and in state ratifying conventions. Three matters arise in reviewing this conceptual history. Why, in the face of waning mass interest in—or even awareness of—national unity after the war, did the idea win such purchase among America's varied groups of elites? What did union mean to these leaders? And what purposes was it intended to achieve? The first question is taken up immediately below: the constitutional framers' unionist outlook owed to a combination of fidelity to the revolutionary generation's "Union of 1776," growing interpersonal ties among elites, self-interested aims, and—most important—fear of disunion. I then turn to an extended study of James Madison's theory of union, in order to analyze coherently the term's meaning and intended purposes. Concluding the chapter is a return to a wide-focus lens on union views in early nineteenth-century America.

Union's Attraction

Much venerated among the constitutional generation was the "Union of 1776," already passing into legend as a touchstone of "UNIVERSAL harmony and concord." Leaders of all stripes recalled this symbol nostalgically during the 1780s, even those who had not actually participated in the revolution. Saluting "that spirit of union" that enabled Americans "to withstand the mighty force of Britain," John Warren worried that "the constitutional authority of the legal representative body of the nation" would be an insufficient substitute "bond of union." Religious invocations of unity continued after the war, as in Benjamin Rush's avowal that "the Union of the States, in its form and adoption, is . . . the work of a Divine Providence," but the framers' deist predilections resulted in fewer evangelical declarations than during the revolution. As Crevecoeur observed in 1782: "It is astonishing to think how pernicious . . . that old maxim has been, that a unity in religious opinions was necessary to establish the unity of law and government."[13]

Vestigial affection for the revolutionaries' achievement also reinforced the attraction of national unity among opponents of the Federalist regime. Among virtually all prominent Americans, paeans to the unanimity of the generation of 1776 only grew over subsequent decades. The Declaration and Constitution would eventually become similar sources of symbolic reverence. But during the

---

12. Storing 1977, 82n; Bailyn 1993, 1:253; 2:609, 599–600.

13. *Pennsylvania Packet*, September 24, 1787; Warren 1783, 19; Rush in Kammen 1987, 45; de Crevecoeur 1963 [1782], 321. On deism see Kramnick and Moore 1996, 34–35, 100–101; Butler 1990, 218–20; on the decline of church leaders' political influence during and after the war see Rhoden 1999, 90–115; Stout 1990, 65–68.

late eighteenth century "the Union" superseded even these as leaders' principal referent of shared loyalty.[14]

Along with this sentimental hold, union ideas had a natural appeal among elites. For despite strong regional differences, personal exchanges were far more frequent after independence. Politicians, lawyers, and wealthier merchants traveled increasingly across town and state boundaries, the first generation of American opinion leaders to do so in significant numbers.[15] Combined with improved communication links first opened in the revolutionary crisis, expanding connections nurtured a tangible sense of shared purposes and goals. Declarations of united fellow-feeling literally described elite relations in the late eighteenth century more than ever before. Americans, wrote John Jay, "were never so cordially united as at this day. By having been obliged to mix with each other, former prejudices have worn off and their several manners become blended."[16] Though Jay referred to "the people of the states," it was leaders who did most of the traveling and fraternal mixing. Ordinary citizens had fewer opportunities for mingling with those from different regions in the late eighteenth century; when they did so, the outcome was not always salutary. In the Continental Army, the broadest melting pot yet created among Americans, tensions between regiments of different states ran perilously high. Officers did little to calm sectional infighting: George Washington himself wrote off New England's soldiers as "an exceeding[ly] dirty and nasty people."[17]

As Washington's comment suggests, even among U.S. leaders separate subcultures remained in force. Members of the Confederation Congress and constitutional convention were as prone to divide along various axes (north-south, large states–small states, planter-merchant) as they were to seek common ground on urgent issues. References to "natural" unity seemed less apt than Luther Martin's conclusion: "The separation from G[reat] B[ritain] placed the 13 States in a state of Nature towards each other." Yet Martin echoed fellow anti-Federalists in fiercely opposing "dissolution of the Union" and even praising the "miraculous Union" in the course of his critiques.[18]

14. See Chatfield 1988, 44, on "the deep loyalty which even disaffected [New England] Federalists expressed for the 'Union of 1776'" in the 1812 crisis. Historians have recently shown that both Declaration and Constitution achieved a "revered position" well after their respective promulgations. "During the first fifteen years following its adoption, the Declaration seems to have been all but forgotten," writes Pauline Maier; only in the 1820s did its popularity "reach a recognizably mature form" (1997, 168–70). The Constitution's slowly evolving appeal is described in Kammen 1987, 13–22, 46 ("the cult of the Constitution did not arise as early, nor so pervasively, as scholars have believed").

15. The Adams family example is instructive: Samuel Adams only left New England once, to attend the Continental Congress in Philadelphia, and was "incredibly homesick for Boston" during his entire stay. His younger cousin John, the second U.S. president, was far better traveled from his late teens on. Miller 1936, 353.

16. *Independent Chronicle* (Boston), October 7, 1779.

17. Abbot et al. 1983–93, 1:336.

18. Farrand 1937, 1:324, 437–38, 445–46. For a time at Philadelphia, Federalists contemplated separate regional unions as "more practicable" than a full union of the states. See Onuf 1988, 79–97, and Banning 1995, 67–68, 120–25.

Sustained references to union, and the interchanges helping foster them, were not only the result of interpersonal exchanges and the nostalgic appeal of independence. Many elite advocates of unity had strong personal interests in view. To some extent, as Charles Beard famously argued, these concerned immediate economic gain. But a Beard-style analysis, in which wealthy notables promoted unity to mask class interests, poorly explains anti-Federalists' own favorable union references alongside their hot denunciations of aristocracy.[19] More likely is that the founders saw their careers and reputations as dependent on maintaining national unity. When Elbridge Gerry declared that "disunion [would] disappoint not only America, but the whole world," his expansive vision suggests a personal identification with the republic's fate, one voiced by many other framers. As historian Douglass Adair explains, "[t]he love of fame" inspired leaders to create "what they conceived to be a more perfect union, and then manage to get it ratified by the reluctant representatives of an apathetic populace."[20]

The specter of self-interest, however motivated, invites a closer look at the split between elites' fervent union usage and mass indifference. As union had belatedly been embraced by a British Ministry striving to reassert superiority and maintain order among restless colonists, so the new American leadership adopted the term partly as a means of control. Officials attempted to gloss over distinctions of status and ward off episodes like Shays' Rebellion by urging their countrymen to consider themselves full participants—"united stakeholders," as Maryland's governor said in 1790—in the nation. No real state apparatus existed to provide strong central enforcement encouraging obedience to national leaders. Federalists' sentimental exhortations of unity were an alternate attempt to foster adherence to a Constitution that, in Wood's phrase, "was intrinsically an aristocratic document designed to check the democratic tendencies of the period."[21]

While plausible, this order-keeping explanation must be qualified to a degree. "Union" had signified rebellion against English assertions of control; American leaders now employing the term well recalled that recent history. (Indeed, many proudly cited Scottish efforts to disunite from England in the 1780s.)[22] Plentiful historical examples exist of revolutionaries turned bourgeois leaders, employing

19. Persuasive responses to the Beard thesis are McDonald 1958 and 1985, 219–24; Appleby 1992, 223–29, 280; Matson and Onuf 1990, 100 and chap. 5.

20. Farrand 1937, 1:515; Adair 1974, 24 (cf. McDonald 1985, 167, 189–91; Nourse 1996, 454–55). See also Franklin's speech urging daily prayers in the convention, where he compared the framers to "the builders of Babel" and warned that "we ourselves shall become a reproach and bye word down to future ages." Farrand 1937, 1:451–52. A thoughtful revisiting of Adair's thesis is in Ceaser 1999, 192.

21. Wood 1969, 513. Cf. Wills 1981, 236–37. On control, the Massachusetts delegate Nathaniel Gorham referred to "the union" as "some general system for maintaining order" early in the convention (Farrand 1937, 1:462). David Waldstreicher provides a richly detailed analysis of Federalist efforts to encourage a restrained spirit of national unity among the general population after 1787 (1997, 85–107).

22. See, e.g., New Jersey Journal (Elizabethtown), July 5, 1786, citing a "letter from a gentleman in Scotland," which noted that "instances are not wanting of infringements on the treaty of union," and promised that "Scotland, disunited from England," would inspire Irish and Scots alike: "now mourn[ing] the union in dust and ashes, [they] shall again lift up their heads and flourish."

the same linguistic or material tools that won them their place. But union pledges ultimately had *failed* the British as a source of obeisance, as no one knew better than the new American leadership.

Indeed, the possibility of similar failures petrified the new republic's leaders. Their repeated expressions of confusion and discouragement soften a portrait of cynical rhetoricians masking their desires for wealth or glory with references to a union of all the people. Elites declared "the population" subject to "monstrous fears of disunion," but their efforts to redress such concerns were equally aimed at comforting one another. The Confederation's virtual collapse, continued tensions with England, the Constitution's near defeat, and the new government's instability contributed a ringing note of urgency to union talk. The "old motto . . . Unite or die" was "never more applicable . . . than at this moment," insisted a New Hampshire writer in 1788. With the question of constitutional ratification reduced to "Union or no Union," Edmund Randolph saw the light: "When I see safety on my right, and destruction on my left . . . I cannot hesitate to decide in favor of the former," he told the Virginia convention.[23] Because Americans appeared so hopelessly divided, unity seemed absolutely necessary; because American leaders so feared imminent disunion, they sought reassurance in its rhetorical opposite. Later, with the republic a surer prospect, union usage would smack more of hubristic excess. But the concept's prevalence in the 1780s often appears as whistling in the dark. Along with the historic appeal of the "Union of 1776," expanded interpersonal contact, and self-interest, political uncertainty thus marks a fourth—and probably the most important—source of early American leaders' affirmations. As James Lewis summarizes, "once the union became the repository of American hopes for the success of the Revolution, disunion—as a consequence of either domestic or foreign pressures—seemed to pose the ultimate danger to the United States."[24]

Beyond the myriad dangers disunion implied, economic and social upheavals surrounding the ratification effort led prominent Americans to advocate closer unity as a means of managing large-scale political change. One example is the debate over organizing western territories, where "Extending the Union" became the popular rationale for an effort of unprecedented magnitude. Individual interests from land speculation to the glories of presiding over a broader empire were surely at play, but leaders also had to make persuasive public arguments for connecting these territories to the whole. In a widely reprinted exchange, Thomas Jefferson's worry that future western states would split from the East was answered by Madison's hopeful expectation that "ties of friendship, of marriage and consanguinity" would prove an enduring foundation for interregional bonds.

23. *Connecticut Courant* (Hartford), February 23, 1787; *New Hampshire Gazette* (Portsmouth), April 16, 1788; Randolph in Elliot 1836, 3:652, 66.

24. Lewis 1998, 10. A more complete look at this fearful inspiration for the founders' unionism appears in the following section on Madison.

Elsewhere Madison was more direct: a "more intimate and permanent . . . Union" would encourage "sympathy between the whole and each particular part"; the resultant "government [with] energy enough to maintain the union of the Atlantic states" would be "equally capable at least, to bind together the Western and Atlantic states."[25]

Union talk was similarly enlisted in the service of initial efforts at national institution-building. John Quincy Adams retrospectively summed up the framers' outlook: "It was only in harmony that . . . political institutions could be founded," and such harmony absolutely had "to preside [in] the soul" of the new republic. Members of the Continental Congress prized unanimity in their deliberations, to the point that their body became "eventually a unanimous consent institution," as Jillson and Wilson show. That Congress's eventual failure necessitated meetings at Annapolis and then Philadelphia; the Constitution's institutional innovations were stridently advanced, in the *Federalist* and elsewhere, as fostering unity of purpose and decision making.[26]

Probably the most important ground for such defense was the first great compromise at the constitutional convention, over balancing states' rights and national interests. Jack Rakove's blow-by-blow survey of disputes over Senate organization, equality of states, and sovereignty's location demonstrates the conclusive place of "general arguments for union" in achieving this agreement, one forged with "little specific reference to the Constitution." Details of debates over organizing the new government are addressed below: the point here is that Federalists' reassuring talk of union, coupled with dire warnings against disunion or "partial unions," provided conveniently ambiguous rhetorical cover and thereby helped the new federal system—defended as the "last best hope for preserving the Union," notes Rakove—to win approval. Ralph Ketcham confirms that "no group could campaign under a 'nationalist' banner with any hope of success." Instead a "composite" of federal and national, as Connecticut's Oliver Ellsworth was first to term it, proceeded under the standard of union.[27] Here especially the concept took on a balancing character, loosely bridging two positions whose partial convergence in 1787 would indelibly color American politics for generations to come.

It was against a backdrop of great uncertainty that the new republic's opinion shapers promoted national union in the 1780s. "No day was ever more clouded

---

25. Hutchinson 1962–91, 8:251; Bailyn 1993, 2:444. On the western territories as a ground for and threat to union, see esp. Onuf 1987, xiii–xiv, 3–5, 16–20, 26–28.

26. Adams in Fliegelman 1993, 39–40; Jillson and Wilson 1994, 160 (cf. 75–76, 89–90). The connection between union and national institutions could be reversed, as where Hamilton sought to concentrate administrative powers in the executive to ensure "unity" and "duration" in government. The fate of his proposals reaffirms the error of equating union with strong central administration. See Flaumenhaft 1992.

27. Rakove 1996, 188, 58; Ketcham 1974, 121; Ellsworth in Farrand 1937, 1:483. On the compromise, see Rakove 1996, 57–70, 188–201; McDonald 1985, 213–19, 226–37; Ketcham 1974, 109–23; Banning 1995, 140–64.

than the present," Washington gloomily observed of dwindling revolutionary hopes in November 1786, as proposals for separate regional confederacies gained strength around the country. A decade later, preparing to leave the presidency, he could more confidently hope "that our Union may be as lasting as time." Washington exemplifies the spirit of most contemporary national leaders, voicing (as Wayne Fields summarizes) two "great themes . . . love of country and 'indissoluble union.'" But such sonorous phrases left many issues unaddressed. Who or what was supposedly united—states, people, or both—and how? When was unity necessary—always, or only in times of national peril? How far did "Union" authority extend, especially in respect to decision makers in the individual states? It was not "plain even to the national men of that day," a pamphleteer recalled in 1861, "either how much, or what sort of union was necessary." [28]

During the Articles' governance, union talk was ubiquitous among elites but largely unexamined: "there was remarkably little discussion in the press or pamphlets of the nature of the union being formed," and even congressional debate on the subject "was very limited and intellectually insignificant." [29] With little opportunity to consider systematically ways of uniting citizens or states, founding leaders hurled "union" into every argumentative gap imaginable. More specificity came at the constitutional convention, where delegates used the term to steer between "confederation"—now a byword for futility—and "nation" or "empire," both dangerously expansive words. The ratification debates highlighted the necessity for well-reasoned definition. "It may perhaps be thought superfluous to offer arguments to prove the utility of the Union," Hamilton wrote in the first *Federalist* paper; yet he and other leaders returned to the subject almost obsessively.

Scholars of American federalism have extensively reviewed the arrangement of parts and whole, and concurrent division of sovereignty, that provided the framework for a national government. Less noticed is that the design of separated powers was interwoven with a comprehensive account of union—of stronger ties among citizens of different regions and outlooks, and between their representatives. This theory of national union was expressed most systematically in the ideas of James Madison, and in fact Madison's unionist outlook underlay in vital ways his immensely influential explication of the American political system. [30] Through his treatment, supplemented in places with other views, we can best recover the meaning and purposes of union among the constitutional generation.

---

28. Washington in Ketcham 1974, 120; Farewell Address draft in Gilbert 1961, 139; Fields 1996, 6; "American Nationality" 1861, 7. Davis 1978 summarizes the uncertainty surrounding the Constitution's declaration of unity (115).

29. Wood 1969, 354; cf. Rakove 1979, xv; Onuf 1988.

30. The extent of Madison's contribution is periodically reevaluated, and at present is at an apogee, the "father of the Constitution" mantle having been fully restored. See, e.g., Ketcham 1974, 139; Rakove 1996, xvi. Stephen Conrad and Samuel Beer separately discuss James Wilson's view of American union, with Beer including a thoughtful contrast of Madison and Wilson on social unity. Beer 1993, 341–77; Conrad 1988.

The preceding section demonstrates both a broad commitment to union among America's founding leadership and the vagueness of their ideal. Such ambiguity stemmed from pressures of practical politics and the term's appeal among elites of all parties. But it also owed to a broader difficulty Madison and other thoughtful framers faced in comprehending, much less winning support for, a new unified political system. In imagining any polity as "meaningful whole" or theorizing its "intelligible web of relations," its founders turned first to "historical experience," particularly "the traditions of a society" and "its public institutions."[31] The fledgling United States had few traditions that were not British, and its national institutions were being thoroughly overhauled.

Early visionaries of political union therefore had to build with materials at hand. Territory, citizens, and political representatives were the components of Madison's theory of union, rather than distinct cultural traditions, venerable institutions, or shared race, language, and religion: all of these latter elements resembled the British versions from which Americans were seeking to differentiate themselves. Madison's complex account rested on popular unity but halted well short of strong democratic association. He acknowledged, without fully addressing, the tension arising from his concurrent reliance on close affective ties among the citizenry and a more restricted, elite-centered political union. Tension similarly hobbled his attempts to blend states' rights and national sovereignty within a unionist framework. Madison's compelling effort to balance all these oppositions, along with his immense public stature after 1787, enshrined his understanding of union at the center of American thought.[32] His model was a remarkably durable one, though (as is taken up in later chapters) competing understandings would emerge. Understanding Madison's vision has important implications for subsequent debates over the extent of political community possible, desirable, and necessary in American society, even to the present day.

Madison's Devotion to Union

In a typically lofty declaration, Jefferson once said of America's eastern and western sections, "God bless them both and keep them in the Union if it be for their good, but separate them if it be better."[33] Madison's unionist commitment

31. Pye and Verba 1965, 7. On the importance of a national history to a popular sense of common obligation, see Miller 1997, 76, and Smith 1986.

32. See, e.g., Remini 1997, 596: "It is interesting that the generation following the revolutionary generation tended to regard James Madison as the great man after Washington . . . [Madison] was seen as the most important individual responsible for the American system of government, [widely viewed] as one of the political wonders of the world."

33. Quoted in Stampp 1978, 23; see also Boyd et al. 1950–, 6:371; 7:26–27; 11:92–94. Differences between Madison and Jefferson on the foundational importance of union are broadly outlined in Koch 1964 [1950], 198–207.

was deeper from the outset. Writing to his college friend William Bradford during the colonial crisis, the young Madison reflected: "When I consider the united virtue of that illustrious [Congress] every apprehension of danger vanishes. . . . I am persuaded that the union, virtue & love of liberty at present presiding throughout the colonies is such that it would be as little in the power of our treacherous friends as of our avowed enemies, to put the yoke upon us." During Virginia's ratification debate Madison exhorted fellow delegates "not to mistake the end for the means. The end is Union." The term appears in almost every one of his *Federalist* contributions; the famous tenth paper, a touchstone for interpreters who find in Madison the roots of American interest-group liberalism, was titled by Madison not "Outcomes of Bargaining" (nor "Number Ten") but "Advantages of Union." Fifty years later, in a posthumously published "Last Political Will and Testament" offering "Advice to My Country," Madison expressed the "advice nearest to my heart and deepest in my convictions[:] that the Union of the States be cherished and perpetuated."[34]

The constitutional period amply displays Madison's unionist persuasion, beginning with his explanation of the issue at hand: "the importance of Union to [the people's] political safety and happiness." Preparing for the convention, Madison examined histories of "ancient & modern confederacies." His reflections produced the Virginia Plan, designed to achieve "some middle ground, which may at once support a due supremacy of the national authority, and not exclude the local authorities." Lance Banning's study of Madison at the convention is an important corrective to commentators' lumping Madison with fervent nationalists: Banning emphasizes Madison's cautious support of a national government in the name of preserving union. Many of Madison's *Federalist* contributions defended the new regime in terms of "invigorating the Union" or warning of the perils of disunion. During the ratifying debates, Madison's political foes also recognized his intended object. At Virginia's convention, Patrick Henry declared, "We have heard the *word Union* from [Madison]. I have heard no word so often pronounced in this House as he did this."[35]

Similar themes abound even as Madison helped establish the polity's first party machinery in the 1790s. His ostensibly states' rights argument in the Virginia Resolutions was predicated on the state's "warm attachment to the Union"; whereas Jefferson favored state nullification of the Alien and Sedition Acts, Madison recommended recourse to the Supreme Court, source of "stability and union." His view of parties was that "the individuals belonging to them . . . intermingled in every part of the whole country" would "strengthen the union of the whole." Madison continued to steer by a unionist star as president. Just before his election, a letter from "One of the People" to a New York newspaper

34. Hutchinson et al. 1962–91, 1:152; Elliot 1836, 3:144; Meyers 1981, 443.
35. Hutchinson et al. 1962–91, 9:3, 383; Banning 1983, 249n, 251, and 1995, 160–91; Rossiter 1961, nos. 14, 15; Bailyn 1993, 2:678. See also Read 1995.

praised Madison as "among the first and most effective agents in casting aside the feeble threats [e.g., from Britain] which so poorly connected the states together, and . . . substituting [an] energetic bond of union." In a private letter to Jefferson, John Adams approvingly summarized Madison's presidency as having "established more Union, than all his three predecessors, Washington, Adams and Jefferson, put together."[36]

Union was Madison's preferred value and was recognized as such by his contemporaries. But as seen above, most leaders talked avidly about unity in the early republic. Essential to realizing the rhetoric was a *theory* of union, a principled treatment of what a political union could be as well as what it should do. Madison sought to fill that gap. His conclusion was that without territorial, affective, and representative unity, the American system would be unrealizable. In the following discussion of Madison's conceptualization of union, more familiar aspects of his political outlook receive relatively little attention.[37] This is necessary for reasons of brevity; it also serves an important historiographic purpose in restoring to our portrait of Madison's thought—and perhaps to constitutional studies more generally—this key theme.

Madison's Theory of Political Union

Though Madison was skeptical about "theoretic politicians," considered much political theorizing "inventions of prudence," and recognized that his own outlook, "like most theories, confessedly requires limitations & modifications," his oft-stated commitment to reasonable persuasion demanded a clear accounting of the union he extolled.[38] Madison's reasoning proceeded in three stages. First, an enduring *territorial* union among the states would ensure liberty, stability, peace, and a host of other political goods. This expanded continental connection rested in turn on *affective* unity between citizens. Engendering "sincere affection"[39] among the American people were ties among *representatives,* between those governors and the citizenry, and even between the national state and civil society, in a complex set of institutional bases for unity. These three mutually supporting pillars were meant to secure the sustainable union he and other founders so prized.

36. Hunt 1910, 9:593; Rives and Fendall 1865, 3:157; *Public Advertiser* (New York), July 2, 1808; Adams in Cappon 1971, 2:508. Madison's relation of parties and unity is in Hutchinson et al. 1962–91, 14:370–72; see also Ketcham 1984, 170–81; Banning 1995, 334–65.

37. Liberty is an obvious example; foremost among the "gross oppositions" (Shapiro 1989) that characterize much founding scholarship is a distinction between individual freedom and civic-republican community. But for Madison liberty (like other leading goods) was best secured in the context of the whole regime's institutional design, not as a separate or prioral value. And that regime had to be united, or individual and collective freedom were imperiled. For an expanded treatment of this issue, see Kersh 1999, 246–47.

38. Rossiter 1961, no. 10, p. 81; Hutchinson et al. 1962–91, 13:73; Rossiter 1961, no. 51, p. 322; Hunt 1910, 9:359n. See also Rossiter 1961, no. 37, p. 238.

39. Madison used this phrase frequently; one example is his 1795 statement on behalf of the House of Representatives, declaring the "pure affection we bear" toward "our Country." Hutchinson et al. 1962–91, 16:165; see also 17:347. Other citations appear in note 56.

Madison's unionist understanding revolved around an idea of balance between local/state and national power, familiarly, and many other inherently conflicting interests as well. The term "union" implies a combination of separate elements, and Madison attempted to bridge a wide assortment of early-republic conflicts through promoting communion among citizens. He did so to achieve several purposes, including enhancing national security against both external and internal threats, building a sense of American identity distinct from the British, and preserving various private and public goods.

A political realist, Madison also recognized that bonds between citizens, leaders, and states could be easily overrun by corrosive passions. While individuals' self-interest contributed to unity and other desirable goods, relying on a market model of exchange among different interests was insufficient to promoting durable political ties. The burden of monitoring and promoting political unity fell on representatives. This process had a maximum boundary as well, as blindly unified citizens posed potential dangers.

United *States:* Territorial Union

Madison's perspective begins where most present-day commentary ends, with union among the states. To most founding-era Americans "the Union" was a *place*, the entity containing the thirteen original colonies and, over time, additional states. Firmly binding this body together was, to Madison, "the immediate object of the federal Constitution." Other confederations, he observed, had proven incomplete in constitutional theory and practice. Ancient Greece would have abided far longer had its component states been "admonished by experience of the necessity of closer union." The United Netherlands, he wrote, still required "a revolution of their government" to "establish their union and render it the parent of tranquility, freedom, and happiness." Given this context, the American republic's fragmentary tendencies were especially troubling. Although today scholars focus on the framers' reapportionment of power between state and central governments, begging the question of how separate states were to interact, the latter issue concerned Madison greatly. His "Vices of the Political System of the U.S.," prepared as a primer for convention delegates, devotes as much attention to states' "want of concert" and lack of "general harmony" as to their "encroachments . . . on the federal authority."[40]

One way to connect the states more permanently, in Madison's conception, was by stressing the benefits of "an united American territory." This goal was hardly obvious, as Commager recalls: "logically there was no more reason the territory [then] embraced in the United States should be a single country than that the territory of South America should be."[41] While contemporaries praised con-

---

40. Rossiter 1961, no. 14, p. 102 (cf. Farrand 1937, 1:465); Rossiter 1961, nos. 18, p. 124; 20, p. 138; Hutchinson et al. 1962–91, 9:349–50.

41. Hutchinson et al. 1962–91, 14:139; Commager 1975, 176.

tinental unity as "natural,"[42] Madison sought to transform accidents of geography into reliable political foundations. His geostrategic arguments—little noted in recent Madison scholarship—provided a substantive rationale for interstate concert, beyond the weaker adhesive powers of self-interest or nature alone.

"Extended republic" familiarly recalls Madison's recipe for restraining factionalism in a polity.[43] But an expanded and united territory also served positive purposes. Madison's most detailed geostrategic view comes in *Federalist* 41, where he sets out "security against foreign danger" as "an avowed and essential object of the American Union." Durable interstate bonds would be "a more forbidding posture to foreign ambition than America disunited, with a hundred thousand veterans ready for combat." The alternative, letting "each state depend on itself for its security," would weaken the whole and spur conflict between the states. Protection against foreign incursions had necessitated standing armies elsewhere, Madison warned. The American states' "due attachment" to their collective union would eliminate that distressing possibility. Internal security was also a vital outcome of closer unity. As president, Madison wrote a Massachusetts Republican party chair in 1809 that "The Union of these States cannot in truth be too highly valued or too watchfully cherished. It is our best barrier against danger from without, and the only one against those armies and taxes, those wars and usurpations, which so readily grow out of the jealousies and ambition of neighboring and independent States."[44]

Security was only one aspect of Madison's geostrategic account. Noting the "propensity of all communities to divide when not pressed into a unity by external danger," Madison sought to bolster interstate bonds in peaceful ways as well. Territorial union of states would provide a structural base for westward development, widely seen as desirable (except among some New England Federalists) by the 1780s. Madison and other leading Virginians provided crucial support for this effort by ceding to the United States their state's western territorial claims. An 1861 writer, lamenting the outbreak of civil war, wistfully recalled this "heroic self-sacrifice on the altar of the purest patriotism, which must awaken astonishment in all future generations. . . . For [Virginia's] territory included Kentucky, and most of that which is now Ohio, Indiana, Illinois, Michigan, and Wisconsin."[45]

Some observers, especially in New England, expected future western states to be "so different, and probably so opposite, that an entire separation must even-

42. "An American," probably Tench Coxe, offered a typical argument that "The various parts of the North-American continent are formed by nature for the most intimate union" (*Pennsylvania Gazette*, May 21, 1788).

43. One good treatment of this topic is Onuf 1990, esp. 2384–87.

44. Rossiter 1961, no. 41, pp. 256–58; Farrand 1937, 1:465. Cf. esp. Madison's "Political Observations" (Hutchinson et al. 1962–91, 15:511–33); Stagg 1984–99, 1:53. See also Amar 1991, 486–91; Sorenson 1995, 21–24; and, on the range of foreign threats to American unity in the early republic, Lewis 1998, 14–40.

45. Hunt 1910, 9:355–56; "American Nationality" 1861, 13.

tually ensue," as Rufus King declared at the convention. Madison thought otherwise. Naysayers were "mistaken," he declared as Secretary of State in 1803, "if [they] suppose that the Western part of the United States can be withdrawn from their present Union with the Atlantic part. . . . Our Western fellow citizens are bound to the Union," he concluded, "by the ties of kindred and affection" as well as by "clear and essential interests." As Peter Onuf has shown, organizing the western lands associated "union" with dynamic expansion, further heightening the term's salience. It also helped persuade states' rights advocates of union's benefits, because longstanding disputes over territorial boundaries and trade issues could be resolved by Madison's dispassionate federal "umpire."[46]

Interstate economic exchange provided another rationale for territorial unity, albeit a blessing more mixed than students of early American political economy usually allow. In his early and later career alike, Madison praised the "links and ligaments" forged by "commercial relations among the States" and promoted government-sponsored internal improvements to that end. Yet he also warned consistently against "the jealousies and collisions of commerce" and in a private letter near the end of his life observed that the "rapid growth of the individual States in population, wealth and power" had "tended to weaken the ties which bind them together"—given the "incompatibility of [economic] interests between different sections of the country." Madison's eventual acceptance of large U.S. manufacturing establishments has provided fodder for scholars' charges about his ideological switch from republican to liberal, as reviewed later in this chapter. But "the destination of a strong Union," as Drew McCoy affirms, "always mattered more than the particular economic path to that end."[47]

At the intersection of territorial and economic bonds was ownership of the American land. Madison's acknowledgment, in *Federalist* 10 and elsewhere, that differential property holdings were a source of faction (as was liberty) did not imply that property rights could never serve beneficial ends. The expanding number of landowners, Madison hoped, would see themselves as stakeholders in the national polity. Federal grants of land to states and individuals would also encourage grantees to view their holding as part of a unified American territory. (Thus, in part, his support for policies of expansion, including the Louisiana Purchase—which he supervised as Secretary of State.) Madison's sustained attention to property rights has led commentators to judge him a "bourgeois" defender of modern "atomized" society,[48] but his view was plainly a larger one. The "freeholders of the country" were "the safest depositories of republican liberty," he wrote; the more such owners, the more stable and secure the political system.

46. King quoted in Rakove 1979, 354; Hunt 1910, 7:12–13; Onuf 1983, 33–41, 79–144. Cf. Rossiter 1961, no. 38, p. 239; and Hutchinson et al. 1962–91, 12:373–7.

47. Farrand 1937, 2:451–52; Hunt 1910, 9:517–19, 547; McCoy 1989, 191. See also his 1826 letter saluting completion of the Erie Canal, in Rives and Fendall 1865, 3:524.

48. Matthews 1995, 242, 240; cf. Boesche 1998. See also Foner's more restrained contrast of Madison's protections of property with "the essence of political freedom" (1998, 22).

Madison's view of property, which encompassed "religious opinions," "conscience," and "free use of [one's] faculties," did not simply reinforce some feudal status quo. Rather, his treatises on property usually concern ownership's beneficial impact on territorial unity.[49]

Capping Madison's geostrategic argument for union was his resistance to redrawing state boundaries along sectional lines. Topographic borders originating with British rule served well the purposes of national unity by acting as so many cross-cutting cleavages. Each state included a diversity of population, resources, economic interests, and political orientations. As Daniel Deudney writes, "if the constitutive states lacked the size to be viable autonomous states and the homogeneity to be distinct nations, the union would be viable."[50] This did not imply the obliteration of states' powers, however. Madison again advocated a balanced view, wherein states always retained "the right, and are in duty bound, to interpose . . . and [maintain] within their respective limits, the authorities, rights, and liberties appertaining to them." United in a common government, each state could guard its prerogatives that much better.[51]

Thus Madison enumerated benefits of an enhanced territorial union, heralding in 1784 to fellow Virginian Edmund Randolph the "much greater mutual confidence and amity among the societies [states] which are to obey it, than the law which has grown out of the transactions & intercourse of jealous and hostile nations." But how to *achieve* closer interstate ties? As Randolph commented at the constitutional convention, one need merely "[l]ook at the public countenance from New Hampshire to Georgia" to observe "peril[ous]" disagreements between the states. Promises of greater security and western territorial gains could only moderate interstate friction, as Madison well knew from his own frustrating experiences in the Virginia legislature.[52]

A constitutional dilemma added to this difficulty. The states had been declared "united" in 1775 but without any accompanying explanation of *how* they were joined. Neither "Locke, Jefferson, nor any other theorist anywhere," writes J. G. A. Pocock, had explained how this united relationship was to be conceived, much less instituted. Today this question is viewed as moot, solved in federalist theory. The states were bound together by common, contractual *foedra*, retaining considerable autonomy of their own. But this federal arrangement explains the origin of "united" *states*, not how they could legitimately become *united.*[53]

49. Farrand 1937, 2:203; Meyers 1981, 186 (see also Hutchinson et al. 1962-91, 14:267, 371-72; and Rossiter 1961, no. 49, p. 314). On Madison and broad-based ownership, see Banning 1995, 181-84, 311-21.

50. Rossiter 1961, no. 41, p. 258; Deudney 1995, 206.

51. Hutchinson et al. 1962-91, 17:189; cf. Rossiter 1961, no. 39, Madison's most detailed account of a "federalist" division of power; and his "Report of 1800," Hutchinson et al. 1962-91, 17:347-49; and McCoy 1989, 130-51; Banning 1995, 295-333; Read 1995.

52. Hutchinson et al. 1962-91, 8:4 (cf. Rossiter 1961, no. 43, 277, on states' exhibiting "the affection of friends"); Farrand 1937, 1:26.

53. Pocock 1987, 705-8. A wealth of commentary describes federalist solutions to balancing needs of the whole and rights of the parts: see Beer 1993, 177-90, 245-64; Davis 1978, 75-118; and

Beyond the states' interests in collective action a deeper source of their bond, explained Madison in a striking innovation, was the people inhabiting them. Much has been made by political historians of the framers' "invention" of popular sovereignty, with Madison accorded a leading role.[54] Less often noted is his insistence that placing government's operation in popular hands required an additional condition: a united people. To cement interstate ties, Madison promoted affective unity among their residents.

United *People:* Affective Union

Marvin Meyers neatly captures the importance of affective spirit in remarking that Madison saw national union as a "state of mind among the people of America."[55] In his 1791 essay "Consolidation," which critiques overreaching central power, Madison ties "the mutual confidence and affection" of the states directly to like feelings among their residents:

> If a consolidation of the states into one government be an event so justly to be avoided, it is not less to be desired . . . that a consolidation should prevail in [the people's] interests and affections. . . . The less the supposed difference of interests, and the greater the concord and confidence throughout the great body of the people, the more readily must they sympathize with each other, the more seasonably can they interpose a common manifestation of their sentiments.[56]

Madison's idea of affective union was not a Panglossian hope that Georgians or Virginians would express enthusiastic fondness for faraway New England strangers. Nor did mutual affection imply avid fraternal bonds, arising in republican theory from intense interpersonal relations in a "kinship" society: this was an impossible goal among a people so geographically and culturally diverse. Affective spirit instead drew on Americans' common understanding, based in viewing others as fellows in a civic enterprise whose continued existence was recognized as vital. Enough of this sentiment and the dictum which spread through the convention could be realized: "A Union of the States is a Union of the men composing them."[57]

---

cites in note 27. But none addresses specifically the problem of horizontally joining the constituent members.

54. Morgan 1988, 266–69; Beer 1993, 249–55.

55. Meyers 1981, xlii; cf. Wood 1969, 532–36; Ericson 1993, 64–70 (on Madison and other Federalist authors' "union of sentiments").

56. Hutchinson et al. 1962–91, 14:138–39; cf. Farrand 1937, 1:2 (where Madison compared relations between states to those between people, each originating in "weaknesses and wants" and resting on "advantages of social intercourse"). See also Madison's later speech in Congress, on joining western territories to the Union by "a common affection." Hutchinson et al. 1962–91, 12:377; see also 10:216; 12:373; 17:307–8, 347–50.

57. Rufus King in Farrand 1937, 1:323. On stronger fraternal bonds, see McWilliams 1973, 7 and passim.

"The Union," Madison wrote in an early *Federalist* entry, existed only because "the people of America" were "knit together as they are by so many cords of affection."[58] Without citizens' active sense of mutual connection and attachment to the whole, Madison consistently warned, political disunion would result. The absence of "confidence and credit between man and man" characterizing the Confederation years had caused the "unstable and unjust career of the States," threatening the very "fabric" of the American experiment.[59] Madison's reasoning might be dismissed as tautological—union is necessary to prevent disunion—but attention to context illuminates his point: affective connections among the people were required to secure political bonds between the states.

Madison also offered positive explanations of how affective ties among Americans could more firmly attach the states. Intersubjective bonds may, after all, merely "unite the solitary occupants of [a nation] only by the mutual agreement to leave each other alone." Popular administration of government was a primary source of stronger connections. "The practice of making a common cause, where there is a common sentiment and common interest," Madison wrote in 1792, would permit "the Government to be administered in the spirit and the form approved by the great body of the people."[60]

Specifically, affective spirit was implicit in the operation of three essential institutions. *Separation of powers* was strengthened by the threat of popular disapprobation for any branch usurping its bounds. All citizens, said Madison, would "maintain the various authorities established by our complicated system, each in its respective constitutional sphere," a supervisory function properly inspired by "brotherly affection." (Hamilton was more blunt: "the people, by throwing themselves into either scale, will invariably make it preponderate.") Madison urged popular attentiveness to the ebb and flow of power among branches, insisting that such watchful governance rested on a sense of unity among the people. Their "eyes must be ever ready to mark, their voice to pronounce, and their arm to repel or repair aggressions" on any branch's authority, he wrote.[61]

Second, *legislative government* was similarly dependent on popular affective support. Madison's preference for legislative over executive power was underscored at the Philadelphia convention in his strenuous support for a legislative veto along with his long list of proposed additions to Congress's power.[62] A uni-

58. Rossiter 1961, no. 14, p. 103. For Madison whether "the people" were considered in the aggregate or as individual majorities in each state, a source of considerable debate in federalist theory, was not especially important: "the authority being equally valid and binding, the question is interesting, but . . . of merely speculative curiosity," he explained in 1835 (Hunt 1910, 9:605).

59. Farrand 1937, 3:548. Cf. Hutchinson et al. 1962–91, 9:359; 10:60–61; or Rossiter 1961, no. 40, p. 253, on the Constitution's being "destroy[ed] forever" by "disapprobation of this supreme authority," the people.

60. Baier 1993, 230; Hutchinson et al. 1962–91, 14:372. Cf. his *National Gazette* essay "Charters," reprinted in ibid., 191–92.

61. Hutchinson et al. 1962–91, 14:139; Rossiter 1961, no. 28, 181; Hutchinson et al. 1962–91, 14:218. Skowronek (1982, 20–22) affirms that popular sovereignty in its "purest" form was an original rationale for separating powers in the national government.

62. Farrand 1937, 2:324–26; see also Read 1995; and Sorenson 1995, 125–37.

fied citizenry enabled sound legislative activity. "Consolidation" of the people's "interests and affections," Madison explained, would ensure "that control on the legislative body which is essential to a faithful discharge of its trust."[63] In a system that required a degree of consultation between representatives and constituents, a deeply divided populace would erode legislators' accord to the point of paralysis. The ballot, moreover, rested ultimate responsibility for congressional government in the people's hands: late in his career, Madison issued a qualified endorsement of "an equal and universal right of suffrage."[64]

Third, episodes of *higher lawmaking,* or in Madison's words "occasions . . . deeply and essentially affecting the vital principles of their political system," demanded great popular concert rooted in mutual affective sentiment. The revolution marked a notable instance, as did Constitutional ratification and amendment. Such historic matters as U.S. support for the French Revolution were also among "certain periods" when the people had a "duty . . . to declare their principles and opinions on subjects which concern the national interest." More frequent constitutional revisions would, Madison argued to Jefferson, "engender pernicious factions that might not otherwise come into existence," leading to the "licenciousness" of dissension. But at rare "constitutional moments," in Ackerman's term, broad appeal was indispensable. "Discord alone," Madison concluded, "on points of vital importance, can render the nation weak in itself."[65]

Thus Madison not only saw affective ties among the populace as desirable in the abstract but also placed them in the engine-room of the new government. "With a union of its citizens," he wrote Maryland Republicans in 1810, "a government thus identified with the nation, may be considered as the strongest in the world, [owing to] the participation of every individual in the rights and welfare of the whole." He by no means expected such a spirit to emerge permanently, given his awareness of the "depravity in mankind." But neither was his view purely contractual, treating any joint action as a form of selective benefit-seeking. Scholars misstate Madison's position in insisting that he was "convinced that civic virtue was impossible and popular government dangerous." As Madison wrote in *Federalist* 55, "there are other qualities in human nature [besides selfishness] which justify a certain portion of esteem and confidence," adding that "Republican government presupposes the existence of these qualities in a higher degree than any other form." If the government was truly to be of and by the

---

63. Hutchinson et al. 1962–91, 14:138. "Consolidation" here had a double meaning, as Madison reassured readers that his aim was not to consolidate authority in the national government, as anti-Federalists insisted. The distinction underscores the difference between union and strong central control in Madison's understanding.

64. See "Note to Speech on the Right to Suffrage," Farrand 1937, 3:450; cf. Hunt 1910, 9:359. James Wilson similarly viewed "the right of suffrage" as "a most pleasing bond of union between the citizens" (Wilson 1967, 2:789).

65. Rossiter 1961, no. 49, p. 315; Hutchinson et al. 1962–91, 13:19–21; Stagg 1984–89, 2:263. Cf., on the revolution, Rossiter 1961, no. 14, p. 104; on the convention, Rossiter 1961, no. 37, pp. 230–31; on the French Revolution, Hutchinson et al. 1962–91, 17:242–43. On "constitutional moments" and "higher-track" lawmaking, see Ackerman 1991, esp. 3–7, 165–99, 266–94.

people—if, given the administrative demands summarized above, it was to endure at all—fostering affective sentiment was a foundational step. Otherwise, as Madison observed in a 1791 essay, "the impossibility of acting together might be succeeded by the inefficacy of partial expressions of the public mind, and this at length, by a universal silence and insensibility," resulting in tyranny.[66] Granting that affective union among the population at large was a key to integrating the republic, how was its achievement possible?

Inspiriting "ties of kindred and affection" among citizens implies a tutelary role, and Madison stressed education as a source of shared values, political participation, and mutual affection. His 1815 annual "Message to Congress" recommended a national university, designed in part to foster "national feelings" and in turn "congenial manners," all "contribut[ing] cement to our Union." Popular enlightenment entailed formal education, as Madison—eventual rector of the University of Virginia—repeatedly endorsed. A "popular Government," he wrote from retirement in 1822, "without popular information, or the means of acquiring it, is but a prologue to a farce or a tragedy; or, perhaps, both." As McCoy testifies, Madison's goal was to "broaden, not restrict, the horizons of the laboring classes in order both to enrich their humanity and to enhance the character of their public vision."[67]

Madison also relied on more immediate means of stimulating affective ties. His descriptions of mutual affection imply its emergence from regular social exchanges, spreading from family and neighborly ties to "local organs" conveying "the voice [and] the sense of ten or twenty millions of people."[68] Today such a flow from local associational activity to a broader civic spirit is described in terms of a thriving "civil society": norms of trust and dense social networks facilitate local action, which percolates upward to the national level.[69] But while Madison affirmed local civic engagement along related lines, he did so cautiously. In a time when individuals' attention was overwhelmingly focused on the local level, Madison emphasized connections between local associational activity and a *national* union, a sense of belonging to the collective whole. The goal, in the terms he used in *Federalist* 10, was to ensure that local associations nurtured fellow-feeling, rather than descending into factional disputes. Madison's experiences in the Virginia legislature left him dubious that local activity unmediated by state power would generate greater political participation: instead, he feared, such "engagement" would be limited to fervent interest-group demands.

Americans engaged locally therefore had to be inspired to imagine themselves

66. Stagg 1984–89, 2:263; Boesche 1998, 864; Rossiter 1961, no. 55, p. 346; Hutchinson et al. 1962–91, 14:138.

67. Hunt 1910, 7:13; 8:342–43; Rives and Fendall 1865, 3:276; McCoy 1989, 201. On education, cf. Madison's support for Kentucky's plan of public instruction, which he recommended to other states—in part as a means to closer union. Hunt 1910, 9:103–9.

68. Hutchinson et al. 1962–91, 16:183.

69. See, among a large body of literature, Putnam 1993; Kaufman 1999; and the works discussed in chapter 7.

as part of a larger whole. Political parties were one instrument for doing so; once his initial distaste for party conflict was overcome, Madison actively worked to organize a broad party of citizens "well affected to the Union and to good government."[70] Another was property ownership, along the lines already noted. Most important, though less frequent, were stirring celebrations of national achievement, commemorating events like the revolutionary struggle, the constitutional convention, and the War of 1812 ("Mr. Madison's War," as it was popularly called at the time). These plainly heightened a sense of national belonging: an antebellum writer exulted that the War of 1812 "kindled up such a glow of loyalty and patriotism in the national mind as seemed to consume the last remains of state sovereignty and pride." Madison's modest style and concerns about nationalist excess limited such expressions on his part. But he approved of certain "patriotic emoluments," including (as will be described) Washington's popular tours of the United States, and was not above arranging "discoveries" of British perfidy in 1812 in support of unified American spirit.[71]

If affective unity were thereby achieved, an opposite danger lurked: an overzealously unified mob. "The voluntary consent of a whole people," in Hamilton's enthusiastic phrase, did not always yield fortuitous consequences. While Madison promoted affective exchanges to bind the territorial union, he was wary of the outcome. Too often mass action yielded a "dangerous union," he noted in 1785. Three years later he warned that "the people, stimulated by some irregular passion, or some illicit advantage, or misled . . . may call for measures which they will after be the most ready to lament and condemn."[72]

Madison nowhere clearly spelled out how a "necessary" or "proper" union might degenerate into (or be clearly distinguished from) a "dangerous" one. Unity based in "calm affection" among the populace received his sanction, while mass "combinations" in pursuit of unworthy objects, sparked by "the passions most unfriendly to order and concord," were anathema. The difference seems a matter of semantics, but Madison did consistently downplay an avidly fraternal society, organized around face-to-face exchanges and familial loyalties, in favor of one featuring a restrained sense of mutual affection. To combat the "infect[ious]" threat of self-interested "violent passions," Madison proposed institutional safeguards against the "danger of combining in pursuit of unjust measures."[73] And to Madison's credit, few other unionist thinkers openly acknowledged the possibility of mob unity. Other founders, particularly James Wilson, were more san-

70. Hutchinson et al. 1962–91, 14:371.

71. "American Nationality" 1861, 25. Madison's conduct in the 1812 conflict is best treated in Stagg 1983.

72. Hamilton in Rossiter 1961, no. 85, p. 527; Hutchinson et al. 1962–91, 8:252; Rossiter 1961, no. 63, p. 384. See also Hutchinson et al. 1962–91, 15:93. On Madison as popular "inventor," see Morgan 1988, 267.

73. Rossiter 1961, no. 63, p. 385; cf. Hutchinson et al. 1962–91, 9:354–57; 10:214 (on oppressive majority unions); and Read's like distinction, between "good" and "bad" majorities (1995, 468–70). On safeguards against improper majoritarian combinations, like an extended republic and divided government powers, see Beer 1993, 255–75.

guine about both the possibility and the outcome of social union. Wilson's theory of affective engagement proceeded without the auxiliary precautions favored by Madison. For popular "error" there was "no superior principle of correction," Wilson argued.[74]

Madison never fully overcame the tension between the fact of faction-prone, self-interested individuals and the decisive importance of union among them. Here lies the paradox of popular union, in fact. A spirit of affective unity was a normative necessity, as Madison wrote in 1792: "the people *ought to be* enlightened, awakened, to be united" to ensure the new government's perpetuation.[75] But an all too human propensity to division demanded protections that threatened to corrode shared purposes and ends. A further element was needed, one that somehow ensured that "justice and the general good" would characterize bonded "coalition[s] of a majority of the whole society."[76] How else could a people so frequently—and, at times, deliberately—divided possibly be one?

United *Representatives:* Institutional Union

Madison's answer was representative government. This "great mechanical power," in his phrase, permitted "the will of the largest political body [to] be concentered and its force directed to any object which the public good requires." Here lay the efficient secret of Madison's theory of union: an institutional component to guide territorial and affective facets. Contemporaries shared this view. "It is in their legislatures," wrote one Rhode Islander in 1779, "that the members of a commonwealth are united and combined together into one coherent, living body. This is the soul that gives form, life, and unity to the commonwealth."[77]

Like the extended republic, representative government superficially appears more a matter of division than of unity. Filtering popular views through independent citizen-leaders eliminated any direct connection between masses and government, charged critics like the anti-Federalist "Brutus." Denouncing Madison's *Federalist* 10 defense of representation, he argued that leaders would neither "derive support from the good will of the people" nor gain "public trust," thereby failing "to preserve the union and manage our national concerns." Many like-minded writers feared an unmediated link between united territory and nationalist leaders, an arrangement that "smelt of *oligarchy*" and would leave "the militia to execute the laws of the union."[78]

It is true that Madison's interest lay peripherally, if at all, with strong democratic governance. His account provides only for limited popular participation in most matters, mediated by representatives who would attract the "attachment

74. McCloskey 1967, 2:778; 1:296; cf. 1:268–69, 364. See also Beer 1993, 360–65; Conrad 1988, 42–49.
75. Hutchinson et al. 1962–91, 14:426 (emphasis added). Madison sets out a similar view in several *Federalist* essays, including (in Rossiter 1961) no. 40, pp. 251–55; 41, p. 271; 45, pp. 289–90; 49, p. 313.
76. Rossiter 1961, no. 51, p. 325. Cf. Hutchinson et al. 1962–91, 14:118.
77. Rossiter 1961, no. 14, pp. 100–101; quoted in Wood 1969, 162. Fuller accounts of Madison on representation are in Gibson 1991; Epstein 1984, 147–61.
78. "Brutus" in Bailyn 1993, 1:426–27.

and reverence" of the citizenry.[79] This was the principal means by which the "whole people" would share in day-to-day government. Union's cherished "preservation" was "to be committed to the guardianship of those whose situation will uniformly beget an immediate interest in the faithful and vigilant performance of the trust." A people only sporadically united by self-interest, falling far short of an "active dialogic enterprise of self-governing citizens," should defer political decisions to cooler-headed governors. This prescription, Madison admitted in the *National Gazette,* was at best "mysteriously" consonant with republican liberty.[80]

But officials were also constrained by popular supervision, as Madison said at Philadelphia: "in all cases where the representatives of the people will have a personal interest distinct from that of their constituents, there was the same reason for being jealous of them, as there was for relying on them with full confidence, when they had a common interest." Madison and other framers defended representative government based on leaders' "wisdom to discern, and the most virtue to pursue, the common good of the society." We have seen that Madison tied elemental government functions to united popular vigilance, and that citizens always retained power to "bring back the Constitution to its primitive form and principles." Leaders remained in office only at the sufferance of the people, who held elective powers along with those of "guardians." As Samuel Beer summarizes, "it was the represented who decided who would make [administrative] decisions and whether the decisions they made were satisfactory."[81]

Rather than log-rolling bearers of particular interests, elected representatives (national or state) were conceived by Madison as foundations of institutional unity. In their better moments, leaders would set aside sectional or personal differences in the name of "the true interest of their country." U.S. House members, though sometimes motivated by more venal qualities—"duty, gratitude, interest, ambition" are listed by Madison—were expected in the main to be virtuous rulers. Senators, given their longer tenure and broader districts, would bring a "greater extent of information and stability of character" to the office. Their "display of enlightened policy and attachment to the public good" would win the "affections and support of the entire body of the people."[82] Yet asserting that en-

79. Rossiter 1961, no. 62, p. 382; cf. Hutchinson et al. 1962–91, 10:354–55. As Banning notes, this "natural aristocracy" (Jefferson's term, not Madison's) "should rely exclusively on merit and the people's recognition, not on wealth, or birth, or formal educational attainments" (1995, 372; cf. 251–53.)

80. Rossiter 1961, no. 58, p. 366; Carter and Kobylka 1990, 33; Hutchinson et al. 1962–91, 14:426–27. Compare Madison's 1829 review, for the Virginia convention, of his long-held fears about abuses of power arising from the "selfish" tendency of most individuals to ignore "the aggregate interests of the community" (Hunt 1910, 9:361–62).

81. Farrand 1937, 2:250; Rossiter 1961, no. 57, p. 350; 63, p. 390; Beer 1993, 344 (cf. Bessette 1994, 44–45; Galston 1990, 56). See also Madison's *Federalist* 51 line: "You must first enable the government to control the governed, and in the next place, oblige it to control itself. A dependence on the people is no doubt the primary control on the government; but experience has taught mankind the necessity of auxiliary precautions" (Rossiter 1961, 322). On popular "guardianship," see Hunt 1910, 6:91–93; Rossiter 1961, no. 46, pp. 298–99.

82. Rossiter 1961, no. 10, p. 82; 57, p. 353; 62, p. 376; cf. Ketcham 1984, 117; Rosen 1999, 13–14.

lightened representatives would govern in the public interest did not explain how unity of purpose would emerge among them. Madison apparently counted on a natural centripetal tendency among his fellow rulers, arising from "connections of blood, of friendship, and of acquaintance." When local or sectional interests threatened to prevail instead, constitutional barriers—"effectual precautions for keeping [representatives] virtuous"—again came into play.[83]

If the idea of affectively joined leaders seems absurd today,[84] Madison's own experience suggests that he took it seriously. His closest friendships were rooted in politics. He met Jefferson when both were advisors to Virginia's governor, beginning a collaboration Jefferson's chief biographer termed "one of the greatest in history." Another longtime Virginia companion was James Monroe: though the two split over partisan disputes during Jefferson's second term, they resumed relations when Monroe joined Madison's cabinet in 1811. Legatees such as Edward Coles and William Rives were constant Madison companions during his later years, as the aging statesman schooled them in the value of unity.[85]

Madison also developed close acquaintances with politicians from other regions of the United States—perhaps as a deliberate manifestation of elites' unity. For he conceived ties among leaders as literally "representative" of the nation as well. If enduring personal connections could be formed among members of Congress or other opinion leaders from "north *and* south, east *and* west," as he urged in an 1820 letter, Americans residing in different areas of the country would be more likely to follow suit, at least imaginatively.[86]

Unified, virtuous elites could attract popular allegiance, as the revolutionary and ratifying periods amply testified. Madison hoped that citizens' resulting national outlook would attach to the republic as a whole, building Americans' spirit of "vertical" unity—between individual and nation. Early in the convention Madison insisted on a "necessary sympathy" between citizens and their national "rulers and officers" as the "ground for Union." He took great pains in succeeding years to buttress this "communion of interests and sympathy of sentiments of which few governments have furnished examples." Such ties were promoted in numerous ways, among them the republican assurance that rulers "can make no law which will not have its full operation on themselves and their friends, as well as on the great mass of the society." Another was representatives' tutelary

---

83. Rossiter 1961, no. 49, p. 316. Cf. Murrin (1987b, 600), underscoring Madison's "belie[f] that gentlemen at the nation's capital could identify and pursue the common good." See also Wood 1969, 506–18, 596–600. Stephen Elkin doubts that citizens could "distinguish those who would be public-law makers from hacks," which he finds "the crucial weakness" in Madison's theory of government (1996, 595–96).

84. See the discussion of "civic friendship," and of its absence among most contemporary theorists, in Schwarzenbach 1996, esp. 97–98.

85. Dumas Malone in Alley 1985, 303; on Monroe, see Madison's unusually heartfelt expression of "the long, close, and uninterrupted friendship which united us," in his letter to Monroe after the latter sold his nearby Virginia estate (Rives and Fendall 1865, 4:178); Rutland 1987, 216–17; on Madison's legatees, see McCoy 1989, esp. 323–29. More generally, Louis Hartz identifies an "American instinct for friendship . . . planted beneath the heroic surface of America's political conflict" (1955, 140).

86. Rives and Fendall 1865, 3:164–65.

role: Madison admonished them to "afford an example . . . animating to those [the people] charged with the interests of the Union."[87] A longtime Madison associate, Baptist leader John Leland, expressed Madison's hoped-for sensibility in a letter to George Washington in 1788. "Convinced on the one hand," Leland wrote, "that without an effective national government the States would fall into disunion and all the subsequent evils; and on the other hand fearing that we should be accessory to some religious oppression should any one society in the Union predominate over the rest; yet . . . our consolation arose from the consideration: the plan must be good, for it has the signature of a tried, trusty friend; for a WASHINGTON will preside."[88]

As a concrete source of affective spirit, Madison supported Washington's three extended tours of the eastern and southern United States during the first years of the latter's presidency. One historian concludes that Washington's physical presence "exerted a centralizing pull in every sense of the word. Union, after all, was what he promoted. And union was a matter of sentiment." Washington's presidential tour became a staple among national elites, as several (not including Madison, who feared for his health and perhaps for the reception his diminutive figure would receive) traveled the country as literal representatives of union, "touching every state as if to bring it into sympathetic connection."[89]

Madison did not fully pursue the logic of how unity among leaders, and between citizens and their representatives, might bring about stronger political union. But his expectation appears to have been something like the following: virtuous leaders would attract popular allegiance, helping to cement affective bonds and otherwise stimulate associational activity among ordinary citizens. This popular mobilization would aid in translating local civil society networks into regional and ultimately national organizational activities. Madison's work in developing the early U.S. party system is exemplary here, as touched on above. Madison conceived his party as a means of linking different groups and issues in a single national institution. He wrote a friend in 1819 to affirm that "parties . . . must always be expected in a government such as ours. When the individuals belonging to them are intermingled in every part of the whole country, they strengthen a union of the whole."[90]

Representative government, finally, promised to alleviate two primary difficulties Madison identified with popular unity: *self-interest*, which led to factional combinations for unjust purposes, and *short-term outlook*, as evidenced in the citizenry's "transient enthusiasm" for national objectives.[91] These recall Calvinist-

---

87. Hutchinson et al. 1962–91, 9:357; 17:190; Farrand 1937, 1:50; Rossiter 1961, no. 57, pp. 352–53; Hutchinson et al. 1962–91, 10:213–14; Stagg 1984–89, 2:401–2. On tutelary leadership, see Ketcham 1984, 113–23, 215–31.

88. Quoted in Gaustad 1974, 119.

89. Waldstreicher 1997, 119, 125. On Washington's tours, see Smith 1993, 88–107; Flexner 1974, 228–29, 237, 259–60.

90. Rives and Fendall 1865, 3:157; see also Hutchinson et al. 1962–91, 15:100.

91. Rossiter 1961, no. 46, p. 295, on people's preference for local concerns. Cf. Hutchinson et al. 1962–91, 9:353–57; 12:38; 14:192.

Puritan visions of human nature, viewing man as fallen (because prone to greedy egotism) and mortal (hence grasping at the immediate present, and unlikely to take a longer view). Madison's own comparatively secular attitude is well chronicled,[92] but the parallel is intriguing—particularly given the deep religious associations the term "union" implied.

Thus Madison hoped there would arise, amid a thicket of checks and divisions, a palpable sense of unity among representatives and between leaders and constituents, underpinning the affective and territorial bonds girding the regime. The constitutional convention supplied a model as delegates surmounted "contending interests and local jealousies" with "a unanimity . . . almost as unprecedented as it must have been unexpected." Such unity of purpose would not necessarily emerge—in this as in much else Madison was cautiously hypothetical—but it *could.* Thirty years on, Madison concluded that it had: "the union of so many states," he told the 1829 Virginia convention in his last public speech, "is, in the eyes of the world, a wonder."[93]

Sources of Madison's Unionism

Madison's elaborate account of unified territory, affective bonds among citizens, representative guidance, and institutional guarantees of unity represented a leap beyond other American thinkers of his day. Where might his ideas have come from? The obvious source, to any present-day scholar of American political thought, is either (or both) of the liberal and republican paradigms allegedly influencing virtually all aspects of the framers' political design. Much of the contemporary outpouring of scholarship on Madison follows this familiar dichotomy.[94] Several writers portray Madison as "a quintessential liberal," relying exclusively on "liberal contractarian . . . political first principles" and "deep liberal commitments" and operating within a "broadly liberal consensus." In short, he was "the constant liberal Prince."[95] Elsewhere, though, a number of scholars hold that "Madison was a republican," exhibiting a "basic faith in republicanism" and championing "a community with shared values."[96] Even Lance Banning's admirably nuanced study portrays Madison as "temperamentally unable to decide between his 'liberal' and his 'republican' convictions" and concludes that his

92. Still the best account of Madison's religious views is Ketcham 1960. On Madison's religious studies in college, see Banning 1995, 80–82.

93. Rossiter 1961, no. 37, p. 230; Hunt 1910, 9:364. Cf. Hutchinson et al. 1962–91, 10:208; and his 1829 note to Virginia governor William Giles: "The happy Union of these States is a wonder" (quote in Brant 1941–61, 6:476).

94. For a brief overview of Madison scholarship between the 1970s and 1996, see Kersh 1996, 129. Outstanding studies since include Rosen 1999 and Leibiger 1999.

95. Matthews 1995, 21, 23; Sinopoli 1992, 102, 20, 157. Also see Dahl 1956, chap. 1; Erler 1992; Drukman 1971, chap. 1; Wood 1969, 606–15.

96. Quotes from Greene 1994, 60; McCoy 1980, 259; Carter and Kobylka 1990, 40. Cf. Hanson 1985, 72–83; and the sources cited in Sunstein 1993, 359n. 8. The literature on liberalism and republicanism is enormous; for cogent summary and commentary see Rodgers 1992 and White 1994.

view of liberty drew on both paradigms: "liberty defined as the inherent rights of individuals, [and] also liberty defined as popular control."[97]

Taken alone, each of these portraits appears plausible, raising a serious interpretive difficulty. Liberal pluralist and civic republican traditions mark opposite poles in conventional scholarship. If Madison legitimately may be seen as representative of both, he surely ranks among the more subtle—or, in George Carey's claim, "schizophrenic"—thinkers in history.[98] A degree of this confusion is due to Madison's own opaque writing; as Jefferson quipped, Madison never used three words where ten would do.[99] And some sixty years of public pronouncements provide plentiful fodder for selective reconstructions. Still, most of the fault lies with his latter-day exegetes. Assigning "republican" or "liberal" labels to a theorist or era serves certain useful explanatory purposes. In Madison's case, and that of American founding thought generally, the practice has exceeded its utility.[100] Union, a value central to Madison's political philosophy, is difficult to locate in any single philosophical paradigm.

At the same time, to deny or ignore outside influences is folly. More than most American framers, Madison read past theorists and incorporated portions of their lessons into his own outlook. He investigated many other examples of unions featuring several states. Great Britain, an obvious source, was both a poor model (continuing struggles after 1776 to incorporate Ireland were archly noted by Madison and others)[101] and a union in which Americans had just renounced membership. Other possible analogues, like the United Netherlands, the Achaean League, and the Swiss confederation, were all taken up in detail by Madison and his fellows but found wanting. Political theorists describing (and prescribing) these arrangements were studied by Madison and others for unionist lessons. Therefore, comparison of Madison's union views with those of preceding thinkers is desirable—especially if carried out carefully, with attention to how learning was actually transmitted and what was misunderstood or left out. Ample

97. Banning 1995, 368, 395. Another mostly nuanced account is Rosen 1999, which portrays Madison as a "natural-rights liberal" (3–4, 114–19, 132–33) while later acknowledging the "destructive consequences of classifying Madison according to one or another scholarly category" (178–79).

98. Carey 1995, 80. See also Meyers 1981, xviii, xxxiii–xliii ("how many Madisons shall we find?"); Greene 1994; Elkins and McKitrick 1993, 146–55 ("The Divided Mind of James Madison"); Gutzman 1998, 19–23; Zvesper 1984; Mason 1950, 516 ("Madison was in disagreement with himself"). Other accounts depict Madison as antidemocratic aristocrat (Burns 1963; Matthews 1995, 10, 19, 237–44), staunch populist (T. Miller 1992; Zvesper 1984, 236), among the first modern thinkers (W. Miller 1992, 34–42), and pastoral agrarian (Richard 1994, 166). On Madison as adherent to Scottish Enlightenment philosophy, see Wills 1981, esp. 21–23, and Morrow 1999.

99. Madison's long 1805 paper on American neutrality in the British-French war, intended as the official administration position, was particularly ill-received: one normally friendly Senator commented, "I never read a book that fatigued me more than this pamphlet has done" (Rutland 1987, 185; cf. Ketcham 1971, 50).

100. For a longer look at one such treatment, pointing out the potential for historical error, see Kersh 1993.

101. Ireland, citing American independence, won a measure of legislative autonomy in 1782, after which Madison remarked: "Ireland is reaping a large share of the harvest produced by our labors." Hutchinson et al. 1962–91, 4:432.

room lies between the taxonomic exercises characterizing much present scholarship on the founding and John Adams's half-serious boast that "these facts [are] as new as any political tale that could be brought . . . by special message from Sirius, the dog-star."[102]

Madison himself did little to clear up questions of philosophical influence on his theory of union. His immense reading list implies at least passing familiarity with hundreds of different authors, from the expected (Locke, Hume, Montesquieu) to the all but forgotten (Petty, Gee, Postlethwayt). Madison made scant acknowledgment of any intellectual debts apart from stray references to the "immortal systems" of "a Newton or a Locke"; more typically he dismisses "writers such as Locke and Montesquieu" for "l[ying] under the same disadvantage, of having written before these subjects were illuminated by the events and discussions which distinguish a very recent period."[103]

Fruitful comparisons may be made with several preceding theorists of national union. Madison's territorial argument for uniting states resembles that of writers such as Pufendorf, who saw interstate alliances as dependent on more than immediate external threats. Certain groups of states, which Pufendorf explicitly terms "unions" (*unum*), were distinguished by their willingness to treat important issues as collective matters in peacetime as well as during security crises.[104] Madison's similar insistence that short-term danger was insufficient grounds for unity was epitomized in his dismissal of the Germanic Empire's "deplorable" union.[105]

But Madison continued much farther along this path than had Pufendorf or other preceding writers. His description of interstate relations as transcending mutual protection, through grounding political unity in popular affective ties, takes on new significance given Pufendorf's and later European thinkers' resistance to such a conclusion. A further distinction was that Madison conceived of sovereignty in such a union as divisible, while Pufendorf upheld traditional notions of *imperium in imperio*.[106] Equally important, previous writers treated confederations of states as a subject separate from union among citizens within a state.[107] Madison innovatively erased the distinction between unions of states and of their residents in his connection of territorial and affective unity.

102. Quoted in Bowen 1961, x. Cf. Ackerman 1991, 3: "we must approach [constitutional thought] without the assistance of guides imported from another time and place."
103. Book list at Hutchinson et al. 1962–91, 6:62–115. Quotes from Meyers 1981, 184, and Hutchinson et al. 1962–91, 15:68–69.
104. Pufendorf 1710 [1679], 2:105; 7:502–3, 550–55. For more details see Kersh 1996, 56–64.
105. Rossiter 1961, no. 19, p. 131. Pufendorf similarly singled out the Germanic Empire in his first published work, *Constitution of the Germanic Empire* (1667).
106. For Madison on divided sovereignty, see esp. his "Notes on Nullification," Hunt 1910, 9:594–602; cf. his long letter to Jefferson after the convention, at Hutchinson et al. 1962–91, 10: 209–11, and Rossiter 1961, nos. 34, 39, 40, and 44. The originality of "Madisonian" federalism is well treated in Ostrom 1991, 70, 243–47. On precedent writers, particularly including Bodin and Pufendorf, see Antholis 1993, 265–380.
107. Rousseau, for example, after reviewing the extensive political philosophy of "domestic" union, turned to political "confederations," or unions among states. Sketching the outlines of a

Lockean liberalism, still routinely cited as the principal influence on founding thought in everything from religion to rhetoric, seems an equally oblique referent for Madison's ideas of union. Private ownership as a source of shared interests leading to political union is a core liberal idea; it is conceivable that Madison's views of labor and property were derived from Locke's at least in part. Locke and other Enlightenment liberals also were leaders in rejecting the Reformation fusion of religion and politics, driving a wedge that helped to diminish union's religious implications in American politics. Madison's most "liberal" moments come in his promotion of religious toleration.

Madison's view of the genesis of American union during the revolution and constitutional convention also recalls Lockean descriptions of the founding of states, with one vital difference. For Locke an initial political union was a spontaneous contractual expression by "all," or at least a great majority, of the citizenry.[108] Madison recognized it as the work of a smaller "patriotic and respectable" body, which then was ratified by the people.[109] The difference transcends mere procedural concerns and points up Madison's wariness of immediate popular action, particularly when not properly informed by reason and affection. Madison also devotes close attention, where Locke did not, to strengthening popular bonds after the initial founding, further distinguishing their approaches.[110] Nor, finally, was Madison's view of union "liberal" in the sense of prioritizing personal (or collective) liberty; as we have seen, he occasionally advised limits on individual liberty as necessary to protect a unified political order.

Madison also failed to follow a civic-republican script emphasizing avid citizen participation in small units of face-to-face governance. He did seek to balance federal and local authority but never extolled a "ward system" of government as Jefferson did (once). Madison's cautious hope that "sufficient virtue" would exist "among [Americans] for self-government"[111] was a pale echo of Cicero or Machiavelli's portrait of robust civic *virtu* in Sparta, Rome, or Florence.[112] To some analysts, this hesitation to embrace public virtue marks Madison as definitively "modern"; others see him as the last republican, operating amid "different cultural

---

planned treatise on the latter, Rousseau declared "[t]his subject is entirely new," and that "its principles have yet to be established" (Rousseau 1968 [1762], 143n; cf. 188).

108. Locke 1988 [1690], chap. 7, §87; chap. 19, §§211, 212; chap. 8, §§99, 102 ("Politick Societies all began from a voluntary Union"), 122. For related commentary see Lloyd Thomas 1995, 25–27.

109. Rossiter 1961, no. 40, p. 253; compare Madison's observation to Edmund Randolph, that if the Constitution had been the work of "an obscure individual, instead of a body possessing public respect and confidence," it "never" would have won adoption. Hutchinson et al. 1962–91, 10:355.

110. For Locke, citizens' act of uniting is restricted to an original act of political founding, and "their Union" is reserved for the body thus created. Nowhere does he indicate that legislators, or citizens bound by the social contract, should aspire to broad consensus on the basis of common interests—apart from a worst-case determination that "the Legislative" had usurped its constitutional bounds. (Locke accordingly issued a "Call to the Nation for Unity" during the Glorious Revolution.) See Locke 1988 [1690], chap. 19, §§211–22; chap. 8, esp. §112. A longer discussion of this point is at Kersh 1996, 39–42; see also Wood 1983, esp. 163.

111. Rossiter 1961, no. 55, p. 346; and see text accompanying note 82.

112. Machiavelli relates *virtu* to a "more united" citizenry at 1950 [1531], I.i.107. See generally Pocock 1975, esp. 189–232.

realities than the ones that succeeded his age."[113] Absent evidence that Madison relied to any meaningful extent on classical republican views of civic virtue, as either a support or a foil for his views, such debates lose relevance.

One republican thinker writing closer to Madison's own time was Jean-Jacques Rousseau. Though Rousseau has not seriously been suggested as Madison's philosophical ancestor,[114] a possible connection lies in his brief for ultracommunal ties and related concern that "particular interests begin to make themselves felt and sectional societies begin to exert an influence over the greater society."[115] Stretching Rousseau's perspective a bit, one might describe his *Social Contract* "lawgiver" as a model Madisonian representative, a guarantor of popular agreement.

In places Madison's language directly recalls Rousseau's, as when the latter recommends that "if there are sectional associations, it is wise to multiply their number and to prevent inequality among them," or, anticipating Madison's *Federalist* 51 line on nonangelic men and necessary government: "All justice comes from God, who alone is its source and if only we knew how to receive it from that exalted fountain, we should need neither governments nor laws." Whereas the more moderate Madison stopped well short of such Rousseauan declarations as "everything that destroys social unity is worthless," his own conviction of union's importance, and his horror at disunion, implies a tacit endorsement of the principle.[116]

But Rousseau's outright hostility to such central features of a Madisonian political union as the extended republic and legislative representation diminishes the force of such a comparison. Moreover, direct influence seems unlikely, as Madison's sole reference to Rousseau was to refute the latter's *Paix Perpetuelle*, where Madison dismisses Rousseau as a "visionary philosopher."[117] If reading Rousseau confirmed the civic-republican idea that close fraternal sentiment underlies a successful polity, Madison turned the notion in a very different direction.

The connection between colonial-era religious union rhetoric and American revolutionaries, as explored in chapter 1, also had little impact on Madison's unionist thought. Though Madison was quite familiar with biblical teachings, his opposition to establishmentarian efforts in Virginia and elsewhere, and his protection of minority religions against what he saw as overbearing regional sects, led him to downplay this source of authority. As early as 1774, he inveighed against the "[u]nion of religious sentiments," which, he wrote William Bradford, "begets a surprising confidence . . . tend[ing] to great ignorance and corruption all of which facilitate the execution of mischievous projects."[118]

What of a related argument that Madison drew on ethnonationalist or other-

---

113. Wills 1981, 278–70; see also cites at note 96.

114. The closest anyone comes is at Meyers 1981, xxiv–xxxiii. Matthews uses a comparison of Jefferson and Rousseau to distinguish both from Madison (1995, 270–71).

115. Rousseau 1968 [1762], 150.

116. Ibid., 73, 80, 181.

117. Meyers 1981, 193.

118. Hutchinson et al. 1962–91, 1:105.

wise ascriptive views in promoting a political union of Anglo-American white males? Such accounts were available in the eighteenth century and beyond; Johann Herder and other early Romantic philosophers located political unity in shared cultural traits. Some American thinkers during the founding era advanced such arguments, but not Madison. A view of the United States as a nationalized Christian community was anathema, given his battles for religious toleration and liberty of conscience. Though Madison was not a champion of enlightened inclusion in modern terms, his only reference to common "blood" came in a *Federalist* mention of "mingled" *patriot* blood—a source of unity achieved through service in the Revolutionary War, rather than through birth into a particular ethnic or cultural group.[119] Again, the difficulty of distinguishing Americans from Britons likely inclined Madison and other framers against an ethnically-based union. His vision was instead one of civic unity, based on allegiance to fellow citizens and rulers and on institutional promotion of this end. (The limits of Madison's inclusive spirit are taken up in a following section.)

More substantial attributions—the extended-republic argument to Hume and separation of powers to Montesquieu are most familiar—were important aspects of Madison's theory of union but were auxiliary to the central thrust. Montesquieu's central unionist claim, that a small-scale republic was required to combat the chaos of heterogeneous interests and opinions, was rejected outright by Madison in his *Federalist* 10 acknowledgment of the inevitability of factional dissent in any confederation, however limited its population.[120] Madison's debt to Hume has provided considerable grist for scholarly mills since Douglass Adair published his influential study in 1974. But from a unionist perspective, Madison's purpose in extending the republic evidently differed from Hume's.[121]

Even if each step in Madison's logic owes something to an intellectual precursor, no single paradigm or theorist appears to have wielded significant philosophical influence. Showing that his views were primarily derived from others would require demonstrating a substantial connection, one beyond occasional points of symmetry or evidence that Madison read a particular author. The most one can say after examining precedent unionist theories[122] is that Madison found stray aspects of liberal, classical-republican, and other schools useful, applied these in patchwork fashion, and paid little or no attention to any philosophy as a holistic paradigm. Like other leading voices during colonial and founding

---

119. Rossiter 1961, no. 14, p. 104.

120. On Montesquieu's theory of a limited republic, see Beer 1993, 219–23.

121. On Hume's influence, see Adair 1974, 97–106; Wills 1981, 21–23, 29–45, 53–54, 183–84, 210–30; Rosen 1999, 107–8; Matthews 1995, 74–75, 177. Persuasive arguments that Madison's account of representative government bore at most a "superficial resemblance" to Hume's are in Morgan 1986, 102; McCoy 1989, 48–50. For his part, Madison described Hume as "foremost among these bungling lawgivers" whose attempts at constitution-making were "sadly defective." Rives and Fendall 1865, 4:58.

122. A sustained examination of possible unionist "precedents," beginning with Aristotle, is in Kersh 1996, 21–66.

times, Madison was not sounding unionist ideas drawn mainly from liberal or republican sources, nor even a blend of these. Perhaps "multiple traditions" did organize early American thoughts about union and most other political virtues.[123] But if so these traditions operated in fragmentary, piecemeal ways not often recognized in conventional scholarship.

Two further points should be made about the interpretive-paradigms approach to conceptual study. First, the complex ideological outlook of Madison and other founders recedes in importance amid scholars' emphasis on past philosophical influences. American thinkers appear as passive registers for various bodies of imported thought: liberal, republican, Scottish Enlightenment, and so forth.[124] But far more is obscured than illuminated in striving to demonstrate Madison's "commitment to his particular Calvinistic-Lockean frame of reference," or Americans' "skewed, neorepublican sort of pseudo-liberalism."[125] The framers' actual intentions are lost amid extensive efforts to match American pronouncements to their supposed inspirations—a curious state of affairs, especially given the primacy of national self-determination among the objects Madison, like his fellow leaders, thought he was securing.

Second, paradigmatic accounts of founding ideology overlook concepts that do not fit neatly into their frame of reference, however important they might otherwise have been among American thinkers. Union is a leading example. Chapter 1 traced a pattern in ante–Revolutionary War references to communal union that, as noted there, fails to follow the liberal/republican script of a transition from classical to modern usage. Madison, it seems, developed his ideas of union from a blend of political experience, wide reading dominated by no single paradigm, and synthetic imagination. When we view his and other framers' ideas in a less encumbered way, still in their historical context but without trying to locate them definitively in one or another ideological camp, then union's centrality becomes plain.

With interpretations mounting beyond comprehensible limits, the benefit in such taxonomic exercises diminishes. Indeed, in recent years some participants have relaxed their guard and admitted a paradigmatic pluralism, in Isaac Kramnick's apt phrase, as determinative.[126] Now all influences are recognized as im-

---

123. Smith 1997 is the leading statement of this view.

124. See, from the republican side, Pocock's exploration of early American ideas "in search of *manifestations* of the problems of the republican perspective" (1975, 506–18; emphasis added). Pangle's equally dismissive response portrays American republicanism as wholly derived from Lockean rationalism: he explains that "we must not forget that the founders were not themselves philosophers" (1988, 11; cf. Huyler 1995).

125. Matthews 1995, 35; Berthoff 1997, 235–36.

126. Kramnick 1990, 294; cf. 1–42, 260–95. Ian Shapiro's charge in another context applies here: "both sides are to a degree co-opted by the terms of reference of what they attack and the resulting arguments begin to look remarkably like one another, professed differences to the contrary notwithstanding" (1990, 296). Cf. the "liberal republicanism" identified by Sunstein 1988; Ackerman 1991, 29–32; and Smith 1997, 471, or the "half-classical, half-liberal" founders portrayed in Carl Richard's study (1994, 238).

portant, an advance for antidogmatism but hardly one for clarity. Murkiness can only increase, given the internal complexity and ambiguity of each paradigm. Madison's own words are apposite: "My doubts . . . proceed from the danger of turning the controversy too much into the wilderness of books . . . [by] writers such as Locke and Montesquieu &c."[127] Comparison to inherited bodies of thought helped to illuminate perennial problems and provide a ground for their solution, by posing the "right questions" for political thinkers. But to these Madison and fellow framers offered their own, often distinctive answers.[128]

*

James Madison was a unionist. Viewing his political thought and activity through this explanatory prism helps explain his outlook on a range of issues at the constitutional convention and thereafter, far better than do the sprawling templates of liberalism, nationalism, civic republicanism, and so forth. Madison's briefs for local representative leadership (as in the Alien & Sedition Acts fracas), contrasted with his support at the convention for strengthening the central government, is a source of the "two Madisons" scholarship mentioned earlier. Both, however, were part of a steady vision of stable political union, which was (in Banning's words) a "vital 'mean' between state sovereignty and an excessive concentration of authority in distant, unresponsive hands."[129]

This balancing ethic is evident in every element of Madison's theory of union. Unified territory joined discrete, self-governing parts; efforts to enhance mutual affection among Americans were balanced by protections against popular excess; and representative leadership was hedged with oversight by the people they governed. Madison's legislative career consistently displayed this inclination to the mean, from his early work in the Continental Congress (e.g., offering a compromise version of the first system of national revenue) to his steering carefully between War Hawks' fervor and New England Federalists' isolationism in 1812.[130] Such moderation (a term Madison used often) served the republic well in its early years and did much to establish union as the first in an important line of balancing terms in American political talk.

127. Hutchinson et al. 1962–91, 15:59. Cf. Madison's first "Helvidius" essay, which explicitly considered the influence of Locke and Montesquieu on constitutional thought before concluding, "let us quit a field of research which is more likely to perplex than to decide, and bring the question to other tests of which it will be more easy to judge" (ibid., 68).

128. Galston 1990, 64. See also Lutz 1992, 111–40; Howe 1989, 580–81; Lienesch 1988, 121–26. Embracing universal paradigms is hardly an error confined to modern-day scholars, of course. A writer styling himself "Ghost of Aaron [Burr]" anticipated present debates in 1807 by groaning that "Republicanism means anything and everything," a fact that led him to conclude that "In short, sir, these gentry can prove black white, and white black" (*Baltimore Whig*, December 21, 1807).

129. Banning 1995, 350. On "two Madisons" studies, see note 98 and text accompanying.

130. On the revenue compromise, see Rakove 1996, 37–38; on Madison's "principled realism" in foreign affairs—another testament to his balanced approach to political science—see Russell 1995, 716–21.

Sustainable Union: Consequences

Commitments have consequences, and Madison's considerable political weight greatly extended the influence of his unionist vision. As contexts changed, the limits of his theory became evident. Later chapters will demonstrate that this sustainable-union ideal was eventually harnessed to secessionist ideas and that it partly thwarted Reconstruction efforts after the Civil War. Here follows a brief examination of how Madison's commitment to union shaped his views in ways we can only regard now as unfortunate.

Beyond a nagging inconclusiveness on certain essential topics, such as how affective unity was to emerge, Madison's account of union raises two major concerns. First, he largely bypassed questions of how to join partially excluded and dominated groups to the polity. In a political view oriented around affective bonds among the mass of Americans, connections between majority Anglo-Europeans and other groups populating the country required spelling out. Madison's attention in this regard was largely limited to protection of minority interests: his *Federalist* 10 checking and balancing is meant to ensure that no interest, especially property, is unjustly opposed.[131] But *integration* into the union that served as the source of so many vital goods is quite another matter. Madison's virtual silence on this point is less a problem with the logic of his theory of union—in principle he could have limited affective bonds to various subsets of the population—and more the failure to address a set of issues that remain among the thorniest perennials in American society.

Madison was not loath to take on controversial questions, generally speaking. His penchant for stability and compromise did not preclude unwavering efforts to secure religious tolerance, an unpopular position in early 1780s Virginia. His promotion of the Constitution similarly led him into the teeth of home-state opposition. But when it came to inclusion of nonwhite peoples in the union he so prized Madison backed away, despite his condemnation of slavery.

Madison did affirm unity with certain outsiders—"respectable European" immigrants, most notably. Such "foreigners of merit & republican principles" were to be "invite[d] . . . among us," he wrote, for reasons encompassing ideology ("maintain[ing] the character of liberality" attributed to America); prudence ("when they come among us . . . their adopted country soon takes the place of a native home"); and practicality ("respectable" immigrants were "the most desirable class of people," given their skills and "fortunes").[132] Such expansiveness illustrates the degree to which the founders' idealized union excluded[133] others— American Indians and both free and enslaved blacks. Madison appears to have

---

131. The notable exception is enslaved blacks, as discussed below.

132. Farrand 1937, 2:236; Rives and Fendall 1865, 3:120; Farrand 1937, 2:270–71. On early American elites' immigration views, including that of Madison, see Baseler 1998, 271–344.

133. "Excluded" misstates the case subtly: slaves and Indians were denied citizenship rights, but were included in the population in that they were governed by, and decisively subordinate to, federal and state officials. See Smith 1997, 17–18.

considered Native Americans only rarely, and then only in terms of stock stereotypes, terming them "savages" or, as he addressed a gathering of Sac, Fox, and Osage leaders at the White House, "my red children." Indians appeared to him as separate from white Americans' territorial and affective union, both figuratively and literally. Madison referred in his 1812 war message to "inhabitants of the shadowy borderlands," dwelling on "our extensive frontiers." [134]

Other framers, living in closer proximity to Native Americans than did Madison, might have seen matters differently. Before the war for independence some expressions of intimacy were voiced, as when Florida's colonial governor described Seminoles as "interwoven with us." [135] But this outlook was drastically affected by the revolutionary conflict. Though tribal responses to the war included neutrality and occasional alliances with the rebel Americans, the conventional postwar view was that all Indians had been firm—and brutal—supporters of the British side. The "middle ground," in historian Richard White's term, that had existed between Anglo-Americans and Indians was all but destroyed by the war and this widespread belief afterward. [136] In part due to the war's recency, then, though also owing to expansionist desires and ethnocentric prejudice, most of Madison's fellow political leaders shared his conception of Indians as completely outside the new political union. [137]

African Americans were similarly excluded from union membership, though Madison devoted far more attention to slaves and free blacks than he did to Indians. Madison's antislavery views; his resigned awareness of whites' "existing and probably unalterable prejudices," which led him to conclude that "it appears impossible for two such distinct races to occupy the same country in amity & peace"; and his status as slaveholding Virginia planter led to a jumbled set of pronouncements on slavery, which he termed "this great evil under which the nation labors," and on race relations. Unlike Jefferson's tentative "scientific" racist writings, notes Drew McCoy, Madison "never referred to any intrinsic inadequacy

134. Quoted in Brant 1941–61, 6:69; Hunt 1910, 8:198–200. Cf. Hutchinson et al. 1962–91, 11:271; Rives and Fendall 1865, 3:64–66; and Brant 1941–61, 1:45–48 (on Madison's childhood "dread of Indians").

135. Quoted in Calloway 1995, 255. The closest that Anglo-Americans and Indians came to living on at least quasi-equal terms was in the Great Lakes Region from the colonial period through the late eighteenth century. There a "middle ground" was established, as Richard White (1991, 212–308) describes in rich detail. Into the early nineteenth century, some tribes also mingled freely with American and European frontiersmen in the "borderlands" along the Missouri Valley and parts of the Rio Grande Basin until whites' "unlimited appetite for land" (and a consequent policy among Osage and other tribes to kill Anglo-American migrants on sight) crippled any chance of preserving the "syncretic societies" of Indian and white American. Adelman and Aron 1999, 823–39 (quotes at p. 839); Faragher 1998, 304–18.

136. White 1991, esp. 413–57; see also Prucha 1984, 36–38; Dowd 1992, 47–65; Calloway 1995, 272–83, 292–98. A Continental Congress committee concluded that Native Americans "were aggressors in the war, without even a pretense of provocation." Ford et al. 1904–37, 25:683.

137. Jill Lepore's recent book portrays King Philip's War, in 1675, as "a critical step in the evolution toward an increasingly racialized ideology of the differences between Europeans and Indians" (1998, 7). See also Merrell 1989; Smith 1997, 106–10, 131–34, 144–46. For a sustained look at Jefferson's Indian policies, and personal views, see Wallace 1999, esp. 206–40 (during Jefferson's presidency), and Onuf 1999.

of the blacks." Rather, he saw African Americans as inevitably viewed by most whites as outside the national whole, a view strengthened by the contentious debates already swirling around racial issues.[138] Madison's deep concern to preserve union and interregional accord inclined him toward "diffusion" of slaves into the West "beyond the region occupied by or allotted to a White population" and, eventually, "removal" of free and newly manumitted African Americans via Liberian colonization.[139]

McCoy calls Madison's a "conservative" position, based both on his underlying pessimism about the possibility of changing mass white attitudes and on his vain faith in an eventual resolution of "an evil that cannot as yet be removed." To many, particularly free blacks and slaves who preferred their birthplaces to Liberian exile, it must instead have appeared a thoughtlessly expedient one, possibly even a disguised effort to strengthen slavery's hold in the South. The latter seems unlikely, given Madison's strenuous opposition to the institution. William Lee Miller's summary serves well here: "Although James Madison would oppose slavery as a moral evil all his life . . . both in thought and in action, he did so in the context of other beliefs and commitments that subordinated that conviction."[140] Miller does not enumerate these, but clearly one principal commitment was to national union. The tragic irony was that Madison's effort to preserve racial homogeneity in the name of unity did little to alleviate cleavages among whites; conflicts raged for decades over the place of slave and free blacks in America.

Madison's political colleagues similarly considered African Americans as outside the circle of unity, though few bothered to defend in print such an apparently self-evident point. Into the 1820s, even strenuous antislavery statements (except those by Quakers) usually featured recommendations for "removal" to the western territories or Africa. Occasional references to black "brethren" typically arose in the context of necessity, not mutuality, as in free blacks' service as Revolutionary War soldiers or, later, party voters. A Republican paper in New York, flushed with electoral victory in 1808, saluted the "firm, united, and happy" nation while chiding "deluded Africans" who had "sold your suffrage privileges for the smiles of federalism"—that is, voted Federalist. Support Republicans in the next election, the editorial concluded, and "your country [will be] proud to acknowledge you as brethren, or [else conclude] that you are determined to continue 'slaves by choice.'"[141]

---

138. McCoy 1989, 307. Delegates from South Carolina and Georgia were already threatening disunion at the constitutional convention, leading even antislavery New Englanders to agree to compromise "because two states might be lost to the Union" (Farrand 1937, 1:595–96).

139. Rives and Fendall 1865, 3:134; cf. Hunt 1910, 9:85, 265–67. McCoy (1989, 253–322) and W. Miller (1992, 171–84) provide thorough treatments of Madison's views on slavery; also worthwhile is Matthews 1995, 205–10. An excellent study of Jefferson on race and slavery is Onuf 1998.

140. McCoy 1989, 276–78; Rives and Fendall 1865, 3:134. On Madison's support of "diffusion," leading some historians to term him proslavery, see McCoy 1989, 265–74. W. Miller 1992, 180.

141. Jordan 1968, 540–48; *Public Advertiser* (New York), May 2, 1808. On the general prevalence of "a nationalist ideology that could comprehend nothing but a wholly white America," see Waldstreicher 1997, 302–48 (quote at p. 305). In a little-noted 1780 private letter, Madison proposed en-

A second major oversight in Madison's theory concerns questions of obligation. In the cause of perpetuating political union, certain responsibilities presumably were required of the constituent parts. But it is difficult to determine from his account what these were. States had to remain in the union and observe "the constitutionality of Federal acts," as Madison's arguments against nullification reconfirmed.[142] Citizens' unionist obligations were little mentioned, apart from a general expectation that they would exhibit affective spirit. Formally obliging the people to comprehend their mutual bonds, while minimizing opportunities to act "wrongly" on these, was a daunting order. Encouraging allegiance to (and monitoring of) elective representatives and their political decisions seems as far as Madison was able to go in this regard.[143]

Even national representatives were not explicitly required to act virtuously or observe the public interest in order to further a necessary sense of political union. Madison clearly hoped they would do so; his writings and work in the national government were in part intended as inspirational example. Otherwise, he saw institutional restraints as securities against failure. Through Madison's lifetime, this arrangement appeared adequate. But as discussed in chapters 4 and 5, when northerners sought to reshape the moral promise of union to more inclusive ends, the lasting influence of his balanced ideal contributed to their disappointing failures.

UNION AND THE EARLY REPUBLIC: 1789–1820s

According to the Constitution's chief architect, several American political verities were predicated on political union. National defense required unity among the states, warding off multiple horrors: foreign invasion, a standing army, and possibly a tyrannical sovereign. Enduring territorial union in turn demanded popular coherence. Without a significant degree of affective union, the government could be neither established nor changed; once in motion, it would function poorly without popular unity, though many operations could be supervised by united representatives. Displays of accord among these national leaders would, Madison and other framers hoped, help fellow-feeling to emerge among the people.

Madison's conviction about the importance of national unity led him to develop a political theory in support of it and to spend much of his life working to effect this vision. Most other politicians of the time were content to invoke the

---

listing African Americans in the Revolutionary War: "would it not be as well to liberate and make soldiers at once of the blacks?" he wrote a colleague, Joseph Jones. Hutchinson et al. 1962–91, 2:209.

142. Madison's most detailed assessment of the nullification issue is in "Notes on Nullification" (Hunt 1910, 9:573–607; quote at p. 576).

143. Madison does offer a general account of citizens' obligation to national or local government; Sinopoli (1992, 103–11) provides a summary. But the obligation to pursue affective ties and thereby uphold political union is largely unaddressed.

term and trust in its realization. Through the Federalist Era, and in the early years of Jefferson's presidency, talk of national union seems principally to have been the province of American leaders. Newspaper references to union include several advertisements targeting elites—as when a New York hotelier boasted in print of hosting wealthy guests from "all parts of the Union." The word also cropped up in diplomatic circles: Colombia's army commander, exhorting independence from Spain in 1806, saluted the "enduring Union" of "the Americans, our neighbors," adding that "Union will [also] assure to us permanent and perpetual happiness."[144]

Among some creative thinkers, energetic efforts to realize union in practice were mounted in the years after 1789. Engineers and architects viewed Madison's account of territory-based union literally. Pierre L'Enfant, designing the layout of Washington, D.C., in 1792, deliberately sought to embody national unity in the territory of the new capital. As an architectural historian notes, "L'Enfant's main and most obvious symbolic objective, clearly spelled out in the system of state avenues and state squares and circles, was the structure of the United States as a union of states." L'Enfant's intention may be obscure today, but it was recognized at the time. A New Yorker writer celebrated the "Federal City" as designed to "melt down the distinctions of southern and northern, of eastern and western, and make them feel for ever as members of one common undivided community."[145] Abstract space was also invested with representations of American unity. In 1809 a War Department clerk named William Lambert proposed a new prime meridian, running through the center of Washington, D.C. His aim was "to symbolize both the Union's political coherence and its independence" so that Americans would not have to rely on "foreign territories" in calculating their longitude. Lambert was praised as "a patriot" by President Monroe, and his plan was rushed through Congress; some American cartographers employed Lambert's "American meridian" until 1884, when Greenwich was adopted as the international standard.[146]

Within a few months of the Constitution's ratification, David Ramsay and Jedediah Morse published full-blown histories of the nation's brief existence that were expressly designed to "inspire Americans to think in national terms and give their loyalties to a nation state." Other writers penned poems, allegories, and sermons in praise of American union. Philip Freneau, later a founder with Madison and Jefferson of the first national political party, declared in prose and poetry that Americans' "union chain" was "by heaven inspired." Four Connecticut au-

144. *American Minerva*, July 6, 1802; *New York Commercial-Advertiser*, October 2, 1806.

145. Schirmer 1999, 135; "Hancock" in *Public Advertiser* (New York), February 24, 1808. Such monumental representations of unity continued well into the nineteenth century: the Capitol dome, for example, begun in 1850, features near the apex a circle of thirty-six columns—one for each state at the time.

146. Edney 1994, quotes at pp. 384, 392–93. Jedediah Morse, in his monumental 1789 *American Geography*, had earlier recommended a Philadelphia prime meridian. On Morse's labors to "create and foster a uniquely 'American' identity," including in the realm of national geography, see Short 1999, 30–40.

thors collaborated on the twelve-part epic *Anarchiad,* which was filled with dark visions of disunion and concluded, in case readers missed the point, "the voice of UNION calls . . . 'YE LIVE UNITED, OR DIVIDED DIE.'"[147]

Especially prominent in this lexical labor was Noah Webster, for whom "political harmony" depended on creating a "uniformity of American language," a project he described as no less important than the Constitution's framing. Webster insisted in his *Dissertations on the English Language* that a shared vocabulary was elemental to U.S. citizens' self-conception as part of a larger whole; an "American tongue" free of British taint represented a great stride in that direction. As linguist Charles Kreidler summarizes, "Webster was the foremost person in the 1780s and 1790s to see the value of a standard language [as] something which would unify the country and differentiate it from the former mother country. . . . Webster, more than anyone, envisioned a uniform language as the instrument for cultural, and thence political, cohesion." Among the terms Webster singled out in his *Dissertations* as essential to Americans' "national attachments" was "Union."[148]

Webster, L'Enfant, and other elites saw urgent purposes in their didactic activity, as opinion leaders' fervent union talk had attracted only sporadic popular echoes after 1789. Although elites may have sought solace in praising an "era of good feelings" in the early nineteenth century, political turmoil was plentiful. Republican/Federalist clashes during Jefferson's administration echoed well into Madison's, culminating in the Hartford Convention of 1814. A short-lived boost in the mass public's unionist sentiment came with the conclusion of "Mr. Madison's War" in 1815; a Philadelphia editorial that year noted the "curious . . . political calm, which now prevails throughout the United States. . . . Apparently the people at large are contented and united." But populist reaction to a Compensation Act doubling congressional pay the next year, followed by an economic depression beginning in 1819 and the Missouri crisis of 1819–21, renewed American leaders' concern about popular indifference or even opposition to national unity.[149]

Thus sustaining the legitimacy of union was a leading difficulty facing political elites throughout the decade following ratification. As Robert Wiebe attests, "the real danger to the union . . . was apathy." Education was one way to encourage national sentiments among a late-eighteenth-century American populace seemingly indifferent to union's charms. American history textbooks accordingly drew on Noah Webster in admonishing schoolchildren to seek "common affec-

147. Thelen 1998, 381; Freneau in Pattee 1902, 1:147; *Anarchiad* cited and described in Waldstreicher 1997, 59–60. On "the emergence of an American literature that both signals and helps solidify that national identity," see Barnes 1997 (quote at p. 597).

148. Webster 1789, 19–27, 35–36, 288–90; Kreidler 1998, 102. A similar though more critical view of Webster's aim is in Kramer 1988, 222–24.

149. *Aurora* (Philadelphia), July 6, 1815. On the events mentioned briefly here, see Knupfer 1991, 90–102, and Freehling 1990, 144–54 (both on Missouri); Banner 1970 and Chatfield 1988 (both on the Hartford Convention); Lewis 1998, 14–68, 126–54; Formisano 1974; Waldstreicher 1997, 293–302; McCormick 1990; and McWilliams 1973, 200–209.

tion," setting out a secular catechism: "The Union of these States is the production of the spirit of harmony and compromise. Do we remember how much our fathers surrendered to compose [it], and shall we refuse to surrender any thing to preserve it?" Hugely popular nationalist artworks, particularly those of the Hudson River School beginning in the 1820s, reinforced such lessons through national tours.[150]

But stronger unionist encouragement was needed in the early republic, as a famous European visitor would later affirm. "Patriotism and religion are the only two motives," Tocqueville wrote early in *Democracy in America*, "which can long urge all the people towards the same end."[151] These twin sources of inspiration, along with institutional activities beginning to realize imagined connections as concrete advantages, heightened the popular appeal of union ideals as the nineteenth century began.

A resurgence of religious thought and practice, dating from the Second Awakening early in the nineteenth century, expanded union's resonance in the public mind. Low-, middle-, and high-brow theologians all utilized the term, mingling political references in ways recalling their colonial predecessors. "Crazy" Lorenzo Dow, the best-known and most-traveled revival preacher of the day, mixed appeals to "unity of all Christians" and "union among Americans" in his sermons, which when published went through seventy editions. The more traditional sermons of Lyman Beecher featured "exhortations for national union with God" that were "unsurpassed" during the early nineteenth century, according to one historian. Concluded a typical Beecher lecture, "The integrity of the Union demands exertions to produce in the nation a more homogeneous character, and bind us together with . . . [common] habits and institutions." And Horace Bushnell, among the most intellectual of antebellum clerics, oriented his theology around an idea of organic unity stretching from God to individual, family, town, and nation, based on a "pious bond of intimate union" at each intersection.[152]

Religious leaders admonished congregants to seek unity with one another outside the church as well, in a society that often seemed impossibly disorderly. Nathan Hatch notes that "the rhetoric of unity was omnipresent in American churches" precisely because "the first third of the nineteenth century experienced a period of religious ferment, chaos, and originality unmatched in American history." Ministers and independent reformers saw part of their charge as "inculcating those religious beliefs and values that could serve to hold the society together." Tenuous social bonds could be tightened, according to these ecumenical

150. Wiebe 1984, 202; Pierce 1930, 255–56 (cf. Ruth Elson: "the first duty of schoolbook authors in their own eyes was to attach the child's loyalty to the state and nation"—1964, 282). A good summary of American artists' "landscapes of nationalism" is in Miller 1993.

151. Tocqueville 1969 [1835–40], 2:19.

152. Dow 1814, 14–16 (on covenants and Christian unity), 146–49 (on society), 175–76, 247–48 (on "the bond of Union") (see also Hatch 1989, 36–40); Nagel 1971, 44; Beecher in Foster 1960, 223; Bushnell 1847, 70–73; 84–91.

unionists, by extending Christian values to the political order. Politicians searching for sources of stability—and personal electoral appeal—readily agreed, filling their speeches and platforms with pious union references. "We hold sacred the Union of the states," the Pennsylvania Senate formally declared in early 1809. "We will adhere and cling to it, in prosperity and adversity . . . and pledge ourselves to each other, to our common country, and to our God, that we will, as citizens and as legislators, exert every energy of body and soul, to preserve and transmit to posterity unimpaired, the present happy Union of the states." [153]

Along with promoting religious ties as a means to common sentiment, nineteenth-century political elites sought to inspire wider patriotic identification with national union. These efforts are most apparent today in printed accounts of July 4 and election-day celebrations. The Fourth was a regular occasion for unionist spirit by the early nineteenth century, when standardized observances were staged throughout the United States. Citizens gathered at the town hall or another civic site for a public ceremony, featuring a notable local or visiting politician's speech, inevitably invoking national union at length. The dignitaries then repaired to a dinner featuring numerous patriotic toasts, generally reprinted in the next issue of the local newspaper. Usually the first or second toast was to national union, often in the most extravagant terms imaginable. "The Union of the States," offered William Carmichael at Monroe, Georgia's 1827 celebration. "May the brain be palsied that would meditate its severance." Not to be outdone, the next guest quoted "our sterling Governor" in declaring "I would lay down my life to preserve this Union but a single day." Notably, national union was often toasted separately from "the United States" and "the General Government." [154]

National elections were more complicated occasions for unionist sentiment. Party members in each state were regularly treated to newspaper headlines and oratory celebrating glorious victory (or exposing the corrupt forces behind their defeat) in other locations around the country, reinforcing their conception of belonging to a larger whole. But these were partisan reports, after all, and the corrosive effects of party spirit worried some national-minded leaders. Thus victors magnanimously extended a hand "in union . . . to members of the Federalist vanquished" and spokesmen for the losers enjoined followers not to "go to the altar and offer up an oath of eternal hatred against our opponents. That would be . . . dividing every family from itself. We are sent here to do good; and what more beneficial object can we accomplish, than the restoration of social harmony?" David Waldstreicher masterfully dissects the "partisan antipartisanship" of the early nineteenth century, showing how "local partisan activity" was frequently "justified by a larger goal of national unanimity." [155]

---

153. Hatch 1989, 63–64 (see 49–122 more generally); *Pennsylvania Herald and Easton Intelligencer*, March 8, 1809. Note the echoes of marriage vows and of the Declaration.

154. *Georgia Journal* (Milledgeville), July 24, 1827.

155. *Aurora* (Philadelphia), December 7, 1804; *Commercial Advertiser* (New York), January 28, 1805; Waldstreicher 1997, 201–15 (quotes at pp. 201–2). See also Bassett 1999 on the "canopy of patriotism" alleviating "bitter partisanship" in Vermont (36).

Newspapers, beginning to reach beyond elite audiences in the early nineteenth century, offered more regular opportunities to encounter unionist themes. Editorial comment often followed Madison's tripartite conception of united territory, people, and representatives. Savannah, Georgia's Republican paper opened its first issue (in 1802) with a long rumination on "how men unite to preserve liberty." The next piece, reprinted from the *National Intelligencer*, extolled the present U.S. Congress for exhibiting "a greater unity of sentiment, views, and opinion, than has existed at any other period for the last ten years." The editor later turned to territorial unity, exhorting "Georgians" that "the spirit of improvement is diffusing itself over the eastern, northern, and western parts of the union, and will you remain unmoved by its influence?"[156] Public lectures and oratory, often reprinted in newspapers, provided further opportunities for drumming home unionist themes. Henry Adams captured the practice well in his history of the period:

[Henry] Clay's maiden speech [in the U.S. House, 1810] marked the appearance of a school which was for fifty years to express the national ideals of statesmanship, drawing elevation of character from confidence in itself, and from devotion to ideas of nationality and union, which redeemed every mistake committed in their names. In Clay's speech almost for the first time the two rhetorical marks of his generation made their appearance, and during the next half century the Union and the Fathers were rarely omitted from any popular harangue.[157]

An early peak in these unionist "harangues" came in the Missouri crisis of 1819–21, the most serious sectional challenge to national harmony in the republic's short history. President Monroe, midway through his proudly proclaimed Era of Good Feelings, praised "the union which has prevailed" and urged "a like accord in all questions touching . . . the happiness of our country." Partisans on all sides hewed to this call. Theodore Dwight, antislavery editor of the *New York Advertiser*, declared that even Missouri's admission as a slave state was endurable: "As for dividing the Union, that is out of the question. THEY DARE NOT DO IT." And leaders in Richmond, Virginia, the hotbed of opposition to the Compromise, after its passage saw "the Union" as "too precious to be threatened" by continued belligerence. Monroe's Federalist opponents similarly expressed "sincere hope," in the words of one Maryland writer, that "the compromise will take place, and I am confident that by this means harmony will be restored. . . . May heaven avert such a calamity [as] dissolution of the union."[158]

Concerns about disunion arose from the nature of national politics in the early republic. Even as memories of the nation's uncertain future under the Articles of

156. *Georgia Republican and State Intelligencer* (Savannah), August 21, 1802; July 7, 1803.

157. Adams 1930, 5:190.

158. Monroe in Lott 1994, 44; *New York Daily Advertiser*, February 24, 1820; *Richmond Enquirer*, March 7, 1820; *Maryland Gazette and Political Intelligencer* (Annapolis), February 17, 1820.

Confederation faded, a spreading democratic ethic in the political and religious realms after 1790 contributed to a sense of instability among national leaders. Union appeals provided at least some rhetorical security in response. The duties of governance demanded a balancing ideal like union: in one succinct description, American national politics in the early nineteenth century comprised "two parties triangulating three regions, two foreign powers, and two levels of government—state and national. The flexibility this system required made mediating and nonpartisan gestures not just an ideological preference but a practical necessity."[159] Most such "gestures" among national elites were expressed in unionist terms. Prominent among these were issues concerning federalism—the "two levels of government"—in the early republic.

Calibrating the relative authority of state and federal governments in the name of maintaining political union became second nature to American statesmen after ratification (and to other opinion leaders as well: newspapers are full of editorials counseling restraint in both spheres, well into the 1890s). As noted in the introduction, Americans had both strategic and principled reasons for adopting a federal approach to national union. Tactically, Madison and other unionist founders recognized that the state governments were prized by residents and state leadership. Even had they wished it otherwise, it was impossible to win ratification without strong assurances of continued state autonomy in certain matters. The founding generation sought vital changes in American administrative organization, but not total revolution: existing economic and social systems were built on local attachments, and few attempts were made to upset these to any great degree.

On a more positive note, American thinkers embraced a federalist idea of dual authority as a source of potential strength. A "partnership" of power, many framers recognized, could provide a functional division of labor—a concept very much in vogue in the late eighteenth century, thanks to Adam Smith and the early industrialists he helped inspire. This expectation, that dual authority could enable each level to perform better, became a dominant theme in founding thought. Arendt cites John Adams in this respect: "When he wrote 'Power must be opposed to power, force to force, strength to strength, interest to interest, as well as reason to reason, eloquence to eloquence and passion to passion,' he obviously believed he had found in this very opposition an instrument to generate more power, more strength, more reason and not to abolish them."[160] The view that constant mutual suspicion between the two levels of government was not necessary proved to be accurate in the long run, as federal relations in various realms (fiscal, regulatory, administrative) featured mostly peaceable political exchanges.

Scattered examples can be found among the founders and nineteenth-century American nation-builders of more ardent champions of a unitary state. But this

159. Waldstreicher 2000, 14–15. On Americans' unionist foreign policy in the early republic, as it concerned the dissolution of the Spanish empire in the United States, see the insightful study by Lewis 1998.

160. Arendt 1963, 152. On this theme, see also Epstein 1984 and Zvesper 1999.

was a very subdued minority voice, compared to an overwhelming trend toward reaffirming the federalist nature of national union. (It appears all the more subdued compared to contemporaneous statements of unitary nationalism in France and, later, Italy.)[161] Affirmation of a federal relationship was lexical in speeches and newspaper editorials, theoretical in the unionist understanding of Madison and Lincoln among others,[162] and political in institutional design. One result, as seen in chapter 3, was American thinkers' affinity for blending civil society and state functions, spheres often conceived as separate today.

*

An 1830 convention of the national Episcopal Church, meeting to draft a "prayer for the whole people," ran into difficulty. The original "O Lord, bless our nation" drew "so many objections [from] the laity to the word 'nation'" that it was replaced with "union." Two aspects of this story are pertinent here. Well into the nineteenth century, "union" remained distinct from "nation" in the minds of many Americans.[163] And national elites—here, heads of the country's most exclusive church—were actively concerned with issues of conceptual nuance.[164] Both points were legacies of the constitutional era, when union's political salience was reestablished by leaders' ardent use of the term.

The central standing of union ideas in American mass discourse was not fully established until the Jacksonian and early antebellum period, judging from the frequency and breadth of union usage. As the term proliferated, Madison's combination of institutional protection, affective sentiment, and enlightened, unity-minded representative leadership continued as the leading theoretical basis of national union. Succeeding chapters will suggest that Madison and fellow unionists during this period did their work too well, imposing a vision bounded by time and circumstance on a polity that soon little resembled that of the early republic.

161. Mazzini, the theorist of Italian nationalism, strongly opposed federalism as a retrogressive force that threatened to drive Italy "back towards the Middle Ages," as he wrote in 1831. Hence he and other Italian nationalist revolutionaries sought inspiration in the French rather than the American example. See Haddock 1999, 323, 332.

162. Madison noted critically in 1824 that "the word 'consolidate,'" in the constitutional convention, "there and then meant to give strength and solidity to the union of the states. In its current and controversial application, it means a destruction of the States by transferring their powers into the government of the Union." Rives and Fendall 1865, 3:412–13.

163. Bryce 1896, 3. Compare Ellsworth at the constitutional convention, proposing to "drop the word *national,* and retain the proper title 'the United States'" (Farrand 1937, 1:335); or the National Republican Party changing its name to "Whig" in the early 1820s, because "the adjective *national* . . . conveyed suspicions of upper-class pretension" (Saxton 1990, 24). Henry Adams's study of early national history noted that delegates "made no reference to the nation; the word itself was unknown to the Constitution, which invariably spoke of the *Union* whenever such an expression was needed." Adams 1909, 2:85.

164. This concern was noted, often with frustration, by British observers. Colonial Georgia's Chief Justice Anthony Stokes began his history of colonial America (written after the revolution) by observing: "For some time before the Civil War broke out in America, the popular leaders there affected to call the . . . King's Governments on the Continent, 'Colonies,' instead of 'Provinces,' from an opinion they had conceived, that the word Province meant a conquered country. . . . [But] Colony or Plantation does not import a conquest, but rather the contrary" (1783, 3).

CHAPTER 3

Nrational Unity and
Nation-Building, 1820s–1850s

The late political discussions and events, have tended to loosen those
bonds of fraternal affection which once united the remotest parts of our
great empire. . . . Too many of our youth are growing up in the dangerous belief that these [sections] are incompatible and contrasted. . . . It
is our special aim to revive in its full force the benign spirit of Union,
to renew the mutual confidence in each other's good will and patriotism,
without which the laws and statutes, and form of government of these
states, will exist in vain.

> —South Carolina Union and States' Rights Party,
> letter to Andrew Jackson, 1831

AMONG THE TRAPPINGS of nationhood in early-nineteenth-century America was a growing tourist industry, as Europeans arrived in expanding numbers.
Several visitors, most famously Tocqueville, published accounts of their travels;
one was Thomas Hamilton, a young Londoner whose 1833 tour left him won-
dering how America remained a single country at all. "It is abundantly clear," he
wrote in *Men and Manners* (1843),

> that the seeds of discord are plentifully scattered throughout the Union.
> Men of different habits, different interests, different modes of thought;
> the inhabitants of different climates, agreeing only in mutual antipa-
> thy, are united. . . . A union on [those] principles resembles that of a bag
> of sand, in which the separate particles, though held together for a time,
> retain their original and abstract individuality.

Hamilton proceeded to "look for a moment at this Union," finding such rampant
disagreement that he declared, "they are animated by no sentiment of brotherhood and affinity." And yet, he marveled, people in all regions talked incessantly
of their "considerable" national unity. This was no "singular opinion of some
eccentric individual" but of "men of great intelligence in different parts of the
Union" who displayed "a perfect harmony of opinion as to the results of separation"—namely, disaster. Americans universally "seemed to regard this word as
the ark of their safety." Primly, Hamilton concluded: "In such cases, it might

charitably be wished, that their ark was a stronger sea-boat, and better calculated to weather the storms to which it is likely to be exposed."[1]

Observers a century and a half later share Hamilton's incredulity that such an obviously divided people were so vehemently given to pronouncing themselves united. With the decline of "consensus history" after the early 1960s,[2] scholarly accounts of an antebellum America unified in any significant respect are rare.[3] Struggles over slavery, merchant capitalism, democracy, land reform, tariffs, immigration, and a hundred other issues make up our picture of the "violent and competitive society" of Jacksonian and later antebellum years, characterized principally by "multiple conflicts: racial, political, economic, and religious." Emerging popular politics frequently took the form of mob action or violent protest. Summarizes Gordon Wood: "Government was weak, the churches were divided, and social institutions were fragmented." Period union talk, if noticed at all, is portrayed as a false rhetorical veneer that made a dangerously friable society more so. In Anne Norton's influential study, northern leaders' "conception of the Union . . . evok[ed] a particularist, sectional notion of nationality" and "effectively excluded the North from political discourse with the South."[4]

Union's manifold appearances in American talk from the late 1820s to the early 1850s suggest the presence of stronger national feeling than prevailing accounts of period antipathy acknowledge. Even sectional partisans like John C. Calhoun could legitimately avow, as he did in his last public speech, a consistent "devotion to the Union."[5] Perhaps Americans, aware their country was coming apart, paid greater lip service to maintaining unity. But this explanation must be qualified by a tremendous chorus of celebratory unionist assessments. With Andrew Jackson and successors consciously deploying the presidency as an instrument of national unity, clerics imploring divine grace on behalf of a rightly constituted Union, and orators like Daniel Webster ardently extolling the term, the blend of providential and patriotic proved irresistible.

As seen in chapter 2, opinion leaders worried during the early years of the

---

1. Hamilton 1843, 179–80.

2. Higham notes that historians once saw "harmony and unity in [antebellum] America" (1984, 97); see, e.g., Randall 1947, esp. 62 (on the avoidable "blunders" leading to war); Hartz 1955; Boorstin 1965; Handlin 1951; Donald 1960; and Nagel 1964.

3. Few post-1960s accounts depict a period consensus; one tentative attempt is Samuel Huntington's portrayal of the "Middle Period" from 1820 to 1860 as a time of "diversity and yet common purpose," one "when the United States could least well be characterized as a disharmonic society" (1981, 224–25; though cf. 91–92). David Potter details a "curious overlap of the national and sectional forces" from the late 1840s to 1861 (1976, 18). Lewis (1998, 218–20) describes "the unionist logic of the Founders" as "disavowed by the public and discarded by policymakers" after 1828.

4. Foner and Mahoney 1990, 3; Howe 1997, 61; K. K. Smith 1999, 51–83 (on rioting in the antebellum period); Wood 1992, 359; Norton 1986, 26. See also Sellers 1991, esp. 332–95; Morrison 1997 (on the centrality of sectionalist differences to political development in the 1840s and 1850s); Grant 1997, esp. 122–23; Sydnor 1948, 134–221, 294–330 (on antebellum southern sectionalism in the 1820s to 1840s); and Elazar 1992, 127–40.

5. Lence 1992, 590. Calhoun's ideas of union are taken up in detail later.

nineteenth century about ordinary Americans' indifference to national union. Concerns about popular cohesion remained plentiful during the 1830s, 1840s, and 1850s in the face of nullification and secessionist strains developing around slavery. But fears that the general public was aloof to unionist appeals faded: from Jackson's presidency forward, everyone used the term. A common household soap and most of the railroad stations serving the westward-thrusting tracks were alike named Union, as was the Polk Administration's party organ (*The Washington Union*), the first American workingmen's magazine (*The Union*, founded in 1836), and dozens of U.S. newspapers, with at least one in practically every antebellum state. Radicals from utopian socialists to left-wing artisans, in David Davis's depiction, "all appealed" for closer national unity, affectively understood as "intimate, fraternal bonds that should somehow replace the 'stern reality of actual life.'" As for more genteel reformers, a "visible, organized union" of teetotalers, constituting the largest formal organization yet established in the United States, was formally christened the American Temperance Union in 1836. From San Francisco's Union Party to moderate South Carolinians' Union and States' Rights Party, numerous state and national parties expressed their unionism in their titles. African Americans in the North appealed to "a community of interests" between black and white Americans, one that "will bind us all, indissolubly one united people." "By getting to know each other better, the various parts of the Union have drawn closer," Tocqueville observed of Jacksonian America. "There is no French province where the inhabitants know each other so well as do the thirteen million men spread over the extent of the United States. . . . They all get closer and closer to one common type."[6]

Figures 2 and 3 graphically demonstrate a rise in union usage during the early 1830s, when leaders' oratory and the nullification crisis combined to anchor the term in the American political vernacular. Based on a broad sample of period newspapers, magazines, diaries, and congressional speeches, as described in the appendix, figure 2 depicts this jump in union talk. Similarly, figure 3 shows that union accounted for about 10 percent of national references (among a group including, inter alia, "country," "land," and "America") from the turn of the century to the 1820s. This proportion more than doubled after 1830, and by 1832 union was the most commonly used term for the national whole.

Amid these universal paeans to union, alternative conceptions emerged. Departures from Madison and fellows' qualified sustainable-union ideal took two forms: challenges to the representative component, as a deferential style in politics and culture faded after Andrew Jackson's election, and, more ambitiously, new concepts of union, variously centered around common ethnicity or shared moral aims. These competing accounts of union's meaning, and divergent purposes

6. *Middlesex Gazette* (Conn.), December 26, 1827; Davis 1986, 131; Temperance Society national secretary quoted in Sellers 1991, 265; *Colored American* (Philadelphia), August 25, 1838; de Tocqueville 1969 [1835–40], 384.

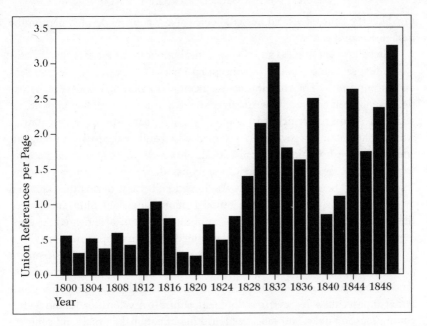

FIGURE 2. Union references, 1800–1850

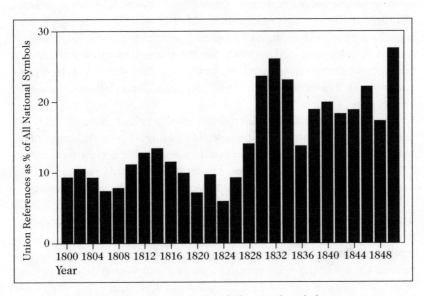

FIGURE 3. "Union" as proportion of all national symbols, 1800–1850

to which the concept was addressed, helped shape political development in the mid-nineteenth century.

Antebellum union ideas and their practical implications are this chapter's focus. A first section considers the concept's primary meanings from the late 1820s until around 1850. The constitutional generation's vision of a praiseworthy national union was embraced by Americans of all persuasions—though not necessarily for Madison's principled reasons. The idea that virtuous representatives would uphold union in governance was gradually abandoned. Sparked by religious and patriotic exhortations, unionist ideals also took on ethnocultural tones in some quarters. Assertion of American unity based on pride in common descent, "more perfect" because more purely Anglo-Saxon, became during the 1840s and 1850s a second major conception of national union. Elites sometimes encouraged this version, though many deplored its implications—and all lamented the waning of their own authority, which accompanied the term's popularization.

Union's appeal provided an important basis for expanding central government activity, as explored in this chapter's second section. National administrators defended a range of aims in the name of unity, including elaborate programs of internal improvements, western development, efforts to develop broader and swifter communication links, and subsidized printing of national journals and congressional speeches. Not all of these actually contributed to "cementing the union," as advertised: territorial expansion, for example, was also a source of sectional and partisan dispute. And unionists in the Madisonian vein were generally careful to balance recommendations for central government growth with continued assurances of state and local authority. But the extensive administrative activities that did exist should call into question familiar scholarly accounts of the national government's "embarrassingly irrelevant"[7] functions during Jacksonian and antebellum years.

Americans' enthusiasm for this collective ideal was limited by other commitments, though less than might be expected. Two prominent challenges to national unity—individualism and sectionalism—are taken up in a third section. Although each appeared incompatible with unionist aims, in practice the theorists and spokesmen of each ideology tempered their outlook with references to union. This phenomenon is examined through attention to two representative figures. A complex connection between individualism and unity was present in the thought of Ralph Waldo Emerson, avatar of self-reliance—but one who also invoked national union with surprising regularity. Equally incongruous were political testaments featuring appeals to national unity alongside stout defenses of sectional or states' rights. John Calhoun's theoretical attempts to blend the two themes are examined as exemplary here. Ultimately apparent in this section is the integrative force of unionist ideals, even when measured against the powerful fragmentary forces at work in antebellum America.

7. Berthoff and Murrin 1973, 278.

Religion and a qualified patriotism, we saw earlier, were the primary sources of union's initial popularity among Americans. The two became more intertwined in the service of national unity as the antebellum period wore on. U.S. Rep. Samuel Gordon, a New York Democrat, declared in 1847: "Next to the Christian religion, the people of these United States, from north to south, from east to west, all cherish and adore this holy and sacred Union of ours." President Polk, touring New England the same year, termed union "an altar at which we all may worship." A Kentucky editor went him one better, demanding that "we continu[e], as our fathers did before us, to worship in the temple of Union." North Carolina independence day revelers echoed counterparts throughout the country in toasting "The 4th of July—our political Sabbath."[8] With political rhetoric, voting blocs, and policy preferences all shaped in important ways by Protestant evangelicals, the connection had compelling force.[9]

Political elites found the religious-patriotic nexus spilling in unanticipated directions, however. A democratic ethic deeply infused early-nineteenth-century American Christianity as the "direct reign of God in the hearts of men" was contrasted with corrupt earthly hierarchies of wealth and power. Religious populism grew from a basic evangelical commitment to voluntary choice of one's life and destiny, creating—as historian James Moorhead notes—"a potential rationale for assault against all arbitrary barriers and customs that impeded the society of free people."[10] As references to a sacred, voluntary union of believers multiplied, American churchgoers applied the term similarly to their secular concerns. Much as during the colonial era, only now in a culture featuring a stronger democratic ethos, mass support for closer congregational unity inspired popular demand for participation in the political realm. "As men gain the courage of their convictions in matters of the spirit, so do they incline towards making their views known on questions of the day," affirmed a New Orleans newspaper.[11] A democratic approach to unity among believers was reinforced among citizens, if unintentionally, by politicians' passionate praise of the term.

Along with promoting religious ties as a means to national feeling, antebellum political elites reasserted the sustainable understanding of union, often invoking Madison and other framers to bolster the value's patriotic appeal. As president the "committed Unionist" John Tyler, for example, frequently quoted Madison

8. Luker 1991, 3; *Cong. Globe*, 29th Cong., 2d sess., 1847, 388; Polk in Cutler 1986, 48; *Louisville Courier* (Ky.), July 4, 1849. *Tarboro Press* (N.C.), July 9, 1842. Most churches held services on the Fourth, and the proceedings were often reported in newspapers in the general accounts of public celebrations.

9. Carwardine 1993, 51ff.; on antebellum religious-political ties, see also Maclear 1959, 44–62; Conkin 1995; Butler 1990, 268–84; Baker 1983, esp. 270; and Mead 1963, 58–67.

10. Moorhead 1978, 12. Even Deism, once the creed of genteel skeptics, became "a way for various workingmen to express their social and intellectual independence from elite [religious] authority" (Wiebe 1984, 160). On the democratic spirit infusing nineteenth-century religion see esp. Hatch 1989 and Conkin 1995, 226–82.

11. *Orleans Gazette & Commercial Advertiser*, October 29, 1837.

on the benefits and importance of national union, and titled his administration's house journal *The Madisonian* in case anyone missed the connection.[12] Tyler's Democratic counterparts proved equally devoted to the term, including Andrew Jackson himself. Jackson's response to Calhoun and fellow nullifiers in 1832 on behalf of "our more perfect union" repeatedly cited "our revolutionary fathers" in support. His address appeared in newspapers throughout the country and was later packaged with the Constitution, Washington's Farewell Address, and the Declaration in a book that was reprinted into the 1860s.[13]

Perhaps even more esteemed than Jackson among leaders promoting union in the mid-nineteenth century was Daniel Webster, whose hugely popular public appearances (where he usually insisted on being introduced as "Daniel Webster of the Union" or "of the United States" rather than as Massachusetts Senator) drew audiences as large as 50,000 and countless more readers. As Herbert Croly noted a half century later, "Webster taught American public opinion to consider the Union as the core and the crown of the American political system. His services in giving the Union a more impressive place in the American political imagination can scarcely be over-estimated."[14] A survey of Webster's unionist oratory displays its strong appeal—one which ironically, given Webster's own gentry sensibilities, helped to doom the older elite-centered conception of political union. Webster's mix of populist rhetoric and representative guidance prescribed a desirable approach to a more inclusive union, at least in principle. But most middle-class whites' opposition to social bonds outside their ascriptively defined circle meant that Webster's warnings against ethnocultural exclusivity went unheard, even as his inspirational unionism attracted a widening crowd of adherents.

Webster and the Decline of Gentry Union

Where scholars ascribe multiple personalities to Madison, Webster's basic conviction is indisputable. "I am a unionist," the New Englander stated in his 1830 "Reply to Hayne," which at well over 100,000 reprints was "the most widely read and most influential utterance" of the antebellum years. Period increases in popular union usage owed partly to Webster's oratory, which invigorated and extended the concept beyond a vague referent for territorial America. Webster's unionism was informed by two basic commitments, which originally were mutually reinforcing but came increasingly into conflict over time. His prominent place in the representative-led political union led him to endorse Madison's carefully structured account of national unity. Separately, Webster's concern about such "purveyors of disunion" as southern would-be nullifiers inspired him to

---

12. Crapol 1997, 468, 474–78, 487. The "power of the spoken word" in antebellum times is amply illustrated by Kimberly Smith, who terms the period from the 1820s to the 1850s "the dominion of voice" (1999, esp. 92–117).

13. Linfield 1862, 90, 115 (on "our fathers," see also 83, 90, 109, 113, 119–21).

14. Adams 1930, 5:190; Croly 1909, 75. On Webster's introductions, see Remini 1997, 596.

mount passionate defenses of unity that eventually transcended all bounds.[15] Logically the two views could not be simultaneously supported; it is a measure of the range of meaning union represented in the antebellum years that Webster could promote both a circumscribed and hyperbolic understanding for as long as he did.

Like most Whigs, Webster opposed Jacksonians' major democratizing reforms, from state constitutional conventions to proliferation of elected officials. He even resisted the growth of national political parties, though he reluctantly acknowledged the Whig organization as a source of fierce loyalty that might be translated into popular support for the Union. Mass interpersonal "attractions" fell far short of the reasoned exchanges informing sound governing decisions, Webster asserted in a Madisonian vein: "sudden movements of the affections, whether personal or political, are a little out of nature." Union itself he saw as a fragile value, susceptible to abuse in the wrong hands. "The spirit of union is particularly liable to temptation and seduction," he warned fellow Senators in 1838.[16] Judging by his reluctance to use them, Webster also mistrusted manifest-destinarian themes, a principal spur to popular union sentiment in other orators' rhetoric.

Webster's efforts to stuff the democratic genie back into an eighteenth-century bottle proceeded from the founders' balanced understanding of a sustainable union. Madison's deliberate separation of mass affective expressions from political power mediated the connection between united popular opinion and institutional decisions through the agency of representative government, in a way that appealed strongly to his successors in office. Only very rarely, as they saw it, could even an unusually unified populace achieve wide enough agreement to actually exert authority. Ideally governance would remain top-down in operation, as exemplified when a group of notables, meeting in secret at Philadelphia, had pledged the nation to forming a "more perfect union" and assured the populace that their leadership would secure that aim. Thus Webster promoted a restored connection between territory, interpersonal affection, and political representation.[17] Social harmony and stability would be maintained through expanding popular fealty to national unity. At the same time, supervisory control over the

15. Wiltse and Berolzheimer 1986–88, 1:381; Shewmaker 1990, 86 (cf. Kammen 1986, 88). Some biographers note a "transition from state-rights Federalism to pro-tariff nationalism," based on Webster's opposition, along with most New England Federalists, to the War of 1812. Current 1990, 2–3.

16. Wiltse and Berolzheimer 1986–88, 1:141; 2:269, 282. Cf. 1:270, where Webster declared: "Neither individuals nor nations can perform their part well, until they understand and feel its importance, and comprehend and justly appreciate all the duties belonging to it."

17. The strong personal connection between Webster and Madison further reinforced Webster's "Madisonian" ideas of unity. In May 1830, for example, Madison remarked in a letter to Webster that the American system of unified governments was "so unexampled in its origin, so complex in its structure, and so peculiar in some of its features" that ordinary "political vocabulary" did not "furnish terms sufficiently distinctive and appropriate" to describe it (Rives and Fendall 1865, 4:85). For more on Webster's fealty to Madison's political outlook, see Remini 1997, 232–33, 333–34, 596; and Howe 1979, 90 (Madison as "patron saint" to Webster and other Whigs).

levers of government should remain in representative hands, reinforcing political union among fellow leaders.

Webster's great Senate speeches, as well as public orations at places like Plymouth Rock, Bunker Hill, and Faneuil Hall—the last commemorating the simultaneous July 4 deaths of Jefferson and Adams, on the fiftieth anniversary of independence—were instrumental in connecting American unionism and territory, and inculcating a sense of a common homeland. His second appearance at Bunker Hill in 1843 epitomized the genre: "Woe betide the man who brings to this day's worship feeling less than wholly American. This column [indicating the Bunker Hill monument] stands on Union." Webster identified the ground itself, "sacralized" by revolutionaries, as the basis of national cohesion. Elsewhere he drew less abstract connections between land and national unity, in conjunction with fellow Senate luminary Henry Clay. Compromise tariff plans, combined with an "American System" of internal improvements and land credit, were the Whigs' (partly successful) solution to sectional battles over land reform during the early 1830s. Their program also multiplied the "bonds of commerce" across regions, a strategy employed since the 1780s to win support for national unity. As Tocqueville summarized the results: "In step with the progress of American industry, all the commercial links uniting the confederated states are tightened, and the Union, which at first was the child of their imagination, is now a part of their habits."[18]

When Democrats dismissed internal improvements as Whig pork-barrel attempts to claim credit for "local goods," Webster defended them as sources of unity. Responding to Senator Hayne, he said: "He may well ask what interest has South Carolina in a canal in Ohio. On his system, it is true, she has no interest. On that system, Ohio and Carolina are different governments and different countries. . . . We look [instead] upon the states, not as separated but as united." Webster proceeded to join interest and affective interchange in classic Madisonian fashion. "Carolina and Ohio," he insisted, "are parts of the same country, states, united under the same general government, having interests, common, associated, intermingled." Webster's emphasis on ordered unity proscribed aggressive territorial expansion, whatever the material gains. He objected to Polk's Mexican "land grab," for example, as upsetting the "united equilibrium" so difficult to maintain. "Instead of aiming to enlarge [America's] boundaries, let us seek, rather, to strengthen its union."[19]

Territorial associations were one means of expanding affective spirit, and thus popular support for national unity,[20] without threatening gentry control of ad-

18. Wiltse and Berolzheimer 1986–88, 1:257; de Tocqueville 1969 [1835–40], 385. On territory and shared memories, see Smith 1996, 453–55. Complexities of land reform and Clay's compromise are sorted out well in Feller 1984, who also demonstrates how various antebellum conflicts of politics and principle were muted in the name of union.

19. Wiltse and Berolzheimer 1986–88, 1:303–4; Dalzell 1973, 85. On Webster's "antiimperialism," see C. R. Smith 1999, 2–4, and Peterson 1987, 346, 369–70.

20. The popularity of territorial-union themes continued well into the 1850s. In 1855, for example, a Kansas editor declared: "We consider this [Mississippi] river a greater security for the prosperity of

ministration. More effective reinforcement for elite authority came in identifying union directly with American political leaders, an effort promoted by Madison (and legitimated by Washington) and later associated with people's tribune Andrew Jackson. In his half-dozen most celebrated speeches, and in a trip through the South in 1847, Webster sought to epitomize union as had his predecessors. The effort was largely successful: as Wayne Fields writes, Webster's tours "made [him] the representative of union."[21] His oratory rang with personal associations, beginning with the closing of his "Reply to Hayne": "When *my* eyes shall be turned to behold for the last time the sun in heaven, may *I* not see him shining on the broken and dishonored fragments of a once glorious Union." Webster employed this self-identification with unity regularly thereafter, as in this 1838 speech on the subtreasury bill:

> If I am born for any good, in my day and generation, it is the good of the whole Country. . . . So far as depends on any agency of mine, they shall continue united States, united in interest and affection; united in everything in regard to which the Constitution has decreed their union.[22]

The personal meaning Webster and other elites evidently found in the quest for national unity reinforced their growing inclination to view union as an end in itself, and also heightened their tormenting fears at the prospect of disunion.[23]

This connection between self and union made Webster all the more inclined to follow Madison's model to its conclusion, securing unified territory and promoting popular affection by channeling related measures through political representatives. But several obstacles inhibited the exercise of elite leadership in the founders' mode. For one, as a wave of state constitutional revisions indicated, Americans were far less inclined to cede governing power to national leaders by the 1820s. Webster himself was partly responsible for this change: his unionist credentials were firmly grounded in an association between united people and protection of their personal liberties against all would-be usurpers. "Liberty and Union, now and forever," Webster's best-known lines concluded. None

---

the Union, than all the compromises which our legislators have ever formed. It is the compromise of nature and destiny, and cannot be repealed. Through its channel there is a unity of interest, of which the people will not deprive themselves." *Kansas Herald of Freedom* (Lawrence), April 28, 1855.

21. Fields 1983, 16. Cf. Howe (1979, 213): "the Webster cult . . . provided a father figure in whom devotees could feel a measure of security." Webster sought to appear as a "man of the people," in part through the slightly mocking claim that his *brother* had been born in a log cabin. Webster's life was recorded by none other than Horatio Alger, in a cheery biography titled *From Farm Boy to Senator.* On Webster's southern tour, see Fuess 1929 and Peterson 1987, 428–30.

22. Wiltse and Berolzheimer 1986–88, 1:348 (emphasis added); 2:284–85. Cf. ibid., 577: "For myself I propose, Sir, to abide by the principles and the purposes which I have avowed. I will stand by the Union, and by all who stand by it." James Polk inherited the personal-representative mantle in the late 1840s, traveling "north for union" on a three-week tour designed to "solicit [Americans'] continual regard for the Union" (Cutler 1986, xvii).

23. Strozier's psychobiographical study of Lincoln makes a book-length argument to this effect, taken up in chapter 4. A more measured account of political/personal unity is Gebhardt 1993, 184–99.

should dare "separat[e liberty] from that Union, by which alone its existence is made sure." [24]

As state legislatures passed increasingly into middle-class hands, Webster and fellow leaders were left with only the federal government as a counterweight to popular control. And a foundational principle in all American unionists' lexicon was a balanced commitment to state and national authority. Webster's inclination to boost federal power ran only to cautious intimations that the "very end" of national administration was to "do that for individuals which individuals cannot do for themselves." Even these qualified statements brought fierce states' rights responses from "Calhounites and Jacksonians alike," as Wiebe details. Madison openly objected to any departure from his delicate arrangement of mutually reinforcing state and federal realms: "This idea of an absolute separation & independence between the government of the U.S. and the state governments as if they belonged to different nations alien to each other" was "tainted reasoning," he warned in 1830. Cohesive affective sentiment, not a unity imposed by the central state, was the soundest basis for a national common life. Commentary in North and South continued to stress, as in a Boston editor's review of James Polk's inaugural address, "state rights principles *and* deep devotion to the Union." [25]

Despite the best efforts of these and other leaders, the traditional association of union with American elites seemed increasingly anachronistic as the nineteenth century progressed. Political essayist Henry Flanders observed in 1843 that the American "middle classes" had come to conceive of themselves an "influential agent in the administration of the [national government], watch[ing] with eager interest its course and . . . act[ing] boldly and greatly in its service." Only when "accepted" as partners in governance, Flanders concluded, "will they call themselves 'united.'" With popular movements overrunning elite authority in realms from religion to commerce to arts to public discourse itself, Webster and his colleagues saw their control fade in a swamping of traditional deference. They found it little consolation that their own praise of the masses had swelled the tide. "The voice of the people is the voice of God," declared figures from George Bancroft to John C. Calhoun. Who could be surprised if the speakers then demanded greater influence in "the great democratic family of the Union"? [26]

By the mid-1840s Webster recognized that governance by national elites was increasingly a quaint fiction. [27] American leaders "could not suppress," he ac-

24. Wiltse and Berolzheimer 1986–88, 1:339–40.

25. Ibid., 2:305; Wiebe 1984, 248; Hunt 1910, 9:390; *Boston Post* editorial, which *The Banner* (Athens, Ga.), March 11, 1845, reprinted as "generally entitled to our approbation." On Webster and limited national power, see Remini 1997, 319, and on his dubious outlook toward Jacksonian democracy, see ibid., 450–51.

26. Paludan 1972, 33; Bartlett 1967, 47 (Bancroft); Lence 1992, 31 (Calhoun); *Watchtower* (Cooperstown, N.Y.), November 12, 1827 (on "democratic family"). On the decline of gentry control, see esp. Wiebe 1984, 130–252; compare Altschuler and Blumin 1997, 880 ("the institutionalization of political leadership in the party era did not entirely efface older, deferential relations"), and K. K. Smith 1999, 54–56.

27. This is not to suggest that elite political leadership disappeared altogether in the antebellum United States, only that national leaders' ability to command deference declined substantially. *Local*

knowledged publicly, "either the thoughts, or the hopes, which arise in men's minds." One might expect that as union talk passed more and more into popular currency, national leaders desperate to preserve their privileges might have disavowed the term much as they abandoned such other terms as "the People."[28] But sectional rifts were widening, touched off by disagreement over Mexican War spoils and fueled by slavery. Unionists once again issued anguished alarms about national disintegration, voiced with an urgency not seen since the nullification controversy in the previous decade. Thus threatened, Webster and fellow elites adopted an unconditional unionism as their core political good, surpassing all other considerations. Its adherents spoke in capital letters: "let the truth sink deep into all American minds," Webster urged in 1850, "that it was the WANT OF UNION among her several states which finally gave the mastery of Greece to Philip of Macedon." Rhapsodized Walt Whitman, "UNIONISM, in its truest and amplest sense . . . [is] the foundation and tie of all, as the future will grandly develop."[29] Such fervent unionist oratory during and after Jacksonian times overwhelmed the Madisonian sense of restrained unity, especially the "representative control" aspects. It also pointed in other directions the constitutional generation had not countenanced.

Ethnocultural Union and Its Targets

As outlined in the previous chapter, Madison's fear of "dangerous" mob unity, his moral outlook, and the imperative of separating the majority of Americans from their British roots all combined to mute ethnocultural or manifest-destinarian themes in his unionist vision. Webster, Clay, and some other prominent antebellum leaders also largely eschewed such appeals, but the barriers were repeatedly breached as the term's religious and patriotic associations spread. Fueled by rising immigration and expansion into Mexican territory, notions of a national union limited to a divinely chosen, homogeneous white American "race" attracted many adherents from the 1830s onward.

As already mentioned, Protestant leaders were principal authors of the connection between national union and divine destiny. Some also contributed to an associated ethic of intolerance toward minorities and other "strangers." Though state-sponsored churches were all defunct by the end of Jackson's reign, clerics demanded government prohibition of nonorthodox sects, buttressing their pleas with nativist impugnings of Mormons, Catholics, Freemasons, and other infidels. These exclusions were frequently explained in terms of outsiders' deleterious effects on union, an argument that slipped easily from religious to political

---

party activists and other professionals (lawyers, doctors, and so forth) were politically prominent in almost every community. See Formisano 1974, 475–86, and Altschuler and Blumin 1997, 880–81.

28. Shewmaker et al. 1983–87, 2:52; Rodgers 1987, 102 (Webster's role is described at p. 104).

29. Wiltse and Berolzheimer 1986–88, 2:607 (and cf. 551); Whitman in Stovall 1939, 467. Compare Jürgen Gebhardt's perceptive account of Webster and other leaders' "tormenting . . . fear that the new nation would break apart," and consequent position that "the Union's existence was now meant to sanction *any* constitutional pragmatism" (Gebhardt 1993, 184–85).

applications. Lyman Beecher's assurances that "God appointed" northern Whigs to "produce in the nation a more homogeneous character" encouraged resistance to exogenous "impurities" in divine and earthly matters alike. Stephen Colwell's 1853 tract on "true Christianity," replete with arguments for state prohibition of "[a]ny other religions inconsistent with Christianity," was a classic sectarian defense. Colwell's certainty that America was a nation appointed to carry out God's work on earth, and his insistence that only a tightly drawn circle of "true Christian Americans" could fulfill this awesome responsibility, exemplified the destinarian outlook.[30]

Unionists already attuned to the potent source of appeal contained in religious-political connections readily promoted more strident versions. Manifest destinarian rhetoric, affirming Americans' Anglo-Saxon, Protestant roots and the divine right of "united white people" to govern the entire continent, provided a compelling rationale for some whites to take up the union banner. Jacksonian Democrats like presidential spokesman John O'Sullivan were especially active in popularizing the destinarian basis of unity; though most Whigs originally followed Webster in minimizing such views, many adopted them after Clay's presidential loss in 1844, widely believed among partisans to have been caused by Whig candidates' failure to attract nativist support.[31] Prominent members of both parties subsequently insisted on an ethnoculturally defined "Union of Whites," as a Kentucky Whig leader described the country in 1849. This strain in antebellum thought is described by scholars today in terms of a "full-fledged civic ideology" and marks a second major understanding of Americans' more perfect union.[32]

Manifestly excluded among those valorizing a union of "strong Anglo-Saxon men" were a variety of groups in the antebellum republic. As we saw earlier, Native Americans were largely ignored in white elites' first steps toward intercolonial union or viewed as a threat spurring colonists' efforts at mutual defense. Frederick Jackson Turner testified that "the unifying tendencies of the Revolutionary period were facilitated by the [British American colonists'] previous cooperation in the regulation of the Indian frontier."[33] Ethnocultural ideas further doomed the potential place of Native Americans as members of the national union. An "era of removal," beginning in the late 1820s, featured little of the discomfort expressed by revolutionaries and constitutional framers at excluding longtime residents from national membership. Among Jacksonians and later antebellum whites any such guilt was conveniently alleviated in "scientific" doctrines elevating whites to a higher cultural plane.

30. Beecher 1820, 236–37; Colwell in Butler 1990, 285–86.

31. Anbinder 1992, 12–13; Remini 1997, 598–99; Holt 1999, 211–12. On antebellum Whigs' organicist thought, which anticipated social Darwinian themes in some ways, see Howe 1979, 69–72, 81–82. Whigs' mixture of general and ethnocultural appeals is detailed in Holt 1999, 250, and Smith 1997, 206–12.

32. *Louisville Journal*, April 6, 1849; Smith 1988, 232 (cf. Lind 1995, 46–56; Holt 1992, 88–150; Higham 1988, 3–11; Foner 1998, 77–79. See also the description of the "Union Degree" oath taken by members of the nativist Order of the Star-Spangled Banner, in Cantrell 1992, 133–34.

33. Taylor 1972, 12.

As Jackson's reign dawned, departing President Adams spoke for many national elites in casually telling his Cabinet that "Indians' disappearance from the human family would be no great loss." Indian Commissioner Thomas McKinney, a few months before, cited "that law of nature immutable" which "decreed that without a systematic removal policy, they [American Indians] must perish." The Indian Removal Act, which passed Congress in 1830, and the formal ouster of the Cherokees from Georgia in the *Worcester v. Georgia* controversy provided institutional confirmation of this view.[34] Even those opinion leaders who publicly opposed removal—Webster, for example—never contemplated including Indians in the circle of national unity. In debating western settlement, when Webster asked rhetorically "How did [white settlers] come there? How did this great number of persons get onto the public lands?" Native Americans were ignored. Privately Webster was equally dismissive: he wrote a friend in 1826, "I believe there is as little in the languages of the tribes as in their laws, manners, and customs, worth studying or worth knowing."[35]

Native Americans' own testimony demonstrates that by Jackson's presidency few harbored any illusions about their place in the American Union. Black Hawk, the Sauk chief whose 1833 autobiography went through five editions the year it was published, represents one strong view during the antebellum years. Of his forced "tour" (as a sort of war trophy) through West Virginia and western Maryland, Black Hawk recalled "[I] was astonished to find so many whites living in the hills! I have often thought of them since my return to my own people: and am happy to think that they prefer living in their own country, to coming out to ours, and driving us from it." His tribe's "Great Father," he went on, had set "the Mississippi [as] the dividing line between his red and white children, and . . . he did not wish either to cross it." In revealing moments like these Black Hawk and other tribesmen seemed painfully aware that white Americans' attempts to define their union depended in part on clearly delineating boundaries, and that "we Indians . . . are outside that Union." Most Native American testimony concurred, from colonial times well into the nineteenth century. An Oneida chief in 1775 told Connecticut's governor that "us Indians . . . cannot intermeddle in this dispute between two brothers [i.e., the Americans and English]. The quarrel seems to be unnatural. You are two brothers of one blood. . . . Let us Indians be all of one mind, and live with one another; and you white people settle your own disputes." Josiah Quinney, a Mahican invited to address a New York July 4 gathering in 1854, referred to his white audience as "a strange race," compared to all the different Indian tribes in the northeast, "bound together, as one family, by blood, marriage, and descent."[36]

34. Merrell 1989; Adams in Sellers 1991, 279; *Worcester v. Georgia*, 6 Peters 515 (1832); Hurtado and Iverson 1994, 207. Cf. Kerber 1975, 271–88; Prucha 1984, chaps. 7–9; Smith 1997, 181–85, 235–42; Berkhofer 1979, 157–66.

35. Wiltse and Berolzheimer 1986–88, 2:207; letter quoted in Remini 1997, 259. On similar Anglo-American dismissals of Mexicans, during conflicts from the 1835–36 border disputes over Texas to the 1853 Gadsden Treaty, see Weber 1997, esp. 13–21.

36. Jackson 1955 [1833], 168, 175; Force 1837–46, 2:1117; Calloway 1994, 40.

African Americans were similarly construed, by most whites in the 1820s to 1850s, as outside the circle of national unity. Antislavery references from this period (as in earlier decades) almost never referred to blacks as "fellow Unionists," in an otherwise common phrase, but dwelt instead on the evils of slavery. By the time of Jackson's election, members of Congress and other political notables had begun sounding racist themes at length. One typical example was Rep. Charles Miner of Pennsylvania, who devoted his speech during a debate on slavery in the District of Columbia to denouncing blacks as "a degraded caste [that] will gradually disappear" and a "great nuisance to the community." A South Carolina Senator put the point more starkly, insisting that "free negroes . . . of all the spectacles of squalid wretchedness to be found on the face of the habitable globe . . . exhibit the most wretched and revolting. They are, in every view of moral dignity, a libel upon the human race." Nor would enslaved blacks, despite "the progress they have made . . . in the school of slavery, under the dominion of a superior race," be fit for unity with the white majority. African Americans' own unionist rhetoric is taken up at length in the following chapter; note for now that white Americans' antebellum ethnocultural claims built on a long tradition of anti-black sentiment.[37]

In contrast to Native American Indians or blacks, white women believed themselves to be—and were plainly considered by most white men as—part of the American social whole. Though their civic standing was anything but definite—as extensive legal and informal norms of disempowerment made clear—their place in the rhetoric of destinarian unity was secure. Webster, thundering in 1851 that "there is but one question in this country now[:] can we so preserve the union of these States . . . by the silken cords of mutual, fraternal, patriotic affection?" in his affirmative answer pointed to "the people of western New York. . . . Here, too, are women, educated, refined, and intelligent"—and therefore fellow Unionists.[38]

Women were specifically identified with national union in three related (and only loosely political) respects. First, a common metaphor—especially among Whigs—was the correspondence between intimate familial unity and that of the larger polity. Repeated assertions of interdependence among different classes, regions, and interest groups routinely drew parallels to the union of wife and husband. A *Philadelphia Gazette* response to nullification in 1831 wove wedding vows into the declaration that "this [national] union has been accepted by every member thereof 'for better, for worse.'" Implicit in such accounts was a related metaphor: sexual union, which had been delicately avoided in most public comment since colonial times but which surely helped account for the term's resonance. Second, union itself was frequently identified as a "feminine" value precisely be-

---

37. *Register of Debates*, 20th Cong., 1829, 175–87 (quotes at pp. 181, 186); Senator McDuffie reported in *Richmond Enquirer*, June 14, 1844.

38. Wiltse and Berolzheimer 1986–88, 2:581–82. On antebellum barriers to women's political participation, see Smith 1997, 230–35; Ryan 1991; Faragher and Stansell 1975; Kleinberg 1999, 83–88 (on minority women).

cause of its connection with the domestic, familial sphere. Union suggested traits and activities generally associated with women—cooperation, affection, association. In 1849 Virginia governor Henry Wise praised "our womanly virtue, Union." Anne Norton similarly finds that antebellum femininity "was emblematic of *communitas*," limiting the correlation to the South in her intriguing argument that southerners identified with dispossessed blacks, women, and Indians in their drive for separation. But northern union talk was similarly stocked with such metaphors.[39]

Women also symbolized unity in the toasts ubiquitous on July 4 and other national celebrations, such as presidential inaugurations. "Who are we?" asked an eminent doctor of Lawrence, Kansas, in his Independence Day oration of 1855. "Were not our *mothers*, as well as fathers, of Anglo-Saxon blood?" Almost every ceremony in this genre concluded with a toast to American women, and on many occasions a patriotic poem or ditty composed by local women was published in newspaper accounts of the day's commemorative activities. As David Waldstreicher describes, women's "effective expansion of nationalism and containment of partisanship helped obscure the contradictions of a male-dominated, competitive, nationalist political culture." He reprints a characteristic period couplet in support:

Among the men what dire divisions rise,
For *union* one—and one *no* union cries;
Shame on the sex which such disput[e] began,
Ladies are all for UNION, to a man.[40]

Women's response to such gallant sentiments is unrecorded, but it seems clear from other testimony that women activists supported the idea of national unity. Anne Royall, a Jacksonian Democratic pamphleteer and, after 1832, a newspaper publisher, wrote often on "the benefits of Union," especially during the nullification crisis, and in one editorial reported that "ladies, too, are enamored of the states['] national cohesiveness." Though testaments are less plentiful, it also is likely that most women conceived of themselves as full members of the national union, despite their circumscribed citizenship status. "This is a Union of females, as well as males," affirmed a "Lady" writing to the *Painesville Telegraph* in 1844.[41]

In sum, ethnocultural union doctrine was less "bounded" by women than at least partially, and often directly, incorporative of them. (Indeed, the party featuring the highest proportion of women participants was the Nativists, whose women's auxiliary associations, such as the American Benevolent Republican Association, included thousands of women counted as "coadjutors in the

39. *Gazette* editorial reprinted in *Hartford Courant*, July 9, 1831; Wise 1899, 184; Norton 1986, 174.

40. *Kansas Herald of Freedom* (Lawrence), July 7, 1855; Waldstreicher 1997, 241 (and see generally 232–41).

41. Royall in *Paul Pry*, February 18, 1822; *The Huntress* (Washington, D.C.), July 7, 1837 (her final issue of the latter, on July 24, 1854, echoed Madison's "Last Political Will and Testament": "[My] prayer is that the Union of these States may be eternal"); *Painesville Telegraph* (Ohio), October 12, 1844. On Royall's career, see James 1972, esp. 312–78.

cause.")[42] With respect to inclusion in the national union, it seems inaccurate to apply the categorical description "Other" to women as is done to Native Americans or blacks. To be sure, the inclusive words of Webster and other leaders may be pointedly contrasted with women's struggles to gain formal political equality, as at the 1848 Seneca Falls Convention. And white women's place in the union was most often construed in apolitical terms: outside partisanship, above the "political world of the nineteenth century [which was] in part constructed in contrast to the feminine sphere of the home."[43] Whether the communal union language of the mid-nineteenth century achieved any worthy political ends for dominated groups or merely masked ascriptive practices is further addressed in a study of African Americans and national unity in chapter 4.

Catholics and southern Europeans were also sporadically excluded from antebellum ethnic-union doctrines, though less emphatically than were Indians or African Americans. Increasing immigration to the United States, rising steadily from 151,000 arrivals in the 1820s to 2.3 million during the 1850s, was another impetus to blending religious and cultural meanings of union. A common Anglo-American Protestant culture was often contrasted to "the mongrel races of Europe." Such views were promoted most avidly by Know-Nothings and other nativists in the 1850s, but they also appeared earlier among a range of groups—including New England academics, as in Edward Everett's much-reprinted 1824 Harvard Phi Beta Kappa oration on "American Union, European Diversity," and American clerics, who boasted of U.S. denominations' "bond of unity" in contrast to the quarreling sects of Europe. "In Europe," declared Everett,

> international alienation, which begins in the diversity of language, is carried on and consummated by diversity of government, institutions, national descent, and national prejudices. . . . While, on the other hand, throughout the vast regions included within the limits of our republic, not only the same language, but the same laws, the same national government, the same republican institutions, and common ancestral associations prevail. Mankind will here exist and act in a kindred mass, such as was never before congregated on the earth's surface . . . all her nations and tribes amalgamated into one vast empire, speaking the same tongue, united into one political system, and that a free one![44]

While few legislative restrictions were placed on immigration, many states tied voting rights to citizenship and created stringent naturalization requirements.

42. See Dinkin 1995, 34–35 (quote at p. 34).

43. Foner 1998, 72. On women as "other," see, e.g., Norton (1986, 6–7) on the antebellum American polity's "series of exclusions, the absence of blacks, of Indians, of women." Women's inclusion in the abolitionist movement is detailed in Jeffrey 1998, 96–170.

44. Ahlstrom 1972, 472 (on clerics abroad); Everett 1824, 47–48. Everett's formulation was characteristic of most cultural-union references into the 1840s; only with the rise of Know-Nothings' aggressive anti-immigrant policies were crudely nativist depredations regularly voiced. As Walzer (1990) notes, nativists mainly sought to restrict immigrants' rights, especially suffrage, not curtail all immigration.

And with the rise of Know-Nothingism in the 1850s, open hostility to immigrants' "un-American" ways and "the foreign man's hostility to uniting his loyalty to ours," as a *Chicago Tribune* commentary complained in 1852, became more common.[45]

National administrators in all three branches took up ethnocultural themes as well. Several Supreme Court decisions formalized the union of white Protestants, with American Indians explicitly excluded in such cases as *Cherokee Nation v. Georgia* (1831) and African Americans written out most notably in *Dred Scott v. Sandford* (1857).[46] Chief Justice Roger Taney wrote in the latter: "Citizens in the several States, became also citizens of this new political body: but none other; it was formed by them, and for them and their posterity, but for no one else. . . . It was the union of those who were at that time members of distinct and separate political communities into one political family, whose power [was] to extend over the whole territory of the United States." Three decades earlier John Marshall had declared America's "Indian tribes" to be "a people with whom it [is] impossible to mix."[47] Similar exclusionary-unionist doctrines were standard fare among presidents from Jackson through Buchanan. Jackson's association with Indian "removal" was among the most abiding features of his career, both prior to and during his presidency; his successor Van Buren praised the "happy results" of Jackson's "enlightened" efforts in this regard, adding that "our national Union is made more secure by removal of the tribes to the commodious country set aside for them in the West."[48]

Congressional debate also featured ethnocultural unionist appeals, appearing in unvarnished form especially during consideration of the Mexican war and of immigration. One statement early in Jackson's term came from Virginia Senator Benjamin Leigh, a fellow Democrat: "It is peculiar to the character of this Anglo-Saxon race of men to which we belong, that it has never been contented to live in the same country with any other distinct race, upon terms of equality." A quarter century later Leigh's Whig counterpart, Benjamin Toombs of Georgia, was more succinct: American unity was forged "by white men for white men, by our race for our race." Northern members of Congress sounded similar themes, as in

45. *Chicago Tribune*, March 10, 1852. On federal immigration policies during the period from 1820 to 1860, see Schuck and Smith 1985, 92–95, 112–16; Kleppner 1990, esp. 43–46 (on suffrage); Smith 1997, 225–28; and (for criticism of the scholarly "myth" about open immigration before 1875) Neuman 1993.

46. 30 U.S. 1 (1831); 19 How. 393 (1857). Both cases garnered immense national attention at the time: within a few months of the *Cherokee Nation* decision, for example, Supreme Court clerk Richard Peters published a widely advertised book featuring lawyers' arguments before the Court and several appendices, including treaties between the United States and Cherokees, relevant Georgia laws, and "Chancellor Kent's opinion on the case." Peters 1831; see advertisements for the book in, e.g., *Connecticut Mirror*, all issues, June–August 1831.

47. 19 How. 393, 406 (1857); *Johnson v. McIntosh*, 8 Wheat. 543, 590 (1823). Cf. Marshall's similar sentiments in *Cherokee Nation*, 30 U.S. 1, 8–9, 26–27, 31–33 (1831). On the exclusionary impact of these cases, see Berkhofer 1979, 156–65; Scheckel 1998, 110, 120–23 (on Marshall's decisions generally); and Smith 1997, 263–71 (on *Dred Scott*).

48. Richardson, 1896–99, 3:629. On nineteenth-century presidents' exclusionary rhetoric, see Fields 1996, 192–203.

Michigan Senator Zachariah Chandler's speech opposing Cuban annexation in 1860: "do you want these people in your Union? Are you prepared . . . to bring such a set of criminals into the Union?" Congress twice considered establishing territorial enclaves for immigrants (Irish in 1818, and Germans in 1848), but neither plan passed.[49]

The appeal of racist and other ethnocultural themes among antebellum white Americans of all stations has been thoroughly examined, especially in recent years.[50] The incorporation of these themes in unionist arguments both narrowed the scope of union membership (though other thinkers struggled against an exclusive understanding) and marked one facet of the term's democratization. Gentry leaders during the constitution-making and Federalist era had indulged far less often in restrictive definitions of union among white Anglo Protestants. From Jackson's presidency on, the ethnocultural and sustainable views of union—though divergent in principle—were more readily mingled. This potent combination, spreading to both parties and among Americans throughout the country, took on additional life as the unconditional unionism advocated by Webster and others spread, especially after the Mexican conflict in 1847–48.

Whatever else their effects, ethnocultural ideas of unity almost certainly strengthened the term's popular salience. But when most Americans lauded their national union, judging from newspaper references, they were less often celebrating a particular tribal identity than a sense of shared membership in a worthy polity.[51] A substantial majority of unionist references, voiced by Webster and workingmen alike, invoked "the Union" as itself a vital source of national belonging. The political system of federalist authority, the single territory comprised by the United States, the various institutions described in the Constitution and the history of its peaceful establishment: these were essential constituents of national unity, as expressed by many antebellum Americans. Such a sense of identification with the polity led union usage to be registered in institutional practices as well as newspaper editorials and Senate oratory.

INSTITUTIONAL UNION

Contrary to conventional scholarly wisdom about American development, during the first half of the nineteenth century the national government undertook an ambitious set of administrative activities. These often were carried out jointly

49. Leigh in Stephanson 1995, 27; *Cong. Globe,* 33rd Cong., 1st sess., Appendix 1854, 351; 35th Cong., 2d sess., 1860, 1089. On territorial enclaves, see Hollinger 1995, 91.

50. See, e.g., Saxton 1990, 23–159; Horsman 1981, 158–59; Hietala 1985; Smith 1997, 198–242; and Berkhofer 1979, 44–61.

51. Comments explicitly lauding "a union of whites" were comparatively rare in the newspapers I examined for the period from 1828 to 1850. Far more common in papers of different parties and U.S. regions was continued praise of—or anxiety for—"the safety and perpetuity of our glorious Union," as a *Richmond Enquirer* editorial put it (April 6, 1846). After 1850, with the rise of Know-Nothings and proto-Darwinist doctrines, ethnocultural unionist themes were more frequently sounded.

with state and local officials or in a mixed-enterprise arrangement with private actors; most were also contested by opponents, and on occasion (as with a national banking system, or some internal-improvements bills) reversed. Neither caveat erases the significance of national-state functions. To dismiss this extensive activity as "embarrassingly irrelevant" requires comparison to a standard that is inapplicable to the social and political conditions of the antebellum republic.[52]

Not all observers have missed this development. Writers closer to the events of the time saw matters differently: *Harper's* correspondent Henry Loomis Nelson noted in 1892 that by the 1830s "the Federal sovereignty was present everywhere—in the post offices, in the harbors, in the custom-houses. Its councils became the most interesting in the country, and ambitious public men worked through service to the State for promotion to Washington. Moreover, the government which was organized as the common agent for the thirteen States . . . soon came to be a creator of States." Tocqueville, comparing the U.S. national government to that of France and Spain, wrote that the American "union is more centralized than the two governments of the continent" in certain respects. More recently, a few scholars have sought to alter the conventional portrait of a "national state [which] barely existed."[53] Contributed here is one plausible rationale for much early federal activity: preserving and strengthening national union.

Evidence of the unionist roots of institution-building appears in the rhetoric surrounding Clay's "American System" as well as that of less ambitious developers. Clay invariably defended his overlapping policies of public works as "eminently advantageous to all parts of the union, and injurious really to none." His opponents occasionally ceded this point, as when Maryland's Rep. William Giles, a states' rights Democrat, admitted, "if new territory is to be acquired," by "whom is it to be purchased? By the whole Union. From whence comes the treasure to meet these extraordinary expenses? From the common treasury of the Union." Such rhetorical claims found confirmation in the nature of nineteenth-century institutional activity. True, numerous attributes common among European national governments were absent in the United States, such as a professional civil service or extensive redistributive programs. But the American state was notably active in other important ways: expanding and consolidating new territory, extending lines of communication, defending the republic in wartime and preserving domestic stability, removing "undesirable" groups of people from settled areas, and facilitating white settlers' movement into frontier regions.

---

52. Berthoff and Murrin 1973, 278; cf. Goetzmann 1995, 47 (summarizing a "rising tide of works that do not see a solid nation state emerging in America until at least the middle of the Civil War"); Steinmo 1994; Bensel 1990. Skowronek provides a somewhat more nuanced portrait, noting that the "unobtrusive" and "innocuous" central-government activities could "make it seem as if there was no state in America at all," but that government operations were "remarkably serviceable within the context of early American society" (Skowronek 1982, 23, 34).

53. Nelson 1892, 241; Maletz 1998, 606 (cf. de Tocqueville 1969 [1835–40], 117); Foner 1998, 54. A comprehensive summary of older and new-institutionalist scholarship on the early republic is in John 1997.

Common to all these policies was a homogenizing, bonding, unifying rationale—and effect. William Freehling describes the thrust of antebellum state and national government activity as "the knitting of spread-out communities into a national culture." Though the pace of administrative activity varied and insistence on limited government (especially among southern Democrats) remained a staple of political debate, the antebellum state carried out a dynamic range of functions, many of these both inspired by and serving to buttress ideas of national union.[54]

Before adding detail to this picture, I offer an observation about the mutually constitutive connection between union ideas and institutional development. Union's political value was invoked to justify certain national-government functions, such as territorial defense and expansion. As these activities were institutionalized, they in turn became a focus of national loyalty, serving as sources of more cohesive national unity. Independently examining institutional development and political ideas, standard practice among social scientists, misses this vital interplay. Indeed, recognizing the link between concept and public function enriches our understanding of the antebellum American state. Rather than the "political state" alone, typically described as the "legitimate monopoly of organized force qua its formal organization . . . with the central goal of policing citizens' productive competition," Hegel's term, the "state proper"—which as Sibyl Schwarzenbach describes "includes something more: the customs, manners, and moral consciousness of a people historically united together in a tradition"—is more accurate.[55]

The following paragraphs develop a portrait of America's "state proper," focusing on the purposes and accomplishments of government power. Relating administrative activities explicitly to their unionist inspiration provides a perspective on institutional development more useful than irresolvable debates over whether the state was "strong" or "weak" relative to some Platonic (or Prussian, etc.) standard. Madison posed the question well in 1787: "whether or not a government commensurate to the exigencies of the Union shall be established; or, in other words, whether the Union itself shall be preserved."[56] Many American political actors during the first half of the nineteenth century strove to answer this challenge in the affirmative.

Foreign Policy

Though foreign policy is almost entirely overlooked in most histories of antebellum America,[57] it was a vital locus of central-state activity and simultane-

---

54. Hopkins 1959–92, 9:159 (see also his 1843 "Speech at Memphis," 9:801–3; and 1830 "Speech at Cincinnati," 8:242–44); Giles in *Cong. Globe*, 29th Cong., 2d sess., 1847, 388; Freehling 1994, 152. On Clay's American System as preserver of union, see Knupfer 1991, 130–49, and Lewis 1998, 190–93.

55. Schwarzenbach 1996, 118. Hegel is among the European theorists who viewed America's state as "anomalous"; his cursory inspection included only administrative powers, however. See Paolucci 1978.

56. Rossiter 1961, no. 44, p. 288.

57. As Howe (1997, 60) laments. Lewis (1998) demonstrates the paramount place of unionist concerns in the foreign policy of the early republic—but ends his study in 1829.

ously of Americans' imagining themselves part of a larger whole. Referring to "the powers appertaining to [our] foreign relations," John C. Calhoun explained in his *Discourse on the Constitution and Government* that "to the rest of the world, the States composing this Union are now, and have ever been known in no other than their united, confederated character. Abroad—to the rest of the world— they are but one."[58] It is no coincidence that two of the nation's leading union- ists—Madison and Daniel Webster—each served as secretary of state.

There were, of course, numerous reasons for attending to America's place in the world besides constructing a stronger union at home. But certain interna- tional strategies are best interpreted in unionist terms. Mlada Bukovansky's study of Americans' neutrality declarations in several European conflicts during the early nineteenth century is instructive. "Why," asks Bukovansky, "did a weak and divided state, stubbornly . . . but with entirely inadequate material resources for the task, cling to a [neutrality] policy that was opposed and consistently chal- lenged by far stronger powers?" Her answer involves leaders' efforts to promote "a principled conception of [national] identity." The "U.S. polity had to be con- ceived of as a whole before it could be used as a venue for the pursuit of various interests or aims. The process by which American identity was conceptualized— and its underlying ideas—was as critical to the constitution of state identity as the existence of the territory and the people, since the same territory and peo- ple could have continued to exist as a colony or perhaps become a very differ- ent type of state."[59] In short, remaining neutral toward Britain and France (and, later, other powers) defined the United States as beyond the sphere of either, providing a rallying point for citizens to imagine themselves as part of a single nation.

Similar defenses were offered in support of notable diplomatic efforts of the time, such as the Monroe Doctrine. Webster praised this "bright page in our history" as "elevat[ing] the hopes, and gratify[ing] the patriotism of the people." Monroe himself couched his doctrine of noninterference in explicitly unionist terms, as Fields summarizes: "Union, institutional coherence, harmony, and pub- lic happiness were what vindicated America's claims over an 'unsettled' Europe." The Doctrine was the strongest statement of U.S. sovereignty in the interna- tional sphere ever attempted by an American political leader; its stated purpose was "the advancement of the Union toward perfection." Even if the actual aims mainly involved more mundane material concerns, leaders clearly believed they had an appreciative audience for assertions of national power.[60]

Domestic Policies

At least since Italian republics of the early Renaissance, political officials have distinguished between national-state activity in foreign policy and local repub-

58. Lence 1992, 143.

59. Bukovansky 1997, 210 (emphasis added).

60. Wiltse and Berolzheimer 1986–88, 1:224 (cf. Webster in *Annals of Cong.*, 18th Cong. 1st sess., 1824, 1085, 1087); Fields 1996, 187.

lican governance in the domestic realm.[61] Americans upheld this divide to an extent, but even at home the national state was more ambitious than is ordinarily recalled today. In investigating this activity we begin where Madison's sustainable-union design did: with U.S. territory. The nineteenth century saw Americans—including Madison himself, as secretary of state and then president—support this vision through aggressive policies of acquiring new lands and improving existing ones. The nation added territory at an astounding rate between 1800 and 1850, with federal purchase and war spoils transforming the United States from a collection of Atlantic settlements to a continental empire. Most expansionists cited as one of their central aims enhancing unity, from zealous supporters like Jackson to such restrained advocates as John Quincy Adams, who saw new land as contributing to "union, the ark of our salvation."[62] As the country spread under the acquisitive eyes of Jackson and his successors, union usage advanced along with settlers, investing space with symbolic order. Jingoistic boasts displayed union talk at their center, further popularizing the term. John O'Sullivan, coiner of the Manifest Destiny catchphrase, contrasted "our great, pacific and friendly Union" to "Mexican conceit and imbecility" in urging Texas's annexation in 1845. A southerner's representative view of the Mexican War directly linked expansion and affective feeling:

> The association of men from all parts of the Union, under such circumstances, will be fruitful of good offices, kindly acts, lasting friendships, fraternal feelings, which will last while life endures. When the war is done, and these principles and feelings, hallowed by victory, are carried to the remotest corners of the confederacy, by the return of the citizen soldiery, what an additional cement will it form to the Union!

Opponents of expansion interpreted union commitments differently, though little less ardently. The "forcible addition of foreign territory," thundered Whig Congressman Washington Hunt in 1846, was "so far from forming a 'more perfect union,' it could end only in discord and disunion. The mere attempt would at once destroy all national harmony."[63]

With territorial growth outstripping the organizational abilities of settlers or state governments, federal officials of both parties helped plan and subsidize a vast set of what were then termed "internal improvements." These ranged from roads, canals, and, later, railroads to a series of lighthouses along the Atlantic coast, erected "in the absence of local will or resources."[64] Timely federal aid and

---

61. On this history see Viroli 1992.

62. Adams in Lott 1994, 57–59 (quote at p. 58). Compare his predecessor Monroe: "expansion of our population and accession of new States to our Union have had the happiest effect on all its higher interests . . . .Consolidation and disunion have thereby been rendered equally impractical" (Richardson 1896–99, 4:214).

63. Stephanson 1995, 43–44; McCardell 1990, 234; *Cong. Globe*, 29th Cong., 2d sess., 1846, 72.

64. Zelinsky 1996, 172. John C. Calhoun, in a Senate floor speech, captured the prevailing spirit among political elites, declaring that "Internal Improvements" was "a subject every way so intimately

land grants for railroad and telegraph construction, John Fiske retrospectively observed, had "made our vast country, both for political and for social purposes, more snug and compact than was New England during the founding." The "National Road," built early in Monroe's presidency to connect the mid-Atlantic region and the Ohio Valley, was accompanied by the construction of hundreds of smaller routes, many with national funds. Between 1820 and 1840, notes one historian, "so many miles of road were built, largely at state and federal expense, that few additional major arteries were cut east of the Mississippi until the twentieth century." These projects were typically defended, as Rep. Beecher declared of the national road in 1825, as a way to "bind the extremities of the nation in closer ties, strengthen mutual confidence, attach the people to their Government, and promote the general strength and prosperity of our common country."[65]

Merchants and farmers seeking quicker routes to market, real estate speculators, stock jobbers, and swarms of other beneficiaries supported public works projects. Opponents usually varied with party, as out-parties sought to block these rich sources of patronage until they recaptured power in the state legislature or Congress. Whigs and northern leaders more often tended to support internal improvements, but many Democrats and southerners were fervent advocates of projects benefiting their state or region. Andrew Jackson, usually portrayed as a states' rights foe of improvements, in fact approved more federal spending for this purpose during his presidency—more than $10 million—than all the previous administrations combined. (Jackson did prominently oppose many improvements projects, but as Richard Ellis shows these were usually programs narrowly targeting specific local communities.) Several of Jackson's counterparts in southern statehouses also looked favorably on public works: "Across the South, strict-constructionist Democrats found themselves steadily outvoted by friends of internal improvements." And when Democratic leaders like Presidents Polk and Buchanan vetoed public works bills, they couched their denials in unionist terms. Congress's 1846 bill, explained Polk, would "lead to a consolidation of power in the Federal Government," violating the federalist balance of nation and states underpinning sustainable-union ideas; it would also "engender sectional feelings and prejudices calculated to disturb the harmony of the Union" and "destroy the harmony which should prevail in our legislative councils."[66]

Targeted economic gain undeniably helped explain the popularity of im-

connected with the ultimate attainment of national strength and the perfection of our political institutions . . . it would make the parts adhere more closely; [and] form a new and most powerful cement." Lence 1992, 309.

65. Fiske 1888, 60; Mayfield 1982, 64; *Register of Debates,* 18th Cong., 2d sess., 1825, 192.

66. Ellis 1987, 19–25; Summers 1987, 100; Polk in Richardson 1896–99, 2:314. McWilliams (1973, 247) notes that Jackson's "opposition to 'internal improvements' was more ambiguous than many believe. . . . He supported those improvements he thought likely to cement the Union." On the "scramble for resources" among Democrats as well as Whigs, see Silbey 1991, 186–87. On southern support for federally aided improvements, see Rubin 1994, 384, 387, 398. Rubin chides antebellum historians for viewing "the early nineteenth century through the prism of the Civil War" and thereby "highlight[ing] a strain of [southern anti-federal] radicalism that rarely dominated."

provement plans. But federal largesse was the result of more than pork-barrel lobbying. Congressional and executive officials were joined by newspaper editors throughout the country in saluting the beneficent effect of improvements on national unity. "We call the Pacific Railroad a national work," wrote the *St. Louis Democrat*, "because we consider it national in its location, national in its advantages, and, above all, national in its binding and strengthening influences. . . . [T]he extremes of this country are literally bound together, by 'bars of iron.'" Similarly, Daniel Webster cited "the instance of the Delaware breakwater" in his famous reply to Hayne. The giant artificial harbor "will cost several millions of money," he noted. "Would Pennsylvania alone ever have constructed it? Certainly never, while this Union lasts, because it is not for her sole benefit. Would Pennsylvania, New Jersey and Delaware have united to accomplish it at their joint expense? Certainly not, for the same reason. It could not be done, therefore, but by the general government."[67] In specific cases, such arguments may have helped win a close vote or swing community opinion in favor of such activity. Americans' suspicion of the central state ran especially high during the 1830s and 1840s, and not only in the South;[68] assurances of national programs' providential effects on unity helped in some cases to overcome critics' qualms and allow advances in transportation and communication to proceed.

Once in place, public works were energetically regulated by national and state actors in the antebellum republic. Ports, highways, canal and river traffic, and railroads were all monitored in various ways, with Congress and the executive bureaucracy wielding oversight responsibility upheld by the courts. As William Novak notes, antebellum administrators were "not simply reflectors or instruments or facilitators of natural evolutions in the market or civil society. They were creative and generative." In the case of levying customs duties, for example, American national authorities wielded more power vis-à-vis state governments than did their European counterparts. Federal officials also worked with their state colleagues to regulate corporate conduct, severely limiting the accessibility and duration of corporate charters, for example.[69]

In 1845 a Georgia writer described U.S. internal improvements and territorial organization as "Union-promoting" labors. To these examples may be added such programmatic activities as extending postal delivery across the continent, via a Post Office Act that also subsidized newspapers and other sources of popular information on public affairs;[70] developing a pension system for Revolution-

67. *Democrat* editorial reprinted in *Kansas Herald of Freedom* (Lawrence), April 28, 1855. Webster in Wiltse and Berolzheimer 1986–88, 1:309.

68. In James Morone's pithy summary, "the Jacksonians introduced new state capacities while articulating an antistatist faith" (1990, 93).

69. Novak 1996, 236; cf. 161–237 generally. On customs duties, see Maletz 1998, 606; on corporate regulation, see Dodd 1934, 367–414, and Bruyn 1999, 28–29 (demonstrating concern for "the community" and "the public good" as rationales for regulation).

70. *Southern Banner* (Athens, Ga.), November 18, 1845. For details on postal expansion, see John 1995.

ary War veterans and expanding it in 1818, 1832, and 1836;[71] financing and otherwise promoting national newspapers, congressional speeches, and related sources of popular information on public affairs;[72] establishing widespread public education, described as "education for patriotism" and "a growing spirit of nationalism";[73] surveying and enforcing boundaries between the states; determining the makeup of U.S. citizenship through immigration and naturalization powers; supporting numerous nascent national voluntary organizations;[74] and, notoriously, forcing the resettlement or marginalization of nonwhites (along with the "Indian removal" policies, more than 13,000 former slaves were "repatriated" to Africa with federal financial support before the Civil War).[75]

Another example of unionist-defended federal activity was the development of western territories and lands. Patricia Nelson Limerick notes that "from the beginning of Western development, federal goodwill . . . has been one of the West's principal resources. When other resources faltered or collapsed, federal support often turned out to be the crucial remaining prop to the economy." National officials also attended to smaller details during the Jacksonian and antebellum years, including paying for tours by popular patriotic figures. During General Lafayette's 1825 travels, as Bassett describes, "celebrations were held in each town, and . . . the federal government picked up the tab."[76]

National administrators worked with (and sometimes against) state officials on many of these programs. And compared to the New Deal or Great Society distributive state, these early federal functions appear attenuated. But a decisive increase in administrative capacity is evident after 1820. As the social critic Orestes Brownson noted in 1831: "We are making more rapid strides towards . . . centralization and the bureaucratic system than even the most sensitive nullifyer [sic] has suspected." Of most importance here is that federal officials frequently defended their activities as advancing "the spirit of national union," as a Democrat-appointed customs inspector put it in 1844.[77]

Evidence that the mass of Americans were not isolated from these national government functions is plentiful in newspapers of the day. Many papers, in every region of the United States and in small hamlets as well as large cities, carried regular accounts of congressional and executive action. The *Hartford Daily Courant,* for example, from its inception in September 1837 featured a "Report

71. A comprehensive study of this program, and the expanding federal bureaucracy required to administer it, is in Jensen 1996.

72. See Freehling 1994, 153; John 1997, 372–73; Brown 1996.

73. Butts and Cremin 1953, 217. See also Branham 1996, 626 ("The overriding mission of early public schools was the moral and civic development of their pupils, as schools explicitly sought to forge a 'National Character' by imparting knowledge of and allegiance to national principles.")

74. Skocpol 1997a.

75. Redky 1969.

76. Limerick 1987, 138; Bassett 1999, 37. Also see McCormick 1986, who details a long list of federal "riches" bestowed on Americans during the first half of the nineteenth century.

77. Brownson in Morone 1990, 92–93; cf. John 1997, 373–80, and Elazar 1962 (on intergovernmental cooperation before the Civil War). Inspector quoted in Jourdan 1889, 39.

from Congress" almost every day the body was in session—often covering half of the front page, which was usually the only page (of four total, until it expanded late in the 1850s) not dedicated to advertisements. Editors also took the national legislature to task for inactivity, in terms strikingly familiar today. A small-town North Carolina editor insisted in 1842 that "Congress had better abandon all paper expedients, and go in the straight forward way to work. . . . Nothing but this is required to restore full confidence in the Government itself, and to bring back confidence . . . between section and section of the Union." A decade earlier, the *American Spectator* commented on the "do nothing aspect" of congressional affairs: "this session of Congress," the *Spectator*'s Washington correspondent noted, "is likely to pass away without even the appearance of business. . . . There would be some consolation in a mere show of work, though no work were actually done; but cool, deliberate, preconcerted indolence is always a little provoking."[78]

Thus even those Americans who only occasionally glanced at a newspaper were aware of the national government's power to act and the clamor from many quarters of the country for its doing so. "This is a time when the eyes of the people are directed to the seat of Government," editorialized the *Connecticut Mirror* in 1831, with no burning national issue in mind; the claim was a generic one. Antebellum readers consistently encountered enthusiastic statements about national deeds, such as a widely reprinted oration commemorating the laying of the Washington Monument's cornerstone: "Let us seize this occasion to renew to each other our vows of allegiance and devotion to the American Union . . . the all sufficient centripetal power, which shall hold the thick clustering stars of our confederacy in one glorious constellation forever!"[79]

A more nuanced account of what was missing or lagging in nineteenth-century American state development draws on Skowronek's "absence of a sense of the state." Some observers lamented this at the time, including a Maine cleric: "So invisible is our government, so void of all symbols that set forth its presence and its majesty, so rarely have we come into contact with its civil and military officials, so silently fall its blessings like the noiseless sunbeams or the gentle dew, that we have not appreciated its beneficent agency, nor rendered it the affectionate loyalty which is its due." Most of the political class, however, was freely given to praising the agency of "the Union," as already noted.[80]

In fact, a missing "sense of the state" seems more pronounced among scholars today than among antebellum Americans. These modern writers acknowledge the extent of national administrative activity, but still hold that a culture of suspicion about centralization, many Americans' local orientation, and institutional competition from state officials limited federal authority in some signifi-

78. *Tarboro Press* (N.C.), January 15, 1842; *American Spectator,* December 1830. Statistical evidence of U.S. newspapers' "nationalization" of political news in the 1830s is in Kernell 1986.

79. *Connecticut Mirror,* January 8, 1831; *Hartford Daily Courant,* July 13, 1848.

80. Skowronek 1982, 5–6, 19 (emphasis added); Maine reverend Samuel Harris in Moorhead 1978, 130.

cant way. It is difficult, given the roster of national activity, to specify exactly *what* was missing, but one possibility is welfare-state functions, which for many contemporary analysts are virtually synonymous with state activity.[81] With no substantial public provision of such goods as poor relief or health insurance, the nineteenth-century American state indeed appears "exceptional." This outlook may account for the "popular notion," as Massachusetts state official Herbert Heaton sarcastically noted in the 1940s, that "until the fourth of March, 1933, the United States was the land of laissez faire."[82] Where welfare-state functions did exist in the antebellum United States, they supported unimpeachably patriotic causes. Federal pensions for Revolutionary War veterans, as previously mentioned, were the first American entitlement programs.

Specific evidence that national actors at the time distinguished between institutional activity designed to unite the white majority and policies viewed as unnecessarily aiding the indigent or otherwise unworthy came in 1854, when Dorothea Dix convinced Congress to set aside some ten million acres for financial aid to benefit indigent mentally ill and other "needy Americans." Franklin Pierce vetoed the bill as "subversive of the whole theory upon which the union of these states is founded." Pierce's response owed something to specific political circumstances, but he also explicitly contrasted national programs consistent with prevailing ideas of union and other functions—welfare for the "needy," in this case—that failed to uphold such a "theory."[83]

Attention to this patchwork central state—active in some respects, virtually absent in others—helps explain how citizens of this "great anomaly among Western states" managed to develop a strong sense of common identity and a robust civic infrastructure despite a small federal bureaucracy. Historians point to parties as the "real" source of connections across sectional divisions, the "glue that held the political nation together."[84] There is something to that claim, as detailed later in this chapter. But strong party identification translated feebly or obliquely into support for the federal regime, especially when the opposing party held control. Fealty to "the Union," in contrast, justified a set of national institutions able to "hold otherwise atomistic and self-interested individuals together in an organized society," a function generally associated with the national state.[85]

Order and equilibrium, the vital products of political institutions, were widely perceived as endangered in antebellum America. The idea of union, embodied

81. See, e.g., Wuthnow 1991, 290.

82. Heaton quoted in John 1997, 354–55. Under the pre-20th Amendment electoral calendar, March 4 was FDR's first day in office.

83. *Cong. Globe*, 33rd Cong., 1st sess., 1854, 1061 (see 1060–70 for full Pierce message, and Senate reaction following). For more detail, and a claim that the antebellum federal government *did* undertake certain welfare-state functions, see Trattner 1988, esp. 351–52.

84. Skowronek 1982, 24–31 (quote at p. 6); Silbey 1991, 126. Cf. Skocpol 1992, 71–87; McCormick 1990; Bender 1978, 83–89). For a critical accounting of parties' overstated importance, see Altschuler and Blumin 1997.

85. Shepsle 1989, 2.

in the territorial United States and an administrative state primarily undertaking projects designed to "cement the whole," became a source of loyalty and stability in its own right. Most Americans' loyalty in the mid-nineteenth century, as expressed in countless newspaper editorials and private declarations, was not to any government per se, national or local. Rather, people declared a commitment to the idea of unity, which much federal activity sought (or was claimed) to uphold. National activity in foreign and domestic spheres was rationalized in terms of union, and ratified especially in the "great compromises" (those of 1820, 1833, and 1850) that were inevitably defended as "preservers of Union." A Washington, D.C., editor wrote in 1820 that "the spirit of compromise was necessary in forming the Union: and, however long the Union may continue, the spirit of compromise will always be found necessary to preserve it."[86] Assertions of the concept's value, repeated in oratory, textbooks, newspapers, and conversations, became a powerful if intangible source of allegiance. Without the concrete bonds this strenuous promotion of unity engendered during the first half of the nineteenth century, it is difficult to imagine the republic undertaking, much less surviving, the Civil War.

One related point on the import of this early U.S. state development. The institutional connections traced above grew partly out of Madison's tripartite vision of unity, but nineteenth-century actors forged more elaborate connections between the American national state and what we now call civil society: the collection of voluntary associations and other types of civic activity that, in Robert Hefner's description, "mediate the vast expanse of social life between the household and the state." Hefner also notes that most students of civil society, in the United States and elsewhere, view a "healthy civil society" as a "counterbalance" to national state power.[87] Among Americans in the early republic, however, the two realms were more often viewed as mutually supportive. The national government in most depictions was not portrayed as separate from or as "floating above" state and local authorities; rather, the work of both was considered to be mutually reinforcing. The two great exceptions here concerned slavery and tariff issues, with one or the other the source of most extended paeans to "states' rights" before the 1850s. These and other sectional issues are investigated later in this chapter.

In enacting internal improvements and other federal policies defended as contributing to union, Jacksonian and later antebellum officials bolstered the connection between state and society. One effect of the institutional activities just outlined was to provide central-government resources to aid the growth of local organizations, such as the numerous associations that sprang up around canal, road, and later railroad construction. Thanks in significant part to state advocacy and funding, these organizations grew into early national associations,

---

86. *Indiana Whig*, December 15, 1855; *National Messenger* (Georgetown), February 14, 1820. On this "spirit" of compromise, see the wonderfully detailed study by Peter Knupfer (1991, esp. 86–157).
87. Hefner 1998, 17.

Table 2. Supreme Court cases mentioning "Union," 1790–1860

Years	Total cases	Relevant cases	Percentage of total relevant cases
1790–99	15	14	3.5
1800–1809	18	12	3.1
1810–19	39	24	6.1
1820–29	81	61	15.5
1830–39	99	80	20.4
1840–49	106	81	20.6
1850–59	167	121	30.8
Total	525	393	100

Source: Lexis database of Supreme Court cases.
Note: Column 1 indicates the total Lexis count of cases including one or more "Union" references. I examined each case to determine if the reference was indeed to *national* union, was instead to a place-name (e.g., Union Bank), or was otherwise irrelevant. Column 2 reports the total "relevant references" count of all those cases including at least one mention of "the Union" or national union. Column 3 gives the proportion of relevant cases by decade. A similar exercise is performed for terms referring to "tyranny" in nineteenth-century federal and some state court decisions in Likhovski 1997; see 205–7 for commentary.

a process described by Tocqueville in the case of a "free trade" group organized to discuss tariff issues.[88] Even relatively limited early U.S. government activity, then, helped engender a more vigorous civil society as local networks were built across regions and sometimes across the entire United States. In turn, symbiotic relationships developed between national associations and the government that sponsored them, helping produce a more active national state. This book's conclusion explores the connection in more detail, but note that as early as the 1830s, American political leaders had forged initial links between state and civil society in the service of collective goals. They did so primarily in the name of strengthening national union, though a host of other purposes were likely also involved.

Further confirmation of the national government's role in advancing unity came in a series of Supreme Court decisions over the first half of the nineteenth century. Table 2 displays the Court's growing tendency to employ unionist terms in its decisions. Though many of these were rote references to "the Union," justices also struggled to define the terms of union in ways usually consonant with Madison's balanced ideal. The overall effect of the Court's repeated incantation of union was a potent symbolism, as the nation's supreme lawmaking authority repeatedly affirmed—in the words of Chief Justice Taney, in an 1839 decision—the "intimate union of these states, as members of the same great political family . . . [sharing] deep and vital interests."[89]

88. de Tocqueville 1969 [1835–40], 192. See also the overview in Skocpol 1997a.
89. *Bank of Augusta v. Earle*, 38 U.S. 519, 590 (1839).

Consonant with ongoing efforts of union-minded officials to construct political reality through language, many of the Court's union references appeared in cases adjudicating matters of federalist balance. The Constitution's loose definition of the respective powers of state and national government led to—invited, one may almost say—numerous conflicts over jurisdiction and sovereignty, which are still subjects of intense debate.[90] The complex issues surrounding antebellum federalism are treated in a wealth of studies;[91] I wish to point out the role that unionist ideas played in Court rulings about the location of sovereignty, ranging from minor matters like state boundary disputes to severe trials, as in the 1829–33 nullification controversy. Confusion reigned even on basic definitional matters, as John Marshall's opinion in an obscure 1814 case testifies: "The members of the American confederacy *only* are those States contemplated in the Constitution. . . . the word 'State' is used in the Constitution as designating a member of the Union, and excludes from the term the signification attached to it by writers on the law of nations."[92]

Madison and other framers' balanced unionist understanding, upholding state rights *and* federal authority, was a touchstone for Court decisions. John Marshall and fellow justices repeatedly quoted such standbys as Hamilton's *Federalist* 82 assertion that "the state governments and the national government" were best viewed "in the light of kindred systems and as parts of ONE WHOLE."[93] Marshall is still sometimes portrayed as an aggressive nationalist, given that his decisions established the national Court as the ultimate arbiter of judicial questions. But most of the relevant Marshall Court decisions balanced expanded federal authority with elaborately specified limits on national power, beginning with the famous example of *Marbury v. Madison.* The succeeding Taney Court—portrayed today as a purveyor of "centrist federalism"—similarly framed opinions in the name of "strengthening the Union." Legal historian David Kopel notes that Taney's colleague (and later successor as Chief Justice) Joseph Story, in his influential *Commentaries on the Constitution* (1833) and a series of related opinions, "almost singlehandedly created the doctrine of an indissoluble Union."[94]

My focus on the commitment of Supreme Court justices and other Jacksonian-era officials to a balanced, Madisonian account of national union overlooks a

90. On constitutional construction, see Lutz 1988, 153–54; continuing federalist conflicts are summarized in Amar 1998, 128–29.

91. See, e.g., Ostrom 1991; Elazar 1962, 1972b; M. Diamond 1992.

92. *Hepburn & Dundass v. Ellxey,* 2 Cranch 452, 454 (1814). On state boundaries, one example among many is *Burgess Poole v. Fleeger,* 36 U.S. 185 (1837); the decision delicately affirmed each state's rights to set its geographic boundaries—but with Congressional consent (209–10).

93. Rossiter 1961, no. 82, p. 555; Marshall citing Hamilton in *Cohens v. Virginia,* 19 U.S. 264, 295 (1821).

94. *Marbury v. Madison,* 1 Cranch 137 (1803); Story 1987 [1833]; Kopel 1998, 1389. The conclusion that Marshall consistently strived to uphold a "Madison-style" balance of national, state, and local powers is extensively defended in Hobson 1996, esp. 122–24 (on *McCulloch v. Maryland*), 141–47, 164–80, 200–206, 247 (critiquing accounts that overstate Marshall's nationalism); for a complementary earlier account see Boudin 1932, 267–316. On *Marbury v. Madison* as a similarly "balanced" decision, see esp. Van Alstyne 1969, 1–6. The Taney Court's "centrist" position on federalism issues in the 1830s and 1840s is well described in Whittington 1999, 90–93.

range of political and legal subtleties, to be sure. Various parties in the nullification controversy, or other antebellum issues, defined the relative powers of state and nation in profoundly different ways. But a common thread in all conversations—between Calhoun and Webster, between Marshall or Taney and their various critics on and off the Court, and so forth—was parties' insistence that they acted in the service of national unity. This reinforced union's earlier balancing function, wherein nationalists like Hamilton employed the term in part as a means of avoiding explicit central-government designations likely to alarm anti-Federalist opponents of ratification. In the 1830s and 1840s, union ideas retained a convenient vagueness about the location of government powers among other issues, permitting states' rights adherents to share common rhetorical goals with free-soilers to the north and west. Though period unionist views and practices may be seen now (as they sometimes were by other nations at the time) as pugnacious jingoism, manifest-destiny claims also reflected deep anxieties on the part of their promoters. Thomas Hietala's detailed study locates "anxious aggrandizement" at the root of many destinarian boasts.[95] As in the revolutionary and constitutional periods, disunion cast a long shadow over antebellum political rhetoric.

Implicit in much antebellum union talk were a pair of fears that haunted unionists even as the term spread. One was self-interest, now recast as individualism; the "spirit of individualism . . . ushered in by General Jackson," worried an Indiana Whig, "threatens at every turn the affection united Americans must needs display."[96] Even more ominously, the old American bugaboo of states' rights and sectionalism threatened to split the United States into multiple parts, a fate dreaded since the "more perfect Union" was ordained. These threats to affective, representative-centered American union are taken up serially in the following section. Both individualism and sectionalism have been thoroughly treated elsewhere as a feature of antebellum politics;[97] my purpose is to assess the effects of each on union ideas and vice versa. To do so, I take up at length the public arguments of individualism's greatest American analyst, Ralph Waldo Emerson, and the Ur-sectionalist, John C. Calhoun. Both attempted to reconcile an ostensibly alien value with national unity, respectively posing strong individuality and sectional differentiation as constituents of national union. Their unionist references may be dismissed as superficial posturing, but at a minimum they testify to the value's central place in the antebellum United States.

CHALLENGES TO UNION: INDIVIDUALS AND SECTIONS

An essay contest on "Why I Love the Union," held at the Pleasant Hill (N.C.) Female Academy in 1842, was "a surpassingly successful event" in the school's

95. Hietala 1985.
96. *American Whig Review* 6 (February 1844): 67.
97. See, e.g., Bensel 1984 (on sectionalism), and Sellers 1991 and Arieli 1964 (on individualism).

short history, the local newspaper editor (and contest judge) beamed. "Every con-
testant mustered praise . . . in the most creative manner, of the American union
spirit," and not a "single fear for Union's permanency" was expressed, at least
none that the editor-judge noticed. Such a sunny outlook was "refreshing," his
write-up concluded, "when compared with so many shudderings, from our Federal spokesmen, about the perils of disunion on every hand." [98] The discrepancy
between a small-town editor's complacent view of national unity and the concerns he attributed to national leaders is telling. Even as most Americans proudly
extolled their common spirit and perpetual union, some were wrestling with
forces they saw as corroding the bonds of affection.

Individualism and the Emersonian Solution

Tocqueville's landmark description of the democratic individual was drawn,
significantly, from his direct observations of Jacksonian America. "[N]ot only
does democracy make men forget their ancestors," Tocqueville warned, "but also
clouds their view of their descendants and isolates them from their contemporaries. Each man is forever thrown back on himself alone . . . shut up in the solitude of his own heart." Most American politicians were openly alarmed at popular apathy and strenuously promoted unity in response. "What is an individual
man?" Henry Clay pleaded. "An atom, almost invisible without a magnifying
glass. . . . Shall a being so small, so petty, so fleeting, so evanescent, oppose itself
to the onward march of a great nation, to subsist for ages and ages to come?"
Prominent cultural figures were equally concerned. Nathaniel Hawthorne, for
one, in his best-known works drew a tragic conflict between individualism and
unity. In Hawthorne's work, concludes one commentator, "the things that unite
people are more precious than the things that separate them. . . . Those of Hawthorne's characters who deny the affectional impulses in themselves are transformed into fiends." [99]

Threats of fiendish ends hardly dampened the individualism of the mid-
nineteenth century. In an industrializing society only beginning to develop the
continent, the necessity for both self-sufficient citizens and unified organization
among them was vast. But merely identifying this need did little to inspire anyone to think in terms of union. As John William Ward writes, "the question how
society was to harness for its own good the will of the self-determined individual did loom large." [100] The traditional answer, representing unity in the person
of national heroes, worked only up to a point. James Monroe's presidential tour
of New England and the mid-Atlantic states was intended, as he wrote Madi-

---

98. *Tarboro Press* (N.C.), May 7, 1842.
99. de Tocqueville 1969 [1835–40], 508; Clay in Howe 1979, 148; Bartlett 1967, 108–9.
100. Ward 1955, 190. Bender (1979) emphasizes the social fragmentation, isolation, and anonym-
ity characterizing New York and other major cities during this period; a more balanced treatment is
in McWilliams 1973, 229–34. A good short survey of 1820s–50s American individualism is in Curry
and Valois 1991, 26–43.

son, "to provide an occasion for the people to demonstrate the new spirit of unity animating the nation." His effort was judged as less than successful by many reviewers at the time.[101]

A more considered response to the problem of encouraging unity among individualists was undertaken by Ralph Waldo Emerson, renowned oracle of self-reliance. Emerson's union applications were more challenging than celebratory and also more political in nature than is normally perceived. Though novel in certain respects, his approach to joining disparate, autonomous individuals closely mirrored Madison's view. Emerson also was uncommonly influential in the expanding American public sphere, inasmuch as he "had become the professional embodiment of Man Thinking . . . the people liked him because he did their thinking for them." Thomas Augst notes that "for ordinary Americans . . . attending lectures given by Emerson and others were crucial means of finding practical moral guidance" on such subjects as "the kinds of social bonds to which we will commit ourselves."[102]

Emerson's championing of autochthonic American arts and manners often featured invocations of national union. Religious overtones were usually present as well: his Transcendentalist vision spanned religious and political community, like many antebellum ministers. But Emerson avoided the sacrosanct tone of much period union talk. In 1842 he satirized Americans as "waking up to the idea of Union, and already we love Communities, Phalanxes & Aesthetic Families, & Pestalozian institutions. [National unity] is and will be magic. Men will live & communicate & ride & plough & reap & govern as by lightning and galvanic & ethereal power." For Emerson existing society—"the rhetoricians' Union"—and "true union" were incompatible. His concentration on rigorous self-understanding supplied a critique of extant society, which, he charged, "is frivolous, and sheds its day into scraps." Instead a new order was to be effected, "renovate[d] on the principle of right and love."[103] Well-formed individuals, Emerson assured his audiences, could bring about a democratic national union worthy of the name and counter the forces of apathy and atomism.

Emerson closely linked political solidarity and self-sufficiency, asserting mutual reinforcement in tendencies today posed as irreconcilable. Alongside a conviction that self-reflection was the key to full personal development, Emerson held that affective interaction among sound individuals provided an essential

101. Ammon 1990, 372, 377 (for a more positive account of Monroe's 1817 tour, see Waldstreicher 1997, 298–302).

102. Cayton 1987, 618; Augst 1999, 89. Cf. McWilliams 1973, 280–82; Curry and Valois 1991, 39 (on Emerson as "accurately refect[ing] nineteenth-century American attitudes"); and Sellers 1991, 375–80 (on Emerson as "high priest of middle-class culture"). Emerson himself answered any objection that he was a poetic, not political, thinker: "It is not possible to extricate oneself from the questions in which your age is involved" (Gilman 1960–82, 14:385). Even before the "American Scholar" address in 1837, Emerson "had been deeply involved in social and political matters for years" (Richardson 1995, 269). Compare Shklar 1998, 49, 101.

103. Gilman 1960–82, 8:250–51; Edman 1926, 332, 417. "True union" is described in his "American Scholar" address, see Emerson 1903–4, 1:113–15.

grounding for the republic.[104] Which took precedence for him, individual or united whole? Most scholars tack hard toward the former. George Fredrickson, for example, locates a pure "radical individualist" strain in Emerson's pre–Civil War thought. Sacvan Bercovitch's assessment seems more apt: Emerson was "devoted at once to the exaltation of the individual and the search for a perfect community."[105] This recognizes that Emerson's exhortations to individualism were integrated into his vision of union among self-sufficient persons. It is difficult to distinguish the two tendencies, much less determine which he saw as preeminent.

Affective sentiment, in Emerson's conception, often appears a means to greater individuality. He depicted fraternal fellowship as a source of enhanced personal happiness and fulfillment, further developing individuality. Yet the self's ultimate authority was qualified. Only the "strong individual," Emerson's greatest biographer notes, "can frankly concede the sometimes surprising extent of his own dependence." A dialectic of support between individual and social whole derived from Emerson's faith in personal transformation. Individuals were not passive vessels shaped by powerful outside forces; neither were they chiefly the product of personal reflection and will. Each self was a work continually in progress, responsive to a composite of influences—including social connections. As Emerson noted in 1829, "the power of the individual depends upon the power of society"; thirteen years later he described his "union ideal—in actual individualism, actual union." Even "Self-Reliance" displays Emerson's conviction that a more tightly bound society, voluntarily composed of vigorous individuals, was a legitimate and desirable goal.[106]

Primary features in Emerson's interpolation of individualism and unity recall Madison's understanding of political union. Through identification with national territory, Emerson concluded, Americans would apply their individuality to the service of a greater whole. As he wrote in "Society and Solitude": "Our American people . . . are feeling our youth and nerve and bone. We have the power of *territory* and of sea-coast, and know the use of these. . . . Our eyes run approvingly along the lengthened lines of railroad and telegraph; we are adding to an already enormous territory. . . . We value ourselves on all these feats." Emerson's theme has little to do with Madison's more prosaic hopes that unified territory would better protect property values and political stability; instead it builds on and extends the notion that Americans would affirm common pride in land, their "sovereign glory." Knowledge and love of the land inspired a greater respect for self, as an inhabitant of such vital, extensive ground. Myra Jehlen sum-

104. See, e.g., ibid., 1:73–74: "The reason why the world lacks unity, and lies broken and in heaps, is because man is disunited with himself." See also Edman 1926, 417, or Gilman 1960–82, 7:304.

105. Fredrickson 1965, 10–15; Bercovitch 1985, 40. Bercovitch traces Emerson's interpolation of self and nation to Puritan foundations; compare the analysis in Newfield 1996.

106. Richardson 1995, 88; Gilman 1960–82, 8:251; Edman 1926, 52–56. Compare his essays "Spiritual Laws," esp. 98–101, and "Over-Soul." On "exalted individualism," see Gilman 1960–82, 9:424.

marizes Emerson's complex view: "Literally inspired by the land's physical ema-nations, the abstract individual becomes an American, and it is as an American that he becomes not only singular but representative. The representativeness of the autonomous individual in turn provides a basis for community that comes from within, rather than as an external and limiting obligation."[107]

Emerson occasionally traced Madison's outline further, upholding affective exchange as a bond of unity. Joined by common residence on American territory and by their status as living expressions of that land, a "nation of friends" might become "the basis of a State." One would naturally wish to associate with others bearing the salutary character of democratic individuals, an association Emerson saw as reaching its highest historical fulfillment in the United States. This wind-ing together of self-reliant, affectively joined individuals and American territory was, for Emerson as for Madison, secured by rightly formed leaders, expected to govern as "moral . . . wise men."[108] Here Daniel Webster was Emerson's exem-plar, one of his "Representative Men."[109]

Given his praise of Webster and a handful of other notables, some commen-tators view membership in Emerson's "true union [of] sentiment" as open only to "American gentry."[110] But this overlooks his profound democratic commit-ment, made clear in both poetry (his "America is a poem in our eyes" prefigures Walt Whitman's sweeping inclusive themes) and prose, as in his 1845 antinativist screed: "in this Continent, asylum of all nations, the energy of Irish, Germans, Swedes, Poles, & Cossacks & all the European tribes,—of the Africans, & of the Polynesians, will construct a new race, a new religion, a new State, a new litera-ture." As Judith Shklar attests, "democratic political experiences . . . quite often gave his essays their intellectual purpose and direction." Here one difference between Emerson and other unionists becomes apparent. Madison and heirs like Webster saw the American many as a collective force for political or social good—but only via the filtering work of their greater-souled representatives. Emerson held that virtually anyone, white or black, native-born or immigrant, could achieve the excellence of character that supported a well-constituted pol-ity. "Here is Man," he noted in 1844, "and if you have man, black or white is an insignificance." Ignore this fact, he told a Concord audience the same year, and "the Union is already at an end."[111]

While Emerson was a more committed democrat than Madison or most founding leaders, tensions between affirming the diverse American polity and organizing a strong national union are apparent in his thought. Emerson was

107. Emerson 1903-4, 7:283 (emphasis added); Jehlen 1986, 14-15; cf. 76-122.
108. Edman 1926, 418-19; Gilman 1960-82, 10:55.
109. Emerson's longstanding admiration for Webster was first expressed in his Phi Beta Kappa poem of 1834, reprinted in 1884 as "Webster" (Emerson 1903-4, 9:398). See also Gilman 1960-82, 3:308-9 (Webster as "a true genius"), 8:362-63, and 10:393-96.
110. See, e.g., Patterson 1997, esp. chaps. 5-6; Marr 1988, 68-70 (quote at p. 70).
111. Edman 1926, 287; Gilman 1960-82, 9:299, 125 (compare his dismissal of racial thinking at 13:288); Shklar 1998, 49; Emerson 1903-4, 2:133.

chiefly concerned with joining self-conscious individuals, not different groups as such, and though he nowhere insisted on Anglo-Saxon bloodlines as criteria of membership in the American union, he sometimes hinted at hierarchical cultural views. In the essay "Considerations by the Way" Emerson expressed a desire to "tame, drill, divide and break up, and draw individuals out of" the diverse "immigrant masses" before turning to their re-collection as members of the Union. His opposition to the Mexican War was muted by a strangely passive providentialism: "It is very certain that the strong British race . . . must overrun [Texas], and Mexico and Oregon also, and it will in the course of the ages be of small import by what particular occasions and methods it was done." Emerson's most sustained reflections on race came in his 1856 book *English Traits*, which rejected the idea of "pure races" as "legend" and emphasized the value of racial "mixture."[112]

In 1846, amid increasing disputes over the status of newly annexed territories, Emerson further distanced himself from the conventional, hyperpatriotic understanding of American union while still evincing hope for his alternate conception. "Cotten [*sic*] thread holds the Union together, unites John C. Calhoun and [abolitionist] Abbott Lawrence. Patriotism is for holidays and summer evenings with music and rockets, but cotten thread is the union." In the bleak years immediately before the war, Emerson would relinquish the notion of an America "without falsehood or patchwork, but sincerity and unity." But throughout the 1830s and 1840s he staunchly held that a viable national union could be composed of strong, autonomous individuals. As an exemplar of this ideal he pointed to the abolitionist movement (which he joined in 1844), citing its "assertion of the sufficiency of the private man" as a basis for "mass movement" leading to worthwhile collective endeavor.[113]

Emerson's professional work also exemplified democratic unity. Thousands of middle-class Americans attending Emerson's lectures or reading his hortatory essays were moved, writes Augst, to a greater "capacity for self-care . . . the jump start of the moral senses on which political engagement . . . in a democratic community depends." Emerson's focus on unity among the wider population rather than fellow elites was right in line with Jacksonian ideals; less realized in practice was his hope that the American masses would yield great-souled individuals uniting voluntarily for enlightened aims. But his interest in the connection between abstract whole and the existential reality of each member of society provided a means of accommodating strong self-awareness within a better constituted nation.[114]

112. Emerson 1903–4, 6:248–49; Stephanson 1995, 53; Emerson 1903–4, 5:49–50 (see also ibid., 11:138–44, on "Emancipation").

113. Gilman 1960–82, 9:425, 267; Emerson 1903–4, 3:251–52. Compare Emerson's warning in 1846, at a Massachusetts "abolition celebration": addressing abolitionists directly, Emerson said "they have yet lessons to learn. . . . I shall esteem them, as they cease to be a party, and come to rely on that which is not a part, or a party, but is the whole." *National Anti-Slavery Standard*, July 16, 1846. And see Lawrence Friedman's affirmation that abolitionists' "blend of conviviality and austere piety" led them to precisely such an achievement of individual growth through joint moral labors. Friedman 1982, esp. 3.

114. Augst 1999, 114.

Calhoun and a Union of Sovereign Sections

On its face the concurrent-majority theory of John C. Calhoun, centrally featuring interposition, nullification, and a strong brief for states' rights, constitutes an especially strong challenge to doctrines of national unity. Calhoun is primarily remembered today as "contributing more to sectional mistrust than any other man." Calhoun's *Disquisitions* and *Discourse,* the extended reflections on government he completed shortly before dying in 1850, are routinely cited as the culmination of southerners' intellectual justification for secession.[115] Yet an examination of the works and his related speeches reveals Calhoun's fundamental concern for preserving national unity, alongside (*through,* he insisted) the theory of concurrent majorities. Even for this champion of sectional rights, in short, union retained signal importance. This commitment was sometimes acknowledged at the time. One defense of Calhoun against charges of disunionism came in an 1849 Kentucky editorial, classing Calhoun with "Washington, Madison, and Jefferson" *against* "those who would be certain to cut asunder . . . the bonds that now bind the Union together." Despite a history of sharp debates between them, Webster's emotional eulogy of Calhoun emphasized the South Carolinian's "patriotism" and "love for Union."[116]

As with individualism, sectionalist sentiment is logically viewed as a vital source of difference and therefore as a key component of disunion. Calhoun saw matters otherwise. Somewhat like Emerson's union of strong individuals, sovereign states retaining significant autonomy could best constitute Calhoun's well-formed union. State authority was guaranteed through the concurrent-majority concept, permitting individual states or sectional coalitions to nullify certain federal laws[117] judged to be unconstitutional. Again, this appears to be a direct challenge to unionist aims. But Calhoun's two sustained excursions into political philosophy (written mainly at the end of his career) each proceed by explaining basic elements of the concurrent majority, including its nullification feature,[118] and

115. Treatments of Calhoun as arch-secessionist include Taylor 1961, vii (Calhoun as "the symbol of southern nationalism"); Current 1987, 144–46; Wills 1999, 165–68; and Lind 1995, 127. For more balanced accounts, see Peterson 1987, 252–64, 334–48, 476–78; Freehling 1990, 266–68, 282–85, 516–19 (Calhoun as "the extremist who had ever sought to save South and Union too); Ericson 1993, 75–87; and Knupfer 1991, 179–80, which traces Calhoun's complex passage from ardent Union supporter to a position, by 1850, when "Calhoun was no longer a unionist of the first fire. He had been sounding the alarm for the Union for the previous twelve years; he had already concluded that the old Union, wholly federal and not at all national, had been subverted by northern aggression against the compact of 1787."

116. *Louisville Courier,* July 9, 1849; Webster's eulogy is from the *National Intelligencer,* April 2, 1850. That his remarks were not empty funeral pieties is affirmed by Calhoun biographer John Niven (1988, 344), on "the depth of Calhoun's allegiance to the Union," recognized "only [by] Webster." A dissenting period view came from Calhoun's onetime comrade Henry Clay, who denounced him as separatist in a March 10, 1838, Senate speech. See Hopkins 1959–92, 9:158–62.

117. Even in his most forceful statement of nullification, his February 1833 Senate speech on the tariff, Calhoun carefully specified the class of federal laws subject to state interposition, powers reserved by the tenth amendment to the states. See Lence 1992, 405–9.

118. Useful summaries of concurrent-majority theory are in Current 1987, 132–35; Ericson 1993, 75–89. Erwin Levine (1972, 13) views "Calhoun's concurrent-majority principle" as "hand-in-hand with the pluralist interpretation of American society by Madison" and places both Madison and Calhoun "in the pragmatic school of American political thought."

then defending the theory as an essential source of national unity. As he wrote early in the *Disquisitions,* "the concurrent majority . . . tends to unite the most opposite and conflicting interests, and to blend the whole in one common attachment to the country." Pure majoritarianism, by contrast, would leave embittered minorities feeling "antipathy" toward one another and toward the whole. Similar rationales for incorporating minority groups in the nation are advanced today, most notably by Lani Guinier.[119]

Why such an emphasis on union in Calhoun's account? His testaments to state sovereignty imply that he included national unity as a sop to critics, an afterthought intended to deflect opposition. Yet union was as central to Calhoun's theory of government and human nature as to the work of any other thinker of the time. The *Disquisitions* begin with an account of "man's social nature," "irresistibly impel[led] to associate with his kind." Calhoun's subsequent defense of concurrent majorities builds on this natural inclination to association, and at several points returns to spell out the doctrine's beneficial effects on unity among American citizens and between their states. His first topic in the *Discourses* is an almost comically lengthy discussion of the precise meaning of "union," as opposed to "nation" or "federation," attacking both the contemporary "general use of the term" and the view set out in certain of the *Federalist Papers.* A typical passage reads: "It could not have been intended, by the expression in the preamble—'to form a more perfect union'—to declare, that the old was abolished, and a new and more perfect union established in its place . . . although it may more strongly intimate closeness of connection, it can imply nothing incompatible with the professed object of perfecting the union—still less a meaning and effect wholly inconsistent with the nature of a confederated community."[120]

Calhoun's numerous constitutional blueprints for securing equal power across states or sections almost always featured national unity as a guiding purpose. His account of a dual executive—one elected by the North, one by southerners—was advertised entirely in terms of "insur[ing] harmony and concord between the two sections, and, through them, the government." This in 1850, with Calhoun dying and no longer active in public life. "The [dual] presidential election," he went on, "would make the Union a union in truth—a bond of mutual affection and brotherhood—and not a mere connection used by the stronger as the instrument of dominion and aggrandizement."[121]

Even read skeptically, Calhoun's aim appears more complicated than a pure

119. Lence 1992, 37 (compare the *Discourse*'s tracing of centralized powers to a "tendency to unite for sectional objects," at pp. 260–61). Among much recent commentary linking Guinier's theory to that of "the South Carolina Machiavelli," see Hench 1998, 786 (quote). Richard Ellis's nuanced treatment of the nullification crisis notes Calhoun's elaborate denials of disunion throughout (Ellis 1987, 64–66).

120. Lence 1992, 5, 86, 98–99. George Fitzhugh, another unlikely southern unionist, similarly began from premises of humans' social nature (creating, in his account, an "inegalitarian . . . organic" society). Fitzhugh 1960 [1857], 12–13. On Fitzhugh's strong opposition to secession, and "dread" of disunion, see Woodward introduction in ibid., xi.

121. Lence 1992, 227.

defense of states' rights or slavery. His occasional references to the disunionist consequences of southern mistreatment seem at least partly strategic, designed to sway moderates against abolitionists and mercantilists. But Calhoun's many positive references to national unity suggest that he also found union a desirable good, for many of the reasons asserted by Webster or, earlier, Madison. Like them, Calhoun lists national security ("So imperious was the necessity of union, and a common government to take charge of their foreign relations, that . . . without it, the States never would have been united. The same necessity still continues to be one of the strongest bonds of their union"); a loyal and engaged citizenry; virtuous leadership; and protection of other values, prominently including liberty. Even in his "nullifying" 1833 Senate statement on the tariff, he concluded with a promise that readjusted rates would "be followed by greater stability, and will tend to harmonize the manufacturing with all the other great interests of the country, and bind the whole in mutual affection." [122]

Moreover, as Calhoun readily acknowledged, southerners benefited from inclusion in a strong national union. Commercial development was promoted through internal-improvement policies in the South as in the rest of the country, provided that tariff policies were altered to benefit rather than harm regional economic interests. His last years in the Senate were primarily spent on securing federal support for South Carolina and the rest of the region, most notably a railroad connecting the South and west. [123]

Calhoun's departure from sustainable-union views concerned not the value of unity but the means to its preservation. Like Madison he advocated a balance of local and national forces, [124] but he set the fulcrum much closer to the former. Calhoun's argument that the states retained considerable "sovereign power" and that "the Union" was a compact among these entities was not dramatically different from Madison or other founders. Indeed, Calhoun identified the "league" under the Articles as an insufficient source of unity, and he defined a "more perfect union" as the necessary alternative to the Confederation. [125]

At the same time, these subtle points of divergence between Calhoun's account and those of leading unionists were not insignificant. While Madison had directly linked union of the states to ties among all their residents, Calhoun more

---

122. Ibid., 143, 397; cf. 42 (on the need for "protection," provided by a unified citizenry, outweighing even the good of liberty), 48 (on necessary "elements of moral power" in a republic, "harmony, unanimity, devotion to country, and a disposition to elevate to places of trust and power, those who are distinguished for wisdom and experience").

123. Ibid., 473. Calhoun's early Senate speeches on the tariff, until the 1828 "Tariff of Abominations" appeared to him to overstep federal authority and unfairly benefit New England merchants, were fervently pro-union: in 1816 he explained that "encouragement of manufactures" was "calculated to bind together more closely our widely spread republic. It will greatly increase our mutual dependence and intercourse" (ibid., 308–9).

124. From Calhoun's *Discourse:* "consolidation and disunion are, equally, destructive of [constitutional] government—one by merging the States composing the Union into one community or nation; and the other, by resolving them into their original elements, as separate and disconnected States." Lence 1992, 102; cf. his related discussion at 138.

125. Ibid., 116, 240–47, 266–69; on the Articles, see ibid., 118.

freely distinguished between the "political union" of states established by the Constitution and a "social union" "composed of individuals united by . . . a social compact." For later thinkers like Lincoln, this analytical separation of the two constituents of union—the states (*e pluribus unum*) and "We, the People"— was a crucially destructive move. But in the 1830s it was not clear whether the whole American people or separate states had originally contracted to form the Constitution; the matter had been argued at length in the Philadelphia convention but was never decisively settled. In Madison's theory, the states through their residents formed the union. This "one people" conception provided legitimacy for John Marshall to uphold federal courts' right to overrule state decisions, an important "nationalist" turn in the early republic. Calhoun's defense of state supremacy in speeches during the tariff controversy (1828–33), boldly claiming Madison himself in support, sent shock waves through American leadership. From retirement at Montpelier, Madison called it "a preposterous and anarchical pretension."[126]

Webster's response, in his two replies to Senator Hayne (Hayne was widely recognized as Calhoun's stand-in in the Senate debate; as vice president, Calhoun was present but silent), was to attack the idea that states as sovereign communities had originated the Constitutional compact. "The people, Sir, erected this government," Webster countered, dressing the point with a "for the people, by the people" phrase that Lincoln would revive some three decades later. American national unity was in no way dependent upon continuously renewed consent by the states, he avowed.[127] Webster's strident response is now sometimes cited to support inevitable-conflict accounts, identifying a clear path to secession dating from sectional quarrels of the late 1820s. By asserting "consolidation" as an acceptable principle and dismissing Calhoun's union of sovereign states, the argument goes, Webster helped destroy any ground of common understanding. But in fact he left ample room for reconciliation, as had Hayne and as would Calhoun over the next two decades. The desirability of national union was the constant theme; disagreement over whether the United States was a collectivity of states or people was carried out, until the late 1850s, fully within a unionist context. As Webster said in his famous reply to Hayne, he sought "no enlarge[d] powers of the [national] government," but would "rejoice in whatever tends to strengthen the bond that unites us, and encourages the hope that our Union may be perpetual."[128]

Implicitly informing Webster's view was a fact that many northerners and moderate southerners preferred to gloss over: that sectional differences grew in

126. McCoy 1989, 132. On the connection between nineteenth-century debates over state and federal sovereignty and similar issues in the present day, see Kaczorowski 1997.

127. Wiltse and Berolzheimer 1986–88, 1:330, 340.

128. Ibid., 1:304; cf. 315–16. Polk similarly told a Maine audience in 1847: "However much we may differ about local or temporary questions of policy, on the question of the Union, we are all united" (Cutler 1986, 48).

vital part from southern slavery. As Herbert Croly later wrote, "what was a good American to do who was at once a convinced democrat (e.g., antislavery) and a loyal Unionist? . . . The thing to do was to shut your eyes to the inconsistency [and] denounce anybody who insisted on it as unpatriotic." Calhoun was not so squeamish, offering some of the most elaborate proslavery arguments among American political thinkers. As he told the Senate in 1837: "Abolition and Union cannot coexist. . . . To maintain the existing relations between the two races, inhabiting that section of the Union [e.g., the South], is indispensable to the peace and happiness of both. It cannot be subverted without drenching the country in blood." Calhoun moved on to self-proclaimed "higher ground" via a description of slavery as a "positive good," given blacks' inferiority and other insuperable differences between the "two races."[129] Unionists throughout the country required none of the latter arguments (though these certainly appealed to those endorsing an ethnocultural sensibility) to accept the thrust of Calhoun's statement. Fear of a blood-drenched, disunited country was inspiration enough for many to minimize their opposition to the "slave power."

In important places, Calhoun's account is inconsistent with unionist ends as Madison or Webster understood them. His proposals for unprecedented institutional safeguards for states' rights, a dual executive, and the like contributed in principle as well as practice to the slow separation of state and national loyalties, as David Ericson has noted. And his insistence on national recognition of slavery's legitimate existence in the South disturbed unionists like Webster, though few moved to oppose Calhoun directly. Most significant, Calhoun's unionism—unlike that of Webster or Jackson, among other national leaders of the day, but resembling Madison's in this regard—had an outer limit. Carey McWilliams puts the point well: "Willing to withdraw from the Union in the last extremity, he [Calhoun] hoped always to preserve it."[130] Ultimately, that Calhoun's vision includes such strong appeals to union, and that his departure from the traditional view of unity primarily concerns the metaphysical basis of sovereignty, suggests the ameliorative effect on sectionalism represented by union sentiment.

Expanding this discussion beyond Calhoun, it is emphatically not the case that national-union sentiment was largely absent in the South, even in the late 1850s.[131] A New Orleans editor remarked during the Missouri crisis that "all Louisianans" were indifferent as to the fate of slavery in Missouri: instead they "are deeply, vitally interested in conserving the union of the states entire." Future president John Tyler, in an 1837 address at Yorktown, Virginia, exhorted his fellow southerners to "exorcise the spirit of sectional feeling. . . . I would point to a common country—a common glory, and a common destiny." As president,

129. Croly 1909, 75; Lence 1992, 472–75.
130. Ericson 1993, 89; McWilliams 1973, 262.
131. For a contrary argument (focused on Georgia) that sectional differences, beginning as early as the nullification crisis, inspired unanimity among white southerners in support of secession, see Carey 1997; compare the works at note 4, particularly Morrison 1997 and Sydnor 1948.

Tyler remained a passionate unionist, and subsequently spoke out against secession as late as 1860. Historian Edward Crapol notes that "at no time in these patriotic flourishes did Tyler betray the slightest concern that the pursuit of national greatness might undermine states' rights and lead to a strong centralized government. . . . Clearly, Tyler was untroubled by this contradiction because he was operating on the Madisonian assumption that the federative system was uniquely able to expand indefinitely across unsettled space without the danger of consolidation."[132]

Farther south, and also well into the 1850s, others praised union in similar terms. George Fitzhugh remained a unionist "until the final hour." Jefferson Davis, of all people, could still proclaim in late 1859 that "Our principles are national; they belong to every State of the Union . . . our principles are written in living light; all proclaiming the constitutional Union, justice, equality, and fraternity of our ocean-bound domain, for a limitless future." Leading Alabama industrialist Daniel Pratt ran his 1855 campaign for the state senate on a platform of internal improvements and national union; even after the war Pratt was remembered as a "Whig of the Henry Clay and Daniel Webster school, [whose] patriotism embraced the Union." Raleigh's largest newspaper, reporting on an unusually "animated and extensive" Fourth of July celebration in 1856, found no "fear for the Union" amid "an outpouring of joy and thanksgiving for the blessings and privileges inaugurated on the 4th of July 1776."[133]

It is certainly plausible that Calhoun and other southerners voicing unionist themes primarily sought to harness the term's power in the service of their slaveholding interests. A self-proclaimed Georgia "unionist," saluting the Compromise of 1850, praised at length the "fruits of national union" but concluded that "should Congress, at any time exhibit its intentions to war upon our [slave] property . . . we stand ready to vindicate those rights in the Union so long as possible, and out of the Union, when we are left no other alternative." Southerners, as Kenneth Stampp has shown, protected their "peculiar institution" by threatening disunion whenever abolitionists attacked.[134] The relative weight of instrumental and genuine union talk is difficult to assess; one associated factor is how separatist-minded these union-praising southerners actually were.

Assertions that the South was a "region that was apart and different from the rest of the nation" are a staple of American political history, and show little sign of abating.[135] Looking at actual rhetoric from the time, Calhoun and other

132. *Orleans Gazette & Commercial Advertiser,* March 17, 1820; Crapol 1997, 474–75.

133. Genovese 1995, 111; Davis in Elazar 1992, 105; Pratt in Evans 1997, 17 (see generally on Pratt's 1855 campaign); *Raleigh Standard,* July 9, 1856. Davis, stoking the Lost Cause myth in 1881, wrote that in 1861, "still striving for peace and union, we waited [to threaten secession] until a sectional President . . . was about to be inducted into office" (1881, 1:84–85).

134. *Georgia Journal & Messenger* (Macon), November 13, 1850; Stampp 1956.

135. Lynn 1960, 53. Anne Norton similarly notes that "the meaning of America, variously conceived [by historians], invariably results in the exclusion of the South" (1986, 3). Norton's own thesis is that North and South featured distinct "national identities," with the South's resultant "alienation from the Union" (esp. 14–15).

southern stalwarts are noteworthy in their defensive account of the South, focusing on northern misunderstanding and maltreatment rather than on a separate southern identity. David Potter's unmatched study of the prewar period concludes that by 1861 a variety of causes had given "to southern society a degree of homogeneity and to southerners a sense of kinship." But, Potter continues, "a sense of kinship is one thing, and an impulse toward political unity is another. If one searches for explicit evidence of efforts to unify the South politically because of cultural homogeneity, common values, and other positive influences, rather than as a common negative response to the North, one finds relatively little of it." Consider also Drew Gilpin Faust's account of the "southern nationalist" movement, which concludes that not until the South actually declared independence in 1861 did "there exist a widespread and self-conscious effort to create an ideology of confederate nationalism to unite and inspire the new nation."[136]

Calhoun's praise of the South, in his congressional speeches and works of political theory alike, usually honored values he saw as distinguishing (white European) Americans from other peoples, not southerners from northerners. Though it was "odious to make comparison" between regions, he admonished the Senate in 1837, he was moved to list worthy personal qualities among southerners as well as "our brethren in other sections of the Union." "I appeal to all sides whether the South is not equal in virtue, intelligence, patriotism, courage, disinterestedness, and all the high qualities which adorn our nature."[137] Reading through newspapers from the 1830s through the 1850s, it is striking how often quotidian news from southern states is reported in northern papers, and vice versa. In little more than a page of one ordinary New Orleans paper, the *Picayune* of April 19, 1837, mention is made of events in New York City (three times); Boston (twice); Claremont, New Hampshire; Baltimore; Newburgh, New York; "the good people of New Haven"; Louisville; and "the rising population of Portland, Maine." That the two sections were increasingly diverging from 1820 on, as historians now insist, is not immediately obvious from a survey of daily expressions of opinion in either. At the time in the South or North, separatist sentiment appeared less frequently than optimistic references to national unity. As the *Picayune* noted later the same year: "We might advert to some unfortunate divisions among [America's] inhabitants . . . but we look above them. It is true they ought not to exist, and should, by harmony of arrangement, be prevented for the future."[138]

Another common strain in the Jacksonian and antebellum years was charges in each section of "disunionist" intentions or actions by some party or parties in the other. Though these statements certainly indicate mutual mistrust, they also

---

136. Potter 1976, 461 (cf. 448–84; Marmor 1988, 234–47; McWilliams 1973, 264–70; and Freehling 1990); Faust 1988, 14 (cf. Boucher 1921; McCardell 1990, esp. 336–38). George Rable argues that southerners, especially after the war began, drew on "the political culture of national unity, with its patriotic appeals and symbols" (Rable 1994, 300).

137. Lence 1992, 473.

138. *The Picayune* (New Orleans), July 6, 1837. On sectional divergence and the "irrepressible conflict," see Wilson 1974 and Morrison 1997.

testify to the continued appeal of union, both as a positive good and a foil. A South Carolina speaker offered a July Fourth toast (in 1849) to "The *Union*. We hope our Northern brethren will not let the family circle be broken to satisfy the wishes of a few jealous abolitionists." On the antislavery side, the devoutly abolitionist *Liberty Standard* warned in 1844 that southern "slaveholding policies . . . unless arrested by the united power of [the] whole country, must result in the dissolution of our Union." Since "the origin of our national history," a New York editor insisted in 1856, "The North has been steadily loyal and devoted to the Union, while every formidable opposition to it has derived its impulse and power from the South." And so forth. At times, reading the charges and countercharges, it can appear that the idea of union itself was the only force holding the country together. Other antidotes to sectionalism existed as well, however.[139]

While antebellum politics was a staging ground for fierce partisan contests, parties were also an important source of American unity. At least until the mid-1850s, national political parties served as cross-cutting cleavages diminishing sectional differences. Common ground between southern and northern Democrats or Whigs could sometimes seem sparse, but election season (and in the nineteenth century it was nearly always election season somewhere in the United States) usually dissolved regional differences in a flurry of partisan activity. James Morone affirms this point about parties and unity in his *Democratic Wish:* "The contending factions of a heterogeneous nation were united through their participation in the party processes."[140]

Partisanship was also a threat to national unity, of course. Independence Day rituals, for example, sometimes split into separate celebrations by the two major parties. But a prominent feature of antebellum national parties blunted such separatism. As Tocqueville memorably described, American parties of the time tended to agree on "the most essential points," leading to "consensus" on major issues. A central source of this agreement was partisans' avid unionist rhetoric. The preceding chapter depicted local political leaders' emphasis on national unity, even while promoting their party's cause at the expense of the other. This tendency remained a prominent feature of antebellum politics. Every president from Jackson to Lincoln "mention[ed] sectional and party divisions as threats to national unity" in their inaugural addresses, David Ericson notes, but "they almost always do so only to discount the nature of those threats." All the major parties after 1820 idealized union and listed its preservation and "perfection" as a leading programmatic aim. As Henry Adams wrote, looking back on the prewar period in his magisterial history: "The Union and the Fathers belonged to

---

139. *Charleston Courier* (S.C.), July 9, 1849; *Liberty Standard* (Hallowell, Maine), January 4, 1844; *New York Tribune*, October 9, 1856.

140. Morone 1990, 85; cf. Holt 1978, 138 ("Between the late 1820s and early 1850s . . . as long as men had placed loyalty to their own party and defeat of the opposing party within their own section ahead of sectional loyalty, neither the North nor the South could be united into a phalanx against each other"); and Silbey 1991, 130–40.

no party, and might be used with equal advantage by orators of every section."
Whigs were most closely associated with national unity, partly because of Webster's oratory but also given their activist view of the federal government's role in
promoting it. Among Democrats as well, party spirit was closely tied to "sentiment for the Union," as Jean Baker describes. Even if the shared purposes promoted through party activity were limited to winning elections, they were a real
means of overcoming sectional antagonism and raising Americans' consciousness of national unity.[141]

Common to both Calhoun and Emerson was a conviction that national union
could be enhanced by attention to the separate constituents—states and individuals, respectively—of the whole. State, regional, and national identity were often in conflict, for individuals and collectivities alike, and these differences were
powerful throughout the antebellum period. That they ended in civil war may be
taken as the last word on the subject. But thirty-three years passed between Calhoun's initial nullification statement and the first shots on Fort Sumter, a period
featuring a series of major compromises and other efforts to minimize or overcome differences. Sectional differences could be sources of creative tension as
well as of undying enmity.

Though their audiences, argumentative styles, and political outlook on many
issues were all quite distinct, Emerson and Calhoun display similar accounts of
union in important respects—again, while both were promoting ostensibly fragmentary doctrines. Each suggested that through diverse interests, pursuits, and
ideas the citizenry might achieve more unified well-being. Such "commonality"
may appear to conflate vastly divergent conceptions under the very loose rubric
of a shared vocabulary term. But both defined union along roughly Madisonian
lines, as already outlined; for both, attention to rightly constituted parts was essential to unifying the nation. Each thinker also portrayed union as a desirable
rationale, one end toward which self-reliant individuals (Emerson) or sovereign
states (Calhoun) were advancing. A Democratic Party circular from the 1830s
pithily summarizes the antebellum tendency to connect these doctrines to national unity, praising "the freedom of the individual in the social union, [and] the
freedom of the State in the Federative Union."[142]

Only when specifically contrasting the two thinkers' ideas about how union
might arise from diverse elements is a meaningful theoretical divergence apparent. Calhoun drew on an argument still familiar today, one more commonly
associated with Adam Smith than with antebellum Americans. In a polity as
in a factory, differentiation among regions or individuals produces increased exchange, yielding greater total output and joining separate parts more closely in

---

141. de Tocqueville 1969 [1835–40], 175; Ericson 1997, 732; Adams 1930, 5:191; Baker 1983, 317–27.
For a strong argument that Whigs (and, later, Republicans) were consistently nationalist and statist,
in contrast with local-minded Democrats, see Gerring 1998.

142. Cited in E. Foner 1998, 54.

the name of socioeconomic efficiency. Calhoun's treatment of tariff questions, for example, follows this division of labor reasoning.[143] Emerson's understanding of how political diversity could inspire closer unity derives instead from what a modern commentator calls "agonistic respect" among differentiated parts. At least in smaller, everyday matters of governance, conflict might be a basis for, rather than an obstacle to, political unity. Differing ideals, defended stoutly, could inspire mutual respect among citizens (Calhoun and Webster, for example), breeding in turn the virtuous friendship essential to ruling—and being ruled—well. This view would later be expressed by Abraham Lincoln as well, as explored in subsequent chapters.[144]

"The Union is no longer desirable"

Between Jackson's election in 1828 and the heated aftermath of the Compromise of 1850, amid a succession of crises over nullification and slavery, Americans' commitment to national unity demonstrated remarkable endurance. Prevailing ideas of union were decidedly altered, taking on unconditional and, in some quarters, ethnocultural tones. In contrast to Madison and other founders' conception, political elites were no longer viewed as the principal agents of unity, and underlying principles of restraint, balance, and affective ties were considerably frayed. But the effects of antebellum turbulence on a unionist persuasion were less telling than the tendency of that persuasion, expressed in all corners of the republic, to alleviate the myriad centrifugal forces at work in the United States.

After 1850 that tendency could seem spent, as the concept's correspondence to institutional or political reality appeared in decline. Flights of unionist fancy verged on the untenable: expostulated one Boston writer, "upon that Union, which makes us one people, hangs our prosperity and our importance abroad; and, more than we are accustomed to think, the progress of the age. And not interest alone, but the eternal order of things would seem to bind us in Union."[145] Extraordinary benefits were claimed in union's name, and an endless array of policies defended as vital to its preservation, from the Fugitive Slave Law to a uniform commercial code.[146] This sprawl bore little resemblance to the restrained,

143. Lence 1992, 50, 233–36. Compare Calhoun's 1846 Senate speech on the Oregon Question, reprinted in the *Southern Banner* (Athens, Ga.), April 7, 1846.

144. Connolly 1993, 153. Emerson's account is in, inter alia, Emerson 1903–4, 4:39–48; 11:135–41. On Calhoun and Webster, see, e.g., the sharp but respectful Senate exchanges between the two on the subtreasury bill in 1838, *Cong. Globe*, 25th Cong., 2d sess., Appendix 1838, 243–50, 632–41. Calhoun said that "there never has been, between the senator (Webster) and myself, the least personal difference . . . which, considering how often we have stood opposed on deep and exciting questions, may be regarded as not a little remarkable" (243).

145. *Boston Post*, May 16, 1861.

146. Webster in 1838 declared a code of uniform commercial regulation "in my opinion, indispensable to the safety of the union of the states . . . [without it] our union can hereafter be nothing, while it remains, but a connection without harmony, a bond without affection; a theatre for the angry contests of local feelings, local objects, and local jealousies." Wiltse and Berolzheimer 1986–88, 2:282–83.

balanced account of union advanced by Madison, or to any consistent theory whatsoever. Webster implicitly admitted as much: "Instead of groping with those [secessionist] ideas so full of all that is horrid and horrible, let us come out into the light of day; let us enjoy the fresh air of Liberty and Union."[147]

The compromises underpinning union were becoming, by 1850, less palatable to ardent abolitionists in the North and proslavery diehards in the South. Balancing acts by national leaders, like Franklin Pierce's tortured "integrity of the Union" speech on New Year's Eve, 1855, met with increasing scorn from members of the radical wing on both sides. Thus the concept's appeal began to erode. Looking back in 1872 on the immediate prewar period, Radical Republican historian Henry Wilson wrote: "Many, indeed, under the pleas of fraternity and loyalty to the Union, palliated and apologized . . . but the numbers were increasing every hour, as the struggle progressed, who could no longer be deceived by these hollow pretenses."[148] In 1850, Frederick Douglass charged that for Webster and fellow Whigs "UNION is above all earthly blessings; and to save it, they are willing to sacrifice liberty, justice, and all manly independence."[149] The same year, the Fugitive Slave Law's reaffirmation by Congress proved to be Emerson's personal Rubicon:

Nothing seems to me more bitterly futile than this bluster about the Union. A year ago we were all lovers & prizers of it. Before the passage of that law . . . we indulged in all the dreams which foreign nations still cherish of American destiny . . . [now] frankly once for all the Union is sunk, the flag is hateful, & will be hissed. . . . The Union! o yes, I prized that, other things being equal; but what is the Union to a man self condemned. . . . It [seemed] incredible that even the passage of the Law would make the Union odious, but . . . the Union is no longer desirable.

Emerson's vitriol continues for eighty-six manuscript pages, concluding: "As soon as the Constitution enacts a criminal law, disunion already exists." Throughout Emerson refers not only to the "rhetoricians' Union" for which he had always reserved scorn but also to his idealized "Union, a delectable thing . . . the destiny of America."[150] Exacerbating his sourness was the Fugitive Slave Law's support from Webster, whom Emerson had previously upheld as the avatar of his self-sufficient unionist. Now "all Webster's 'Union' talk was merely rhetoric and ju-

147. Wiltse and Berolzheimer 1986–88, 2.550. Cf. 484: "I am not going into metaphysics, for there . . . we should find 'no end, in wandering mazes lost,' until after the time for the adjournment of Congress."

148. Wilson 1872, 2:406; *Salem Register* (Mass.), January 3, 1856, which reprinted most of Pierce's speech and then denounced it at length. Still smoldering days later, the editor sneered "we trust that the next President will be man enough to deal with [southern proslavery] Disunionists" and called for "a politician of the Madisonian and old Constitution stamp."

149. Blassingame 1979–94, 2:258.

150. Gilman 1960–82, 11:348–49; cf. "The Fugitive Slave Law," Emerson 1903–4, 11:206–9; Gilman 1960–82, 11:410, 360–63.

venile enthusiasm, sentimentalism. . . . In Concord in 1776 he would without question have been a refugee."[151]

Webster's efforts to preserve the territorial Union and with it a spirit of national unity, which contemporaries like Edward Everett saw as the key to "national gratitude" and consequently the presidency,[152] appeared insufficient to many after 1850. Others retrospectively find them venal. Charles Sellers suggests that Webster utilized the concept principally to serve the New England capitalists to whom his political career literally was indebted. The "rhetorical defense of the nationalist union," he writes, was mounted by Webster as "hired gun of wealth and power."[153] Sellers's own historiographical interests are apparent here: his rehabilitation of Jacksonian Democrats as progressive populists requires a Manichean portrait of Webster and other Whigs as uncontrolled, rapacious capitalists. Doubtless Webster's applications of union talk were instrumentally inspired in places. But the intersections he drew between national union, political stability, industrial advancement, and property rights, along with other personal liberties, were too complex to single out a particular end as preeminent. Moreover, Webster's union talk suggested further inclusive purposes.

Webster, along with other unionist Whigs like Clay, Seward, and Horace Greeley, generally opposed nativist policies, citing their deleterious effects on Americans' affective spirit. He rejected anti-immigration platforms despite their electoral appeal in mid-1840s Boston, instead declaiming "all we desire, whoever come, is that they will Americanize themselves; that forgetting the things that are behind, they will look forward [and] . . . prove themselves worthy and respectable citizens." (As Daniel Walker Howe observes, this assimilationist ethic of forgetting was at odds with the customary Whig fealty to history.) In a move equally unpopular among his banker backers, Webster opposed Massachusetts's attempt to collect an "importation tax" on immigrants, insisting on federal precedence and "the loyalty of [Massachusetts] to the Government of the Union."[154] Whig resistance to nativism and racism was far from bedrock, as some found electoral and perhaps personal appeal in ascriptive themes.[155] But Webster's and other leaders' expansive defenses of union aroused hope in unexpected quarters. Surprisingly, black Americans also found promise in the term.

151. Emerson's bitter description is at Gilman 1960–82, 11:405–6. Other famous denunciations came from John Greenleaf Whittier, whose poem "Ichabod" depicted Webster as a fallen angel; and Theodore Parker, for whom "the Anglo-Saxon race never knew such a calamitous ruin [as Webster's]. . . . His downfall shook the continent. Truth fell prostrate in the street." Quoted in Shewmaker 1990, 78. An earlier critic was John Quincy Adams: see Hessler 1998, 198.

152. Wiltse et al. 1974–86, 7:244, 148.

153. Sellers 1991, 102; contrast Peterson 1987, 37–38, 155–56, 266–67; Remini 1997, 603–18.

154. Current 1990, 3; Howe 1979, 202–3; *Alien State Tax Case,* in Shewmaker 1990, 197–202.

155. On Whigs' mixed ascriptive commitments, see Howe 1979, 17–18, 85, 112, 201–4, 248–55, and Smith 1997, 206–12.

CHAPTER 4

Conceiving a More
Moral Union, 1850s–1865

Can the white and colored people of this country be blended into a common nationality, and enjoy together, in the same Union, under the same flag, the inestimable blessings of life, liberty, and the pursuit of happiness, as neighborly citizens of a common country? I answer most unhesitatingly, I believe they can.

—Frederick Douglass, "The Present and Future
of the Colored Race in America," 1863

THE 1850S APPEAR IN RETROSPECT as a time of unremitting crisis in the United States, with clashes over the Compromise of 1850 and the Kansas-Nebraska Act of 1854, rising references among northerners to the potent "Slave Power," and the turmoil of 1857—*Dred Scott* and the "Lecompton constitution" struggles over admitting Kansas as a state—all pointing inexorably to civil war. Yet islands of calm periodically soothed the national mood. In early 1851, a long San Francisco newspaper article analyzed the "actual possibilities of disunion," concluding that "upon the whole we cannot see that any very imminent peril threatens the Union . . . the country and its institutions have a fair chance of much longer continuance as a united people than some are ready to allow." For much of 1858–59, political discourse was less concerned with impending schism than with celebrating restored harmony. In a fairly typical issue of a Kentucky newspaper, one correspondent saluted the "peace and quiet [now] prevailing in the country," and an editorial urged readers to attend a "most excellent" local "programme" featuring "a new national song, called 'The Union Forever,' [that] has been written especially for the occasion." Even in the deep South, views were similar: "the perpetuity and destiny of our sacred Union find their conclusive proof and illustration in the bosom of nature," wrote a Mississippian in an 1858 *DeBow's Review*. "The political storms that periodically rage are but the clouds and sunshine that give variety to the atmosphere . . . [Americans] move harmoniously on to plant a hundred States and consummate their civic greatness." Historian Ludwell Johnson concurs with these snapshot judgments, describing even southerners after 1857 as relatively complacent:

Excitement over Kansas had disappeared. Territorial slavery was now an abstraction only tenuously connected with the real world. However important the contestants, the debates between [Stephen] Douglas and the Southern rights champions aroused little public interest. Times were good. The cotton crop of 1858 was the second largest in history. . . . In short, the section's healthy and dynamic economy helped to counterbalance the anxiety aroused by the slave controversy. The South had lived with the latter for some time now and still had prospered. A conservative mood prevailed.

John Brown's October 1859 raid on Harper's Ferry, and his support in the North afterward, largely ended this "mood." But it is important to underscore that calm here, especially given our latter-day inclination to view the entire period from 1850 to 1861 as a prelude to civil war.[1]

Examining public discourse during the late antebellum years, most in evidence is not a dissolution of national sentiment in either North or South but a divergence in union pronouncements. Ethnocultural claims (gaining force during the early 1850s, especially as the Know-Nothing movement peaked in 1854) inspired in response a "growing sentiment," as one historian describes, "that mere survival of the United States did not constitute a patriotism lofty enough to command respect."[2] The association of union with principled ends—here termed "moral union"—by the late 1850s constituted a third major understanding of the term, alongside the ethnocultural and sustainable versions outlined in earlier chapters. Rhetorical conflicts before 1861 over "union vs. disunion" were often specifically about whether national unity would be sustained at all costs or invested with more principled (usually antislavery) meaning, even at the risk of losing some constituent parts.[3]

This chapter sketches the development of a moral unionism in the United States, focusing primarily on the years 1850 to 1865. I first trace the rise of a principled account of national unity among antebellum African Americans. After examining blacks' general patterns of union usage during the period, I focus in the second section on a representative figure, Frederick Douglass. Beginning from a disunionist position, Douglass moved toward a strong (if qualified) endorsement

1. *Alta Californian* (San Francisco), January 15, 1851; *Louisville Courier* (Ky.), January 20, 1858; Gilpin 1858, 164–65; L. H. Johnson 1978, 56–57. Historians' tendency to "ignore" quieter years like 1853 "in their rush to get to the more exciting events of 1854" is noted in Holt 1978, 137. Freehling (1990) provides the most persuasive argument that a "road to disunion" stretched back well before 1860: see esp. his summary remarks at pp. 449–52 and 473–74. I sidestep here the long controversy over whether the war was "inevitable," tracing instead the continued prevalence of unionist sentiment—in all sections—until 1861.

2. Moorhead 1978, 15.

3. The risk of disunion was frequently downplayed, perhaps most often by northern abolitionists seeking to call proslavery southerners' bluff. Carl Schurz, the Wisconsin abolitionist and Senator, in an October 1860 speech loftily dismissed "arguments of the opponents of the Republicans that we are endangering the perpetuity of the Union." Schurz related a comic sketch, portraying a group of southern medical students in Pennsylvania "stampeding" back South in winter 1859 and then returning "quietly this fall to the boarding-houses and washer-women of Philadelphia." To laughter and applause, Schurz concluded, "Thus ended one great attempt at the dissolution of the Union." *Daily Advertiser* (Galena, Ill.), October 20, 1860.

of a reformed national union—as a basis for ending slavery and eventually including blacks as full-fledged members.

The third section takes up Abraham Lincoln's complex view of union. Lincoln promoted a principled unionist doctrine but stopped short of endorsing inclusion of blacks until late in the Civil War. His account exemplified no few white northerners' conviction after 1850 that a unified polity was no end in itself, but a means to securing moral values—though these were sometimes vaguely defined. Both Douglass and Lincoln were critical of the ethnocultural and unconditional currents of late-antebellum union talk, but rather than dismiss the underlying notion each labored to reform the ideal. The results of their and others' efforts are assessed in a fourth section, on union references during wartime. After Fort Sumter the divergent strands of 1850s union thought were collected into a single, concentrated vision of union's redemption through war.

AFRICAN AMERICANS AND ANTEBELLUM UNION

Free blacks[4] employed the power of words—often the principal power they had—to declare themselves united, in two primary respects. First, some African Americans termed their own interrelations a union, in an early example of "black nationalism" in the United States. Blacks' efforts to carve out a separate union, like southerners' later attempts to do the same, mark an important turn in the concept's history. Previous concepts of political union had encompassed the whole national sphere. Union usage among some free blacks in the antebellum period prefigured the concept's eventual transformation, as traced in chapter 6, into a referent for multiple smaller-scale collectivities organized along class, ethnic, occupational, and regional lines.

Amid these scattered efforts toward separatist unity, many other African Americans expressed a commitment to full participation in the national union. This group evidently saw the idea of union among all Americans as meliorist, ultimately implying full black membership in the polity. Their insistence on blacks' legitimate place in the national whole responded directly to ethnocultural claims about the racial boundaries of unity. African Americans' cautious celebration of union's inclusive implications was one of the strongest moral interpretations of a "more perfect" union conceived during the prewar period. This understanding, advanced by Frederick Douglass along with some white abolitionists, represents a third major conception of national union.

4. And, possibly, enslaved ones: evidence is sketchy, with even the best accounts of slave culture, like Sterling Stuckey's (1987, esp. 3–97), only occasionally able to reconstruct records of slaves' speech. The "slave reminiscences" conducted in the 1920s and 1930s are unreliable records of common speech during the slavocracy's reign. Most of those testifying were slaves relatively briefly and had been exposed in Reconstruction and its aftermath to black and white speakers whom the typical slave would never have encountered. As Frederick Douglass wrote, "there comes no *voice* from the enslaved. We are left to gather his feelings by imagining what ours would be" (Blassingame 1979–94, 2:337).

The opening section analyzes blacks' union references, drawing on leading African-American and abolitionist periodicals, including *The Colored American, The Liberator, The North Star,* and *Freedom's Journal;* the writings of Frederick Douglass, the most eloquent advocate for black rights between the 1830s and 1860s; and records from a series of state and national Negro Conventions and like gatherings from the 1820s onward.[5] After detailing blacks' positive applications of the concept I explore the probable basis for such usage.

Separatists and Integrationists: "Dissolution is not a solution"

Though fraternal sentiment among American blacks was originally affirmed in terms like "society" or "association," by the 1820s union references appeared in official petitions, contributions to abolitionist presses, and personal letters. This development recalls the term's evolution among white British Americans during colonial times. Facing a larger, hostile paternalist power that referred to its own interrelations as a Union, blacks—like American colonists decades before—first utilized the term as a call to resistance and then proposed a Plan of Union, at a national convention.[6] Among antebellum black separatists as for colonial American spokesmen, union described a good devoutly sought yet distressingly distant. Some advocated a separate, unified "nation within a nation," as Martin Delany urged in 1852; this early variant of a black-nationalist theme would reappear in varying guises for decades thereafter.[7]

As white racism became more virulent around 1820,[8] African Americans increasingly urged their own cohesion. David Walker in his fiery "Appeal" warned fellow blacks in 1829 that remaining "dis-united, as the colored people are now," was "the reason our natural enemies are enabled to keep their feet on our throats." At the first Negro National Convention a year later, delegates formally "rejoiced," with a sidelong glance at national unity, "that the bond of brotherhood, which rivets a nation together in one indissoluble chain, has collected so large a portion of *our* people together."[9] Similar calls were heard at most subsequent gatherings of free blacks. "We want *union* and *action,*" demanded an assembly of the "Colored Freemen of Long Island" in 1841. Michigan's statewide Negro Convention resolved the same year that "the time has come for us to be united in sentiment and action." African Americans in Philadelphia warned against "fractional effort"

5. "The history of the Negro Conventions from 1830 to 1861 is, in many respects, a history of the thought—as well as the action—of what was even then America's greatest racial minority" (Bell 1969, 2).

6. The proposal was for a "Union of the Colored People of the Free States" organized through the "National Council of the Colored People." Like Franklin's Albany Plan, it won delegates' approval, in this case at the Rochester National Negro Convention in 1853. *Proceedings of the Colored National Convention at Rochester* (1853), 4–14.

7. Delany 1969, 209, and cf. 12–14. On pre-1860s expressions of "national" African-American unity, see Pease and Pease 1974, 251–77; Bruce 1995; Moses 1978, 26–27, 32–47; and Stuckey 1987, 172–73, 183–90.

8. See esp. Nash 1988; cf. Thomas 1996, chap. 5; and Pease and Pease 1974, 18, 22–23.

9. Walker 1995 [1829], 20; *Anglo-African* (New York), October 1859, 4. On Walker's "Appeal" and black unity, see generally Hinks 1997, and Stuckey 1987, 98–137.

and urged "union, peace, order and tranquillity" as "the strength and spirit of our future prosperity." Especially outspoken in this vein was Samuel Cornish, whose newspaper *The Colored American* was replete with insistences that blacks' joint activities "must be inscribed all over with this motto, Union, Union, Union!"[10]

Slavery was a primary spur to fraternal declarations among free blacks. All upheavals surrounding the institution, from abolitionist Elijah Lovejoy's 1837 lynching ("the blood of the martyred Lovejoy calls upon us an oppressed people, to become more united in sentiment and effort") to the Fugitive Slave Act ("recent events . . . call trumpet-tongued for our union"), were met with urgent appeals for African-American unity. Frederick Douglass, dedicating the inaugural issue of his *North Star* to the bondsmen, wrote: "What you endure, we endure. We are indissolubly united, and must fall or flourish together."[11] Many free blacks emphasizing these ties bitterly invoked a shared slave past, either their own or that of siblings or parents.

Testimony from escaped slaves suggests a similar black-unionist spirit. Douglass wrote in his *Life* that "it is my opinion that thousands would escape from slavery, who now remain, but for the strong cords of affection that bind them to their friends." Though fraternal and familial bonds were purposefully broken by masters, rendering slave communities an "agglomeration of atoms" in W. E. B. Du Bois's phrase, one consistent source of mutuality was religion. Here again the colonial American context is analogous, as Christian rituals (modified, in some cases, by African spiritual practices) provided both a basis for and a language of union. Slaves' Sunday night prayer meetings, for example, conferred "strength derived from direct communion with God and with each other. . . . But above all, the meetings provided a sense of autonomy—of constituting not merely a community unto themselves but a community with leaders of their own choice." Du Bois chronicled a "religious frenzy" among slaves, concluding in Emersonian fashion that worship brought "the slaves together in a special kind of communion, which brought out the most individual expressions and yet disciplined the collective."[12]

Free African Americans similarly found shared social purposes in religious gatherings, but with a strong political dimension prohibited among slaves. Black unionism was rooted in religious universalism—the shared "union in Christ" that had been a leading source of colonists' imagined connections before the revolution. In black ministers' political pronouncements in sermons and in the frequent religious references in free blacks' policy tracts, a shifting outlook is apparent over time. In the early years of the nineteenth century African Americans

---

10. *Liberator* (Boston), November 26, 1841; Aptheker 1962, 233; *Hazard's Register* (Philadelphia) 9 (March 16, 1833): 186; *Colored American,* April 1, 1837. Cf. *Freedom's Journal* (New York), December 19, 1828.
    11. *Liberator,* December 29, 1837; *Proceedings of the Colored National Convention at Rochester* (1853), 2; *Freedom's Journal,* March 16, 1827; *North Star* (Rochester, N.Y.), December 3, 1847.
    12. Douglass 1968 [1845], 58; Du Bois 1970 [1909], 49; Genovese 1975; 238; Du Bois at ibid. Cf. Fogel 1989, 173–75; Stuckey 1987, 30–33, 83–97; Franklin 1992, 34–67.

favored theological avowals of universality, as in Benjamin Banneker's comment to Jefferson in 1791: "one universal Father hath . . . not only made us all [black and white] of one flesh, he hath also, without partiality, afforded us all the same sensations and endowed us all with the same faculties . . . however diversified [we are] in situation or color, we are all in the same family and stand in the same relation to him." Other blacks at the time echoed masters' religion: "Slaves should . . . bear their worldly condition for the glory of God, obeying their masters with fear and trembling, in a singleness of your heart, as unto Christ." [13]

During the 1820s, and especially after Nat Turner's rebellion in 1831, black nationalists struck a more militant, chiliastic tone. Typical was Peter Osborne's "with the Declaration of Independence in one hand and the Holy Bible in the other, I think we might courageously give battle to [slavery]." A benevolent God who counseled patience and universal fellowship in the face of earthly oppressions was, if not precisely dismissed, expanded to include a more vengeful deity who would exact due payment. "Some may ask," David Walker wrote in his *Appeal*, "what is the matter with this united and happy people [of white America]? . . . But has not the Lord an oppressed and suffering people among them? . . . Will he let the oppressors rest comfortably and happy always?" In the 1840s, Henry Highland Garnet, Maria Stewart, and other black biblical exegetes alarmed slavery's southern supporters, many of whom had painstakingly worked out a Christian theology sanctioning slavery, by exhorting the bondsmen: "Neither God, nor angels, nor just men, command you to suffer for a single moment. Therefore it is your solemn and imperative duty to *unite* and use every means . . . that promises success." [14]

The declarations by Walker, Garnet, and other advocates of a "union apart" did not nullify most blacks' inclination to view a more general union of all Americans in a positive light. As figure 4 indicates, blacks employed national-union references at a steady clip throughout the antebellum years. Depicted here, as in earlier chapters, are union references per page of newspapers surveyed, along with supplementary sources described in the appendix. I began in 1838, rather than 1800 (or 1776), because of the difficulty in locating an adequate sample of black-owned newspapers and other written records for earlier years.

Blacks' antebellum references to American national unity were usually phrased without irony or reproach. Few African Americans favored the sarcastic wordplays of white abolitionists like Fanny Kemble, whose excoriations of "this Union of profligacy and cruelty" [15] were characteristic of many in the movement, including Garrison himself ("No Union with Slaveholders," urged *The Liberator*'s mast-

13. Boyd et al. 1950–, Sec. of State Series, 1:141; Davis 1975, 43; cf. generally 41–44. See also Garrison's comment: "there is power enough in the [Christian] religion . . . to unite in fellowship the most hostile, and to equalize and bless all its recipients" (1832, 154).

14. Osborne in *Liberator*, December 1, 1832; Walker 1995 [1829], 3; Garnet 1865, 47 (emphasis added). Stewart in Richardson 1987, 39, 65–74. On antebellum black nationalism generally, see Adeleke 1998.

15. Quoted in Genovese 1975, 96.

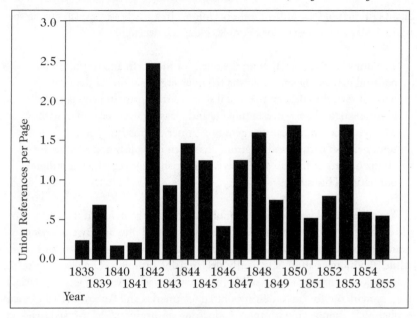

FIGURE 4. African Americans' union references, 1838–55

head for most of the journal's existence). Instead, even such eloquent antislavery black leaders as Frederick Douglass applied the term in mostly positive ways. Among most black Americans, even in the face of such brutal rebuttals as the *Dred Scott* decision, ideas of national union appear to have been at least a partial source of inspiration. Perhaps some free blacks considered their inclusion in "the Union" so implausible as to be an unrewarding target of satire. Many others, cognizant of this virtue's place in the pantheon of antebellum American values, were inclined to appeal to it, as with liberty and equality. For a detailed accounting of this salutary usage, consider the writings and speeches of Frederick Douglass, a fearless ridiculer of empty rhetoric.

DOUGLASS AND A MORE MORAL UNION

Douglass is taken as exemplary here given his prominence among free blacks and his "legendary popularity" among many northern whites.[16] After his escape from slavery he initially took a stridently disunionist line. In the spirit of Garrison's trademark "No Union with Slaveholders," Douglass initially offered tren-

16. Stephens 1997, 175–76 (also noting that "Douglass sp[oke] to ecstatic, overflow multiracial audiences almost wherever he went, [and] the mainstream press of his day also took his influence far beyond abolitionist circles"). On Douglass as "Representative Man" among African Americans, see Blight 1989, xii.

chant critiques of "the present unholy Union." In a Rochester speech during the fugitive-slave controversy, for example, Douglass declared:

> The union of the government; the union of the north and south, in the political parties; the union, in the religious organizations of the land, have all served to deaden the moral sense of the northern people, and to impregnate them with sentiments and ideas for ever in conflict with what, as a nation, we call the genius of American institutions. . . . [T]his sentiment, so natural and so strong, has been impiously appealed to, by all the powers of human selfishness, to cherish the viper which is stinging our national life away.[17]

Yet after several years of such admonitions ("It is the union of the white people of this country," he said in 1848), Douglass around 1850 underwent what contemporaries called a "radical change of mind."[18] Even as Garrison and other white abolitionists more adamantly declared for disunion, Douglass began to voice unionist themes, at first subtly (in an 1850 speech: "All the facts in [blacks'] history mark out for [us] a destiny, united to America and Americans") and then explicitly. "I cannot go with the . . . doctrine of disunion," he avowed, back at Rochester in 1855; two years later he said "the dissolution of the Union is the worst step that could be taken. I have no idea of surrendering so easily" and quoted, to stirring effect, a popular Methodist hymn:

> Oh, we have been wid ye,
> and we still is wid ye,
> and we will go wid ye *to the end*.[19]

After 1850 Douglass spoke frequently of topics like "the loyalty and patriotism of *all* [the nation's] people" and insisted that the "friendship and affection of her black sons and daughters . . . will be an element of strength to the Republic too obvious to be neglected and repelled." While also heralding blacks' "becoming a nation, in the midst of a nation which disowns them, and for weal or woe this [black] nation is united," he denounced "one of the faults of the colored race— their clannishness [and] their desire to live together." Both inter- and intra-racial

---

17. Blassingame 1979–94, 2:268–70, and cf. 95, 221–35, 252, 258, 295; his powerful speech to New England's leading abolitionist society, reprinted in *National Anti-Slavery Standard,* July 25, 1844, 30; and the "Parody" at the end of his autobiography, on "heavenly union" (Douglass 1968 [1845], 124–26). Douglass's anti-union sentiment before 1845 is well treated in Lampe 1998.

18. Blassingame 1979–94, 2:222, 350n. 17. Douglass himself, commenting in 1860 on his reversal, said "when I was a child, I spake as a child." Ibid., 3:365. See also the brief contrast of Douglass and black nationalists like Garvey in M. Ellis 1993, 714–17.

19. Blassingame 1979–94, 2:524; 3:162. Douglass explained why "I cannot go with the American Anti-Slavery Society in its doctrine of disunion" in a long 1855 address at Rochester (ibid., 3:40–43). He reiterated the point in *Frederick Douglass's Newspaper* later that year (August 31, 1855).

unity were desirable, he concluded, apparently seeing nothing mutually exclusive in the two positions.[20]

Even Douglass's most searing critique of the antebellum republic, his "What to the Slave is the Fourth of July?" speech in 1852, concludes on a more positive note than is generally remembered. "I do not despair of this country," he declared. "There are forces in operation, which must inevitably work the downfall of slavery." Douglass did not enumerate these "forces" in any detail, but given his other pronouncements of the time, it is plausible that blacks' inclusion in the political union, and possibly closer social unity between blacks and whites, were prominent examples. In this vein Douglass ended his speech with a well-known biblical passage: "of one blood, God made all nations of men to dwell on the face of the earth." Douglass elsewhere repeatedly pressed the view during the 1850s and 1860s that a multiracial Union, constructed "without regard to color, class, or clime," was a worthier goal than black emigration or "colonization," as even sympathetic whites were promoting. "We shall never leave you," he said in Boston during the war. "In the very extreme difference of colors and features of the negro and the Anglo-Saxon shall be learned . . . the fullness and perfection of human brotherhood."[21]

Douglass's purpose appears not to have been principally strategic, aimed at pleasing a white northern populace overwhelmingly attuned to unionist ideas. For he advocated pan-American unity before black audiences as well, and typically enjoyed a favorable reception. In 1857 Douglass defended the Union as "antislavery" in a two-day debate in New York City before a crowd evenly divided between black and white. His opponent, black abolitionist Charles Lenox Remond, observed wryly of his disunionist position that "no one here appears to agree with it" and failed to appear for most of the second day's contest.[22] Douglass's popular overseas tours, before fervently antislavery audiences, featured similar proclamations. In Glasgow, Scotland, in 1860, Douglass said "Union is named as one of the objects for which the constitution was formed, and it is one that is very excellent; it is quite incompatible with slavery." The following year, with war all but formally declared, Douglass sounded practically Websterian:

> All natural relations conspire to make the United States one country, under one government, and one general code of laws. Nature seems to have frowned upon separation, and welded the sections together so strongly as

20. Blassingame 1979–94, 3:577 (cf. 2:427, 452–54); 2:477–78. On Douglass's "multiracial abolitionism," see Stephens 1997, 176–77, and Moses 1978, 83–86. A harsher portrait of Douglass as "like a man trapped between races" is in Freehling 1990, 89–90.

21. Foner 1950, 2:203 (from Acts 17:26); 3:508. Douglass's opposition to Delany and others' plans for emigration is chronicled in Boxill 1999, 29–44; Stuckey 1987, 222–26; and Franklin 1992, 99–102.

22. Blassingame 1979–94, 3:151–62. The roots of Remond's "argument against the Union" are traced in Bacon 1998, 64–65.

to defy permanent separation to the people who inhabit it. To the mighty rivers and fertile fields that bind it together, civilization, commerce and science have flung over it a net-work of iron, making the sections one and indivisible. . . . Dissolution is not a solution of our present troubles.[23]

What inspired a clear-eyed strategist like Douglass to affirm the value of national unity in a republic so hostile or indifferent to his antislavery aims? Douglass's shift away from disunion is passed off in some accounts as the consequence of his 1847 break with Garrison.[24] But his valorizing such an ostensibly antithetical principle owed to more than personal squabbles. Other black leaders also expressed support for the concept, suggesting that a unionist outlook among African Americans had a surer foundation than desperation or fantasy. Even emigration-minded Henry Highland Garnet offered a resigned version: "It is too late to make a successful attempt to separate the black and white people in the New World. America is my home, my country, and I have no other."[25]

Affective Connection?

In the Madisonian outline upheld by antebellum leaders from Emerson to Webster, political union developed from affective exchanges among the populace. Douglass at times invoked his personal connections to white comrades in the abolitionist struggle. At issue is whether affective encouragement from whites might have been a source of his and other blacks' unionist sensibility. Some studies of African-American communities demonstrate that black culture deeply influenced whites (especially in the South, where blacks and whites mingled far more extensively than in the North) in everything from speech patterns to ideology.[26] This suggests a means by which affective ties might have emerged: it is hard to imagine that any majority culture could absorb as much from a minority group as, for example, Virginia's whites did from African Americans without feeling genuine affection for them. W. E. B. Du Bois looked back wistfully from the 1890s South of Jim Crow segregation to a time "before and directly after the War, when . . . there were bonds of intimacy, affection, and sometimes blood relation, between the races. They lived in the same home, shared in the same family life, often attended the same church, and talked and conversed with each

23. Blassingame 1979–94, 3:361, 427. On the Glasgow trip, see McFeely 1991, 203–5.

24. See Quarles 1938; Martin 1984, 4, 20–21, 47; and Huggins 1980, 117–20.

25. Garnet quoted in Draper 1969, 34. Compare his 1850 comment: "Even to me my country is lively—how much more so it must be to those of her sons around whom she throws her arms of protection." *Non-Slaveholder,* October 1, 1850. Even separatists like Delany occasionally referred to blacks' common nationality with whites; the dedication to his book advocating black emigration was to "the American people, North and South," from "their most devout and patriotic fellow-citizen" (1969, 1). On the "shifting position" between "patriotism . . . and separatism" among the antebellum "black elite," including Delany, see Marx 1998, 351 (quote); Boxill 1999, 23–29; and Kinshasa 1988.

26. See esp. Sobel 1987; Fogel cites other historians' attention—exaggerated, in his view—to the cultural "power of the slaves" (1989, 187; see generally pp. 186–98).

other." Other aspects of plantation life in the South—shared Christian worship, collective gatherings at holidays and harvest times, and even sexual "unions" between slaves and masters—contributed in different ways to the sense of shared purposes and destiny that resembled, if often grotesquely, the affective sense undergirding American unity.[27]

But mutual respect was the key to affective relations, in Madison and others' depiction. And this was painfully absent in southern exchanges between blacks and whites. As J. W. Loguen, a minister and fugitive slave, wrote his former master in 1860: "Have you got to learn that human rights are mutual and reciprocal, and if you take my liberty and life, you forfeit your own?" Here lies the most obvious objection to characterizing the tie between southern blacks and whites as "affective." Eugene Genovese captures the nuances of this conclusion:

A special sense of family shaped Southern culture. In its positive aspect, it brought white and black together and welded them into one people with genuine elements of affection & intimacy that may yet, as a black historian has prayerfully suggested, blossom into a wholesome new relationship. But in its overwhelming negative aspect—its arrogant doctrine of domination and inherent cruelty towards disobedient "children"—it pitted blacks against whites in bitter antagonism & simultaneously poisoned the life of the dominant white community.[28]

It is exceedingly difficult to conceive that a meaningful sense of unity, interpersonal or political, could emerge from such hostility.

Among northern whites and free blacks more genuinely affective ties can be chronicled in some instances, particularly within abolitionist circles. Gerrit Smith, for example, wrote Douglass in 1850 that "nothing [stands] in the way of a complete and glorious union [between whites and blacks]. Let us have toleration . . . let us unite in the spirit of love." But far more common even among antislavery devotees were figures like Horace Greeley, who alongside his abolitionist and black-suffrage positions dismissed blacks as "indolent, improvident, servile and licentious . . . incapable of achieving social equality with whites." As Tocqueville noted, "race prejudice seems stronger in the states that have abolished slavery than in those where it still exists."[29] Many northern whites encountered African Americans primarily through the warped prism of minstrel shows, which along with print caricatures of blacks produced, as Jean Baker notes, "a standard black countenance as different from the newly named Caucasian as to

27. Du Bois 1989 [1903], 149; cf. Genovese 1975, 133. Fogel and Engerman (1974) find a general commitment to keeping slave families intact and laborers materially contented (the psychological dimension is a different story, of course). Norton 1986, 232.

28. *Liberator*, April 27, 1860; Genovese 1975, 74.

29. Greeley quoted in Isley 1947, 104; Smith quoted in Blassingame 1979-94, 2:235; Tocqueville 1969 [1835-40], 343.

be regarded easily as the visage of a debased species. . . . The effect, in a society that increasingly associated language with nationhood, was to widen the chasm between a responsible white citizenry and a feckless black population unable to pronounce even the words of freedom." Prominent in this pseudo-"black dialect" was a rendering of Union as "Onion," as Baker points out.[30] Thus free blacks in the North likely gained little reinforcement for their unionist references from the collective attitudes of white Americans. Individual abolitionists like Smith contributed a measure of encouragement, as previously suggested, but affective exchange requires a sense of reciprocity and personal obligation, again. The Madisonian vision of a corporate body of affectively joined individuals and geographic sections did not require passionate mutual feeling, but even on this qualified view blacks were rebuffed by most whites' opposition to extending the unionist embrace.

Douglass likely recognized that Webster and other orators were not especially concerned with African Americans, except as a potential source of sectional conflict, when they employed union rhetoric at its loftiest. National leaders' eyes were on what Daniel Elazar describes as "the tragic dilemma of union or chaos," not their dispossessed countrymen.[31] Indeed, even self-styled emancipation men frequently looked to other means of squaring universalist convictions with oppressive institutional practice. The solution many leading political figures favored was colonization. Though almost farcical in its ambitious aims, given its limited resources, the American Colonization Society (ACS) was active enough in the North to draw extended fire from most free black spokesmen. In the South, the fearful reaction the ACS triggered among slaveholders was one catalytic factor in the war, in historian William Freehling's estimation. For all its star-studded membership the ACS achieved little, in part because of lack of support from the majority of whites. Nor, significantly, did many African Americans support the colonization movement: Douglass insisted in 1852 that "contact with the white race, even under the many unjust and painful restrictions to which we are submitted, does more for our elevation and improvement, than the mere circumstance of being separated from them could do."[32]

On examination, the possibility that affective encouragement from whites, in North or South, inspired Douglass and other blacks' positive references to national unity seems too remote for contemplation. We turn again to the question:

---

30. Baker 1983, 225 (see pp. 212–49 generally).

31. Elazar 1992, 134. On Webster's disinterest in slavery or other issues concerning blacks, see Kersh 1996, 230–31. See also Potter (1976, 340) on Stephen Douglas: "He did not think that the choice between slavery and some other form of insubordination for an inferior people was important enough to make an issue of it at the risk of disrupting the Union." New York's Republican Congressman (and abolition supporter) Michael Hoffman, in contrast, commented that "the Negro question" was "the Rock on which the Ship Union will split" (Henretta 1996, 158).

32. Freehling 1990, 159–61, 254, 422; Foner 1950, 2:173, 108. In all, between 1820 and 1860 some 7,500 blacks were "removed," almost all to Liberia, by the ACS; more than half made the journey in exchange for manumission. The total represents less than 2 percent of blacks living in America circa 1860.

facing paternalist domination and other brutal indignities in slaveholding states and, in nominally "free" states, white prejudice along with nationally sanctioned plans for erasing blacks from the continent, how could Douglass and other African Americans even appear to place faith in national union?

Douglass's Moral Union

Ultimately, while excluded in fact from American governing and social institutions, Douglass and most other free African Americans found promise in the moral possibilities implicit in a "more perfect" union. In Douglass's terms, "the Union, under the constitution . . . gives me many facilities for doing good." This righteousness inherent in unionist ideals far surpassed the concept's actual embodiment, given most antebellum politicians' meager efforts to match moral rhetoric with institutional change. Still, the principle of national unity offered a strong platform for criticizing American slavery. As Douglass said in 1856: "I am a believer in the Union . . . because I believe it can be made a means of emancipation. . . . The forms of the Union are good enough. If [only] the people were as good as those forms and appliances which form and characterize Union." Samuel Cornish similarly praised "the principles of the Union" as a potent source of abolition.[33]

Douglass's moral understanding of union featured three constituent themes, also evident in the thought of other prominent antebellum blacks. One was *ethical commonality:* like many African Americans since the republic's origin, Douglass insisted that blacks' ethical outlook be recognized as identical to that of "the true meaning of our [American] creed." Maria Stewart, speaking in 1832 before an audience of white Boston women, emphasized her (and, by extension, fellow blacks') moral understanding, even in the face of enforced ignorance: "I possess nothing but moral capability—no teachings but the teachings of the Holy Spirit." Another was *unadulterated equality.* "Note how [the Constitution] starts," Douglass repeated in lecture hall after lecture hall. "'We the people of the United States'—not we the horses, not we the white people, but 'we the people, in order to form a more perfect union.'" In thus invoking "more perfect," he explicitly associated the idea of union with the inclusion of *all* residents, white and black. Any deliberate exclusion on the grounds of race should be viewed as a moral shortcoming, he affirmed. A third was *mutual relationship:* Douglass repeatedly insisted that black and white Americans would eventually be joined in a common nationality, eliminating "the idea that [blacks are] forever doomed to be a stranger and a sojourner" in the United States. African Americans should be viewed, he wrote in 1853, "as citizens, as brothers, as dwellers in a common country." The claim of mutuality was a particularly innovative moral-unionist move:

33. Blassingame 1979–94, 3:43, 120; *Colored American,* April 1, 1837.

until that point majority Americans had not been judged morally deficient for excluding certain people from their national union.[34]

Throughout the 1850s this moral tenor was unwavering in Douglass's applications of union. "The more unitedly you can attach us to your institutions, the more reason you give us to love your government, the more you strengthen the country in which you live," he told a mostly white audience in Troy, New York, in a message widely dispersed in print among northern whites and blacks. If unity was a source of moral strength, the swiftest way to realize it was by ending slavery. "The slaveholder [is] ill at ease," Douglass warned in 1853, "for deep down in his own dark conscience comes a recurring voice—'thou art verily guilty concerning thy *brother.'*" This religious-fraternal outlook, a staple of unionist thought since colonial times, allowed Douglass to feel "hopeful" and "have faith" that "slavery will come down." As historian Peter Walker notes, "the political Union was an arena in which a providential [antislavery] moral drama was being enacted. And without a Union, this morality play was impossible."[35]

In fact Douglass could draw only to a limited degree on support for his moral-union view from religious leaders in 1850s America. Most Protestant congregations, despite their standing as an obvious potential source of opposition to slavery and support for a reformed idea of national unity, were loath to adopt a strong stance in this respect. Partly their reluctance owed to familiar sustainable-union insistence that compromise between North and South was essential to preserving a united country. Underpinning such views was an old theological doctrine, termed "the principle of automatic harmony" by historian Sidney Mead. Churches could concentrate on converting and inspiring believers because, the doctrine held, a society of Christians would be "naturally united," with no possibility of corrosive disagreement among fellow communicants. Thus whatever encouragement union ideas might have had for moral-reform efforts remained mostly latent among religious thinkers. Numerous churches, and other religious institutions like the YMCA, explicitly forbade discussion of "controverted points" (i.e., slavery). This restriction, James Moorhead notes, was "scrupulously observed by leaders who excluded the slavery question from the revival hall."[36]

Possibly in response, Douglass's revised understanding of union drew less on religious doctrines than on a deep-rooted political persuasion among antebellum Americans. Whatever their famed pragmatism, when it came to fundamental values leaders and citizens abandoned moderate phraseology. *All* men were created equal; liberty and justice for all; union and liberty, now and forever. That taste for universalist affirmation informed union talk from the 1820s on, owing

34. Stephens 1997, 180; Stewart in Richardson 1987, 45; Blassingame 1979–94, 3:153; Boxill 1999, 30; Foner 1950, 2:258. Douglass laid the foundation for his morally principled view of union, and indeed of all political and social matters, in his 1849 lecture "Of Morals and Men" (ibid., 2:170–74).

35. Blassingame 1979–94, 3:93; 2:478; Walker in Curry and Valois 1991, 33. Bernard Boxill notes that Douglass's "own experience convinced him blacks could acquire the moral power to compel whites to accept them as full and equal members of the nation" (1999, 22, and cf. 35–44).

36. Mead 1963, 100; Moorhead 1978, 21.

to the influential words of Jackson and Emerson and, later, the unconditional union of Webster and other prominent politicians. Such statements of principle committed unionists to extraordinary efforts to overcome division, including turning a blind eye to slavery. Douglass sought to redirect the force of inspirational union talk to encourage fuller inclusion. His stress on the moral promise of national union and his push to reinterpret the meaning of "more perfect" unity helped to consolidate a strain of principled unionist thought that had been implicit in the hyperbolic lines of Webster and other ardent union-praisers. The "just force of admitted American principles," as Douglass put it in 1853, provided a basis for moral appeals to union.[37]

When Webster or other unconditional unionists declared "all American hearts united," or hailed "this people" as exhibiting a "sense of fraternal affection, patriotic love, and mutual regard . . . for every one,"[38] antebellum African Americans surely did not take the expressions at face value. But free blacks otherwise diverged over how far to accommodate existing oppressive circumstances in their desire to be united to the whole. A few drew a stark line, like the fugitive slave who prayed "Heaven grant, that not a shred of the current religion, nor a shred of the current politics of this land, may remain. *Then* . . . white men will love black men, and gladly acknowledge that all men have equal rights. Come blessed day—come quickly." Others favored resolutions like that of delegates to the 1856 Ohio Convention: "We are not Africans, but Americans, as much so as any of your population . . . American is the only title we desire."[39] Some black speakers, including Garnet and Stewart, maintained reservations not prevalent among whites celebrating national union. Maria Stewart repeatedly denounced "the unfriendly whites" who "stole our fathers from their peaceful and quiet dwellings [in Africa]." Yet she simultaneously appealed to "my white brethren to awake . . . though you should endeavor to drive us from these shores, still will we cling to you all the more firmly." "We love our native country, much as it has wronged us; and in the peaceable exercise of our inalienable rights, we will cling to it," declared Philadelphia blacks in 1838. African Americans' political and personal identity alike was ineluctably constituted in terms of "the ties of affection which every human being must feel for his native land"—and, by extension, its fellow inhabitants.[40]

Participation in the American Union as citizens, joined (politically and affectively) to one another and to whites, was a goal Douglass and many fellow African Americans supported. Blacks' unionist claims were couched in the language of moral reason, appealing to norms of individual flourishing and emancipa-

37. Foner 1950, 2:243.
38. Wiltse and Berolzheimer 1986–88, 2:606, 540.
39. Boardman 1947, 49; Aptheker 1962, 385. See also delegates' resolution to the 1835 annual Negro Convention, "to recommend as far as possible, to our people to abandon the use of the word 'colored' . . . concerning themselves, and especially to remove the title of African from their institutions, the marbles of churches, and etc." (*Liberator,* August 1, 1835).
40. Richardson 1987, 63; Aptheker 1962, 178, 385.

tion and looking beyond unsatisfying unconditional-unionist blandishments. As with other sacrosanct values, principled declarations of a more inclusive national union could be profoundly improved in practice. Whether they *would* be, whether Douglass's morally endowed union would be fulfilled and, in his words, "the character of this country redeemed,"[41] is discussed in subsequent sections.

LINCOLN AND A MORE MORAL UNION

Along with Douglass and other blacks, a few white political leaders proclaimed that only a Union dedicated to a particular set of propositions was worth preserving, not unity at any price. Outspoken abolitionist and U.S. Senator Benjamin Wade, for example, told an Ohio political meeting that he was "attached to the Union" but "on just principles." Wade was "for peace and union *with freedom* but for neither without it."[42] A similar view was promoted by Abraham Lincoln, who from his early career saw "a unified America" as a compelling matter "practically and . . . intellectually." His struggle to reconceive the value in morally progressive terms while remaining generally faithful to the framers' outline was criticized by both impatient abolitionists and proslavery southerners. During the war, however, Lincoln's moral-unionist outlook came to epitomize what Douglass called "something incomparably better than the old Union."[43] Lincoln's inclination to revise concepts of national union evolved gradually: only during the Civil War did he directly associate a more moral union with the status of black Americans. But his vision of national unity pointed the way to Douglass's more radical views.

Lincoln, Unionist

Like Washington, Webster, and a few other leaders before him, Lincoln came to be considered the personal incarnation of national union. One such idealization was drawn by Emerson, who after his deep disillusionment of 1850 had written off "moral Union" as limited to "comparatively low and external purposes, like the cooperation of a ship's company." By 1859 he was sounding elegies for "The Union already old." Yet the war promised a "national moral cleansing," and Emerson hopefully portrayed Lincoln as a new "Representative Man" in an 1862 *Atlantic* essay. Two years later in the lecture "Social Aims" he described renewed possibilities of "fraternity in this land," naming Lincoln as the inspiration. Such treatments continue into the present; as David Donald writes, Lincoln continues to "live in memory as the nation's martyred President who freed the slaves

---

41. *Liberator,* September 22, 1832.
42. Reported in *Ashtabula Sentinel* (Ohio), June 10, 1855.
43. Blassingame 1979–94, 4:91.

and saved the Union."[44] Thus a mass of secondary opinion must be sifted in addressing the question: What was national union to Lincoln?

According to one strand of commentary, Lincoln viewed union in intensely personal terms. Some describe his vision of unity as a sort of "sublim[e] . . . religious mysticism," as Whig-turned-Confederate Vice President Alexander Stephens recalled. Historian G. S. Boritt likewise sees union as "carry[ing] a certain aura" in Lincoln's thought, a theme Charles Strozier propounds at book length, suggesting that Lincoln's inability to resolve his "ambivalent quest for union—with his dead mother, his bride, his alienated father—gave meaning to the nation's turbulence as it hurtled towards civil war." To bridge this public-private divide, Lincoln "turned outward and attempted . . . to solve for all what he could not solve for himself alone" and was finally able to "purposely shape his heroic image to fit a nation longing for unity and greatness."[45]

Other scholars find union less central in Lincoln's political purview. Several writers hold that Lincoln's defenses of "the white Union" were "a technical point," a "shibboleth," a convenient rhetorical cover for avoiding strong antislavery or reconstruction policies. Self-interest is also alleged as a factor, as when Lincoln's proposed "Union Party" retitling of the Republican Party is depicted as a cynical stratagem to ensure his reelection.[46]

This explanatory range, while often insightful in particulars, falls short of explaining Lincoln's understanding of political unity for by now familiar reasons. In each angle of approach Lincoln's union ideas are obstructed by the analyst's deeper purpose. The result: "union" becomes a marker for other concerns (Lincoln's psychological state, or his antipathy to black rights, and so forth) and remains unexamined as a distinctive source of political meaning in its own right. Without taking up each interpretive strain at length, recall that "Lincoln had *arguments* for Union, not just a kind of mystical attachment to it." Moreover, Lincoln's frequent repetition of the term over time indicates that the concept held far more than instrumental interest. With little help from main scholarly currents in evaluating his union ideas, let Lincoln himself be our guide: "I only ask all who are eager for the truth, that . . . they will turn to my own words and examine for themselves."[47]

Such an examination suggests, first of all, that Lincoln was not forced into a hasty consideration of national unity by imminent civil war. His public observations on the subject date from the late 1830s and were refined over the subsequent

44. Gilman 1960–82, 12:447; 14:228; *Atlantic Monthly* 10 (November 1862), 639; Edman 1926 [1841, 1844], 332; Richardson 1995, 552–53; Donald 1978, 160.

45. On religious mysticism, Stephens in Howe 1979, 296; Boritt 1988, 99. Cf. Wilson 1962, chap. 3 ("The Union as Religious Mysticism"); Neely 1991, 230–32. On psychological union, Strozier 1987, 233; 1988, 230. Cf. 1987, xii–xiii, 202–32; Anderson 1988; Forgie 1979, esp. 6–8; and Bellah et al. 1985, 146–47 ("what saved Lincoln from nihilism was the larger whole for which he felt it was important to live and worthwhile to die").

46. On union as excuse, quotes from Harding 1981, 223; Du Bois 1989 [1903], 13. Du Bois is the fountainhead and still best expression of this argument; see also Fredrickson 1975, and Harding 1981, esp. 215–36. On union as disingenuous/pragmatic, see the summary in Holt 1992, 331–33.

47. McPherson 1992, 4; Basler 1953–55, 1:315; 2:525.

quarter century. As he testified before the war: "I have often inquired of myself what great principle or idea it was that kept this Confederacy so long together."[48] Lincoln's "overriding concern for union"[49] originally related to a comparatively abstract matter rather than to the strains of the late antebellum years. His first major address, "The Perpetuation of Our Political Institutions" (1838), set out the problem: encouraging popular devotion to "constitutional maintenance," or retaining the founders' vision of united America in a much altered polity. Lincoln identified a trend of declining local solidarity and the consequent difficulty of encouraging feelings of mutual obligation and trust across larger spaces and between strangers. Unlike many antebellum leaders, Lincoln was wary of promoting unity by affirming ascriptive or romantic-nationalist themes. Lincoln's comparative advantage (though one he would gladly have forsworn) in pondering alternate approaches was his relative obscurity until the late 1850s; this allowed his thinking to develop in response to the efforts of unionist predecessors. His eventual national prominence provided a platform for his union ideas, fashioning them into the moral instrument for which Douglass, Emerson, and others had longed. But all essential elements of Lincoln's union theory were in place long before the war began.

As his frequent references to Webster and to "the fathers" testify, Lincoln rethought the nature of American national community in the light of existing union ideals. Among his adaptations was linking the concept directly to other foundational goods, particularly equality. Lincoln also largely dismissed the notion of widespread friendship or affection between citizens, which appeared to him as an untenable fiction in the late 1850s. He thus replaced the affective basis for union with a complex combination of rule of law, deliberative competition, and popular sovereignty.

Lincoln came of age politically in the early 1840s, a period marked by the oratorical flights of fellow Whig Daniel Webster. Little wonder that aspects of Lincoln's account of union resemble Webster's, as well as Madison's. As a major Whig spokesman in the 1856 presidential campaign, Lincoln quoted Webster so often that one newspaper accused him of plagiarism. Lincoln's ardent arguments for perpetuating the Union were principally drawn from Webster, as was his strongest union metaphor, a "house divided," with which he first won national attention in 1854. The last line of Lincoln's legendary "Lost Speech," delivered two years later at the Illinois Republican Convention, repeats Webster's "Liberty and Union, now and forever" lines from the "Reply to Hayne." Paul Erickson concludes that Lincoln's unionist "faith" derived from "the works of Daniel Webster, [from] his . . . prophetic vision of disunion."[50]

48. Basler 1989 [1946], 577.
49. Rawley 1963, 9; cf. Holt 1986.
50. Basler 1953–55, 2:341; Erickson 1986, 114. On Lincoln's reliance on Webster, see Howe 1979, 284 (on plagiarism charge); Donald 1995, 163, 270; Current 1983, chap. 4; and Wills 1992, 122–33, who finds that "Lincoln used [Webster's] style and arguments . . . as models all through his political life." Lincoln's posthumous eulogies helped to rehabilitate Webster, even as Fugitive Slave Law outrage

Yet such influences went only so far, as Lincoln plainly stated. "I do not mean to say we are bound to follow implicitly in whatever our fathers did. To do so, would be to discard all the lights of current experience—to reject all progress—all improvement," the new president declared in 1860. Lincoln wrestled throughout his career with the burden of "supporting and maintaining an edifice that has been erected by others," as might any ambitious person. One field of improvement on Jacksonian-era luminaries, and even the "deathless names" (Lincoln's term) of the founding,[51] was unionist ideas and related policies. Lincoln treated the unconditional-union claims of Webster and others as excessive, given his own insistence on precise language. In speeches and letters drafted with such care that he warned editors "I do not wish the sense changed, or modified, to a hair's breadth," Lincoln expressed union in simple figures: marriage, family, divided houses. Lincoln painstakingly shaped his public statements to draw on the tremendous potency union had attained in Americans' political talk, but he did so via subtle lexical techniques. His speeches, according to one analyst, exhibit a "tension between unity and division," through the devices of alternating parallelism—blending ideas by linking them serially—and antithesis, or presenting opposing ideas in alternating contrast. While a certain confusion over the term's status remains evident—like everyone else at the time, Lincoln freely mingled references to "the Union" and small-u valuational union, suggesting at once a concrete good, a political territory, and a psychological disposition—Lincoln's usage was considerably more deliberate than that of his effusive contemporaries.[52]

Not only in linguistic style did Lincoln depart from previous generations. Where Webster and other antebellum unionists were content to rest on established doctrine, Lincoln systematically reevaluated the concept. How, as he summarized the problem before New Jersey's state senate in 1861, could "citizens of the United States" best be "united by a purpose to perpetuate the Union"?[53] In Lincoln's conception the outlines of Madisonian theory remained, but the core of each linked aspect was hollowed out and invested with a different meaning. Territorial union was reinforced by a sense of "integrity" rather than geostrategic considerations. Unity among American citizens relied not on natural affection

retained some force. Lincoln's self-description as representing "original principles" in "Jeffersonian, Washingtonian, and Madisonian fashion" is in Basler 1989 [1946], 449. On the connection between Lincoln and Madison, see McCoy 1995.

51. Basler 1989 [1946], 575, 82–83. The founders' appeal for Lincoln has attracted much scholarly comment, viz. Strozier's argument that Lincoln "idealiz[ed] the nation's founders" in part as "an attempt to establish parental surrogates" (1987, 55); or Dwight Anderson's "psychobiography," portraying the founders as Lincoln's slain "fathers"—an Oedipal theory Anderson himself admits is an "oddity" (1988, 254). Herman Belz's (1986) position seems most plausible: that Lincoln drew on the framers to buttress his arguments and as a source of constitutional validation for his actions. As Lincoln wrote (Basler 1989 [1946], 575): "If we would supplant the opinions and policy of our fathers in any case, we should do so upon evidence so conclusive, and argument so clear, that even their great authority, carefully considered and weighed, cannot stand."

52. Basler 1989 [1946], 545; Forgie 1979, 39. On "union" images, see inter alia Basler 1989 [1946], 571, 748; on Lincoln's style, cf. Weaver 1953, 108–10; Wills 1992, 52–62.

53. Basler 1989 [1946], 575.

but expanded political participation, guided by enlightened self-interest, and an association of union with strong moral values, particularly equality. And "institutional union" was carefully balanced between popular sovereignty and legal precedent, with virtuous representatives barely in sight.

Lincoln's Territorial Union

Lincoln's account of national union began, by now traditionally, with American territory. "A nation may be said to consist of its territory, its people, and its laws. The territory is the only part which is of certain durability. . . . It is of the first importance to duly consider, and estimate, this ever-enduring part," the new president told Congress in 1861. The American land, he concluded, was "advantageous [only] for one united people."[54] Despite this familiar emphasis, Lincoln was engaged in a different territorial-unity enterprise. Madison and Jackson's generations were occupied with separation and expansion, first breaking with Britain and then obtaining through various means territory from British, French, Spanish, Mexican, and Native American holders. The founders and their early-nineteenth-century legatees, as described in chapter 2, freely played on fear of outside (especially British) aggression to bolster their geostrategic arguments, and defended territorial acquisitions on the grounds of enhanced security.

In contrast, freshman Congressman Lincoln's first notable act was to oppose Polk's Mexican policy. With some other Whigs, including Webster, his "fear [was] that expansion and war with Mexico, like slavery, would destroy the moral core of national identity." And long after other Whigs rejoined the expansionist fold—indeed, long after the Whig party's demise—Lincoln's continued attention to territorial union revolved around *maintaining* existing territory, and thereby keeping the United States one. "The question," Lincoln told Congress in his first public statement on the war, was "whether a constitutional republic, or democracy—a Government of the people by the same people—can or cannot maintain its territorial integrity against its own domestic foes."[55] This was not a geostrategic matter of protection from external danger, Lincoln made clear. "All the armies of Europe, Asia and Africa combined, with all the treasures of the earth, with a Buonaparte for a commander, could not by force, take a drink from the Ohio." His account instead featured commercial rationales ("separate our common country into two nations . . . and every man of this great interior region is cut off from sea-ports"), arguments from propinquity ("physically speaking, we cannot separate"), and principle.[56] The last drew on a robust conception of "territorial integrity."

Integrity, in Lincoln's carefully specified terms, connoted both "integrated"—joined as a single whole—and the moral rectitude also commonly associated

---

54. Ibid., 676.
55. Thelen 1998, 382; Basler 1989 [1946], 598. On Lincoln and constitutional maintenance, cf. Kahn 1992, 32–36, and Jaffa 1982 [1959].
56. Basler 1953–55, 1:108; Basler 1989 [1946], 678, 586. Cf. ibid., 617.

with the idea. "The Union must be preserved in the purity of its principles," Lincoln told campaign crowds in 1856. Only then could Americans claim "integrity of its territorial parts." He first construed territory in principled terms two years earlier during the Kansas-Nebraska debates, with a crescendo of rhetorical questions opposing slavery in the territories: "Is not Nebraska, while a territory, a part of us? Do we not own the country? And if we surrender the control of it, do we not surrender the right of self-government? It is part of ourselves . . . when all the parts are gone, what has become of the whole? What is there left of us? What use for the General Government, when there is nothing left of us?"[57]

Investing territory with "integrity" drew on the quasi-sacral authority conferred by tradition. This notion was not new among U.S. officials: Justice Story, for example, in his 1833 constitutional study wrote that "Time and long and steady operations are indispensable to the perfection of all social institutions." Webster's orations at anniversary celebrations of symbolic American places dramatically reinforced the point. Lincoln's innovation was to insist (following abolitionists like Douglass) that territory could only remain a legitimate source of "one national family" when it was *free* land, upholding the "purity" of the Union's "principles." Free-soil ideology dated to the colonial era, but it was Lincoln and fellow Republicans who popularized the idea of principled territorial union, ensuring that "the goals of Union and free soil were intertwined, and neither could be sacrificed without endangering the other."[58] Similarly transfigured in Lincoln's account was union among the people, whose status as bearers of mutual affection was exchanged for that of active citizens, most notably those "who gave their lives that [the] nation might live."[59]

Sources of Popular Unity

Lincoln's first inaugural address culminated, in line with Madison's original schema, by proceeding from territorial-union arguments to invoking "bonds of affection" among Americans. "We are not enemies, but friends. We must not be enemies," Lincoln implored, offering the vision of a renewed "chorus of the Union." This familiar affective-unionist theme in fact marks an exception in Lincoln's public statements and undoubtedly was a product of the circumstance surrounding its delivery—the threshold of national division. Elsewhere Lincoln rarely attempted even such minimalist appeals to personal bonds among Americans of different regions, appeals that had been so common among antebellum speakers from Webster to Stephen Douglas to Jefferson Davis. Lincoln's occasional references to mutual affection were universal rather than national in scope. Deploring lynchings of black workers during the July 1863 New York draft riots, he said: "The strongest bond of human sympathy, outside of the family re-

<hr>

57. Basler 1953–55, 2: 341; Basler 1989 [1946], 305.

58. Story 1987 [1833], 717; Foner 1970, 225 (cf. 11–40); cf. Potter 1976, 227–32. For a thoughtful overview of such moralizing in the American constitutional tradition, see Powell 1993a.

59. Basler 1953–55, 7: 23.

lation, should be one uniting all working people, of all nations, and tongues, and kindreds."[60]

Lincoln's habitual omission of affective language was very likely purposeful. It stemmed from the sources of popular ties, as Madison and other thinkers conceived of these. As early as his Lyceum Speech (1838) Lincoln acknowledged what most antebellum leaders did not: that popular public spirit was evident only occasionally, as during patriotic celebrations and, for more sustained periods, during national crises like the War of 1812, the nullification crisis, or the Kansas conflict. Recognizing that affective sentiment was otherwise sparse, especially among mutually suspicious northerners and southerners in the 1850s, Lincoln rarely extolled this theme, in contrast to most other leaders at the time.[61] Even when he did look back nostalgically, as in an 1854 eulogy for the "peace and quiet" preceding the turmoil surrounding the Kansas-Nebraska Act, he did not claim that Americans were once united in sentiment or purpose, but merely that "the nation was [then] looking to the forming of new bonds of Union."[62]

Lincoln's skeptical attitude toward affective unity owed partly to sectional divisions evident in the pre-Sumter years. Yet he seems by present-day "shadow of a coming war" standards oddly oblivious to the looming conflict. In an 1856 campaign speech he concluded, "all this talk about the dissolution of the Union is humbug—nothing but folly."[63] Lincoln's writings suggest other sources of resistance to sentimentality about a "nation of friends." Though saluting the "spirit of mutual concession—that spirit which first gave us the Constitution, and which has thrice saved the Union,"[64] by the 1850s Lincoln was much less inclined than his Whig forebears to compromise other values for unity's sake. Union might be achieved on faulty premises, as he tartly noted in 1852: "This immense, palpable, pecuniary interest, on the question of extending slavery, unites the Southern people, as one man. Moral principle is all, or nearly all, that unites us of the North. . . . Right here is the plain cause of their *perfect* union and our *want* of it."[65] Fellow-feeling could produce wholly unequal relations, moreover:

60. Basler 1989 [1946], 588, and cf. 310, where Lincoln refers to a "national feeling of brotherhood" but in the context of "concession and compromise." (This also reasserted union's balanced connotation.)

61. Compare, e.g., Stephen Douglas's hailing the "bonds of friendship" between "all Americans, united." Opening the third of his 1858 debates with Lincoln, Douglas asserted that past generations—including "the leaders of the Whig party and the great Democratic party"—agreed "to bury, for the time being, their partisan dispute and unite to save the Union." Concluding, he again appealed to past comity: "I would that we should do as our fathers did, who made the government. There was no sectional strife—there was no warfare between sections in Washington's army. They were brothers." Holzer 1993, 140, 155, 168.

62. Basler 1989 [1946], 309.

63. Basler 1953–55, 2:355 (see also p. 349). Cf., on Lincoln's failure to recognize the war as "inevitable," Bruce 1992, 25–26. The range of leading figures, including Generals Sherman and Lee, who committed similar errors of judgment suggests that the "foreshadowings" of civil war are far clearer in retrospect.

64. Basler 1989 [1946], 310.

65. Ibid., 349. On compromise, see especially Lincoln's stern statements in early 1860, including his letter to a southerner, in Basler 1953–55, 4:149–52.

"Much is said by Southern people about the affection of slaves for their masters and mistresses; and a part of it, at least, is true."[66] His point was not that slavery had redeeming features, but that affection was both an improbable and an insufficient source of a praiseworthy national union. In Lincoln's repeated attempts to "address a few words to the Southern people," this natural occasion for sentimental-affective language instead brought strict, judgmental calls to "reason" and "justice."[67]

In place of affective unity, Lincoln proposed three sources of popular ties. His earliest substitute was reason and its cousin "tolerance," addressed at greatest length in his Lyceum Address. These were insufficiently appealing bases of political attraction, however, and Lincoln eventually turned elsewhere for a substitute to rhetorical embraces of Americans' mutual affection. A shrewd and hard-nosed legislative operator, Lincoln relished the partisan combat that marked mid-nineteenth-century American politics—for example, retaining in his cabinet Salmon Chase, a potential 1864 presidential foe. Within limits (secession clearly being well outside them), Lincoln saw legally circumscribed political conflict as a second basis for citizens' fellow-feeling.

Lincoln recognized that conflict is an unavoidable part of any joint endeavor, and made a virtue of this necessity. Anyone who has "engaged in athletic competition," he observed informally to his secretary John Hay, could well appreciate the shared feelings of "accomplishment" and "respect" derived from "joining in the game." The same sentiments arose from good-faith political deliberation. His Senate debates with Douglas were a classic example, displaying (as Potter attests) that "the right to fight for one's ideas involved an obligation to fight fair and to recognize a democratic bond with other fighters for other ideas." It is too much to say that Lincoln replaced affection with agonistic respect as a basis for union; at most it provided a partial substitute. But his view departed decisively from those of prior politicians. Madison and other founders' tutelary outlook suggests the limited "respect" they had for Americans collectively; why should the many be expected to honor this virtue in one another? Webster, though like Lincoln a master trial lawyer, in politics was more inclined to appeasement than to promoting competition.[68]

Lincoln's praise of "cold, calculating, unimpassioned reason" and of the respect arising from political conflict do not mean, as some biographers conclude, that the human desire for affective relations was a "mystery" to him. His predecessors' efforts to inculcate affection on a national level were estimable but insufficient. "Passional attraction" yielded a stunted and temporary bond, he wrote in 1859, one valued only by "our *professed* lovers of the Union." To this Lincoln

---

66. Basler 1989 [1946], 530. Affective relations between masters and slaves in the antebellum South are considered at greater length in Kersh 1996, 221–32.

67. Basler 1989 [1946], 526. Cf. ibid., 291, 479.

68. Hay quoting Lincoln in Jourdan 1889, 140; Potter 1976, 333. Compare Emerson's view of conflict as a source of unity, discussed in chapter 3.

counterposed the calm, permanent ties found in "family relation[s]" and "regular marriage." "Passion has helped us," he observed in 1838, "but can do so no more." Even as his contemporaries reiterated "the need to move beyond reason to the 'affections'" to reunite the whole, Lincoln proposed a third basis for unifying the people, one consonant with a more moral understanding of national union.[69]

Frederick Douglass's approach to a more moral union, as outlined, sought to establish the assertion in American popular understanding that "the Union" was morally flawed as long as some members of the polity were unjustly excluded. Lincoln also, though more cautiously, insisted on a union dedicated to a particular proposition: equality. The "central idea in our political public opinion" was, Lincoln said over and over, "the equality of all men."[70] Commentators from Karl Marx forward have credited Lincoln with redefining ideas of equality, but this was not in fact the thrust of his "second American revolution."[71] Lincoln's conception merely reasserted doctrines sounded by Jefferson and others during the founding era. As he testified: "Little by little . . . we have been giving up the old for the *new* faith. Near eighty years ago we began by declaring that all men are created equal: but now from that beginning we have run down."[72]

Instead Lincoln's innovation lay in his nuanced association of equality and union—a connection that appeared unlikely on its face. "Union" implied stability, compromise, even stasis; equality retained a strong revolutionary flavor, especially in the supercharged ideological environment before and during the war. In the antebellum period, indeed, speakers promoting equality were portrayed by most northern and southern whites as agents of *dis*union, given southerners' (reasonably accurate) view of egalitarian doctrines as "abolitionism, pure and simple." Accordingly an either/or relationship between equality and union was frequently posited during Lincoln's time. Said Stephen Douglas: "we should unite to save the Union before we should quarrel as to the mode in which it was to be governed." Similar judgments are reached today: Paul Kahn, in his generally brilliant discussion of Lincoln and constitutional maintenance, concludes at one point that "to Lincoln, union is more important than truth," given that "it would not be enough, for example, for the seceding states to affirm the same true principles at their foundation. Full vindication of the moral truths of equality and liberty would not justify a failure to maintain the community."[73]

Yet without the commitment to inequality inherent in slaveholders' ideology "the community" might not be in danger to begin with. Lincoln by the mid-1850s consistently stated that union was a dependent virtue, no longer defensible in

69. Basler 1989 [1946], 84, 571–72, 84; Kahn 1992.

70. Basler 1953–55, 4:267–68; 2:385. Cf. Basler 1989 [1946], 335–36, 361, 577.

71. Marx in Padover 1972, 264; Kendall and Carey 1970; Boritt 1988, 94–95; Jaffa 1982 [1959], 221–28; Wills 1992, 120–24; Ellis 1992. But cf. Wood 1992, 40.

72. Basler 1953–55, 2:275–76.

73. "Mississippi man" quoted in *Cincinnati Enquirer,* July 7, 1855 (cf. Garnet 1865, 37); Holzer 1993, 140; Kahn 1992, 142 (cf., inter alia, Donald 1995, 170).

merely its own right. The thrust of his "House Divided" speech, for example, was that "under the guise of allaying controversy and establishing national unity, the Democratic party had constantly pushed slavery into new territory and had thwarted all efforts aimed at control and ultimate extinction of the evil." Two months before the war began, Lincoln declared that he "would rather be assassinated" than preserve a Union open to expanded slavery.[74]

Lincoln thus treated the ostensibly divergent values of equality and union as mutually reinforcing. In one debate with Douglas, Lincoln insisted that returning to the moral principles ("the practices, and policy") of the Declaration would mean "we shall not only have saved the union, but we shall have so saved it as to make, and to keep it, forever worthy of the saving." He opposed the "Crittenden Compromise" in 1860, which conceded certain territories to the South (and thus to slavery) in exchange for continued national unity. As the president-elect wrote his ally William Seward, who supported the legislation, "[it] acknowledges that slavery has equal rights with liberty, and surrenders all we have contended for. . . . A year will not pass, till we shall have to take Cuba as a condition upon which [the southern states] will stay in the Union."[75]

Lincoln's idea of equality was closely connected with property and free labor, as Howe notes: "Equality meant, in the first instance, an equal opportunity to work for one's living and an equal right to retain the fruits of one's labor." Viewing a nation of affectively joined friends as a dim prospect, Lincoln hoped instead that Americans would respond to a vision of their common entitlement to the political goods of participation, economic rewards, and the like. Ensuring broad popular welfare, on his view, was a natural extension of each individual's desire to advance free of artificial obstacles. Lincoln urged this as a universal precept, applicable in both North and South. He viewed southern society as also reflecting devotion to equal opportunity—at least for white men. As Jürgen Gebhardt summarizes: "[E]specially in the South, the republican 'ideal of equal opportunity' . . . was of great significance for social mobility and social self-understanding of whites on all social levels."[76]

Lincoln's association of equality and union rested on a foundation of mutuality among the people, eliminating hierarchies of authority. As will be seen, until wartime he barely acknowledged the implications of this idea for black rights. But Lincoln's promotion of moral union did imply elimination of the restraints on antislavery activity associated with sustainable-unity claims. If the Union had to be preserved at all costs, as a generation of orators had argued, black rights were out of the question, given the need for compromise with the slavocracy. In contrast, Lincoln's relation of equality and national union strengthened the

74. Basler 1989 [1946], 24; Basler 1953–55, 4:240.

75. Basler 1953–55, 3:9; 4:155, 172. Lincoln's strategic partisan reasons for opposing the compromise plan are treated in L. H. Johnson 1978, 68–70.

76. Howe 1979, 297 (on Lincoln and free labor, see also Foner 1970, 38, 296; 1998, 67–68, 91–92); Gebhardt 1993, 174–75.

former value. From the war for Union, as Foner writes, "emerged the principle of a national citizenship whose members enjoyed equal protection of the laws, regardless of race." Looking back from the vantage point of 1892 at the war's central lessons, former Union soldier Jacob Polson Cox declared that "the unity of the American people is the necessary condition of human progress on this continent."[77]

Union's value was also enhanced by its association with equality, in a number of ways. For one, when connected to equality and other prized goods, national unity became a more alluring prospect in some Americans' eyes. This was certainly the case among abolitionists: with equality as a stated purpose of the war, wrote Douglass after the Emancipation Proclamation, "now . . . [w]e are fighting for unity; unity of object, unity of institutions, in which there shall be no North, no South, no East, no West, no black, no white, but a solidarity of the nation." Others found the connection appealing as well. "The Union now stands for *something*," cheered the moderate *Cincinnati Enquirer* in 1862. "Equality *and* union; it has that old Dan'l Webster ring." Lincoln also tied the union's durability to the Declaration's assurance of universal equality. "The purpose" of the constitutional convention, he explained, "was to form a more perfect union." And "more perfect," he made clear, involved dedication to the "principle of equality" in "the good old [Declaration], penned by Jefferson." If the national union was founded in 1776 with a pledge of equal rights for all, both secession and slavery were illegal—and the Union was perpetual.[78]

Second, as Anne Norton points out, the American messianic streak traceable to Puritan thought retained currency in Lincoln's time. Lincoln drew on this "city on a hill" tradition in insisting that the Union should be preserved in order to demonstrate to Old World observers the viability of equality and other democratic principles—"the last, best hope of earth."[79] If anything, southerners like Calhoun and Fitzhugh claimed America as the shining republican example more ardently than did their northern counterparts, all the while insisting that slavery was perfectly consistent with prized national ideals.[80]

In his reworking of a biblical proverb, in which "the Union, and the Constitution, are the picture of silver" and "[t]he assertion of that [equality] principle . . . has proved an 'apple of gold' to us," Lincoln set out the relation between union and equal liberty. "The picture was made for the apple, not the apple for the picture. So let us act, that neither picture, or apple, shall ever be blurred, or

77. Foner 1998, 97; Cox 1892, 383.

78. Blassingame 1979–94, 4:93; *Cincinnati Enquirer*, March 10, 1863; Basler 1989 [1946], 587; Basler 1953–55, 4:433–35.

79. Norton 1986, 19–32, 304–14. Cf. Lincoln, in his first inaugural, urging "firm reliance on Him, who has never yet forsaken this favored land" (Basler 1989 [1946], 588). On Lincoln's relation of religious providence and national unity, see also Morel 2000, 67–68, 208–10.

80. Fitzhugh 1960 [1857], 248–49. C. Vann Woodward's introduction to this edition calls it "ironical" that Fitzhugh was "made a symbol of Southern intransigence and militant disunionism. He actually deplored nullification . . . and dreaded disunion." Ibid., xxx–xxxi.

broken."[81] Presenting Union and Constitution as foundations of equality invested national unity with a moral standing never so explicitly conferred on it. When we consider this achievement together with Lincoln's attempt to realize political union on a wider scale than had before been attempted, the thrust of his conceptual revision becomes clear. If the people were to be more closely bound together, it would have to be as moral equals. The extent to which Lincoln specifically included black Americans in his vision of a more equal union is taken up below; first we examine Lincoln's revisionist conception of the third "pillar" of Madisonian union, the representative/institutional dimension.

Institutional Union: Rule of Law and Popular Sovereignty

Madison's elaborate treatment of representative leadership, national unity, and governance included protective reserves against the temporary absence of virtuous leaders, as noted earlier. Lincoln instead abandoned the expectation. "Politicians," the latter declared in his Lyceum Address, were "a set of men who have interests aside from the interests of the people, and who, to say the most of them, are, taken as a mass, at least one long step removed from honest men." The few outstanding exceptions were likely to prove even more dangerous. From early in his career Lincoln warned against the political "genius" turned tyrant, who "thirsts and burns for distinction; and, if possible . . . will have it, whether at the expense of emancipating slavery, or enslaving freemen." Simultaneously, he denounced "that lawless and mobocratic spirit . . . which is already abroad in the land; and is spreading with rapid and fearful impetuosity, to the ultimate overthrow of every institution, or even moral principle, in which persons and property have hitherto found security."[82] With leaders and followers alike tending to venality, erasing any possibility of Madison's "special understanding" between governors and governed, where to turn?

"Reverence for the Laws"

Rule of law was Lincoln's preferred substitute for enlightened representatives as the "institutional" agent of political union. Recognizing that "the strongest bulwark of any Government, and particularly those constituted like ours," was "the *attachment* of the People," in 1838 he urged "every American" to "swear by the blood of the Revolution, never to violate in the least particular, the laws of the country." Such "reverence for the laws" would enhance citizens' sense of mutual connectedness, Lincoln argued in later years. Legal securities ensured protection of both equality and private property. More grandly, Lincoln in 1862 described even the Civil War as a "struggle to preserve the rule of law, the constitutional Union."[83] This view culminated in his claim (just quoted) that "a na-

---

81. Basler 1989 [1946], 513. The biblical reference is to Proverbs 25:11.
82. Ibid., 68, 71.
83. Ibid., 80–83; Paludan 1988, 27. Cf. Basler 1989 [1946], 354–59, 396–98, 417–20, 585–86.

tion may be said to consist of its territory, its people, and its laws," which neatly restated the Madison triad of territory, people, and representatives.

While Lincoln's "reverence for the laws" echoed founding rhetoric, in the mid-nineteenth century rule of law was not a widely hallowed ideal. Laissez-faire ruled in federal and state lawmaking alike, as Lawrence Friedman's histori-cal overview attests. Webster, the period's best-known constitutional lawyer, rarely extolled law as such, apart from sentimental salutes to the Constitution in public addresses; Andrew Jackson or any of his immediate successors never de-livered a speech like Lincoln's first wartime message to Congress, fully a third of which was devoted to justifying the legality of his presidential actions.[84]

An emphasis on law implied relocation of representative power in the Su-preme Court, but Lincoln clearly thought otherwise. From his first inaugural ad-dress: "The candid citizen must confess that if the policy of the whole govern-ment upon vital questions, affecting the whole people, is to be irrevocably fixed by decisions of the Supreme Court, the instant they are made . . . the people will have ceased to be their own rulers, having to that extent practically resigned their government into the hands of that eminent tribunal."[85] The Court played a key part in affirming basic American principles, including union,[86] but Justices were fallible, requiring review by "higher" sources. The first of these was the Consti-tution itself, which Lincoln viewed as "the standard of what law should be." An-other "higher law" locus was Christianity. As president Lincoln regularly invoked aid from a heavenly "ruler," "lawgiver," or "Supreme Government," counterposed to "human counsel."[87] Constitution and God had each long been associated with American unity, and Lincoln's shift in emphasis from wise representatives and affectively joined people to equality and the rule of law depended heavily on re-asserting this history. The "cult of the Constitution" and paeans to union by re-ligious leaders both proliferated during the nineteenth century, confirming and strengthening Lincoln's view. Boston minister A. L. Stone's wartime sermon suc-cinctly combined these themes: "Strike for Law and Union, for Country and God's great ordinance of Government."[88]

In Lincoln's view legal securities were far more reliable restraints on popular excess than was political leaders' tutelage. Yet reducing the importance of politi-cians and the people alike while proclaiming reverence for law bordered on the

84. Basler 1989 [1946], 594, and cf. 629–30, 699–708, 720–23. Friedman 1973, 165–66, 295–99. Madison's *Federalist* no. 49 is the most comprehensive founding-era account of "reverence for the laws."

85. Basler 1989 [1946], 586.

86. Through "good laws" and "suitable provisions for the establishment of courts of justice," the Supreme Court declared in 1855, "the people [will] think and feel, tho' residing in different States of the Union, that their relations to each other were protected by the strictest justice. . . . [Thus] men unite in civil society." *Dodge v. Woolsey*, 59 U.S. 331, 354 (1855).

87. Reid 1989, 8; Basler 1989 [1946], 655, 762, 610, 728.

88. Quoted in Paludan 1988, 346. On the Constitution as symbolic linchpin of union during the war, see Kammen 1993; on Lincoln's "connection between God and the Union," see Paludan 1988, 339–74 (quote at p. 346); cf. Donald 1995, 514–15, and Niebuhr 1964.

disingenuous, considering the roles of the former as lawmakers and the latter as law-approvers. With "higher law" securities in place, Lincoln advanced an ideal closer to unfettered popular rule than had any other American political figure, Thomas Jefferson's aside on the ward system notwithstanding. Discarding the complex mechanism that linked a people united in friendship to a set of political representatives, in 1858 Lincoln rhetorically asked "What does Popular Sovereignty mean?" "Strictly and literally it means the sovereignty of the people over their own affairs—in other words, the right of the people . . . to govern themselves."[89]

Popular Sovereignty and Representation

Lincoln's early comments on popular rule were vague and sonorous, probably owing to his focus on legal protections. The essence of the American "experiment," he said in 1838, was "the capability of a people to govern themselves." A decade later his views had become more specific. Speaking in the House on "the will of the people," he professed "the one great living principle of all Democratic republican government" to be "the principle that the representative is bound to carry out the known will of his constituents." Lincoln viewed national legislators not as independent paragons of political wisdom, but as delegates requiring instruction. His advice to ordinary citizens:

> Send up members of Congress from the various districts, with opinions according to your own, and if they are for [my preferred measures], I shall have nothing to oppose; if they are not for them, I shall not . . . attempt to dragoon them into their adoption. Now, then, can there be any difficulty in understanding this? . . . [I am] in favor of making Presidential elections and the legislation of the country distinct matters; so that the people can elect whom they please, and afterwards, legislate just as they please. . . .
> In leaving the people's business in their hands, we cannot be wrong.[90]

This speech came in the midst of the debate over war with Mexico, an event that galvanized Lincoln's thinking on popular sovereignty. As in the later "people's contest" over which he presided, reports of dead and suffering soldiers powerfully illustrated the extent of central government claims on American citizens.[91] Recognizing that those claims at times required the ultimate personal sacrifice, Lincoln constructed a blueprint for a deliberative collectivity of competent self-governors.

Lincoln made clear that this "revolution" in popular sovereignty was tied to a united citizenry. Self-rule was among "these glorious institutions," he told the

---

89. Basler 1989 [1946], 472.

90. Ibid., 235–39, and cf. 587–88, 602. Debates over whether elected representatives should be "delegates," as Lincoln suggests here, or "trustees" in the Burkean tradition continue today.

91. Lincoln's "people's contest" line is at Basler 1989 [1946], 607.

Army of the Potomac after Antietam, whose "benefits [are] conferred on us by a united country."[92] Jacksonians' praise of "the People: the 'dear, dear people,' the 'sovereign people'" had helped popularize union talk among the many, as we saw earlier. Lincoln certainly had an ear for winning adages, but his was a more considered position than simple pandering. His developing ideas of popular sovereignty were tested in the 1858 Senate campaign, with Douglas arguing that the principle "recogniz[es] the right of each state to do as it please[s]." This states' rights idea of sovereignty, with its traditional appeal, won Douglas acclaim on the territorial question. Lincoln, portraying the position as "a congenial political strategy for advancing the interests of slavery," dismissed Douglas's view as "squatter sovereignty," a mere "patchwork of local peoples" separately forging "dozens of locally convenient compromises," and responded with a sweeping account of popular rule encompassing all Americans. Douglas in turn seized on this definition. "I care more for the great principle of self-government, the right of the people to rule . . . than I do for all the negroes in Christendom." The line clarified the difference between the two and almost certainly hurt Lincoln's immediate electoral fortunes. It also brought into sharp relief Lincoln's attempts to realize in practice a more moral union.[93]

Expanding popular sovereignty necessitated a revised account of representation, described in chapter 2 as the efficient core of Madison's theory of union. For Madison, representation entailed "refin[ing] and enlarg[ing] the public views," a function that included leaders' handing down opinions to a consenting people, synthesizing scattered popular opinions and re-presenting them in more considered, coherent form, and—on extraordinary occasions like the founding—interpreting the people's collective will.[94] Hence Madison had called on an *enlightened* people to be their own governors, reserving an important activist role for leaders like himself. Lincoln shared the goal of popular enlightenment, and took more seriously the notion that each citizen was a potential "lay theorist" of politics. His advances on Madisonian expectations are summarized in the famous "government of the people, by the people, for the people" phrase. "Of" and especially "for" fit well with the words, at least, of gentry leaders. But "by" the people? Paradoxical as it may seem, Lincoln's expectation was that a people could become representative of itself.[95]

To better understand this notion of self-representation, consider another environment where the idea appears: the courtroom. There experts familiar with the process, vocabulary, and structures of power represent the accused, steering them (for a price) through the system. Unless called to the stand, the defendant

92. Ibid., 656.

93. Rodgers 1987, 83; Howe 1979, 287; Basler 1989 [1946], 440; Rodgers 1987, 11. On the 1858 outcome see Heckman 1967, 137–43, and Donald 1995, 227.

94. Rossiter 1961, no. 10; cf. nos. 36, 51, 57.

95. The famous phrase is found in Basler 1989 [1946], 734. Skepticism about self-representation is expressed in Ricoeur 1965, esp. 247–65.

literally has no voice. Yet occasionally defendants choose to represent themselves, especially when their faith in the courts is weak. As Lincoln's presidency dawned, the "system" of political union had collapsed: secession marked "a new kind of national crisis, brought on by the people themselves instead of their legislators." Congressional representatives supposedly laboring in a spirit of comity had disbanded. As Lincoln then asked, "Why should there *not* be a patient confidence in the ultimate justice of the people? Is there any better or equal hope, in the world?"[96]

Popular Sovereignty and Union

In an antebellum polity marked by torchlight parades, passionate partisanship, huge turnouts for political speeches, and record voting levels, it could appear that political activity was integral to human existence.[97] Lincoln's views of popular sovereignty occasionally approached such a characterization, although he offered no civic-humanist encomiums about political activity as the best life. Rather, his commitment to popular rule connected individual and national identity. Building on the idea of territorial integrity, Lincoln based citizen participation in the nation's temporal continuity. People living on—inheriting—the ground consecrated by their forebears' deeds were obligated to uphold past standards of political life, demanding a degree of involvement in the work of self-government.[98] Lincoln made this point most powerfully in wartime addresses like that at Gettysburg, striking chords among war-era listeners whose commitment to the public order starkly required blood, but the seeds were present as early as the late 1830s.

Conceiving personal identity in political-participatory terms did not obviously translate into a heightened commitment to national union. Lincoln seems to have adapted to this end Madisonian assumptions about interpersonal affection to citizens' attitudes toward civic engagement. Participation in governing would inspire a shared sense of purpose; political activity was, Lincoln insisted, "an important principle to rally and unite the people . . . [this is] a fundamental idea, going about as deep as anything."[99] Establishing common laws and otherwise exercising sovereignty (being "in the game") aroused individuals' spirit of mutuality. Rather than a subject of everyday politics, the citizen in Lincoln's vision became an architect of the political order, which in turn was seen as constitutive of his or her[100] personal identity. Emerson's voluntary association of vig-

96. Potter 1976, 552; Basler 1989 [1946], 586-87.

97. See Gienapp 1982, esp. 15, 32-45, 62-66; Silbey 1991, 125-28; and Formisano 1999. Compare the critical account in Altschuler and Blumin 1997.

98. In 1838 Lincoln described political activity as a "task of gratitude to our fathers, justice to ourselves, duty to posterity," a responsibility facing "every young man . . . to the last generation." Basler 1989 [1946], 77. On this topic see also Kahn 1992, esp. 54.

99. Basler 1953-55, 6:424.

100. From Lincoln's first campaign statement, issued in 1836: "I go for all sharing the privileges of the government, who assist in bearing its burthens. Consequently I go for admitting all whites to

orous fellows is a model, though there is no evidence that Lincoln had read his New England contemporary.[101]

By the time Lincoln was elected president he clearly believed, as evidenced in informal talks to audiences ranging from inaugural well-wishers to Union regiments, that political participation promised the citizen considerable benefits. The contrary idea, that government was a complicated business best carried on by those with remarkable foresight and fortitude, had a long pedigree in America. (As, in some quarters, did the view that it was the province of incompetent knaves.) But Lincoln suggested that political activity could be personally rewarding for most residents. This was a view he arrived at slowly, over the course of his political life. Whereas the founders had envisioned a community of at most metaparticipation, and Webster had reluctantly joined the cry for mass activity in government without contributing much practical or theoretical support, Lincoln came to see relatively unmediated participation in politics as a necessary source of national unity. In an 1854 aside, Lincoln compared American ideals to those of "most [other] governments"; he might have been contrasting his own view with that of the founders. "*They* said, some men are too ignorant, and vicious to share in government. Possibly so, said we; and, by your system, you would always keep them ignorant, and vicious. We proposed to give all a chance; and we expected the weak to grow stronger, the ignorant, wiser; and all better, and happier *together*."[102]

In this way Lincoln remained faithful to a basic tenet guiding unionist philosophy since the early republic: that citizens had actively to express an ethic of mutual responsibility for the polity to remain united in any meaningful sense. His doubts about interpersonal affection led Lincoln to emphasize popular participation in governance instead, in hopes of inspiring a sense of common purpose and also an agreement on higher principles, most notably equality. Lincoln related popular sovereignty and equal rights on occasion, especially in his debates with Douglas and subsequent speeches. In 1858 Lincoln asked, "If the Negro is a man, is it not to that extent a total destruction of self-government to say that he too shall not govern himself?"[103] His views on equality for African Americans—and blacks' inclusion in a union of sovereign citizens—would become much more publicly apparent during the Civil War. Though the war was not an im-

---

the right of suffrage, who pay taxes or bear arms (by no means excluding females)" (Basler 1989 [1946], 58).

101. Lincoln's recorded reading lists run more to literary works, particularly Shakespeare, than to political philosophers (besides the American constitutional framers). Lincoln consciously built on the founders' views—yet (recall arguments in earlier chapters about originality and influence) very rare in contemporary scholarship are surveys of European or other non-American influences on Lincoln's thought.

102. Basler 1989 [1946], 279.

103. Basler 1953–55, 3:16–19, 94–95, 179, 221–22, 235 (on Mexicans and sovereignty), 279–80, 405–25, 446–47, 454–55.

mediate inspiration for Lincoln's unionist ideas, it was a spur to realizing changes long present in theory.

African Americans, Equality, and Union

Issuing the *Dred Scott* majority opinion in 1857, Chief Justice Taney stated what Lincoln later impugned as the "amended" view of the Declaration.[104] "The general words," admitted Taney, "would seem to embrace the whole human family, and if they were used in a similar instrument at this day would be so understood. But it is too clear for dispute, that the enslaved African race were not intended to be included."[105] Lincoln was outspoken in response: his opposition to the decision formed the heart of his "House Divided" speech, among others. Lincoln's very different interpretation of the founders' views on equality and union is evident in a campaign speech he made shortly preceding the famous debates with Douglas:

> [T]hey cannot carry themselves back into that glorious [revolutionary] epoch and make themselves feel that they are part of us, but when they look back . . . they find that those old men say that 'We hold these truths to be self-evident, that all men are created equal,' and then they feel that that moral sentiment taught in that day evidences their relation to those men, that it is the father of all moral principle in them, and that they have a right to claim it as though they were blood of the blood, and flesh of the flesh of the men who wrote that Declaration, and so they are. That is the electric cord in that Declaration. That links the hearts of patriotic and liberty-loving men together. . . . [L]et us discard all this quibbling about this man and the other man—this race and that race and the other race being inferior, and therefore they must be placed in an inferior position—discarding our standard that we have left us. Let us discard all these things, and unite as one people throughout the land, until we shall stand up once more declaring that all men are created equal.

Lincoln spoke primarily of European immigrants but evidently referred to African Americans as well: "If one man says it [the Declaration] does not mean the Negro, why not another say it does not mean another man?" Extending the Declaration's familiar passage to include different races, and emphasizing that *all* Americans should "unite as one people"—these were novel public positions for a national political party leader.[106]

---

104. "If Judge Douglas and his friends are not willing to stand by [the Declaration], let them come up and amend it. Let them make it read that all men are created equal, except negroes" (Basler 1989 [1946], 422).

105. 19 How. 393, 410 (1857). Lincoln's views of *Dred Scott* are in Basler 1953–55, 2:494; 3:255.

106. Basler 1989 [1946], 401–3.

Though a body of scholarship dismisses Lincoln's emancipatory intent,[107] he is sometimes read today as exhibiting a "growing radicalism" on issues of black rights.[108] Specific to our purposes is whether this "radical" outlook extended to including African Americans in a reformulated union. In numerous speeches shortly before and during the war, including the immediately preceding long excerpt, Lincoln made clear that the Declaration's "all men" clause encompassed blacks. Union membership in Lincoln's understanding, however, entailed more than vague references to "shared humanity," particularly given his stress on the benefits of political participation.

In 1858 Lincoln said "there is a physical difference between the white and black races, which I suppose, will forever forbid the two races living together upon terms of social and political equality." These words came in the heat of a senatorial race in which Lincoln was repeatedly badgered by Douglas and others on racial-purity issues, a tactic that probably cost him the election.[109] LaWanda Cox holds, plausibly, that Lincoln's white-supremacy rhetoric during the Douglas debates "was a formulation that accepted rather than championed white dominance," and that there is "a larger consistency between the presidential and prepresidential Lincoln" than most scholars admit.[110] Less clear is whether longstanding white opposition to integration was so enduring that Lincoln dared not proceed beyond private musings on black equality.

The evolution of Lincoln's position from the 1850s through the war indicates otherwise. While in 1855 he could still write that he along with "the great body of the Northern people do crucify their [antislavery] feelings, in order to maintain their loyalty to the constitution and the Union," his views were already changing. In 1857 he repeated before several audiences his powerful affirmation of free labor and equality. Responding to Douglas's race-baiting, Lincoln defended the "natural right" of any "black woman [to] eat the bread she earns with her own hands" and concluded "in this . . . she is my equal and the equal of all others." At the 1859 Wisconsin Agricultural Fair the not-yet-declared presidential candidate avowed:

> From the first appearances of man upon the earth, down to very recent times, the words "stranger" and "enemy" were quite and almost synonymous. . . . To correct the evils, great and small, which spring from want

107. E.g., Fredrickson 1971, 149–51; Harding 1981; DiLorenzo 1998, 244–48; Donald 1995, 269–70 (though cf. 373–77, 526–27, 541–42, 583–85); see also sources cited in Cox 1981, chap. 1, n. 30.

108. Quote from Current 1988, 383. Lincoln's views on black inclusion are assessed in Cox 1981, chaps. 1–3, and Johannsen 1991, 7–55; see also Howe 1979, 292–93; McPherson 1990, 51–56, 134–52; 1995; Smith 1997, 249–51, 272–73, 279–82; and Jones 1999, 11–16, 22–33 (especially good on Lincoln's evolving position), 188–91.

109. Holzer 1993, 189. The words from Douglas that inspired the remark: "I believe this Government was made on the white basis. . . . I am in favor of confining citizenship to white men, instead of . . . inferior races."

110. Cox 1981, 20–21. For similar views about Lincoln's consistently principled support for black rights, see Oates 1984, 104–10, and C. R. Smith 1999, 35–41.

of sympathy and from positive enmity, among *strangers,* as nations or as individuals, is one of the highest functions of civilization. [Such corrections] make more pleasant, and more strong, and more durable, the bond of social and political union among us.

Lincoln did not identify free or slave blacks as the "strangers" to be embraced. Yet it is no great speculative leap to read this meaning into his words, especially given the prominence of slavery issues in 1859. His annual message to Congress in 1862 addressed blacks' inclusion even more clearly, concluding, "It is not 'can *any* of us *imagine* better?' but 'can we *all* do better?' Object whatsoever is possible, still the question recurs 'can we do better?'"[111]

Succeeding public and private statements, especially after Lincoln dropped his support for colonization in 1863, suggest his inclination to conclude that African Americans should be full-fledged constituents of a reconstructed union. Lincoln wrote in 1863 to his chief commander in Louisiana that the state should "adopt some practical system by which the two races could gradually live themselves out of their old relation to each other, & both come out better prepared for the new." Anticipating objections from "pro-slavery men," he noted that "even they have strong enough reason to . . . place themselves under the shield of the Union." The same month, addressing white soldiers who "say you will not fight to free negroes," he chided that "some of them seem willing to fight for you" and concluded "there will be some black men who can remember that, with silent tongue, and clenched teeth, and steady eye, and well-poised bayonet, they have helped mankind on to this great consummation; while, I fear, there will be some white ones, unable to forget that, with malignant heart, and deceitful speech, they strove to hinder it." In 1864 Lincoln wrote Louisiana's new governor: "I barely suggest for your private consideration, whether some of the colored people may not be let in [to the franchise]. . . . They would probably help, in some trying time to come, to keep the jewel of liberty within the family of freedom."[112]

Lincoln's last public address, delivered to a White House crowd serenading his return from Appomattox, leads one historian to "suspect that many were disappointed in that audience . . . for Lincoln spoke not in the vein of celebration but of heavy conviction." After previewing his reconstruction policy, Lincoln warned against saying "to the blacks . . . 'This cup of liberty which these, your old masters, hold to your lips, we will dash from you, and leave you to the chances of gathering the spilled and scattered contents in some vague and undefined when, where, and how.'" Instead, Lincoln urged, "recognize, and sustain the new government of Louisiana." Thus "the colored man, too, in *seeing all united for him,* is inspired."[113]

Here we may contrast Lincoln with unionists such as Webster or Madison,

111. Basler 1953–55, 2:320; Basler 1989 [1946], 444, 493, 688.
112. Basler 1989 [1946], 715, 722–24, 745.
113. Ibid., 801, 800 (emphasis added).

both of whom largely ignored questions of blacks' place in the national whole. Lincoln by 1857 was openly including African Americans within the Declaration's guarantee of equality—and hinting, especially after the war began, at their legitimate place as members of the political union. An essential part of the latter assurance was Lincoln's controversial decision to enlist blacks in the Union Army—assuring them an especially deep form of community membership, the right to die for it. Frederick Douglass heralded the decision: African American soldiers would, he wrote, "rise in one bound from social degradation to the plane of common equality with all other varieties of men."[114] Black suffrage, as Lincoln privately endorsed in 1865, was a similarly strong guarantee.

Lincoln's "advoca[cy] of the more and more immediate realization of the promise of [black] equality" fell short in practice. The limits of his leadership are evident in the postwar situation W. E. B. Du Bois later described: "the races . . . liv[ing] for many years side by side, united in economic effort, obeying a common government, sensitive to mutual thought & feeling, yet subtly and silently separate in many matters of deeper human intimacy."[115] Recall, however, that Lincoln viewed affective exchange even between whites as an unpromising source of unity; political union, not "deeper human intimacy," was his aim in 1865. During the last two years of the war (and of his life), Lincoln's commitment to promoting a change in African Americans' status was far deeper than would be any nationally prominent white political leader's over the rest of the century, save perhaps Charles Sumner. No less astute an analyst than Douglass concluded in 1876, with the reversal of Reconstruction's gains well underway, that "measuring [Lincoln] by the sentiment of his country, a sentiment he was bound as a statesman to consult, he was swift, zealous, radical, and determined: because of his fidelity to Union and liberty, he is doubly dear to us [African Americans]." Dorothy Wickenden affirms more recently that "in strikingly similar terms, Abraham Lincoln and Frederick Douglass described a more perfect union, one they together helped to construct."[116]

Lincoln's insistence on *principled* union, and his simultaneous drawing back from the unconditional usage most other politicians adopted, was immensely influential. As the war proceeded, moral unionism was established alongside the old sustainable meaning, and ethnocultural claims became less common, especially after black soldiers joined Union ranks. Unconditional-union claims retained currency, of course; Lincoln's own secretary of state, William Seward, regularly asserted that "no one of us ought to object when called upon to reaffirm his devotion to the Union, however unconditionally." The phrase resonated

114. *Douglass' Monthly*, February 1863, 225. Cf. Taney's decision in *Dred Scott*, explicitly banning "the African race" from this right by noting their exclusion from state militias. 19 How. 393, 410, 415–16.

115. Current 1988, 383; Du Bois 1989 [1903], 86–87.

116. Blassingame 1979–94, 4:436, 440 (cf. 3:606–8); Wickenden 1990, 112. See also Kahn 1992 (53–58) on Lincoln's "moral communitarianism."

beyond the North: "unconditional unionist" became loyalist southerners' self-description during the war, among those "who opposed secession and who never voluntarily aided the Confederacy."[117] But Lincoln's effort to relate union to equality and other moral values won a degree of acceptance, thanks to his great prominence in public life and sacralized status after death. In one telling example, the formerly disunionist abolitionist J. W. Bliss proposed to Sumner "in Lincoln's vein" the doctrine "we mean both *Emancipation* and *Union* . . . the one for the sake of the other and both for the sake of the country." McPherson cites numerous examples of Union soldiers saluting "Lincoln's great evocation of Union war aims," particularly liberty and equality, as well as "the perception that the abolition of slavery was inseparably linked to the goal of preserving the Union."[118]

By no means did everyone referring to "the Union" during or after the war have Lincoln's valuative meaning in mind. One popular ditty among northern soldiers following the Emancipation Proclamation went:

"De Union!" used to be de cry
For dat we went it strong;
But now de motto seems to be,
"De nigger, right or wrong."

Less frivolous critiques made a similar point. Responding to Lincoln's annual message to Congress in 1864, Rep. Yeaman of Kentucky insisted that "we are the most unconditional of Union men," and that "the real character of our unionism has not been understood. . . . Our unionism is not pro-slavery and it is not anti-slavery. The spirit, the chief element, the life of our unionism is a thorough, profound, and elementary condemnation of the theory and practice of *secession* . . . and an equally profound conviction of the unity and oneness of our national Government." Yeaman concluded that "this is a just definition of our unionism; it rises far above the negro as a race, and far above the whole subject of slavery . . . [to] the record of ideas and principles."[119]

Ultimately Lincoln did much to place union on a coherent and principled foundation, as the war propelled the concept to an even more central valuative role among Americans. By insisting, even if only cautiously, on blacks' inclusion in territorial and political union, he staked much of his own prestige on the revised understanding. That prestige soared to uncharted heights with Lincoln's

---

117. Seward in Smith 1997, 275; Abbott 1997, 39n. 5.
118. Quoted in Stampp 1992, 136; McPherson 1997, 104–30 (quotes at 104, 117).
119. Donald 1978, 156; *Cong. Globe*, 38th Cong., 1st sess., 1864, 195. Compare a *Chicago Times* "review" of Lincoln's Gettysburg address: "It was to uphold this constitution, and the Union created by it, that our officers and soldiers gave their lives at Gettysburg. How dare he, then, standing on their graves, misstate the cause for which they died . . . ? They were men possessing too much respect to declare that Negroes were their equals, or were entitled to equal privileges" (November 23, 1863).

martyrdom, temporarily cementing national union's identification as a morally informed instrument.

One significant oversight marks Lincoln's account of unified America. While he cast deliberative conflict over political issues as a positive source of interpersonal connection, he did not address the deep diversity, and ensuing clashes of values and purposes, characterizing the U.S. polity. Madison sought to alleviate enduring conflicts by extending the republic and balancing multiple interests; Webster by promoting compromise and stirringly declaring differences of opinion, economic station, religious views, and ethnic background overcome. But by Lincoln's presidency the territory left to extend into was shrinking fast; his grim declaration in 1863 that "I do not believe any compromise, embracing the maintenance of the Union, is now possible" [120] evidenced his attitude to that Whig tradition.

Lincoln's presidency was almost completely colored by war, a consequence of which was that ordinary tolerations of difference were severely restricted. Witness the violations of habeas corpus, deportation of administration critics like Rep. Clement Vallandigham, and so forth. [121] Wartime exigency may explain why Lincoln's presidential speeches and writings include little regard for bringing divisive forces, whatever their genesis, into the tent of union. Yet even in earlier peaceable times, Lincoln's muted, respectful account of conflict depended on participants' accepting their roles in the game. He based political unity on a particular set of beliefs and values, rejecting most dissenting views. J. David Greenstone describes this as a clash of foundational liberal tenets: the principle of toleration (as upheld by Douglas, for example, in insisting on states' equal right to accept or reject slavery) was overridden by Lincoln's insistence on democratic equality. What to do about those unwilling to enter into the "game" of deliberative political conflict, like secession-minded southerners? Wage war on them. In mid-nineteenth-century America, facing outbreaks of sectional and economic conflict and experiencing increasing immigration from a wider variety of shores, a more creative approach to joining diverse elements was needed. None was forthcoming from Lincoln, an oversight that may have helped speed the postwar decline of moral unionist claims. But before addressing that development, we turn to how union ideals—in moral, ethnocultural, or sustainable versions—operated from 1861 to 1865.

WARTIME UNION

The Civil War's outbreak altered most features of American politics, including ideas of political union. As the conflict began, eminent Ohio lawyer Robert

120. Basler 1989 [1946], 720.
121. On these events, see Rawley 1974, 60–64 (habeas corpus), 92–93, 124–26 (Vallandigham).

Breck predicted "now . . . men in both sections" would "examine for the first time . . . the vessel which has borne them, to understand the great timbers and braces that hold it together."[122] Most evident in such reviews, as seen in innumerable northern statements during the war, is a sense that "true" unity was finally being achieved through common suffering. War resolved the tensions between a sustainable "union at any price" and the moral ends others sought to associate with the term. Historian James Moorhead notes that "by any standard of judgement, the metamorphosis of feeling in April 1861 was remarkable . . . [even] those who had talked of sundering the nation suddenly bowed in reverence before the ark of the Union. As a symbol of political and religious meaning for all Protestants, the Union had been rehabilitated, and suffused with new moral vitality."[123]

As the North-South conflict began there was, for the first time since the 1780s, no confusion over union's meaning. The antebellum period, in contrast, was portrayed as a time "when it was not very distinctly understood what Unionism meant." The term stood for reabsorption of the seceding states into the whole—ardently desired in the North, furiously resisted in the South—and was also synonymous with the loyal states and the army comprising many of their residents. The *New York Times* set the tone early, editorializing a week after Sumter that "the South's attack has made the North a Union." This correspondence was codified in endless ways, from songs, poems, sermons, and speeches to bloodshed. Lincoln was among many northern politicians contributing a strong moral tone to this surge of union talk, declaring in his initial proclamation requesting troops that the war was joined "to maintain the honor, the integrity, and the existence of our National Union."[124]

Nagging antebellum (like founding-era) fears that Americans' unionist spirit was flagging were answered by the unifying effects of war. Southern secession provided common ground for moral unionists and those urging unity at any price, as a New York weekly noted: "All other questions are now merged in one: Have we a Government? Is the Union of these states a solid reality, or only an airy vision?" Boston minister G. E. Ellis insisted in 1864, in Lincolnian terms, that the war's "purpose is to put the maintenance of our American National Unity foremost in resolve . . . the question of territorial integrity and unity takes precedence over all others. The purpose is, that the law of the nation shall extend over the whole of it, whatever may befall the inhabitants or the peculiar institutions of any rebellious portion of it." Edmund Wilson has aptly termed northerners' wartime rhetoric "patriotic gore," and a good deal of it was spilled on be-

---

122. Breck 1862, 10.
123. Moorhead 1978, 41.
124. *Cong. Globe,* 37th Cong., 3d sess., 1863, 1082; *New York Times,* April 15, 1861; Basler 1953–55, 4:332. Ardent unionist references filled newspapers everywhere outside the South, including the staid *Farmers' Cabinet* (Amherst, N.H.), which devoted its first column for weeks after Fort Sumter to patriotic poems extolling, e.g., "the great union that blesses our land" (May 24, 1861).

half of national union after April 1861. Within a few weeks criticism developed among northerners (especially Democrats) about the *means* Lincoln elected to prosecute the war, a chorus that intensified after the Emancipation Proclamation. But virtually no one outside the South publicly disagreed that the principal object of the war was restored national union.[125]

Why Northerners Fought

The bombardment of Fort Sumter made it plain that antebellum bonds of national unity were insufficient to prevent secession. This fact certainly colors the compromises and other practical manifestations of unionism outlined in previous pages. "How 'national' can our Union [be] said to have been," soberly wondered a Boston writer in 1861, "now that it has been so easily sundered?"[126] Yet this sundering provoked a profound response, in the form of innumerable northerners' stated readiness to go to war in defense of this value. Elisha Hunt Rhodes, concluding a long diary entry about how cold, wet, and miserable his recent soldiering had been, brightened momentarily: "It is all for the Union. . . . God help us—all I want is to see the Union restored." Many modern analysts are skeptical of Rhodes and other northerners' unionist explanations for why they fought; Heather Cox Richardson chronicles recent arguments "that Civil War soldiers did not fight for ideas." Yet ample evidence supports past historians' conclusion that "for many in the North preservation of the Union was an end in itself. They did not rush to the colors to get a higher tariff or a Pacific railroad . . . but to protect the sacred Union."[127]

James McPherson's exhaustive recounting of Civil War soldiers' stated reasons for volunteering, fighting, and reenlisting emphasizes—against the grain of recent scholarship—the "patriotic convictions" expressed on both sides. Of the 647 Union soldiers whose diaries and letters McPherson examined, nearly three quarters affirmed their motivation in unionist terms, like one Illinois colonel: "We are fighting for the Union, a high and noble sentiment." A lieutenant in an Ohio brigade saw national union as the basis of other values, again in Lincoln's style: "without Union & peace our freedom is worthless," he wrote his wife in 1862. Southern soldiers also invoked their "country" in battle, and one South Carolinian insisted that slavery was "a bond of union stronger than any which holds the north together." Men fought for a variety of reasons, as McPherson amply chronicles, but he persuasively locates love of country and an insistence on reunion as prominent among these.[128]

125. *Independent* (New York), April 25, 1861; Ellis 1864, 10; Wilson 1962. Congressional Democrats were especially harsh Lincoln critics, few more avid than Kentucky Senator Garrett Davis, who was nearly expelled from the Senate for urging a popular "revolt" against the administration. Details, including Davis's statement, in *Cong. Globe*, 38th Cong., 1st sess., 1864, 344.

126. *Boston Post*, October 7, 1861.

127. Rhodes 1991, 61; Richardson 1999, 399; L. H. Johnson 1978, 80.

128. McPherson 1997, quotes at pp. 98, 135, 20; figures on motivation at pp. 100–101; on patriotic/unionist inspiration see generally pp. 90–103, 168–78. Compare generally Frank 1998, which

Those closer to the event similarly saw national unity as a leading source of soldiers' conviction. Ulysses Grant's unusually frank memoirs include an episode in which his Illinois regiment was about to be mustered into service for three years after an original ninety-day tour of duty. Many soldiers, now fully aware of the realities of war, refused to sign on for such a long spell, wrote Grant: "they felt that this change of period released them from the obligation of re-volunteering." Grant invited the local Congressman, a well-reputed orator, to address the reluctant regiment. His speech "breathed a loyalty and devotion to the Union which inspired my men to such a point that they would have volunteered to remain in the army as long as an enemy of the country continued to bear arms against it," Grant reported. "They entered the U.S. service almost to a man." In 1887 John Fiske referred to "the trumpet-call which [led] them [Union soldiers] on to death for that Union which was Webster's highest inspiration." Jacob Polson Cox, in his 1892 *Atlantic* article "Why the Men of '61 Fought for the Union," recalled that "amongst Northern people . . . even among the unthinking, there was an attachment to the Union which became a contagion of patriotism when the struggle really began. . . . The grand outburst of devotion to the flag, from east to west, settled once for all the question whether we were strong enough to nullify the acts of nullification, and to restore the Union." [129]

Beyond the motivation of soldiers to fight, more common locations of northerners' union sentiment—newspapers, congressional speeches, pamphlets, Supreme Court decisions—spilled over with references to "the sacred union of our fathers." The war's beginning occasioned clear relief among many unionists. A *Princeton Review* study of "American Nationality," later reprinted in pamphlet form, spoke for many in October 1861: "the guns of Fort Sumter were heard, through the telegraphic wires, with strange thrills, by every man and woman and child. . . . Patriotism, which seemed to have died, now revived; it superseded the love of ease, of gain, of life; and the bond of national unity asserted its legitimate supremacy over the strongest affections of family and kindred." Many women may well have taken umbrage at the implied distinction between unionist spirit and family "affections," given their wartime work on behalf of the Union Army. Existing women's reform and welfare organizations like the National Loyal League addressed their efforts to the Union cause. Essayists favorably described these activities and women's support for "the sacred Union" in general; some pamphlets, such as "A Few Words in Behalf of the Loyal Women of the United State by One of Themselves," were circulated nationally. [130]

A unionist outlook accounts, at least in part, for the statements and actions of millions of northern soldiers and supporters before and during the conflict. Less

---

analyzes more than a thousand letters and diaries in seeking to comprehend why Civil War soldiers fought; Mitchell 1993, 115–26; Baker 1983, 327–44.

129. Grant 1962 [1885], 61–62; Fiske 1877, 86; Cox 1892, 391–92.

130. "American Nationality," 1861, 32–33; Freidel 1967, 2:769 (full pamphlet at pp. 766–86). On Union women's war service, see Jeffrey 1998, 217–21, and Mitchell 1993, 75–80.

apparent is why abolitionists and other northern opponents of the slavocracy were willing to fight on behalf of a reunited country. The historian Roger Ransom supplies the likeliest answer: "The possibility that a powerful nation, independent of the United States and controlled by an oligarchy of slaveholders, would exist if the South left the Union was not lost on contemporaries in the Northern states." Hence union as such likely played a secondary part in abolitionists' calculations, but it was nonetheless cited as a valued aim. Such an outlook affirmed Douglass's prewar outlook, now spreading throughout the abolitionist movement. Garrison, after years of preaching "disunion and peace," declared in 1861 that "there is not a drop of blood in my veins, both as an abolitionist and as a peace man, that does not flow with the Northern tide of sentiment," and later expressed hope "that a *cleansed* national Union will soon be restored." [131]

Union's appeal even remained palpable in parts of the wartime South. Until hostilities commenced, strong unionist voices could still be heard throughout the region; these were termed "Union Shriekers" by opponents. Most of these men, including such prominent figures as John Janney, the president of the Virginia Convention that voted for secession, "renounced a lifetime of staunch Unionism at the last minute." [132] During the war, all Confederate states included small but significant segments of pro-Union residents. Most of these were demarcated geographically: mountainous areas of western Virginia and North Carolina, eastern Tennessee, northern Georgia and Alabama, and the Arkansas foothills together contributed some 75,000 native whites to the Union Army (of an estimated 100,000 total southern Union soldiers). Wartime provisional Union governors like Andrew Johnson of Tennessee and Arkansas's Isaac Murphy also hailed from mountain regions. Another group of southern union supporters was spread along the Atlantic and Gulf coasts, from New Orleans through coastal Florida, Georgia, the Carolinas, and Virginia. [133] Along with their military and political support for the Union cause, southern unionists in a few instances founded pro-Union newspapers, spreading a message of reconciliation and antisecession (and, in a few cases, antislavery) through a region otherwise hostile to the term. Though most papers were bought by Union soldiers, some discontented Confederates were apparently encouraged by these publications to support unionist causes. [134]

Again, these southern unionists were a small fraction of the region's population during the war. Most others endorsed attempts to construct a separate southern nationality, carefully described in terms other than union: confederacy, asso-

131. Ransom 1999, 38; Garrison in Rawley 1974, 19–20; *Non-Slaveholder*, June 10, 1861.

132. Rubin 1994, 381. Janney publicly accepted his own designation as a "Union Shrieker," declaring at an 1860 gathering: "I am willing to be placed in the same category with . . . the authors of the Constitution, who made a more perfect Union—[and] with George Washington, who, in 1796, uttered a shriek for the Union, the echoes of which will never die" (ibid., 406).

133. Current 1992, 218. Two excellent studies of wartime southern Unionists, in Atlanta and East Tennessee respectively, are Dyer 1999 and Fisher 1998.

134. On wartime newspapers, see esp. Abbott 1997.

ciation, republic, and so forth. The degree to which the Confederacy attracted southern patriotic sentiment is contested by historians to this day.[135] Not so their temporary loathing for "the very *thought* of Union; the word itself remains in my throat, like a carbuncle[;] I cannot say it," as a Richmond writer put it in 1863.[136] But as the war ended two years later, southerners en masse renewed their rhetorical support for national union. Chapter 5 takes up this remarkable development, along with the reversal of Lincoln's moral unionism during Reconstruction. First, however, is a look at another important aspect of union ideas during the war.

Institution-Building

The previous chapter demonstrated the relevance of union concepts to antebellum national-state development. The war years brought an exponential increase in the volume of state activity, further exhibiting the interplay of ideas and institutions. Daniel Elazar describes Lincoln's administration as "a veritable 'New Deal' of concentrated expansion of the role of government." These efforts, including creation of an Agriculture Department in 1862, federalizing taxation and other commercial powers, railroad expansion, confiscation of Confederate property including slaves, and homestead and land-grant acts, have been well reviewed elsewhere.[137] Important for our purposes is the extent to which these organizational developments were connected to, or justified in terms of, preserving national unity.

Congressional actors described most of their extensive wartime legislative output as in the service of union, a claim hard to distinguish from the more generic "aiding the war effort." During debates on a Pacific railroad, a U.S. House member from California described established practice: "the Government unites its capital with individuals to build [the] work . . . and that kind of enterprise and capital united is what we have to rely upon to secure the accomplishment of this work." Acts to conscript soldiers into the Union Army were especially ground for unionist declamations, from supporters like Samuel Fessenden (who described the bill as "legislation by the help of which we hope soon to see a cemented Union") and foes including Ohio Rep. Samuel Cox, who insisted that the bill would secure "no Union, but . . . a despotism of power." Congressional exchanges on everything from creation of a national currency to presidential in-

135. In the wartime Confederacy, moreover, a familiar tension between states' rights and southern nationality reappeared during the war. One southerner, writing as a "South Carolinian," insisted on "the right of the State" to exempt local police from military service and reminded readers that "South Carolina for 40 years has been an illustrious example [of] her great idea of State Sovereignty." *Charleston Daily Courier,* December 13, 1864.

136. *Richmond Enquirer,* March 14, 1863. On the creation of a "southern nation," see cites at note 136, chap. 3.

137. Elazar 1972b, 43; cf. McPherson 1990, vii–viii, 3–42; Richardson 1997, esp. 86–91 (on the expanding federal role in the economy); and Paludan 1994, 106–18.

demnification were similarly punctuated by repeated promises that the measure would assure "the chief purpose[,] the restoration of the Union." Certainly these claims were "rhetorical," but that does not dismiss their defenders' seriousness—especially not in a book contending, as this one does, that legislative objects were invested with unionist meaning because of union's immense appeal among the citizenry.[138]

Lincoln's executive contributions to this legislative invigoration of the machinery of central government were small, mostly limited to signing laws and giving rein to activist cabinet members.[139] Indeed, struggles with Republicans in Congress led him to set off on his own Union Party–building efforts. Still, when Lincoln's attention turned from the battlefield to issues of restoring union between the sections, his principled view of national unity dictated strong institutional safeguards. Here the relation between Lincoln's unionist ideas and administrative action becomes apparent.

In affirming new federal practices, Lincoln had to respond to the familiar charge that expanding central powers threatened to circumscribe personal liberty. The result would be quite the opposite, he insisted. Homestead and land-grant college laws promised the means for individual self-improvement—and for realizing "man's duty . . . to assist in ameliorating mankind." Central-government efforts abetted rather than restricted individual economic and sociopolitical ends. Loosening fetters on political participation, epitomized in ending slavery, would similarly lead to more personal freedom, not less. Lincoln made this clear in his hint to new Louisiana governor Michael Hahn, previously noted, that African Americans be granted suffrage.[140] Expanded voting rights, educational opportunities, property ownership, and for that matter centralized banking, making small-business loans far easier to obtain, were all defended by Lincoln as bases of popular sovereignty. No less an observer than Karl Marx testified to the import of these changes: Lincoln, the "single-minded son of the working class," led "the reconstruction of a social world." The change, "workingmen of Europe feel sure," would "initiate a new era of ascendancy for . . . the working classes."[141]

Lincoln promoted expanded federal powers where these demonstrably helped secure other prized goods, like union and equality. His was not the vision of a Mazzini or Bismarck, explicitly seeking to further nationalist spirit through administrative centralization. As Howe attests, postwar U.S. tendencies toward state-building "ushered in an era very different from anything Lincoln could have expected or wanted. His objective, in the broadest sense, was to defend and

138. *Cong. Globe,* 37th Cong., 3rd sess., 1863, 1246, 1267, 1269, 1083. An overview of the wartime Congress's activities is in Rawley 1974, 31–53.

139. See Donald (1956, 192), who argues that Lincoln "had remarkably little connection with the legislation passed during the Civil War."

140. Basler 1989 [1946], 573, 745.

141. Marx quoted in Padover 1972, 237.

extend the 'mixed' society of small entrepreneurs, market-oriented farmers, young men working for others until they could save enough to set up for themselves, and striving professionals like himself."[142] This vision depended not on a set of national institutions penetrating deeply into everyday life, but on a people as widely engaged in political affairs as possible.

142. Howe 1979, 297.

CHAPTER 5

The Terms of Reunion

The Union never made war upon the South. It was not the Union, my countrymen, that slew your children; it was not the Union that burned your cities. . . . Every one of these wrongs was inflicted by a diabolical sectionalism in the very teeth of every principle of the American Union. So, equally, I affirm that the South never made war upon the Union. There has never been an hour when nine out of ten of us would not have given our lives for this Union.

> —Confederate Senator Benjamin Hill,
> "Davis Hall Speech," Atlanta, 1867

RALEIGH, NORTH CAROLINA, seems an unlikely place for a post–Civil War tribute to the idea of national union. During the war, Raleigh's local leaders and Confederated citizens, like those in other southern cities, rooted out public references to the word. Union Square, the city's center since 1792, was instead called "Capitol" or "Central" Square. The Union Station signboard was repeatedly defaced and finally stolen, leaving "trains [to] arrive at an anonymous depot," as a traveler sourly observed in 1863. Into early 1865 editorials avowed that "very few of our people prefer a union with our northern foes. Ninety-nine hundredths of them can never again . . . be content under the same government with the North."[1]

Yet only weeks after Appomattox the term was back in vogue. War's end was greeted with banners and "illuminations" throughout Raleigh, from the Christian Commission's doorfront placard "Peace, Union and Liberty Forever" to a Confederate lieutenant's daughter heading the July 4 parade with a sign reading "We will teach our children to love the Union." Provisional Governor Holden's June 1865 inaugural address was a model of conciliation, concluding: "Remember that all that you have, and all that you can hope to be, and all of good that is in reserve for your children, are indissolubly bound up with the American Union. The unity of government which constitutes us one people should be more dear to us than ever, on account of the sufferings through which we have passed." Northern visitors from 1865 onward noted, with qualifications, the spread of "North Carolina Unionism" throughout the population and even among prominent former secessionists. The swift and widespread renewal of union talk among North

---

1. Battle 1893, 24; Connor 1929, 291; *Raleigh News,* August 22, 1863; *Daily Conservative* (Raleigh), April 6, 1865. Compare, among many like examples throughout the South, the proposed changes to Union County, Georgia, and Union District, South Carolina, as reported in the *Charleston Daily Courier,* December 10, 1864.

Carolinians—and whites throughout the South—marks one of the strangest turns in the concept's career.[2]

For more obvious reasons, union retained extraordinary value among northerners after 1865. Leaders and masses alike heralded the war's outcome with such declarations as "there has been in the history of no people the witness to a higher unity."[3] The past was also mined for evidence of a moral union, or reshaped to yield it. George Bancroft, publishing in 1866 the ninth volume of his monumental history of early America, dedicated it "reverently on the altar of freedom and union," extending and deepening what had been his principal theme since volume 1.[4]

This surging postwar union talk receives little attention among scholars today, for the story of post–Civil War political development is directed elsewhere. From a fragile collection of mutually suspicious states, the United States became a *nation*. "Begun to preserve the old Union, the Civil War brought into being a new American nation-state," in Eric Foner's representative claim.[5] This conventional account has two components: (1) weak prewar ideas of national unity were replaced by a robust sense of nationalism among most Americans, and (2) a "laissez-faire, individual enterprise state" was "now transformed into a nation" with strong central administrative direction.[6] Both argumentative prongs are misguided.

Rather than ushering in a new regime of state-centered nationalism in place of a tenuous prewar union, the years following the war featured an intense conflict over the terms of restored unity. At the heart of this struggle, which involved such vital issues as how to reintegrate southerners and whether African Americans were members of the national union, was a contest among the unionist views laid out in preceding chapters. A morally informed account of union, as developed by Lincoln and Douglass, was advanced by Radical Republicans and their supporters, notably including black leaders. Southerners and moderates from other sections responded with a reworked version of prewar balanced, sustainable-union views, complete with guarantees for states' rights (often defended in ethnocul-

2. *Daily Standard* (Raleigh), May 12, 1865; *Daily Progress* (Raleigh), July 6, 1865; Holden speech in *Daily Standard,* June 29, 1865; Andrews 1866b, 240. The *Standard,* founded by Holden during the war, was a Unionist paper, reviled by other Raleigh journals (see, e.g., *Raleigh Register,* April 5, 1862).

3. Mulford 1882, 328.

4. Bancroft 1897, 1:3; 9:5. On Bancroft as romantic nationalist, see Thelen 1998, 382–83. Francis Parkman and Henry Adams similarly if less explicitly oriented their respective studies of pre-Jacksonian North America around the fitful progress of national unity. See Vitzthum 1974, 3–41, 207–20. Novelists also wove themes of political and moral unity into their postwar works: Melville's *Battle-Pieces,* Henry James's *Bostonians,* and Henry Adams's *Democracy* are examples.

5. Foner 1998, 98; compare, e.g., Nichols 1961, 147–53, 175; Foner 1988, xxvi, 451–69; McPherson 1990, vi–viii; Sandel 1996, 39; Richardson 1997; Grant 1998, 172 ("the old nation had already become extinct" with the outbreak of war). A more judicious account comes from Bruce Ackerman, who describes a "new, *more nation-centered,* configuration marked strongly by presidential leadership" (1998, 157; emphasis added).

6. Nichols 1961, 147.

tural terms, though now avoiding reference to slavery) as the surest means of permanently restoring national unity.

Thus old-style unionist arguments by no means receded in the wake of a "Second American Revolution" supposedly featuring, among other aspects, "intense new nationalism" and unprecedented central-state authority.[7] Instead a powerful desire for renewed national unity deeply influenced postwar U.S. political vocabulary and institution-building. This chapter chronicles both the debates over union's postwar definition and the concept's effects in the polity. Battles surrounding the three landmark constitutional amendments and associated congressional acts of 1865–69 mark the apex of Americans' moral understanding of a more perfect union. Yet even these measures were defended (and opposed) in terms of securing union and reintegrating the southern states. Moreover, this principled achievement spurred many in the South to insist even more firmly that the prewar "Union as it was" be restored, excepting the slave system.

These southern demands drew on a massive recurrence of sustainable-union views across the United States. Support for morally informed union was already dwindling by 1867–68. The postwar terms of union were subsequently solidified in a form closely resembling the balanced account set out by Madison or Webster. Southerners' positive response to this compromise position—especially after Reconstruction officially ended, in 1877—engendered an outpouring of sentimental praise for national unity throughout the country.

Implicated in these shifting rhetorical conditions were institutional efforts at establishing a reunited country. On one hand, congressional Republicans' civil-rights achievements were largely dismantled, as southerners asserted white rule and local control as the price of reunion. On the other hand, state and national actors alike sought to cement national unity in enduring forms. Two examples of the latter are traced at length in the following sections: Supreme Court efforts to codify the postwar terms of unity in jurisprudence; and the implicit agreement reached among several states, after 1877, to honor the restored Union by scheduling U.S. House elections—long a jealously guarded state prerogative, much like presidential primary dates today—on a single common date in early November.

The resumption of familiar terms of union, with accompanying limits on centralized authority, eventually turned certain groups against the ideal, as explored in the next chapter. But union's continued salience after the war was far more widespread than contemporary accounts of a new, nationalist American regime acknowledge. The Reconstruction period temporarily gave rise to a "new birth of freedom," as many have noted.[8] It witnessed a renewal of union affirmations as well.

---

7. "Second American Revolution" was originally coined by Charles and Mary Beard: see Ransom 1999, 28–30. "Nationalism" quote from Foner 1998, 98. My argument here is not that *no* "revolution" in the American polity was wrought by the war, but that traditional union ideas remained in force—and helped shape postwar developments.

8. Most recently Akhil Amar, from whom this quote is taken (1998, 284–94; see also McPherson 1990, 41).

WAR AND FORGETTANCE:
RENEWED SOUTHERN UNIONISM, 1865 – 67

During the Civil War most southern unionists kept their loyalty to themselves, whatever they might otherwise have been doing to effect sectional reconciliation. Favorable references to "union" earned penalties as grave as death in the wartime South.[9] Such virulent reactions received ample notice in the North as the war drew to a close, fueling concerns about one of the conflict's primary objectives— restoring national unity. Longtime abolitionist William Whiting grimly commented that "to suppose that a Union sentiment will remain in any considerable number of men, among a [southern] people who have strained every nerve and made every sacrifice to destroy Union, indicates dishonesty, insanity, or feebleness of intellect." An anonymous contributor to the *Liberator,* possibly Douglass, remarked at the end of 1864, "now, whoever lives to see this rebellion suppressed . . . will also see the South characterized by a sullen hatred towards the National Government. It will be transmitted from father to son, and will be held by them as 'sacred animosity.'"[10]

Postwar animosity most southerners expressed in spades, but not toward the idea of union. Political historians today depict the region's whites as bitterly resistant to reconciliation: Richard Bensel's study of postwar state building, to take a prominent example, details "militantly separatist" tendencies among southerners lasting long after war's end.[11] Yet well into the 1880s, much more common among southerners than vestigial appeals to the Confederacy were fervent calls for inclusion and reunion that transcended mere sloganeering in intensity and breadth. Many such statements were qualified, but the general expression was of a desire for renewed unity; many in the North responded positively as Reconstruction proceeded. An insistence on local autonomy that drew northern ire, and eventually fire, when associated with slavery proved more palatable when expressed in the context of national reunion.

Postwar Southern Usage

In a startling reversal, virtually overnight "union" again became a favorable symbol among southerners. Southerners early in 1865 were still fulminating about

9. *New York Times,* April 15, 1861. On wartime treatment of loyalists, see Crofts 1989; Fleming 1905, 112–16 (specifying "unionist" usage among Alabamans during war); Chesebrough 1993; and Olsen 1980, 159 (on the fate of unionists in North Carolina).

10. Whiting in Hyman 1967, 92; *Liberator,* December 23, 1864 (on the latter, cf. Blassingame 1979–94, 4:158–65).

11. Bensel 1990, 15–17, 377–79, 414–15 ("the fundamental issue facing the nation during the latter half of the nineteenth century was southern separatism"), 422–26, 436. Bensel misconstrues opposition to central state authority as "separatism" plain and simple. This error stems partly from over-reliance on planter testimony; this group was superseded after 1865 by a "banker-merchant-farmer-lawyer-doctor governing class" more favorable to sectional harmony. Quote from Shannon 1948, 44; cf. Woodward's bold claim (1951) that the planter class was "destroyed" by the war, and Rabinowitz's (1992, 18–27) balanced summary.

"the odious name, [the] crust and sham and shell and pretensive Union." But barely three months later came a sea change. M. P. O'Connor, a Democrat seeking nomination to South Carolina's constitutional convention in 1865, contrasted "the spectacle South Carolina to-day presents, prone and exhausted" with the future "State in her new and restored relation to the Union . . . [where] the fortunes of all constitute the fortunes of the State." The forthcoming "blessings of harmony, union, and prosperity," he continued, even qualified the war as "a permanent national blessing," despite its "great evil and much disaster." The *Richmond Enquirer,* described by the *Cincinnati Gazette* as "especially famous during the war in denouncing the Northern people, and inspiring the rebels," announced in its first postwar issue "Let the dead bury their dead—let the past, with all our errors as well as yours, be forgotten" and reminded "our countrymen, both North and South" of "the early pledges of the fathers of the Republic," securing "the bonds of restored friendship and brotherly love."[12] Across the South, judging from newspaper testimony, carpetbaggers and Radical Republicans were reviled, but not so the latter half of what was then termed "reconstruction and reunion."[13] Indeed, Yankees and Republicans were routinely pilloried as "radical opponents of both Union and Constitution"—underscoring the positive valence of these ideals.[14]

Figure 5 provides empirical evidence of union's postwar appeal among citizens of the short-lived Confederacy between 1865 and 1890. As in preceding chapters, a sample of (southern, in this case) newspapers was plumbed for all national references to union.[15] The term's substantive meaning changed among southerners during this period, as laid out in the following pages. The vast majority of references after the war, however, were positive, ushering in a broad resumption of unionist rhetoric from 1865 onward.

Among southerners the union banner was waved most vigorously by wartime loyalists, whose new "Unconditional Union" organization in 1866 was one of numerous Union parties in the region.[16] African Americans in the region also

12. *Charleston Daily Courier,* January 14, 1865, and September 1, 1865; *Richmond Enquirer,* November 7, 1865. The *Enquirer,* unlike some southern papers, retained its Confederate editor after the war.

13. Among the rare examples of explicitly anti-union sentiment came in a popular song skewering everything from the Freedmen's Bureau to New England cuisine—one that originated as a poem satirizing grumbling ex-Confederates. Reprinted in *Collier's,* April 4, 1914, 25.

14. See, e.g., *Mobile Daily Advertiser and Register,* March 9, 1866. Carl Degler traces a similar argument among southerners in the secession period: "it was the North that had changed and in doing so threatened the South and the Union created in 1787. That interpretation has been given only occasional credence by historians, primarily because it repudiated . . . values highly esteemed by Whig historians" (Degler 1987, 7).

15. The *Charleston Daily Courier* was taken over by Unionist management for several months after Charleston fell in February 1865 (the new editor declared it "a truly and thoroughly loyal Union newspaper" in its first issue thereafter, on February 21). Thus I altered the list of newspapers included in my count in the Appendix, removing the *Courier* between 1865 and 1870 and substituting available issues of the *Virginia Gazette* (Williamsburg), which retained its antebellum editor and, for the most part, prewar tone.

16. Between 1865 and 1868, these included: Andrew Johnson's ill-fated National Union party in 1866 (Democrats settled for the slogan "The Union as It Is—The Constitution as It Was"); loyalists'

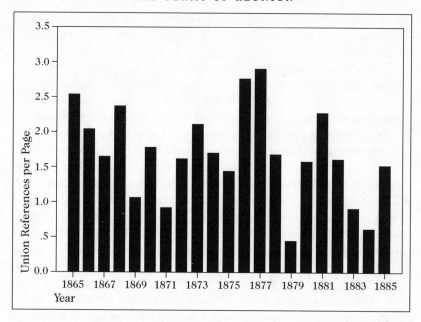

FIGURE 5. White Southerners' union references, 1865–85

linked national unity and freedom in the early postwar period. A September 1865 convention of North Carolina blacks, mostly made up of former slaves, publicly stated: "We can conceive of no reason that our God-bestowed freedom should now sever the kindly ties which have so long united us to the whole. . . . Now that freedom and a new career are before us, we love this land and the people more than ever before."[17] The term appeared among diehard white Democrats as well, though sometimes in the context of defiance. The editor of Wilmington's daily paper wrote after July 4, 1866, that "the South would have been glad to have united with the North in honest and grateful rejoicings of this national holiday," but southerners' "cheerful concessions were responded to by renewed exactions, evincing . . . a determined purpose to degrade them." Such mixed accounts were also recorded in private. Gertrude Thomas, a Georgia planter's wife and later

efforts to organize in 1866–67 under the banner of "Unconditional Unionists"; moderate southern Republicans' "National Union Republican" ticket in 1868, meant to counteract Radical tendencies— and hastily matched in South Carolina and other states by Democrats' "Union Reform" party, which courted blacks and disaffected Republicans. Most Union parties in the Deep South were fronts for Democratic organizations, combating northern Republicans who had followed Lincoln in adopting the term to broaden their political base during the war. In border states, however, "'unionist' Congressmen represented real attempts to find a middle way between the two major parties." Quote from Bensel 1990, 225n; also see Foner 1988, 185, 266, 414; Fleming 1905, 400, 402–5; Perman 1984, 9, 20, 45; Baker 1983, 344–52.

17. Quoted in Ashe 1925, 2:1027. Andrews (1866a, 131) emphasized that the gathering "was really a convention of colored men, not . . . engineered by white men." A detailed study of patterns in blacks' postwar union usage appears in chapter 6.

a spokeswoman for early Progressive reform movements, wrote in a May 1865 diary entry:

> The war is over and again we become a part of the United States—how united will depend alone upon treatment we receive from the hands of the North. It will prove to their interest to be very discreet. . . . Treated as members of one family—a band of brothers, in time we may have a common interest—but pressed too hard upon, our property taken from us— a desperate people having nothing to lose, the South may again revolt.[18]

But on numerous occasions, even former Confederates extolled national unity in ways that masked the war's bitter enmity. Alabama's Willard Warner, a U.S. Senator after the war, privately wrote an Ohio general in May 1865: "All the [southern] people submit utterly, and a large portion cheerfully, and the work of reconstruction and reconciliation will be easy if not hindered by a vindictive policy . . . in three years our country will be nearer a union of feeling than before the war."[19]

Northerners traveling in the South during the first months after the war recorded this union talk with deep suspicion. Political journalist E. P. Whipple wrote early in 1866 that "Southern politicians" had "adapted themselves with marvelous flexibility to the changed condition of things . . . and begin to declaim in favor of the Union, even while their curses against it were yet echoing in the air." Massachusetts lawyer Sidney Andrews, after spending fall 1865 in Georgia and the Carolinas, decried the region's "sham Unionism": "There may be in it the seed of loyalty, but woe to him who mistakes the germ for the ripened fruit! . . . [H]ow full of promise for the new era of national life is the Unionism which rests only on this foundation?"[20]

These northern reports resemble many historical accounts today, dismissing white southerners' union talk as a disingenuous cover for the perpetuation of prewar defiance. But an examination of southern rhetoric suggests that economic or other self-serving interests account for only part of the story. Also apparent was a genuine unionist orientation related to the psychology of defeat. By 1868 many southerners were again explicitly working to reestablish national unity on their own terms. But in the chaotic months after Appomattox, solidarity with their former foes was an important source of personal and regional regeneration. Why did southerners initially readopt the language of national union?

Union Resurgent: Self-Interest

Ockham's razor prescribes that we search no farther than material self-interest in accounting for the resurgence of favorable union terminology among south-

---

18. *Daily Journal* (Wilmington, N.C.), July 6, 1866; Burr 1990, 260. By 1870 Thomas more freely expressed sentiments of reconciliation (Burr 1990, 336, 373).

19. Reprinted in *Cong. Globe*, 41st Cong., 2d sess., 1870, 2813.

20. Whipple 1866, 506; Andrews 1866b, 240–41.

erners. The region's near total economic collapse—and perhaps the age-old injunction to "buy low"—sent northerners streaming south from 1865 onward. Though later despised as carpetbaggers, these investors were readily, if not always warmly, received in the war's immediate aftermath. Some southerners undoubtedly shaped their language in accordance with "frantic effort[s] to attract outside capital." Similarly, former Confederates seeking a federal pardon for wartime activity had personal reasons for holding, or appearing to hold, intersectional amity in highest regard.[21]

Reunion-minded northerners, while encouraging material ties, worried about their durability. Union soldier turned journalist Russell Conwell reported that "southerners seemed to treat northern men with respect, not out of any true fraternal feelings, but mostly because of their money."[22] One example he likely had in mind was George Fitzhugh, whose postwar writings Conwell copied into his travel journals. Fitzhugh, once a fire-eating defender of the slave economy and harsh critic of capitalism, now reappeared as a Chamber of Commerce booster. Plainspoken as before the war, Fitzhugh declared in 1867: "We of the South wish to be friends with the North. We are trying to conciliate her, and to attract immigration, skill, and capital from the North."[23]

Southerners struggling for an economic foothold realized at least some benefits in adopting the language of national unity. C. Vann Woodward, like other New South chroniclers, finds that businessmen and industrialists aping northern practices were "the only Southern spokesmen who commanded national attention in that era." More pointedly, in a typical period observation George Templeton Strong noted that his acquaintances feared investing in the South in large part because of the region's expected hostility to reconciliation and continued "social discord." As Carl Schurz warned in 1865: "no safe investments can be made in the south as long as Southern society is liable to be convulsed by anarchical disorders." What better than soothing unionist assurances to mollify such fears?—even, on this cynical view, if few below the Mason-Dixon line believed a word of their own avowals.[24]

This argument falters somewhat on investigation. Little economic assistance was in fact forthcoming over the first decade and a half after surrender; union references did not decline as a result. Context also belies a purely self-interested explanation. Southerners registered hopes for restored unity in places where their potential benefactors could not see them: in letters, private political meetings, and personal diaries. In one example, North Carolina wartime Confederate hero and postwar Democratic Governor Worth praised his handpicked successor, Thomas

21. Quote from Foner 1988, 380. See generally ibid., 137–42, 379–409, and Rabinowitz 1992, 5–71. On carpetbaggers' motives for moving south, see Current 1988, chaps. 2–3. On pardons, see Coulter 1947, 32–33.

22. Quoted in Silber 1993, 47; cf. 45–48 generally on northerners' mixed feelings about "the redemptive power of money and investments."

23. Quoted in Wish 1943, 332. On Fitzhugh's postwar career, see esp. Wiener 1979.

24. Woodward 1968, 110; Strong 1952, 4:158–59; Hyman 1967, 294. Cf. the "Report from the South" in *Nation*, April 5, 1866.

Ashe, in a private letter to another conservative Democrat as "an old Union Henry Clay Whig."[25] It may be that many privately pledged their troth to union in an effort to reassure one another of the prospect of economic relief. But the object of such utterances often had little to do with personal or regional material gain. At least during the months immediately after the war, many southerners invoked national union in the context of psychological healing and continuity.

Regenerative Union: Healing the Wounds of War

Social responses to shattering military defeat have taken a wide range of forms, from mass depression and even suicide through bitter vows of vengeance, bewildered dislocation marked by a search for continuity with the past, identification with the victorious foe, and denial or avoidance.[26] Former Confederates exhibited all of these, including a brief attempt at guerrilla resistance, in seeking avenues to solace.[27] Published sources suggest that a favored source of alleviating postwar distress was the vocabulary of intersectional union. The term recurrently appears as a metaphorical balm for southerners' postwar misery, as in a regional leader's 1867 declamation: "[A]ll the curses that we have suffered originated, not in adherence to the principles of our Union, but in a departure from those principles." Return to those principles, he vowed, and "we shall have peace; then we shall have Union; cordial, equal Union."[28]

In a more subtle manifestation of healing, opinion leaders in the region recalled Lincoln's "southernness" following his death—often while heralding his commitment to national unity. Among many eulogists who before 1865 had cast Lincoln as a traitor or, synonymously, "northern to the core," Thomas Nelson Page located "the key to Lincoln's passion for preserving the Union in the fact of his Southern birth." Henry Grady's "New South" declaration presented Lincoln as "the sum of Puritan and Cavalier, for in his ardent nature were fused the virtues of both." One southern biographer went farther, linking the South's greatest hero to his erstwhile White House antagonist in the claim that Robert E. Lee and Lincoln were cousins.[29]

Religion provided a related source of catharsis, and a long tradition of union talk from southern pulpits resumed as the war concluded, keeping the idea in popular focus. Pleas of forgiveness for wartime sins were regularly accompanied by invocations of secular as well as divine union. Tennessee's presiding Episcopal bishop is representative: in his 1866 address to the state's diocesan convention,

25. Quoted in Connor 1929, 302n. 13. Also see, e.g., Childs 1947, 232, 240, and Burr 1990, 274–385.
26. For a particularly able treatment of this theme, concerning Japanese recovery after World War II, see Dower 1999.
27. Postbellum southerners "seemed fascinated with" suicide, but few of those who expressed the wish in print carried it out in practice. Foster 1987, 37, 48. On General E. P. Alexander's guerrilla plan to fight on after Appomattox, see Donald 1978, 173.
28. Hill 1909 [1867], 371.
29. Walt Whitman, the dead president's most eloquent mourner, similarly described Lincoln as "essentially, in personnel & character, a Southern contribution." Johannsen 1991, 3; Page quoted at ibid. Grady in Watson 1909, 9:377.

Bishop Quintard described the church as "at unity in itself; [it] has . . . always been a strong bond of union between the North and the South, the East and the West, because her children all speak the same thing, and in essentials are perfectly joined together in one mind. . . . The various denominations look to [the church] to be the first to reunite the bonds of religious fellowship throughout the land." A similar symbolic function was later served, as Nina Silber shows, in personal "romantic reunions"—intersectional marriages, widely and usually favorably reported in North and South alike.[30]

Southerners eager to blot out the painful present frequently sought solace in the past, a tendency later associated with "Lost Cause" nostalgia. But separatist yearnings for Confederate success are scarcely evident before the 1880s, as Foster attests in detail. In the immediate postwar years, historical memories instead tended toward rosy evocations of prewar harmony between the sections. "The Union" was, asserted a *Richmond Dispatch* writer in 1868, "a community where before the war prevailed a degree of harmony, content, abundance, peace, and happiness [unequalled] on the face of the earth."[31]

Materially speaking, certain functions performed by "the Union" provided a tangible reminder of prewar stability. The federal system in 1865 in many respects resembled its pre-Sumter analogue, providing through the war a continuity of government services "that made union worthwhile until all else failed and which . . . ultimately [did] much to make union possible once again," as Daniel Elazar writes.[32] Mail service, judicial decisions by both northern and southern federal courts, and even territorial acquisition and consolidation (eight new territories and four new states, as well as Alaska, were added between 1861 and 1868) were all continued during and fully restored shortly after the war. These services constituted a direct everyday reminder of shared purposes—hardly sufficient to halt the damning of Yankees, but certainly a foundation for postwar reconnections.

A stronger sense of regeneration was conveyed by Andrew Johnson's plan to restore Confederate states, their boundaries unaltered, to Union membership. Sustained military rule in the South, Johnson asserted along with most Democrats in Congress, "would have envenomed hatred rather than have restored affection."[33] This promised reestablishment of territorial unity "made the word

30. Quintard 1866, 38; Silber 1993, 39–40, 64–65, 116–18. The national denominations were also negotiating their own reunion between northern and southern dioceses after the war: in those that remained divided well into Reconstruction, especially Baptists and Methodists, the ability to act as brokers of reunion was severely limited. See Ahlstrom 1972, 695–97 for details of postwar church schisms.

31. Foster 1987; *Richmond Dispatch* (Va.), April 8, 1868. See also Mobile *Daily Advertiser,* June 17, 1866.

32. Elazar 1972a, 52. Compare Fredrickson (1965) and Bensel (1990, 17; 94–365 passim), who stress the profound break in American state development occasioned by the war. Accepting this portrayal does not deny that certain elements of central-government activity were maintained, however; and, as Elazar points out, much of the federal system was reestablished with very few changes.

33. Richardson 1896–99, 6:356. For details on Johnson's plan, see Nichols 1961, 160–66, and Donald 1978, 170–71.

[union] again acceptable to Southern tongues," a Georgia journalist recalled in 1884. Much as the rapid reinstatement was criticized (and eventually blocked) by Republicans at the time, it did encourage a sense of intersectional identification among the region's residents. The Louisianan or South Carolinian whose state was quickly reintegrated into the whole was more likely to respond to exhortations of unity—out of a grudging gratitude, if not forthright patriotism. Given that union had been so closely bound to territory for so long, the move appeared logical; as early as July 1865 a moderate-left Republican like Massachusetts Congressman George Boutwell could cautiously recommend restoring some southern states "to their ancient relations to the Union," largely to capitalize on the "affection" that ideally would result from this "renewed territorial integrity." Epitomizing this spirit was a summer 1866 "National Union Convention," symbolically held in Philadelphia and inaugurated by delegates from South Carolina and Massachusetts, entering the hall arm in arm.[34]

As a revised social and political order evolved in the postwar South, uncertainties abounded in a once relatively settled, hierarchical regime. Union, an idea evoking the good old days, was a buffer of constancy against a sea of change. Its use seems part of a general regional unwillingness to face up to postwar realities or to squarely confront secession and its legacy. "The Union as it was" slogan, among other things, denied any inexorable rise of sectional conflict and secession before 1861. History served southerners, in the period immediately after surrender, as a source of artificial comfort rather than understanding, and promises of restored unity were a pillar in this gimcrack edifice. Thus—because of a need for healing and continuity at least as strong as desires for material gain—southerners quickly resumed talk of national unity in 1865–66.

NORTHERN UNIONISM, 1865–68

Against southerners' "Union as it was" declarations, northerners in the first months of peace offered triumphant comparisons of tenuous antebellum national unity with that forged by the war. In Republican journalist William Grosvenor's jumbled metaphor, "no chemical union had ever taken place; for that the white-hot crucible of civil war was found necessary. To keep up the fire until antagonistic elements are refined away and a perfect union is effected is needful," requiring "exalted statesmanship . . . [that] can push boldly out of the narrow range of precedents and established forms into the deep water of first principles and permanent truths." The term "sacred Union," occasionally heard in the antebellum years, was a postwar mantra. Former Colorado governor William Gilpin, for example, devoted an entire book to demonstrating the "geographical, social, and

34. Atlanta *Constitution*, July 5, 1884; Boutwell in Hyman 1967, 260. On the National Union Convention, see Ackerman 1998, 179–80, and Donald 1978, 196.

political Mission of the North American People," which he defined as "plant[ing] States of" the "sacred Union . . . onward to that [Pacific] ocean" and which concluded "Hail to the sacred union of [the] states!" Few spokesmen agreed on how to establish this permanent unity, however. As Eric Foner attests, "'Unionism' possessed such divergent meanings in 1865" as to produce "considerable misunderstanding between North and South" as well as within each section.[35]

Most piercing amid the clamor of northerners' postwar union talk were chauvinistic declarations that the South would be reintegrated—if at all—on whatever terms the North desired. Apart from this chest-pounding, two more subtle themes may be identified. *Organic* unionists drew on emerging Darwinist thought to identify a "natural" connection among all Americans, secured by a robust central state. Partisans of a *moral* union, as introduced in the previous chapter, saw their position as validated by the Emancipation Proclamation and war's outcome, and insisted that "something incomparably better than the old Union," in Frederick Douglass's words, should be conceived and realized.[36] After briefly describing each of these views, I examine their joint culmination in the Radical Republican effort to invest union with meaningful moral content in the postwar constitutional amendments and Reconstruction Acts.

Organic Unionism

The years after 1865 saw the first sustained appearance in the United States of union ideology in organicist dress. A group of influential intellectuals, among them Francis Lieber, Elisha Mulford, and John Hurd, identified a natural solidarity among all Americans (usually, though not always, explicitly limited to whites). These writers invested the "organic" metaphor with a dual biological implication: the American polity lived and grew through time, and membership in the society was defined in innate terms rather than by civic contributions or other qualities. Ethnicity or "blood," in period vernacular, was said to be the carrier of culture.

Many northerners, for reasons ranging from ethnocentric pride to concern over reintegrating the seceding states, found appealing the idea of an American "organism, a political body animated by a life of its own." Francis Lieber, from his postwar Columbia University perch, was the doctrine's leading spokesman, demanding that Americans feel "an organic unity with one another, as well as being conscious of a common destiny."[37] Politicians, judges, and other institutional

35. Grosvenor 1865, 118; Gilpin 1873, 1, 63, 217; Foner 1988, 185. Another term redefined in the postbellum era was "reconstruction," which "southerners . . . frequently used during the war" to mean restoration of the prewar status quo minus slavery; writes a Dunning School historian, northern usage was so "grotesquely different as to cause the term to be abhorred afterwards for generations" (Coulter 1947, 22).

36. Douglass cited in chapter 4, note 43. On postwar Darwinist thought in the United States, see Degler 1991, 15–31, and Fredrickson 1971, 235–55.

37. Economist Robert Thompson, quoted in Curti 1946, 176; Lieber 1881, 2:227 (cf. 225–43). Other intellectuals took up the call, some even more fervently than Lieber. "Dr. Lieber . . . allows no

elites readily adopted organic-union themes. An otherwise unexceptional 1866 U.S. Senate debate on black suffrage in the District of Columbia featured quotes from *Social Statics* and this conclusion from Kentucky's senior Senator: the "white races" in America could "become amalgamated . . . in one nationality and harmoniously move on under the same Government to fulfill a united and common destiny, because they [are] all of the shemitic [*sic*] race, of the same color, and essentially of the like physical, mental, and moral organization." Judge John Jameson spoke for thousands in the North when he defined the United States in 1867 as "such a unity of blood, of interest, and of feelings" that it would "fly together by a [natural] force of attraction that is practically irresistible." President Ulysses S. Grant, eponymously represented in his election materials as "*Union Saving* Grant," sounded organic-unity themes in his first inaugural address. Even a habitual skeptic like Herman Melville caught the drift, insisting in 1866 that southerners were "a people who, having a like origin with ourselves, share essentially in whatever worthy qualities we may possess."[38]

The popularity of these organic ideas owed also to northern adherents' nagging concern about reunion, a fear apparent in even the airy metaphysics of Elisha Mulford, who devoted pages to demolishing the very idea of "confederacy." Mulford dismissed this "sham unity" as "the embodiment of the evil spirit, in which there is the destruction of the being of the nation, the organic and moral unity and continuity of society, and the subversion of the whole to selfish ends." As at Babel, "the [confederacy's] builders are driven away . . . with confusion and division." Southerners had not committed any ordinary wrong by seceding; their act had "violated the very laws of nature."[39] Unity and division were repeatedly counterposed by organic thinkers, reflecting the continued impact of war.

Buttressed by Darwinian theories, traditional ethnocultural doctrines of national union were fitted to a "scientific" organic interpretation without much difficulty. United American territory implied natural "boundaries encircling the whole," Lieber wrote. Biological determinism enhanced the basis for affection among Americans of different regions by assuring an Anglo-Saxon base of homogeneity. This was also meant to answer Confederate leaders' wartime attempts to identify southerners as "Normans" as against the "Saxons" of North

---

corresponding weight to the fact that [national] institutions have their only ground in the organic unity of the people," wrote Elisha Mulford in *The Nation*, his 1870 book intended "to ascertain and define the being of the nation in its unity and continuity." Mulford 1882, 114n. 1, v.

38. *Cong. Globe*, 39th Cong, 2d sess., 1866, 80; Jameson in Rodgers 1987, 162; Melville 1866, 266. Herbert Spencer, a foundational source of the organic metaphor, described social development in organic-unity terms: "This union of men into one community, this increasing mutual dependence of units which were originally independent . . . this growth of an organism of which one portion cannot be injured without the rest feeling it" (Spencer 1910 [1865], 408).

39. Mulford 1882, 341, 325. The religious reference was also characteristic of the day, though Mulford may have overdone matters by his book's end, declaring the Bible as of "immediate worth" mainly because it "reveal[s] the foundation of the unity and continuity of the first nation in history" (ibid., 389). On postwar and Gilded Age religious patriotism, see Foster 1996.

and West.[40] Issuing a flurry of organic credos, the Order of the American Union revived Know-Nothing agitation against Catholics during its 1870–78 existence.[41]

A more troubling obstacle for organic thinkers was the longstanding balance of national and state authority central to sustainable-union doctrine. At times Lieber and others called for a stronger national state—a "head" or "brain," in organicist parlance. In an anxious 1867 essay about "the difficulties attending the problem of reconstruction," Carl Schurz declared that the "organism of the Republic" would again be "a harmonious whole" only "if its central organ ha[s] the power, as well as the duty, to guarantee to the people of the different States . . . republican government." Others writing in the organic vein similarly promoted the central government as an instrument of postwar unity. Publications such as the *Nation* prepared the way with fiery manifestoes dismissing the loose balance implied by federalist union: "This territorial, political, and historical oneness of the nation is now ratified by the blood of thousands of her sons. . . . The prime issue of the war was between nationality one & indivisible, and the loose & changeable federation of independent States."[42]

These organic thinkers were among the leading postwar advocates of a national state "commensurate with," in Mulford's words, "a more perfect, when more *permanent,* American union." Yet this group also advertised its aim as renewing and securing union's traditional balance. Lieber, for example, drew a careful distinction between "nationalization" and "centralization": the latter he posed as a dangerous "concentration of all the rays of power into one central point," compared with "nationalization[,] the diffusion of the same life-blood through a system of arteries, throughout a body politic." As David Donald summarizes, Lieber's was "a doctrine of compromise . . . Lieber exalted American nationalism—but encouraged autonomy for local and particularistic interests."[43] Thus the prewar understanding of sustainable union retained currency in some unlikely places.

Moral Union

Following Lincoln's death, proponents of the martyred president's ideas of a more inclusive national identity vowed to realize his principled vision, or their version of it. Most were fellow Republicans, many considerably more radical than Lincoln on questions of blacks' inclusion in the union and severity of punishment for secession. One dominant theme was the unsatisfactory nature of old territorial/affective ideas of union, as voiced by Wendell Phillips.

No technicality and peculiarity of territory will make us a nation. We lie all around loose. Hitherto we have been only a herd of States hunting for

40. Lieber 1881, 2:53. On southern Normans, see Faust 1988, 10–11.
41. Higham 1988 [1955], 30.
42. Schurz 1867, 371, 375; *Nation,* July 13, 1865.
43. Mulford 1882, 107; Lieber 1881, 2:101–5; Donald 1978, 219.

our food in company. . . . What I want is a government so broad, so impartial, so founded on an average of national interests, that no local prejudice, no local malignity, no local wealth, can hold up its hand against
the peaceful exercise of the citizenship under its flag.[44]

Like organic nationalists, Phillips and other Republicans seeking a morally
improved union saw the central state as a key to their aim. Orestes Brownson
mixed organic and moral purposes in many of his writings, extolling a stronger
government to "render effective the solidarity of the individuals of a nation, and
to render the nation an organism . . . to combine men in one living body, and
to strengthen all with the strength of each." Richard Yates, a House Republican
from Illinois, summarized Radical views in his speech opposing "musty precedent": "It seems that the doctrine of State rights or State sovereignty, which was
undoubtedly the father of secession and the cause of the war . . . is certainly the
gateway to the dissolution of the Union." Yates urged "a new spirit of inquiry"
into the "relative powers of the General Government and of the States." "More
fully than other Republicans," Foner summarizes, "the Radicals embraced the
wartime expansion of federal authority, carrying into Reconstruction the conviction that federalism and state rights must not obstruct a sweeping national effort
to define and protect the rights of citizens."[45] Could the postwar national state
live up to this charge?

Perfecting the Union: Radical Reconstruction
The collection of congressional legislation passed between 1865 and 1869,
comprising three constitutional amendments and several related civil-rights and
enforcement acts, is the high-water mark for moral union's realization—for conceiving a "more perfect" union as more *inclusive,* especially of African Americans.
This was, Rogers Smith writes, "the most radical hour in American history."
Bruce Ackerman concludes that the Fourteenth Amendment and attendant accomplishments constitute a "re-founding" of the United States, a moment when
"nineteenth-century Americans were prepared to set aside their racist prejudices
long enough to support the Republican vision of a Union that made birth-right
citizenship, and not skin color, the fundamental bond that sustains our identity as a People." Republicans, in Eric Foner's account, erected a "powerful
national state" as a means of "guaranteeing blacks equal standing in the polity
and equal opportunity in a free-labor economy."[46] I will take up both the moral-
accomplishments claim and the related assertion that congressional Republicans significantly strengthened the central government in order to carry out
their aims.

44. *Boston Commonwealth,* December 4, 1869.
45. Brownson 1866, 15 (cf. 37–46); *Cong. Globe,* 40th Cong., 2d sess., 1868, 347; Foner 1988, 231.
46. Smith 1997, 283; Ackerman 1998, 198, 182; Foner 1988, 237.

Historians continue to disagree over whether these "radical" legislative accomplishments represent truly far-reaching changes in the South and the United States generally or amount to a missed opportunity for progress, limited by adherents' unwillingness to push their advantage. My interest is in a specific part of that debate: how proponents *defended* the changes they proposed. Did Republican (or Democratic) constituents and newspaper readers view the legislation, and their leaders' votes on ratification, in moral terms, that is, as a referendum on black equality? In actuality, most participants at the time, sometimes even including leading radicals like Sumner and Stevens, promoted the amendments and related acts in terms of restoring national union—not principally as blows for freedom and equality. Ackerman is correct in stressing popular support as a key feature of this legislative achievement. But its general acceptance was achieved, in most localities, by appealing to Americans' desire for reunion. Radicals and other supporters of this legislation were able politicians; it is not surprising that they couched their arguments for black rights in the most palatable terms possible. But by emphasizing national unity and constitutional fidelity, they helped set the stage for the subsequent erosion of the civil rights gains secured by the amendments and related legislation. Only by investigating period developments through a rhetorical lens does a defense for this unorthodox perspective become apparent.

The Thirteenth Amendment, to abolish slavery, is the first such development. Some advocates openly promoted the measure as a vital source of blacks' freedom or of ending "this organized system of iniquity, [which] send[s] reason reeling from her throne," as a Michigan House member put it. But as often, supporters heralded the amendment as a means to strengthen unity. Andrew Johnson's annual message to Congress in 1865 is an example: "The adoption of the amendment reunites us beyond all disruption; it heals the wound that is still imperfectly closed; it removes slavery, the element which has so long perplexed and divided the country; it makes of us once more a united people, renewed and strengthened, bound more than ever to mutual affection and support." Addressing southern recalcitrants directly, Johnson added that "the evidence of [your] sincerity in the future maintenance of the Union shall be put beyond any doubt by the ratification of the proposed amendment."[47]

This is thin gruel where defense of freedmen is concerned. Johnson, whatever else his motives, was playing to his audience (it was certainly not Johnson's support for the Thirteenth Amendment that enraged Radical Republicans, but his subsequent efforts to immediately restore southern states ratifying the measure). And the president was one of many sounding a unionist line. A California House Republican insisted "pass the Resolution . . . or consent to see the Union of our fathers destroyed, its hitherto proud name become a hissing and a reproach, and its people no longer free."[48] Why this ground for the amendment's defense? One

47. *Cong. Globe,* 38th Cong., 1st sess., 1864, 2952; Richardson 1896–99, 6:358.
48. *Cong. Globe,* 38th Cong., 1st sess., 1864, 2949.

reason was the strong appeal of union among constituents, compared to that of black rights. Another part of the answer has to do with tactics of the amendment's *opponents,* as expressed in Congress and countless editorial pages during 1864–65. Kentucky's Robert Mallory, for example, in a long June 1864 House speech outlined two main objections to the proposed amendment: (1) "its tendency . . . is to strengthen the resistance to the restoration of the Union"—by inflaming southern opinion, and (2) "it is in conflict with the theory and spirit of the Constitution, and subversive of the principles and basis of the Union" because "it seeks to draw within the authority of the Federal [government] a question of local or internal authority." Responses to such arguments had to insist that the amendment would promote national unity. Hence Republican Rep. Ingersoll, speaking after Mallory, asserted that the amendment's passage would mean "there shall be no more slavery and no more oppression, no more tyranny and no more injustice, and our voices may go up together in one grand diapason which will ascend to heaven over a country reunited."[49] One eventual effect of the debates taking such a form was to return American union ideas to Madison's balanced turf: a people united by "mutual affection" rather than insistence on equality and other principled ends.

Stronger moral language was sounded in debates on the Civil Rights Bill (enacted in April 1866) and the Fourteenth Amendment (introduced in June of the same year). Frederick Douglass commented when the latter was ratified that "liberty and union have become identical." But the most powerful jeremiad on behalf of black citizenship and suffrage was Sumner's great two-day oration *opposing* the amendment as insufficiently radical:

> To save the freedman from this tyranny, with all its accumulated outrage, is your solemn duty . . . [and] the only sufficient guarantee is the ballot. Let the freedman vote, and he will have in himself under the law a constant, ever-present, self-protecting power. . . . [I]t is plain that the equal rights of all will be established. Amid all seeming vicissitudes the work goes on. Soon or late the final victory will be won. I believe soon. . . . There is a Christian Providence which watches this battle for right, caring especially for the poor and downtrodden who have no helper. The freedman still writhing under cruel oppression now lifts his voice to God the avenger. It is for us to save ourselves from righteous judgement . . . [and] in saving the Republic we elevate it. . . . Our country will cease to be a patchwork where different states vary in the rights they accord, and will become a Plural Unit with one Constitution, one liberty, and one universal franchise.[50]

On the House side, leading Radical spokesman George Julian offered an equally fiery speech in defense of a stronger amendment. Julian mixed moral injunctions

49. *Cong. Globe,* 38th Cong., 1st sess., 1864, 2987–88, 2991.
50. Foner 1950, 3:214; *Cong. Globe,* 39th Cong., 1st sess., 1866, 685–86.

on blacks' behalf with warnings of disunion, an old recipe in American political debate. "[I]mpartial suffrage in the South" was required, said Julian, "on the score of justice and gratitude to the negro, the peace and well-being of society, and the stability of the Union itself." Warming to his theme, Julian concluded: "The people *are* ready . . . [a]nd if the voice of the loyal millions could be faithfully executed today, treason would be made infamous, traitors would be disfranchised, and the loyal men of the South, irrespective of color, would hold the front seats in the work of reconstruction. Do you doubt this? If there is real union among Union men everywhere . . . it is in their absolute determination to make sure the fruits of their victory."[51]

These Radicals aimed to improve ideas of national unity by enhancing their moral stature. They invoked the constituent parts of "moral union," as described in the previous chapter: *ethical commonality* ("The freedmen among us," Sumner declared, "have the same organs, dimensions, senses, affections, passions, and above all, the same sense of wrong"); *unadulterated equality* ("the Equal Rights of All," said Sumner, "is the Great Guarantee, without which all other guarantees will fail. This is the sole solution of our present troubles and anxieties. This is the only sufficient assurance of peace and reconciliation"); and *mutual relationship* (here Sumner and other Radicals were more tentative, but did vaguely address the theme: "Parties [southern freedmen and whites] that have been estranged are brought into harmony. They learn to live together. They are kind to each other . . . and this mutual kindness is a mutual advantage").[52]

Analysts today treat Sumner and fellow Radicals' equal-rights oratory as the motivating force behind the Reconstruction Amendments and Acts.[53] But their unstinting moral views were often on the losing side, as in the long Sumner quotation above. African-American equality was not the principal theme sounded in debate, even on the Fourteenth Amendment. A day after Sumner concluded his stirring speech, fellow Republican Senator (and close ally) Henry Wilson took the floor. His defense made only passing reference to equality or other moral ends; Wilson instead warned that without constitutional securities southerners would "rally and unite . . . against the national Government." He appealed to "the interests of [you] loyal millions" in response: "They fought four years to get out of the Union; the nation fought four years to keep them in. . . . The flag of united America floats over their strongholds, over city and hamlet . . . for all the purposes of governmental authority over the people of those States the Union is entire and complete."[54] Here a version of chauvinistic unionism, rather than appeals to shared moral values, was the ground on which Reconstruction was promoted. More participants at the time followed Wilson's line than Sumner's. Apart from Radical leaders, one finds few explicit defenses of,

51. *Cong. Globe*, 39th Cong., 2d sess., 1866, 3209, 3211.
52. *Cong. Globe*, 39th Cong., 1st sess., 1866, 675, 674, 685.
53. See, e.g., Kaczorowski 1985; Ackerman 1998; and Smith 1997.
54. *Cong. Globe*, 39th Cong., 2d sess., 1866, 702.

or even allusions to, the "transformative aims" now attributed to the legislation's advocates.

As debate over the Fourteenth Amendment wore on, fewer proponents in Congress or editorial columns attempted a clear moral defense. Instead, support was repeatedly sought on behalf of restored unity. West Virginia's Republican Rep. Milton Latham, in a sardonic speech during the run-up to final passage, left no doubt about most speakers' theme:

> We are told from day to day with much seeming sincerity . . . that the Union when restored must be restored upon a basis which will make it as permanent as the everlasting hills and as invulnerable as the throne of the Eternal, and with such safeguards [e.g., the Amendment] that even treason will no longer be possible within its jurisdiction. I need not refer to particulars or quote authorities or precedents upon this point to show that I state the case fairly. To attempt to do so would be but to recite a hundred speeches made upon this floor during the present session, and the daily editorials of a thousand newspapers . . . those [Americans] who really love their country and are devoted to their Government are almost ready to believe that the long-looked for millennium will be ushered in with the reconstruction of the Union.[55]

Defenders of the amendment, Latham lamented, had adopted renewed national union as their promised goal—presumably at the expense of strong moral gains on behalf of blacks. This is not to suggest that Radical leaders did not have black equality as their aim, but that virtually all supporters advocated the Reconstruction legislation in unionist terms. If, *pace* Ackerman, we are above all to honor the intent of "the People" in interpreting the amendments, the way they were presented to most Americans is of considerable importance.

Table 3 suggests that Latham was largely on target. This table sorts the various arguments in support of the three postwar amendments (or closely related versions thereof), both in congressional debates and in newspaper editorial commentary. For the former, I surveyed a sample of substantial (at least two columns in the *Congressional Globe*) speeches by supporters of the amendments and noted all reasons each speaker put forward on behalf of passage and ratification. The latter came from my regular sample of newspapers: when I came across commentary defending any of the amendments, again I coded it by category. The analysis yielded 447 separate rationales; the table provides percentages represented by

55. *Cong. Globe,* 39th Cong., 2d sess., 1866, 2883. Latham went on to examine the Amendment section by section, measuring whether each would "promise a restoration of the Union on principles which promise security to the country and do justice to the . . . loyalists of the South" (ibid., 2885). State legislative battles over black suffrage and civil rights were similarly pitched. Even in a relatively radical state like Wisconsin, as Richard N. Current's case study demonstrates, the "proposed Fourteenth Amendment became a test not only of Republicanism [i.e., party support] but also of patriotism, of true Unionism." Current in Mohr 1976, 153.

Table 3. Rationales for supporting reconstruction amendments, 1865–69

Rationale	Percentage supporting
Black rights: mutuality	1.3
Black rights: free labor/personal liberty	6.5
Black rights: equality/suffrage	9.8
"Evils of slavery" (generic)	14.1
Adherence to Constitution/republicanism	19.7
Support for GOP/party unity	5.6
Deference to Congress	3.8
"Fruits of victory"	9.8
Restore union/harmony/concord	18.9
"Perfecting" union	4.9
Other	5.6

Source: Debates in *Congressional Globe* and northern newspaper discussion of the three amendments.
Note: $N = 447$.

each type (so, for example, I counted six arguments that the amendment in question would enhance black/white mutual relations, representing 1.3 percent of the total). For some speeches, like Sumner's long defense of the Fourteenth Amendment in February 1866, virtually all the categories in the table were mentioned. (Rep. Kellogg, speaking in 1864, said "there are so many reasons and so many arguments that might be urged on behalf of this measure that I hardly know where to begin.")[56] Although this approach does not reflect the relative importance or intensity of arguments, it provides insight into how American opinion makers actually "pitched" the amendment to their fellow elites, constituents, and readers.

From table 3 we see that less than one-fifth of statements supporting the amendments had to do with various aspects of African-American civil rights, most often equality. Nearly as many (14 percent) pointed to the iniquity of slavery in a generic sense. Around a fifth were grounded in the Constitution and/or "republicanism"; these were often linked in arguments of the time. A quarter of supporters cited restored or improved national union. Just under 10 percent invoked the victorious North's right to remake the country; Michael Les Benedict calls this the "Grasp-of-War" theory.[57] The "deference to Congress" figure does not represent briefs for separated-powers originalism; most often anti-Johnson rancor informed a claim that the work of Congress should be supported.

Hence, it appears, the basis for the three postwar amendments—the ground

56. *Cong. Globe,* 38th Cong., 1st sess., 1864, 2952.
57. Benedict 1974, 72–76.

on which these were presented to the electorate—did not signify a reordering of fundamental regime principles, as Ackerman and others suggest. Instead, familiar rhetorical purposes were most often advanced: preserve the Union and Constitution, confirm the republican "experiment" (still a favored trope) begun by the framers, cement Republican Party unity. The justification for formally enfranchising blacks and ending slavery had more to do with perpetuating the union than with establishing a more morally perfect one. This cautious, conservative foundation for the civil rights changes brought about by congressional Reconstruction was all the easier to overturn when a different set of union-preserving values was subsequently advanced.

That reversal of postwar guarantees to blacks has been widely documented by contemporary historians. Yet it remains puzzling: Why, in the aftermath of total defeat, was the South permitted so rapidly to reassert traditional privileges and practices within the "reformed" Union—of whites' self-determination and domination of blacks? Reassertion, as defined here, came in two stages. One was formal reintegration as states, epitomized by southern elections of state legislators, governors, and members of Congress (in the late 1860s, for most states). Then followed the Redemption program, beginning in the mid-1870s, of dismantling federal intervention, slashing African Americans' political power, rewriting state and local laws governing labor rights and racial codes, and otherwise retaking local political control. Explaining this "lustration" sequence has occupied political historians virtually since Reconstruction concluded; among those who accept that southerners indeed reversed most congressional Reconstruction gains,[58] answers fall into three leading schools of thought.

First is an economic argument, set out by Eric Foner and dating back to W. E. B. Du Bois. Liberal commitments to property rights and associated opposition to labor radicalism, this perspective holds, led wealthy Republicans and non-southern Democrats to oppose Reconstruction reforms as unacceptable redistributive policies. Their fear was that workers would view the abolition of slavery as legitimating the abrogation of property rights by the U.S. government. Thus northern capitalists and their supporters forged connections with southern planters to dismantle short-lived civil rights gains, in an "alliance of land and capital" justified in free-labor terms.[59]

Other scholars see stubborn sectionalism among southerners, and northerners' fearful response, as the reason behind the Bourbon Redeemers' swift readmittance to full national privileges and virtually complete local dominance. Three advocates of this view are George Rable, Robert Kaczorowski, and Richard Bensel, who from very different angles of approach find that massive southern resis-

58. Ackerman suggests, with qualifications, that "there was no moment in the late nineteenth century in which a mobilized national majority repudiated the Reconstruction amendments" (1998, 471–74).
59. Foner 1988, 124–75, 460–99, 516–53, 575–601; Foner 1998, 100–101, 113; Du Bois 1962 [1935].

tance to national authority and emancipation was the impetus behind northern compromises on civil rights and otherwise remaking the South.[60]

A third important explanation, also originally voiced by Du Bois, was reaffirmed by Harold Hyman and recently given compelling voice by Rogers Smith. Racism, with the scientific patina conferred by Social Darwinism, best accounts for why northerners softened their Reconstruction aims. "Something happened," writes Hyman. "Northern whites lost their penchant for being their [African-American] brothers' keepers." White commitments in both sections to "theories of racial hierarchy," Smith concludes, spurred the "official retreat from radical political reconstruction."[61]

None of these three versions appears fully satisfactory. It seems unlikely that with war's memories still smoldering, the mass of northerners would accept rapid readmittance of the South on free-labor or white-supremacy grounds alone; both of these forces demonstrably existed before the war as well. And recalcitrant southern separatism, much less "guerrilla warfare," would seem to arouse northern ire more than encourage a spirit of conciliation. Instead another factor was also at play: the appeal of union. Commitment to a long cherished understanding of national unity, ardently promoted by southern spokesmen, underlies northern acceptance of southern states' reinstatement. Southerners by 1867 consistently promoted union as a balancing ideal, again combining national governance and local autonomy. Their aim was to achieve reunion at least partly on their own terms, and they were largely successful in promoting their preferred meaning and winning acquiescence from most northerners. Resurgent free-labor and racist views are partial, but not sufficient, causes. Unionist ideals had a vital role in Reconstruction's reversal, in short, by inspiriting the coalition that dismantled strong nationalist promises. To pursue this claim, we turn now to the evolution of southern union views amid Radical Reconstruction's advance.

RESISTING THE STATE: SOUTHERN UNIONISM, 1867–76

As Radical legislation proceeded, the disparate threads of southern union usage chronicled earlier—healing, nostalgia, personal and regional revitalization—were drawn into a more coherent conceptual meaning. In the tradition of Madison, Webster, and other notable past unionists, a prominent figure served as union's chief interpreter among southerners. Georgia's Benjamin Hill, a leading Whig before the war and subsequently a Confederate Congressman and U.S.

60. Bensel 1990, cites at note 11; Kaczorowski 1985, xi–xiii, 28–30, 49–50, 225–27; Rable 1984 (depicting Reconstruction as a potential revolution, defeated by southerners' "guerrilla warfare" counterrevolutionary tactics).

61. Hyman 1967, xvii–xx, xxiv–xxii, xxix–lxi (quote at p. xxvi); Smith 1997, 287–89, 291–95, 303–4 (quote at p. 291); Du Bois 1962 [1935]; Donald 1978, 201–11.

Senator, in July 1867 spoke in Atlanta's Davis Hall before a mixed audience of northerners—mostly military officers—and southern gentry. Decades later, portions of his "Davis Hall speech" were still memorized by schoolchildren, much as Webster's "Reply to Hayne" peroration was before the war. Clark Howell, successor to Henry Grady at the helm of the *Atlanta Constitution,* in 1909 recalled: "the speech of 'Ben' Hill came like dawn after an agonizing and intolerable night. . . . No[thing in] Southern oratory, from the closing of the war to the present day, can approach [it] in sheer eloquence, in force, in immediate effect or in splendid bravery."[62] Of more relevance here, Hill's speech forcefully linked union with local rights and opposition to government centralization, a connotation that retained currency into the 1890s. The reassertion of this balanced understanding soon came to dominate unionist vernacular in the region and eventually in the reunited nation.

Hill opened with a paean to union—in his words, "cordial reunion, and earnest fraternal association of all portions of the country." How, he asked, "shall that great desirable object be completely accomplished?" In answer he set out a series of "axioms in American politics never to be questioned." The first was the extraordinary importance of national unity. Hill's praise was as fulsome as any of the treacly oratory of Webster's day: "The American Union constituted, when formed, and yet constitutes, the wisest, noblest, and grandest contribution ever made by the human intellect to the science of government." Hill also examined the concept analytically, first dismissing superficial definitions. "Most people think that by American Union you mean the fact that the people of this country, inhabiting a given territory . . . now composing thirty-eight states, extending from ocean to ocean and from lakes to gulf, live under one and the same government and have the same flag." This "fact-based" understanding was woefully inadequate, he said, equally valid for declaring "a Russian despotism, a German empire, a Mexican anarchy" to be a union.[63]

Far more than a "mere fact," union was "a principle." Here Hill faced the old problem of what sort of good national unity was; he sidestepped the issue, declaring the "principle" synonymous with "a system of government." This system rested in turn on certain "great features," foremost among which was the balance of powers wielded by national and local authorities. "There shall be a *general* government for *general* affairs and a *local* government for *local* affairs. That is the first underlying and indispensable principle of the American system of union," Hill proclaimed. Recalling Lincoln's treatment of the concept, Hill mingled the argument for bifurcated power with respect for "a land of law" and allusions to the union's "perpetuity."[64]

62. Howell in Watson 1909, 9:72–73. On Hill's popularity, see also Conway 1966, 141 (Hill as "Moses of the South"); Pearce 1928, 143–48.

63. Hill 1909 [1867], 357–59.

64. Ibid., 359–61, 373. On continuity, see Hill's quote at the opening of this chapter.

The remainder of Hill's speech laid out a union catechism that would become drearily familiar to northern reformers seeking to employ the national state on behalf of black rights and other morally principled purposes. Federal measures first had to be certifiably free of "sectionalism," now mostly exhibited by Republican Radicals but admittedly a broader problem in the past ("the grand point . . . is that the late war was between two sectional parties. The Union . . . was no party to that war save as a weeping, bleeding victim"). The postwar place of freedmen was of comparatively little importance, Hill further insisted ("The whole African race, whether slave or free, were not worth the American Union"). Above all, again, central government "meddling" with sectional privileges was to be resisted: "Invade the states and you invade the Union." [65]

Though echoing traditional southern states' rights (and anti-black) themes in his stress on local self-government, Hill carefully avoided the fire-eaters' arguments—unlike Alexander Stephens, who championed a modified version of nullification and proslavery doctrines at book length the following year. Stephens faithfully insisted that Constitution and Union were no more than "compacts" among sovereign states. [66] Hill better caught the prevailing postwar spirit in elevating "union" well beyond a limited arrangement among separate entities. In a subsequent speech Hill expressly disavowed "the old theories of the democracy," asserting that unbending insistence on states' primacy "will not do now." He sidestepped Stephens's elaborate defenses of slavery, describing the institution instead as an unfortunate "mistake," though one hardly worth the resultant "shed[ding of] white blood" and "wast[ing of] white treasure." Ultimately, Hill's view of national union is closer to the sustainable account of Madison and Webster than to Stephens's warmed-over Confederate doctrines. In locating union simultaneously on immediate and general planes, Hill offered a restatement of the balanced philosophy developed by Madison and reshaped by Lincoln. What neither of these thinkers would have countenanced was Hill and fellows' strenuous opposition to most government activity, on the national as well as local level. [67]

Strengthened federal powers were a negative inspiration for Hill and like-minded southern unionists. A particular target was the first Reconstruction Act, passed a few months before Hill's speech. Even Radical Republicans later ac-

---

65. Ibid., 361–73.

66. Stephens 1868–70, 1:420–23 and passim for states' rights defense. Stephens eventually saw the writing on the wall, declaring in an 1878 speech on "States' Rights and Union" that even during the war he was certain that "so long as the Mississippi runs—philosophy and reason and everything taught that this grand country and people . . . must be joined by some kind of union or other. How, I did not know, but that the grand picture should be carried out I believed." Stephens quoted in *Chicago Tribune*, July 5, 1878.

67. Hill in *Atlanta Constitution*, February 24, 1872; Hill 1909 [1867], 368. Lincoln would also likely have objected to, though not been surprised by, Hill's adjectival emphasis on "white." Hill's own racism appears to have lessened somewhat over time: a vehement opponent of black suffrage in 1867, he later emerged as leader of the more moderate "New Departure." Conway 1966, 191–92; Foner 1988, 293–94, 415, 425.

knowledged that the Act had unnecessarily stirred up localist sentiment in the South. It was "utterly indefensible on principle," said George Julian of Massachusetts, "completely at war with the genius and spirit of democratic government. Instead of furnishing the Rebel districts with civil governments, and providing for a military force adequate to sustain them, it abolished civil government entirely, and installed the army in its place. It was a confession of Congressional incompetence."[68] Hill's Davis Hall oration made only veiled references to the ongoing political drama, but the specter of expanded federal authority was a probable inspiration for his deployment of "union" in opposition to administrative centralization. State building was objected to here and in Hill's subsequent writings on abstract, principled grounds: individual self-development was hindered by government "interference." Union, in Hill's influential formulation, became an anti–central government totem.

Thus, with customary qualifications about dissenters, a portrait of white southerners' union ideas during the Radical portion of Reconstruction takes shape. Focusing initially on a need for healing and nostalgic denial, Hill and subsequent southern spokesmen encouraged the association of union sentiment with full reabsorption into a vaguely defined whole, encompassing all white Americans (excepting the architects of Radical legislation). Vital to this vision was space for southerners to manage local affairs, and particularly to determine the status of blacks in the region. To the extent that this replicates many southerners' unionist outlook before Sumter, albeit now formally free of slavery's taint, it seems especially surprising that northerners soon acceded in the definition.

A UNION OF HEARTS: NORTHERN USAGE, 1870–77

Mississippi's U.S. Senator R. Q. C. Lamar, writing to a constituent in 1874, reported on his investigation among northern colleagues "to find out, if I could, whether there was any point upon which they could be approached successfully by the South—to ascertain if there was any ground upon which harmony, concord, peace & justice between the sections could be established." He feared confirmation of southerners' "instinct" after the "Radical triumph" that northerners recognized "no common union, no brotherly feeling—no bond of association." But among many, "even the *Republicans* in the North West" and New England, he found "a strong desire among them, & they declared it to be universal among the Northern people" for unity even on southern terms—for example, dismantling of federal powers in favor of local control. Despite a discernible "apprehensi[on] and distrust of reactionary measures," a "basis for union" was evident: "the

68. Julian in Hyman 1967, 377.

Southern states relieved from misgovernment & for the restoration of the whites to the control of their own affairs."[69]

Lamar's "report" attests to a dominant northern view during and especially after Radical Reconstruction. Institutional guarantees to blacks by 1868 encompassed not only emancipation but also suffrage and other legal securities. But northerners had affirmed union as their principal war aim, and those scarred deeply by its breakdown were fundamentally committed to preserving postwar accord. As Hill and other southerners developed their terms of union in 1867–68, northern opinion leaders proved willing to accept most of these. Not southern separatism but the willingness of former Confederates to set aside talk of disunion governed the breakdown of Reconstruction aims in which African-American rights and state-building were concerned.

This is a sweeping description of a complex set of attitudes, to be sure. Historian Robert Sawrey's close study of the Reconstruction debate in Ohio provides supporting evidence, tracing a development that was repeated in most northern and western states. Ohioans like others in the region set a high standard in 1865, demanding "that the South give proof of future loyalty before readmission, that the Confederate debt not be paid [by the United States], that the freedmen control and benefit from their own labor, and that the antebellum leaders not be allowed to dominate postwar politics in the South." Andrew Johnson initially seemed amenable to such terms, but after his resistance "Congress quickly adopted as the core of the Fourteenth Amendment most of what Ohio Republicans believed necessary for *complete and secure reunion*." However, Sawrey continues, "their expectation that the nation would quickly be reunited was almost immediately dispelled when southerners resoundingly rejected the amendment." This led to "ambivalence" about congressional Reconstruction policies and eventually capitulation: "in 1868, with public interest generally waning and new groups of southerners following the requirements of military Reconstruction, Ohio Republicans carried the state for Grant and proclaimed Reconstruction a qualified success . . . [all] remaining problems were now deemed incapable of threatening the country."[70]

At work in Ohio and elsewhere in the late 1860s and 1870s, helping to blunt Radical aims, was a sentimental "romantic reunion" sensibility. This took on strength throughout the North and West as objections to centralizing policies emerged in the South. With slavery formally buried, many northerners more readily accommodated southern concerns about the national/local balance of power. To the stream of Benjamin Hill–inspired rhetoric coloring postwar southern ideas of union northerners responded enthusiastically. Amid the flowering of

69. Lamar in Russell 1955. Cf. President Hayes to his frequent southern correspondent Horace Austin in 1875: "The 'let alone policy' seems now to be the true course . . . nothing but good will now exists toward you" (quoted in Foner 1988, 558).
70. Sawrey 1992, 145; emphasis added.

renewed intersectional union sentiment, the unity-based defense of Radical Reconstruction legislation came home to roost.

Sentimental Reunion

As Radical gains slowed after 1868 and then turned to stalemate, an overwhelmingly sentimental discourse of reunion spread across the North. Boston provided an early example with its "mammoth" National Peace Jubilee in 1869, attended by guests from "all parts of the Union" and designed "to symbolically reconcile the divided nation." "Let us make it our first duty and pleasure," intoned New York's governor-elect Lucius Robinson in 1876, "now that the conflict is over to exclude all inordinate excitement and passion and to forgive offences. Join hands as friends and patriots, having a common interest in the good government of our common country . . . [under] the flag of the Union." John Fiske, in his landmark *Harper's* piece on "Manifest Destiny," reassuringly saluted "the good sense and good faith with which the Southern people, in spite of the chagrin of defeat, have accepted the situation, and acted upon it" as "something unprecedented in history, [which] calls for the warmest sympathy and admiration on the part of their brethren of the North."[71]

Even longtime foes of slavery were increasingly charitable toward their onetime antagonists. Wrote Charles Sumner to House Speaker Blaine in 1872, "Can we not after seven years commence a new life, especially when those once our foes repeat the saying 'Thy people shall be my people, and thy God my God[?]'" Herman Melville, the prototype of New England abolitionism, imagined hopefully in 1866 that "in the generation next to come, Southerners there will be yielding allegiance to the Union, feeling all their interests bound up in it, and yet cherishing unrebuked that [passionate] feeling for the memory of the soldiers of the fallen Confederacy." Carl Schurz, a staunch prewar abolitionist and chronicler of anti-Yankee sentiment among southerners after the war, published in 1885 *The New South*—during the height of southern "Redemption," with hard-won civil rights gains being furiously dismantled throughout the region.[72] Yet Schurz's tone throughout this work, and especially when he refers to relations between the sections, is laden with sentimentality. "Southerners," he concluded, "are as loyal to the Union as the people of any part of the country." The region's principal desire was to "strengthen . . . [this] united country."[73]

Such a spirit was widely popularized in national magazines like the *Atlantic*,

71. Branham 1996, 637 (on Peace Jubilee); Robinson in *Raleigh News*, November 14, 1876 (his speech was reprinted widely, in North and South); Fiske 1885, 84.

72. Sumner in Russell 1955, 375–77; Melville 1866, 262. Sumner was anticipated by fellow abolitionist Gerrit Smith, who in 1867 declared "I long for a heart-union between the North and the South," but feared "it cannot be enforced" (quoted in Silber 1993, 45). On Redemption's reversals, see Franklin 1969, 324–43; Smith 1997, 371–85.

73. Schurz 1969 [1885], 14, 18. Of Schurz, W. E. B. Du Bois wrote: "No man was better prepared dispassionately to judge conditions in the South" (1962 [1935], 133). Schurz's "Radical" credibility declined steadily as Reconstruction continued, however: see Trefousse 1969, 454–59.

Harper's, and *Scribner's,* which declared as its editorial policy "to increase the sentiment of union throughout our diverse sisterhood of states." An 1878 yellow fever epidemic among southerners occasioned a flood of sympathy: *Harper's* editor saw "one of the great consolations of so melancholy a situation" that "it alleviates sectional hostility [and] tends to confirm the union of hearts, without which that of hands is fruitless." Southern writers like Joel Chandler Harris (author of the "Uncle Remus" stories), Mary Noailes Murfee, and Thomas Nelson Page contributed sanitized tales of prewar harmony and sectional reconciliation. Page testified that he had "never wittingly written a line which [I] did not hope might tend to bring about a better understanding between the North and the South, and finally lead to a more perfect Union."[74] These articles and books won a huge audience among white Americans, and were a spur to the praise of unity filling the editorial columns of newspapers from Maine to California. As Sawrey notes, "very few in Ohio advocated a vindictive policy toward the South. . . . The overriding concern was to reunite the country and ensure a secure, peaceful future."[75]

One manifestation of spreading sentimental ties was a host of invitations to southern leaders, including some former Confederates, to speak at northern cities' Fourth of July celebrations. In Evansville, Indiana, local leaders declared that the 1878 Fourth promised to be "the most extensive and successful [celebration] ever given." Two southern dignitaries were scheduled to appear: South Carolina Governor Wade Hampton and Georgia's General Gordon, one of Lee's leading adjutants during the war. Gordon became ill and had to cancel his trip but sent a message read to "great approval" among the crowd: "I send you the gratitude of a full heart for your kindness to me, with congratulations over the complete restoration of all the States. The hearts and homes of the South are open [to you]. . . . The whole South earnestly unites with you in saluting this day, with all its memories of the past and pledges for the future."[76]

Romantic-reunion tales in both sections prominently featured women, aptly so inasmuch as matters of sentiment were traditionally considered feminine territory. Women were protagonists in the drama of reconciliation, both in fiction (often seen smoothing gruff male antagonism between former sectional foes) and reality (as brides in much-publicized intersectional marriages, and schoolteachers hailed as "the kindly personification of the 'good Yankee'"). Organic nationalists shifted between descriptions of "the delicate, ladylike, body of the Union" and what Lieber termed "pulsing organic unity" and "manly organic nationality." An association of national unity and feminine virtues had always existed, given the term's connotations of marriage and familial intimacy, but the sentimental discourse of Reconstruction exponentially increased its salience.[77]

74. Donald 1978, 269 (*Scribner's* and Page quotes); *Harper's* 57 (November 1878): 936.
75. Sawrey 1992, 20–21.
76. Reported in the *Chicago Tribune,* July 5, 1878.
77. Lieber 1881, 2:141, 203; Silber 1993.

Women's place in the reconstructed national union primarily remained of this symbolic type, even as blacks and other historically marginalized groups won political gains. In 1865, Susan B. Anthony wryly wrote Elizabeth Cady Stanton that "the church folks called a Union meeting . . . last Sunday night for general expression of all the people—but alas priests took the platform, read the Bible, gave the hymn, said the prayer, and called out one man [only] to speak" on national unity.[78] With the passing of the abolitionist movement after 1863, as Julie Jeffrey notes, "the traditional outlets for these women's voices were gone." By the time of Florence Kelley and Jane Addams, although women remained excluded from basic political rights like full citizenship and voting, they were again central to the realm of affective/social union—one still firmly shut to African Americans, as detailed in chapter 6. As postwar associational life blossomed, white women formed myriad "unions" in the civil-society sphere. Most prominent was the Women's Christian Temperance Union (familiarly known to members as "the Union"), founded in 1874 and eventually growing to nearly 170,000 members.[79]

White southerners welcomed the romantic spirit of reunion and, as Reconstruction drew to a close, actively joined in it. An 1876 *Raleigh News* editorial, misreporting a presidential triumph for Tilden, exulted "The Banner of Reconciliation—the symbol of a fraternal union in its purity . . . has been glorified by [this] magnificent victory; and let us bear it aloft triumphantly in all the coming years, until the last vestige of enmity engendered by the war shall disappear." Newspapers that barely a decade before had soberly reprinted a Confederate official's declaration "that devilish word [union] is the foulest curse in this [southern] country" trumpeted now the theme of union restored. "[T]he bonds of sectional fraternity [are] knit anew," editorialized the Petersburg (Virginia) *Index-Appeal*. "Again—at last—we rest in peace and union."[80]

Despite subsequent outcries at the "Great Swap" that elevated Hayes to the presidency, favorable references to national unity steadily issued from the South into the 1890s. Henry Grady, in a famous 1886 "New South" address to the New England Club, closed by quoting Daniel Webster's speech before the same group, four decades before: "[C]lasping hands, we should remain united as we have been for sixty years, citizens of the same country, members of the same government, united, all united now and united forever." Two years later, Jefferson Davis—in his last speech—could declare: "The past is dead; let it bury its dead . . . make your place in the ranks of those who will bring about a consummation devoutly to be wished—a reunited country."[81] Other signs of approval were regis-

78. Anthony to Stanton, April 19, 1865, Elizabeth Cady Stanton papers, Library of Congress.

79. Jeffrey 1998, 231. On the WTCU, see Bordin 1981, esp. 94–120, and Parker 1997. Women's continued political disfranchisement during Reconstruction is chronicled in Smith 1997, 311–16, 337–42.

80. *Raleigh News*, November 5 and 9, 1876; July 6, 1864; *Index-Appeal* (Petersburg, Va.), November 7, 1876.

81. Grady in Watson 1909, 9:385; Davis quoted in Foster 1987, 73. Compare, in 1874, the extraordinary spectacle of a Democratic Senator from Mississippi delivering a moving eulogy to Charles Sumner (detailed in Murphy 1973, 112–20).

tered in institutional form. Every southern town had a Union Democratic Club, generally referred to as the "Union Club," and the region's dwindling Republican population found companionship in the (also dwindling) network of Union Leagues, their southern organizational wing.[82]

In 1878, *Harper's* editorialized that the war's "cause was a true union, the union which rests upon right understanding and common friendly feeling" and called for "a consideration of the newer duties and relations which the contest opened." And within a few years, Union and Confederate veterans were meeting regularly on battlefields in what President Cleveland described, in a letter saluting former combatants' "reunion" at Gettysburg, as a "fraternal meeting." Such events increasingly turned the war into a romantic memory experienced "less as a divisive conflict and more as a shared experience that had brought them closer together," as historian Susan-Mary Grant summarizes. Former Union general Joshua Chamberlain described the war's legacy as "a rushing tide of memories which divided us, yet made us one forever." Such fraternal reenactments continue into the present—a practice, notably, not replicated in convivial reunions of Americans and their foes at Normandy or Da Nang, or even Lexington and Concord.[83]

Recalling this sentimental turn in both sections, W. E. B. Du Bois grimly characterized the late 1870s as marked by a "growing spirit of kindliness and reconciliation between the North and South," a spirit he lamented as a death knell for blacks' inclusion in the civic life of either section.[84] Similar alarm is apparent earlier, in the attitudes of African Americans toward an ideal once seen as a source of immense promise. Chapter 6 explores blacks' postwar turn away from union talk. But first an extended look at the institutional aftermath of Radical efforts to lay the foundations of a more moral union. As a period of supposed consolidation of central government powers, the postwar years proved considerably less distinct from the prewar American regime than is often claimed today.

UNION AND POSTWAR INSTITUTIONAL CHANGE

Recall the dominant scholarly view introduced early in this chapter: that the war was a decisive watershed in U.S. history, ushering in a new American political regime best described as a "nation-centered model." The Civil War, asserts historian James McPherson, "changed the U.S. as thoroughly as the French Revolution changed France." "After the searing experience of Civil War," writes Ackerman, "Americans did become more of a nation."[85] Evidence for this change is mar-

82. Social pages of most southern papers were filled with such gatherings; see, e.g., the *Richmond Times* of October 27, 1886, announcing a Union Club rally along with upcoming meetings of the "Social Union of the Baptist Church" and the local chapter of the WCTU. This seems unremarkable until we recall that "union" was a term of absolute opprobrium only a short time before.

83. *Harper's* 57 (July 1878): 460; *New York Times*, July 3, 1887; Grant 1998, 175; Chamberlain in ibid. Thanks to Rogers Smith for pointing out the (lack of) modern analogues.

84. Du Bois 1989 [1903], 47.

85. McPherson 1990, vi; Ackerman 1998, 23.

shalled along two fronts: the massive growth of central-state activity during the war and Reconstruction, and period lexical changes signifying a rise in national-ist outlook among most Americans. I take up the latter point first, given this study's emphasis on political rhetoric; but in both cases, viewed through a union-ist prism, matters look rather different.

Rhetorical Nationalism

No study of which I am aware makes the specific case that Americans turned from a language of localism and states' rights to one emphasizing nationalism during and immediately after the war, but a set of related claims is identifiable. First, a few authors propose that "union" references dwindled or disappeared swiftly after Appomattox. Wayne Fields's landmark study of presidential oratory, for example, claims in passing that "almost immediately after the Civil War the word 'peace' took on the preeminence previously reserved for 'union.'"[86] The evi-dence assembled in this chapter should confirm instead that union talk retained substantial currency long after the war's end.

Second, historians and political scientists note, again on an anecdotal basis, the replacement of references to "the Union" with "the Nation." But this devel-opment was not as clear-cut as a few representative instances suggest. McPher-son, for example, contrasts Lincoln's first inaugural address, "in which he refers twelve times to 'the Union,'" to his Gettysburg speech, which invoked "the na-tion" five times and "the Union" not once. Here, McPherson suggests, is decisive evidence of a metamorphosis in political speech. Yet consider Lincoln's second inaugural address, delivered some fifteen months after he spoke at Gettysburg. Here he used both terms: union three times and nation twice. More to the point, Lincoln presented national unity as his controlling theme, as Fields writes: "The Second Inaugural vindicated no other American ideal or virtue save Union."[87]

For empirical defense of this point, consider figure 6. Here the same sample of American newspapers used throughout this work is examined for evidence of changes in references to "union" and to "nation" over time. (As in fig. 3, I counted all national referents during this period: along with "union," also "nation," "America," "the republic," and so forth.) The figure indicates a rise in postwar references to "nation," but certainly not enough to indicate the emergence of a new American spirit of vigorous nationalism, especially with references to "union" still running high. Eventually these proportions would change but not for another quarter-century after 1865, when (as chapter 6 details) a sharp distinc-tion between "union" and "nation" or "America" did prevail.

A third type of evidence in this vein involves a shift in grammatical usage,

---

86. Fields 1996, 22–23.
87. McPherson 1990, viii (a similar point is made by Donald 1978, 215; Grant 1997, 105; and Jones 1999, 12); Fields 1996, 141 (though note that Lincoln also "vindicated" equality, in his searing conclu-sion to the speech; see Morel 2000, 175–82).

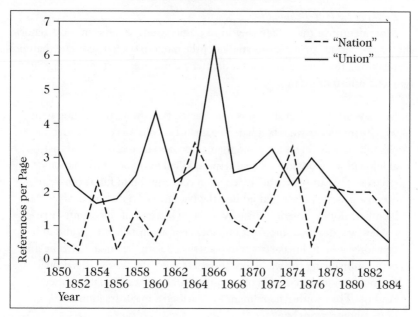

FIGURE 6. Comparison of "nation" and "union" references, 1850–84

from "United States *are*" before the war to the singular "United States *is*" afterward.[88] Such a change does appear to have occurred during the 1870s–90s. But based on my reading of newspapers and speeches of the time, I suspect that this was part of a grammatical rather than a consciously political shift away from traditional British English practice. Period examples abound of plural subjects that were reassigned the singular verb: "the Supreme Court are" became "the Supreme Court is," also over the latter third of the nineteenth century. Likewise athletic teams: typical is a July 1878 *Chicago Tribune*'s sports-page note that "the Columbia College crew have met their English competitors."[89] By 1889, the *Tribune* was reporting "Washington gives an imitation of [base]ball playing and Chicago wins." Compare British vernacular, which continues in the older style, writing "Liverpool continue their battle" or "Tottenham *are* victorious" today.[90] My guess is that, for reasons better assessed by linguists than by political historians, a slow adaptation took place at the time. Absent harder empirical evidence, it might be argued that the move from plural to singular "United States" inspired a more general change, but the possibility seems far-fetched.

88. E.g., Donald 1978, 215: "A small shift in grammar tells the whole story . . . after 1865 only a pedant or an unreconstructed Southerner would dream of saying 'the United States *are*.'" See also McPherson 1990, viii; Wills 1992, 145; and Foster 1996, 123.

89. *Chicago Tribune*, July 6, 1878, and July 7, 1889. Earlier Americans applied the plural to numerous subjects later treated as singular: Thomas Galloway, writing to Benjamin Franklin in 1770, noted that "the [British] Ministry *are* much mistaken . . ." (Labaree et al. 1959–, 17:177).

90. See, e.g., *The Independent* (London), March 2, 2000, 30–31.

Building the Post-Bellum State

More definitive than these rhetorical observations, at least in most scholar-ship of the period, are extensive studies of the modern centralized state that took shape during the Civil War. Martin Shefter summarizes wartime changes in na-tional administration:

> In the years 1861–65 a state was constructed that dwarfed anything with which Americans were familiar. President Lincoln was commander-in-chief of an army in which more than 2,000,000 men served, and that, along with its Confederate counterpart, killed 600,000 of the nation's citizens. This army eventually relied on conscription to fill its ranks, an exercise of state power that ignited the New York Draft Riot of 1863, the bloodiest riot in American history. In large sections of the country mar-tial law was declared, the right of habeas corpus suspended . . . and mili-tary force used to break strikes in plants producing war materiél. The im-petus of financing the war led to the enactment of a system of national taxation and to the creation of a national debt and a national currency. . . . And the Thirteenth Amendment . . . released a major fraction of the na-tion's laborers from bondage.[91]

Add to this impressive roster a "Southern Leviathan," Richard Bensel's descrip-tive term for central-state authority in the Confederacy,[92] along with the Re-construction legislation discussed early in this chapter, and the case for a nation, not a mere Union, seems solid. Even Stephen Skowronek, whose intricate study demonstrates the "patchwork" growth of administrative-state institutions be-tween 1877 and 1920, characterizes the Civil War as "the great departure in Amer-ican institutional development," when "new national administrative institutions first emerged free from the clutches of . . . localistic orientations."[93]

On this Jacobist-style premise, as American national state development pro-ceeded during and after the war, a traditional unionist sense of linked "island communities" was eradicated by the encroaching federal bureaucracy.[94] The state's coercive, impersonal administrators and insensitivity to citizens' desires and needs overrode both local political ties and the affective sense binding Amer-icans in a common project. Patricia Mayo writes (in the European context) that state actors "conce[ive] society as a mass of unorganised individuals who should be ruled from above by uniform methods of administration, combined with a re-fusal to allow for the existence of the natural and informal group . . . or for the diversity essential to all true forms of growth."[95]

91. Shefter 1994, 113–14. Compare, e.g., Curry 1968; Bensel 1987; 1990; Eisenach 1990, 193–95; and Foner 1998, 98–100.
92. Bensel 1987. Details on southern administrative capacity and centralization of authority are at pp. 81–125.
93. Skowronek 1982, 5–6.
94. See, inter alia, Wiebe 1967 and Donald 1978.
95. Mayo 1974, 150.

Extraordinary wartime centralization and expansion of U.S. national capacity was followed, however, by an equally extensive dismantling of many of the administrative features Shefter and others list. Both Union and Confederate armies, together making up the largest fighting force in the world at the time, melted away. In Skowronek's summary: "As the Prussian revolution in military organization swept Europe, the American army was being swept back into obscurity as an Indian patrol."[96] New concentrations of industry and capital succeeded the war, to be sure, but no regulatory apparatus to control these appeared for forty years or more. Welfare-state functions on anything approaching a national scale were only hesitantly attempted in the 1880s and were limited to two objects of great nostalgic sentimentality among Americans: Union soldiers and destitute mothers. It is, in short, difficult to conjure out of these a "consolidating," or even nascent, spirit of *étatisme* remotely like that exhibited in most European nations at the time.

Historians' claims for a new postwar regime also invoke congressional Republicans' great civil-rights accomplishments, as outlined earlier in this chapter. Extending full national citizenship to all white and black males;[97] securing suffrage for a fifth of the male population; eliminating slavery, the "central institution of southern society and U.S. largest concentration of wealth";[98] and empowering the national government to supervise these activities all mark a genuine advance in American state development. But also important is how blunted these administrative instruments quickly became. White supremacy was fully restored in the south within a few years after the last troops were withdrawn in 1877. Black citizens were systematically stripped of social, civil, and political rights achieved barely a decade before. And an empowered new state did nothing in the remainder of the nineteenth century to exercise its vaunted power of extending national citizenship (to, say, Asian Americans or women). Even national public education, which was financed lavishly by the wartime Congress, was systematically removed from federal control in both North and South during the 1870s, with the Education Department reduced to a minor section within the Interior Department.[99] The postwar "Leviathan," devoted to internal improvements, a national financing system, and party patronage, functionally resembled its limited prewar analogue in most respects as the nineteenth century drew to a close.

Instead of fading away after 1865, union ideas' resounding popular resurgence helped limit the development of a stronger, more independent national government in the three decades following the war. The extent of this influence is impossible to measure in any rigorous way. Instead my attempt to substantiate the powers of rhetoric takes the form of two short case studies: Supreme Court de-

96. Skowronek 1982, 86–87; quote at p. 87.
97. Ackerman views this as a key transformative act: "Whereas before, We the People consisted of a union of states that defined their own citizenship criteria, it now consisted of a union in which the People of the Nation imposed fundamental criteria of citizenship on the people of each state" (1998, 236).
98. Foner 1998, 99.
99. Smith 1997, 321–24.

cisions formally restricting national government in the name of an "equilibrium" with states' rights, and an example where a move to national standardization (of House elections) *was* achieved in the late 1870s–80s—but explicitly on states' own terms.

Reconstruction-era States' Rights: Supreme Court Doctrine

In the wake of Benjamin Hill's Atlanta speech, states' rights supporters again began speaking out in southern, and eventually national, councils. As early as 1870 leading Republican Carl Schurz devoted the better part of a Senate speech to the topic, concluding:

> I am for State-rights as the embodiment of true and general self-government, and I am convinced that this is the prevailing sentiment among the American people. It would be a sad day for this Republic if it should cease to be so. It is true the exigencies of the civil war have quite naturally developed a tendency to accumulate and centralize power in the hands of the National Government . . . but as soon as the pressure of necessity ceases, as soon as it becomes apparent that the great problems for the solution of which we are struggling may be solved just as well by the simple operation of local self-government as by the interference of the National power, then the tide will just as certainly set in the opposite direction.[100]

As in Madison or Webster's day, one key to securing national union in its sustainable form was to deliberately balance local and federal authority. One agent of the postwar balancing effort was a newly activist Supreme Court.

When Salmon Chase's march through the upper echelons of American politics stalled a step away from the presidency, his 1864 appointment as Chief Justice left him no less inclined to weigh in on national issues. After Appomattox U.S. federal courts, having mostly honored existing bounds of center-periphery relations from the early nineteenth century onward, were faced with specifying the nature of ties between national and state governments and among the people represented by each. Assigned a stream of postwar cases[101] hinging, as Chase put it privately to a friend, on "what this Union is . . . that nobody [seems to] know or can persuasively explain," he seized in late 1868 the unlikely subject of Texas indemnity bonds as ground for codifying "state," "union," and relations between the two. Where orators, pundits, and sermonizers still differed, legal reasoning would triumph.

As in any judicial opinion Chase left undeclared his intellectual inheritance,

---

100. *Cong. Globe*, 41st Cong., 2d sess., 1870, 2062–63 (cf. 474–75, 2817–19). Schurz, like many commentators of the time, cited the Article IV "republican form of government" guarantee in defense of local powers.

101. E.g., *County of Lane v. Oregon*, 7 Wall. 76 (1869); *Walker v. Villavaso* (id., 124); *Smith v. Cockrill* (id., 756); *The Ouachita Cotton* (id., 521). Chase in Jourdan 1889, 43; on Chase's jurisprudence generally, see Benedict 1997.

but his words in *Texas v. White* suggest a distinct debt to Madison and Lincoln. The Chief Justice's opinion opens with a long excursus on "the correct idea of a State," apparently required because "the poverty of language often compels the employment of terms in quite different significations . . . hardly any example more signal is to be found than in the use of the word we are now considering." Concisely replicating Madison's tripartite account of union, Chase explained that a state could denote a "people or community of inhabitants united more or less closely in political relations," a "territorial region, inhabited by such a community," or a "government under which the people live." At "other times," Chase affirmed, "it represents the combined idea of people, territory, and government." A national union, it followed logically from this definition, was "the union of such states . . . [which] make[s] of the people and states which compose it one people and one country." Belying a rich history of dispute, Chase concluded: "The use of the word in this sense hardly requires further remark."[102]

If Madisonian in the generalities, Chase proved attentive to antebellum disputes over unionist doctrine in the specific American case. "The Union of the States," he declared, echoing Lincoln's famous response to Douglas,

> never was a purely artificial and arbitrary relation. It began among the Colonies, and grew out of common origin, mutual sympathies, kindred principles, similar interests, and geographical relations. It was confirmed and strengthened by the necessities of war, and received definite form, and character, and sanction from the Articles of Confederation. By these the Union was solemnly declared to "be perpetual." And when these Articles were found to be inadequate to the exigencies of the country, the Constitution was ordained "to form a more perfect Union." It is difficult to convey the idea of indissoluble unity more clearly by these words. What can be indissoluble if a perpetual Union, made more perfect, is not?

Yet, Chase went on, this perpetual, indissoluble national union was indelibly grounded in the principle of local self-government. Quoting his own opinion in the recent *Lane County v. Oregon* case, Chase explained: "Without the States in Union, there could be no such political body as the United States." He proceeded to reiterate at length a dual-autonomy thesis, concluding that "the Constitution, in all its provisions, looks to an indestructible Union, composed of indestructible States." Thus a state such as Texas consented to both obligations and guarantees of Union membership upon admission, an act that "was something more than a compact; it was the incorporation of a new member into the political body."[103]

Though the Court later issued occasional "nationalist" decisions,[104] this

102. *Texas v. White et al.*, 74 U.S. 700, 720–21 (1869).
103. Ibid., 724–25; *Lane County*, 7 Wall. 71, 76 (1869).
104. See, e.g., *Knox v. Lee*, 79 U.S. (12 Wall.) 457, 556 (1871) (United States as a "National Government . . . the only government in this country that has the character of nationality").

balanced theme remained consistent beyond Chase's nine-year reign as Chief Justice. The 1876 case *United States v. Cruikshank* [105] remained for years a pillar of dual federalism, while three years earlier in the *Slaughter-House Cases* the Court rejected application of the Bill of Rights (and, for good measure, all natural rights of humankind) to the states, also on grounds of protecting exclusive state powers.[106] In summary, the postwar Court both during and after Chase's tenure treated the increasing centralization of government powers as an implicit challenge to reconstructed ideas of national union. One signal effort, in *Lane County*, revived the Tenth Amendment doctrine that substantive powers are explicitly reserved to the states. Chase's opinion is a model of subtlety, casually shoehorning the term "expressly" back into the Tenth Amendment—an effort originally rebutted by Madison himself.[107] Chase's definitive, ringing tones in *Texas v. White* obscured a raft of questions accompanying his reassertion of sustainable unity. Like generals readying for the previous war, Chase was chiefly concerned with preventing any renewed challenge to the whole.

The Supreme Court's halting response to efforts at boosting federal authority, as expressed most clearly in *Texas v. White*, grew out of a concern to preserve national union. An older tradition of dual federalist precedent [108] was softened somewhat, but enough was retained to support a conventionally balanced understanding of union. Even when the Court tentatively sought to defend national governance, its words are telling. In 1879, for example, struggling to sort out "the relations which subsist between the State and national governments," the Justices could have been quoting Ben Hill:

> The true interest of the people of this country requires that both the national and state governments should be allowed . . . to exercise all the powers which respectively belong to them. . . . State rights and the rights of the United States should be equally respected. Both are essential to the preservation of our liberties and the perpetuity of our institutions. But, in endeavoring to vindicate the one, we should not allow our zeal to nullify or impair the other.[109]

The Court's conceptualization of postwar national unity patched together preceding generations' ideas, with the most powerful contributor the old balanced arrangement of part and whole. The result reinforced—and conferred institutional sanction upon—Americans' sentimentalized yearning for consensus.

105. 92 U.S. (2 Otto) 542 (1876).

106. *Slaughter-House Cases,* 83 U.S. (16 Wall.) 36 (1873). Cf., inter alia, *Hurtado v. California,* 110 U.S. 516 (1884).

107. 7 Wall. 71, 76.

108. On the "large body" of dual-federalist precedent binding Court decisions during this period, see Smith 1997, 295–97, 328–37, and Benedict 1997, 484–87.

109. *Ex Parte Siebold,* 100 U.S. 371, 394 (1879).

Where the rhetorical efforts of past leaders had been too cautious to promote a principled sense of national solidarity, attempts to register a moral union in formal jurisprudence were no more successful. Simultaneously, separate affirmations of a renewed dual-autonomy view were underway in the states themselves. The federal courts' effort to balance national and state powers in the name of unionist ties was echoed by state legislatures—provided they were free to act voluntarily.

Creating a National Election

In February 1872, the still Republican-dominated Congress voted to require all states to hold House elections on a single day in November.[110] As is virtually forgotten today, over the republic's first century the date of congressional elections varied widely by state. For reasons similar to presidential-primary date jockeying today, many states jealously guarded their right to schedule all elections, as guaranteed in Article I of the Constitution.[111] The 1872 law, passed while Reconstruction tensions still ran high, was simply ignored by many state officials. A few years later, however, after military "occupation" ended, many states in the South and elsewhere honored reunion by signing on to the standard national election date. This little-remembered episode provides an intriguing example of *state*-inspired movement toward nationalization, in the name of sentimental reunion.

A few words of background on this issue need to be said. Colonial-era contests had been scheduled arbitrarily, but the formalization of national elections in the 1780s led state legislatures to adopt a regular calendar. States chose very different election dates, however. New York scheduled elections for state and federal offices on the last Tuesday in April; Maryland voters gathered on the first Monday in October. The North Carolina Assembly's first formal act, in 1789, was to designate House races on "the first Thursday and Friday in February"; for obscure reasons, the date was moved the next year to "the last Thursday and Friday in January."[112] These schedules also ranged across different years. States divided almost equally between House contests in odd- and even-numbered years into the 1860s.[113] Many states' "1866" elections for the 40th Congress, for example, did not occur until 1867—including California, whose September 4, 1867 election

110. This section is based on a larger research project, carried out jointly with Jeffrey Stonecash; thanks to him for allowing presentation of a portion of it here.
111. *U.S. Constitution*, Article I, Section 4: "The Times, Places, and Manner of holding Elections for Senators and Representatives, shall be prescribed in each State by the Legislature thereof. . . ." Largely ignored for more than a century, this clause has recently become a central feature of the debate over term limits for House and Senate members.
112. Dinkin 1982, 91–92; Clark 1906, 25:1, 64; see also Bancroft 1879, 690–705, and Argersinger 1992, 43–44.
113. For early Congresses, the period of balloting also varied: polls were open for one day in most states, but some extended elections to two or three days, and others longer still. Essex County, New Jersey, voters in the 1780s had a full ten weeks to cast their House ballots. Kelly 1991, 26; Argersinger 1992.

occurred long after the 40th convened for two early special sessions in March and July 1867, sessions that consequently included no California House members.[114]

Initial pressure for a national election date came at the presidential level, in the 1840s. (Presidential election schedules also originally varied by state.) The inspiration was widespread fraud in voting for presidential electors in 1840 and 1844: in midwestern and mid-Atlantic border states, organized gangs of repeat voters went from state to state, following the electoral calendar. In response, Congress in 1845 established a uniform date for electing electors, the "first Tuesday after the first Monday in November" so familiar today.[115] In the next presidential election—1848, won by Zachary Taylor—all thirty states obliged, scheduling the presidential contest on the appointed day.

A quarter century elapsed before the same date was officially adopted for House elections, by the 47th Congress in 1872. Several states had already synchronized their House contests with the presidential schedule, but almost half (seventeen of the thirty-seven states in 1872) continued to hold House races at different times. Among this group, the new legislation had little effect. The 47th Congress's compromise decision permitted exceptions when a state's constitution already prescribed a different day. All seventeen states that had previously scheduled House elections on dates other than the presidential November Tuesday continued that practice in 1872 and 1874, and most did so for years thereafter. As table 4 demonstrates, the movement to consistency lagged considerably, in contrast to the unanimous response to the 1845 law on presidential elections.

To summarize, when Congress enacted uniform scheduling in 1872, seventeen states (46 percent of the total) held House races on dates other than the Tuesday after the first Monday in November. Five years later, in 1877, only three had shifted: Connecticut and Vermont in 1875 and California in 1876. Over the next few electoral cycles, thirteen of the fourteen remaining holdouts signed on to the November date. Of particular interest here is this group of thirteen. What accounts for their belated compliance, and in such close temporal proximity?

Political scientists and historians have mostly ignored this puzzle with respect to House elections.[116] I investigate three possible reasons for standardization here. The first, and probably most obvious, is formal-institutional: Congress passed a law. But the long lag in many states' response—over a decade, in sev-

114. Kelley 1978, 135–36. California's scheduling got even stranger in succeeding years. In the "1872" election cycle, to the 43d Congress, three House races were held in 1871, four in 1872, and four more in 1873. The last four were for the 44th Congress (opening in 1875), but were held *before* the 43d met for its first session. See the 1873 *Evening Journal Almanac* (Albany, Weed, Parsons & Co.), long footnote on p. 49.

115. 5 Stat. 721, *U.S. Statutes* (1872); Kelly 1991, 95–96.

116. Allan Bogue suggests that most of his fellow historians see elections "as more or less meaningless. . . . Electoral politics is but a grand puppet show in which societal elites pick the lawmakers—one will serve to mislead and mulct the populace as well as another" (Bogue 1986, 120). Two works that acknowledge the vital importance of these schedules in nineteenth-century politics are Ackerman 1998, 124–25, 201–2, 218, 462n. 35; and Holt 1986 (on the House electoral calendar's influence on Lincoln's Civil War strategy).

Table 4. Year when states formally moved House elections to first Tuesday after first Monday in November

State	Year uniform date adopted
California	1876
Colorado	1880
Connecticut	1875
Georgia	1877
Indiana	1881
Iowa	1879
Louisiana	1878
Maine	1960
Nebraska	1878
New Hampshire	1878
North Carolina	1878
Ohio	1885
Oregon	1892
Rhode Island	1877
Texas	1881
Vermont	1875
West Virginia	1886

Source: Dates are based on annual reports in four sets of political almanacs. Some of the information provided there is sketchy, especially in the cases of Louisiana, Texas, Oregon, and Rhode Island. Annual national political almanacs list the month and year of each state's elections for governor, state legislature, and House seats: I used the *Whig Almanac,* the *Tribune Almanac,* the *Argus Almanac,* and the *Evening Journal Almanac.* These provide electoral information in different ways, and cover different years, necessitating reliance on several sets; also, few libraries have complete collections of any single edition.

Note: Only those states that had not already adopted that date before 1872 are listed.

eral cases—calls this view into question, especially compared to the unanimous and instantaneous response to presidential-election standardization thirty years before.

A more plausible claim is that House elections became "national" as part of a post–Civil War trend toward centralization and nationalization, along the lines outlined earlier in this chapter. On this view, Congress in 1872 was ratifying a process already well underway, and the states obligingly fell into line. A third possibility is that the adoption of a uniform election date reflected widespread sentimental commitment to national reunion. States' recognition of this common standard was one of several symbolic gestures meant to alleviate the trauma of the war and divisions of Reconstruction, and to express solidarity for functioning as a single political union. Taking the latter two hypotheses as most promising, here is the "nationalization" vs. "balanced-union" debate in miniature.

Nationalization

The vast scholarly literature on the growth of an American national state makes no reference to the timing of congressional elections. But this issue fits the accounts of Bensel, Ackerman, and other analysts already cited. Might a standard House election date have been part of the postwar trend they describe, toward a stronger central government and more coordinated interstate activity?

Perhaps, but under examination the claim proves so general as to seem almost specious. One problem in applying a "nationalization" thesis to a particular event is that no agreement exists on when the trend began or peaked. A recent essay by Richard John places the origins of nationalization in the early republic, during the so-called Era of Good Feelings (1800–1828). From a different analytic direction, Thomas Bender chronicles historians' multiple claims about the "breakdown of local community" and commensurate move to "a centralized, formalized national society." As Bender shows, this threshold is variously located in "the 1650s, 1690s, 1740s, 1820s, 1850s, 1880s, and 1920s."[117] With such a dizzying array of transition points to "nationalization," almost any event in U.S. history could be explained in these terms.

Even looking exclusively at the post-Reconstruction period when standard House election dates were adopted, evidence for "nationalization" is thin. Skowronek, as previously noted, describes a "patchwork" pattern of central-state administrative expansion from 1877 to 1920; he observes that such institutions as the military and civil service were slow to centralize nationally.[118] There is no reason to believe that state legislatures felt special pressure to adopt a uniform election date any more speedily, especially given the concurrent efforts by Hill and other southerners to reassert state and local privileges.[119] States were often reluctant to participate in nationalizing activities, in sum. In a close analogy, direct election of U.S. senators—similarly involving states' relinquishing a cherished prerogative—was first enacted by the House in 1893[120] and proposed long before that. Only after a swell of Progressive-Era outrage was it actually achieved, however, via the Seventeenth Amendment in 1913.[121]

Asserting that the states conformed as part of a nationalizing trend thus seems too broad an explanation, providing no nuanced insight into the convergence after 1877. The impetus for state after state abandoning independent, local control and signing on to a standard House election date is no clearer when explained in generic "nationalization" terms. Might a more immediate triggering event have been at work? Looking again at table 4, a pattern appears among individual states that may be accounted for in more specific terms.

117. John 1997; Bensel 1990, 2 (though cf. Elazar 1972a); Bender 1978, 50–51.
118. Skowronek 1982, 37–162.
119. Wiebe 1967, 2–10.
120. 387 Stat. 384, *U.S. Statutes* (1893).
121. Kobach 1994, 1971–77; Kelley 1978, 141.

Support for (Re)Union

The outpouring of goodwill following Reconstruction's close helped elevate the common November election date to a symbolic norm,[122] particularly in the South but also among northern and midwestern states. Extensive research into all seventeen of the states that changed their schedules after 1872 would be required to prove this claim definitively, but changes within selected states suggest that the "union of hearts" sentiment chronicled above, cresting after 1877 and southern "redemption," played a significant role. The process by which House elections on the first Tuesday following the first Monday in November became a norm, spreading from state to state, was a function of Americans' postwar spirit of reunion.

On this explanation, the congressional law of 1872 mandating standardized House elections was initially ineffective not because nationalizing trends were slow to spread, but because it was passed amid the bristling tensions of Radical Reconstruction. Given such a context, those southern states that traditionally scheduled House contests apart from the standard November Tuesday (North Carolina, Georgia, Louisiana, Texas, and the border state of West Virginia) were loath to alter their practice. "Line up with the Yankees?" asked a North Carolina state senator rhetorically in an 1872 *Raleigh Observer* column on the proposed change. "Not *this* son of the South."[123] Depicting U.S. authorities as "wretches," "ravenous partisans," and a "race of animals,"[124] southerners during Reconstruction saw any federal regulation of state/local issues, including elections, as anathema. A congressional act mandating uniform House voting had little chance of winning their allegiance.

Southerners' determined opposition to federal influence was echoed by state legislators in the North and Midwest, though many were also responding to a strategic imperative. The "October States" of Indiana, Iowa, and Ohio, for example, enjoyed their bellwether House elections status no less than Iowa and New Hampshire guard their prerogative in presidential primary scheduling today. Then as now, states were hesitant to move electoral contests "because they hope[d] to share in the disproportionate influence typically enjoyed by those states that chose . . . earliest," as Leonard Stark observes in the presidential-primary context.[125] Interstate electoral calendar competition is not an innovation of the late twentieth century. And northerners were made all the more adamant in this policy by perceived southern intransigence. October voters in Iowa, or Californians who picked their House members in September, might piously sec-

122. On the influential power of norms to inspire swift changes in established institutional forms, see Lessig 1996.

123. *Raleigh News,* June 4, 1872.

124. *Raleigh News,* November 18, 1876.

125. Stark 1996, 331; cf. 354–55. A large literature addresses states' right to schedule presidential primaries, though little attention is paid to the 1870s–90s House uniformity question. See, e.g., Claude 1969 and Stark 1996 (which briefly alludes to uniformity of House elections).

ond an Ohioan's claim that "the *South* is not yet tamed; I see no cause for rushing to join our election to [the majority of states']." [126]

The strength of these convictions apparently was overcome by the rush of emotion favoring reunion, highest after the withdrawal of federal troops from the South. Against a flood of unionist sentiment, election schedules were no more immune than other former bulwarks of separation. Despite the 1872 congressional act mandating a common date, North Carolina's legislature had expressly voted in 1874 to elect House members in August.[127] Before the next off-year election [128] in 1878, the legislature unanimously approved a switch to the national date and wrote the rule into the new state constitution. This was a "new and excellent election law," one Democratic-leaning historian observed a few years later; at the time, the *Raleigh News* urged: "Time for a formal change . . . [to] join our brethren in one United vote." [129]

In the North, convergence around the new norm of uniform elections similarly appeared a way to honor reunion. Iowa legislators, and presumably residents in general, long protective of their October bellwether status, approvingly noted the North Carolina debates in the press,[130] and within months took up a proposal to change their date as well. Though Iowa's state elections remained an October tradition into the mid-1880s, and were thereafter scheduled in early January, House elections were moved in 1879 to the first Tuesday following the first Monday in November, on which date they remain today. As in the southern states, congressional imperatives appeared to have little direct influence. Instead the animating impulse was the "romance of reunion."

The aftermath of civil war in the United States saw profound changes in American economic, political, and social life. But these changes did not extend to a wholesale reconception of the Union as a "nation," as is routinely claimed today. Prewar notions of national unity remained in force—not because the potential for change was absent but because a wide swath of the population, pushed by southern political leaders, insisted on (or acquiesced in) reasserting an older, cherished meaning. Neither intellectuals' attempts to establish an "organic union" with greater central-state authority nor a concentrated effort by Republican leaders to realize the normative promise of a "more perfect union" could be sustained. During the latter 1870s the force of sentimental-union rhetoric cemented the

126. Quoted in *Raleigh News*, May 20, 1875.
127. Ashe 1925, 2:1165.
128. North Carolina, like a few other states, after 1860 held presidential and House elections simultaneously in November during presidential years, but scheduled House elections at different times during off years.
129. Hamilton 1919, 2:193; *Raleigh News*, September 14, 1878. See also the mid-1880s pamphlet "For the Old North State," Cushing Biggs Hassell papers, Box 2, Duke University.
130. *Iowa State Register* (Des Moines), January 11, 1879.

term's continued place in the polity. Texas Senator Maxey, at an Independence Day 1881 celebration in Galveston, summarized the prevailing mood. Among the founders, Maxey recalled, "it became apparent to [those] wise statesmen, that a more perfect union would have to be established, or that which they had would fall to pieces." After reviewing at length developments in the understanding of federal and state "duties and rights," Maxey confidently concluded: "With the cause of discussion removed, the Union is stronger today than it ever has been, and it will continue to grow stronger and stronger as the years roll by."[131]

As it happened, this return to familiar unionist roots helped spur the term's decline. First African Americans and organic nationalists, and later workers, labor leaders, and businessmen, all abandoned the term—in a fashion similar in its ubiquity to the decline in union talk among revolution-era Americans. This time, however, its fate was not a temporary displacement (as during 1764–74, chronicled in chapter 1) but permanent disappearance.

131. *Galveston Daily News,* July 5, 1881.

CHAPTER 6

The Ends of Union,
1877–1898

We are not one people, not as we once were . . . our unity is shattered
to pieces, and cannot conceivably be put back again. The age of Union
is done; we await an age of Uncertainty in its stead.

—David Garnett, "Reflections on a Century Soon Past," 1895

Although the individual, in a merely mechanical sense, is part of a wider
whole than ever before, he has . . . lost that conscious membership in
the whole upon which his human breadth depends: unless the larger life
is a moral life, he gains nothing in this regard, and may lose.

—Charles Cooley, *Social Organization*, 1929

FOLLOWING HIS WARTIME efforts as organizer and leader of a San Francisco
black regiment, Philip A. Bell opened a weekly newspaper in 1865. Bell had
moved west from Cincinnati a decade earlier, inspired by the same "golden
dream" that brought so many others to California. His paper, *The Elevator*, featured along with the usual mix of local gossip and U.S. and international news
an unusual number of editorials: Bell wrote powerfully and often, on a wide range
of topics. He quickly became an influential figure in San Francisco's black community and, indeed, among political commentators of all races.[1]

The Elevator's early issues were filled with patriotic exclamations as well as
more thoughtful exhortations to national unity. Bell regularly published short
editorial treatises titled "Union," praising "this much needed consummation" in
terms like "the great moral nursery of society—the true standard by which to
measure its purity and foundation on which to maintain it. It [union] is the guide
in life to warn us against the quicksands and quagmires which beset us on every
hand . . . [it] ennobles the head and softens the heart of all within its realm." But
by mid-1873, touched off especially by the "Great Slaughter" of blacks at Colfax,
Louisiana, Bell's faith in pan-American union was in decline. Six weeks after Colfax, he published another editorial headed "Union," this time urging unity among
"*our* people—the colored citizens of San Franciso and the State at large—[has]

1. Little surviving material on Bell exists; for biographical information I drew on his own accounts
in *The Elevator* (San Francisco), esp. his piece commemorating Salmon Chase on May 10, 1873. See
also March 1, 1873, and June 15, 1872.

any nation, community, or class, ever stood more in need of union—social, religious, and political, than we do?" Bell had long advocated greater unity among African Americans, and did so all the more fervently after 1873. But he no longer referred to national union in any respect.[2]

Bell's personal pattern of union usage was mirrored by that of other blacks, and eventually by the country as a whole. From its postwar reaffirmation among Americans of all stripes, union sentiment declined in clusters: first among blacks and their Radical Republican allies, subsequently among whites in the North and West, and finally in the South. By the late 1890s the term had passed into virtual disuse. A long history of vernacular and valuative centrality ended rather abruptly, without much notice or immediately obvious cause. By the early twentieth century, the word appeared as outmoded as the political epoch it had so deeply marked. Union's disappearance from popular usage is not in itself remarkable, given the fate of many political words. But the term's rapid and thorough decline not long after it returned so powerfully following the war is difficult to account for.[3] This chapter explores the end of union talk among Americans, and considers the consequences for period ideas of national unity.

Figure 7 displays the overall pattern of union usage between 1852 and 1900. A sharp decline is evident in the term's appearance in American newspapers during the 1880s, a decrease mirrored in presidential and congressional speeches as well as other examples of popular opinion. In the 1890s, union references dwindled further and had all but vanished by century's end.

At face value, the term's virtual disappearance from American political talk by the 1890s upholds claims voiced at the time, that the war and Reconstruction had "solved" the problem of national unity.[4] As noted in previous pages, historians make a similar argument about the end of the Civil War: union had served its rhetorical purposes, and the now permanently reunited country moved on to other issues. This strikes me as an unsatisfactory conclusion about 1890 as well as about 1865. The notion that a concept disappears from usage when it has achieved its apotheosis contradicts most of U.S. history. Talk of democracy did not decline among middle-class white men during or after Jacksonian times, after expanded suffrage opened the public sphere to them. African Americans still avidly discussed freedom after emancipation. Not a single word in the Constitution was altered between 1804 and 1865, yet as Michael Kammen demonstrates, the document was invoked in every political crisis, and in plenty of minor issues, during that period.[5] Finally achieving a goal, whether a personal accomplishment or a collective end like securing a seemingly permanent national union, seems far

---

2. *The Elevator,* July 26, 1873; April 26, 1873; June 21, 1873 (cf. May 3, 1873; November 21, 1874).

3. Rodgers 1987 chronicles the disappearance of other terms once central to American political vernacular.

4. Theodore Roosevelt, for example, declared in 1890 that "politically this question of American nationality has been settled once for all" (Roosevelt 1918 [1897], 239).

5. Kammen 1987.

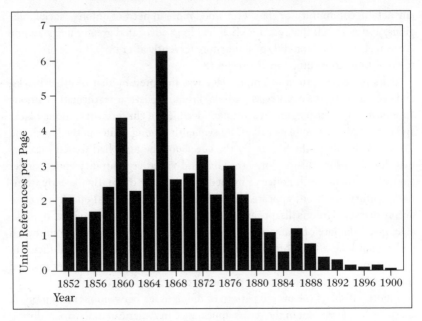

FIGURE 7. Union references, 1852–90

more likely to result in its more fervent application than in its disappearance from common use.

Moreover, the notion that national unity was "achieved" by 1890 (much less 1865) appears far-fetched. No more secessionist movements sprang up after the war's conclusion, but the breadth and intensity of conflict over other domestic issues—industrialism and labor conditions, immigration, tariff levels, silver coinage, and so on—left Americans internally divided along innumerable fault lines. In the past such tensions usually inspired a surge in union talk; not so after 1885. Longtime assurances that the United States constituted a "sacred union," as noted in chapter 5, faded as well. No such reference turns up in my reading (or in a large database of period American documents) after 1890.[6]

A close inspection of disappearing union rhetoric, and the surrounding context, points to a set of influences that deeply corroded traditional bonds. Rather than a widespread positive belief that national unity was no longer a concern, the main sources of its decline in popular speech were negative. Three contributing factors are most pertinent, none of which derived from a new nationalist sensibility. First, most African Americans and white Radical Republicans abandoned

6. See the "Making of America" database of period books, available online: "sacred union" was used sixteen times to denote the American nation between 1865 and 1885, and none thereafter (search from 1885–1920). Interestingly, in 1914 France's President Raymond Poincaré applied "union sacrée" to the French people as World War I dawned; the term became immensely popular, particularly through the efforts of nationalist politician and novelist Maurice Barrés. Byrnes 1999, 263–64.

the term in the 1870s, once union's "balanced" reassociation with states' rights (and therefore white supremacy in the South) was confirmed. Second, as the labor movement expanded rapidly following a high-profile 1877 railway strike, a twofold effect on union ideas can be charted. Bitter, divisive conflicts between capital and labor, and an attendant sense of class differences in the United States, helped diminish a sense of shared purposes even among native whites. Such unity had always been a contested matter, as previous chapters detail, but a qualitative difference is apparent in examining attitudes during the 1880s and 1890s. Also in response to the emergence of mass unionism, the term "union" increasingly became associated with organized labor. By the 1890s, "the union" more often referred to an AFL local or Knights of Labor chapter than to the United States or the national population. With workers and labor leaders reserving the term for their collective enterprise, and business interests viewing "union" as "the very *word* of perfidy . . . [an] offensive idea on its face,"[7] these substantial segments of the populace turned to other terms—"America," most notably—to denote their national idea.

A third source of union sentiment's decline was immigration. As conflicts between workers and owners shattered postwar complacency about the enduring nature of American national unity, an "unprecedented influx" of immigrants sparked the most powerful expressions of ethnocultural sensibilities in the nation's history.[8] These exclusionary impulses led to rearguard unionist declarations, but an overwhelming sense of "alien radicalism" invalidated their force. To be sure, similar reactions were heard during the immigration surge during the late 1840s and 1850s, as chapter 3 chronicles; and taken alone, neither 1880s immigration, the rise of the labor unions, nor reformers' disappointment might have ended union's vernacular dominance in the United States. But together their effect was decisive.

This combination of certain groups' distaste for union talk, the term's association among many others with labor unions, and a fast diminishing sense of a comprehensible "American people" united in traditional ways appears to have sealed the concept's doom. The passing of union from national social and political conversation did not mean the end of struggles for closer bonds among Americans, of course. But the complex blend of meanings represented by the term was demonstrably altered after Reconstruction ended and the mighty industrial engines of the Gilded Age became the central feature of American life. In the 1890s a fervent nationalism, rooted in imperialist impulses, ethnocentrism, and jingoistic patriotism, swept the country. Balanced ideas of "sustainable union" (and of antinativist moral union) had helped to blunt such expressions in earlier years; this barrier was now eroded.

Perhaps unionist ideals and rhetoric would have dwindled in any event. But this chapter seeks to comprehend the causes as specifically as possible. The his-

7. *New York World,* December 4, 1881.
8. Smith 1997, 357.

tory of union's displacement and disappearance has important implications for those seeking to reinaugurate a sense of national unity in the United States today, as explored in the conclusion. First we turn to a close chronicling of the end of American dreams of a more perfect union.

THE END OF MORAL UNION:
AFRICAN AMERICANS IN RECONSTRUCTION

An extraordinary swell of hope following emancipation and black soldiers' inclusion in the Union Army inspired a freshet of union rhetoric and, it appears, ideational commitment among African Americans during the latter Civil War years. "The promise of union waxed strong," one black editor nostalgically recalled in 1875. The first black-owned newspaper outside the North was established in New Orleans during the war; its Creole founders called it "L'Union" because, as the inaugural issue explained, "it [union] is our law, our conviction!" The ardor with which free and, after 1862, newly emancipated African Americans took up unionist rhetoric reinforced the point nationwide. With the war's outbreak, petitions from blacks flooded War Secretary Cameron and other federal and state officials' desks. "We are all anxious to fight for the maintenance of the Union and the preservation of the principles promulgated by President Lincoln," wrote one would-be soldier. Another, on behalf of all "loyal Union colored Americans and Christians," assured Cameron of "our most willing aid to deliver our loyal colored brethren and other Unionists."[9] Union Army generals' foot-dragging in response is well chronicled elsewhere; once permitted to fight, blacks overwhelmingly declared themselves "in defence of the Union, and Democracy" and, as one black soldier wrote home, did "ardently desire the maintenance of the national unity, for which [we] are ready to sacrifice [our] fortunes and lives. . . . At the call of General Banks, [we] hastened to rally under the banner of Union and Liberty."[10]

As the war drew to a close, African Americans and their political allies expected that these gains would be expanded in statutory and affective realms, in line with the "moral union" advocated by Lincoln, Douglass, and Radical Republicans. Blacks in Norfolk, Virginia, in 1865 established the "Union Monitor Club," the state's first civil-rights organization for former slaves. This along with numerous voluntary societies in other states helped make up the American Freedmen's-Aid Union, whose credo promised "no distinction of race or color." Few expected the road ahead to be trouble-free; as the New Orleans *Tribune* acknowledged, "the

9. *The Nationalist*, November 10, 1875; *L'Union* (New Orleans), September 27, 1862 [my translation]; Aptheker 1962, 460; *Liberator*, September 12, 1862.

10. Aptheker 1962, 483; *Liberator*, April 1, 1864. For a history of black Union soldiers, see Paludan 1988, 65, 208–14, 217, 222; Glatthaar 1992, 138–62. The black regiment raised by Philip Bell in San Francisco was never called to duty, a fact that sent Bell to Washington in protest; after meeting with Sumner and Salmon Chase, Bell received a commission as a special Treasury Department agent.

black man had to fight the battles of Union and Freedom with his musket; he will have to fight them too with the ballot." But the expectation of eventual "acceptance into a reborn Union of all Americans" was plain. At times this rhetoric spilled in peculiar directions, as when Beverly Nash, a black delegate to South Carolina's postwar constitutional convention, avowed that "we recognize the Southern white man as the true friend of the black man. . . . In [all] public affairs, we must unite with our white fellow-citizens. They tell us that they have been disfranchised, [and] we tell the North that we shall never let the halls of Congress be silent until we remove that disability."[11]

Strong initial encouragement came from Radical Republican plans for a more moral postwar union. Along with the congressional activities of Sumner, Wade, and others, longtime abolitionists like Wendell Phillips had begun advocating "amalgamation of the races" during the war, as in this 1863 Massachusetts Fourth of July speech: "I have no hope for the future . . . but in that sublime mingling of races, which is God's own method of civilizing and elevating the world [loud applause]. Not that amalgamation of licentiousness, born of slavery . . . but that gradual and harmonizing union, in honorable marriage, which has mingled all other races, and from which springs the present phase of European and Northern civilization." In states from Massachusetts to Iowa, local Radicals pledged support for integrative measures. African Americans responded cautiously: "a perfect Union," said the South Carolina minister E. J. Adams in 1867, "cannot be secured without equal suffrage."[12]

Yet soon after the landmark Reconstruction legislation was passed this unionist outlook faltered, both among blacks and among their Republican supporters. From the early 1870s onward African Americans referred less and less to their inclusion in a reunited whole, judging from black-owned newspapers, diaries, and the oratory of Douglass and other leaders, including the black Members of Congress serving between 1869 and 1879. Set against a backdrop of Reconstruction gains—political officeholding at the local and national levels, universal citizenship and suffrage for black males, and the raft of formal civil-rights guarantees in the postwar constitutional amendments as well as various national statutes—African Americans' short-lived inclination to join in the jubilant postwar celebration of unity is counterintuitive. As William Lloyd Garrison said in 1870, in a pun celebrating the election of Jefferson Davis's black Senate successor, Hiram Revels, African Americans "might well rejoice and be filled with all jubilation, for they were having their *Revels* in the Senate of the United States."[13]

11. Foner 1988, 111; Hyman 1967, 224; New Orleans *Tribune*, April 2, 1865; Nash quoted in Franklin 1969, 316.

12. Phillips quoted in Lind 1995, 291; *Charleston Courier* (S.C.), March 22, 1867. On Radical activities in individual states, see the separate essays in Mohr, ed. 1976. David Montgomery's essay on Pennsylvania sets the tone: "On the subject of civil rights for Negroes in Pennsylvania . . . [t]he conventional view of historians that the Republicans advocated civil rights and Negro suffrage for the South but shunned them for the North may be true of the conservative Republicans, but it is not true of the Radicals" (in Mohr 1976, 56).

13. Reported in *Commonwealth* (Boston), April 23, 1870, 15.

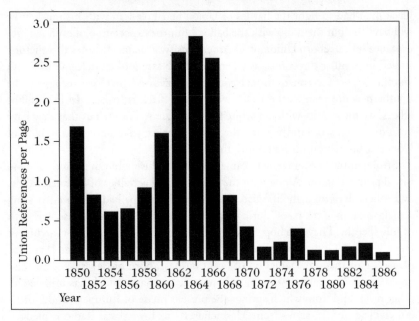

FIGURE 8. African Americans' union references, 1850–86

But the spirit of fraternal exchange was evidently fading even as Garrison spoke. In the flush of postwar optimism it may briefly have appeared true, as Eric Foner writes, that "'freedom' meant inclusion rather than separation" and that African Americans' "animating impulse" was originally to seek full membership in the national union. But most blacks soon realized that anything like affective recognition was not forthcoming. Many freedmen, persuaded that federal intervention was the only security for newly won rights, recognized instead that union retained its traditional balanced connotations—including an antistatist ethic. Hence union talk disappeared early among black leaders as well as the rank and file. Frederick Douglass was left to predict a more general passing of union sentiment in America, a prophecy that would remain unfulfilled for two decades.[14]

Figure 8 displays union references in a sample of black newspapers and congressional oratory from 1845 to 1880; compare figure 7 above for frequency and nature of use more generally in postwar North and South. (As noted in chapter 4, the scarcity of existing copies of black-owned newspapers, especially before the Civil War, renders this figure less reliable than others in this study.)

Exploring this pattern casts light on a broader controversy over freedmen's prospects during Reconstruction and beyond. Historians of the subject have long differed sharply, with one school finding "no . . . specific changes either in the status of former slaves or in the conditions under which they labored." Others

14. Foner 1988, 110; Douglass in Martin 1984, 17n.

point to political gains represented by the postwar amendments and congressional acts, particularly the Civil Rights Act of 1866, along with (more disputed) economic advances in identifying "genuine progress toward racial integration during Reconstruction," especially in politics and government.[15]

The swift decline of postwar union talk among African Americans, even during the height of Radical Reconstruction, suggests that sweeping formal-legal gains could not alleviate many blacks' sense of exclusion conveyed, in W. E. B. Du Bois's words, by "the atmosphere of the land, the thought and feeling; the thousand and one little actions which go to make up life. In any community or nation it is these little things which are most . . . essential to any clear conception of the group life taken as a whole."[16] Why these "little things" might have so definitively destroyed hopes of affective participation is not immediately clear. For at least equally deep exclusionary sentiments marked the antebellum years—a period, as we saw earlier, in which union ideology enjoyed much wider currency among black opinion leaders.

Three points are worth noting by way of unraveling this postwar development. The first is comparative, drawing on the observation from chapter 4 that before 1865 the abolitionist movement served as a rare beacon of inclusionary promise in a personal, immediate way. With postwar declarations like that of W. L. Garrison that "my vocation, as an Abolitionist, thank God, is ended," this vital spring of support for blacks' unionist impulses was quickly receding. The trend was capped barely four years later when the American Anti-Slavery Society disbanded following passage of the Fifteenth Amendment.[17] Most white Republicans after the war poorly filled this informal but vital function of personally expressing affective connections between blacks and whites. Party members such as the Union officer who, after the 1863 Battle of Nashville, characterized the "great cause" as "giv[ing] freedom, unity, manhood, and peace to all men, whatever birth or complexion," mostly changed their tune after (or during the course of) the 1867 elections, in which Republicans suffered heavy losses across the North and West. Thereafter, notes Foner, "looming on the horizon was a new Republican self-image, in which devotion to the Union and fiscal responsibility would overshadow civil and political equality."[18] The sentimental "union of

15. Gerteis 1973, 5; Foner 1988, 371. Cf., on (temporary) gains, Ayers 1992, 67–72, 132–59; McPherson 1991, 11–22, 131–52; Smith 1997, 298–300. On hostile stasis, see Gillette 1979; Williamson 1984, chaps. 2–3. Foner's massive synthesis neatly reconciles the two views by presenting the freedmen's outlook alongside that of planters or Republicans. From this perspective advances in black civil rights are appreciated in full, while setbacks seem especially painful. His attention to "the centrality of the black experience" and the "complex series of interactions among blacks and whites" (xxiv–xxv) does not include acknowledgment of union talk's early disappearance among African Americans.

16. Du Bois 1989 [1903], 147. See also Rabinowitz 1992, 325–41, and Bentley (1955, 214): "what the freedmen . . . needed in 1865 was not just an act of Congress and the guardianship of a federal agency, but a change in the mores of a nation."

17. The American Freedmen's Union Commission announced "The Beginning of the End" of its activities in 1868: see McPherson 1964, 401–5. Quote in Foner 1988, 26.

18. Officer quoted in Glatthaar 1992, 159; Foner 1988, 315. White southerners saw matters differently, mixing nostalgia for the old order with revilement of the new. Virginia journalist Edward Pol-

hearts" rhetoric chronicled in the previous chapter was largely a whites-only af-
fair, further discouraging union-minded blacks.

Even Reconstruction's monumental legal achievements left African-American
leaders with a bitter aftertaste, as Republicans executing the historic changes
excluded black Congressmen from their councils. Richard H. Cain, a black U.S.
House member from South Carolina, told the 43rd Congress that

> [t]here was a time, not very far distant in the past, when this antagonism
> was not recognized, when a feeling of fraternization between the white
> and the colored races existed, that made them kindred to each other. But
> since our emancipation, since liberty has come, and . . . only since we have
> proceeded to take hold and help advance the civilization of this nation—
> it is only since then that this bugbear is brought up against us again.[19]

Inspirational Garrison-style stands for genuine equality, preceding Union and
Constitution where necessary, were rarely heard among Republicans after 1867;
the ailing Sumner was the sole consistent exception. Prominent Radical leaders
sounded themes hardly in keeping with the prewar personal assurances of a Gerrit Smith. "I am thoroughly sick of niggers," complained Benjamin Wade privately in 1867. Thaddeus Stevens told fellow House members that "negro equality . . . does not mean that a negro shall sit on the same seat or eat at the same
table with a white man. That is a matter of taste which every man must decide
for himself."[20]

Here then is a first distinction of note. While racism pervaded society both
before and after the war, the message of personal acceptance conveyed by abolitionists was muted after 1865. As Maine's Lot Morrill soberly told fellow Senators in 1866: "We have made the negro slave an American citizen, [but] we seem
to start back from contact with him as if his touch were moral and political pol-
lution."[21] Abolitionists' pre-Reconstruction contribution to blacks' sense of inclusion, even against a sea of prejudice and indifference, had virtually disappeared.
Blacks readily recognized the trend. In his long dissection of "The Attitude of the
Republican Party to the Colored American," the California black leader W. H.
Hall gloomily cited Republicans' "lack of sincere and noble sympathy in [our]

---

lard, for instance, recalled antebellum abolitionists as "desir[ing] to do for [the slave] such kindly
offices as they would for any suffering people," while postwar Radical Republicans exhibited "a positive and most offensive disease—manifesting for the Negro a singular affection . . . and intent on
making him the political pet and idol of America" (quoted in Hyman 1967, 247).

19. Cain in *Cong. Record*, 43rd Cong., 1st sess., 1874, 565. Compare his speech two weeks later (ibid.,
901–3). Another black Representative, Mississippi's John Lynch, saw a later beginning to "serious
troubles between the two races" in his state, after "Northern Democratic victories in 1874" (ibid., 4955).

20. Stevens in *Cong. Globe*, 39th Cong., 2d sess., 1866, 252; Wade quoted in Trefousse 1963, 311–
12; cf. his comments in *Cong. Globe*, 36th Cong., 1st sess., Appendix (1860), 355. On white Republican hostility, among leaders and constituents, cf. Sawrey's study of Ohio (1992, esp. 3, 88, 117).

21. Morrill continued: "The bond of our national unity is not expressed by the epithets 'rights of
states,' 'state sovereignty' . . . but in unity of faith in human rights, unity of spirit and purpose for the
development and protection of individual rights." *Cong. Globe*, 39th Cong., 2d sess., 1866, 40–41.

behalf." P. B. S. Pinchback, who briefly served Louisiana as the first black governor in U.S. history, observed shortly before taking office in 1872: "As a race [we] are between the hawk of Republican demagogism and the buzzards of Democratic prejudices." Eventually a wry sarcasm appeared among some African-American speakers. "At the Judgement Day," wrote a black Kansas editor, "there will be many white Christians who will refuse to go into heaven, because there will be Negroes admitted."[22]

A second explanation for this lack of rhetorical commitment to national unity after the 1860s is closely related. Within a few years after the war blacks turned inward, displaying "remarkable political unity" as a group. For African Americans "as a class," said black U.S. Senator Blanche K. Bruce, "in union, not division, is strength." The black-owned *Charleston Advocate* summarized "the general outlook" in 1867: "Each class should be duly represented, that whites may act for whites, and colored for colored." In the religious arena, still a mainspring of African-American common life, a "wholesale withdrawal of [southern] blacks from biracial congregations" signaled a more general drawing apart. A Tennessee cleric reported after the war that "mixed churches are doomed by the voluntary action of the negroes themselves, who prefer to worship in their own temples, with their own people and under the inspiration of their own preachers."[23]

A "thriving institutional structure," encompassing black-run schools, churches, charities, stores, and the like, was the beneficial result of this segregative trend. Historian August Meier outlines at length a more problematic outcome:

> [T]he Negro leaders . . . were fundamentally struggling for integration into American society, for the elimination of segregation of any sort. Yet in creating a racial equal-rights organization . . . they appeared to be creating a segregated movement in itself, to be fostering the very thing they were attacking. Independence and self-help were commonplace virtues in American culture, and no one could deny that in union there is strength. Yet the appeal for racial solidarity smacked of self-segregation, of a sort of nationalism, of furthering the system of "color caste." This paradox is one of the central themes in American Negro thought on the race problem.[24]

As Meier details, such withdrawal has been one response by African Americans (and other minorities) to majority-culture hostility since the founding era: chapter 4 traced similar "black nationalist" themes in the antebellum years. Interpretive differences have arisen in Meier's wake over assessing the extent and nature

22. *The Elevator* (San Francisco), February 8, 1873; Pinchback in Taylor 1980, 223; *The National Reflector* (Wichita), January 18, 1896. On Radicals' general movement away from ideals of racial justice, see Trefousse 1969, 460–67.

23. Bruce in *Cong. Globe*, 44th Cong., 1st sess., 1876, 2103; *Charleston Advocate*, May 11, 1867; Foner 1988, 398 (on black political unity), 89 (on black religious separatism; cf. ibid., 89–92); Rabinowitz 1980, 224 (cf. 198–204, 223–25).

24. Foner 1988, 95; Meier 1966, 7–8.

of Reconstruction-era separatism.[25] But as far as African Americans' postwar public talk is concerned, segregation appears to have been a reality: already in the late 1860s "union" usage was present most often among blacks in a self-help context. African Americans in Racine, Wisconsin, regularly scheduled "a kind of Union meeting of all the colored people in the city," for example; and the Washington, D.C., *National Leader* featured the refrain "unite and make a sacrifice for the good of all, or do the reverse and go to the wall."[26]

To what degree such separatist attitudes actually inhibited blacks' acceptance into majority-white American society is impossible to ascertain. Their effect was surely weak compared to the majority of northern as well as southern whites' resistance to inclusion: African Americans' exclusion from postwar membership in the reunited nation was not a chicken-or-egg matter. But in comprehending the difference between common union usage among blacks before the war and its virtual absence soon afterward, this expanded tendency to voice themes of self-segregation deserves mention. As Howard Rabinowitz shows, African Americans' challenges to other customary practices after the war played an important part in codifying official segregation, promulgated by white officials, during the 1890s.[27]

Where African Americans appeared to prefer separatism to accommodation, heightened white hostility was one byproduct at the time. A South Carolina editor wrote in response to perceived black self-segregation: "Let us [then] have a thorough understanding and union of the whole *white* people . . . not forgetting either the worthy exceptions among the negroes who have identified themselves with us, or any others who may see fit to cast their lines in with us."[28] Would white South Carolinians, or Ohioans or Vermonters, have articulated different views if African Americans had avoided a "separatist" strategy? Perhaps not, but some whites might have had more difficulty justifying exclusionary sentiments and practices after Reconstruction.

A third possible contributing factor to blacks' collective decision to eschew union usage is the postwar organic-union talk described in chapter 5. A Darwin-admiring white editor of the San Francisco *Chronicle* (drawing an angry reply from Bell in *The Elevator*) allowed that blacks were "with us in sympathy, in interest, in habit, in language, in religion" but that their "distinct blood" and racial "antagonism" made them "the Nemesis of American unification and progress." Such organic imagery centered on blood and race may not always have specifically singled out African Americans as excluded, but the implications were clear enough. A contributor to a black-owned New Orleans paper dissected the organic metaphor in 1867: "Strange that all their talk of Anglo-Saxon bodies politic should ignore the *black man;* he is the *veins* . . . of the American political organ-

25. See esp. Foner 1988, 544–47.
26. *Wisconsin Afro-American,* October 8, 1892; *The National Leader,* February 16, 1889, 4.
27. Rabinowitz 1980, 226–58, 330–39.
28. Newberry (S.C.) *Herald,* November 3, 1870.

ism!"[29] Into the 1850s, even as blacks' prospects for equal treatment as members of the polity appeared especially dim, a degree of hope had been held out by Webster, Lincoln, and others' nonexclusive union themes, as demonstrated in chapter 4. Now white elites' invocations of Anglo-Saxon organicism mingled with the postwar ascendancy of Social Darwinist doctrines, providing intellectual cover to committed segregationists and raising the argumentative bar for integrationists.

Faced with such attitudes, black spokesmen insisted grimly on the political and civil rights guaranteed by law while affirming repeatedly that no "social equality"—affective union, in essence—was sought with whites. A certain subversive irony marks many such statements, as Rep. John Lynch's "I have never believed for even a moment that social equality could be brought about even between persons of the same race," but most African Americans seemed wearily to accept his congressional colleague Joseph H. Rainey's observation that white House members, and presumably their constituents, "have a feeling against the negro in this country that I suppose will never die out."[30] Unmet rising expectations, to echo Tocqueville's famous explanation of the French Revolution, are apparent in such expressions of frustration. African Americans' hopes for inclusive definitions of national unity soared during and immediately after the war; however, they were soon dashed. In 1865, Connecticut held the first state referendum on black suffrage, only to reject it overwhelmingly. Such blows must have fallen doubly hard at the time, as blacks realized that inclusion in the reunited land was as distant as ever and became more aware that sectional unity was cemented by the return of white domination.

Among southern freedmen and former masters, even the skewed sense of cross-racial fellowship that existed under slavery was deeply diminished after 1865. The geography of blacks' postwar settlement testifies to this change: where emancipated slaves remained on a plantation to labor as sharecroppers, their cabins were located as far from the "Great House" as possible, rather than in tight proximity as before. As discussed above in chapter 4, a limited version of Mecham Sobel's "world they made together" applies to antebellum black-white relations. Although governed by a profoundly unequal power calculus, a sense of shared destiny arguably existed on both sides.[31]

Now a sullen hostility characterized most interaction between African Americans and southern whites, at least as far as the printed record reveals. As one southern editor wrote in 1865: "The Law which freed the negro, at the same time freed the master, all obligations springing out of the relations of master and slave,

29. San Francisco *Chronicle*, February 10, 1873 (cf. *The Elevator*, February 15, 1873); New Orleans *Tribune*, March 24, 1867.

30. Lynch in *Cong. Globe*, 43rd Cong., 2d sess., 1875, 1145; Rainey in *Cong. Globe*, 43rd Cong., 1st sess., 1873, 218. Cf. Rainey's definition in a subsequent speech to the House: "Social equality consists in congeniality of feeling, a reciprocity of sentiment, and mutual, social recognition among men, which is grading according to desire and taste, and not by any known or possible law." *Cong. Globe*, 43rd Cong., 2d sess., 1875, 1228.

31. Sobel 1987; Genovese 1975, esp. 74.

except those of kindness, cease mutually to exist." And "kindness," as Foner writes, "proved all too rare" at the time. Even occasional attempts to bridge the gulf, such as Oxford, Mississippi's white citizens declaring "Why Negroes Should be Educated," were couched in an insulting paternalism: "Do we not owe it [education] to them as a debt of gratitude? . . . And is it not a small return for all [slaves' prewar service] that we are asked to make?"[32] The region's wartime Unionists were no better on this score: the "six principles of Southern Unionism," as set out in the *Raleigh Standard*, gave pride of place to "unqualified opposition to what is called negro suffrage."[33] Though southern Republicans initially evoked national unity in their appeals to black voters, the practice had dwindled by 1868.[34]

The return of union's antistatist connotations in the 1870s only made the term less attractive where African Americans were concerned. Among the few remaining scholarly verities about Reconstruction[35] is that blacks' fate lay in important part with Republicans' ability to maintain federal protection and secure economic support for freedmen in the former Confederacy. Southerners' embrace of union as a counterweight to federal power, described in chapter 5, contributed to the idea's lack of purchase among southern blacks.

Especially after what African Americans viewed as the "devil's compromise" of 1877, the onset of Jim Crow regulations confirmed that a "swelling sense of national unity between North and South was accomplished at the expense of the Negroes." Among the few remaining symbols of national unity with currency among blacks was the Union League, whose officers were a principal source of recruiting black soldiers during the war. Most local Leagues remained integrated during Reconstruction, but in the late 1870s Union Leagues were forcibly dismantled throughout the South. Strict racial separation codes subsequently eroded any enduring hopes of African Americans' inclusion in an increasingly sentimentalized union. As Du Bois observed of black and white early in the century, "there stand in the South two separate worlds. . . . [T]he separation is so thorough and deep that it absolutely precludes for the present anything like that sympathetic and effective group-training and leadership of the one by the other." Even Booker T. Washington's writings and speeches, with their peculiar blend of stern

---

32. Foner 1988, 131; *Selma Times*, June 12, 1866. Cf. the planter Henry W. Ravenal's journal entry on the subject in Childs 1947, 239–40. Far more common than paternalistic kindness after the war was an out-and-out "policy of violence" by whites toward blacks. As Vandal (1991, 182) writes: "For many, violence became not only a means to oppose [Reconstruction] changes, but also an instrument of self-preservation, a way to re-establish common values and a new sense of community." See generally Rable 1984; Franklin 1969, 326–28; and Fitzgerald 1989, 213–18.

33. Raleigh *Standard*, August 3, 1865.

34. On Republican union rhetoric, consider the Loyal League's "catechism," promoted among freedmen: the initial version advised blacks to vote for "the Union Republican Party," but "Union" was dropped after 1867 (Fleming 1905, 13). This owed in part to Democrats' skillfully framing issues of black-white relations in terms of *social* union: sexual relations, marriage, social correspondence, and so forth.

35. A mid-1960s wave of revisionism is described in Donald 1984, xi–xv, 2–11; the changing interpretive ground before and since is summarized in Foner 1988, xix–xxvi, and Amar 1998, 302–4.

self-reliance and naive denial ("the pleasant relations that have continued to exist between us and the white people in [the North] . . . now extend throughout the South," he said of the early 1880s), never referred to national union, much less blacks' part in it; at most Washington alluded vaguely to "the whole nation."[36]

Hence irony and tragedy intermingle in the unionist outlook of African Americans after the Civil War. Cautiously receptive to the idea of national union while a majority of their number were still enslaved, blacks displayed little patience for such talk after a strong promise of freedom had been won and then swiftly dismantled. Postwar bonds between whites in North and South were strengthened in several ways: developing economic exchanges; forging cultural linkages, often around religious themes; and vocally affirming the benefits of reunion, often in sentimental fashion. Social, economic, and political ties among the sections were all promoted either by explicitly excluding, or at best while ignoring, African Americans. Compounding this cruel development was the fact that railroads, the technological guarantor of territorial unity, were the original location for the restrictions of Jim Crow laws. Historian Rayford Logan provides an appropriate summary: blacks by the early 1880s occupied "a separate wing [of the] edifice of national unity," where "on the pediments . . . were carved Exploitation, Disenfranchisement, Segregation, Discrimination, Lynching, [and] Contempt."[37]

Radical Republicans and the End of Moral Union

Radical Republicans, the most avid postwar promoters of African-American civil rights and of a stronger national government, began backing away from both causes after the exhausting battles of 1867–69. The muting of Radical support for black rights was examined in chapter 5. As for state power, Foner attests that "while hardly abandoning the broad conception of national power engendered by the Civil War, Republicans proved reluctant to promote the state's expansion into new realms . . . even among Republicans, doubts about the activist state persisted."[38]

Yet a measure of the Radical spirit evidently remained, as expressed in their linguistic practices. During the 1870s most remaining Radical stalwarts (several party leaders, such as Julian, Wade, and Ohio Rep. James Ashley, lost their seats in Congress, while Stevens and Sumner died in 1868 and 1874 respectively) also ceased referring to "the Union" or otherwise praising national unity. It is not clear whether their erstwhile black allies' disinclination to use the term had any effect

36. Meier 1966, 24, and 3–25 passim; Du Bois 1989, 80; Washington 1986 [1901], 153 (and on "nation," see for example 166). On the Union League, see especially Fitzgerald 1989 (southern Leagues' forced dismantling by hostile southern whites, many organized as Klansmen, is discussed at pp. 200–52); Saville 1994, 162–88; and McPherson 1964, 123, 207–8, 378–79.

37. Logan 1965, 313 (see generally pp. 23–61, on consolidation of white supremacy in the South during the 1870s–80s).

38. Foner 1988, 451.

on, for example, Ben Butler or Michigan Senator Zachariah Chandler's subsequent avoidance of union talk. But a glance through the speeches of these and other Radicals indicates an inability to imagine the postwar United States as anything resembling a "more perfect" union on their preferred moral terms. Meanwhile, most other members of Congress—notably including lapsed Radicals like Carl Schurz and Lyman Trumbull—indulged freely in the rhetoric of sentimental union.[39]

Union's rhetorical rejection by African Americans and Radical Republicans marks the first mass turning away from the term since the decade before the revolution, apart from southerners' hiatus during the war. Most abolitionists had opposed—indeed, had been shocked by—Garrison's call for disunion, with even outspoken movement leaders like Frederick Douglass turning to moral-union doctrines instead. Now blacks' resistance to union talk was scarcely noticed amidst whites' "union of hearts" sentiment dominating the end of Reconstruction. There is no evidence that the moral disillusionment captured in blacks' and Radicals' rhetorical disenchantment had wider influence in the polity. But it is conceivable that the absence of a weighty normative thrust, as was previously contributed to postwar ideas of union by Douglass, Lincoln, and other advocates of civil rights, played a part in the term's wider abandonment.

Beginning a decade later, most other Americans would follow the lead of blacks and their Radical allies and abandon references to national union. The trend is reflected in miniature by U.S. presidents' inaugural addresses. From Washington onward, every president through Garfield (1881) included paeans to "the Union" in their inaugural statement, usually as a central theme. Garfield devoted less space than some of his predecessors to the theme, but he was typical in providing an abbreviated history of national unity, from the framers (who "established a National Union, founded directly upon the will of the people") through national development ("twenty-five States have been added to the Union") and civil war ("the Union emerged from the blood and fire of that conflict purified and made stronger") to the future ("Let all our people, leaving behind them the battlefields of dead issues, move forward . . . in their strength of liberty and the restored Union"). Grover Cleveland's first inaugural address, in 1885, broke this trend, including no references to union or unity. Benjamin Harrison, his successor, commented in passing about Reconstruction that "the divergent interests of peace speedily demanded a 'more perfect union.'" Then Cleveland in 1889 again departed from tradition—as did his successors, well into the twentieth century, none of whom mentioned union in their addresses.[40]

Two main influences spurred union's decline among the majority of whites: (1) a co-optation of the term by organized labor (and its foes), to the point that by the 1890s "union" usually signified a labor or trade association; and (2) from

39. On Schurz and Trumbull as increasingly moderate, see Trefousse 1969, 454–59.
40. Lott 1994, quotes at pp. 164, 167 (Garfield), p. 180 (Harrison).

around 1880 onward, a combination of spreading class conflict and dramatic rises in immigration that rendered older notions of affective ties and improvable unity all but moot.

THE END OF RHETORICAL UNION: *LABOR* UNION, 1880s–90s

From around 50,000 trade union members in 1880, the United States during the "Great Upheaval" of the mid-1880s witnessed a remarkable rise in organized labor. Total union membership topped one million in 1886, and though a drop accompanied the collapse of the Knights of Labor a few years later, mass labor unionism was a significant presence in American politics and society from the mid-1880s on.[41] Nationwide strikes also increased exponentially during this period, beginning with widespread railroad work stoppages in late summer 1877. A series of labor actions, sometimes including riots, culminated in the "great strike year" of 1886, when nearly 1,500 strikes involved more than 400,000 workers. Trade unions, as a *New York Times* correspondent noted a year later, were "now the center of America's attention; they have become a central question wherever men gather to discuss public affairs."[42]

This is a familiar Gilded Age story. My contention here is that extensive trade union organizing, strikes, and other newsworthy activities in the 1880s and 1890s helped establish "union" as a referent for *labor* unions, rather than for the country as a whole. This argument is based in important part on chronology. From around 1880 onward there was a notable boost in the use of "union" as a referent for organized labor both in the particular sense, as in the American Railway Union or United Brotherhood of Carpenters and Joiners, and the general, whereby "union" signified the labor movement overall. Henry George's campaign for New York mayor in 1886, on the "Central Labor Union" ticket, "was watched by the whole country"; newspaper reports at the time referred to George as "the Union candidate" or "unions' man," without apparent confusion over meaning.[43] As noted in figure 7, this was precisely the period during which union usage in its national sense began to decline, with a marked drop after 1886—the year of labor's "Great Upheaval."

American references to trade unions date to 1827, when a group of Philadelphia laborers formed the Mechanics' Union of Trade Associations. Like most workingmen's organizations of the time, including the first "General Trades Union," formed in New York in 1833, it was short-lived. The term itself came into

41. U.S. union membership statistics are in Docherty 1996, 252–53, and Davis et al. 1972, 220.

42. *New York Times*, February 27, 1887. Figures on strike trends are from Montgomery 1979, 20 (table 1). On labor more generally during this period, see Foner 1947–64, vol. 2; Dubofsky 1994, esp. 1–35; and Laurie 1989. For a skeptical view that the "Great Upheaval" was "more the ideal than reality," see Weir 1997, 421–23, 435.

43. Quote on George campaign from Perlman 1928, 178; see also Weir 1997. Labor unions' expanding prominence among all Americans was furthered by numerous political campaigns on behalf of trade-union candidates and platforms, including presidential contests from 1872 onward.

use in the organized-labor sense around the same time in England, amid the early stirrings of the Industrial Revolution. It is unlikely that it constituted much competition for rhetorical preeminence before the 1870s, however. The first national U.S. labor union, the National Typographical Union, was formed only in 1852, and as late as 1877 the total number of national unions was less than ten. Amid a wide range of Reconstruction-era organizations denoted by "union," from the Women's Christian Temperance Union to the Klan-affiliated Constitutional Union Guard, there is no reason labor entities would stand out.[44] But their dramatic growth in the 1880s established trade unions as America's largest type of organized group. This expansion, along with tumultuous conflicts between workers and management, cemented union's new place in the national consciousness as a referent for labor.

Union's increased prominence in this sense can be traced through newspaper and other popular and official sources. Casual references in a wide variety of journals, by the late 1880s, to "Union men," "unionist ideas," and the like, now in the context of organized labor, indicate a general linguistic shift. "Unionism has now become a thing of vast proportions," wrote labor activist John Swinton, going on to salute "the power and the genius of Unionism," the "spirit of the Union," and "Unionism" as "the very grandest embodiment of the supreme principle of Fraternity." More objective observers also referred to labor activities in ways formerly associated with national unity, as in this 1886 *Chicago Tribune* editorial: "The visit of the Chicago Knights Templar to St. Louis this week in such large numbers shows how strong must be the bond of union that unites the members of the order."[45]

Labor leaders consciously promoted "union," and related terms like "federation" and "association," to denote their organizations. The Knights of Labor adopted as an unofficial slogan Edmund Burke's maxim "when bad men combine, the good must associate, else they will fall, one by one"—strongly reminiscent of American revolutionaries' "united we stand, divided we fall" credo. Knights leader Terence Powderly drew the connection directly, as in a speech in 1880 to assembled Knights: "To the subject of co-operation do I invite your attention, and I liken it unto the Revolutionary war . . . co-operation requires every Washington of labor to be up and doing." Powderly also illustrated his massive 1889 biography-cum-manifesto, *Thirty Years of Labor*, with pictorial images of national unity, such as an elaborate "E Pluribus Unum" design and Franklin's old "Join or Die" snake symbol.[46] The 1895 American Federation of Labor's national convention announced that "we [are] banded together. The words union, fed-

---

44. The National Labor Union (NLU), formed in 1866, drew far less attention in nonlabor newspapers than did the strikes and other labor activity of the 1880s, especially after Haymarket in 1886. NLU members were deeply divided internally, and the organization collapsed in 1872. Hattam describes it as "an unsuccessful attempt to unify the heterogeneous and fragmented labor movement after the Civil War" (1990, 87).

45. Swinton 1895, 76, 84, 136, 150; *Chicago Tribune*, September 24, 1886.

46. Powderly 1889, 123 (Knights motto), 464 (cooperation quote), 327.

eration impl[y] it." Swinton described the formation of the American Railway Union in terms clearly reminiscent of national-union talk, spicing his description with organic imagery of "the new Union":

> The Union took shape some time in 1893; it was quietly planted, without musical accompaniment, in soil which had been prepared for it; it grew like those trees of the Oriental magicians which can be seen growing as you look at them. After a short while branches of it appeared in hundreds of places; they could be counted . . . upon the Northern lakes, along the Mississippi, where roll the Missouri and Yellowstone, in and over the mountains, westward far as flies the American flag. No other Union had ever grown as grew this Union. . . . It had become evident that the new Union was needed, and that multitudes had awaited its formation.

As had many political parties earlier, labor leaders adopted the union label as their party standard, with the Union Labor Party and United Labor Party competing for members. Even smaller locals joined the trend. A fledgling Kansas organization named itself the United American Mechanics and listed its "avowed objects" in nationalist (and nativist) terms: "to maintain and promote the interests of Americans and shield them from the depressing effects of foreign competition; to assist Americans in obtaining employment; to encourage Americans in business . . . and to uphold the public school system of the United States and prevent sectarian interference therewith. Only American-born citizens are eligible to membership."[47]

Labor writers further mimicked past advocates of national union, including Lincoln. A labor local could not "be a union in the full sense of the word," economist Selig Perlman testified, "unless it has educated the members to put the *integrity* of the collective 'job-*territory*' above the security of their individual job tenure. Unionism is, in this respect, not unlike patriotism which may and does demand of the citizen the supreme sacrifice, when the integrity of the national territory is at stake."[48] This association between labor unions and territory went deeper. Into the 1880s, members of the NLU and Knights of Labor "accepted the republican assumption that propertied independence was a necessary precondition of civic participation" and excluded day laborers and unskilled workers from both their membership and (in principle) the national polity.[49]

Labor activists promoting nationwide fraternity and cooperation also echoed

---

47. AFL convention quote in Hall 1898, 103; Swinton 1895, 146–47; *Emporia Daily Gazette* (Kansas), June 9, 1893.

48. Perlman 1928, 273.

49. Hattam 1990, 92; Shefter 1994, 165. Racial and ethnic minority workers were also often denied union membership. Distinctions between skilled and unskilled workers were nominally the difference between "trade" and "labor" unions, though the divide was partly bridged after the AFL included both from the late 1880s on. See Antoine Joseph's detailed account of skilled workers' creation of a system of ethnic stratification (1989).

traditional sustainable-unionist views in their emphasis on voluntarism. Powderly was a strong voice for "self-help," urging in an 1880 speech to the national Knights convention that "everything should not be left to the state or nation."[50] At the same time, however, correspondence between postwar balanced-union ideals and labor views only went so far. Powderly and other prominent labor figures like Samuel Gompers advocated stronger government activity on various fronts, most notably control of currency and credit terms, and in some cases even nationalization of the growing trusts.[51]

Workers streaming into labor's ranks embraced the union label with gusto as well. Members of a Detroit coopers' union reasserted Daniel Webster's now-classic association between liberty and union in an 1880 parade, bearing a banner that read:

Each for himself is the bosses' plea
Union for all will make you free.

A San Francisco Labor Day celebration was characterized in a local labor newspaper as dominated by "patriotism . . . [e]verywhere the nation's flag and the nation's colors were on view"; the correspondent concluded that "Unionism that is founded on patriotism and order cannot be stamped out." A labor reporter after a successful Colorado strike explained that "'unanimity' is a word made from the same root from which 'union' is derived. [The strike's] strength was in union; from this [experience] came *perfect union.*"[52]

Business leaders, bankers and other vendors of capital, and industry's supporters in the press and academy also took up the term—not, of course, with the same favorable implication. "Unionism [is] my greatest distress . . . it is *destroying* the country," fumed railroad titan James Hill in 1884. Businessmen and their allies associated labor with violent protest: "Their influence for disruption," complained southern industrialist N. F. Thompson, "is far more dangerous to the perpetuation of our Government . . . than would be the hostile array on our borders of the army of the entire world combined."[53] Unions were routinely denounced by labor's opponents as foreign-dominated, in reference to urban immigrants who frequently constituted the majority of a city local's members.[54]

50. Powderly 1940, 268.
51. Hattam 1990, 98.
52. Shefter 1994, 118; Neather 1996; 93; *National Labor Tribune* (Pittsburgh), July 2, 1887.
53. Hill quoted in (New York) *Judge*, September 20, 1884; Thompson in Garraty 1968, 145. On anti-union spirit among business leaders, see Foner 1988, esp. 518. Rosenzweig 1983 (15–16, 23–24) provides fine-grained detail of industrialist hostility to trade unions in Worcester, Massachusetts, at the time (including "routine" firings of any laborers even suspected of union activity).
54. See, e.g., the *Nation*'s 1887 editorial entitled "The Composition of the Trades-Unions": after compiling detailed statistics on national origins of Illinois's 54,247 union members, showing only 21 percent to be "Americans," the editors concluded, "a great many people have been asking with some anxiety . . . [about] the extent to which native-born Americans are wrestling with the labor problem by means of strikes and boycotts." *Nation*, May 12, 1887.

They also were portrayed as outmoded and inefficient in an age of technological innovation. Among committed Taylorites, for example, David Montgomery reports that trade unions appeared as "reactionary obstacles to efficiency and progress."[55] The likelihood that most businessmen—many emerging as important opinion leaders in an age that accorded unprecedented respect to industrial activity and capitalist finance—would continue to refer to "the [American] Union" as the source of their national feeling was diminished, as their opposition to "the [labor] unions" mounted.

To return to the notion of conceptual displacement introduced in chapter 1, union's association with organized labor represents co-optation of the term. Timing was essential in effecting this rhetorical "capture." Had the American labor movement achieved greater gains earlier, such co-optation might well have occurred sooner—or we might be talking today about "labor federations" or "labor associations" rather than labor unions. But amidst the titanic labor-capital struggles and expanding class consciousness of the Gilded Age into which these gains emerged,[56] the potential for conceptual displacement was ripe. Notes Eric Foner in another context, "public discourse in the late nineteenth century fractured along class lines."[57] Traditional national-union ideals fractured right along with it.

This phenomenon had consequences deeper than a shift in usage from one meaning to another. As industrial capitalism and its attendant crises, shocks, and grinding conflict increasingly dominated the U.S. economy after Reconstruction, traditional conceptions of agrarian land-centered, affective harmony inevitably faded. Distinctions between urban and rural life, between capitalist and laborer and agricultural producer, and between manager and worker all abraded longstanding notions of a national union of like-minded, similarly situated individuals. Older notions of binding people of various sections and regions, differentiated mainly in terms of the territory they inhabited, receded before an American society "in the process of becoming an economic and political community created out of a diversity of economically functional groups. From this the United States ceased to stress the reputation of the individual citizen but rather the functional group to which he/she belonged."[58] A unionist ideal long tied, in the conception of Madison and later Emerson, Douglass, Lincoln, and many others, to meaningful connections among individual Americans appeared increasingly quaint in a society stressing the economic and other distinctions among such differentiated groups.

Beginning around a decade after African Americans and their Radical Republican supporters largely ceased using "union" in its national sense, many

55. Montgomery 1987, 213; and see pp. 214–56 generally.
56. For overviews of period capital–labor conflicts, see Trachtenberg 1982, 71–73; Foner 1947–64, 2:11–29, 103–31, 178–88, 200–234, 243–46, 261–78; and Edwards 1979, 49–71.
57. Foner 1998, 124.
58. Munslow 1992, 12. See also Klein 1993, 42–43: the 1880s "organizational revolution revamped the basic structure of American civilization, so that a society of individuals was transformed into a society of organizations."

in America's burgeoning industrial sector did the same. Fragmentation seemed endemic during the 1880s; one historian notes that many in American society, capitalists and laborers alike, "recognized that new conflicts might rend society more effectively than had the Civil War."[59] And in this period there was no massive mobilized force of unconditional unionists, or strong national political parties, devoted to keeping the nation whole. Indeed, the inclination of many Americans to do so was vanishing in the face of another powerful current in the late nineteenth-century United States: the "new immigration," as it was quickly dubbed at the time.

THE END OF SUSTAINABLE UNION:
IMMIGRATION AND NATIONAL UNITY, 1880s–90s

Virulent antiforeign sentiment became a national norm during the 1880s and 1890s, as a tremendous immigration wave brought "numbers of new arrivals [that] vastly exceeded what any established nation had ever undergone."[60] Nativist depredations were nothing new in American public discourse, but previous outbursts—most notably the Know-Nothing agitation of the 1850s and also Federalist attempts to circumscribe immigration in 1798—occurred amidst a "relatively cosmopolitan outlook" characterizing many framers' and antebellum Americans' view of immigrant arrivals. Prominent unionists from Madison to Lincoln were consistent supporters of immigration, or at least expressed a more generally felt "American confidence in an effortless process of ethnic integration," well into the 1870s.[61]

Now, in contrast, anti-immigrant feeling took hold throughout the United States. The *New York Times* complained in 1887 about "the great tide of immigration," whose "result has been to bring a great mass of undesirable population and to produce considerable discontent"; the unnamed columnist concluded that "it should first of all be clearly understood that the policy of promoting immigration to this country is at an end." Writing in 1892, MIT president Francis Walker contrasted Americans' previous "proud" attitudes toward immigration, "contemplated as one of the main sources of the nation's wealth and power," with "a considerable change" during the previous decade in "the feelings of our people regarding immigration." The 1880s, confirms historian John Higham, featured "sweeping indictment[s] of immigrant influence," as "a baffled need for unity as-

---

59. Munslow 1992, 12. To Eric Foner, the 1880s–90s were "two decades of labor conflict the most violent the country had ever known" (1988, 585).
60. Smith 1997, 358.
61. Ueda 1997, 41; Higham 1984, 32 (and cf. 1988 [1955], 4–11). See also Spalding 1994; Smith 1988, 238 (earlier "liberal policy" on immigration "was tinged by republican and ethnocentric reservation, but these had limited impact in comparison with later years"); and discussions in chaps. 3–4.

serted itself in nativistic aggression."[62] Beginning with the 1882 Chinese Exclusion Act, Congress passed a series of laws limiting immigration—the first such statutory restrictions since the short-lived Alien Acts of 1798. Social Darwinist themes became common among politicians, writers, and other opinion leaders of the period; their targets included Chinese immigrants, described by Republican Rep. William Higby as "nothing but a pagan race"; central and eastern Europeans, portrayed as "the thronging Goth and Vandal" barbarians who had "trampled Rome"; and those perennial targets of racist abuse, Native Americans and blacks.[63]

Historians account for this xenophobic surge in a variety of ways. Nativist impulses were sparked by capital/labor conflicts, often associated with "foreign anarchists" as at Haymarket; economic uncertainty in the wake of the 1873–78 depression; and the disappearing western frontier, traditionally considered an outlet for new arrivals. Also causally prominent in contemporary accounts, and most relevant for our focus on a disappearing sentiment of national unity, were the increased absolute numbers and the novel national origins of immigrants after 1880. In numerical terms, immigration trends remained steady from the 1850s through the 1870s, at around 220,000 arrivals each year. A dramatic rise began in 1880, peaking temporarily in the early 1890s at some 550,000 immigrants per annum. The decade from 1881–90 counted some 5.25 million arrivals, a total greater than all combined immigration from 1781–1860.[64] As with the mounting labor strife of the time, this increase coincides with Americans' declining references to union.

Along with a rise in numbers, the new emigrants' place of national origin shifted markedly to the south and east. Historian Reed Ueda identifies "two distinct ethnically defined stages" of immigration, the first lasting from the early eighteenth century to the 1870s and featuring predominantly Irish and German arrivals, along with others of northern and western European ancestry. Second-stage immigrants hailed from southern and eastern Europe, particularly Italy, Russia, and Austria-Hungary (comprising Czechs and Slovaks, Poles, Jews, Serbs, Croats, Slovenes, and Magyar Hungarians). In 1880, around 225,000 immigrants arrived from these regions; that figure surpassed a million in some subsequent years. By the early twentieth century some 90 percent of new arrivals were from southern and eastern Europe, a figure period writers (in books with titles like *The Immigration Problem*) contrasted worriedly with the 95 percent of

62. *New York Times,* July 14, 1887; Walker 1892, 127–28; Higham 1988, 35–67 (quotes at pp. 39, 53). Compare Kraut 1982, 148–65 (on the "new immigrants" confronting "substantial and escalating hostility in the period 1880 to 1921": quote at p. 148).

63. *Cong. Globe,* 37th Cong., 2d sess., 1862, 555; Thomas Bailey Aldrich quoted in Summers 1997, 117. On the social-Darwinist/racist basis of much anti-immigration spirit at the time, see Smith 1997, 351–71. Higham downplays the racial aspects of 1880s nativism, while emphasizing a connection to the "new swell of discontent" accompanying the "labor convulsion of the day" (Higham 1988, 53–55).

64. Figures from Bean, Cushing, and Haynes 1997, 125 (table 4.2).

immigrants hailing from northern Europe before 1883. Asian immigration also increased after 1880, though this remained a small percentage of the total into the twentieth century.[65]

In response to these profound changes in numbers and ethnic origin—further fueled by economic uncertainty and a general postwar sense of dislocation—xenophobic rhetoric, legislation, and occasionally mob action spiraled. Henry James summarized the patrician view, sniffing after a stroll on Boston Common that "no sound of English in a single instance escaped their lips; the greater number spoke a rude form of Italian, the others some outland dialect unknown to me. . . . The types and faces bore them out; the people before me were gross aliens to a man, and they were in serene and triumphant possession." Working-class opposition was less effete: immigrants were widely seen as directly competing with natives for jobs and were denounced accordingly. Leading labor newspapers like the *National Labor Tribune* featured headlines like "Keep the Chinese Out" and "The Huns Must Go," the latter directing "non–English-speaking" workers to "find their way speedily . . . on board the first ships bound for Europe." New England laborers founded the Immigration Destruction League, a sister organization to midwesterners' virulently anti-immigrant American Protective Association, which was founded in 1887.[66]

Broad histories of U.S. political culture frequently represent this Gilded Age and subsequent Progressive resistance to immigration as a short-lived way station on the way to "Euro-America," in Michael Lind's phrase. Accounts of rapid assimilation and inclusion, as exemplified in this representative telling, hold that the United States "absorbed [southern and eastern European] immigrants, eventually granted them their rights, and [saw] them take their places as 'Americans' despite the existence of considerable nativist hostility and prejudice against them."[67] I would instead note the sustained ethnocultural outlook accompanying expanded immigration after Reconstruction, a trend that continued until 1924 (when immigration was sharply restricted by statute) and arguably even up to World War II. From the 1880s onward politicians, editors, and other opinion leaders devoted sustained attention to the new "type of immigrants to these shores," cited by a Dwight, Illinois, Fourth of July speaker as a "danger" more "menac[ing]" than that posed by slavery and secession two decades before. "[T]he hostile machinations of the worst type of foreignism," he warned, could

65. Ueda 1997, 45–46; Jenks and Lauck 1911, 24. Figures on national origins from Kraut 1982, 20–21. See also Higham 1988; Alba 1990.

66. James in Lind 1995, 78; *National Labor Tribune*, November 29, 1887, and May 5, 1888; Gaustad 1974, 216–17. In a rare poll of workingmen from the mid-1880s, taken in Wisconsin, more than 50 percent of the laborers surveyed agreed that immigration had "hurt" their livelihood. Reported in Higham 1988, 46. Anti-immigrant bias was a regular theme in 1880s newspaper accounts of Fourth of July celebrations, a point confirmed in my sample (see, e.g., *Chicago Tribune*, July 5, 1882) and also by Rosenzweig (1983, 71–74).

67. Lind 1995, 55–95; Omi and Winant 1986, 17. Tellingly, such historical accounts began to appear in great numbers after World War II: see, e.g., Warner and Srole 1945.

only be resisted by forcing new arrivals to "merge themselves into a common whole and lose their race identity." Similar language appeared consistently in the highest reaches of state and national government. Theodore Roosevelt warned that "if they remain alien elements, unassimilated, and with interests separate from ours, they are mere obstructions to the current of our national life." Chinese immigrants, declared Oregon's Radical Republican Senator George Williams during debates on Reconstruction, "are a people who do not or will not learn our language; they cannot or will not adopt our manners or customs and modes of life; they do not amalgamate with our people; they constitute a distinct and separate nationality."[68] Such nativist outpourings, more extensive in breadth and duration than those of antebellum years, were another primary factor in the decline of national-union ideals.

Even strong supporters of immigration utilized racial categorizations, although they emphasized the likelihood of their speedy eradication under the benevolent influence of "Americanization." Sociology professor Edward Steiner, himself an emigré, devoted most of his career after 1880 to studies of his fellow "new immigrants" from central and eastern Europe; he described these people as "more of an alien than that older class which was related to the native stock by race, speech, or religious ties." But "external racial characteristics," Steiner assured a generation of students and readers, were "in most cases but chalk marks on a blackboard, so easily are they washed away. . . . The crowd on Rivington Street in New York looks less Jewish than that in Warsaw, and the Bohemians in Chicago look so like 'us,' that in spite of the fact that I have some training in detecting racial marks, I am often puzzled and mistaken."[69]

Compounding the effects of labor strife and immigration on Americans' unionist outlook was the intertwining of these two phenomena. As the Massachusetts minister Samuel Loomis said in 1887, "not every foreigner is a workingman, but in the cities, at least, it may almost be said that every workingman is a foreigner." The association of "union" with *foreign* labor, a specific target of nativist abuse especially amid the rocky U.S. economic climate of the late 1870s, further diminished the traditional inclination to employ a collective referent like "the Union."[70]

Earlier conceptions of national union rested (if often tenuously) on a commitment to affective bonds between U.S. residents, as chronicled in previous chapters. Economic and ethnic separation, it seemed to many in the late nineteenth century, were overwhelming Americans' interpersonal connections. Economist Simon Patten characterized the splintering "imagined community" in 1896: "Each class or section of the nation is becoming conscious of an opposition

68. *Chicago Tribune,* July 5, 1891; Roosevelt 1918 [1897], 245; *Cong. Globe,* 40th Cong., 3d sess., 1869, 901.
69. Steiner 1906, 292–94.
70. Quoted in Rosenzweig 1983, 17.

between its standards and the activities and tendencies of some less developed class. . . . Every one is beginning to differentiate those with proper qualifications for citizenship from some other class or classes which he wishes to restrain or exclude from society."[71] Older unionist visions based on bridging different territorial realms had helped to blunt sectionalism, as we saw in chapter 3, though residents of North and South might have had somewhat divergent understandings of "the Union" they praised. Such traditional conceptions were overshadowed in the face of widespread sentiments that "the country is coming apart," as a contributor to the *Cleveland Plain Dealer* wrote in 1889. The multiple factors of immigration, labor conflict, rhetorical co-optation, and mass abandonment of "the Union" as a significant symbolic term together presented a burden too great for advocates of balanced, federalist union to bear.[72]

Southern Departure

Much of the new immigration, as well as the majority of working-class conflict, was centered in large cities of the North and Midwest. With relatively few immigrants in the South, and the region's economy expanding during most of the 1880s and 1890s, officials in most southern states sought to attract immigrants even as their counterparts elsewhere in the United States advocated restriction. The *New Haven Register* of April 26, 1888, under the incredulous headline "The South Wants Immigrants," reported the formation of a Southern Immigration Association, based in New York City. Thus southern nativist expressions were (as ever) mainly directed at African Americans, not the "new immigration." The notion that American whites were affectively united appears to have retained more legitimacy in the South. Organized labor similarly achieved less purchase in southern "right to work" states than in the more industrialized North. The reduced appeal of labor's alternate "union" designation, and the relative paucity of new immigrants arriving in the region during the 1880s–90s—combined with the favorable terms of union promoted by Benjamin Hill and other southern notables—implies a slower decline among southerners' references to national unity. And indeed such a lag is visible. Figure 9 breaks down postwar unionist trends by region, comparing southern usage to that in the rest of the country.

Even among white southerners, however, by the end of the 1890s adherence to an older idea of union had mostly vanished. As historian Edward Ayers testifies, "the decade of the nineties . . . shattered the carefully tended illusions of white unity and black docility."[73] The fact that the old national-unity ideal lived on longest among those who had sought in 1861 to bury it is an ironic epitaph to

71. Patten in Foner 1998, 133.

72. *Cleveland Plain Dealer*, March 5, 1889. John Higham's authoritative study of nativist attitudes similarly concludes that during the 1890s, as "consciousness of racial, national, and ethnic differences radically intensified," the "willingness of Americans to live with a divided heritage and an ambiguous national identity declined" (1984, 192–93).

73. Ayers 1992, 305.

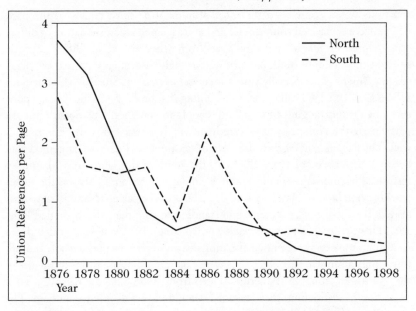

FIGURE 9. Comparison of northern and southern whites' union usage, 1876–98

our unionist story. I turn in conclusion to what developed in its place as a referent for collective purposes in the late nineteenth century.

ONE AMERICAN NATION, INDIVISIBLE

Chapter 5 explored and rejected conventional claims that the Civil War marked
a broad popular turn from older ideas of national unity to a stronger nationalist sensibility. A more persuasive case for a "new nationalism" may be made for
the 1880s–90s, the period when union talk faded into irrelevance. Ethnocultural
praise of Anglo-Saxon superiority, jingoistic support for imperialist ventures,
and a heightened sense of American "destiny" combined, historian John Lukacs
writes, to spark a "rapid crystallization of a passionate nationalism" culminating in the Spanish-American War of 1898. For Lukacs, the war marks a decisive
"change . . . in the national vision of the destiny of the United States," rooted in
a "change in mentality" he describes as "a concordance of Darwinism and of
racism and of Protestant Christianity."[74]

Mutually reinforcing racism and Christianity in the name of national unity
was nothing new in U.S. political discourse, as we have seen. But the central
place of xenophobia, imperialism, and intolerance in late nineteenth-century in-

74. Lukacs 1998, 73–76.

vocations was a contrast to the most prominent unionist credos of the past, which had emphasized compromise and at least some accommodation of difference. Moreover, for the first time apart from actual armed hostilities, patriotic spirit in the late nineteenth century was strongly associated with martial virtue among Americans, especially young men and even boys. Stuart McConnell describes a "full-fledged cult of military training that broke out in the 1890s," sponsored by groups ranging from public schools to churches.[75] National symbols, particularly the American flag, were increasingly associated with militarism as well. The flag, an 1895 *Nation* editorial on "Sentimental Jingoism" lamented, had become "a war symbol above all else to the youth of this land," and "the newer festival of Memorial Day must end in a similar perversion." This was the age of patriotic holidays, as Flag Day was also added to the calendar, and of new rituals like the Pledge of Allegiance and standing to sing the "Star-Spangled Banner." Heightened prominence was accorded songs like "America," which dated to 1831 but took on more muscular nationalist connotations in the 1890s. Indeed, it was only after 1889 that objections were first raised by Americans to the use of the "borrowed" tune for "America" (taken from "God Save the King/Queen"). "A nation of distinction, they reasoned, should have a distinctive anthem. The song's borrowed melody seemed to some at odds with the emergence of the United States as a world power."[76]

Such late-century nationalist celebrations are most visible in July 4 celebrations, which appear (judging, as throughout this book, from newspaper coverage) noticeably larger, more boisterous and boastful than those of the past. Sorting through dozens of reports on Independence Day gatherings large and small from the mid-1880s into the 1890s, two points seem clear: national union, long the mainstay of Fourth orations and toasts, was almost never mentioned after 1885; and patriotic outbursts swelled during this period beyond previous descriptions. "Yesterday's [Fourth] celebration eclipsed anything of the kind ever attempted here before," crowed the *New Haven Register* in 1888. That same year the celebration at Tammany Hall, which had hosted like events for decades, prompted a New York correspondent to enthuse: "The natal day of the nation has seldom been honored on a more magnificent scale, and never with more of the genuine spirit of patriotism." Other celebrations were also occasions for self-congratulation: the turn of the century was greeted by a *New York Times* headline heralding "The United States the Envy of the World."[77]

The emergence of the United States as an international power after 1898 further inspired such hyperpatriotic sentiment. Past ideas of union had been invoked to justify territorial expansion, as we saw earlier, but these manifest-destiny visions were limited almost exclusively to the North American continent. Prewar visions of an overseas U.S. empire, mostly confined to American aggrandizement

---

75. McConnell 1996, quote at p. 114.
76. *Nation*, December 19, 1895, 440–41; Branham 1999, 17.
77. *New Haven Register*, July 5, 1888; *New York World*, same date; *New York Times*, January 1, 1900.

in Mexico in the mid-1840s, amounted to little. In historian Roy Nichols's summary, "the only acquisitions of territory [before the Civil War], beyond the continental limits of the United States, were one guano island . . . in the Caribbean, and three similar islands in Polynesia, from which could be secured fertilizer for exhausted Southern acres."[78]

The post–Civil War tenor of U.S. foreign policy was initially isolationist. George Washington's old warning against "entangling alliances" was still sounded into the 1880s, as a St. Louis newspaper editorial confirmed in 1881. The "world outside our borders," the author avowed, "is a violent and dangerous place . . . [it is] wise that the U. States concentrate on our own affairs, in particular cementing our reunion." Ardent expansionist William Seward acted secretly in 1867 to secure Alaska ("Seward's Folly") and the Midway Islands, neither of which aroused any noticeable patriotic sentiment. In contrast, the 1890s incursions in Cuba, Puerto Rico, Hawaii, the Philippines, and elsewhere attracted considerable attention and were generally popular. The result, as one critic described it at the time, was "a combination of Uncle Sam puffery and Nervous Nelly fright . . . it is appalling to watch this once unified people bestir themselves in such a Great Power fashion."[79]

As the last comment suggests, U.S. imperialist ventures attracted opposition in some quarters. In another sad irony marking union's decline from American political discourse, these critics employed sustained ethnocultural unionist arguments in objecting to the annexation of Cuba, the Philippines, Puerto Rico, Guam, and Hawaii. South Dakota's Senator Richard Pettigrew summarized a host of arguments in citing "the founders" and their "union of sovereign states" in declaring "an unwritten law that no area should be brought within the bounds of the Republic which did not, and could not, sustain a race equipped in all essentials for the maintenance of a free civilization." Hawaiian natives were unfit for unity with the Anglo-American majority, Pettigrew continued: "If we adopt the policy of acquiring tropical countries, where republics cannot live, we overthrow the theory on which this Government is established." William Graham Sumner, spinning out his Social Darwinist theories from New Haven, explained "the first condition of the Union; viz., that all the states members of it should be on the same plane of civilization and political development; that they should all hold the same ideas, traditions, and political creed." It was "fundamentally antagonistic" to this unionist "system to hold dependencies which are unfit to enter into the Union." Concluded Sumner, "We [whites] are all united. The negro's day is over. He is out of fashion . . . [and] we cannot treat him one way and the Malays, Tagals, and Kanaks another."[80]

Sumner's comment underscores the "causal relationship," in historian Freder-

78. Nichols 1961, 49.
79. *St. Louis Globe,* February 19, 1881; *Alta Californian* (San Francisco), March 29, 1899. On the tenor of 1890s imperialism, see also Merk 1995 [1963], 231–60; Lukacs 1998; Beisner 1986, 96–144; and Campbell 1976, 177–318.
80. *Cong. Record,* 55th Cong., 2d sess., 1898, 6228; Sumner in Bannister 1992, 277, 286, 293.

ick Merk's estimation, that existed between "the racism of the decade 1885–95 and the imperialism of the late 1890s; that racism was the climate in which imperialism flourished." African Americans, who were already all too aware of their isolated position outside the national mainstream, developed such a thesis at the time. College professor William Scarborough, in a widely circulated 1894 address, excoriated "the wrongs inflicted on a weak and defenseless people like the Hawaiians by a strong power like our own." Scarborough went on to marshal "strong evidence of the fact [that this] is a question of color and nationality. It is an ethnological question as well."[81]

This ethnocultural unionism, however, was a minor motif, as even more sober and thoughtful commentators sounded a more boisterous, nervous nationalist spirit. Herbert Croly's instant classic *The Promise of American Life*, published early in the twentieth century, was a comparatively qualified treatment of U.S. values and mores; the author dismissed much period patriotism as influenced by "an easy, generous, and irresponsible optimism." Croly also included a detailed analysis of older unionist ideas, characterizing "the pioneer period" (1830s–70s, by his reckoning) as exhibiting "a natural community of feeling and a general similarity of occupation and well-being." Reconstruction's aftermath, he wrote, marked "the gradual disintegration of this early national consistency" in the face of industrialism, professional specialization (destroying older tendencies to communally mix public and private affairs), and a new style of detached political leadership. But even Croly eventually exemplified the new outlook. Croly's solution to "impaired social and economic homogeneity," once "the essential quality of fruitful Americanism," was a complicated mix of regulatory activity, carried out by a greatly empowered national state; expert leadership in politics and other professions; and active imperialism abroad. "The American nation, just in so far as it believes in its nationality and is ready to become more of a nation, must assume a more definite and a more responsible place in the international system."[82]

In summary, the combination of anxiety over a splintering nation, impossible to bring together in traditional ways, and shrill confidence in rising U.S. presence internationally inspired Americans' new conceptions of national unity as the nineteenth century concluded. To comprehend these fully would require another book-length treatise; I offer here instead a briefer look at two rhetorical registers of nationalism at century's end. First, fears of domestic disruption occasioned greater support for the U.S. national state, as evidenced in my summary of Croly's views. Second, in place of "union" as a national referent, boasts about the rising power of "America" were heard in every section of the country.

One still finds among the mass of Americans little overt preference for a stronger central government in the late nineteenth century. But the widening

---

81. Merk 1995 [1963], 241; *Christian Recorder* (Philadelphia), March 15, 1894.

82. Croly 1909, 7, 104–5, 289 (for Croly's insistence that his views were not "a sanctimonious paraphrase for . . . political aggrandizement in the Western Hemisphere," see 300–307). A judicious treatment of Croly on foreign policy is Stettner 1993, 72–74, 122–43.

cleavages in U.S. society drove many influential thinkers to embrace new guarantors of stability, and the national state was one potential source. This seems to have been an "any port in a storm" argument for most adherents, rather than a testament to a sweeping new statist sensibility. Shrewd political observers, like *Atlantic Monthly* correspondent Charles Clark, affirmed that Republicans' halfhearted "national policy" in the 1880s was opposed by Democratic and other adherents to "the old doctrine of state rights." With state rights ostensibly "dead" as a sectional issue, Clark noted, political thinkers were "gradually crystallizing a new theory of [national] state duties and individual responsibility."[83]

Within a few years, theorists like Croly and John Dewey were openly advocating the expansion of national government activity. Federal administrative development was synonymous with "nationality" for Croly, who traced the theme from Greece through medieval Europe and into the American present, of which he declared: "Only by faith in an efficient national organization and by an exclusive and aggressive devotion to the national welfare, can the American democratic ideal be made good." Croly further avowed that "popular interests have nothing to fear from a measure of Federal centralization, which bestows on the Federal government powers necessary to the fulfillment of its legitimate responsibilities." Croly's view was embraced by such notable figures as Theodore Roosevelt, who drew extensively on the book (and subsequent correspondence with Croly) in promulgating his "New Nationalism" principles in 1910–12. Croly's proposed augmentation of federal power was not universally embraced; some reviewers took issue with the specifics of his call for greater centralization.[84]

Generally speaking, the notion of the state as an overarching focus for diverse Americans' interpersonal connections seems to have become widely appealing in the late nineteenth and early twentieth century. Much like the original knitting together of the colonies through reassuring words during the years before independence, and the popular union oratory of Webster that helped secure the early republic thereafter, a rhetorical commitment to the national state is apparent among some U.S. opinion leaders at the time. Daniel Rodgers summarizes this outlook:

[A]s the wartime victory over the forces of disintegration was obscured by economic conflicts . . . [and] by a mounting ethnic cacophony and intensifying racial violence, it was no easy task to find the unitary nation for which so much blood had flowed. It was the middle-class heirs to the old Whig-Protestant longings for unity who felt the pain of fragmentation most acutely. Elbowed out, or so they feared, by a swelling tide of immigrants . . . many of the late 19th century Protestant middle class's most influential talkers took refuge not in orthodox faith but in abstract

83. Clark 1889, 227.
84. Croly 1909, quotes at pp. 270, 278; see more generally pp. 215–88. On the book's reception, see Levy 1985, 132–36; on Croly and Roosevelt, see Goldman 1952, chap. 9.

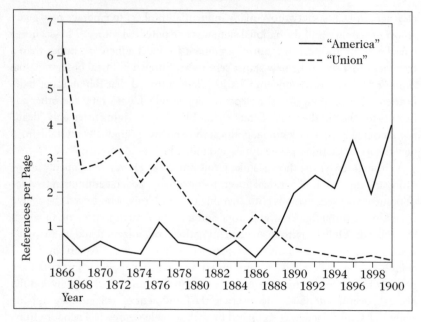

FIGURE 10. Comparison of "America" and "union" references, 1866–1900

words . . . in the hope that some trick of consciousness or words—loyalty, community, or State—would pull the "intolerably confused" character of "mere facts" into unity. . . . Through talk of the state, held together by a sovereignty no discordant social fragment could resist, they found a way of bringing an increasingly pluralistic, fragmenting polity back together, if not in fact, at least in the mind's eye.[85]

Implicit here is these speakers' vanished faith that traditional ideas of a balanced union might satisfy this need for cohesion. Rather than a skein of bonds among the people themselves, national unity seemed to depend on an abstract, impersonal entity, imposing common values and purposes from above. Though not part of our story here, this intellectual support for stronger administrative activity would initially find expression in the Progressive movement and later in the New Deal.[86]

More compelling among most of the population than intellectual reformers' talk of "the State" was a comparatively new term denoting national themes in the late nineteenth century: "America." "Nation" references also increased during the 1890s—the July 4, 1889, *Chicago Tribune* gushed "Today the Nation, with a big 'N,' is 113 years old"—but the rise of "America(n)" surpassed these. Figure 10 pro-

85. Rodgers 1987, 169–71.
86. On this point, see for example Morone 1990, 115–19; and Sandel 1996, 216–21.

vides empirical evidence of the swift rise of "America" as the principal national referent, drawn as usual from editorial comment in newspapers and journals and from congressional floor speeches. "America" references are compared with "union" references from 1866–1900, per page of newspaper and other materials examined.

From the nation's early years through Reconstruction, "American" had usually appeared as a descriptive adjective for U.S. residents. Beginning in the 1890s, and especially after 1898, the term erupted everywhere in denoting the ambitious new player on the world stage. Grover Cleveland's second inaugural address defined "true Americanism" as "American manliness and fairness" and cited "American character" and "American achievement" in saluting the "American people." Theodore Roosevelt, while governor of New York, penned a treatise "What 'Americanism' Means," reprinted across the country (and reissued repeatedly after he became president). Roosevelt thunderously concluded with a long quote from a Wisconsin congressman, Richard Guenther: "America first, last, and all the time. America against Germany, America against the world; America, right or wrong; always America. We are Americans."[87]

As Roosevelt and numerous other commentators made clear, immigrants were to undergo "Americanization," requiring instruction in the "American creed." Like southerners bearing banners after the Civil War declaring their fealty to Union, immigrants sought publicly to integrate themselves into the popular understanding of national unity: "We are Americans through and through by the spirit of our nation," read a Czech contingent's banner at the forefront of a Cleveland parade. Americanism was not limited to the most blatant champions of Anglo-Saxon "civilizing influence." John Swinton, the sometime Socialist and labor newspaper editor, exulted in 1895: "Where in all the world was there ever a match for our country. . . . Its name, America!" Subsequent years featured efforts to institute an annual "Americanization Day," which was celebrated sporadically and peaked in 1915 with observances by more than 150 towns and cities.[88]

In certain respects the popularization of "America" as referent for nationalist spirit resembled some versions of the antebellum unionist outlook. Territorial aggrandizement—now Cuba and the Philippines, then Mexico and Native American Indian territories—was joined to praise of Anglo-Saxon racial identity, all leavened by the destinarian assurances of prominent Protestant clerics (once Lyman Beecher, now Josiah Strong). But 1890s "Americanism" demanded a qualitatively different style of patriotism than was implied in the union ideas prevailing in the first half of the century—especially the sustainable-union views of a polity built on affective bonds and far-sighted representatives balancing local and national administration. As Foner describes, "government and private organiza-

87. Lott 1994, 192–95; Roosevelt 1918 [1897], 248 (quote from the year 1891). By way of contrast, consider Carl Schurz in 1872: "Our country right or wrong! When right, to be kept right; *when wrong, to be put right!*" Quoted in Curti 1946, 1 (emphasis added).

88. Park and Miller 1921, 273; Swinton 1895, 293; Branham 1996, 628.

tions in the 1890s promoted a unifying, coercive patriotism." Even those expressing strong ethnocultural-union views in antebellum times had hewn to the balanced, compromise accommodation inherent in unionist ideas.[89]

Chapter 5 argued that older ideas of national unity retained their currency well after the Civil War, fading not with postwar nationalism but in the face of corrosive economic, social, and political changes during the 1880s and especially the 1890s. Such a claim has relevance for present-day scholarly efforts to demarcate more accurately distinct periods in U.S. history. Americans' turning point to industrial-capitalist modernity remains contested, with students of American political development variously supporting decisive changes in 1865, 1877, and the 1890s. This study of union's rhetorical decline (and the corresponding rise of "America") lends support to the last case, summarized by historian Martin Sklar: "the 1890s marked a turning point in the nation's history, [and] developments thenceforward to World War I made United States society into something significantly different from what it had been before."[90]

The Ends of Union

Associated in the North with organic wholes and then intertwined hearts, and in the South with regeneration and eventually renewed calls for states' rights, union represented a rhetorical refuge from the highly charged struggles of Reconstruction and the early Gilded Age. As such it sometimes seemed free of substantive political content: a positively valued concept, source of continuity and possible improvement amid a sea of change. "The Union idea, noble, strong . . . floats above the fungus of party disputes," a Kansas writer enthused in 1873.[91] But the term carried potent political meaning. During the 1870s southerners recast union as a protest ideal, a critique of the new and the aggressively national. A vast majority of northerners reacted positively to this usage and affirmed a sentimental reunion between the sections, which helped blunt efforts to turn the U.S. administrative state to principled purposes.

Disillusioned by this experience, African Americans were first to abandon the union ideal, along with their Radical Republican supporters. Eventually others joined this rhetorical exodus, and by the mid-1880s other terms increasingly were used to denote the whole. Though this change was slower in coming than most commentators recognize—"union" did not fade into archaic irrelevance with the Civil War's end—by the 1890s it had done so, dwindling among all Americans

89. Foner 1998, 134. Knupfer 1991 is the definitive statement of antebellum extremists' willingness, if sometimes grudgingly, to compromise in the name of national unity.

90. Sklar 1991, 174. See also Faulkner 1959, esp. 1–22, for an early statement of this view ("The 1890s separated not only two centuries but two eras in American history," at 1); Neather 1996; and Lukacs 1998. A separate debate in political science concerns whether the 1890s, and especially 1896, marked an electoral "realignment" in U.S. history, on the order of 1860 or 1932: while I would not endorse that conclusion (for a strong opposing view see Mayhew 2000), the general account of an "intense burst of punctuated change in the 1890s," affecting political, economic, and social sectors alike, seems on target. See Burnham 1999, 2256 (quote), 2247–57 more generally.

91. *Lawrence Weekly Journal* (Kansas), February 13, 1873.

to almost nil. Among representatives of the national government, both presidents (as we saw earlier) and members of Congress similarly dropped "union" from their political vernacular. The holdout was Supreme Court Justices, some of whom continued regularly to invoke a "more perfect Union" and related themes in their opinions into the twentieth century—in keeping, perhaps, with the Court's attention to precedent.[92] Examining remaining references in the early twentieth century, it is evident that the term had ossified into a referent for bygone days.

The demise of "union" as a meaningful political term, and of the communal ideals it represented, was scarcely noted. This was a quiet burial, in a lexical potter's field. Was anything significant lost in its passing? A few candidates for commemoration come to mind. The comparatively humane sense of national unity, and the possibility of a more moral basis for union, set out by previous generations of leaders was scarcely voiced during the tumult of the 1880s–1900s. A stress on "improving" existing territory and building affective bonds, and on self-conscious leadership on behalf of national unity, was muted alongside the muscular chauvinism of subsequent patriotic appeals. Also lost amid imperialist ventures and other sources of national glory was the sense (or at least publicly voiced commitment) that American unity could be meaningfully improved. How, in contrast, could the bracing bonds of an Anglo-Saxon people, dedicated to spreading their civilizing influence over the globe, possibly be bettered? Meliorist appeals of the older sort—conceptions of a *more perfect* union—were largely absent from American political and social discourse at least into the first decade of the twentieth century.

A more significant loss concerns one of union's primary rhetorical functions. The term's near universal appeal, as noted throughout this work, permitted a wide range of policies and positions to be advanced in the name of strengthening national unity. This had negative consequences aplenty, but also permitted separate elements to be more or less peaceably combined, and addressed in American political debate: Hamiltonian nationalism and Jeffersonian localism; Jacksonian southerners' state rights views and Whigs' internal improvements carried out by the central government; individual rights and communal obligations; local civil-society efforts and government assistance; and so forth. By treating these themes in the context of sustained union, Americans could balance—if often precariously—political views otherwise perpetually in tension. With the term's disappearance from common use, other concepts subsumed the constituent elements of union, but the vital balancing function was lost. The consequences are further discussed in the conclusion of this volume.

Aspirations to American national unity in other forms hardly ceased with union's passage into anachronism. Progressive thinkers like Croly and Dewey

---

92. See, inter alia, *In re Debs,* 158 U.S. 564, 578–79 (1895); *Minnesota v. Hitchcock,* 185 U.S. 373, 386 (1902); or *De Lima v. Bidwell,* 182 U.S. 1, 254 (1901), where one Justice wistfully remarked "there never was any doubt in those [founding] days as to what that ['more perfect Union'] meant."

urged a "new nationalism" and "Great Community" in place of the individual-ism, economic rapacity, and ethnocultural excesses they viewed with horror. Such thinkers' efforts to arouse a democratic American solidarity required, first of all, that leaders "fashion their fellow-countrymen into more of a nation . . . informed by genuinely national ideas and aspirations," in Croly's terms. But Progressives' efforts sounded, and looked, very different from the unionist visions of the eigh-teenth and nineteenth centuries. Imperial Americanism abroad, combined with the growth of an activist welfare and regulatory spirit at home, manifestly re-quired a national government commensurate with these projects. "Nation" (or "America") and "state" became more nearly synonymous; the Progressives sought to encourage American solidarity from the national center, with the federal state providing top-down inspiration.[93]

An iconic moment comes in Woodrow Wilson's 1916 Flag Day proclamation, initiating the holiday in order to resist "influences which have seemed to threaten to divide us in interest and sympathy." "In the words of Abraham Lincoln," Wil-son wrote, "let us on [this] day rededicate ourselves to the Nation, 'one and in-separable,' from which every thought that is not worthy of our fathers' first vows . . . shall be excluded." The spirit was certainly Lincoln's, as were all the words but one: Lincoln had said "Union," but Wilson substituted "Nation."[94]

93. Croly 1909, 212 (cf. 207–14, 279–88); Bond in Wigginton 1991, 333. On Progressives' com-munal outlook, see also Morone 1990, 112–15. Morone's conclusion includes an intriguing hint of the consequences of lost unionist vocabulary: "Like the colonists and the Jacksonians, the Progressives promised a return of unity and virtue if power was restored to the people. When their people failed to materialize, Progressive democracy was undone" (1990, 115).

94. Wilson 1926, 2:189–90.

Political Union in Modern America

[America's] very heterogeneity makes the quest for unifying ideals and a common culture all the more urgent. And in a world savagely rent by ethnic and racial antagonisms, it is all the more essential that the United States continue as an example of how a highly differentiated society holds itself together.

—Arthur Schlesinger Jr., *The Disuniting of America*, 1991

SCHLESINGER'S INVOCATION of the United States as exemplary has a long history in American letters, dating from the "city on a hill" sermon John Winthrop delivered upon the *Arbella*'s arrival in Massachusetts Bay. And such a model is surely needed in an age when prominent geopolitical developments center on issues of political union: Europe's effort to construct one; former Soviet states' post-Union attempt to negotiate relations with Russia and each other; splintering confederations in Indonesia, Yugoslavia, and elsewhere; Quebec's attempts at secession; and so on around the globe.

Yet it is not readily apparent what the contemporary United States actually offers in terms of unionist example. Part of the difficulty in confidently affirming how this polity "holds itself together" is that Americans' own collective ties are increasingly frayed. (Schlesinger's book is titled *The Disuniting of America*.) Influences tending to diminish American unity operate both from outside and within the country's borders. Among the former are globalization, a sprawling term optimistically advertised as "transnational democracy" but more often indicative of a dwindling inclination among U.S. corporate chiefs to view their business concerns as concurrent with national interests; a world divided into "clashing civilizations," necessitating closer integration with the "Western" countries sharing common "values, norms, institutions, and modes of thinking" and a commensurate diminution of national self-determination; and a complex of attitudes sometimes summarized as "cosmopolitanism," whose adherents "look beyond a province or nation to the larger sphere of humankind."[1] Within the United States, forces eroding citizens' national outlook and attachments include the proposed wholesale "devolution" of national responsibilities to state and local levels,

---

1. Huntington 1996, 41 (and on "Western civilization" more generally, see pp. 81–101, 183–206); Hollinger 1995, 84 (on cosmopolitanism); cf. the classic treatment in Meinecke 1970 [1907]. On globalization, see Held 1999, for a relatively positive view (the potential growth of "transnational democracy" is charted at pp. 89–91, 104–8); accounts stressing globalization's negative implications are Devetak and Higgott 1999 and the essays in Hurrell and Woods 1999.

much incanted at present; surging assertions of cultural pluralism and related expressions of "group rights," often inspired by continuing ethnic and racial discrimination; and that old target of unionist concern, individualism. The sum of these trends is, in David Hollinger's nuanced account, an American polity that increasingly resembles "a multitude of constituencies united less by a sense of common destiny than by a will to use the state as an instrument of their particular agendas."[2]

Some of these developments feature admirable, even liberating aspects, and it is possible that their emerging combination will render notions of political union in the United States or other nation-states irrelevant. But in recent years these trends have attracted as much concern as applause, often based on an insistence that can only be described as unionist (or neo-unionist). Thus a liberal thinker like Sibyl Schwarzenbach can note, "in the face of" profound "disintegrative tendencies," that "particularly in our time, the problem of social unity—of what it is that generally binds persons together in a just society—is emerging as of critical importance once again."[3] Both communitarian champions of local self-rule[4] and liberals like Schwarzenbach, committed to protect minority-group rights,[5] increasingly ask a fundamental question: How can the U.S. polity be united to ensure its stable perpetuation while balancing constituent members' multiple sources of identity and allegiance?

This and related issues of national political union have yet to attract the sort of detailed analyses that are devoted in overwhelming number to other themes, such as democracy, justice, or rights. Such a study would seem all the more profitable given that journalists, politicians, and other citizens are joining scholars in lamenting the loss of a viable sense of national unity. "Middle-class Americans," concludes a comprehensive 1998 study of that group, "are desperate that we

2. Hollinger 1995, 147. On devolution, see Bogdanor 1999, esp. 188–91, and Schambra 1998; among a huge literature on group rights and multiculturalism, see Young 1990 and Kymlicka 1995; for opposing views of individualism in modern America, see Lasch 1978 and Gans 1988.

3. Schwarzenbach 1996, 98. Two recent landmark studies of U.S. political history respectively invoke a "more perfect union" at their work's beginning (Ackerman 1998, 32) and end (Smith 1997, 506).

4. Amitai Etzioni writes that "societies in which different communities pull in incompatible directions on basic matters are societies that experience moral confusion.... We need—on all levels, local, national—to agree on some basics" (1993, 10, 25, 32). Michael Sandel's *Democracy's Discontent* similarly envisions, if cautiously, "a common life at the level of the nation" and enlists Lincoln on behalf of the morally informed "political community and civic engagement that liberty requires" (1996, 202, 21–24).

5. Most liberal thinkers have long been skeptical of calls to solidarity or fraternity (for a summary statement see Kymlicka 1995, 173), but seem more inclined to affirm national union of late. Even such a favorite communitarian target as John Rawls asserts, in his lengthy *Political Liberalism* treatment of "overlapping consensus" on the national level, that political philosophy's *raison d'être* is to seek a resort "when our shared political understandings break down" (1993, 4). And longtime liberal fears about "moral homogeneity" (Waldron 1989, 582–90) and solicitude for the "diversity ... threatened when community is sought as part of a national agenda" (Hirsch 1986, 444) have recently been muted in favor of teleological appeals to union. See, among other prominent liberal scholars writing in this vein, Smith 1997, 488–506; Gray 1993, 312–18; Kymlicka 1995, 187–92; Ackerman 1991, 314–22; Macedo 1999; and Ackerman and Alstott 1999, 43–44, 184–87.

once again become one nation." Former U.S. Senator Bill Bradley, to cite a characteristic elite example, declares that "revitalizing our national community" is "America's central problem."[6] Such recurring emphasis on "once again" and "*re-*vitalizing" reflects a consistent theme: both within and beyond the academy, contemporary calls for union invariably appeal to the nation's past. Communitarian writers frequently contrast present-day levels of social cooperation and affective sentiment with a far more cohesive early republic of numerous small communities, with either the founding or Tocqueville's (Jacksonian) America the favored historical touchstone for comparison.[7] Liberal accounts, such as Theda Skocpol's insistence that the federal government has long been involved in stimulating voluntary associations, appeal to historical evidence as well. And Senator Bradley, writing for a nonscholarly audience, traces Americans' communal spirit to colonial New England and "the general store of Tocqueville's America."[8]

This backward-looking tendency stems from a mix of factors. Among these are a Whiggish belief that the present is indelibly marked by the past and that solutions to current difficulties might be located in national origins; the conviction that constructing a political union embracing *all* residents is only possible when precedent injustices and errors are chronicled and overcome; and/or the peculiarly American habit of treating virtually all major political issues as a matter of constitutional adjudication, entailing the testimony of the framing generation and subsequent opinion leaders. Whatever the specific reason, past efforts to establish unity are an object of legitimate concern, given the insights they might reveal.

Yet historians have been little more inclined than political theorists to address the topic of national union, or even American nationalism. This oversight owes something to the recent turn away from national or consensus themes, as described in the introduction, in favor of specialized attention to one or more groups' social and cultural experience during a portion of the U.S. past. Higham, writing in 1999, notes that "there is no agreement about a theory of America [among historians] . . . we find quite widely in today's academic world a sourly negative and cynical attitude toward any broadly national project." Yet he also identifies "a new sense" among historians "that national identity has been too long neglected," so this void may eventually be filled.[9]

Drawing useful lessons—for the present-day United States, let alone other nations or confederations—from the American experience with forging and

---

6. Wolfe 1998, 321; Bradley 1998, 107–8.

7. A recent, book-length example is Sandel 1996.

8. Skocpol 1997a; Bradley 1998, 110. Similar approaches are taken by scholars studying the unification of present-day Europe: see, e.g., Tassin 1992, who traces European "political unity" to the "ruins of the Greek *polis* and the Roman Empire" (1992, 174).

9. Higham 1999, 324–25. On scholarly inattention to nationalism in the U.S. context, see Grant 1997, 98–99 ("the dominant nation of this century remains on the sidelines in nationalism studies") and Waldstreicher 2000.

sustaining common bonds among constituent members' demands, first of all, detailed investigation into that experience. This would seem to require both a full-fledged theory of political union and a recognition of the implications aris-ing from union ideas' long history in American political discourse. Of these two tasks—analyzing national unity in rich theoretical detail and drawing unionist parallels from the U.S. past—this book is best suited to the second. If we accept that Americans (or Europeans, Indonesians, and so forth) indeed have an urgent need for a thorough examination of the obstacles to their national unity and ele-ments that might better secure it, there follows here a small advance on that task: assessment of the implications of past efforts to construct a more perfect union. With the obvious caveat that the complex history of American union ideas does not yield "lessons" for all relevant concerns in the present, several separate obser-vations are taken up in turn here, organized under three rubrics: (1) union's de-cline as a central concept in American political talk; (2) nineteenth-century union-ists' inclination to connect the spheres of civil society and national union; and (3) fruitful past avenues to uniting diverse elements in the United States.

UNION'S CONCEPTUAL DEMISE

From colonial times through the 1880s, union ideas helped to structure the way Americans conceived their society, in terms of both its political arrangements and their own place in the national whole. With the concept's disappearance from popular use, what might be called a unionist persuasion faded as well, though el-ements of it remained and were expressed in other ways: "America," "nation," and so forth. Aspirations to mutual belonging on a broad scale did not vanish, but the longtime basis for expressing (and understanding) those aspirations did. Over time a new vocabulary of national attachment grew in the place of "union," centered primarily on economic exchange and mutual pursuit of self-interest along with assurances that Americans' fellow-feeling could best be enhanced by experts heading a strong national state. Herbert Croly, among the most per-ceptive analysts of American nationalism in any age, nonetheless epitomized the spirit of his own in setting out a "truth to which patriotic Americans should firmly cleave": that "the modern nation . . . constitutes the best machinery as yet developed for raising the level of human association. It really teaches men how they must feel, what they must think, and what they must do, in order that they may live together amicably and *profitably*."[10]

In choosing, consciously or not, to value one political/moral vocabulary over another, a people subtly redirects its national course. The abandonment of union concepts after the 1890s also influenced institutional practices, though in ways

10. Croly 1909, 284 (emphasis added).

that are difficult to specify in detail. To this end, we may identify various tensions that emerged in sharp relief in U.S. politics after the passing of a strong unionist commitment among national elites and the mass of citizens. Three of these seem particularly noteworthy: a perceived divergence of individual and communal purposes, as the long-familiar "liberty *and* union" couplet disappeared from popular use;[11] a growing distinction between the national state (dubbed "big government" in the 1920s) and civil society; and the emergence of a crude patriotism, expressed as a propensity to demand "100 percent Americanism" of citizens. All three features were at times central to twentieth-century U.S. politics.[12] They became more prominent after union's conceptual demise, as amply evidenced during and after the 1890s.

Numerous cultural, social, and institutional developments contributed to these features of the political landscape, to be sure, and all three phenomena are traceable in earlier American history as well. But, as stressed in earlier chapters, a general commitment to preserving union had long restrained some of the potential excesses of individualism, autonomous government activity (either at the national or state/local level), and jingoism. All three emerged in sharper relief after 1890, arguably because of the disappearance of union ideas' balancing influence. Consider earlier Americans' tendency to view the national state and civil society as integrated, as discussed in chapter 3 (and in a separate section below). This connection lost much of its force during the twentieth century, as hostility to "big government" mounted with the growth of national administrative capacities and as policymakers and activists turned their attention from strengthening networks of civic engagement to regulatory solutions. All three types of change might well have occurred even had "union" retained its central appeal in American political conversation, but the coincidental timing is suggestive. Sandel notes that "as the welfare state developed, it drew less on an ethic of social solidarity and mutual obligation and more on an ethic of fair procedures and individual rights."[13] One facet of this development, emphasized in previous chapters, is that earlier generations of national leaders routinely defended national programs in terms of enhancing unity. With this longtime language of commonality lost, diminishing the connection between institution and national identity, the distance between government actions and popular support grew untenably large.

A few general observations about conceptual change may also be derived from union's rhetorical demise. Alongside commonplaces about any core political con-

---

11. Croly, for one, bade it a happy farewell: no more "glowing proclamation[s] about the inseparability of liberty in general from an indestructible union" (1909, 76).

12. Sandel explores the "erosion of community" and other aspects of twentieth-century individual/communal tensions in detail (1996, quote at p. 208); see also Wiebe 1967, 44–111. On patriotism, see Gary Gerstle's account of the post–World War I United States, when "virtually every group seriously interested in political power" was forced "to couch their programs in the language of Americanism" (1989, 8, and chaps. 2–4).

13. Sandel 1996, 346.

cept—that its meaning is contested and its application is conditioned by time, place, social system, and speakers' intent—a further claim is possible.[14] A foundational concept like "union" can help shape political agendas by enabling issues to be discussed, or ignored, in certain ways. Such an idea's *decline* from centrality, the union example suggests, will also affect political practice and the attendant social order. That political concepts' intelligibility depends upon the prevailing institutional order, which structures the context for meaning and usage, is a familiar truth. But that institutional arrangements can in turn be influenced by a vital concept, and also by its decline from use, is a more unusual finding. The history of union ideas in American political discourse appears to bear it out; such an assertion may merit further theoretical investigation.

Recognition that words have potent effects—that political outcomes are dependent on conceptual contests, as well as material interests or institutional orders—thus may be essential to actors in any polity as well as to fuller historical understanding. In short, conceptual change is not merely the realm of linguistic archaeologists. Shifting union ideas deeply affected political participants in late eighteenth-century America, for example, including both colonists struggling to find common themes and British officials who well understood the power of words. Specifically, as chapter 1's account of union's revolution-era history suggests, terminological conflict, communicative breakdown, and a swift conceptual reordering (from union with Britain to union among Americans) were basic to conceiving a more united people. Similar effects are apparent in the nineteenth century, as evidenced by the extensive debates over the term's meaning and application to a host of issues, from slavery to tariff rates. And when "union" passed from the American political vernacular, its absence was significant.

Acknowledging this past has a cautionary side as well. Concepts and the rhetoric inspired by them, it appears from the history of union talk, can influence political development. At the same time, such effects are extremely complex. No small group of political actors or theorists could control the conceptual development of union, as American elites repeatedly learned, especially in the aftermath of Andrew Jackson's election. Awareness of the import of language, though essential to understanding events, rarely confers predictive, much less decisive, power over events and outcomes. This seems a compelling reminder for theorists contrasting "good" and "bad" (because progressive or malign) styles of building political unity or nationalism in the present.[15] It also counsels caution among those promoting other American concepts, especially those related to constitutional development abroad.[16] When registered in actual political experience, these ideal types are transformed in often unpredictable ways.

14. A rich history of various American "contested truths" is in Rodgers 1987; that ideas are historically contingent is argued in, e.g., Richter 1995.
15. See, e.g., Nielsen 1997; Tamir 1993, 83–84, 163–67; and Mason 1999.
16. Bruce Ackerman describes (and critiques) the "triumphalism" characterizing recent "constitutional prescriptions" by many U.S. legal scholars and other consultants to countries abroad (2000, 634–35).

The importance of examining conceptual demise like that "union" underwent in the 1890s has further potential implications. Only ideas of union could be examined in detail here, but that term's history invites speculation about other concepts that served to balance conflicting political elements in the twentieth century, as union did in the nineteenth. One such example might be "liberal." In 1936, Democratic Party delegates meeting in Philadelphia to renominate Roosevelt and Garner ratified a party platform "dedicated to a government of liberal American principles . . . as conceived by the founders of our nation." Republican nominee Alfred Landon, though running hard against the New Deal on most fronts, also praised "the liberal idea . . . [as] a hallmark of American policy." Four years later, Roosevelt's third victory rested on a platform that concluded with an "appeal to all the liberal-minded men and women of the nation to approve this platform and go forward with us." Liberalism was synonymous with "the American system of government, the only system under which men are masters of their souls."[17]

As with "union," conflicts soon erupted over legitimate applications of "liberal." Self-proclaimed liberals like Friedrich Hayek and Herbert Hoover strenuously disagreed with not only the principles of New Deal liberalism but also the use of "liberal" by FDR and followers. "True liberalism," Hoover insisted during Roosevelt's second presidential term, was directly opposed to the New Deal, which instead constituted a form of "national regimentation." As historian Alan Brinkley notes, "nothing, in fact, so irritated many conservatives of the 1930s and 1940s as the New Deal's appropriation of the word 'liberal.' The real liberals, they insisted, were the enemies of New Deal statism, the defenders of individual rights against the 'social engineering' and 'paternalism' of the left."[18]

Such high-stakes disagreement testified to the importance "liberal" held in American public discourse. It captured—and influenced—the spirit of the times during the middle third of the twentieth century, as had "union" for most of the nineteenth century. By 1950, literary critic Lionel Trilling could plausibly claim, in his influential *The Liberal Imagination,* that "in the United States at this time liberalism is not only the dominant but even the sole intellectual tradition," a notion given historical legitimacy five years later by Louis Hartz in his likewise acclaimed *The Liberal Tradition in America.*[19] Much as "union" had bridged competing notions of localism and stronger national government, during and after the New Deal "liberal" was a synonym for compromise. The term stood for a political program (or orientation) falling well short of socialism but encouraging considerably more government activism, especially in the area of welfare provision, than Americans were accustomed to before the 1930s. "Liberal" in America stood midway between Marx and Spencer, to adapt a phrase. The successful assertion of this balancing ideal was important in consolidating a national

17. Porter and Johnson 1966, 363, 388; Landon in D. B. Johnson 1978, 119.
18. Brinkley 1998, 283 (includes Hoover quote).
19. Trilling 1950, ix; Hartz 1955.

state identified with activist social welfare ideals, among a people widely defining themselves as liberal.

Eventually the principles the term represented and then the very word "liberal" would come under fire, to the point that political speech (outside the academy, at least) now features the word in an overwhelmingly pejorative sense.[20] No detailed history of this development has yet been attempted, but such a study would turn in important ways on the notion of conceptual demise.

CIVIL SOCIETY AND *NATIONAL* UNITY

Intellectuals and political officials seeking to promote a closer sense of unity among diverse, pluralist Americans (or other democratic peoples) today have a ready prescription: encourage citizens to organize in local, preferably face-to-face associations to pursue their shared goals. Through voluntary, neighborly cooperation, arising from activities as varied as bowling leagues, PTA meetings, and volunteer service, individuals form interpersonal ties that engender civic sentiment and political participation. Much as financial capital provides the wherewithal for successful economic interchange, the "social capital" created by local activity will help a national community to endure.[21]

As upheld by a wide range of thinkers, this perspective is long on specifics about local involvement. Robert Putnam, whose work is at the center of the recent civil-society revival, investigates rotating credit associations, social norms like reciprocal trust, and a host of other immediate sources of civic engagement in his investigation into successful democratic citizenship. Putnam chooses the bowling alley, "a community-based institution if there ever was one," as an emblem of declining civil society.[22] His overwhelming emphasis on local activity is widely shared, both in relevant scholarship and in government efforts at policy devolution.

Absent in Putnam's and most other civil-society studies is how networks of neighborly cooperation translate into anything like a robust sense of *national* belonging: how local activity might actually enhance collective engagement and citizen commitment to the nation. Apart from rote references to Tocqueville's account of civic responsibility growing from small-scale associational life, or Louis Brandeis's line about local democratic "experiments" being replicated at the federal level, most commentators simply assume that a national spirit will emerge from an expansion of social capital in neighborhoods.[23] Specific connec-

---

20. James Dao writes that the "'liberal' label . . . has become a political dirty word over the past two decades" (*New York Times*, October 27, 1999, A22). See also Beatty 1996, 96–98 ("liberal" as "the kiss of death in American politics") and Foner 1998, 324.

21. See, e.g., the essays in Novak 1996; Etzioni 1993; Putnam 1993; and Barber 1998. A useful summary of scholarship on social capital is in Foley and Edwards 1997.

22. Putnam 1993, 163–85; see also Putnam 2000. Quote in Wolfe 1998, 233.

23. In Sandel's representative formulation: "Practicing self-government in small spheres . . . impels citizens to larger spheres of political activity as well" (1996, 347).

tions between local participation and national civic renewal are drawn only vaguely, if at all.

Some writers emphasizing local activity also verge on contempt for efforts to build stronger national ties. Political scientist William Schambra urges (in an essay suggestively titled "All Community is Local") that researchers and activists "direct our gaze away from the failed project of national community and focus once again on the churches, voluntary associations, and grass-roots groups that are rebuilding America's civil society one family, one block, one neighborhood at a time."[24] On such a view, the nation is too far removed from most people's lives (or its governing officials too corrupt, impersonal, and so forth) to nurture a genuine sense of shared purposes and civic spirit.

The preceding chapters suggest instead that any project promoting responsible local citizenship must address issues of national belonging in explicit detail. From the Confederation period to various crises over nullification and other issues in the nineteenth century, the social cohesion underlying political stability (and, eventually, inspiriting Union victory in war) derived vitally from citizens' conscious involvement in a unified community. Membership in a national polity is "a matter of dignity," writes Liah Greenfeld. "It gives people reason to be proud." Without the sense of shared purpose and pride accompanying citizens' self-conception as belonging to a greater whole, the "civic" component of local engagement can dwindle to the point of meaninglessness. As a *New Haven Register* column put it in 1888: "Thousands of men have been found ready to die for the United States. [But] where are the men who would die for Brooklyn, San Francisco, or Chicago? Indeed, where are the men who would live for them?"[25]

The view that individuals exercise local agency in a way that translates automatically into a sense of national belonging is also belied by the preceding chapters of this volume. Conventional portraits of vigorous civic participation at the local level in bygone times seem considerably overdone. Recall Madison and fellow framers' hand-wringing over the mismanagement and malfeasance of local governments; Daniel Webster and other prominent nineteenth-century Senators' resistance to state legislators' efforts to turn them into spokesmen for local interests; the rude justice prevailing in lower courts, sparking assertions on behalf of Supreme Court superiority from John Marshall and later justices; or Abraham Lincoln's rebuttals of "squatter sovereignty" in his 1858 Senate campaign debates with Stephen Douglas. While these leaders recognized the fruits of neighborhood participation, they also actively urged citizens to take a broader view (some did so by touring the United States, in a direct bid to attract attention to national purposes) and proposed federal policies on behalf of national unity. The connec-

---

24. Schambra 1998, 49. Such critiques are usually associated with the Right in America, but for a discussion of leftist community organizations' longstanding "suspicion" of "collaboration across groups and levels of governance," see Weir and Ganz 1997, 161–62. See also Paul Gilbert's overview of scholarship hostile to pretensions of national community (1997, 152–55).

25. Greenfeld 1992, 487–88 (a similar argument appears in Staub 1997); *New Haven Register,* January 7, 1888.

tion between citizens' local activities and spirited attachment to the Union was hardly "natural" in the eyes of these leaders.

A further concern about the civil-society model, when advanced without commensurate attention to national spirit, has to do with local associations' effects in breeding civic engagement. From Madison in the 1780s to Francis Lieber a century later, commentators worried that such associations were rarely incubators for citizens' public spirit, even in a neighborly sense; instead, they warned, organizations mainly served the selfish (usually economic) interests of their members. Madison's *Federalist* account of factions portrayed the myriad small "interests, parties, and sects" dominating state politics as self-promoting and unconcerned with the greater good. Sociologist Jason Kaufman has recently demonstrated empirically that most nineteenth-century local associational activity in the United States was directed not to building social capital, but to "sectional rent-seeking behavior."[26]

Past associations that emphasized civic ends generally did so through a federalist-style organization. As Theda Skocpol demonstrates, most "local" civic groups well back into the nineteenth century drew strength and resources from participation in a broad network of like-minded assemblies, united under a national parent organization. In each of a variety of social realms, from military veterans to mothers' groups, Skocpol identifies a "classic three-tiered voluntary civic association, with tens of thousands of local posts, whose members met regularly, plus state and national affiliates that held big annual conventions." If Kaufman confirms the first portion of Madison's *Federalist* 51 argument about factions, Skocpol may be read as supporting the second part, that on the national level a majority coalition of groups "could seldom take place on any other principles than those of justice and the general good."[27]

Thus one traditional way of maximizing the civic benefits of local engagement—given that people live, work, and act in immediate communities—was to link associations on a broader level. Another way to affirm a spirit of national unity without detracting from beneficial local participation is evident from past American practice. As traced in chapters 2 and 3, unionists treated the national state and civil society not as separate spheres but as instruments of mutual empowerment. This perspective is untenable in much contemporary social science theory, which (in Xu Wang's summary account) "equate[s] the strength of the state with its autonomy from society and with the ability of state elites to ignore other social actors or to impose their will in any simple manner on society." Analysts outside the academy similarly view civil-society activity as a "realm beyond the state."[28]

Despite theoretical inclinations to maintain the strict separation of these spheres, past Americans' more integrative approach to state and society seems

---

26. Madison in Rossiter 1961, 325; Kaufman 1999, 1297.
27. Skocpol 1997b, 114 (see also 1997a); Rossiter 1961, 325.
28. Wang 1999, 231; intro. to Novak 1996, 3; see also Diamond 1994 and Hefner 1998, 20.

worth reexamining. The national state and related organizations such as political parties were essential to fostering exchanges among citizens, from affective bonds to economic ties. Federal resources were also a basis for developing local activity into associational networks across state and regional borders. National actors' efforts to secure civil freedoms greatly advanced the gains registered in this area by African Americans, some other minority groups, and the mass of white citizens over the country's first century. Though limited in its infrastructure and many other respects, the early state was an animating source of local political participation, aiding rather than abrading Americans' developing civil society. The dual-federalist arrangement of U.S. power has evolved since, but setting and enforcing uniform standards, restraining destructive competition among states or interest groups, mediating matters of economic and social justice, and providing for minorities' security all remain primarily national-government responsibilities—as even most apostles of devolution or "subsidiarity" in their calmer hours accept.[29] All these features are also basic to constructing a genuinely improved union.

This sunny portrait of state-society interaction has limits. Stressing a national foundation for Americans' civic ideals can threaten to erase legitimate lines between private and public, or state and society. Wang notes that while "the state helps create, organize, and fund pluralist civil associations, it is also likely to co-opt, preempt, subordinate, and control them." Corrosive effects also work in reverse, as the state can suffer from overly tight connections between its officials and regional or local social networks, as evidenced in the large literature on bureaucratic "capture" by the groups supposedly subject to state oversight.[30] Finally, the above-described factional tendencies of local groups are not necessarily diminished, much less eliminated, when an association operates at a national level.

Acknowledging these concerns, and the fact that the federalist balance between local and national power is constantly under negotiation, highlights the difficulties of promoting federal efforts to enhance individuals' sense of connectedness to the whole. Given the range of alarm about fragmentation, separatism, and other "disunionist" tendencies in the present, however, and considering past Americans' practice of promoting unity via a government/civil society partnership, it seems wise to revisit the zero-sum conception of state and civil society relations prevailing at present.

Some of the American theorists and practitioners featured in earlier chapters imagined—and, to at least a limited extent, instantiated—a public realm that was neither an isolated, separate sphere nor subsumed by the state, but instead was organized in conjunction with state actors and institutions. Perhaps it was easier to conceive of federal-government institutions and local purposes as mu-

29. Michael Grunwald notes a continued tendency among national policy makers to "preempt" states' autonomy, alongside the "mantra" of devolution, but also that "even strict states' rights advocates say Washington's recent tendency to impose uniform laws for complex industries such as banking and telecommunications makes some sense" (1999, 29).

30. Wang 1999, 245.

tually implicated in a time when those institutions were smaller and, indeed, still under construction—or when the public was apparently not so negatively disposed toward the administrative state as is the case today. Social theorist Craig Calhoun, noting the "outright cynic[ism]" widely expressed toward "the legal system, the public schools, the media, and, above all, the government," recognizes that these "domestic institutions [are] central to the real, practical unification of American life . . . we depend on [them] to organize our relations—including relations across lines of difference," in imporant part by providing "cross-cutting linkages among participants" from throughout U.S. society, including "subordinate publics." One step toward reversing such cynicism, as Calhoun implicitly acknowledges, might come in reasserting the connections between civil society and the institutions of governance.[31] Past American actors deployed the language of union as a means to achieving the conditions they saw as crucial to the efficacy of public institutions, a lesson with obvious connotations for the present.

SUSTAINING UNION:
RELIGION, NATIONAL BELONGING, AND DIVERSITY

One widely advertised route to a more united people is fostering local civic participation; the previous section suggested that links between local activity and national-state support are a necessary supplement. A second likely source of stronger unity is national *sentiment*, as both the history of union's rhetorical development and present scholarship testify. If a widespread sense of national belonging among citizens is in fact essential to a polity's health, how to inspire such a commitment? This spirit was long invoked as an important source of Americans' unionist persuasion, inspired initially by broadly common religious values and later augmented by patriotic expressions. Here I address religion and patriotism as present-day phenomena, with frequent references to past generations' attempts to create a more perfect union. The focus of this discussion is on how a spirit of national unity might be enhanced among diverse citizens while minimizing tendencies to religious exclusivity and division or hyperpatriotic excesses. A third section explicitly addresses the issue of achieving greater unity among a people without requiring oppressive "assimilation" of diverse practices and interests. Taken as exemplary—and looking backward once again—is the unionist vision of Walt Whitman.

Religion
Union's extraordinary popular currency for over a century after 1776 owed in important part to the religious overtones the term evoked, as cultural leaders like Lincoln, Douglass, and Emerson well knew. None of these men advocated a holy crusade to achieve closer ties among citizens; indeed, each kept his personal re-

---

31. Calhoun 1998, 34.

ligious views mostly private. But all three extensively drew on biblical rhetoric and divine sanction to advance their visions of union. Encouraging people to imagine themselves as meaningfully connected is always difficult in any large, heterogeneous nation. The American "civil religion," comprising a set of beliefs that the vast majority of residents share and root their principled ideals in, was an uncommonly fruitful basis for such a conception from the early colonial period on.

Similar effects of a qualified promotion of religious values in political culture are discernible today. Efforts to build solidarity across a host of dividing lines invites extended attention to religion, which remains an integral source of broad-based mutual bonds. Among African Americans, whose well-founded suspicion of appeals to national solidarity is apparent throughout national history, the principal agents of inclusive mobilization have been religious themes and leaders—as figures from Douglass to the Reverend Martin Luther King Jr. attest. Those concerned with the worst-off in society and the effect of inequality on social solidarity owe serious investigation to the ecumenical, fraternal effects of religious congregation.

One promising guide for such an understanding, as chronicled in chapter 4, is Abraham Lincoln's example. Lincoln sought to infuse union sentiment with a moral standing explicitly drawn from biblical precepts: his aim was thereby to legitimize, or at least make it harder to ignore, the political equality of different groups—prominently including African Americans. Though Lincoln's attempts to link equality and union in the public mind were attenuated during and after Reconstruction, his efforts did inspire some Union soldiers to view emancipation as a "salient issue" in their support for the "preservation of one nation indivisible," as James McPherson affirms. One Illinois soldier wrote after the Emancipation Proclamation that "it always has been plain to me that this race must be free before God would recognize us . . . now I believe we are on God's side [and] now I can fight with a good heart."[32] To the extent that opinion leaders are concerned to promote principled national solidarity, a set of religious beliefs the vast majority of Americans share and root their ethical understanding in provides one well-grounded source.

But what of the dangers long associated with religious influences in the public sphere, from clashing doctrines to inquisitions against unbelievers? This past leads many modern analysts, inside and outside the academy, to be extremely wary of religious influences in public matters.[33] In the contemporary United States, where religion is highly pluralized and deliberately isolated from most influence on state action, fears of clerical domination seem misplaced. Alan Wolfe's recent "Middle Class Morality Project," which studied citizen attitudes in four representative U.S. communities, concludes that

> most middle-class Americans take their religion seriously. But very few of them take it so seriously that they believe that religion should be the

---

32. McPherson 1997, 117–31; quote at p. 130 (spelling modernized here, as throughout this study).
33. See, e.g., Kramnick and Moore 1996 and Smith 1998.

sole, or even the most important, guide for establishing rules about how *other* people should live. . . . Despite the attention that conservative Christians have commanded in the political realm, there is not much support out there in middle-class America . . . for the notion that religion can play an official and didactic role in guiding public morality.[34]

Tapping the vast reservoir of common religious feeling among Americans and encouraging its application to civic purposes was once a preferred approach to uniting the polity. There seems little compelling reason to shun this source in the present. Although the civic/religious nexus is frequently identified with conservative social policies, some liberal thinkers increasingly acknowledge that "it is time for mainstream suburban congregations—many of which played major roles in the civil rights and antiwar movements—to return to the fray . . . middle-class churches could play a far stronger role as collaborators in a common effort to address *shared* community, regional, and national concerns."[35] In sum, we might do well to recognize and build on the long tradition of intertwined religious invocations and Americans' spirit of unity.

National Belonging

While common religious values are a potential basis of bonds among citizens, a spirit of patriotic belonging provides a more direct means of politically relating individual and collective aspirations. Yet—as with religion—active attempts to foster patriotism inspire immense uneasiness among many thinkers and activists. "In its very nature," as Kai Nielsen summarizes, national sentiment "cannot but be xenophobic, authoritarian, exclusivist, and, where it has the opportunity, often expansionist as well."[36] Here the history sketched above may have particularly valuable relevance. Consider, for example, the Madisonian framework for promoting affective bonds and a restrained sense of national belonging among Americans. Madison's unionist vision, we saw in chapter 2, was largely free of the ethnonationalist impulses then as now coloring public discourse in societies around the globe. He also made scant reference to religious or strong patriotic sources of unity. Instead he relied on three means of inspiriting a sense of national belonging among Americans: territory, affective ties, and institutionally protected bonds between citizens and their political leaders. Elsewhere I have described how these might be adapted to present circumstances in policy form;[37] the point here is that past means of conceiving unionist sentiment are applicable in the contemporary United States, without resort to dangerous versions of patriotic fervor.

34. Wolfe 1998, 55. Wolfe's own surprise at these findings is chronicled at ibid., 58–61.
35. Weir and Ganz 1997, 167.
36. Nielsen 1997, 43; compare, e.g., Mayerfeld 1998, 565–76, and Kateb 1992, esp. chap. 3.
37. Kersh forthcoming.

"Liberal nationalist" adherents come closest in the present to earlier thinkers' faith that it is possible to forge political unity without requiring a supreme commitment to the nation or trampling on individual and group rights.[38] For Tamir and others writing in this vein, national sentiment can derive principally (or even purely, in extreme versions) from a commitment to abstract values—usually equality, liberty, and democracy.[39] Such a position is well grounded in liberal theory, as most modern leading lights in the tradition list primary goods as the desired basis of social exchange: equal respect, for Ronald Dworkin; social justice, for Bruce Ackerman; fairness, for John Rawls.

The conceptual history of American union provides mixed support for such a universal value-based approach to national sentiment. Efforts by leaders like Lincoln or Douglass to identify equality as the basis for national unity, and to insist on tying union membership to individuals' observance of that principle, were mostly unsuccessful, stymied by (among other things) the popular reassertion of balanced ideas of union in sentimentalized form during Reconstruction. It was possible for U.S. citizens to reject black equality after the Civil War Amendments' passage and yet remain full participants in the national union. This history suggests that while abstract moral principles can be a basis for stronger connections among citizens, their appeal is usually limited in practice. Moreover, the relationship between political ideas and the various traditions that inform them is a tenuous one. Union ideas' universal, unconditional application by many antebellum speakers ultimately dissolved the term's connection to specific principles (and institutional practices), as seen in chapter 3.

Note that this objection to liberal-nationalist views has nothing to say about whether principles as such can attract citizen sentiment. Evident in the conceptual history traced above is that union *itself* became for many Americans a dearly held value, defended in antebellum and Reconstruction times even to the detriment of other goods. This impulse to cohere around cohesion, so to speak, is also apparent in modern social movements. Notes philosopher Robert Grant, "the solidarity with fellow-campaigners, the general, group-enhanced consciousness of one's lofty ethical status, the heady sense of being at the cutting-edge of history, of being caught up in something greater than oneself . . . all acquire a significance for the participants which wholly dwarfs the ostensible object or original beneficiary of the exercise." Ideas of union acquired attractive force in the U.S. past seemingly out of all proportion to their actual import or realization. How they did so was difficult to explain, as the Boston writer James Joseph noted with a touch of exasperation in 1854: "Ask him [the 'common man'], *why* he feels

38. See esp. Tamir 1993; also useful are Lichtenberg 1997 and Kymlicka 1995.
39. For Tamir: "The state [is] seen as an embodiment of abstract humanity, representing those universal human qualities that unite all human beings" (1993, 141; cf. 79). Ignatieff (1994, 5) defines his preferred "civic nation" as "a community of equal, rights-bearing citizens, united in patriotic attachment to a shared set of political practices and values." See also Greenfeld 1992, 8–11, 484.

such devotion to Union, and he will go mute. Yet he will [feel] his preference not the less, and go away still whistling 'Union, glorious union.'"[40]

Along with the idea of union as a source of coherence, the polity—referred to as "the Union"—served a similar inspirational role for much of early U.S. history. When northerners fought to preserve the Union, or Webster extolled "this system of Union," the locus of this spirit was a particular set of institutions and practices; the basis of closer unity was Americans' sense of connection with these. Andrew Mason draws a subtle theoretical distinction between citizens' spirit of national identity arising from "belonging together," on the basis of shared ethnic, religious, or other qualities, and "belonging to a polity." The latter, on his terms, involves a person's "identif[ying] with most of its major institutions and some of its central practies and feel[ing] at home in them . . . [and] regard[ing] her flourishing as intimately linked to their flourishing." This aptly describes the ground for American sustainable-union concepts, one not based on a strong sense of shared ethnicity or culture (as ethnocultural unionists urged), nor even a shared conception of the good (in moral-unionist terms), but a shared identity based on belonging to the U.S. polity, familiarly termed "the Union."[41]

While inclusive moral standards did not supply the basis for a long-lasting or especially avid unionist sentiment in the past, neither did an opposite ethnic-chauvinist tendency—decried by liberal nationalists today—automatically gain sway in their place. For many Americans rejected ancestry or ethnicity as an absolute qualification for membership in the U.S. national union. Influential spokesmen like Webster and Madison promoted voluntary national solidarity without resorting to ethnocentric advocacy, advising merely that citizens participate in the polity and broad cultural practices associated with it. These together girded a palpable spirit of fellow-feeling, both in these leaders' conception and as borne out during some periods. This tradition is an important one to recall today, when cultural and ethnic sources of mutuality are routinely treated as synonymous and critiqued in similar terms.[42] The history of union ideas provides at least some concrete evidence that a distinction may be drawn between the two, and that a "mature" spirit of common belonging to the polity may be a genuinely promising basis for a sense of national unity.[43]

Diversity and Union: Whitman's Affirmative View

Madison's framework proved least applicable, as noted in earlier chapters, to the matter of integrating excluded peoples into the national union. Here lies one of the most compelling dilemmas for would-be modern unionists: how to

40. Grant 1995, 133; Joseph quoted in *New Haven Register*, December 10, 1854.

41. On Webster, see, e.g., his 1850 speech "The Constitution and the Union" in Wiltse and Berolzheimer 1986–88, 2:515–51; Mason 1999, 272; cf. 271–76.

42. As Kai Nielsen points out (1997, 49).

43. The term "mature patriotism" is defined and substantiated in Wolfe 1998, 133–79. See also Staub 1997.

achieve political and social integration of minorities without violating group rights or norms of self-determination.[44] The sustainable-union idea of belonging to the polity, as just outlined, suggests a promising basis for integration today, in that a variety of immigrant groups joined the American national whole in the eighteenth and nineteenth centuries without having prized aspects of their traditional cultures automatically stripped away. On another side, however, is the tradition of ethnocultural union, subordinating or excluding many ethnic and racial minorities. As we saw in chapter 6, the unfamiliar national origins and sheer numbers of 1880s–90s immigrants likely contributed to ending the majority of citizens' inclination to describe their political body as a union. The record with respect to African Americans' or Native Americans' inclusion in the whole is even less salutary.

Even amid past professions of *e pluribus unum*, the principal American accounts of cultural diversity were negative, as briefly traced in earlier chapters. Madison and like-minded thinkers recognized the potential explosiveness of differences among the population and advocated a slowly widening range of inclusion, but rarely was diversity per se espoused as a source of union. John Higham describes antebellum Americans' outlook: "the decentralization of society and disjunction of values and traditions made every alternative feasible . . . no [single ethnic group] could present a united front against the rest. . . . Innumerable separations flourish[ed] within a matrix of national unity."[45] Benign though this flourishing may sound, the dominant theories informing the national-unity "matrix" were only vaguely concerned with integrating diverse elements as such into the polity. For an American thinker who offered a more affirmative view, we turn instead to Walt Whitman. Whitman was not as influential a thinker in his time as Madison or cultural leaders like Emerson, and therefore is not featured in earlier chapters. But Whitman's enthusiastic affirmation of diversity and union, even amid civil war, is a provocative standard for thinkers pondering these questions today.

Whitman has lately received a surprising share of attention from political theorists, principally for his democratic vision. In George Kateb's summary claim: "Whitman is a great philosopher of democracy. Indeed, he may be the greatest." Whitman is less familiar as a theorist of union, but no nineteenth-century thinker did more to address the means by which America's many might be conceived of as "one."[46] Certainly his devotion to the value of union was unquestionable. In

---

44. Significantly, scholars wrestling with this question in recent years mainly address issues of *protecting* minority rights, not how different ethnic groups, races, and other minorities relate to each other or how a more inclusive whole might be achieved.

45. Higham 1984, 185–93. See also Wiebe 1975.

46. Kateb 1990, 545. An early testament to Whitman as "democracy's seer" was John Dewey, in his conclusion to "Search for the Great Community." See also, more recently, Norton 1986, 315–29; Rosenblum 1990, 120–21; Mosher 1990; and Reynolds 1995. Two scholars who recognize Whitman as a "philosopher of Unionism" are Fredrickson (1965, quote at p. 66) and Beer, who draws a direct similarity between Lincoln and Whitman (1984, 368; cf. Barton 1928).

both poetry and prose Whitman celebrated an undivided country, as in his "Song of the Exposition" ("Thou Union holding all, fusing, absorbing, tolerating all, / Thee, ever thee, I sing") and in his rambling manifesto *Democratic Vistas:* "The fear of conflicting and irreconcilable interiors, and the lack of a common skeleton, knitting all close, continually haunts me. . . . Nothing is plainer than the need . . . of a fusion of the States."[47]

The latter view recalls the outlook of many antebellum thinkers fearing disunion. But Whitman departed from these both in his analysis of the obstacles inhibiting a united America and in his poetic "solutions." Many modern readers of Whitman find it difficult to comprehend his unabashed paeans to unity, as in his opening-line call in "For You O Democracy" (1860) to "make the continent indissoluble." Critical reactions include outright condemnation; one analyst finds the unity-minded Whitman "more like a Fourth of July orator than a perceptive critic or poet: he was a poor historian and a naive prophet of the future." Others ignore Whitman's politics, erecting a divide between the "poet of the self" and the "bard of democracy" and dismissing his political ideas as Romantic sentimentalism.[48] Even among writers seeking to "recover the political" in Whitman, a somewhat disbelieving attitude prevails: he cannot have meant what he said! Betsy Erkkila accordingly depicts Whitman as an increasingly pessimistic abolitionist in Emerson's style, "anticipating the political state hover[ing] on the brink of disaster and the culture of capital tighten[ing] its grip on the nation."[49]

But opposing slavery was a secondary aim for Whitman, who in his later years would reminisce that "the negro was not the chief thing, the chief thing was to stick together."[50] Only in his faith that wartime turmoil would result in a more inclusive union did Whitman's account resemble that of abolitionists like Douglass. But neither was he yet another nineteenth-century racist thinker. Rather than abolitionist condemnation, Whitman adopted as his basic approach to achieving what he, too, called "sacred Union" a sympathetic embrace of difference. Whitman's affirmative ethic has proven tiresome to many readers, as in D. H. Lawrence's biting dismissal: "ALLNESS! shrieks Walt, going whizz over a Red Indian."[51] Yet Whitman's account of union through diversity was carefully

47. Kaplan 1982, 348; Stovall 1939, 383.
48. Miller 1968, 27; Lewis 1986, 124–25.
49. Erkkila 1989, 159; cf., on the extent of Whitman's political commitment, Trachtenberg 1994; Dougherty 1993; and Larson 1988.
50. Quoted in Fredrickson 1965, 66. More even than slavery, fostering disunion was the South's great misdeed, to Whitman "the foulest crime in history known in any land or age" (quoted in Norton 1986, 323). Cf. his July 17, 1857, editorial in the *Brooklyn Daily Times*, "On the Old Subject—The Origin of It All," opposing colonization in favor of eventual "absorption" of blacks into a thereby "redeemed" country. A year later (May 6, 1858) in another editorial, "Prohibition of Colored Persons," Whitman gamely urged "battling against this [racial] prejudice," ironically denouncing the majority view: "Besides, is not America for Whites? And is it not better so?" Holloway and Schwarz 1932, 44–45, 47.
51. Lawrence quoted in Pearce 1962, 15. Cf. the similar dismissals from Bloom ("the Whitman who will not cease affirming until we wish never to hear anything affirmed again—[he] is done with, and in good time") 1971, 226; Simpson 1990. On Whitman and slavery, see Sanchez-Eppler 1993, 57–63, 71–82.

grounded, in two ways. Whitman's notion of "adhesive" division of labor, knitting together distinct elements through eros, and his notion of shared aesthetic experiences together promised to (in his words) "cohere, and signalize in time, these States."[52] The result marks an innovative and still instructive attempt to honor the full range of *pluribus* in the search for *unum*.

Traditional economic divisions of labor provided that as "the specialized parts become more independent, exchange among them grows, and the total output of material goods and services rises." Lincoln saw U.S. economic relations thus: "the great variety of the local [economic] institutions in the States [are] bonds of union. . . . They make a house united." In reality, as Lincoln knew, prevailing economic divisions between manufacturing North and agricultural cotton-planting South also served to exacerbate differences, eventually contributing to civil war. For Whitman, in contrast, a *social* "division of labor" served as the agent of unity. As Samuel Beer summarizes, Whitman "claims [that] it is not merely diversity, but 'differences which require each other for their mutual fruition' that bring about this passionate union [of two people]. And similarly in wider social relations . . . small friendly associations are formed 'wherein each one plays a role conformable to his character, where there is a true exchange of services.' Such are the complementary services that are exchanged in the social division of labor." Whitman's procession from pairs to small-group associations is replicated as society expands. "With this growing diversity," Beer further notes, "goes an increase in scale and the boundaries of the culture and of the economy are extended . . . the nation-states derive their remarkable cohesion from the same affectual sources as the more intimate groups."[53]

Through this process of social exchange a more genuine national union may be created by the diverse elements making up that nation. Such a view may appear hopelessly optimistic, especially in the later antebellum period. But Whitman even then conveyed an implacable faith that union would arise from the social "division of labor" produced by cultural diversity. An initial example of Whitman's commitment comes in his sweeping egalitarian lists, most famously in "Song of Myself." There representatives of excluded groups, among them the "hounded slave," "half-breed" (who, significantly, "straps on his light boots to compete in the race"), "groups of newly-come immigrants," "prostitute," and "red squaw," are depicted as integral parts of American society. Whitman draws this connection by placing these figures in poetic proximity, interspersing them with majority-culture elites: "the fluent lawyers" and "my Congress in session in the Capitol." By introducing into traditional tableaux "matters hitherto thought unworthy, obscene, contemptible, beyond the range of what was deemed decorous in poetry—or society," Whitman "assert[s] the worthiness" of "unhonored and unnoticed" occupations and people. In displaying a "negro drayman," for example, as free laborer alongside blacksmith and butcher, and declaring that "I be-

---

52. Stovall 1939, 421.
53. Basler 1953–55, 446; cf. 440; Beer 1984, 365–67.

hold the picturesque giant and love him," Whitman suggests in a powerfully immediate way the social exchange-value of each American resident, alike engaged in his or her professional practice.[54]

America's "multitudinous diversities" were not to be forcibly assimilated to some preexisting cultural standard, Whitman insisted: "The diverse shall be no less diverse, but they shall flow and unite."[55] In much nineteenth-century thought the diversity of America appeared as something to be overcome. Emerson's "divide and tame" quotation in chapter 3 is emblematic: through the individuating influences of the dominant national culture a self-reliant collectivity would emerge. Whitman proposed an opposite understanding. While also valuing individuality—"children are taught to be laws to themselves, and to depend on themselves," he said—in the end individualism appears vitally informed by and in turn a source of diversity, another means of uniting differently constituted people, none requiring prior status as "self-reliant."[56]

Presenting blacks as fellow free laborers was one matter, but in embracing runaway slaves as such ("I am the hounded slave, I wince at the bite of the dogs"), exhibiting intimate identification with their plight but suggesting no condemnation or necessity for change, Whitman's outlook is judged problematic by many commentators. In affirming all at face value, Whitman is criticized for exhibiting "a too simple faith in the status quo" and even for taking artistic advantage of the inherent tension in relations between different American groups.[57] But as I read him he was groping toward an alternate purpose. The tentative attempts of Lincoln (or of Seward, Chase, and even Charles Sumner) to include African Americans within the political union relied explicitly upon blacks' mimicking the white cultural and social majority. Whitman, in contrast, through positive portrayals of divergent elements suggests that differences themselves are valuable rather than disorderly. And by insisting that America was both singled out for greatness and unified by its "oceanic, variegated" ensembles,[58] Whitman opened the way to reexamining the balance between accommodating difference and ensuring political stability, an issue still occupying public thinkers today.

Whitman also tapped into the more sublimated, irrational conceptual history of union, bound up with sexuality and bodies. He was the first major cultural figure openly to apply this erotic exchange to the political realm, terming "adhesiveness" between people and groups as a basis for unity. Where Lincoln invoked venerable images of God and Constitution in his appeals to union, Whitman's account of the "fervid comradeship" arising from adhesiveness draws on the "appeal of lovers, the fondness of friends." It is more than a play on words to say

54. Whitman 1992, 33–40; Dougherty 1993, 64–65.
55. Stovall 1939, 92; Whitman 1992, 113.
56. Kateb (1990) asserts that Whitman's democratic unity arises from individualism; compare Rosenblum's critique at 1990, 576–84.
57. Stovall 1939, 40; Chase 1974, 146; Sanchez-Eppler 1993, 39–50. Cf. the balanced assessment in Trachtenberg 1994.
58. Stovall 1939, 436. "Ensemble" was a favorite Whitman word, signaling reconciliation both of diverse groups and of individuals and aggregate.

that Whitman literally seeks to embody the idea of union in his account of erotic exchange.[59]

Whitman related this notion of adhesiveness directly to America's diverse residents, asserting the benefits of "the deep quality of all-accepting fusion." Diversity appears as the hallmark of the United States, characterized by its "large variety of character" and "full ply for human nature to expand itself in numberless and even conflicting directions." In people's diverse social practices Whitman found "an infinite number of currents and forces, and contributions, and temperatures, and cross purposes, whose ceaseless play of counterpart on counterpart brings constant restoration and vitality." To this benefit Whitman added a warning: "Of all dangers to a nation . . . there can be no greater one than having certain portions of the people set off from the rest by a line drawn—they not privileged as others, but degraded, humiliated, made of no account."[60]

Two central sources of adhesiveness in Whitman's understanding, beyond actual erotic exchanges, were based in sentiment. One stemmed from imagined connections across generations and the other was a product of national aesthetic achievements. In numerous places Whitman displays adhesive unity as bridging not only ethnicity and geography but time. His poem "Crossing Brooklyn Ferry" is the finest example, heralding "the others that are to follow me, the ties between me and them, / The certainty of others. . . . It avails not, time or place—distance avails not." The poem is written as an appeal to future generations, "you that shall cross from shore to shore years hence." While Whitman labored to demonstrate the present possibility and rewards of adhesive social exchange, he principally looked ahead in inscribing "a new virtue, unknown to other lands and not yet really known here, but the foundation and tie of all, as the future will grandly develop: 'UNIONISM.'" This "higher" source of unity would specifically arise, he wrote, in a "national literature" that would "cultivate and recognize . . . [i]ntense and loving comradeship, the personal and passionate attachment of man to man."[61]

Whitman's call for a great national literature was nothing novel when he sounded it in the 1860s and 1870s. Emerson's "American Scholar" address was a classic statement, and Longfellow had satirized like appeals a quarter century before. But original in Whitman's version was the insistence that American aesthetic achievement could serve as a bond of national union. The claim is developed in detail in *Democratic Vistas:*

Should some two or three really original American poets (perhaps artists or lecturers) arise . . . from their eminence, fusing contributions, races,

---

59. Whitman 1992, 7. To Whitman, Samuel Beer notes, "Eros is not merely an urge . . . [i]t has a rationale. Eros binds because of what it does and seeks to do" (1984, 373). In Whitman's terms: "adhesiveness or love . . . fuses, ties and aggregates, making the races comrades, and fraternizing all" (Stovall 1939, 397).

60. Stovall 1939, 401, 376, 398.

61. Ibid., 91, 467.

far localities, &c., together, they would give more compaction and more moral identity (the quality to-day most needed) to these States, than all its Constitutions, legislative and judicial ties. . . . There could hardly happen anything that would more serve the States, with all their variety of origins, their diverse climes, cities, standards, &c., than possessing . . . the aggregation of a cluster of mighty poets, artists, teachers, fit for us, national expressers, comprehending and effusing . . . what is universal, native, common to all, inland and seaboard, northern and southern.

It was "not enough," Whitman declared, that national unity "be vivified and held together merely by political means, superficial suffrage, legislation, &c." The "true nationality of the States, the genuine union" was "neither the written law, nor (as is generally supposed) either self-interest, or common pecuniary or ma-terial objects." Rather, it lay in what David Bromwich terms "gratefully shared memory."[62] As in Lincoln's account of political participation, *aesthetic* participa-tion—reading, viewing, hearing and thus engaging in American productions— would resonate nationally, communicating higher purposes and values and ele-vating individuals beyond ordinary personal concerns.

Whitman's notion of aesthetic inspiration also addressed a familiar dilemma, one that had occupied American thinkers since colonial times: reconciling in-dividual and collective aims. This was theoretically accomplished in the mid-nineteenth century by harnessing self-interest to common ends, but Whitman characteristically sought a grander solution. Although most commentators locate Whitman's ultimate allegiance in individualism, he attempted wholesale affirma-tions of both personal and collective identity in a vaguely specified dialectical re-lation. In a footnote to *Democratic Vistas,* he pondered the "serious problem and paradox in the United States" arising from the "oppositions" of "modern Indi-vidualism" and "the fervid and absorbing love of general country": "I have no doubt myself that the two will merge, and will mutually profit and brace each other, and that from them a greater product . . . will arise."[63]

Such conviction was a key to Whitman's aesthetic defense of diversity as a ba-sis for union. As one study of *Democratic Vistas* concludes, Whitman "turns else-where in an attempt to understand how human experience may be shared and community formed without reducing life to a faceless uniformity. . . . [H]e was not entirely amiss in looking to literature, part of whose special prowess it is to seek out the difficult grounds of human commonality." Skilled artists could, in Whitman's vision, inspire the strength of character necessary to produce genuine individuals: "the greatest poet brings the spirit of any or all events and passions and scenes and persons . . . to bear on your individual character as you hear or read," he assured readers in 1855. Simultaneously, Whitman wrote, "a great poem

62. Stovall 1939, 275, 279, 383; Bromwich 1990, 575.
63. Stovall 1939, 389. On Whitman as individualist, see, e.g., Kateb 1990, 570.

is for ages and ages in common and for all degrees and complexions and all departments and sects and for a woman as much as a man and a man as much as a woman." In the end "this idea of perfect individualism it is indeed that deepest tinges and gives character to the idea of the aggregate." To the extent that the realm of law and politics could not contemplate, much less resolve, such a dialectic, great literary works represented "the medium that shall well nigh express the inexpressible."[64]

Such assurances of aesthetic union's viability added up to a dramatic claim, if one with self-serving aspects. It is unclear whether Whitman was being modest or ornerily honest when he declared the material for this shared cultural experience not yet created: "America has yet morally and artistically accomplished nothing," he wrote in 1871. Similarly underdeveloped was how literary achievement would "fraternize [and] tie the races" and yet appeal specifically to Americans, who in Whitman's view "depend far more on association, identity and place, than is supposed." Whitman only hints at an answer, one that draws on territorial-union claims: "To most it is a secret. This something is rooted in the invisible roots, the profoundest meanings of that place [America] . . . to absorb and again effuse it, uttering words and products as from its midst. . . . Here, and here only, are the foundations for our really valuable and permanent verse, drama, &c."[65]

It remains to wonder how Whitman's account of aesthetic union specifically appeals to the political theorist, Shelley's line about poets as the world's unacknowledged legislators aside. For, apart from occasional asides on participation ("I advise you to enter more strongly yet into politics. I advise every young man to do so"), Whitman's views on diversity and union rarely addressed typical political concerns.[66] Such apparent hesitation could lead back to dismissal of the political Whitman, lamenting with critics "Whitman's limits as a political theorist and apologist for America in the nineteenth century." Yet his account of union through diversity invites us to expand the boundaries of "political" analysis. Nancy Rosenblum's is an apt assessment:

[A]esthetic appreciation is ephemeral and has no direct outcome in political beliefs nor in regular support for the political machinery of constitutions, or organized parties, or voting. Yet Whitman's spectacle of diversity *does* have significance for political theory if we are willing to acknowledge the binding power of aesthetic response, and the fact that Burkean traditionalists have no monopoly on this force for attachment. In Whitman's vision, the plain face of democracy takes on its own enchantment; he loved the spectacle of diversity in the same way that Burke loved monarchical plumage.[67]

64. Chase 1974, 145; Stovall 1939, 322, 334, 390, 335.
65. Stovall 1939, 411, 429.
66. Ibid., 415; see also p. 418.
67. Rosenblum 1990, 585.

Those seeking a precise blueprint for connecting marginalized groups and individuals to one another and to the nation will not find it in Whitman—nor anywhere else in American thought before or since. Whitman appears to have anticipated a desire that would only become widely voiced a century or more later: effecting a more genuinely inclusive unity among American residents while honoring the diverse identities of (and within) constituent groups. At the root of his view was an ethic that proceeded well beyond mere tolerance across group or geographic or other boundaries, to an expansive notion of mutual *identification*. Whitman exalted unity, not sameness or homogeneity. His matter-of-fact poetic embrace of free-laboring blacks, women, wealthy city dwellers, immigrants, farmers, and impoverished people presented all as active and equal participants in everyday economic, social, and political life. This concrete view communicated a sense of solidarity matchable only by the century's great orators, had any chosen diversity as their theme. Whitman does not—could not—logically or empirically defend his commitment to adhesive/aesthetic union. Today we call such a posture "antifoundationalist"; Whitman would instead have termed it faith.

> Many will say it is a dream, and will not follow my inferences: but I
> confidently expect a time when there will be seen, running like a half-
> hid warp through all the myriad audible and visible worldly interests of
> America, threads of manly friendship, fond and loving, pure and sweet,
> strong and life-long, carried to degrees hitherto unknown—not only giv-
> ing tone to individual character . . . but having the deepest relations to
> general politics.[68]

Whitman's vision of union through diversity was little honored in his time, as his writings attracted only a few faithful followers compared to the audiences of a Webster or an Emerson. Yet it deserves attention in our own. If a "more perfect" union today is one affirming diverse elements on their own terms, in a process of mutual exchange, aesthetic achievement would seem a critical—if oddly unacknowledged—feature of this process. The gains in African American, Latino, and other minority-group inclusion in the national whole in recent years have in no small part come via the dominant "aesthetic" institutions of our time—not, as Whitman hoped, through poetry but through the mighty American entertainment complex: movies, literature, sports, music, television. A self-acknowledged "black feminist" voice, Oprah Winfrey's, currently wields more influence over Americans' literary choices than "anyone in the country's history," according to a recent study of "Oprah's Book Club."[69] Whitman affirmed those benefits in a way that took more than a century of cultural development to attain. And he did so, significantly, with the express purpose of strengthening national union.

68. Stovall 1939, 432.
69. Max 1999, 26.

Aspirations to realize a "more perfect" national union were a constant feature of American public conversation across the late eighteenth and nineteenth centuries. In what respects was that goal met? A viable national union was sustained, as Madison and other framers dearly hoped it would be, for seventy-five years after the constitutional convention and was swiftly rebuilt after the Civil War. Underpinning this political stability was a sense of unity expressed by most Americans, as far as the public record reveals, that waxed and waned but remained palpable throughout the period. Beyond this accomplishment, neither strong ethnocultural nor principled moral understandings of union were fully realized. The term represented a sterling promise at times, when its proponents encouraged Americans to substantiate fundamental guarantees of liberty and equality by extending the bounds of inclusion of their national union. Others sought to employ the concept for exclusionary purposes and to write various groups (by region, race, religion, gender, ethnicity, and so on) out of the circle of unity.

This mixed history of the effects of union ideas in American political life yields a varied set of conclusions, with double-edged implications. Some past evidence suggests that it is possible to encourage affective bonds and common sentiment without resorting to appeals to ethnocultural intolerance, and that national unity can be advanced in tandem with other cherished ideas, such as universal liberty or equality. Yet equally strong historical experience implies that unionist dreams are fated to vanish before a powerful style of self-interested politics, or that these hopes can become nightmares. For those seeking a robustly unified people in the present, U.S. history (as is so often the case) provides ample materials for both hope and dismay.

Contrasting his version of a desirable national polity to Federalist-era reality, James Fenimore Cooper wrote in 1820 that his preferred "Union must remain, for some years to come, a promise to be fulfilled." [70] Cooper's words recurred among public speakers for decades, until unionist aspirations as such faded away. National union, on the morally progressive dimensions Cooper and many others—most prominently Douglass and Lincoln—encouraged, always remained an unfulfilled promise, a receding dream. James Morone identifies an "elusive," plaintive "call to community and collectivism" as a Sisyphan feature of American politics. Better to discard such "illegitimate" "civic myths" before disappointment (or worse) strikes, a host of writers advise. Rogers Smith warns that American opinion leaders' misleading "narratives of meaningful civic membership" have frequently tended to "cloak the exploitation of citizens by their leaders, demonize innocent outsiders, and foster invidious inequalities among the members of a regime." [71]

70. Cooper 1960, 1:90.
71. Morone 1990, 73; Kymlicka 1995, 189–90; Smith 1997, 33–34 (cf. ibid., 504–5).

Yet advancing hopeful visions of national unity was and can still be a powerfully inspirational act. Compelling accounts of a "Union worthy of saving," in Lincoln's words, took numerous forms in eighteenth- and nineteenth-century America. A basic version remained consistent across time: that a well-constituted union, variously grounded in affective bonds, obedience to law, and universal equality, would help to advance national security, reduce the effects of faction, secure individual liberty, and provide a stable, prosperous future for the residents of all U.S. states and regions. Lincoln, among our greatest national storytellers, told such tales about the benefits of union, emphasizing their moral promise; so did Webster (if usually with himself in the protagonist's role). Even the comparatively restrained Madison spun hopeful parables about his countrymen's solidarity, some much more evocative than his *Federalist* accounts of extended territory and dispersed factions. In 1820 Madison penned a short fictional essay titled "Jonathan Bull and Mary Bull," a thinly disguised allegory of the Missouri crisis then unfolding. Madison did not circulate the piece, but it caused a flurry of interest when published after his death, during the 1850s. Drew McCoy emphasizes the tale's value as an insight into Madison's view of slavery: the point for our purposes is that "in his happy ending, Madison could continue to describe, with obvious pride, an extraordinarily prosperous union."[72] Such a principled, inclusive American union was not realized in Madison's lifetime, or in that of any of the other figures previously examined. But these inspiring leaders continued to assert unionist dreams, offering antidotes to Americans' propensity to seek fellowship in less admirable ways.

Such examples suggest a further, modest option for those concerned about declining communal spirit but equally alarmed at the likelihood that strong-nationalist themes eventually translate into illiberal intolerance and even barbarism. Relating narratives of national union (as of any prized or reviled value) in the American past inevitably colors citizens' views of their mutual bonds in the present and future. Indeed, the political import of "storytelling" is acknowledged by a range of writers, including social scientists and legal scholars.[73] One account of American national unity depicts a people connected by shared (if imperfectly realized) ideals as well as by a historical tradition riddled with fault lines but displaying reserves of nobility. Restrained by institutional protections and featuring at least a few leaders aware of their power to encourage solidarity—and of both the good and ill effects of fraternal sentiment—this union is open to improvement, if not perfection. Competing stories range from accounts of pathological inequality borne of buccaneer laissez-faire and unremitting discrimination to complacent defenses of an Anglo-Saxon (or, more often today, "Western") people united to fulfill the destiny conferred upon them by God. Of these three his-

72. McCoy 1989, 274–76.
73. See Sandel 1996, 350–51 ("Political community depends on the narratives by which people make sense of their condition and interpret the common life they share . . . human beings are storytelling beings"); cf. the qualified affirmation of "story" in legal studies by Farber and Sherry 1997.

torical archetypes, the first seems most accurate. It is also the story that deserves telling, if closer political union in the present is an aim. For divergent narratives will assuredly be spun.

Politics is not physics, as the Victorian thinker Walter Bagehot observed; popular beliefs and impressions decisively influence political outcomes. For those Americans serving as teachers or policymakers, or otherwise occupying public and private institutions charged with the task of incubating civic responsibility, the power to affect national ideals is inherent in our portrayals of the republic's past, present, and future. The qualifiedly "noble" version of Americans' attempts to improve their national union is a tale worth honoring. Two speakers implicitly acknowledging this fact come to mind, connecting unionist dreams in the past and present. Martin Luther King Jr., in his famous 1963 speech at the Lincoln Memorial, expressed the core of his "dream" thus: "the sons of former slaves and the sons of former slave-owners [united] at the table of brotherhood." Some eighty years before, Frederick Douglass looked back at the wartime period from the gloomy aftermath of Reconstruction and recalled union along with emancipation as "moral and humane . . . eternal principles[,] for which our sons and brothers encountered . . . danger and death."[74] Douglass's recognition of the potency of historical memory, King's willingness to imagine an integrated future, and both men's inclination in troubled times to reaffirm the promise of American unity are bridges of enduring span.

74. King 1963; Blassingame 1979–94, 5:170.

Appendix

METHODS AND SOURCES

As noted in the introduction's brief "Note on Method," I supplemented my general reading and political-theory analysis with empirical research, based on a large sample of American newspapers between 1750 and 1900. Newspapers were selected according to the following criteria: *representativeness*, regional and partisan (sources were chosen in rough approximation of a region's population, following the decennial census, and I used the partisan makeup of Congress in each period to guide my selection of Democratic, Whig, Republican, and eventually nonpartisan journals); *longevity* (where possible I used journals published over a long period of time, to ensure some degree of consistency in content and readership); and *completeness* of issues available to researchers today—harder to achieve for black-owned papers and, during some periods, for all papers.[1]

My database was compiled using four issues of each newspaper in my sample for every other year between 1750 and 1900. (In a few instances, I coded newspapers from several consecutive years, for reasons indicated in the relevant tables in the text.) For standardization's sake I tried to use issues published on or near the fifth of January, April, July, and October. I chose these dates to pick up July 4 coverage, for obvious reasons. Because of sporadic availability, especially in the early years, I sometimes had to deviate considerably from those dates. The entire list of papers, grouped by twenty-five–year increments, appears at the end of this appendix.

Coding was based on "page" of news/editorial content—not a standard category across time and different papers. I counted as a "page" those on which at least half the columns were devoted to news or editorial commentary. This permits rough comparability within time periods: newspapers from the 1750s–1820s were almost always four-page broadsheets, usually with four columns per page; by the 1880s papers ran to dozens of pages and had as many as eight columns across. Because newspapers changed dramatically in size, readership, and editorial purposes between the American colonial years and the early nineteenth century (and evolved further during that century), I provide no time series displaying union usage over the entire perod from 1750 to 1900. Instead, the results of my coding are reported for specific chronological segments.

As with any such enterprise, various minor problems of classification arose. Worthy of mention here was how to count "United States" and "U.S.," given their shared root with "union." I split my coding at 1790: before then, the "United" part still carried strong symbolic significance, and "United States" had not yet become the routine official designation for the country. Thus I included these as "union" references. After 1790 I coded U.S. and United States as a separate category, except when the source put unusual stress on the

---

1. Compare the similar analyses of Merritt 1966 and Alexander 1990; and see Brooke 1991.

"United" part. A typical example was a *Raleigh Register* editorial comment: "These '*United* States' may scarcely be called thus; they are as *dis*united as before the Revolution."[2] Because of this change, comparisons of union usage in the years before and after 1790 are misleading; thus no table is included featuring these years. One other coding decision: regularly appearing in newspapers then as now were long "news" items that reprinted a president's or other notable's speech, and at times the speaker would repeat a single referent over and over and over. I counted such instances as a maximum of ten references only.

In a few instances, particularly during the years 1750–75 and for counts of African Americans' union references during antebellum and Civil War years, I supplemented the thin newspaper record with other sources. Those are noted following the newspaper list below. In coding these sources I used ten pages per year, randomly chosen, from each collection of papers or record of congressional speeches. All the collected papers (e.g., of Franklin or Douglass) are in similarly sized volumes, so I counted union references per page. For black Congress members' speeches, I counted references per page in the *Congressional Globe;* that volume's large size may have skewed the average slightly downward.

Following is the list of newspapers I used for coding. Some papers changed their names often during the years covered; the *Mobile Advertiser* (Alabama), for example, was variously titled the *Advertiser, Daily Advertiser and Register,* and *Daily Advertiser* in the mid-1850s. I list these only once, based on the most commonly used title during the relevant period. And where papers were not published (or copies were not available to me) for all of the period indicated, I list starting and stopping date in brackets: thus the *Connecticut Gazette,* which began publishing in 1755 and stopped in 1768, has those dates indicated.

LIST OF NEWSPAPERS USED FOR CODING

1750–75
Boston Evening Post
Boston Gazette
Boston Post-Boy [no issues avail. 1755–63]
Connecticut Courant (Hartford) [beg. 1764]
Connecticut Gazette (New Haven) [1755–68]
Georgia Gazette (Savannah) [beg. 1763]
Maryland Gazette (Annapolis)
New Hampshire Gazette (Portsmouth) [numerous names; beg. 1756]
New York Evening Post (New York) [to 1753]
New York Gazette and The Weekly Mercury (New York) [beg. 1752]
New-York Weekly Journal (New York) [to 1751]
North Carolina Gazette (New Bern) [beg. 1751; no issues avail. 1760–67]
Pennsylvania Gazette (Philadelphia)
Pennsylvania Journal and The Weekly Advertiser (Philadelphia)
South Carolina Gazette (Charleston)
Virginia Gazette (Williamsburg)

1776–1800
American Minerva (New York) [beg. 1793; after 1797 *Commercial Advertiser*]
Aurora (Philadelphia) [beg. 1794]
Boston Gazette [to 1798]
Carlisle Weekly Gazette (Pa.) [beg. 1785]

2. *Raleigh Register,* October 5, 1827.

Charleston City Gazette (S.C.) [beg. 1787]
Connecticut Courant (Hartford)
Freeman's Journal (Philadelphia) [1781–92]
Georgia Gazette (Savannah) [resumed 1788]
Independent Chronicle (Boston)
Kentucky Gazette (Lexington) [beg. 1787]
Maryland Gazette (Annapolis)
Massachusetts Spy (Worcester)
Mercantile Advertiser (New York) [beg. 1792]
New Hampshire Gazette (Portsmouth) [numerous names]
New-Jersey Journal (Elizabethtown) [beg. 1786]
New York Gazette and The Weekly Mercury (New York) [to 1783]
North Carolina Gazette (New Bern) [no issues avail. 1789–84]
Pennsylvania Evening Post (Philadelphia) [to 1784]
Pennsylvania Gazette (Philadelphia) [to 1789]
Richmond Gazette [beg. 1781; no issues 1787–89]
South Carolina & American-General Gazette (Charleston) [to 1783]
Vermont Gazette (Bennington) [beg. 1784]

1801–25

Albany Argus (N.Y.) [beg. 1813]
Arkansas Gazette (Arkansas Post) [beg. 1819]
Augusta Chronicle (Georgia)
Aurora (Philadelphia) [to 1812]
Baltimore Daily Advertiser [1807–19]
Carlisle Gazette (Pennsylvania) [to 1817]
Charleston Courier (S.C.) [beg. 1803]
Connecticut Courant (Hartford)
Commercial Advertiser (New York) [to 1820]
Fayetteville Observer (N.C.) [beg. 1816]
Independent Chronicle (Boston)
Inquisitor and Advertiser (Cincinnati) [beg. 1818]
Kentucky Gazette (Lexington)
Louisiana Gazette (New Orleans) [1804–17]
Maryland Gazette (Annapolis)
Massachusetts Spy (Worcester) [to 1820]
Newburyport Herald (Mass.) [to 1820]
National Intelligencer (Washington, D.C.) [to 1812]
New-York Evening Post [beg. 1801]
Raleigh Register (N.C.)
Richmond Enquirer [beg. 1804]
Salem Gazette (Mass.) [to 1820]
Sentinel of Freedom (Newark, N.J.) [to 1820]
Vermont Gazette (Bennington) [beg. 1816]

1826–50

Baltimore Sun [beg. 1837]
Charleston Courier (S.C.)
Cincinnati Enquirer
Colored American (New York and Philadelphia) [1837–42]

Connecticut Courant (Hartford) [to 1843]
Federal Union (Milledgeville, Ga.) [beg. 1830]
Frederick Douglass' Paper (Rochester, N.Y.) [beg. 1847]
Independent Chronicle (Boston)
Lancaster Examiner (Pa.) [beg. 1830]
Liberator (Boston) [beg. 1831]
Louisiana Courier (New Orleans)
Louisville Journal (Ky.) [beg. 1830]
Maine Democrat (Biddeford) [beg. 1835]
Middlesex Gazette (Conn.) [to 1833]
Mobile Register (Ala.) [to 1848]
New Haven Register (Conn.) [beg. 1840]
New York Evening Post
Painesville Telegraph (Ohio) [1834–46]
Philadelphia Gazette [to 1845]
Picayune (New Orleans) [beg. 1837]
Raleigh Register (N.C.)
Richmond Enquirer
Richmond Whig
Sangamo Journal (Springfield, Ill.) [1831–49]
Tarboro Press (N.C.) [beg. 1832]
Vermont Gazette (Bennington) [to 1848]
Weekly Banner (Athens, Ga.) [beg. 1831]

1851–75
Alta Californian (San Francisco)
American and Commercial Advertiser (Baltimore) [beg. 1857]
Atlanta Constitution [beg. 1868]
Boston Post
Charleston Daily Courier
Chicago Daily Tribune [beg. 1855]
Cincinnati Enquirer
Daily Advertiser (Mobile, Ala.) [to 1861]
Daily Arkansas Gazette (Little Rock) [beg. 1865]
Daily Plain Dealer (Cleveland)
Daily Standard (Raleigh, N.C.) [beg. 1865]
The Elevator (San Francisco) [beg. 1865]
Federal Union (Milledgeville, Ga.) [to 1872]
Frederick Douglass' Paper (Rochester, N.Y.) [to 1863]
Herald (Newberry, S.C.) [beg. 1865]
Idaho World (Boise) [beg. 1865]
Illinois State Journal (Springfield) [beg. 1855]
Independent (New York)
Kansas Herald of Freedom (Lawrence) [1855–73]
Lebanon Courier (Pa.)
Mobile Register (Ala.)
New Haven Register (Conn.)
New Orleans Times–Picayune
New York Times

Philadelphia Inquirer
Raleigh News [beg. 1871]
Richmond Enquirer
Richmond Whig
San Francisco Chronicle [beg. 1865]
Southern Banner (Athens, Ga.)
Workingman's Advocate (Chicago) [beg. 1863]

1876–1900
Alta Californian (San Francisco) [to 1891]
Atlanta Constitution
Baltimore Sun
Bennington Banner (Vt.)
Chicago Tribune
Cincinnati Enquirer
Cleveland Plain Dealer
Daily Arkansas Gazette [to 1889]
The Elevator (San Francisco) [to 1898]
Florida Times–Union (Jacksonville) [beg. 1881]
Galveston Daily News (Tex.)
Idaho Weekly Statesman (Boise) [to 1891]
Iowa State Register (Des Moines)
Leavenworth Evening Standard (Kans.) [beg. 1878]
Milwaukee Sentinel (Wisc.)
National Labor Tribune (Pittsburgh) [beg. 1876]
New Haven Register
New York Evening Post
New York Times
Philadelphia Inquirer
Raleigh News
Richmond Dispatch
Richmond Whig [to 1888]
Rocky Mountain News (Denver)
Washington Post [beg. 1877]
Worcester Gazette (Mass.)

LIST OF OTHER REFERENCES USED IN CODING

1750–75
Samuel Adams Papers
Benjamin Franklin Papers

1825–50 and 1851–76
Speeches by African-American members of Congress
Frederick Douglass Papers

References

Abbot, W. W., et al., eds. 1983–93. *The Papers of George Washington: Colonial Series.* 8 vols. Charlottesville: University Press of Virginia.

Abbott, Richard H. 1997. "Civil War Origins of the Southern Republican Press." *Civil War History* 43.

Ackerman, Bruce. 1991. *We the People: Foundations.* Cambridge: Harvard University Press.

———. 1998. *We the People: Transformations.* Cambridge: Harvard University Press.

———. 2000. "The New Separation of Powers." *Harvard Law Review* 113.

Ackerman, Bruce, and Anne Alstott. 1999. *The Stakeholder Society.* New Haven: Yale University Press.

Adair, Douglass. 1974. *Fame and the Founding Fathers: Essays.* Ed. H. Trevor Colbourn. New York: Norton.

Adams, Henry. 1909. *History of the United States of America during the First Administration of Thomas Jefferson.* 2 vols. New York: Charles Scribner's Sons.

———. 1930. *History of the United States of America during the Administration of James Madison.* 2 vols. New York: Albert and Charles Boni.

Adams, John. 1954 [1766–67]. "Replies to Philanthrop." In G. A. Peek Jr., ed., *The Political Writings of John Adams.* Indianapolis: Bobbs-Merrill.

Adams, John, and Daniel Leonard. 1819 [1775]. *Novanglus and Massachusettensis.* Boston: Hews and Goss.

Adeleke, Tunde. 1998. *UnAfrican Americans: Nineteenth-Century Black Nationalists and the Civilizing Mission.* Lexington: University Press of Kentucky.

Adelman, Jeremy, and Stephen Aron. 1999. "From Borderlands to Borders: Empires, Nation-States, and the Peoples in between in North American History." *American Historical Review* 104.

Ahlstrom, Sidney. 1972. *A Religious History of the American People.* New Haven: Yale University Press.

Alba, Richard D. 1990. *Ethnic Identity: The Transformation of White America.* New Haven: Yale University Press.

Alexander, John K. 1990. *The Selling of the Constitutional Convention: A History of News Coverage.* Madison, Wis.: Madison House.

Alison, Francis. 1758. "Peace and Union Recommended." Philadelphia: W. Dunlap.

Alley, Robert S., ed. 1985. *James Madison on Religious Liberty.* Buffalo, N.Y.: Prometheus Books.

Altschuler, Glenn C., and Stuart M. Blumin. 1997. "Limits of Political Engagement in Antebellum America: A New Look at the Golden Age of Participatory Democracy." *Journal of American History* 84.

Amar, Akhil Reed. 1991. "Some New World Lessons for the Old World." *University of Chicago Law Review* 58.

———. 1998. *The Bill of Rights.* New Haven: Yale University Press.

"American Nationality." 1861. Philadelphia: Peter Walker.

Ammon, Harry. 1990. *James Monroe: The Quest for National Identity.* 2d ed. Charlottesville: University Press of Virginia.

Anbinder, Tyler. 1992. *Nativism and Slavery: The Northern Know-Nothings in the Politics of the 1850s.* New York: Oxford University Press.

Anderson, Benedict. 1983. *Imagined Communities: Reflections on the Origin and Spread of Nationalism.* London: Verso.

Anderson, Dwight G. 1988. "Quest for Immortality: A Theory of Abraham Lincoln's Political Psychology." In Gabor S. Boritt, ed. 1988, *The Historian's Lincoln.* Urbana: University of Illinois Press.

Anderson, Fred. 2000. *Crucible of War: The Seven Years' War and the Fate of Empire in North America, 1754–1766.* New York: Knopf.

Andrew, Edward. 1989. "Equality of Opportunity as the Noble Lie." *History of Political Thought* 10.

Andrews, Charles M. 1931. *The Colonial Background of the American Revolution.* Rev. ed. New Haven: Yale University Press.

———, ed. 1915. *Narratives of the Insurrections, 1675–1690.* New York: *Charles Scribner's Sons.*

Andrews, Sidney. 1866a. *The South since the War.* Boston: Ticknor and Fields.

———. 1866b. "Three Months among the Reconstructionists." *Atlantic Monthly* 17.

Antholis, William John. 1993. "Liberal Democratic Theory and the Transformation of Sovereignty." Ph.D. diss. Yale University.

Appleby, Joyce. 1992. *Liberalism and Republicanism in the Historical Imagination.* Cambridge: Harvard University Press.

Aptheker, Herbert, ed. 1962. *A Documentary History of the Negro People of the United States.* New York: Citadel Press.

Arendt, Hannah. 1963. *On Revolution.* New York: Penguin Books.

Argersinger, Peter H. 1992. *Structure, Process, and Party: Essays in American Political History.* Armonk, N.Y.: M. E. Sharpe.

Arieli, Yehoshua. 1964. *Individualism and Nationalism in American Ideology.* Cambridge: Harvard University Press.

Ashe, Samuel A. 1925. *History of North Carolina.* 2 vols. Raleigh, N.C.: Edwards & Broughton.

Aspiz, Harold. 1994. "The Body Politic in 'Democratic Vistas.'" In Ed Folsom, ed., *Walt Whitman: The Centennial Essays.* Iowa City: University of Iowa Press.

Augst, Thomas. 1999. "Composing the Moral Senses: Emerson and the Politics of Character in Nineteenth-Century America." *Political Theory* 27.

Ayers, Edward L. 1992. *The Promise of the New South: Life after Reconstruction.* New York: Oxford University Press.

Backus, Isaac. 1754. "All True Ministers of the Gospel." Boston: Fowle.

Bacon, Jacqueline. 1998. "'Do You Understand Your Own Language?' Revolutionary *Topoi* in the Rhetoric of African-American Abolitionists." *Rhetoric Society Quarterly* 28.

Baier, Annette C. 1993. "How Can Individualists Share Responsibility?" *Political Theory* 21.

Bailyn, Bernard. 1967. *The Ideological Origins of the American Revolution.* Cambridge: Harvard University Press.

———, ed. 1965. *Pamphlets of the American Revolution.* New Haven: Yale University Press.

———. 1993. *The Debate on the Constitution.* 2 vols. New York: Library of America.

Baker, Jean H. 1983. *Affairs of Party: The Political Culture of Northern Democrats in the Mid-Nineteenth Century.* Ithaca: Cornell University Press.

Ball, Terence, James Farr, and Russell L. Hanson, eds. 1989. *Political Innovation and Conceptual Change.* Minneapolis: University of Minnesota Press.

Bancroft, Charles. 1879. *The Footprints of Time: And a Complete Analysis of Our American System of Government.* Burlington, Iowa: R. T. Rust.

Bancroft, George. 1861–97. *History of the United States of America.* 10 vols. New York: Appleton.

Banner, James M. 1970. *To the Hartford Convention: The Federalists and the Origins of Party Politics.* New York: Knopf.

Banning, Lance. 1983. "James Madison and the Nationalists, 1780–1783." *William and Mary Quarterly* 40.

———. 1995. *The Sacred Fire of Liberty: James Madison and the Founding of the Federal Republic.* Ithaca: Cornell University Press.

Bannister, Robert C., ed. 1992. *On Liberty, Society, and Politics: The Essential Essays of William Graham Sumner.* Indianapolis: Liberty Fund.

Barber, Benjamin. 1998. *A Place for Us.* Princeton, N.J.: Princeton University Press.

Barck, Oscar Theodore, and Hugh Talmage Lefler. 1958. *Colonial America.* New York: Macmillan.

Barnes, Elizabeth. 1997. "Affecting Relations: Pedagogy, Patriarchy, and the Politics of Sympathy." *American Literary History* 26.

Barnes, Viola F. 1923. *The Dominion of New England: A Study in British Colonial Policy.* New Haven: Yale University Press.

Bartlett, Irving H. 1967. *The American Mind in the Mid-Nineteenth Century.* New York: Thomas Y. Crowell Co.

Barton, William Eleazar. 1928. *Abraham Lincoln and Walt Whitman.* Indianapolis: Bobbs-Merrill.

Baseler, Marilyn C. 1998. *"Asylum for Mankind": America, 1607–1800.* Ithaca: Cornell University Press.

Basler, Roy P., ed. 1953–55. *The Collected Works of Abraham Lincoln.* 9 vols. New Brunswick, N.J.: Rutgers University Press.

———. 1989 [1946]. *Abraham Lincoln: His Speeches and Writings.* New York: Da Capo Press.

Bassett, T. D. Seymour. 1999. "Vermont's Nineteenth-Century Civil Religion." *Vermont History* 67.

Bates, Frank Greene. 1898. "Rhode Island and the Formation of the Union." Ph.D. diss. Columbia University.

Battle, Kemp P. 1893. *The Early History of Raleigh, the Capital City of North Carolina.* Raleigh, N.C.: Edwards & Broughton.

Bean, Frank D., Robert G. Cushing, and Charles W. Haynes. 1997. "The Changing Demography of U.S. Immigration Flows." In Klaus J. Bade and Myron Weiner, *Migration Past, Migration Future.* London: Berghan Books.

Beard, Charles A. 1935 [1913]. *An Economic Interpretation of the Constitution of the United States.* New York: Macmillan Company.

Beatty, Jack. 1996. "Victories without Victors." *Atlantic Monthly* 278 (December).

Beecher, Lyman. 1820. "Gospel and Union." *Reformer* 1 (October).

Beer, Samuel H. 1984. "Liberty and Union: Walt Whitman's Idea of the Nation." *Political Theory* 12.

——. 1993. *To Make a Nation: The Rediscovery of American Federalism.* Cambridge: Harvard University Press.

Beisner, Robert L. 1986. *From the Old Diplomacy to the New, 1865–1900.* 2d ed. Arlington Heights, Ill.: Harlan Davidson.

Bell, Howard Holman. 1969. *A Survey of the Negro Convention Movement, 1830–1861.* 2d ed. New York: Arno Press.

Bellah, Robert N., et al. 1985. *Habits of the Heart: Individualism and Commitment in American Life.* Berkeley: University of California Press.

Belz, Herman. 1986. "Abraham Lincoln and American Constitutionalism." *Review of Politics* 50.

Bender, Thomas. 1978. *Community and Social Change in America.* New Brunswick, N.J.: Rutgers University Press.

——. 1979. "The Cultures of Intellectual Life: The City and the Professions." In John Higham and Paul K. Conkin, eds., *New Directions in American Intellectual History.* Baltimore: Johns Hopkins University Press.

Benedict, Michael Les. 1974. "Preserving the Constitution: The Conservative Basis of Radical Reconstruction." *Journal of American History* 65.

——. 1997. "Salmon P. Chase and Constitutional Politics." *Law and Social* Inquiry 22.

Bensel, Richard Franklin. 1984. *Sectionalism and American Political Development, 1880–1980.* Madison: University of Wisconsin Press.

——. 1987. "Southern Leviathan: The Development of Central State Authority in the Confederate States of America." *Studies in American Political Development* 2.

——. 1990. *Yankee Leviathan: The Origins of Central State Authority in America, 1859–1877.* New York: Cambridge University Press.

Bentley, George R. 1955. *A History of the Freedmen's Bureau.* Philadelphia: University of Pennsylvania Press.

Bercovitch, Sacvan. 1985. "Emerson the Prophet: Romanticism, Puritanism, and Auto-American Biography." In Harold Bloom, ed., *Ralph Waldo Emerson: Modern Critical Views.* New York: Chelsea House.

Berens, J. F. 1978. *Providence and Patriotism in Early America, 1640–1815.* Charlottesville: University Press of Virginia.

Berkhofer, Robert F. 1979. *The White Man's Indian: Images of the American Indian from Columbus to the Present.* New York: Vintage.

Bernard, Francis. 1774. *Select Letters on the Trade and Government of America.* London: T. Payne.

Berthoff, Rowland. 1997. *Republic of the Dispossessed : The Exceptional Old-European Consensus in America.* Columbia: University of Missouri Press.

Berthoff, Rowland, and John M. Murrin. 1973. "Feudalism, Communalism, and the Yeoman Freeholder." In Stephen G. Kurtz and James H. Hutson, eds., *Essays on the American Revolution.* Chapel Hill: University of North Carolina Press.

Bessette, Joseph M. 1994. *The Mild Voice of Reason: Deliberative Democracy and American National Government.* Chicago: University of Chicago Press.

Blassingame, J. W., ed. 1979–94. *The Frederick Douglass Papers.* 5 vols. New Haven: Yale University Press.

Blight, David W. 1989. *Frederick Douglass's Civil War: Keeping Faith in Jubilee.* Baton Rouge: Louisiana State University Press.

Bloom, Harold. 1971. *The Ringers in the Tower: Studies in the Romantic Tradition.* Chicago: University of Chicago Press.

Boardman, Helen, ed. 1947. "Letter to the American Slaves." *Common Ground* 7.

Boesche, Roger. 1998. "Thinking about Freedom." *Political Theory* 26.

Bogdanor, Vernon. 1999. "Devolution: Decentralisation or Disintegration?" *Political Quarterly* 70.

Bogue, Allan G. 1986. "Why Has the History of the U.S. Congress Been Unpopular?" *Congress and the Presidency* 13: 119–22.

Bonomi, Patricia U. 1986. *Under the Cope of Heaven: Religion, Society, and Politics in Colonial America.* New York: Oxford University Press.

Bonwick, Colin. 1977. *English Radicals and the American Revolution.* Chapel Hill: University of North Carolina Press.

Boorstin, Daniel. 1965. *The Americans.* 3 vols. New York: Vintage Books.

Bordin, Ruth. 1981. *Woman and Temperance: The Quest for Power and Liberty, 1873–1900.* Philadelphia: Temple University Press.

Boritt, Gabor S. 1988. "Lincoln and the Economics of the American Dream." In Boritt, ed. 1988, *The Historian's Lincoln: Pseudohistory, Psychohistory, and History.* Urbana: University of Illinois Press.

———, ed. 1992. *Why the Confederacy Lost.* New York: Oxford University Press.

Boucher, Chauncey. 1921. "*In Re* that Aggressive Slavocracy." *Mississippi Valley Historical Review* 8.

Boudin, Louis B. 1932. *Government by Judiciary.* New York: W. Godwin.

Bowen, Catherine Drinker. 1961. *John Adams and the American Revolution.* Boston: Little, Brown.

Boxill, Bernard R. 1999. "Douglass against the Emigrationists." In Bill E. Lawson and Frank M. Kirkland, eds., *Frederick Douglass: A Critical Reader.* Oxford: Blackwell.

Boyd, Julian P. 1941. *Anglo-American Union: Joseph Galloway's Plans to Preserve the British Empire, 1774–1788.* Philadelphia: University of Pennsylvania Press.

Boyd, Julian P., et al., eds. 1950–. *The Papers of Thomas Jefferson.* 27 vols. Princeton, N.J.: Princeton University Press.

Bradley, Bill. 1998. "America's Challenge." In Dionne ed. 1998, 107–14.

Bradley, Patricia. 1998. *Slavery, Propaganda, and the American Revolution.* Jackson: University Press of Mississippi.

Branham, Robert James. 1996. "'Of Thee I Sing': Contesting 'America.'" *American Quarterly* 48.

———. 1999. "'God Save the ____!' American National Songs and National Identities, 1760–1798." *Quarterly Journal of Speech* 85.

Brant, Irving. 1941–61. *James Madison.* 6 vols. Indianapolis: Bobbs-Merrill.

Breck, Robert L. 1862. *The Habeas Corpus and Martial Law.* Cincinnati, Ohio: R. H. Collins.

Breen, T. H. 1994. "'Baubles of Britain': The American and Consumer Revolutions of the Eighteenth Century." In Cary Carson et al., eds., *Of Consuming Interests: The Style of Life in the Eighteenth Century.* Charlottesville: University Press of Virginia.

———. 1997. "Ideology and Nationalism on the Eve of the American Revolution: Revisions *Once More* in Need of Revising." *Journal of American History* 84.

Bremer, Francis J. 1994. *Congregational Communion: Clerical Friendship in the Anglo-American Puritan Community, 1610–1692.* Boston: Northeastern University Press.

Breuilly, John. 1982. *Nationalism and the State.* Chicago: University of Chicago Press.

Brinkley, Alan. 1998. *Liberalism and Its Discontents.* Cambridge: Harvard University Press.

Brodhead, John Romeyn, ed. 1858. *Documents Relative to the Colonial History of New York.* 15 vols. Albany, N.Y.: Weed, Parsons.

Bromwich, David. 1990. "Whitman and Memory: A Response to Kateb." *Political Theory* 18.

Brooke, John L. 1991. "Talking and Reading in Early America." *Reviews in American History* 19.

Brooks, Christopher K. 1996. "Controlling the Metaphor: Language and Self-Definition in Revolutionary America." *Clio* 25.

Brown, Richard D. 1996. *The Strength of a People: The Idea of an Informed Citizenry in America, 1650–1870.* Chapel Hill: University of North Carolina Press.

Brown, William Wells. 1867. *The Negro in the American Revolution: His Heroism and His Fidelity.* Boston: Lee and Shepard.

Brownson, Orestes A. 1866. *The American Republic: Its Constitution, Tendencies, and Destiny.* New York: P. O'Shea.

Bruce, Dickson D. 1995. "National Identity and African-American Colonization, 1773–1817." *Historian* 58.

Bruce, Robert V. 1992. "The Shadow of a Coming War." In Gabor S. Boritt, ed., *Lincoln, the War President: The Gettysburg Lectures.* New York: Oxford University Press.

Bruyn, Severyn T. 1999. "The Moral Economy." *Review of Social Economy* 57.

Bryce, James. 1896. *The American Commonwealth.* New York: Macmillan.

Bukovansky, Mlada. 1997. "American Identity and Neutral Rights from Independence to the War of 1812." *International Organization* 51.

Bumsted, J. M. 1974. "'Things in the Womb of Time': Ideas of American Independence, 1633–1763." *William and Mary Quarterly* 31.

Burnaby, Andrew. 1904 [1775]. *Travels through the Middle Settlements in North America, in the Years 1759 and 1760.* New York: A. M. Kelley.

Burnett, Edmund C., ed. 1921–36. *Letters of Members of the Continental Congress.* 8 vols. Washington, D.C.: Carnegie Institution.

Burnham, Walter Dean. 1999. "Constitutional Moments and Punctuated Equilibria: A Political Scientist Confronts Bruce Ackerman's *We the People.*" *Yale Law Journal* 108.

Burns, James MacGregor. 1963. *Deadlock of Democracy.* Englewood Cliffs, N.J.: Prentice-Hall.

Burr, Virginia Ingraham, ed. 1990. *The Secret Eye: The Journal of Ella Gertrude Clanton Thomas, 1848–1889.* Chapel Hill: University of North Carolina Press.

Burrows, Edwin G., and Mike Wallace. 1999. *Gotham: A History of New York City to 1898.* New York: Oxford University Press.

Burstein, Andrew. 1999. *Sentimental Democracy: The Evolution of America's Self-Image.* New York: Hill and Wang.

Bushe, Charles Kendall. 1798. "The Union: Cease Your Funning." Dublin: James Moore.

Bushman, Richard L. 1967. *From Puritan to Yankee: Character and the Social Order in Connecticut, 1690–1765.* Cambridge: Harvard University Press.

Bushnell, Horace. 1847. *Barbarism the First Danger: A Discourse for Home Missions.* New York: Wm. Osborn.

Butler, Jon. 1990. *Awash in a Sea of Faith: Christianizing the American People.* Cambridge: Harvard University Press.

Butts, R. Freeman, and Lawrence A. Cremin. 1953. *A History of Education in American Culture.* New York: Holt, Rinehart, and Winston.

Byrnes, Joseph F. 1999. "Priests and *Instituteurs* in the *Union Sacrée:* Reconciliation and Its Limits." *French Historical Studies* 22.

Calhoon, Robert. 1991. "Religion and Individualism in Early America." In R. O. Curry and L. B. Goodheart, eds., *American Chameleon: Individualism in Trans-National Context*. Kent, Ohio: Kent State University Press.

Calhoun, Craig. 1998. "The Public Good as a Social and Cultural Project." In Walter W. Powell and Elisabeth S. Clemens, eds., *Private Action and the Public Good*. New Haven: Yale University Press.

Calloway, Colin G. 1995. *The American Revolution in Indian Country: Crisis and Diversity in Native American Communities*. New York: Cambridge University Press.

———, ed. 1994. *The World Turned Upside Down: Indian Voices from Early America*. Boston: Bedford Books.

Campbell, Charles S. 1976. *The Transformation of American Foreign Relations, 1865–1900*. New York: Harper and Row.

Caney, Simon. 1992. "Liberalism and Communitarianism: A Misconceived Debate." *Political Studies* 40.

Cantrell, Gregg. 1992. "Southerner and Nativist: Kenneth Rayner and the Ideology of 'Americanism.'" *North Carolina Historical Review* 69.

Cappon, Lester J., ed. 1971. *The Adams-Jefferson Letters*. New York: Simon & Schuster.

Carey, Anthony Gene. 1997. *Parties, Slavery, and the Union in Antebellum Georgia*. Athens: University of Georgia Press.

Carey, George W. 1995. *In Defense of the Constitution*. Indianapolis: Liberty Fund.

Carter, Bradley Kent, and Joseph Kobylka. 1990. "The Dialogic Community: Education, Leadership, and Participation in James Madison's Thought." *Review of Politics* 52.

Carwardine, Richard J. 1993. *Evangelicals and Politics in Antebellum America*. New Haven: Yale University Press.

Cayton, Mary K. 1987. "The Making of an American Prophet: Emerson, His Audience, and the Rise of the Culture Industry in 19th-Century America." *American Historical Review* 92.

Ceaser, James. 1999. "Fame and *The Federalist*." In Peter McNamara, ed., *The Noblest Minds: Fame, Honor, and the American Founding*. Lanham, Md.: Rowman and Littlefield.

Chase, Philander D., ed. 1985–99. *The Papers of George Washington: Revolutionary War Series*. 9 vols. Charlottesville: University Press of Virginia.

Chase, Richard. 1974. "The Theory of America." In Arthur Golden, ed., *Walt Whitman*. New York: McGraw-Hill.

Chatfield, John Hastings. 1988. " 'Already We Are a Fallen Country': The Politics and Ideology of Connecticut Federalism, 1797–1812." Ph.D. diss. Columbia University.

Chesebrough, David B. 1993. "Dissenting Clergy in Confederate Mississippi." *Journal of Mississippi History* 55.

Childs, Arney R., ed. 1947. *The Private Journal of Henry W. Ravenal, 1859–1887*. Columbia: University of South Carolina Press.

Chilton, Bruce D. 1996. "Inclusion and Noninclusion: The Practice of the Kingdom in Formative Christianity." In Jacob Neusner, ed., *Religion and the Political Order*. Atlanta, Ga.: Scholars Press.

Christie, Ian R. 1998. "A Vision of Empire: Thomas Whately and 'The Regulations Lately Made Concerning the Colonies.'" *English Historical Review* 113.

Clark, Charles Worcester. 1889. "The Spirit of American Politics as Shown in the Late Election." *Atlantic Monthly* 63.

Clark, J. C. D. 1994. *The Language of Liberty, 1660–1832*. New York: Cambridge University Press.

Clark, Walter, ed. 1906. *The State Records of North Carolina.* 25 vols. Goldsboro, N.C.: Nash Brothers.

Claude, Richard P. 1969. "Nationalization and the Electoral Process." *Harvard Journal of Legislation* 6.

Cochran, Clarke E. 1989. "The Thin Theory of Community: The Communitarians and Their Critics." *Political Studies* 37.

Cohen, Charles L. 1997. "The Post-Puritan Paradigm of Early American Religious History." *William and Mary Quarterly* 54.

Colley, Linda. 1992. *Britons: Forging the Nation, 1707–1837.* New Haven: Yale University Press.

Commager, Henry Steele. 1975. *Jefferson, Nationalism, and the Enlightenment.* New York: Braziller.

Condit, Celeste Michelle, and John Louis Lucaites. 1993. *Crafting Equality: America's Anglo-African Word.* Chicago: University of Chicago Press.

Conkin, Paul K. 1995. *The Uneasy Center: Reformed Christianity in Antebellum America.* Chapel Hill: University of North Carolina Press.

Connolly, William E. 1974. *The Terms of Political Discourse.* Lexington, Mass.: D. C. Heath.

———. 1993. *The Augustinian Imperative: A Reflection on the Politics of Morality.* Newbury Park, Calif.: Sage.

Connor, R. D. W. 1929. *North Carolina: Rebuilding an Ancient Commonwealth, 1584–1925.* Chicago: American Historical Society.

Conrad, Stephen A. 1988. "Metaphor and Imagination in James Wilson's Theory of Federal Union." *Law and Social Inquiry* 13.

Conway, Alan. 1966. *The Reconstruction of Georgia.* Minneapolis: University of Minnesota Press.

Cook, Karen Severud. 1996. "Benjamin Franklin and the Snake That Would Not Die." *British Library Journal* 22.

Cooper, James Fenimore. 1960. *The Letters and Journals of James Fenimore Cooper.* 4 vols. Ed. James Franklin Beard. Cambridge: Harvard University Press.

Coulter, E. Merton. 1947. *The South during Reconstruction, 1865–1877.* Baton Rouge: Louisiana State University Press.

Countryman, Edward. 1986. *The American Revolution.* London: I. B. Tauris & Co.

Cox, Jacob Polson. 1892. "Why the Men of '61 Fought for the Union." *Atlantic Monthly* 69.

Cox, LaWanda. 1981. *Lincoln and Black Freedom: A Study in Presidential Leadership.* Columbia: University of South Carolina Press.

Crapol, Edward P. 1997. "John Tyler and the Pursuit of National Destiny." *Journal of the Early Republic* 17.

Crofts, Daniel W. 1989. *Reluctant Confederates: Upper South in the Secession Crisis.* Chapel Hill: University of North Carolina Press.

Croly, Herbert. 1909. *The Promise of American Life.* New York: Capricorn Press.

Current, Richard N. 1983. *Speaking of Abraham Lincoln.* Urbana: University of Illinois Press.

———. 1987. *Arguing with Historians: Essays on the Historical and the Unhistorical.* Middletown, Conn.: Wesleyan University Press.

———. 1988. *Those Terrible Carpetbaggers: A Reinterpretation.* New York: Oxford University Press.

——. 1990. "Daniel Webster: The Politician." In Kenneth Shewmaker, ed., *Daniel Webster: "The Completest Man."* Hanover, N.H.: University Press of New England, 1990.

——. 1992. *Lincoln's Loyalists: Union Soldiers from the Confederacy.* Boston: Northeastern University Press.

Curry, Leonard P. 1968. *Blueprint for a Modern America: Non-Military Legislation of the First Civil War Congress.* Nashville, Tenn.: Vanderbilt University Press.

Curry, Richard O., and Karl E. Valois. 1991. In R. O. Curry and L. B. Goodheart, eds., *American Chameleon: Individualism in Trans-National Context.* Kent, Ohio: Kent State University Press.

Curti, Merle. 1946. *The Roots of American Loyalty.* New York: Columbia University Press.

Cushing, Harry Alonzo, ed. 1968. *The Writings of Samuel Adams.* 3 vols. New York: Octagon Books.

Cutler, Wayne, ed. 1986. *John Appleton's Journal of a Tour to New England Made by President Polk in June and July 1847.* Nashville, Tenn.: Vanderbilt University Press.

Dahl, Robert A. 1956. *A Preface to Democratic Theory.* Chicago: University of Chicago Press.

Dalzell, Robert F. 1973. *Daniel Webster and the Trial of American Nationalism, 1843–1852.* Boston: Houghton Mifflin.

Darsey, James. 1997. *The Prophetic Tradition and Radical Rhetoric in America.* New York: New York University Press.

Davis, David Brion. 1975. *The Problem of Slavery in the Age of Revolution, 1770–1823.* Ithaca: Cornell University Press.

——. 1986. *From Homicide to Slavery.* New York: Oxford University Press.

——. 1990. *Revolutions: Reflections on American Equality and Foreign Liberations.* Cambridge: Harvard University Press.

Davis, David Brion, and Steven Mintz. 1998. *The Boisterous Sea of Liberty: A Documentary History of America from Discovery through the Civil War.* New York: Oxford University Press.

Davis, Jefferson. 1881. *Rise and Fall of the Confederate Government.* 2 vols. New York: D. Appleton & Co.

Davis, Lance E., et al. 1972. *American Economic Growth.* New York: Harper & Row.

Davis, S. Rufus. 1978. *The Federal Principle: A Journey through Time in Quest of a Meaning.* Berkeley: University of California Press.

de Cillia, Rudolf, et al. 1999. "The Discursive Construction of National Identities." *Discourse and Society* 10.

de Crevecoeur, J. Hector St. John. 1963 [1782]. *Letters from an American Farmer.* New York: Vintage.

de la Guard, Theodore [Nathaniel Ward]. 1969 [1647]. *The Simple Cobler of Aggawam in America.* Lincoln: University of Nebraska Press.

Degler, Carl N. 1987. "Thesis, Antithesis, Synthesis: The South, the North, and the Nation." *Journal of Southern History* 53.

——. 1991. *In Search of Human Nature: The Decline and Revival of Darwinism in American Social Thought.* New York: Oxford University Press.

Delany, Martin. 1969. *The Condition, Elevation, Emigration, and Destiny of the Colored People of the United States.* New York: Arno Press.

Deudney, Daniel H. 1995. "The Philadelphian System: Sovereignty, Arms Control, and Balance of Power in the American States-Union, circa 1787–1861." *International Organization* 49.

Devetak, Richard, and Richard Higgott. 1999. "Justice Unbound? Globalization, States, and the Transformation of the Social Bond." *International Affairs* 75.

Diamond, Larry. 1994. "Toward Democratic Consolidation." *Journal of Democracy* 5.

Diamond, Martin. 1992. *As Far as Republican Principles Will Admit.* Ed. William A. Schambra. Washington, D.C.: AEI Press.

Dickinson, H. T. 1998. "Britain's Imperial Sovereignty: The Ideological Case against the American Colonists." In H. T. Dickinson, ed., *Britain and the American Revolution.* New York: Longman.

DiLorenzo, Thomas J. 1998. "The Great Centralizer: Abraham Lincoln and the War between the States." *Independent Review* 3.

Dinkin, Robert J. 1982. *Voting in Revolutionary America.* Westport, Conn.: Greenwood Press.

——. 1995. *Before Equal Suffrage: Women in Partisan Politics from Colonial Times to 1920.* Westport, Conn.: Greenwood Press.

Dionne, E. J., ed. 1998. *Community Works.* Washington, D.C.: Brookings Press.

Docherty, James C. 1996. *Historical Dictionary of Organized Labor.* Lanham, Md.: Scarecrow Press.

Dodd, Edwin Merrick. 1934. *American Business Corporations until 1860.* Cambridge: Harvard University Press.

Donald, David Herbert. 1956. *Lincoln Reconsidered.* New York: Knopf.

——. 1960. *An Excess of Democracy: The American Civil War and the Social Process.* Oxford: Clarendon Press.

——. 1978. *Liberty and Union: The Crisis of Popular Government, 1830–1890.* Boston: Little, Brown.

——. 1984. *The Politics of Reconstruction. 1863–1867.* 2d ed. Cambridge: Harvard University Press.

——. 1995. *Lincoln.* New York: Simon & Schuster.

Dougherty, James. 1993. *Walt Whitman and the Citizen's Eye.* Baton Rouge: Louisiana State University Press.

Douglass, Frederick. 1968 [1845]. *Narrative of the Life of Frederick Douglass, An American Slave.* New York: Liberty Press.

Dow, Lorenzo. 1814. *All the Polemical Works of Lorenzo Dow.* New York: J. C. Totten.

Dowd, Gregory Evans. 1992. *A Spirited Resistance: The North American Struggle for Unity, 1745–1815.* Baltimore, Md.: Johns Hopkins University Press.

Dower, John W. 1999. *Embracing Defeat: Japan in the Wake of World War II.* New York: Norton.

Draper, Theodore. 1969. *The Rediscovery of Black Nationalism.* New York: Viking Press.

——. 1996. *A Struggle for Power: The American Revolution.* New York: Times Books.

Drukman, Mason. 1971. *Community and Purpose in America.* New York: McGraw-Hill.

Du Bois, W. E. B. 1962 [1935]. *Black Reconstruction in America.* New York: Russell & Russell.

——. 1970 [1909]. *The Negro American Family.* Cambridge: MIT Press.

——. 1989 [1903]. *The Souls of Black Folk.* New York: Penguin Books.

Dubofsky, Melvyn. 1994. *The State and Labor in Modern America.* Chapel Hill: University of North Carolina Press.

Duché, Jacob. 1775. *The American Vine: A Sermon . . . before the Honourable Continental Congress.* Philadelphia: James Humphreys.

Dulany, Daniel. 1765. "Considerations on the Propriety of Imposing Taxes. . . ." New York: J. Holt.

Dyer, Thomas G. 1999. *Secret Yankees: The Union Circle in Confederate Atlanta.* Baltimore, Md.: Johns Hopkins University Press.

Edes, Peter, and John Gill, eds. 1769. "Letters to the Ministry from Governor Bernard, General Gage, and Commodore Hood." Boston: Edes & Gill.

Edman, Irwin, ed. 1926 [1841, 1844]. *Emerson's Essays: First and Second Series.* New York: Thomas Y. Crowell.

Edney, Matthew H. 1994. "Cartographic Culture and Nationalism in the Early United States." *Journal of Historical Geography* 20.

Edwards, Jonathan. 1741. "Distinguishing Marks of a Work of the Spirit." Boston: S. Kneeland and T. Green.

———. 1747. "An Humble Attempt to Promote Explicit Agreement and Visible Union. . . ." Boston: D. Henchman.

Edwards, Richard T. 1979. *Contested Terrain: The Transformation of the Workplace in the Twentieth Century.* New York: Basic Books.

Eisenach, Eldon J. 1990. "Reconstituting the Study of American Political Thought in a Regime-Change Perspective." *Studies in American Political Development* 4.

Eisgruber, Christopher L. 1994. "Political Unity and the Powers of Government." *UCLA Law Review* 41.

Elazar, Daniel J. 1962. *The American Partnership: Intergovernmental Cooperation in the Nineteenth-Century United States.* Chicago: University of Chicago Press.

———. 1972a. "Civil War and the Preservation of American Federalism." *Publius* 1.

———. 1972b. *American Federalism: A View From the States.* 2d ed. New York: Crowell.

———. 1992. *Building towards Civil War: Generational Rhythms in American Politics.* Lanham, Md.: Madison Books.

———. 1996. "From Statism to Federalism: A Paradigm Shift." *International Political Science Review* 17.

———. 1998. *Covenant and Civil Society: The Constitutional Matrix of Modern Democracy.* New Brunswick, N.J.: Transaction Books.

Elkin, Stephen L. 1996. "Madison and After: The American Model of Political Constitution." *Political Studies* 44.

Elkins, Stanley, and Eric McKitrick. 1993. *The Age of Federalism: The Early American Republic, 1788–1800.* New York: Oxford University Press.

Elliot, Jonathan, ed. 1836. *Debates in the Several State Conventions on the Adoption of the Federal Constitution.* 2d ed. 5 vols. Philadelphia: Lippincott.

Ellis, George E. 1864. "The Nation's Ballot and Its Decision." Boston: William V. Spencer.

Ellis, Mark. 1993. "Black Leadership in the United States: Douglass, Garvey, and King Compared." *Ethnic and Racial Studies* 16.

Ellis, Richard E. 1987. *The Union at Risk: Jacksonian Democracy, States' Rights, and the Nullification Crisis.* New York: Oxford University Press.

Ellis, Richard J. 1992. "Rival Visions of Equality in American Political Culture." *Review of Politics* 54.

———. 1993. *American Political Cultures.* New York: Oxford University Press.

Elson, Ruth Miller. 1964. *Guardians of Tradition: American Schoolbooks of the Nineteenth Century.* Lincoln: University of Nebraska Press.

Emerson, E. W., ed. 1903–4. *The Complete Works of Ralph Waldo Emerson.* 12 vols. Boston: Houghton-Mifflin.

Emerson, Ralph Waldo. 1983 [1836]. *Nature.* In *Emerson: Essays and Lectures.* New York: Library of America.

Engeman, Thomas S., et al. 1988. *The Federalist Concordance*. Chicago: University of Chicago Press.

Epstein, David. 1984. *The Political Theory of* The Federalist. Chicago: University of Chicago Press.

Erickson, Paul D. 1986. *The Poetry of Events: Daniel Webster's Rhetoric of the Constitution and Union*. New York: New York University Press.

Ericson, David F. 1993. *The Shaping of American Liberalism: Slavery, Nullification, and Ratification*. Chicago: University of Chicago Press.

——. 1997. "Presidential Inaugural Addresses and American Political Culture." *Presidential Studies Quarterly* 27.

Erkkila, Betsy. 1989. *Whitman the Political Poet*. New York: Oxford University Press.

Erler, Edward J. 1992. "James Madison and the Framing of the Bill of Rights: Reality and Rhetoric in the New Constitutionalism." *Political Communication* 9.

Etzioni, Amitai. 1993. *The Spirit of Community: Rights, Responsibilities, and the Communitarian Agenda*. New York: Crown Publishers.

Evans, Curt J. 1997. "He 'Dared Maintain' His Views: Daniel Pratt's 1855 Senate Race." *Alabama Review* 50.

Evans, Elizabeth. 1975. *Weathering the Storm: Women of the American Revolution*. New York: Charles Scribner's Sons.

Everett, Edward. 1824. *An Oration Pronounced at Cambridge*. . . . Boston: Oliver Everett.

Fagg, David W. 1971. "Unite or Die." *North Carolina Historical Review* 48.

Faragher, John Mack. 1998. "'More Motley than Mackinaw: From Ethnic Mixing to Ethnic Cleansing on the Frontier of the Lower Missouri, 1783–1833." In A. Clayton and F. Teute, eds., *Contact Points: American Frontiers from the Mohawk Valley to the Mississippi, 1750–1830*. Chapel Hill: University of North Carolina Press.

Faragher, John Mack, and Christine Stansell. 1975. "Women and Their Families on the Overland Trail to California and Oregon, 1842–1867." *Feminist Studies* 2.

Farber, Daniel A., and Suzanna Sherry. 1997. *Beyond All Reason: The Radical Assault on Truth in American Law*. New York: Oxford University Press.

Farrand, Max, ed. 1937. *The Records of the Federal Convention of 1787*. 4 vols. New Haven: Yale University Press.

Faulkner, Harold U. 1959. *Politics, Reform, and Expansion: 1890–1900*. New York: Harper.

Faust, Drew Gilpin. 1988. *The Creation of Confederate Nationalism: Ideology and Identity in the Civil War South*. Baton Rouge: Louisiana State University Press.

Feller, Daniel. 1984. *The Public Lands in Jacksonian Politics*. Madison: University of Wisconsin Press.

Ferenbacher, Don E. 1989. *Constitutions and Constitutionalism in the Slaveholding South*. Athens: University of Georgia Press.

Ferguson, S. B., and David F. Wright, eds. 1988. *New Dictionary of Theology*. Downers Grove, Ill.: Intervarsity Press.

Fields, Wayne. 1983. "The Reply to Hayne: Daniel Webster and the Rhetoric of Stewardship." *Political Theory* 11.

——. 1996. *Union of Words: A History of Presidential Eloquence*. New York: Free Press.

Finke, Roger, and Rodney Stark. 1989. "How the Upstart Sects Won America: 1776–1850." *Journal for the Scientific Study of Religion* 28.

——. 1992. *The Churching of America, 1776–1990: Winners and Losers in Our Religious Economy*. New Brunswick, N.J.: Rutgers University Press.

Finzsch, Norbert, and Dietmar Schirmer, eds. 1998. *Identity and Intolerance: National-*

ism, Racism, and Xenophobia in Germany and the United States. New York: Cambridge University Press.

Fischer, David Hackett. 1989. *Albion's Seed: Four British Folkways in America.* New York: Oxford University Press.

Fisher, Noel C. 1998. *War at Every Door: Partisan Politics and Guerrilla Violence in East Tennessee, 1860–1869.* Chapel Hill: University of North Carolina Press.

Fiske, John. 1877. "The Adoption of the Constitution." *Atlantic Monthly* 60 (November).

——. 1885. "Manifest Destiny." *Harper's* 78.

——. 1888. *The Critical Period of American History.* Boston: Houghton Mifflin.

Fitzgerald, Michael W. 1989. *The Union League Movement in the Deep South: Politics and Agricultural Change during Reconstruction.* Baton Rouge: Louisiana State University Press.

Fitzhugh, George. 1960 [1857]. *Cannibals All! or, Slaves without Masters.* Ed. C. Vann Woodward. Cambridge, Mass.: Belknap Press.

Flaumenhaft, Harvey F. 1992. *The Effective Republic: Administration and Constitution in the Thought of Alexander Hamilton.* Durham, N.C.: Duke University Press.

Fleming, Walter L. 1905. *Civil War and Reconstruction in Alabama.* New York: Columbia University Press.

Flexner, Thomas. 1974. *Washington: The Indispensable Man.* New York: Mentor.

Fliegelman, Jay. 1993. *Declaring Independence: Jefferson, Natural Language, and the Culture of Performance.* Stanford, Calif.: Stanford University Press.

Fogel, Robert William. 1989. *Without Consent or Contract: The Rise and Fall of American Slavery.* New York: W. W. Norton.

Fogel, Robert William, and Stanley L. Engerman. 1974. *Time on the Cross: The Economics of American Negro Slavery.* New York: W. W. Norton.

Fogleman, Aaron S. 1998. "From Slaves, Convicts, and Servants to Free Passengers: The Transformation of Immigration in the Era of the American Revolution." *Journal of American History* 85.

Foley, Michael W., and Bob Edwards. 1997. "Escape from Politics? Social Theory and the Social Capital Debate." *American Behavioral Scientist* 40.

Foner, Eric. 1970. *Free Soil, Free Labor, Free Men: The Ideology of the Republican Party before the Civil War.* New York: Oxford University Press.

——. 1988. *Reconstruction, 1863–1877: America's Unfinished Revolution.* New York: Harper & Row.

——. 1998. *The Story of American Freedom.* New York: W. W. Norton.

Foner, Eric, and Olivia Mahoney. 1990. *A House Divided: America in the Age of Lincoln.* New York: W. W. Norton.

Foner, Philip S. 1947–64. *History of the Labor Movement in the United States.* 3 vols. New York: International Publishing Co.

——, ed. 1950. *The Life and Writing of Frederick Douglass.* 5 vols. New York: International Publishers.

Force, Peter, ed. 1837–46. *American Archives.* 6 vols. Washington, D.C.: P. Force.

Ford, W. C., et al., eds. 1904–37. *Journals of the Continental Congress.* 31 vols. Washington, D.C.: U.S. Government Printing Office.

Forgie, George B. 1979. *Patricide in the House Divided: A Psychological Interpretation of Lincoln and His Age.* New York: W. W. Norton.

Formisano, Ronald P. 1974. "Deferential-Participant Politics in the Early Republic's Political Culture, 1789–1840." *American Political Science Review* 68.

——. 1999. "The 'Party Period' Revisited." *Journal of American History* 86.

Foster, Charles I. 1960. *An Errand of Mercy: The Evangelical United Front, 1790–1837.* Chapel Hill: University of North Carolina Press.

Foster, Gaines M. 1987. *Ghosts of the Confederacy: Defeat, the Lost Cause, and the Emergence of the New South.* New York: Oxford University Press.

——. 1996. "A Christian Nation: Signs of a Covenant." In John Bodnar, ed., *Bonds of Affection: Americans Define Their Patriotism.* Princeton, N.J.: Princeton University Press.

Frank, Joseph Allan. 1998. *With Ballot and Bayonet: The Political Socialization of American Civil War Soldiers.* Athens: University of Georgia Press.

Franklin, John Hope. 1969. *From Slavery to Freedom: A History of Negro Americans.* 2d ed. New York: Vintage.

Franklin, V. P. 1992. *Black Self-Determination: A Cultural History of Black Resistance.* 2d ed. Brooklyn, N.Y.: Lawrence Hill Books.

Fredrickson, George M. 1965. *The Inner Civil War: Northern Intellectuals and the Crisis of the Union.* New York: Harper & Row.

——. 1971. *The Black Image in the White Mind: The Debate on Afro-American Character and Destiny, 1817–1914.* New York: Harper & Row.

——. 1975. "A Man but Not a Brother: Abraham Lincoln and Racial Equality." *Journal of Southern History* 41.

Freehling, William W. 1990. *The Road to Disunion: Secessionists at Bay.* New York: Oxford University Press.

——. 1994. *The Reintegration of American History: Slavery and the Civil War.* New York: Oxford University Press.

Freidel, Frank. 1967. *Union Pamphlets of the Civil War.* 2 vols. Cambridge: Harvard University Press.

Friedman, Lawrence J. 1982. *Gregarious Saints: Self and Community in American Abolitionism, 1830–1870.* New York: Cambridge University Press.

Friedman, Lawrence M. 1973. *A History of American Law.* New York: Simon & Schuster.

Fuchs, Lawrence H. 1990. *The American Kaleidoscope: Race, Ethnicity, and the Civic Culture.* Hanover, N.H.: University Press of New England.

Fuess, Claude Moore. 1929. "Senator Webster Goes South." *Massachusetts Historical Society, Proceedings* 62.

Gage, Thomas. 1931–33. *The Correspondence of General Thomas Gage.* 2 vols. Ed. C. Carter. New Haven: Yale University Press.

Galston, William A. 1990. "The Use and Abuse of the Classics in American Constitutionalism." *Chicago-Kent Law Review* 66.

Gans, Herbert J. 1988. *Middle American Individualism: The Future of Liberal Democracy.* New York: Free Press.

Garnet, Henry Highland. 1865. *A Memorial Discourse.* Philadelphia: Mitchell Publishers.

Garraty, John A. 1968. *The New Commonwealth, 1877–1890.* New York: Harper & Row.

Garrison, William Lloyd. 1832. *Thoughts on African Colonization.* Boston: Garrison & Knapp.

Gaustad, Edwin Scott. 1974. *A Religious History of America.* New York: Harper & Row.

Gebhardt, Jürgen. 1993. *Americanism: Revolutionary Order and Societal Self-Interpretation in the American Republic.* Trans. Ruth Hein. Baton Rouge: Louisiana State University Press.

Gellner, Ernest. 1983. *Nations and Nationalism.* Ithaca: Cornell University Press.

Genovese, Eugene D. 1975. *Roll Jordan Roll: The World the Slaves Made.* New York: Vintage.

——. 1995. *The Southern Front: History and Politics in the Cultural War.* Columbia: University of Missouri Press.

Gerring, John. 1998. *Party Ideologies in America, 1828–1996.* New York: Cambridge University Press.

Gerstle, Gary. 1989. *Working-Class Americanism.* New York: Cambridge University Press.

Gerteis, Louis S. 1973. *From Contraband to Freedman: Federal Policy toward Southern Blacks, 1861–1865.* Westport, Conn.: Greenwood Press.

Gibson, Alan. 1991. "Impartial Representation and the Extended Republic: Towards a Comprehensive and Balanced Reading of the Tenth *Federalist* Paper." *History of Political Thought* 12.

Gienapp, William E. 1982. "'Politics Seem to Enter Into Everything': Political Culture in the North, 1840–1860." In S. Maizlish and J. Kushma, eds., *Essays on American Antebellum Politics.* College Station: Texas A&M University Press.

Gilbert, Felix. 1961. *To the Farewell Address: Ideas of Early American Foreign Policy.* Princeton, N.J.: Princeton University Press.

Gilbert, Paul. 1997. "The Concept of a National Community." *Philosophical Forum* 28.

Gilje, Paul A. 1996. "The Rise of Capitalism in the Early Republic." *Journal of the Early Republic* 16.

Gillette, William. 1979. *Retreat from Reconstruction: 1869–1879.* Baton Rouge: Louisiana State University Press.

Gilman, William H., ed. 1960–82. *Emerson: Journals and Miscellaneous Notebooks.* 16 vols. Cambridge, Mass.: Belknap Press.

Gilpin, William. 1858. "The Great Basin of the Mississippi." *DeBow's Review* 24.

——. 1873. *Mission of the North American People.* Philadelphia: J. B. Lippincott.

Gitlin, Todd. 1995. *The Twilight of Common Dreams: Why America Is Wracked by Culture Wars.* New York: H. Holt.

Glatthaar, Joseph T. 1992. "Black Glory: The African-American Role in Union Victory." In Boritt 1992.

Goetzmann, William H. 1995. "The Uncertain Landscapes of Nationalism." *Reviews in American History* 23.

Goldman, Eric F. 1952. *Rendezvous with Destiny: A History of Modern American Reform.* New York: Knopf.

Grant, Robert. 1995. "Must New Worlds Also Be Good?" *Inquiry* 38.

Grant, Susan-Mary C. 1997. "Making History: Myth and the Construction of American Nationhood." In G. H. Hosking and G. Schopflin, eds., *Myths and Nationhood.* London: Hurst & Co.

——. 1998. "Representative Mann: Horace Mann, the Republican Experiment, and the South." *Journal of American Studies* 32.

Grant, Ulysses S. 1962 [1885]. *Personal Memoirs of U.S. Grant.* Ed. P. Stern. New York: Premier.

Gray, John. 1993. *Post-Liberalism.* New York: Routledge.

Greene, Francis R. 1994. "Madison's View of Federalism in *The Federalist.*" *Publius* 24.

Greene, Jack P. 1969. "Political Mimesis: A Consideration of the Historical and Cultural Roots of Legislative Behavior in the British Colonies in the Eighteenth Century." *American Historical Review* 75.

——. 1986. *Peripheries and Center: Constitutional Development in the Extended Polities of the British Empire and the United States, 1607–1788.* Athens: University of Georgia Press.

——. 1987. *The American Revolution: Its Character and Limits.* New York: New York University Press.

——, ed. 1975. *Colonies to Nation, 1763–1789: A Documentary History of the American Revolution.* New York: W. W. Norton.

Greenfeld, Liah. 1992. *Nationalism: Five Roads to Modernity.* Cambridge: Harvard University Press.

Greenstone, J. David. 1986. "Political Culture and American Political Development: Liberty, Union, and the Liberal Bipolarity." *Studies in American Political Development* 1.

Grosvenor, William M. 1865. "The Law of Conquest the True Basis of Reconstruction." *New Englander* 29.

Gruber, Ira D. 1969. "The American Revolution as a Conspiracy: Understanding the British View." *William and Mary Quarterly* 26.

Grunwald, Michael. 1999. "Everybody Talks about States' Rights." *Washington Post National Weekly Edition,* 1 November.

Gutzman, K. R. Constantine. 1998. "'Oh, What a Tangled Web We Weave': James Madison and the Compound Republic." *Continuity* 22.

Haddock, Bruce. 1999. "State and Nation in Mazzini's Political Thought." *History of Political Thought* 20.

Hall, Fred S. 1898. *Sympathetic Strikes and Sympathetic Lockouts.* Studies in History, Economics, and Public Law 26. New York: Columbia University.

Hall, Timothy D. 1994. *Contested Boundaries: Itinerancy and the Reshaping of the Colonial American Religious World.* Durham, N.C.: Duke University Press.

Hamilton, J. G. de Roulliac. 1919. *History of North-Carolina.* 3 vols. Chicago: Lewis Publishing Co.

Hamilton, Thomas. 1843. *Men and Manners in America.* London: William Blackwood and Sons.

Handlin, Oscar. 1951. *The Uprooted.* Boston: Little, Brown.

Handlin, Oscar, and Lilian Handlin. 1986–94. *Liberty in America.* 3 vols. New York: HarperCollins.

Hanson, Russell L. 1985. *The Democratic Imagination in America: Conversations with Our Past.* Princeton, N.J.: Princeton University Press.

Harding, Vincent. 1981. *There Is a River: The Black Struggle for Freedom in America.* New York: Harcourt Brace Jovanovich.

Hart, Albert Bushnell, and Edward Channing, eds. 1894. "Plans of Union, 1696–1780." New York: Macmillan.

Hartz, Louis. 1955. *The Liberal Tradition in America.* New York: Harcourt, Brace.

Hatch, Nathan O. 1989. *The Democratization of American Christianity.* New Haven: Yale University Press.

Hattam, Victoria. 1990. "Economic Visions and Political Strategies: American Labor and the State, 1865–1896." *Studies in American Political Development* 4.

Heckman, Richard Allen. 1967. *Lincoln versus Douglas: The Great Debates Campaign.* Washington, D.C.: Public Affairs Press.

Hefner, Robert W. 1998. "Civil Society: Cultural Possibility of a Modern Ideal." *Society* 35.

Held, David. 1999. "The Transformation of Political Community: Rethinking Democracy in the Context of Globalization." In Ian Shapiro and Casiano Hacker-Cordón, eds., *Democracy's Edges.* New York: Cambridge University Press.

Hench, Virginia E. 1998. "The Death of Voting Rights: The Legal Disenfranchisement of Minority Voters." *Case Western Law Review* 48.

Henderson, H. James. 1974. *Party Politics in the Continental Congress.* New York: McGraw-Hill.

Henretta, James A. 1991. *The Origins of American Capitalism: Collected Essays.* Boston: Northeastern University Press.

———. 1996. "The Strange Birth of Liberal America." *New York History* 77.

Henretta, James A., Michael Kammen, and Stanley N. Katz, eds. 1991. *The Transformation of Early American History: Society, Authority, and Ideology.* New York: Knopf.

Hessler, Katherine. 1998. "Early Efforts to Suppress Protest: Unwanted Abolitionist Speech." *Boston Public Interest Law Journal* 7.

Hietala, Thomas R. 1985. *Manifest Design: Anxious Aggrandizement in Late Jacksonian America.* Ithaca: Cornell University Press.

Higham, John. 1984. *Send These to Me: Immigrants in Urban America.* Rev. ed. Baltimore, Md.: Johns Hopkins University Press.

———. 1988 [1955]. *Strangers in the Land: Patterns of American Nativism, 1860–1925.* 2d ed. New Brunswick, N.J.: Rutgers University Press.

———. 1999. "The Redefinition of America in the Twentieth Century." In H. Lehmann and H. Wellenreuther, eds., *German and American Nationalism: A Comparative Perspective.* New York: Berg.

Hill, Benjamin H. 1909 [1867]. "The Stars and Stripes." Vol. 9 in Thomas Watson, ed., *The South in the Building of the Nation.* Richmond, Va.: Southern Historical Pub. Society.

Hinks, Peter B. 1997. *To Awaken My Afflicted Brethren: David Walker and the Problem of Antebellum Slave Resistance.* University Park: Pennsylvania State University Press.

Hirsch, Harold. 1986. "The Threnody of Liberalism: Constitutional Liberty and the Renewal of Community." *Political Theory* 14.

Hobson, Charles F. 1996. *The Great Chief Justice: John Marshall and the Rule of Law.* Lawrence: University Press of Kansas.

Hoffman, Ronald, and Peter Albert, eds. 1989. *Women in the Age of the American Revolution.* Charlottesville: University Press of Virginia.

Hohmann, Hanns. 1998. "Rhetoric in the Public Sphere and the Discourse of Law and Democracy." *Quarterly Journal of Speech* 84.

Hollinger, David A. 1995. *Postethnic America: Beyond Multiculturalism.* New York: Basic Books.

Holloway, Emory, and Vernolian Schwarz, eds. 1932. *I Sit and Look Out: Editorials from the Brooklyn* Daily Times. New York: Columbia University Press.

Holt, Michael F. 1978. *The Political Crisis of the 1850s.* New York: John Wiley & Sons.

———. 1986. "Abraham Lincoln and the Politics of Union." In John L. Thomas, ed., *Abraham Lincoln and the American Political Tradition.* Amherst: University of Massachusetts Press.

———. 1992. *Political Parties and American Political Development: From the Age of Jackson to the Age of Lincoln.* Baton Rouge: Louisiana State University Press.

———. 1999. *The Rise and Fall of the American Whig Party: Jacksonian Politics and the Onset of the Civil War.* New York: Oxford University Press.

Holzer, Harold, ed. 1993. *The Lincoln-Douglas Debates.* New York: HarperCollins.

Hopkins, James F., et al., eds. 1959–92. *The Papers of Henry Clay.* 10 vols. Lexington: University Press of Kentucky.

Horn, James. 1994. *Adapting to a New World: English Society in the Seventeenth-Century Chesapeake.* Chapel Hill: University of North Carolina Press.

Horsman, Reginald. 1981. *Race and Manifest Destiny: The Origins of American Racial Anglo-Saxonism.* Cambridge: Harvard University Press.

——. 1999. "The Indian Policy of an 'Empire for Liberty.'" In Frederick Hoxie et al., eds., *Native Americans and the Early Republic.* Charlottesville: University Press of Virginia.

Howe, Daniel Walker. 1979. *The Political Culture of the American Whigs.* Chicago: University of Chicago Press.

——. 1989. "Why the Scottish Enlightenment Was Useful to the Framers of the American Constitution." *Journal of Contemporary History* 24.

——. 1997. "Jacksonianism and the Promise of Improvement." *Reviews in American History* 25.

Hubbard, William. 1676. "The Happiness of a People." Boston: John Foster.

Huggins, Nathan Irwin. 1980. *Slave and Citizen: Life and Times of Frederick Douglass.* Boston: Little, Brown.

——. 1995. *Revelations: American History, American Myths.* New York: Oxford University Press.

Hunt, Galliard, ed. 1910. *The Writings of James Madison.* 9 vols. New York: Putnam.

Hunter, James Davison, ed. 1996. *The State of Disunion: 1996 Survey of American Political Culture.* Ivy, Va.: *In Medias Res* Educational Foundation.

Huntington, Samuel P. 1981. *American Politics: The Promise of Disharmony.* Cambridge, Mass.: Belknap Press.

——. 1996. *The Clash of Civilizations and the Remaking of World Order.* New York: Simon & Schuster.

Hurd, John C. 1890. *The Union-State: A Letter to Our States-Rights Friend.* New York: D. Van Nostrand.

Hurrell, Andrew, and Ngaire Woods, eds. 1999. *Inequality, Globalization, and World Markets.* New York: Oxford University Press.

Hurtado, Albert L., and Peter Iverson, eds. 1994. *Major Problems in American Indian History: Documents and Essays.* Lexington, Mass.: D. C. Heath.

Hutchinson, Thomas. 1936 [1773]. *The History of the Colony and Province of Massachusetts Bay.* 3 vols. Ed. Lawrence S. Mayo. Cambridge, Mass.: Belknap Press.

Hutchinson, William T. 1959. "Unite to Divide; Divide to Unite: The Shaping of American Federalism." *Mississippi Valley Historical Review* 46.

Hutchinson, William T., et al., eds. 1962–91. *The Papers of James Madison.* 17 vols. Chicago: University of Chicago Press; and Charlottesville: University Press of Virginia.

Huyler, Jerome. 1995. *Locke in America: The Moral Philosophy of the Founding Era.* Lawrence: University Press of Kansas.

Hyman, Harold M. 1967. *The Radical Republicans and Reconstruction, 1861–1870.* Indianapolis: Bobbs-Merrill.

Ignatieff, Michael. 1994. *Blood and Belonging: Journeys into the New Nationalism.* New York: Farrar, Straus and Giroux.

Isley, Jeter Allen. 1947. *Horace Greeley and the Republican Party, 1853–1861: A Study of the New York* Tribune. Princeton, N.J.: Princeton University Press.

Jackson, Donald, ed. 1955 [1833]. *Black Hawk: An Autobiography.* Urbana: University of Illinois Press.

Jacobson, David L., ed. 1965. *The English Libertarian Heritage: From the Writings of John Trenchard and Thomas Gordon.* Indianapolis: Bobbs-Merrill.

Jaffa, Harry V. 1982 [1959]. *Crisis of the House Divided: An Interpretation of the Issues in the Lincoln-Douglas Debates.* 2d ed. Chicago: University of Chicago Press.

James, Bessie R. 1972. *Anne Royall's U.S.A.* New Brunswick, N.J.: Rutgers University Press.

Jeffrey, Julie Roy. 1998. *The Great Silent Army of Abolitionism: Ordinary Women in the Antislavery Movement.* Chapel Hill: University of North Carolina Press.

Jehlen, Myra. 1986. *American Incarnation: The Individual, the Nation, and the Continent.* Cambridge: Harvard University Press.

Jenks, Jeremiah W., and W. Jett Lauck. 1911. *The Immigration Problem.* New York: Funk & Wagnalls.

Jennings, Francis. 1976. "The Indians' Revolution." In Alfred Young, ed., *The American Revolution: Explorations in the History of American Radicalism.* De Kalb: Northern Illinois University Press.

Jensen, Laura S. 1996. "The Early American Origins of Entitlements." *Studies in American Political Development* 10.

Jensen, Lene Arnett. 1998. "Different Habits, Different Hearts: The Moral Languages of the Culture War." *American Sociologist* 29.

Jensen, Merrill, ed. 1967. *Tracts of the American Revolution.* Indianapolis: Bobbs-Merrill.

Jillson, Calvin, and Rick K. Wilson. 1994. *Congressional Dynamics: Structure, Coordination, and Choice in the First American Congress, 1774–1789.* Stanford, Calif.: Stanford University Press.

Johannsen, Robert W. 1991. *Lincoln, the South, and Slavery: The Political Dimension.* Baton Rouge: Louisiana State University Press.

John, Richard R. 1995. *Spreading the News: The American Postal System from Franklin to Morse.* Cambridge: Harvard University Press.

———. 1997. "Governmental Institutions as Agents of Change: Rethinking American Political Development in the Early Republic, 1787–1835." *Studies in American Political Development* 11.

Johnson, Donald Bruce. 1978. *National Party Platforms, 1840–1956.* Urbana: University of Illinois Press.

Johnson, Ludwell H. 1978. *Division and Reunion: America, 1848–1877.* New York: John Wiley & Sons.

Jones, Howard. 1999. *Abraham Lincoln and a New Birth of Freedom: The Union and Slavery in the Diplomacy of the Civil War.* Lincoln: University of Nebraska Press.

Jones, Jacqueline. 1989. "Race, Sex, and Self-Evident Truths: The Status of Slave Women during the Era of the American Revolution." In Hoffman and Albert 1989, 107–43.

Jordan, Winthrop D. 1968. *White over Black: American Attitudes toward the Negro, 1668–1860.* Chapel Hill: University of North Carolina Press.

Joseph, Antoine. 1989. "The Formation of Class Fractions in the Gilded Age." *Ethnic and Racial Studies* 12.

Jourdan, Willis A. 1889. *The American System: A History.* Boston: Lee and Shepard.

Kaczorowski, Robert J. 1985. *The Politics of Judicial Interpretation, 1866–1876.* New York: Oceana Press.

———. 1987. "To Begin the Nation Anew: Congress, Citizenship, and Civil Rights after the Civil War." *American Historical Review* 92.

———. 1997. "The Tragic Irony of American Federalism: National Sovereignty versus State Sovereignty in Slavery and in Freedom." *Kansas Law Review* 45.

Kahn, Paul W. 1992. *Legitimacy and History: Self-Government in American Constitutional Theory.* New Haven: Yale University Press.

Kamensky, Jane. 1997. *Governing the Tongue: The Politics of Speech in Early New England.* New York: Oxford University Press.

Kammen, Michael. 1972. *People of Paradox: An Inquiry concerning the Origins of American Civilization.* New York: Knopf.

———. 1986. *Spheres of Liberty: Changing Perceptions of Liberty in American Culture.* Ithaca: Cornell University Press.

———. 1987. *A Machine That Would Go of Itself: The Constitution in American Culture.* New York: Vintage Books.

———. 1993. *Mystic Chords of Memory: The Transformation of Tradition in American Culture.* New York: Knopf.

Kaplan, Justin, ed. 1982. *Walt Whitman: Complete Poetry and Collected Prose.* New York: Viking.

Kateb, George. 1990. "Walt Whitman and the Culture of Democracy." *Political Theory* 18.

———. 1992. *The Inner Ocean: Individualism and Democratic Culture.* Ithaca: Cornell University Press.

Kaufman, Jason Andrew. 1999. "Three Views of Associationalism in Nineteenth-Century America: An Empirical Examination." *American Journal of Sociology* 104.

Kearney, Hugh. 2000. "The Importance of Being British." *Political Quarterly* 71.

Keating, Michael. 1998. "Reforging the Union: Devolution and Constitutional Change in the United Kingdom." *Publius* 28.

Kelley, Wayne, ed. 1978. *Electing Congress.* Washington, D.C.: CQ Press.

Kelly, Kate. 1991. *Election Day: An American Holiday, An American History.* New York: Facts on File.

Kendall, Wilmoore, and George W. Carey. 1970. *The Basic Symbols of the American Political Tradition.* Baton Rouge: Louisiana State University Press.

Kerber, Linda K. 1975. "The Abolitionist Perception of the Indian." *Journal of American History* 62.

———. 1980. *Women of the Republic: Intellect and Ideology in Revolutionary America.* Chapel Hill: University of North Carolina Press.

———. 1989. "'History Can Do It No Justice': Women and the Reinterpretation of the American Revolution." In Hoffman and Albert 1989, 18–43.

———. 1995. "A Constitutional Right to Be Treated Like American Ladies: Women and the Obligations of Citizenship." In L. K. Kerber et al., eds., *U.S. History as Women's History: New Feminist Essays.* Chapel Hill: University of North Carolina Press.

Kernell, Samuel A. 1986. "The Early Nationalization of Political News in America." *Studies in American Political Development* 1.

Kersh, Rogan. 1993. "The Founding: Liberalism Redux." *Review of Politics* 55.

———. 1996. "Dreams of a More Perfect Union." Ph.D. diss. Yale University.

———. 1999. "Liberty *and* Union: A Madisonian View." *Journal of Political Philosophy* 7.

———. Forthcoming. "Civic Participation and National Belonging." In Stephen Macedo and Elizabeth Lasch-Quinn, eds., *Instituting Civil Society.* Lanham, Md.: Rowman & Littlefield.

Ketcham, Ralph. 1960. "James Madison and Religion—A New Hypothesis." *Journal of the Presbyterian Historical Society* 38.

———. 1971. *James Madison: A Biography.* New York: Macmillan.

———. 1974. *From Colony to Country: The Revolution in American Thought, 1750–1820.* New York: Macmillan.

———. 1984. *Presidents above Party: The First American Presidency, 1789–1829.* Chapel Hill: University of North Carolina Press.

———. 1993. *Framed for Posterity: The Enduring Philosophy of the Constitution.* Lawrence: University Press of Kansas.

King, Martin Luther, Jr. 1963. "I Have a Dream." Los Angeles: John Henry and Louisa Dunn Henry Bryant Foundation.

Kinshasa, Kwando M. 1988. *Emigration vs. Assimilation: The Debate in the African American Press, 1827–1861.* London: McFarland.

Klein, Maury. 1993. *The Flowering of the Third America : The Making of an Organizational Society, 1850–1920.* Chicago: Ivan R. Dee.

Kleinberg, S. J. 1999. "Race, Region, and Gender in American History." *Journal of American Studies* 33.

Kleppner, Paul. 1990. "Defining Citizenship: Immigration and the Struggle for Voting Rights in Antebellum America." In Donald W. Rogers, ed., *Voting and the Spirit of American Democracy.* Urbana: University of Illinois Press.

Klinkner, Philip A., and Rogers M. Smith. 1999. *The Unsteady March: The Rise and Decline of Racial Equality in America.* Chicago: University of Chicago Press.

Knobel, Dale T. 1986. *Paddy and the Republic.* Middletown, Conn.: Wesleyan University Press.

Knollenberg, Bernhard. 1960. *Origin of the American Revolution: 1759–1766.* New York: Macmillan.

Knupfer, Peter. 1991. *"The Union As It Is": Constitutional Unionism and Sectional Compromise, 1787–1861.* Chapel Hill: University of North Carolina Press.

Kobach, Kris. 1994. "Rethinking Article V: Term Limits and the Seventeenth and Nineteenth Amendments." *Yale Law Journal* 103.

Koch, Adrienne. 1964 [1950]. *Jefferson and Madison: The Great Collaboration.* 2d ed. New York: Oxford University Press.

Koenigsberger, H. G. 1989. "Composite States, Representative Institutions and the American Revolution." *History and Theory* 28.

Kohn, Hans. 1944. *The Idea of Nationalism.* New York: Macmillan.

Konig, David Thomas, ed. 1995. *Devising Liberty: Preserving and Creating Freedom in the New American Republic.* Stanford, Calif.: Stanford University Press.

Kopel, David B. 1998. "The Second Amendment in the Nineteenth Century." *Brigham Young Law Review* 1998.

Kramer, Michael P. 1988. "Condillac to Michaelis to Tooke: How Noah Webster Invented a National Language." In Steve Ickringill, ed., *The Early Republic.* Amsterdam: Free University Press.

Kramnick, Isaac. 1990. *Republicanism and Bourgeois Radicalism: Political Ideology in Late Eighteenth-Century England and America.* Ithaca: Cornell University Press.

Kramnick, Isaac, and R. Laurence Moore. 1996. *The Godless Constitution: The Case against Religious Correctness.* New York: W. W. Norton.

Kraut, Alan M. 1982. *The Huddled Masses: The Immigrant in American Society, 1880–1921.* Arlington Heights, Ill.: Harlan Davidson.

Kreidler, Charles W. 1998. "Noah Webster's Linguistic Influences." *Language and Communication* 18.

Kuehne, Dale S. 1996. *Massachusetts Congregationalist Political Thought, 1760–1790.* Columbia: University of Missouri Press.

Kurtz, Stephen G., and James H. Hutson, eds. 1973. Essays on the American Revolution. Chapel Hill: University of North Carolina Press.

Kymlicka, Will. 1995. *Multicultural Citizenship.* New York: Oxford University Press.

Labaree, Leonard W., et al., eds. 1959–. *The Papers of Benjamin Franklin.* 35 vols. New Haven: Yale University Press.

Lambert, Frank. 1999. *Inventing the "Great Awakening."* Princeton, N.J.: Princeton University Press.

Lampe, Gregory P. 1998. *Frederick Douglass: Freedom's Voice, 1818–1845.* East Lansing: Michigan State University Press.

Langford, Paul, ed. 1981–96. *Writings and Speeches of Edmund Burke.* 12 vols. Oxford: Clarendon Press.

Langlands, Rebeccca. 1999. "Britishness or Englishness? The Historical Problem of National Identity in Britain." *Nations and Nationalism* 5.

Larson, Kerry C. 1988. *Whitman's Drama of Consensus.* Chicago: University of Chicago Press.

Larson, Rebecca. 1999. *Daughters of Light: Quaker Women Preaching and Prophesying in the Colonies and Abroad, 1700–1775.* New York: Knopf.

Lasch, Christopher. 1978. *The Culture of Narcissism: American Life in an Age of Diminishing Expectations.* New York: W. W. Norton.

Laurens, Henry. 1769. "Extracts from the Proceedings . . ." Charleston, S.C.: David Bruce.

Laurie, Bruce. 1989. *Artisans into Workers: Labor in Nineteenth-Century America.* New York: Noonday Press.

Lee, Richard Henry. 1829. *The Life of Arthur Lee.* 2 vols. Boston: Little, Brown.

Leibiger, Stuart. 1999. *Founding Friendship: George Washington, James Madison, and the Creation of the American Republic.* Charlottesville: University Press of Virginia.

Lemay, J. A. Leo, ed. 1987. *Writings of Benjamin Franklin.* New York: Library of America.

Lence, Ross M., ed. 1992. *Union and Liberty: The Political Philosophy of John C. Calhoun.* Indianapolis: Liberty Fund.

Lepore, Jill. 1998. *The Name of War: King Philip's War and the Origins of American Identity.* New York: Alfred A. Knopf.

Lessig, Lawrence. 1996. "Social Meaning and Social Norms." *University of Pennsylvania Law Review* 144.

Levack, Brian P. 1987. *The Formation of the British State: England, Scotland, and the Union, 1603–1707.* New York: Oxford University Press.

Levine, Erwin L. 1972. *The Ghost of John C. Calhoun and American Politics.* Saratoga Springs, N.Y.: Skidmore College.

Levy, David W. 1985. *Herbert Croly of the New Republic: The Life and Thought of an American Progressive.* Princeton, N.J.: Princeton University Press.

Lewis, James E. 1998. *The American Union and the Problem of Neighborhood: The United States and the Collapse of the Spanish Empire, 1783–1829.* Chapel Hill: University of North Carolina Press.

Lewis, R. W. B. 1986. *The Presence of Walt Whitman.* Rev. ed. New York: Columbia University Press.

Lichtenberg, Judith. 1997. "How Liberal Can Nationalism Be?" *Philosophical Forum* 28.

Lieber, Francis. 1881. *The Miscellaneous Writings of Francis Lieber.* 2 vols. Philadelphia: J. B. Lippincott.

Lienesch, Michael. 1988. *New Order of the Ages: Time, the Constitution, and the Making of Modern American Political Thought.* Princeton, N.J.: Princeton University Press.

Likhovski, Assaf. 1997. "'Tyranny' in Nineteenth-Century American Legal Discourse: A Rhetorical Analysis." *Journal of Interdisciplinary History* 28.

Limerick, Patricia Nelson. 1987. *The Legacy of Conquest: The Unbroken Past of the American West.* New York: Norton.

Lind, Michael. 1995. *The Next American Nation: The New Nationalism and the Fourth American Revolution.* New York: Free Press.

Linfield, William W., ed. 1862. *The Declaration of Independence. . . .* Randolph, Mass.: Samuel P. Brown.

Lindblom, Charles E. 1990. *Inquiry and Change: The Troubled Attempt to Understand and Shape Society.* New Haven: Yale University Press.

Lloyd Thomas, D. A. 1995. *Locke on Government.* New York: Routledge.

Locke, John. 1988 [1690]. *Two Treatises of Government.* Ed. Peter Laslett. New York: Cambridge University Press.

Lockridge, Kenneth. 1970. *A New England Town: The First Hundred Years.* New York: W. W. Norton.

Logan, Rayford. 1965. *The Betrayal of the Negro: From Rutherford B. Hayes to Woodrow Wilson.* New York: Collier Books.

Lott, Davis Newton. 1994. *The Presidents Speak: The Inaugural Addresses of the American Presidency from Washington to Clinton.* New York: Henry Holt.

Lukacs, John. 1998. "Our War with Spain Marked the First Year of the American Century." *American Heritage* 49 (May/June).

Luker, Ralph E. 1991. *The Social Gospel in Black and White: American Racial Reform, 1885–1912.* Chapel Hill: University of North Carolina Press.

Lutz, Donald S. 1988. *The Origins of American Constitutionalism.* Baton Rouge: Louisiana State University Press.

———. 1992. *A Preface to American Political Theory.* Lawrence: University Press of Kansas.

Lynn, Kenneth S. 1960. *Mark Twain and Southwestern Humor.* Boston: Little, Brown.

Macedo, Stephen. 1999. *Diversity and Distrust.* Cambridge: Harvard University Press.

Machiavelli, Niccolò. 1950 [1531] *The Discourses.* New York: Penguin.

MacLaurin, Lois Margaret. 1927. "The Vocabulary of Benjamin Franklin." Ph.D. diss. University of Chicago.

Maclear, James F. 1959. "'The True American Union' of Church and State: The Reconstruction of the Theocratic Tradition." *Church History* 27.

Maier, Pauline. 1974. *From Resistance to Revolution: Colonial Radicals and the Development of American Opposition to Britain, 1765–1776.* New York: Vintage Books.

———. 1991. "The Transforming Impact of Independence, Reaffirmed: 1776 and the Definition of American Social Structure." In Henretta et al. 1991, 194–217.

———. 1997. *American Scripture: Making the Declaration of Independence.* New York: Knopf.

Maletz, Donald J. 1998. "The Union as Idea: Tocqueville on the American Constitution." *History of Political Thought* 14.

Mann, Horace. 1868. *Horace Mann: Life and Works.* 5 vols. Boston: Horace Fuller.

Marmor, Theodore R. 1988. *The Career of John C. Calhoun: Politician, Social Critic, Political Philosopher.* New York: Garland.

Martin, Waldo E. Jr. 1984. *The Mind of Frederick Douglass.* Chapel Hill: University of North Carolina Press.

Marx, Anthony W. 1998. "Contested Citizenship: The Dynamics of Racial Identity and Social Movements." In C. McNeely, ed., *Public Rights, Public Rules: Constituting Citizens in the World Polity and National Policy.* New York: Garland.

Mason, Alpheus Thomas. 1950. "The Nature of Our Federal Union Reconsidered." *Political Science Quarterly* 40.

Mason, Andrew. 1999. "Political Community, Liberal-Nationalism, and the Ethics of Assimilation." *Ethics* 109.

Mather, Cotton. 1855 [1702]. *Magnalia Christi Americana.* 2 vols. Ed. Thomas Robbins and L. F. Robinson. Hartford: S. Andrus & Son.

Mathews, Donald G. 1977. *Religion in the Old South.* Chicago: University of Chicago Press.

Matson, Cathy D., and Peter S. Onuf. 1990. *A Union of Interests: Political and Economic Thought in Revolutionary America.* Lawrence: University Press of Kansas.

Matthews, Richard K. 1995. *If Men Were Angels: James Madison and the Heartless Empire of Reason.* Lawrence: University Press of Kansas.

Max, D. T. 1999. "The Oprah Effect." *New York Times Magazine,* 26 December.

Mayerfeld, Jamie. 1998. "The Myth of Benign Group Identity: A Critique of Liberal Nationalism." *Polity* 30.

Mayfield, John. 1982. *The New Nation: 1800–1845.* Rev. ed. New York: Hill and Wang.

Mayhew, David R. 2000. "American Electoral Realignments: A Critique of the Classical Genre." Paper delivered at conference on American Political Development, Massachusetts Institute of Technology, May 6.

Mayo, Bernard, ed. 1942. *Jefferson Himself: Selected Writings.* Boston: Houghton-Mifflin.

Mayo, Patricia Elton. 1974. *The Roots of Identity: Three National Movements in Contemporary European Politics.* London: Allen Lane.

McCardell, John. 1990. *The Idea of a Southern Nation: Southern Nationalists and Southern Nationalism, 1830–60.* New York: W. W. Norton.

McCloskey, R. G., ed. 1967. *The Works of James Wilson.* Cambridge, Mass.: Belknap Press.

McConnell, Stuart. 1996. "Reading the Flag: A Reconsideration of the Patriotic Cults of the 1890s." In John Bodnar, ed., *Bonds of Affection: Americans Define Their Patriotism.* Princeton, N.J.: Princeton University Press.

McCormick, Richard L. 1986. *The Party Period and Public Policy: American Politics from the Age of Jackson to the Progressive Era.* New York: Oxford University Press.

———. 1990. "The Jacksonian Strategy." *Journal of the Early Republic* 10.

McCormick, Richard P. 1953. *The History of Voting in New Jersey.* New Brunswick, N.J.: Rutgers University Press.

McCoy, Drew R. 1980. *The Elusive Republic: Political Economy in Jeffersonian America.* New York: W. W. Norton.

———. 1989. *Last of the Fathers: James Madison and the Republican Legacy.* New York: Cambridge University Press.

———. 1995. "Lincoln and the Founding Fathers: A Reconsideration." *Journal of the Abraham Lincoln Association* 16.

McDonald, Forrest. 1958. *We the People: The Economic Origins of the Constitution.* Chicago: University of Chicago Press.

———. 1979 [1965]. *E Pluribus Unum: The Formation of the American Republic, 1776–1790.* 2d ed. Indianapolis: Liberty Press.

———. 1985. *Novus Ordo Seclorum: The Intellectual Origins of the Constitution.* Lawrence: University Press of Kansas.

McFeely, William S. 1991. *Frederick Douglass.* New York: Norton.

McPherson, James M. 1964. *The Struggle for Equality: Abolitionists and the Negro in the Civil War and Reconstruction.* Princeton, N.J.: Princeton University Press.

———. 1990. *Abraham Lincoln and the Second American Revolution.* New York: Oxford University Press.

———. 1992. "The Art of Abraham Lincoln." *New York Review of Books,* 16 July.

———. 1995. "Who Freed the Slaves?" *Proceedings of the American Philosophical Society* 139.

———. 1997. *For Cause and Comrades: Why Men Fought in the Civil War.* New York: Oxford University Press.

McWilliams, Wilson Carey. 1973. *The Idea of Fraternity in America.* Berkeley: University of California Press.

Mead, Sidney. 1963. *The Lively Experiment: The Shaping of Christianity in America.* New York: Harper & Row.

Meagher, Robert E., ed. 1978. *An Introduction to Augustine.* New York: New York University Press.

Meehan, Elizabeth M. 1996. "European Integration and Citizens' Rights: A Comparative Perspective." *Publius* 26.

Meier, August. 1966. *Negro Thought in America, 1880–1915.* Ann Arbor: University of Michigan Press.

Meinecke, Friedrich. 1970 [1907]. *Cosmopolitanism and the National State.* Princeton, N.J.: Princeton University Press.

Melville, Herman. 1866. *Battle-Pieces and Aspects of the War.* New York: Harper and Brothers.

Merk, Frederick. 1995 [1963]. *Manifest Destiny and Mission in American History: A Reinterpretation.* Cambridge: Harvard University Press.

Merrell, James H. 1989. *The Indians' New World: Catawbas and Their Neighbors from European Contact through the Era of Removal.* Chapel Hill: University of North Carolina Press.

Merriman, Roger Bigelow. 1902. *Life and Letters of Thomas Cromwell.* 2 vols. Oxford: Clarendon Press.

Merritt, Richard L. 1966. *Symbols of American Community, 1735–1775.* New Haven: Yale University Press.

Meyers, Marvin, ed. 1981. *The Mind of the Founder: Sources of the Political Thought of James Madison.* Hanover, N.H.: University Press of New England.

Middlekauff, Robert. 1982. *The Glorious Cause: The American Revolution, 1763–1789.* New York: Oxford University Press.

Miller, Angela. 1993. *The Empire of the Eye: Landscape Representation and American Cultural Politics, 1825–1875.* Ithaca: Cornell University Press.

Miller, David. 1995. *On Nationality.* New York: Oxford University Press.

———. 1997. "Nationality: Some Replies." *Journal of Applied Philosophy* 14.

Miller, Edwin Haviland. 1968. *Walt Whitman's Poetry: A Psychological Journey.* Boston: Houghton-Mifflin.

Miller, John C. 1936. *Sam Adams: Pioneer in Propaganda.* Boston: Little, Brown.

Miller, Perry. 1961 [1936]. *The New England Mind: From Colony to Province.* Boston: Beacon Press.

———, ed. 1956. *The American Puritans: Their Prose and Poetry.* New York: Columbia University Press.

Miller, Trudi C. 1992. "What Adam Smith and James Madison Would Say about the American Political Economy Today." *Public Administration Review* 52.

Miller, William Lee. 1992. *The Business of May Next: James Madison and the Founding.* Charlottesville: University Press of Virginia.

Mitchell, Reid. 1993. *The Vacant Chair: The Northern Soldier Leaves Home.* New York: Oxford University Press.

Mohr, James C., ed. 1976. *Radical Republicans in the North: State Politics during Reconstruction.* Baltimore, Md.: Johns Hopkins University Press.

Montgomery, David. 1979. *Workers' Control in America.* New York: Cambridge University Press.

———. 1987. *The Fall of the House of Labor: The Workplace, the State, and American Labor Activism, 1865–1925.* New York: Cambridge University Press.

Moore, Frank, ed. 1855. *Songs and Ballads of the American Revolution.* New York: D. Appleton.

Moorhead, James H. 1978. *American Apocalypse: Yankee Protestants and the Civil War, 1860–1869.* New Haven: Yale University Press.

Morel, Lucas E. 2000. *Lincoln's Sacred Effort: Defining Religion's Role in American Self-Government.* Lanham, Md.: Lexington Books.

Morgan, Edmund S. 1963. "The Revolution Considered as an Intellectual Movement." In Arthur M. Schlesinger Jr. and Morton White, eds., *Paths of American Thought.* Boston: Houghton-Mifflin.

———. 1986. "Safety in Numbers: Madison, Hume, and the Tenth *Federalist.*" *Huntington Library Quarterly* 49.

———. 1988. *Inventing the People: The Rise of Popular Sovereignty in England and America.* New York: W. W. Norton.

Morgan, Joseph. 1749 [1727]. "A Love to Our Neighbors Recommended." Boston: John Green.

Morone, James A. 1990. *The Democratic Wish.* New York: Basic Books.

Morris, Richard B. 1987. *The Forging of the Union, 1781–1789.* New York: Harper & Row.

Morrison, Michael A. 1997. *Slavery and the American West: The Eclipse of Manifest Destiny and the Coming of the Civil War.* Chapel Hill: University of North Carolina Press.

Morrow, Terence S. 1999. "Common Sense Deliberative Practice: John Witherspoon, James Madison, and the U.S. Constitution." *Rhetoric Society Quarterly* 29.

Moses, Wilson Jeremiah. 1978. *The Golden Age of Black Nationalism, 1850–1925.* Hamden, Conn.: Archon Books.

Mosher, Michael. 1990. "Walt Whitman: Jacobin Poet of American Democracy." *Political Theory* 18.

Mulford, Elisha. 1882. *The Nation.* Rev. ed. Cambridge, Mass.: Riverside Press.

Munslow, Alun. 1992. *Discourse and Culture: The Creation of America, 1870–1920.* New York: Routledge.

Murdoch, Alexander. 1998. *British History, 1660–1832: National Identity and Local Culture.* London: Macmillan Press.

Murphy, James B. 1973. *L. Q. C. Lamar: Pragmatic Patriot.* Baton Rouge: Louisiana State University Press.

Murphy, William P. 1967. *The Triumph of Nationalism.* Chicago: Quadrangle Press.

Murrin, John M. 1973. "The American Revolution Considered as a Social Accident." In Kurtz and Hutson 1973.

———. 1987a. "A Roof without Walls: The Dilemma of American National Identity." In Richard Beeman et al., eds., *Beyond Confederation: Origins of the Constitution and American National Identity.* Chapel Hill: University of North Carolina Press.

———. 1987b. "Gordon Wood and the Search for Liberal America." *William and Mary Quarterly* 44.

Nagel, Paul C. 1964. *One Nation Indivisible: The Union in American Thought, 1776–1861.* New York: Oxford University Press.

———. 1971. *This Sacred Trust: American Nationality, 1798–1898.* New York: Oxford University Press.

Nash, Gary B. 1988. *Forging Freedom: The Formation of Philadelphia's Black Community, 1720–1840.* Cambridge: Harvard University Press.

Neather, Andrew. 1996. "Labor Republicanism, Race, and Popular Patriotism in the Era of Empire, 1890–1914." In John Bodnar, ed., *Bonds of Affection: Americans Define Their Patriotism.* Princeton, N.J.: Princeton University Press.

Neely, Mark E. 1991. *The Fate of Liberty: Abraham Lincoln and Civil Liberties.* New York: Oxford University Press.

Neider, Charles, ed. 1975. *The Complete Tales of Washington Irving.* Garden City, N.Y.: Doubleday.

Nelson, Henry Loomis. 1892. "The Growth of the Federal Power." *Harper's* 85.

Neuman, Gerald L. 1993. "The Lost Century of American Immigration Law (1776–1875)." *Columbia Law Review* 93.

Newcomb, Benjamin H. 1972. *Franklin and Galloway: A Political Partnership.* New Haven: Yale University Press.

Newfield, Christopher. 1996. *The Emerson Effect: Individualism and Submission in America.* Chicago: University of Chicago Press.

Nichols, Roy F. 1961. *The Stakes of Power, 1848–1877.* New York: Hill and Wang.

Niebuhr, Reinhold. 1964. "The Religion of Abraham Lincoln." In Allan Nevins, ed., *Lincoln and the Gettysburg Address.* Urbana: University of Illinois Press.

Nielsen, Kai. 1997. "Cultural Nationalism, neither Ethnic nor Civic." *Philosophical Forum* 28.

Niven, John. 1988. *John C. Calhoun and the Price of Union.* Baton Rouge: Louisiana State University Press.

Norton, Anne. 1986. *Alternative Americas: A Reading of Antebellum Political Culture.* Chicago: University of Chicago Press.

Norton, Mary Beth. 1980. *Liberty's Daughters: The Revolutionary Experience of American Women, 1750–1800.* Boston: Little, Brown.

Novak, Michael, ed. 1996. *To Empower People: From State to Civil Society.* Washington, D.C.: AEI Press.

Nourse, Rebecca. 1996. "Toward a 'Due Foundation' for the Separation of Powers: The Federalist Papers as Political Narrative." *Texas Law Review* 74.

Oates, Stephen B. 1984. *Abraham Lincoln: The Man Behind the Myth.* New York: Harper & Row.

O'Callaghan, E. B., ed. 1855. *Documents Relative to the Colonial History of the State of New York.* 6 vols. Albany: Weed, Parsons.

Oliver, Andrew. 1773. Letters in "The Representation of Governor Hutchinson and Others. . . ." Reprinted in Labaree et al., eds., 1959–, *The Papers of Benjamin Franklin* 20: Appendix. New Haven: Yale University Press.

Olsen, Otto H., ed. 1980. *Reconstruction and Redemption in the South.* Baton Rouge: Louisiana State University Press.

Olson, Alison G. 1960. "The British Government and Colonial Union, 1754." *William and Mary Quarterly* 17.

Olson, Lester C. 1991. *Emblems of American Community in the Revolutionary Era: A Study in Rhetorical Iconology.* Washington, D.C.: Smithsonian Institution Press.

Omi, Michael, and Howard Winant. 1986. *Racial Formation in the United States: From the 1960s to the 1980s.* New York: Routledge and Kegan Paul.

Onuf, Peter S. 1983. *The Origins of the Federal Republic: Jurisdictional Controversies in the United States, 1775–1787.* Philadelphia: University of Pennsylvania Press.

——. 1986. "Liberty, Development, and Union: Visions of the West in the 1780s." *William and Mary Quarterly* 43.

——. 1987. *Statehood and Union: A History of the Northwest Ordinance.* Bloomington: Indiana University Press.

——. 1988. "State Sovereignty and the Making of the Constitution." In Terence Ball and J. G. A. Pocock, eds., *Conceptual Change and the Constitution.* Lawrence: University Press of Kansas.

——. 1990. "James Madison's Extended Republic." *Texas Tech Law Review* 21.

——. 1998. "'To Declare Them a Free and Independent People': Race, Slavery, and National Identity in Jefferson's Thought." *Journal of the Early Republic* 18.

——. 1999. "'We Shall All Be Americans': Thomas Jefferson and the Indians." *Indiana Magazine of History* 95.

Ostrom, Vincent. 1991. *The Meaning of American Federalism: Constituting a Self-Governing Society.* San Francisco: ICS Press.

Otis, James. 1764. "Rights of the British Colonies Asserted and Proved." Boston: Edes and Gill.

Padover, Saul. 1972. *Karl Marx on America and the Civil War.* New York.

Paine, Thomas. 1969 [1791]. *The Rights of Man.* Baltimore: Penguin.

——. 1976 [1776]. *Common Sense.* New York: Viking Penguin.

Paludan, Philip Shaw. 1972. "The American Civil War Considered as a Crisis in Law and Order." *American Historical Review* 75.

——. 1988. *"A People's Contest": The Union and Civil War, 1861–1865.* New York: Harper & Row.

——. 1994. *The Presidency of Abraham Lincoln.* Lawrence: University Press of Kansas.

Pangle, Thomas. 1988. *The Spirit of Modern Republicanism.* Chicago: University of Chicago Press.

Paolucci, Henry. 1978. *A Separate and Equal Station: Hegel, America, and the Nation-State System.* New York: Griffon House.

Park, Robert E., and Herbert A. Miller. 1921. *Old World Traits Transplanted.* New York: Harper & Brothers.

Parker, Alison M. 1997. *Purifying America: Women, Cultural Reform, and Pro-Censorship Activities, 1873–1933.* Urbana: University of Illinois Press.

Pattee, Fred L., ed. 1902. *The Poems of Philip Freneau.* 3 vols. Princeton, N.J.: University Library.

Patterson, Anita Haya. 1997. *From Emerson to King: Democracy, Race, and the Politics of Protest.* New York: Oxford University Press.

Paxton, Litty. 1990. "Sustaining the Dream." Unpublished manuscript on file with author.

Pearce, Haywood J. 1928. *Benjamin H. Hill: Secession and Reconstruction.* Chicago: University of Chicago Press.

Pearce, Roy Harvey. 1962. *Whitman: A Collection of Critical Essays.* Englewood Cliffs, N.J.: Prentice-Hall.

Pease, Jane H., and William H. Pease. 1974. *They Who Would Be Free: Blacks' Search for Freedom, 1830–1861.* New York: Atheneum.

Perlman, Selig. 1928. *A Theory of the Labor Movement.* New York: Augustus M. Kelly.

Perman, Michael. 1984. *The Road to Redemption: Southern Politics, 1869–1879.* Chapel Hill: University of North Carolina Press.

Peters, Richard, ed. 1831. *Case of the Cherokee Nation.* Boston: H. & F. J. Huntington.

Peterson, Mark A. 1997. *The Price of Redemption: The Spiritual Economy of Puritan New England.* Stanford, Calif.: Stanford University Press.

Peterson, Merrill D. 1987. *The Great Triumvirate: Webster, Clay, and Calhoun.* New York: Oxford University Press.

Pierce, Bessie L. 1930. *Civic Attitudes in American School Textbooks.* Chicago: University of Chicago Press.

Pocock, J. G. A. 1972. *Politics, Language, and Time: Essays on Political Thought and History.* London: Methuen.

——. 1975. *The Machiavellian Moment: Florentine Political Thought and the Atlantic Republican Tradition.* Princeton, N.J.: Princeton University Press.

——. 1987. "States, Republics, and Empires: The American Founding in Early Modern Perspective." *Social Science Quarterly* 68.

Pole, J. R. 1977. *The Idea of Union.* Alexandria, Va.: Bicentennial Council.

——. 1983. *The Gift of Government.* Athens: University of Georgia Press.

——. 1993. *The Pursuit of Equality in American History.* Berkeley: University of California Press.

Porter, Kirk H., and Donald Bruce Johnson, eds. 1966. *National Party Platforms, 1840–1964.* Urbana: University of Illinois Press.

Potter, David M. 1942. *Lincoln and His Party in the Secession Crisis.* New Haven: Yale University Press.

——. 1960. "Jefferson Davis and the Political Factors in Confederate Defeat." In David Donald, ed., *Why the North Won the Civil War.* Baton Rouge: Louisiana State University Press.

——. 1976. *The Impending Crisis: 1848–1861.* Ed. Don E. Ferenbacher. New York: Harper & Row.

Powderly, Terence V. 1889. *Thirty Years of Labor, 1859–1889.* Columbus, Ohio: Excelsior Publishing.

——. 1940. *The Path I Trod.* New York: Columbia University Press.

Powell, H. Jefferson. 1993a. *The Moral Tradition of American Constitutionalism: A Theological Interpretation.* Durham, N.C.: Duke University Press.

——. 1993b. "The Oldest Question of Constitutional Law." *Virginia Law Review* 79.

Pownall, Thomas. 1766. *The Administration of the Colonies.* 3d ed. London: J. Walter.

Prucha, Francis Paul. 1984. *The Great Father: The United States Government and the American Indians.* 2 vols. Lincoln: University of Nebraska Press.

Pryde, George S. 1950. *The Treaty of Union of Scotland and England, 1707.* London: Thomas Nelson & Sons.

Pufendorf, Samuel. 1710 [1679]. *Of the Law of Nature and Nations.* Oxford: University Press.

Putnam, Robert D. 1993. *Making Democracy Work: Civic Traditions in Modern Italy.* Princeton, N.J.: Princeton University Press.

——. 2000. *Bowling Alone: The Collapse and Revival of American Community.* New York: Simon & Schuster.

Pye, Lucien W., and Sidney Verba, eds. 1965. *Political Culture and Political Development.* Princeton, N.J.: Princeton University Press.

Quarles, Benjamin. 1938. "The Breach between Douglass and Garrison." *Journal of Negro History* 23.

Quintard, Charles T. 1866. "Bishop's Address." *Proceedings, 34th Annual Convention of the Protestant Episcopal Church (Tennessee Diocese).* Memphis: Hutton, Brower & Co.

Rabinowitz, Howard N. 1980. *Race Relations in the Urban South, 1865–1890.* New York: Oxford University Press.

——. 1992. *The First New South: 1865–1920.* Arlington Heights, Ill.: Harlan Davidson.

Rable, George C. 1984. *"But There Was No Peace": The Role of Violence in the Politics of Reconstruction.* Athens: University of Georgia Press.

——. 1994. *The Confederate Republic: A Revolution against Politics.* Chapel Hill: University of North Carolina Press.

Rae, Douglas W. 1981. *Equalities.* Cambridge, Mass.: Harvard University Press.

Rahe, Paul A. 1992. *Republics Ancient and Modern: Classical Republicanism and the American Revolution.* Chapel Hill: University of North Carolina Press.

Rakove, Jack N. 1979. *The Beginnings of National Politics: An Interpretive History of the Continental Congress.* New York: Alfred A. Knopf.

——. 1988. "The Madisonian Moment." *University of Chicago Law Review* 55.

———. 1996. *Original Meanings: Politics and Ideas in the Making of the Constitution.* New York: Alfred A. Knopf.

Randall, James G. 1947. *Lincoln the Liberal Statesman.* New York: Dodd, Mead.

Ranney, John C. 1946. "The Bases of American Federalism." *William and Mary Quarterly* 3.

Ransom, Roger L. 1999. "Fact and Counterfact: The 'Second American Revolution' Revisited." *Civil War History* 45.

Rawley, James A. 1963. "The Nationalism of Abraham Lincoln." *Civil War History* 9.

———. 1974. *The Politics of Union: Northern Politics during the Civil War.* Lincoln: University of Nebraska Press.

Rawls, John. 1993. *Political Liberalism.* New York: Columbia University Press.

Read, James H. 1995. "'Our Complicated System': James Madison on Power and Liberty." *Political Theory* 23.

Redky, Edwin S. 1969. *Black Exodus.* New Haven: Yale University Press.

Reid, John Phillip. 1989. *The Concept of Representation in the Age of the American Revolution.* Chicago: University of Chicago Press.

Remini, Robert. 1997. *Daniel Webster: The Man and His Time.* New York: W. W. Norton.

Renan, Ernest. 1994 [1882]. "Qu'est-ce qu'une nation?" In John Hutchinson and Anthony D. Smith, eds., *Nationalism.* New York: Oxford University Press.

Reynolds, David S. 1995. *Walt Whitman's America: A Cultural Biography.* New York: Knopf.

Rhoden, Nancy L. 1999. *Revolutionary Anglicanism: The Colonial Church of England Clergy during the American Revolution.* New York: New York University Press.

Rhodes, Elisha Hunt. 1991. *"All for the Union": The Civil War Diary and Letters.* Ed. Robert Hunt Rhodes. New York: Orion Books.

Richard, Carl J. 1994. *The Founders and the Classics: Greece, Rome and the American Enlightenment.* Cambridge: Harvard University Press.

Richards, Eric. 1991. "Scotland and the Uses of the Atlantic Empire." In Bernard Bailyn and Philip D. Morgan, eds., *Strangers Within the Realm: Cultural Margins of the First British Empire.* Chapel Hill: University of North Carolina Press.

Richardson, Heather Cox. 1997. *The Greatest Nation of the Earth: Republican Economic Policies during the Civil War.* Cambridge: Harvard University Press.

———. 1999. "Explaining the American Civil War." *Historian* 61.

Richardson, James D., ed. 1896–99. *Messages and Papers of the Presidents, 1789–1897.* 10 vols. Washington, D.C.: Government Printing Office.

Richardson, Marilyn, ed. 1987. *Maria W. Stewart: America's First Black Political Writer, Essays and Speeches.* Bloomington: Indiana University Press.

Richardson, Robert D. 1995. *Emerson: The Mind on Fire.* Berkeley: University of California Press.

Richter, Melvin. 1990. *"Begriffsgeschichte* and the History of Ideas." *Political Theory* 18.

———. 1995. *The History of Political and Social Concepts: A Critical Introduction.* New York: Oxford University Press.

Ricoeur, Paul. 1965. *History and Truth.* Trans. Charles A. Kelbley. Evanston, Ill.: Northwestern University Press.

Riley, Patrick William. 1978. *The Union of England and Scotland.* Totowa, N.J.: Rowman & Littlefield.

Rives, William C., and Philip R. Fendall, eds. 1865. *Letters and Other Writings of James Madison.* 4 vols. Philadelphia: J. B. Lippincott.

Robertson, John, ed. 1995. *A Union for Empire: Political Thought and the British Union of 1707.* New York: Cambridge University Press.

Robinson, John. 1876 [1620]. "Advice to Pilgrim Colonists." In Albert Bushnell Hart, ed., *Era of Colonization, 1492–1689*. New York: Macmillan.

Rodgers, Daniel T. 1987. *Contested Truths: American Keywords since Independence*. New York: Basic Books.

———. 1992. "Republicanism: The Career of a Concept." *Journal of American History* 79.

Roosevelt, Theodore. 1918 [1897]. "What 'Americanism' Means." In M. G. Fulton, ed., *National Ideals and Problems*. New York: Macmillan.

Rosen, Gary. 1999. *American Compact: James Madison and the Problem of Founding*. Lawrence: University Press of Kansas.

Rosenblum, Nancy L. 1990. "Strange Attractors: How Individualists Connect to Form Democratic Unity." *Political Theory* 18.

Rosenzweig, Roy. 1983. *Eight Hours for What We Will: Workers and Leisure in an Industrial City*. New York: Cambridge University Press.

Rossiter, Clinton. 1953. *Seedtime of the Republic: The Origin of the American Tradition of Political Liberty*. New York: Alfred A. Knopf.

———. 1966. *Conservatism in America: The Thankless Persuasion*. New York: Alfred A. Knopf.

———, ed. 1961. *The Federalist Papers*. New York: Penguin.

Rousseau, Jean-Jacques. 1968 [1762]. *The Social Contract*. Trans. Maurice Cranston. New York: Penguin Books.

Rubin, Anne Sarah. 1994. "Between Union and Chaos: The Political Life of John Janney." *Virginia Magazine of History and Biography* 102.

Russell, Greg. 1995. "Madison's Realism and the Role of Domestic Ideals in Foreign Affairs." *Presidential Studies Quarterly* 25.

Russell, Mattie, ed. 1955. "Why Lamar Eulogized Sumner." *Journal of Southern History* 21.

Rutland, Robert A. 1987. *James Madison: The Founding Father*. New York: Macmillan.

Ryan, Mary P. 1991. "Gender and Public Access: Women's Politics in Nineteenth-Century America." In Craig Calhoun, ed., *Habermas and the Public Sphere*. Cambridge: Harvard University Press.

Safire, William. 1991. "Confederacy Rises Again." *New York Times Sunday Magazine*, 29 September.

Sanchez-Eppler, Karen. 1993. *Touching Liberty: Abolition, Feminism, and the Politics of the Body*. Berkeley: University of California Press.

Sandel, Michael J. 1996. *Democracy's Discontent: America in Search of a Public Philosophy*. Cambridge: Harvard University Press.

Saum, Lewis O. 1980. *The Popular Mood of Pre-Civil War America*. Westport, Conn.: Greenwood Press.

Saville, Julie. 1994. *The Work of Reconstruction: From Slave to Wage Laborer in South Carolina, 1860–70*. New York: Cambridge University Press.

Sawrey, Robert D. 1992. *Dubious Victory: The Reconstruction Debate in Ohio*. Lexington: University Press of Kentucky.

Saxton, Alexander. 1990. *The Rise and Fall of the White Republic: Class Politics and Mass Culture in Nineteenth-Century America*. New York: Verso.

Schambra, William A. 1998. "All Community is Local: The Key to America's Civic Renewal." In Dionne 1998, 44–49.

Scheckel, Susan. 1998. *The Insistence of the Indian: Race and Nationalism in Nineteenth-Century American Culture*. Princeton, N.J.: Princeton University Press.

Schirmer, Dietmar. 1999. "Nation-Building and Nation-Buildings: Washington Art and Architecture and the Symbols of American Nationalism." In H. Lehmann and H. Wellenreuther, eds., *German and American Nationalism: A Comparative Perspective*. New York: Berg.

Schlesinger, Arthur M. Jr. 1992. *The Disuniting of America: Reflections on a Multicultural Society.* New York: W. W. Norton.

Schuck, Peter H., and Rogers M. Smith. 1985. *Citizenship without Consent: Illegal Aliens in the American Polity.* New Haven: Yale University Press.

Schurz, Carl. 1867. "The True Problem." *Atlantic Monthly* 19.

———. 1969 [1885]. *Report on the Condition of the New South.* New York: Arno Press.

Schwarzenbach, Sibyl A. 1996. "On Civic Friendship." *Ethics* 107.

Seligman, Adam B. 1992. *The Idea of Civil Society.* New York: Free Press.

———. 1998. "Between Public and Private." *Society* 35.

Sellers, Charles G. 1960. *The Southerner as American.* Chapel Hill: University of North Carolina Press.

———. 1991. *The Jacksonian Revolution: Society, Markets, and Politics.* New York: Oxford University Press.

Shaftesbury, Anthony Ashley Cooper. 1963 [1711]. *Characteristicks of Men, Manners, Opinions, Times.* 3 vols. Gloucester, Mass.: Peter Smith.

Shain, Barry. 1994. *The Myth of American Individualism: The Protestant Origins of American Political Thought.* Princeton, N.J.: Princeton University Press.

Shannon, Jasper Berry. 1948. *Toward a New Politics in the South.* Knoxville: University of Tennessee Press.

Shapiro, Ian. 1989. "Gross Concepts in Political Argument." *Political Theory* 17.

———. 1990. *Political Criticism.* Berkeley: University of California Press.

Shefter, Martin. 1994. *Political Parties and the State: The American Historical Experience.* Princeton, N.J.: Princeton University Press.

Shepherd, James F. 1988. "British America and the Atlantic Economy." In Ronald Hoffman et al., *The Economy of Early America: The Revolutionary Period, 1763–1790.* Charlottesville: University Press of Virginia.

Shepsle, Kenneth A. 1989. "Studying Institutions: Some Lessons from the Rational Choice Approach." *Journal of Theoretical Politics* 1.

Shewmaker, Kenneth, ed. 1990. *Daniel Webster: "The Completest Man."* Hanover, N.H.: University Press of New England.

Shewmaker, Kenneth, et al., eds. 1983–87. *The Papers of Daniel Webster: Diplomatic Papers.* 2 vols. Hanover, N.H.: University Press of New England.

Shklar, Judith N. 1990. "Emerson and the Inhibitions of Democracy." *Political Theory* 18.

———. 1998. *Redeeming American Political Thought.* Chicago: University of Chicago Press.

Short, John Rennie. 1999. "A New Mode of Thinking: Creating a National Geography in the Early Republic." In Edward C. Carter, ed., *Surveying the Record: North American Scientific Exploration to 1930.* Philadelphia: American Philosophical Society.

Silber, Nina. 1993. *The Romance of Reunion.* Chapel Hill: University of North Carolina Press.

Silbey, Joel H. 1991. *The American Political Nation, 1838–1893.* Stanford, Calif.: Stanford University Press.

Simmons, R. C., and P. D. G. Thomas, eds. 1982. *Proceedings and Debates of the British Parliaments Respecting North America, 1754–1783.* 6 vols. London: Kraus International.

Simpson, David. 1990. "Destiny Made Manifest: The Styles of Whitman's Poetry." In Homi Bhabha, ed., *Nation and Narration.* New York: Routledge.

Sinopoli, Richard C. 1992. *The Foundations of American Citizenship: Liberalism, the Constitution, and Civic Virtue.* New York: Oxford University Press.

Skinner, Quentin. 1969. "Meaning and Understanding in the History of Ideas." *History and Theory* 8.

Sklar, Martin J. 1991. "Periodization and Historiography: Studying American Political Development in the Progressive Era, 1890s–1916." *Studies in American Political Development* 5.

Skocpol, Theda. 1992. *Protecting Soldiers and Mothers: The Political Origins of Social Policy in the United States.* Cambridge: Harvard University Press.

——. 1997a. "The Tocqueville Problem: Civic Engagement in American Democracy." *Social Science History* 21.

——. 1997b. "A Partnership with American Families." In Stanley B. Greenberg and Theda Skocpol, eds., *The New Majority.* New Haven: Yale University Press.

Skowronek, Stephen. 1982. *Building a New American State: The Expansion of National Administrative Capacities, 1877–1920.* New York: Cambridge University Press.

——. 1993. *The Politics Presidents Make: Leadership from John Adams to George Bush.* Cambridge: Harvard University Press.

Smith, Anthony D. 1986. *The Ethnic Origins of Nations.* Oxford: Basil Blackwell.

——. 1996. "Culture, Community, and Territory: The Politics of Ethnicity and Nationalism." *International Affairs* 72.

Smith, Craig R. 1999. "The Anti-War Rhetoric of Daniel Webster." *Quarterly Journal of Speech* 85.

Smith, Kimberly K. 1999. *The Dominion of Voice: Riot, Reason, and Romance in Antebellum Politics.* Lawrence: University Press of Kansas.

Smith, Page. 1980. *The Shaping of America: A People's History of the Young Republic.* New York: McGraw-Hill.

Smith, Paul H., ed. 1976 –. *Letters of Delegates to Congress, 1774–1789.* 25 vols. Washington, D.C.: Government Printing Office.

Smith, Richard Norton. 1993. *Patriarch: George Washington and the New American Nation.* Boston: Houghton-Mifflin.

Smith, Rogers M. 1985. *Liberalism and American Constitutional Law.* Cambridge: Harvard University Press.

——. 1988. "The 'American Creed' and American Identity: The Limits of Liberal Citizenship in the United States." *Western Political Quarterly* 41.

——. 1997. *Civic Ideals: Conflicting Visions of Citizenship in U.S. History.* New Haven: Yale University Press.

——. 1998. "'Equal' Treatment? A Liberal Separationist View." In Steven V. Monsma and J. Christopher Soper, eds., *Equal Treatment of Religion in a Pluralistic Society.* Grand Rapids, Mich.: W. B. Eerdmans.

——. 1999. "Legitimating Reconstruction: The Limits of Legalism." Paper presented at Yale University Political Theory Workshop.

Smith, T. J., and L. Z. Jucovy. 1995. *Launching AmeriCorps.* Philadelphia: Public-Private Ventures Press.

Smith-Rosenberg, Carole. 1992. "Dis-Covering the Subject of the 'Great Constitutional Discussion,' 1786–1789." *Journal of American History* 79.

Smout, T. C. "The Road to Union." In Geoffrey S. Holmes, ed., *Britain after the Glorious Revolution, 1689–1914.* New York: St. Martin's Press.

Sobel, Mecham. 1987. *The World They Made Together: Black and White Values in Eighteenth-Century Virginia.* Princeton, N.J.: Princeton University Press.

Sorenson, Leonard R. 1995. *Madison on the "General Welfare" of America: His Consistent Constitutional Vision.* Lanham, Md.: Rowman & Littlefield.

Spackman, S. G. F. 1990. "Lincoln Shadows: Public Issues and Private Meanings during Civil War and Reconstruction." *Journal of American Studies* 24.

Spalding, Matthew. 1994. "From Pluribus to Unum: Immigration and the Founding Fathers." *Policy Review* 67.

Spencer, Herbert. 1910 [1865]. *Social Statics.* New York: D. Appleton.

Stagg, J. C. A. 1983. *Mr. Madison's War: Politics, Diplomacy, and Warfare in the Early American Republic, 1783–1830.* Princeton, N.J.: Princeton University Press.

Stagg, J. C. A., et al., eds. 1984–99. *The Papers of James Madison: Presidential Series.* Charlottesville: University Press of Virginia.

Stampp, Kenneth M. 1956. *The Peculiar Institution: Slavery in the Ante-Bellum South.* New York: Vintage Books.

——. 1978. "The Concept of Perpetual Union." *Journal of American History* 65.

——. 1992. "One Alone? The United States and National Self-Determination." In Gabor S. Boritt, ed., *Lincoln, the War President: The Gettysburg Lectures.* New York: Oxford University Press.,

Stark, Leonard P. 1996. "The Presidential Primary and Caucus Schedule: A Role for Federal Regulation?" *Yale Law and Policy Review* 15: 331–57.

Staub, Ervin A. 1997. "Blind versus Constructive Patriotism." In Daniel Bar-Tal and Ervin A. Staub, *Patriotism in the Lives of Individuals and Nations.* Chicago: Nelson-Hall.

Staunton, Howard, ed. 1874. *The Works of William Shakespeare.* 6 vols. London: George Routledge.

Steele, Ian K. 1998. "Exploding Colonial American History: Amerindian, Atlantic, and Global Perspectives." *Reviews in American History* 26.

Steiner, Edward A. 1906. *On the Trail of the Immigrant.* New York: Fleming H. Revell.

Steinmo, Sven. 1994. "Rethinking 'Rethinking American Exceptionalism.'" In Larry Dodd and Calvin Jillson, eds. *The Dynamics of American Politics: Approaches and Interpretations.* Boulder: Westview Press.

Stephanson, Anders. 1995. *Manifest Destiny: American Expansion and the Empire of Right.* New York: Hill & Wang.

Stephens, Alexander H. 1868–70. *A Constitutional View of the Late War Between the States.* 2 vols. Philadelphia: National Publishing Co.

Stephens, Gregory. 1997. "Frederick Douglass' Multiracial Abolitionism." *Communication Studies* 48.

Stettner, Edward A. 1993. *Shaping Modern Liberalism: Herbert Croly and Progressive Thought.* Lawrence: University Press of Kansas.

Stevenson, Brenda E. 1996. *Life in Black and White: Family and Community in the Slave South.* New York: Oxford University Press.

Stiles, Ezra. 1790 [1761]. "A Discourse on the Christian Union." Brookfield, Mass.

Stokes, Anthony. 1783. "A View of the Constitution of the British Colonies. . . ." London: B. White.

Stone, Lawrence. 1992. "The Revolution over the Revolution." *New York Review of Books* 39.

Storing, Herbert J. 1977. *What the Anti-Federalists Were FOR: The Political Thought of the Opponents of the Constitution.* Chicago: University of Chicago Press.

——, ed. 1981. *The Complete Anti-Federalist.* 7 vols. Chicago: University of Chicago Press.

Story, Joseph. 1987 [1833]. *Commentaries on the Constitution of the United States.* Ed. R. Rotunda and J. Nowek. Durham, N.C.: Carolina Academic Press.

Stout, Harry S. 1990. "Rhetoric and Reality in the New Republic." In Mark A. Noll, ed., *Religion and American Politics: From the Colonial Period to the 1980s.* New York: Oxford University Press.

Stovall, Floyd, ed. 1939. *Walt Whitman: Representative Selections.* New York: American Book Company.

Strong, George Templeton. 1952. *Diaries: The Civil War, 1860–1865.* Ed. Allan Nevins and Milton H. Thomas. New York: Macmillan.

Strozier, Charles B. 1987. *Lincoln's Quest for Union: Public and Private Meanings.* Urbana: University of Illinois Press.

———. 1988. "Lincoln's Quest for Union." In Gabor S. Boritt, ed. 1988, *The Historian's Lincoln.* Urbana: University of Illinois Press.

Stuckey, Sterling. 1987. *Slave Culture: Nationalist Theory and the Foundations of Black America.* New York: Oxford University Press.

Sullivan, William M. 1982. *Reconstructing Public Philosophy.* Berkeley: University of California Press.

Summers, Mark Wahlgren. 1987. *The Plundering Generation: Corruption and the Crisis of the Union, 1849–61.* New York: Oxford University Press.

———. 1997. *The Gilded Age; or, The Hazard of New Functions.* Upper Saddle River, N.J.: Prentice-Hall.

Sunstein, Cass R. 1988. "Beyond the Republican Revival." *Yale Law Journal* 97.

———. 1993. *The Partial Constitution.* Cambridge: Harvard University Press.

Swinton, John. 1895. *A Momentous Question: The Respective Attitudes of Labor and Capital.* Philadelphia: Keller Publishing Co.

Sydnor, Charles S. 1948. *The Development of Southern Sectionalism, 1819–1848.* Baton Rouge: Louisiana State University Press.

Szechi, Daniel. 1996. "A Union of Necessity." *Parliamentary History* 15.

Takaki, Ronald. 1979. *Iron Cages: Race and Culture in Nineteenth-Century America.* New York: Oxford University Press.

Tambini, Damian. 1999. "Nationalism: A Literature Survey." *European Journal of Social Theory* 1.

Tamir, Yael. 1993. *Liberal Nationalism.* Princeton, N.J.: Princeton University Press.

Tassin, Etienne. 1992. "Europe: A Political Community?" In Chantal Mouffe, ed., *Dimensions of Radical Democracy: Pluralism, Citizenship, Community.* New York: Verso.

Taylor, Charles. 1992. *Multiculturalism and "The Politics of Recognition."* Princeton, N.J.: Princeton University Press.

Taylor, George Rogers, ed. 1972. *The Turner Thesis: Concerning the Role of the Frontier in American History.* Lexington, Mass.: D. C. Heath.

Taylor, Joe Gray. 1980. "Louisiana: An Impossible Task." In O. H. Olsen, ed., *Reconstruction and Redemption in the South.* Baton Rouge: Louisiana State University Press.

Taylor, Robert J., ed. 1977–89. *Papers of John Adams.* 10 vols. Cambridge, Mass.: Harvard University Press.

Taylor, William R. 1961. *Cavalier and Yankee: The Old South and American National Character.* Cambridge: Harvard University Press.

Thelen, David. 1998. "Making History and Making the United States." *Journal of American Studies* 32.

Thomas, Clive S. 1991. *American Union in Federalist Political Thought.* New York: Garland.

Thomas, M. Wynn. 1987. *The Lunar Light of Whitman's Poetry.* Cambridge: Harvard University Press.

Thomas, Richard W. 1996. *Understanding Interracial Unity: A Study of U.S. Race Relations.* Newbury Park, Calif.: Sage Publications.

Thornton, John W., ed. 1860. *The Pulpit of the American Revolution: Political Sermons of 1776.* Boston: Gould and Lincoln.

Tocqueville, Alexis de. 1969 [1835–40]. *Democracy in America.* 2 vols. Ed. J. P. Mayer. Garden City, N.Y.: Anchor Books.

Torsella, J. M. 1988. "American National Identity, 1750–1790." *The Pennsylvania Magazine of History and Biography* 112.

Trachtenberg, Alan. 1982. *The Incorporation of America: Culture and Society in the Gilded Age.* New York: Hill & Wang.

———. 1994. "The Politics of Labor and the Poet's Work: A Reading of 'A Song for Occupations.'" In Ed Folsom, ed., *Walt Whitman: The Centennial Essays.* Iowa City: University of Iowa Press.

Trattner, Walter I. 1988. "The Federal Government and Needy Citizens in Nineteenth-Century America." *Political Science Quarterly* 103.

Treadgold, Donald W. 1990. *Freedom: A History.* New York: New York University Press.

Trefousse, Hans L. 1963. *Benjamin Franklin Wade: Radical Republican from Ohio.* New York: Twayne Publishers.

———. 1969. *The Radical Republicans: Lincoln's Vanguard for Racial Justice.* New York: Knopf.

Trilling, Lionel. 1950. *The Liberal Imagination.* New York: Viking Press.

Trumbull, J. Hammond, ed. 1850. *The Public Records of the Colony of Connecticut, 1636–1665.* Hartford, Conn.: Brown & Parsons.

———. 1876. *The True-Blue Laws of Connecticut and New Haven.* Hartford, Conn.: American Publishing Company.

Tucker, Robert W., and David C. Hendrickson. 1982. *The Fall of the First British Empire: Origins of the American War of Independence.* Baltimore, Md.: Johns Hopkins University Press.

Turner, Frederick C., and Everett Carll Ladd. 1986. "Nationalism, Leadership and the American Creed." *Canadian Review of Studies in Nationalism* 13.

Tuveson, Ernest. 1968. *Redeemer Nation: The Idea of America's Millennial Role.* Chicago: University of Chicago Press.

Ueda, Reed. 1997. "An Immigration Country of Assimilative Pluralism: Immigrant Reception and Absorption in American History." In Klaus J. Bade and Myron Weiner, *Migration Past, Migration Future.* London: Berghan Books.

Ulrich, Laurel Thatcher. 1989. "'Daughters of Liberty': Religious Women in Revolutionary New England." In Hoffman and Albert 1989, 211–43.

Van Alstyne, William. 1969. "A Critical Guide to *Marbury v. Madison.*" *Duke Law Journal* 1969.

van Creveld, Martin. 1999. *The Rise and Decline of the State.* New York: Cambridge University Press.

Vandal, Gilles. 1991. "The Policy of Violence in Caddo Parish, 1865–1884." *Louisiana History* 32.

Van Tyne, Claude H. 1922. *The Causes of the War of Independence.* Cambridge, Mass.: Riverside Press.

Viroli, Maurizio. 1992. *From Politics to Reason of State: The Acquisition and Transformation of the Language of Politics, 1250–1600.* New York: Cambridge University Press.

———. 1998. "On Civic Republicanism." *Critical Review* 12.

Vitzthum, Richard C. 1974. *The American Compromise: Theme and Method in the Histories of Bancroft, Parkman, and Adams.* Norman: University of Oklahoma Press.

Waldron, Jeremy. 1987. "Can Communal Goods Be Human Rights?" *Archives Européennes de Sociologie* 27.

———. 1989. "Particular Values and Critical Morality." *University of California Law Review* 77.

Waldstreicher, David. 1997. *In the Midst of Perpetual Fetes: The Making of American Nationalism, 1776–1820.* Chapel Hill: University of North Carolina Press.

———. 2000. "Before, Beneath, and Between Parties: The Nationalization and Racialization of American Politics, 1790–1840." In Boyd Shafer and Anthony J. Badger, eds., *Structure and Substance in American Political History.* Lawrence: University Press of Kansas.

Walker, David. 1995 [1829]. *Walker's Appeal, in Four Articles. . . .* Ed. Sean Wilentz. New York: Hill & Wang.

Walker, Francis. 1892. "Immigration." *Yale Review* 1.

Wallace, Anthony F. C. 1999. *Jefferson and the Indians: The Tragic Fate of the First Americans.* Cambridge: Harvard University Press.

Walzer, Michael. 1990. "What Does It Mean to Be an 'American'?" *Social Research* 57.

Wang, Xu. 1999. "Mutual Empowerment of State and Society: Its Nature, Conditions, Mechanisms, and Limits." *Comparative Politics* 31.

Ward, Harry M. 1961. *The United Colonies of New England: 1643–90.* New York: Vantage Press.

———. 1971. *'Unite or Die': Intercolony Relations, 1690–1763.* Port Washington, N.Y.: Kennikat Press.

Ward, John William. 1955. *Andrew Jackson: Symbol for an Age.* Oxford, U.K.: Oxford University Press.

Warner, W. Lloyd, and Leo Srole. 1945. *The Social Systems of American Ethnic Groups.* New Haven: Yale University Press.

Warren, John. 1783. "An Oration, Delivered July 4, 1783." Boston: John Gill.

Washington, Booker T. 1986 [1901]. *Up from Slavery.* New York: Penguin.

Watson, Thomas E., ed. 1909. *The South in the Building of the Nation.* 12 vols. Richmond, Va.: Southern Historical Pub. Society.

Weaver, Richard. 1953. *The Ethics of Rhetoric.* Chicago: Henry Regnery Co.

Weber, David J. 1997. "Conflicts and Accommodations: Hispanic and Anglo-American Borders in Historical Perspective, 1670–1853." *Journal of the Southwest* 39.

Webking, Robert H. 1988. *The American Revolution and the Politics of Liberty.* Baton Rouge: Louisiana State University Press.

Webster, Noah. 1789. *Dissertations on the English Language.* Boston: Isaiah Thomas and Company.

Webster, Pelatiah. 1783. "A Dissertation on the Political Union and Constitution of the Thirteen United States." Philadelphia: Hartford.

Weir, Margaret, and Marshall Ganz. 1997. "Reconnecting People and Politics." In Stanley B. Greenberg and Theda Skocpol, eds., *The New Majority.* New Haven: Yale University Press.

Weir, Robert E. 1997. "A Fragile Alliance: Henry George and the Knights of Labor." *American Journal of Economics and Sociology* 56.

Wellman, Christopher Heath. 1997. "Associative Allegiances and Political Obligations." *Social Theory and Practice* 23.

West, Samuel. 1776. "Sermon before the Honorable Council." Boston: John Gill.

Whately, Thomas. 1765. "The Regulations Lately Made concerning the Colonies. . . ." London: J. Walter & Co.

Wheeler, Richard. 1994. *A Rising Thunder: From Lincoln's Election to the Battle of Bull Run, An Eyewitness History.* New York: HarperCollins.

Whipple, E. P. 1866. "The President and Congress." *Atlantic Monthly* 17 (April).

White, G. Edward. 1994. "Reflections on the 'Republican Revival': Interdisciplinary Scholarship in the Legal Academy." *Yale Journal of Law and Humanities* 6.

White, Richard. 1991. *The Middle Ground: Indians, Empires, and Republics in the Great Lakes Region, 1650–1815.* New York: Cambridge University Press.

Whitlock, Brand. 1914. *Forty Years of It.* New York: D. Appleton.

Whitman, Walt. 1992. *Leaves of Grass: The Complete Edition.* New York: Penguin Books.

Whittington, Keith E. 1999. *Constitutional Construction: Divided Powers and Constitutional Meaning.* Cambridge: Harvard University Press.

Wickenden, Dorothy. 1990. "Lincoln and Douglass: Dismantling the Peculiar Institution." *Wilson Quarterly* 14.

Wiebe, Robert H. 1967. *The Search for Order: 1877–1920.* New York: Hill & Wang.

———. 1975. *The Segmented Society: An Introduction to the Meaning of America.* New York: Oxford University Press.

———. 1984. *The Opening of American Society: From the Adoption of the Constitution to the Eve of Disunion.* New York: Vintage Books.

Wiener, Jonathan M. 1979. "Coming to Terms with Capitalism: The Postwar Thought of George Fitzhugh." *Virginia Magazine of History and Biography* 87.

Wigginton, Eliot, ed. 1991. *Refuse to Stand Silently By: An Oral History of Grass Roots Social Activism in America, 1921–1964.* New York: Doubleday.

Wilentz, Sean. 1984. *Chants Democratic: New York City and the Rise of the American Working Class, 1788–1850.* New York: Oxford University Press.

Williams, Raymond. 1976. *Keywords: A Vocabulary of Culture and Society.* New York: Oxford University Press.

Williams, Robert A. 1994. "Linking Arms Together." *California Law Review* 82.

Williams, Roger. 1967 [1644]. "The Bloody Tenet of Persecution." Ann Arbor: University Microfilms.

Williamson, Joel. 1984. *The Crucible of Race: Black-White Relations in the American South since Emancipation.* New York: Oxford University Press.

Wills, Garry. 1981. *Explaining America: The Federalist.* Garden City, N.Y.: Doubleday.

———. 1992. *Lincoln at Gettysburg: The Words that Remade America.* New York: Simon & Schuster.

———. 1999. *A Necessary Evil: A History of American Distrust of Government.* New York: Simon & Schuster.

Wilson, Edmund. 1962. *Patriotic Gore: Studies in the Literature of the American Civil War.* New York: Oxford University Press.

Wilson, Henry. 1872. *History of the Rise and Fall of the Slave Power in America.* 3 vols. Boston: J. R. Osgood.

Wilson, Major L. 1967. "'Liberty' and 'Union': An Analysis of Three Concepts Involved in the Nullification Controversy." *Journal of Southern History* 33.

———. 1974. *Space, Time, and Freedom; The Quest for Nationality and the Irrepressible Conflict, 1815–1861.* Westport, Conn.: Greenwood Press.

———. 1988. "Republicanism and the Idea of Party in the Jacksonian Period." *Journal of the Early Republic* 8.

Wilson, Woodrow. 1926. *The New Democracy.* 2 vols. Ed. Ray S. Baker and William E. Dodd. New York: Harper & Brothers.

Wiltse, Charles M., and Alan R. Berolzheimer, eds. 1986–88. *The Papers of Daniel Webster: Speeches and Formal Writings.* 2 vols. Hanover, N.H.: University Press of New England.

Wiltse, Charles M., et al., eds. 1974–86. *The Papers of Daniel Webster: Correspondence.* 7 vols. Hanover, N.H.: University Press of New England.

Winship, Michael P. 2000. "'The Most Glorious Church in the World': The Unity of the Godly in Boston, Mass., in the 1630s." *Journal of British Studies* 39.

Wise, Barton H. 1899. *The Life of Henry A. Wise of Virginia, 1806–1876.* New York: Dunham.

Wise, John. 1710. "The Churches' Quarrel Espoused." New York: William Bradford.

———. 1717. "Vindication of the Government of New-England Churches." Boston: J. Allen.

Wish, Harvey. 1943. *George Fitzhugh: Propagandist of the Old South.* Baton Rouge: Louisiana State University Press.

Wolfe, Alan. 1998. *One Nation, After All.* New York: Penguin Books.

Wolkeck, Marianne, et al., eds. 1986. *The Papers of William Penn.* 5 vols. Philadelphia: University of Pennsylvania Press.

Wood, Gordon S. 1969. *The Creation of the American Republic, 1776–1787.* Chapel Hill: University of North Carolina Press.

———. 1991. "The Creative Imagination of Bernard Bailyn." In Henretta et al. 1991, 16–50.

———. 1992. *The Radicalism of the American Revolution.* New York: Alfred A. Knopf.

———. 1995. "A Century of Writing Early American History: Then and Now Compared." *American Historical Review* 100.

———. 1996. "Not So Poor Richard." *New York Review of Books* 43 (6 June).

———. 1998. "The Bloodiest War." *New York Review of Books* 45 (9 April).

Wood, Neal. 1983. *The Politics of Locke's Philosophy.* Berkeley: University of California Press.

Woodward, C. Vann. 1951. *Origins of the New South, 1877–1913.* Baton Rouge: Louisiana State University Press.

———. 1968. *The Burden of Southern History.* Rev. ed. Baton Rouge: Louisiana State University Press.

Wright, Benjamin Fletcher. 1967. *Consensus and Continuity, 1776–1787.* 2d ed. New York: W. W. Norton & Co.

Wuthnow, Robert. 1991. *Acts of Compassion.* Princeton, N.J.: Princeton University Press.

Yack, Bernard. 1993. *The Problems of a Political Animal: Community, Justice, and Conflict in Aristotelian Political Thought.* Berkeley: University of California Press.

Yazawa, Melvin. 1985. *From Colonies to Commonwealth: Familial Ideology and the Beginnings of the American Republic.* Baltimore, Md.: Johns Hopkins University Press.

York, Neil L. 1998. "The First Continental Congress and the Problem of American Rights." *Pennsylvania Magazine of History and Biography* 72.

Young, Iris Marion. 1990. *Justice and the Politics of Difference.* Princeton, N.J.: Princeton University Press.

———. 1993. "Communication and the Other: Beyond Deliberative Democracy." Paper presented at the Conference for the Study of Political Thought, Yale University.

Zelinsky, Wilbur. 1988. *Nations into State: The Shifting Symbolic Foundations of American Nationalism.* Chapel Hill: University of North Carolina Press.

———. 1996. "The Changing Face of Nationalism in the American Landscape." *Canadian Geographer* 40.

Zuckerman, Michael. 1970. *Peaceable Kingdoms: New England Towns in the Eighteenth Century.* New York: Alfred A. Knopf.

———. 1977. "The Fabrication of Identity in Early America." *William and Mary Quarterly* 34.

———. 1991. "A Different Thermidor: The Revolution beyond the American Revolution." In Henretta et al. 1991, 170–93.

Zuckert, Michael P. 1994. *Natural Rights and the New Republicanism.* Princeton, N.J.: Princeton University Press.

Zvesper, John. 1984. "The Madisonian Systems." *Western Political Quarterly* 37.

———. 1999. "The Separation of Powers in American Politics: Why We Fail to Accentuate the Positive." *Government and Opposition* 34.

Index